ELECTRICAL MACHINES-I

G.C. Garg

F.I.E., (Elec. Engg.); C. Engg. (I)
T.T.T.I. (Holland-Collaboration), Chandigarh
Ex-Registrar, Technical Education, Haryana
Formerly, Head of Electrical Engineering Deptt,
Govt. Polytechnic, Ambala City (Haryana)

Dr. P. S. Bimbhra

Ph.D., M.E.(Hons.), F.I.E. (India), M.I.S.T.E.
Ex-Dean. Ex-Professor and Head,
Electrical and Electronics Engineering Department
Thapar Institute of Engineering and Technology
Patiala-147004

KHANNA BOOK PUBLISHING CO. (P) LTD.

Publisher of Engineering and Computer Books

4C/4344, Ansari Road, Darya Ganj, New Delhi-110002
Phone : 011-23244447-48 **Mobile:** +91-9910909320
E-mail : contact@khannabooks.com
Website : www.khannabooks.com

Dear Readers,

To prevent the piracy, this book is secured with HIGH SECURITY HOLOGRAM on the front title cover. In case you don't find the hologram on the front cover title, please write us to at contact@khannabooks.com or whatsapp us at +91-99109 09320 and avail special gift voucher for yourself.

Specimen of Hologram on front Cover title:

Moreover, there is a SPECIAL DISCOUNT COUPON for you with EVERY HOLOGRAM.

How to avail this SPECIAL DISCOUNT:

Step 1: Scratch the hologram
Step 2: Under the scratch area, your "coupon code" is available
Step 3: Logon to www.khannabooks.com
Step 4: Use your "coupon code" in the shopping cart and get your copy at a special discount
Step 5: Enjoy your reading!

Price: ₹ 429.00

ISBN: 978-93-86173-44-7

Electric Machines-I
by Dr. P.S. Bimbhra, G.C. Garg

First Edition: 2018
Next Print: 2021
Reprint Edition: 2025

To view complete list of books, Please scan the QR Code:

Published by:
Khanna Book Publishing Co. (P) Ltd.
CIN: U22110DL1998PTC095547

Visit us at: **www.khannabooks.com**
Write us at: **contact@khannabooks.com**

Printed in Bharat.

PREFACE

This book is intended to serve as a textbook for the students of Electrical Engineering in general and for those studying in institutions where AICTE model curriculum has been adopted.

In this book, chapter 1 begins with the concept of magnetic circuits. It is because transformers and electrical machines use magnetic circuits for the efficient usage of magnetic fields for the conversion of energy. In Chapter 2, basic concepts about the production of electromagnetic force and torque are presented. In Chapter 3 and 4, dc machines are described in detail so far as their basic construction, armature windings, derivation of emf and torque expressions are concerned. These two chapters also include analysis of different dc machine configurations, like volt-ampere and speed-torque characteristics, speed control and testing of dc machines. In Chapter 5, transformers are described in detail. The features like voltage regulation, losses, efficiency, various types of tests, auto-transformers, harmonics, scott-connections, three-winding transformers etc are explained in this chapter. A large number of numerical problems have been included to reinforce understanding of the subject matter. Objective type questions included at the end of each chapter will help the readers to evaluate their comprehension of the chapter topics.

Errors might have crept in despite utmost care to avoid these and the authors will be grateful if such errors are pointed out along with other suggestions for the improvement of the book.

Authors

CONTENTS

MAGNETIC FIELDS AND MAGNETIC CIRCUITS

1

1.1. INTRODUCTION

The force of magnetism which was invisible was known to ancient people but they considered it to be a purely magical quantity. However with study of development of scientific knowledge, magnetism has attained a place of pride in the field of electrical engineering.

Many of the everyday devices we think of as electrical depend on proper magnetic design as much as they do on proper electrical design. For example in loudspeaker, motors, generators and relays the magnetic circuit is often more important than the electric circuit. The electric circuit serves only to provide the m.m.f. required to establish a certain flux density, which in turn provides the required mechanical forces. Some devices use permanent for this purpose.

The solution of magnetic circuits is more complex than the solution of electric circuits, primarily because of the non-linear B.H. curve. This complicates the evaluation of the answer, the circuit theory remains the same, and here we can make good use of ohm's law analogy.

Problems are basically of two types. In one case, the required flux is given and the m.m.f. required to achieve this flux must be found. This type of problem occurs in the design of motors, generators and transformers. In the other type, e.m.f. is given and flux is to be found. This type of problem is more difficult when more one kind of material is contained in the magnitude path and often requires a trial and error solution.

1.2. MAGNETISM

Working of electrical machines is based on magnetic effects. Machines like motors, generators transformers etc work of magnetic effects of electrical currents In 1820. Danish scientist-Oersted, discovered magnetic effects of electrical current but phenomenon of magnetism and some of the properties of magnetism were known long before. It was known in the ancient time that pieces of lodestone or magnetite (black Iron Oxide Fe_2O_3) a naturally occuring iron ore has the properly attract small pieces of iron. Later on it was discovered that the pieces of lodestone when suspended freely come to rest always long geographical North-South direction. This directional properly is the principle of magnetic compass which is used as an aid to navigation. It was suggested by William Gilbert that the earth itself is a huge magnet and it is due to earth's magnetism that a magnetic compass needle aligns along North-South line.

1.3. MAGNETS

A Substance which attracts then iron pieces is called Magnet and the properly by which thin attraction takes place is called Magnetism. Certain type of iron over (magnetic (Fe_3O_4) possess this properly of attracting small iron pieces and are called Magnets.

Types of Magnets are generally classified as:

(*i*) *Natural magnets* : The iron are (magnetic Fe_3O_4) pieces which possess the properly of attracting small iron pieces are called *natural magnets*. They do not have practical applications.

(*ii*) *Artificial magnets* : The pieces of some magnetic material which attain magnetic properties by artificial means are called *artificial magnets*. The artificial magnets may further be classified as

(*a*) *Temporary magnets* : The magnets (generally prepared from soft iron or nickel) which retain magnetism as long as the magnetising force is applied are called *temporary magnets*. When the magnetising force is removed, they lose almost all their magnetism. They have their wide applications in the field of electrical equipment *e.g.* generators, motors, electric bells, relays etc.

(*b*) *Permanent magnets* : The magnets (generally prepared from hardened steel and certain magnetic alloys such as cobalt-steel, tungsten steel étc.) which retain their magnetism indefinitely, even if the magnetising force is removal, are called permanent magnets. They are extensively used in electrical intruments, ear-phones, loud-speakers etc.

1.4. MAGNETIC MATERIALS

Any substance which has the property of being attracted by or attracting the magnet is known as magnetic material. On the basis of magnetic properties, all materials may be classified into three types.

(*a*) **Ferromagnetic :** The materials which are strongly attracted by magnets such as iron, steal, nickel, cobalt and some of their aloys. Their relative permeability is very high.

(*b*) **Para-magnetic :** The materials which are not strongly attracted by magnet such as aluminium, tin, platinum, manganese etc. Their relative permeability is slightly higher than unity. These are slightly magnetised when placed in a strong magnetic field and act in the direction of magnetic field.

(*c*) **Dia-magnetic :** These are the materials which are slightly repelled by a magnet such as zinc, mercury, lead sulphur, copper, silver etc. Their relative permeability is slightly less than unity. These are slightly magnetised when placed in strong magnetic fields and act in direction opposite to the field.

1.5. BAR MAGNET AND ITS PROPERTIES

It is found that naturally occuring magnets like lodestones are not very strong. However, the pieces of iron or steel of suitable shapes can be made magnets by rubbing them with lodestones or by placing them in strong magnetic fields of electric currents.

If a bar magnet is brought near to a heap of iron fillings, the ends of the magnet show the greatest attraction. These ends of the magnet where the magnetic attraction is maximum are called the poles of the magnet.

When a magnet is suspended freely, is oscillates for a while and then comes to rest approximately along geographic North and South. The end which point towards the geographic north is called north seeking pole or simply the north pole (N). On the other hand the end which points towards the geographic south is called the South seeking pole or simply the south pole (S).

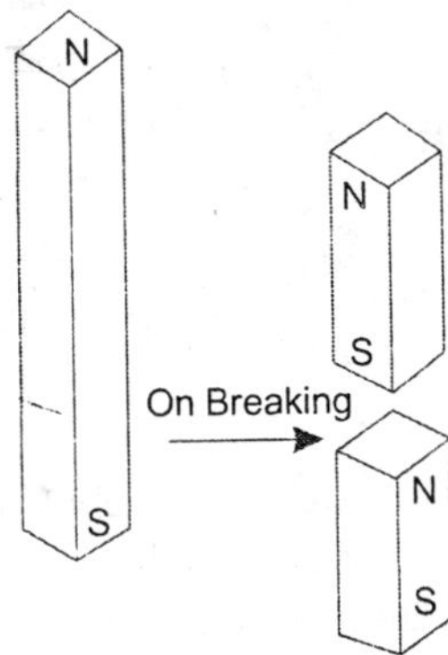

Fig. 1.1

It has been experimentally observed that

1. Like poles repel each other and the opposite poles attract each other.
2. Attractive or repulsive force between two magnetic poles is directly proportional of their pole strength and inversely proportional to equal of the distance between them.
3. Magnetic poles always exist in pairs. An isolated north or south pole can not exist. If a magnet is cut into two pieces, instead of obtaining separate north place and separate south pole, each of the two pairs is still found to be a magnet. The new ends develop polarities opposite to what the ends of two pieces possess as illustrated in Fig.1.1.

If a magnet is cut into two exactly equal parts, pole strength of each part is exactly half of the pole strength of original magnet.

The important difference between electricity and magnetism is that in electricity isolated charge exists whereas in magnetism is an isolated magnetic pole can not exist. In electricity two equal and opposite charges placed at a certain distance apart constitute electric dipole but in magnetism fundamental arrangement is that of two equal and opposite magnetic poles separated by certain distance and this arrangement is called magnet or magnetic dipole.

1.6. MOLECULAR THEORY OF MAGNETISM

This theory was first advanced by Weber in 1852 and later on further developed by Ewing in 1990. The basic assumption theory is that molecules of all the substances are inherently magnets in themselves, each having a north and south pole. In unmagnetised state all these molecular magnets lie in haphazard manner forming more or less closed as shown in Fig.1.2.

According to laws of attraction and repulsion, these closed magnetic circuits are satisfied internally and hence no net external magnetism is exhibited by the iron bar. When such an iron bar is placed in a magnetic field, these molecular magnets start turning around their axes and orient themselves more or less along straight lines parallel to the direction of magnetic field. This linear arrangement of molecular magnets results in North polarity at one end of the bar and South polarity at the other end as shown in Fig.1.3.

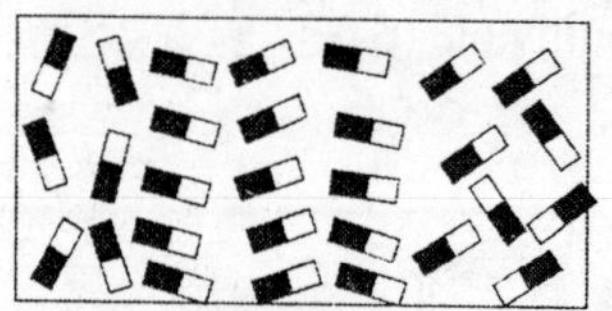

Fig. 1.2

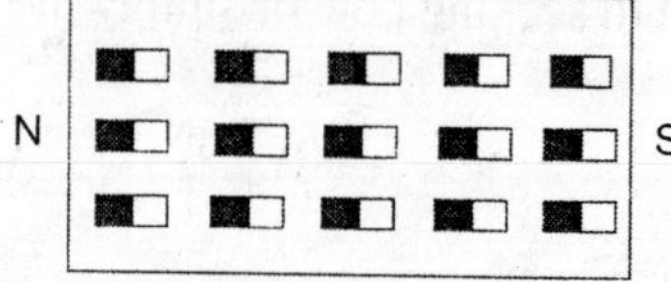

Fig. 1.3

Because of the limited knowledge of molecular structure available at that time, it was not possible to explain:

(*i*) Why molecules themselves are magnets. This objection *i.e.* why molecules of all substances are magnets is explained by Ampere., on the basis that orbital movement of electrons around the nucleus of atoms which constitute flow of current and due to associated magnetic effect of current, molecules act as magnets.

(*ii*) On the basis of molecular theory it was also not possible to explain (a) why certain materials, like water, quartz, silver copper etc. are diamagnetic (b) Iron, nickel, cobalt are ferromagnetic (c) The substance like oxygen aluminium are paramagnetic (d) Also if molecules of all substances are magnets, then why it is not possible to magnetise certain materials like wood, air etc.

All this is explained on the basis of atomic domain theory, according to which in addition to orbital movement of electrons, there is spin movement (rotation about its own axis) which gives rise to magnetic moment. Magnetic moment is either positive or negative. A substance is ferromagnetic if there is excess of negative spin. Substances like wood, or air can not be magnetised as in their case positive and negative spins are exactly equal and hence they cancel each other.

Magnetic Polarity

If a bar magnet is dipped into iron filings, it will be observed that a large quantity of iron filings cluster about the ends of the bar magnet. These ends apparently represent the points of maximum magnetic effect and for convenience are called *poles* of the magnet. A bar magnet has two poles *viz.* north pole and south pole. To determine the polarity of a magnet, it is suspended or piovoted at its centre. The magnet rests in a definite position. One end points in the direction of earth's north pole called north *seeking pole* or simply *north pole*, the other end is called south *seeking pole* or simply *south pole*.

It is observed that if the bar magnet is broken into two pieces each piece will be a complete magnet with two poles at its ends. No matter how many times a magnet times a magnet is broken, every time each piece will have two poles (north and south). Thus, *poles of a magnet cannot be separated.*

The two poles of the magnet have equal strength *i.e.* m water.

1.7. MAGNETIC INDUCTION

If a piece of soft un-magnetised iron is brought near a bar magnet, it also gets magnetized. This phenomenon of inducing magnetism is known as magnetic induction. If south pole of the magnet is brought near the soft iron piece. north pole is induced at the end of the iron piece nearer to the inducing magnet and south pole is induced at the other end of the iron pieces as shown in Fig.1.4.

Fig. 1.4

On the other hand if north pole of the magnet is brought near to the soft iron piece then south and north poles are induced respectively at the nearer and far end of the iron piece.

Coulomb's laws of magnetic force

Quantitative expression for the magnetic force between two isolated point poles was determined experimentally by Coulomb. However, it may be noted here that as the magnetic poles always exist in pairs. it is impossible to get an isolated pole in actual practice. The concept of an rated pole is purely theoretical. poles of thin but long magnets be assumed to be point poles all practical purposes as shown in Fig. 1.5.

Fig. 1.5

It was found that, force between two magnetic poles placed in a medium is

(*i*) directly proportional to their pole strengths.

(*ii*) inversely proportional to square of distance between them.

For example, if m_1 and m_2 represent the magnetic pole strengths of two poles separated by distance r as shown in Fig. 1.6., them magnetic force F between them is given as

Fig. 1.6

$$F = \frac{m_1 m_2}{r^2}$$

or

$$F = K \frac{m_1 m_2}{r^2}$$

where K is the constant of proportionality. The value of K depends upon nature of the medium in which the poles are placed and the system of units employed. In S.I system, the value of K is given by

$$K = \frac{1}{4\pi \mu_0 \mu r}$$

where μ_0 is permeability of free space or air = $4\pi \times 10^{-7}$ Henry per meter, and μr is the relative permeability of the medium with respect to free space or air.

In S.I system pole strength m_1 and m_2 is measured in Webers the, distance r, in metres, and the force F given by the above expression is in newtons.

If
$$m_1 = m_2 = 1 \text{ Weber}$$
$$r = 1 \text{ m}$$

and medium surrounding the poles is air, then is $\mu r = 1$

$$F = \frac{m_1 m_2}{4\pi \mu_0 \mu_r r^2}$$

$$= \frac{1 \times 1}{4\pi \times 4\pi \times 10^{-7} \times 1 \times 1^2} = 62800 \text{ Newtons.}$$

Therefore, a pole is said to be a unit pole or a pole of one weber which when placed in air or vacuum at a distance of one meter from a similar pole of same strength repels it with a force of 62800 newtons.

1.8. MAGNETIC FIELD

The space around the poles of a magnet in which presence of magnetic poles is felt by a unit test pole (of one weber) is called magnetic field. Magnetic field is represented by magnetic lines of force or lines of magnetic flux. The magnetic line of force is defined as the curve along with a unit N-pole would move if free to do so when placed in a magnetic field. The tangent to these lines at any point gives the direction of magnetic field at that point. The lines of magnetic flux has the following properties.

(*i*) Each line of magnetic flux forms a closed loop as shown in Fig. 1.7 *i.e.* a line of flux emerging from any point at North pole of a magnet, passes through the surrounding space to the south pole and returns back to the north pole through the magnet.

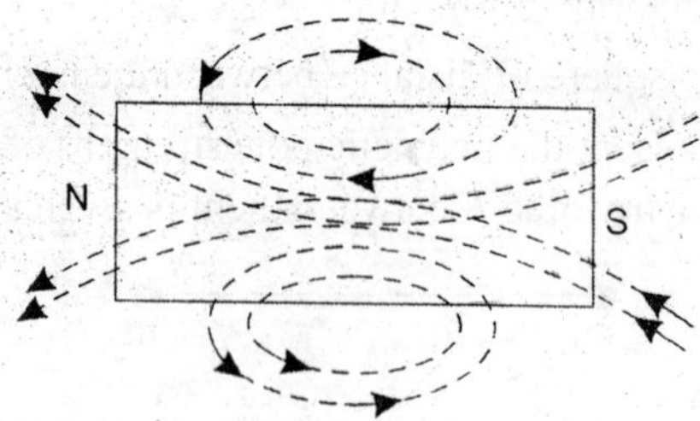

Fig. 1.7

(*ii*) The lines of magnetic flux can not intersect each other.

(*iii*) The lines of magnetic flux tend to contract length wise resulting in the force of attraction between unlike poles as illustrated in Fig. 1.8.

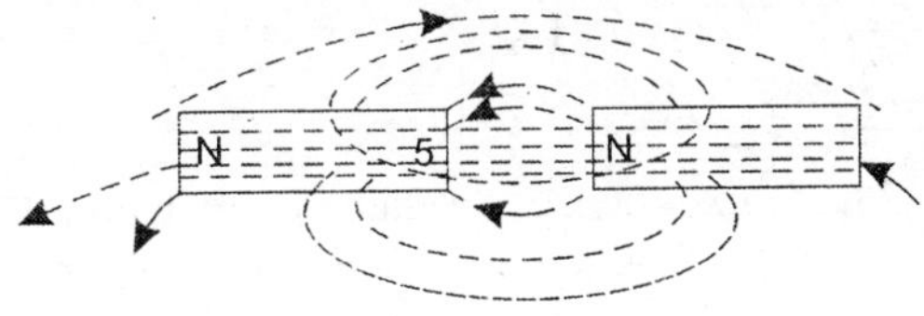

Fig. 1.8

(*iv*) The line of force tend to expand sideways. This property of magnetic lines of force can be used to explain why like poles repel each other as illustrated in Fig.1.9

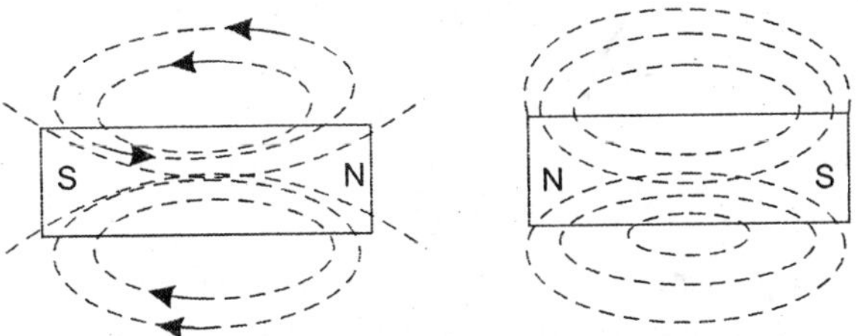

Fig. 1.9

When like poles are brought near to each other, the lines of force in the air gap are in opposite direction and the lines of force from one pole opposes the line of force from the other pole. None of the lines of force from one magnet enters the other magnet and a force of repulsion is exerted between the poles.

(*v*) The lines of force emanate from and terminate on a surface normally.

1.9. EARTH AS A MAGNET

When a magnet is suspended so that it is free to turn, it comes to rest in direction approximately along the geographic north and south. Therefore the suspended magnet is always acted upon by a force which compels it to again along a particular direction *i.e.* geographic north and south. This force is supposed to be due to earth acting as a magnet with its poles near the geographic poles. As the north seeking pole of the magnet points towards the Geographic north, the earth must be having south pole of magnetic earth three. Similarly south geographic pole will be having a north pole of the earth's magnet.

Hence the south pole of earth's magnet is in the northern hemisphere and north pole is situated in the southern hemisphere. The magnetic axis makes an angle of 20° with geographic axis.

Magnetic field of earth is like that of huge bar magnet which may be assumed to be located deep inside the earth. The source of earth's magnetism is not the solid mass of magnetic material located inside the earth. It is guessed that it is the charged metallic fluid which gives rise to current flowing inside the core of the earth. The earth core has a radius of about 3500 km.

It is also suggested that earth's magnetism is due to reaction of earth about its own axis. It is because every substance is made up of charged particles. (protons and electrons) Therefore every substance rotating about an axis will get magnetised.

1.10. UNIFORM FIELD

It is the field within which a unit pole experiences the same force at all points and the direction of such a force is same everywhere. In such a field the lines of force are straight and parallel. The magnetic field of earth is uniform over a fairly extended area.

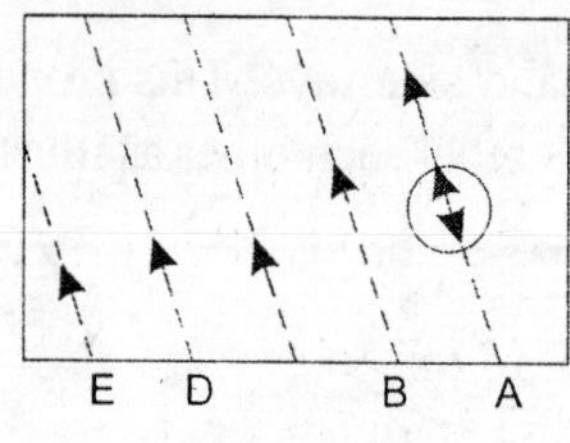

Fig. 1.10

Horizontal magnetic field of earth can be plotted on a paper practically. In order to do so, fix a drawing sheet and remove all the magnets from near to it. Mark off points A, B, C ....on the paper as shown in Fig. 1.10. Place a magnetic needle so that its one pole is vertically above one of the points and mark a point just below the other pole of needle. Now place the needle such that its first pole is exactly over the new point marked and thus obtain a third point. In similar way other points can be obtained. Join all such points. Curve so obtained is a line which represents earth's magnetic field. If earth's magnetic field is plotted at B, C and D, it will be observed that these lines are parallel.

1.11. MAGNETIC FIELD OF A BAR-MAGNET

The space around a magnet is called magnetic field. It is represented by magnetic lines of force. Magnetic line of force is a curve along which a unit north pole moves in the magnetic field. In actual practice it is not possible to have a single pole, the lines of force can be obtained practically by means of a compass needle whose north pole will be moving along the lines of force as represented in Fig.1.11.

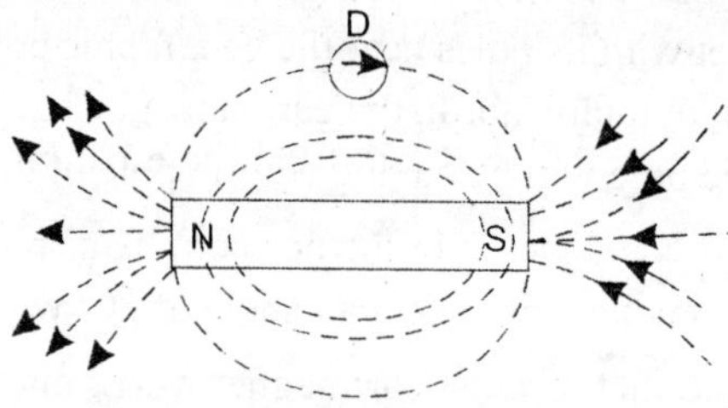

Fig. 1.11

In Fig.1.12, the lines of force over much greater area are shown. Here the magnet is placed with its south pole towards the east at right angles of the magnetic meridian (A vertical plane passing through axis of a freely suspended magnet). Near the magnet, the magnetic field is mainly due to the magnet itself, but as the distance from the magnet increases, field due to magnet decreases and earth's magnetic field pro-dominates as the magnetic field of earth is uniform, the magnetic lines of force due to earth magnetic field are parallel.

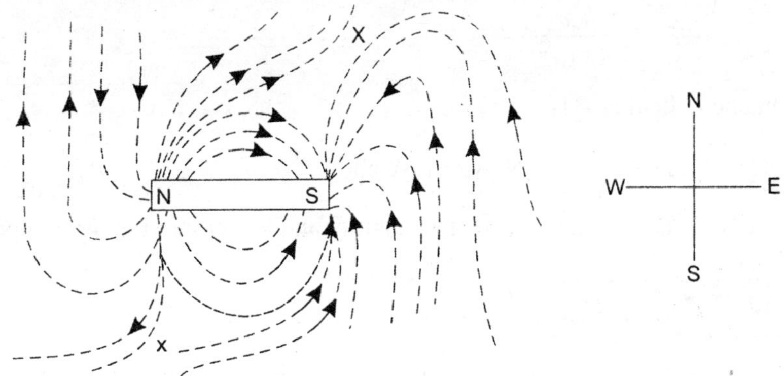

Fig. 1.12

The direction of earth's field is opposite to that of the bar magnet.

At certain points marked as X magnetic field of the bar magnet is equal and opposite to horizontal component of earth's magnetic field, such points are called neutral points. *Therefore, the neutral points are the points where the field due to magnet is completely neutralised by the horizontal component of earth's magnetic field.*

If the bar magnet is placed with its north pole towards geographic north in the magnetic meridian, the resultant field as shown in Fig.1.13.

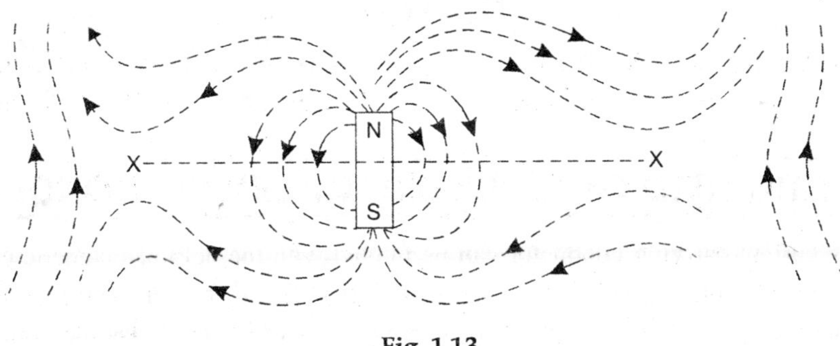

Fig. 1.13

1.12. MAGNETIC FIELD STRENGTH (H) OR INTENSITY OF MAGNETIC FIELD

Intensity of magnetic field at a point is defined as the force experienced by a unit north pole at that point. Suppose it is required at a point P which is at a distance of r meters from a pole of m webers as shown in Fig. 1.14.

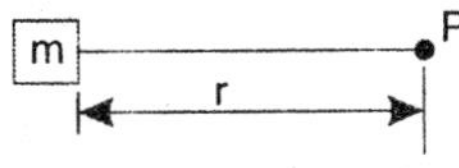

Fig. 1.14

Force experienced by a unit north pole of one web when placed at P

$$F = \frac{m \times 1}{4\pi \mu r^2}$$

∴ Intensity of magnetic field at P is

$$H = \frac{m \times 1}{4\pi \mu r^2} \text{ Newtons / Web.}$$

Intensity of magnetic field at a point is a vector quantity and is measured in newton per weber.

1.13. LINES OF INDUCTION

Lines of magnetic flux travel from north pole to south pole externally and continue to travel through the magnet and finally reach the north pole again forming the closed curve as shown in Fig. 1.15.

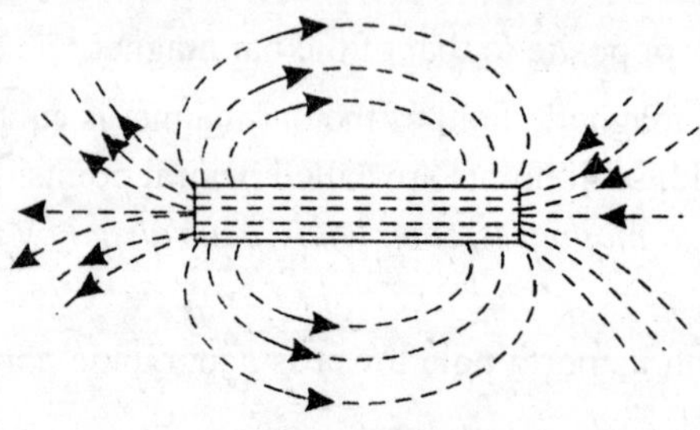

Fig. 1.15

The portion of the curves within the magnetic material are called lines of magnetic induction whereas the portion of the curves outside magnetic material are called lines of magnetic force.

1.14. MAGNETIC FIELD OF A CURRENT CARRYING CONDUCTOR

Magnetic field of a current carrying conductor can be plotted with the help of magnetic compass and placing the conductor carrying current in the card board. It is found that magnetic filed around the current carrying conductor consists of number of lines of force which encircles the conductor when current is passed through the conductor in the upward direction of lines of force is anticlockwise as observed from the top of the conductor as shown in Fig. 1.16.

When the current is passed through the conductor in down ward direction the direction of lines of force is found to be clockwise as observed from the top of the conductor as shown in Fig.1.17.

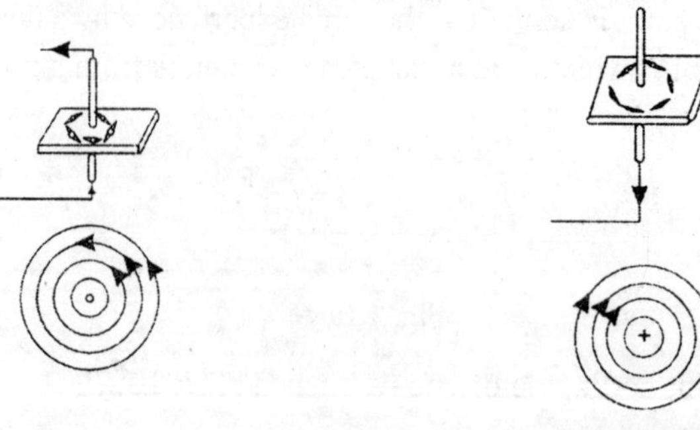

Fig. 1.16 Fig. 1.17

1.15. DIRECTION OF MAGNETIC FIELD AROUND A CURRENT CARRYING CONDUCTOR

The direction of magnetic field around a current carrying conductor can be determined by any one of the following rules.

(*i*) **Right Hand Rule :-** If the conductor current is held by the observer in his right hand so that the thumb points in the direction of current, then encircling fingers will give the direction of magnetic lines of force around the conductor as shown in Fig.1.18.

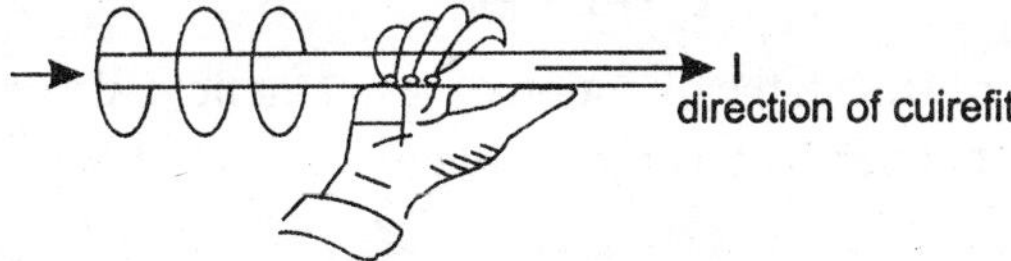

Fig. 1.18

(*ii*) **Cork Screw Rule :-** If a right handed cork screw is held with its axis parallel to the conductor pointing in the direction of current and the head of the screw is turned in such a direction that the screw moves in the direction of flow of current, then the direction in which the head of the screw is rotated gives the directior of magnetic lines of force around the conductor as illustrated in Fig. 1.19.

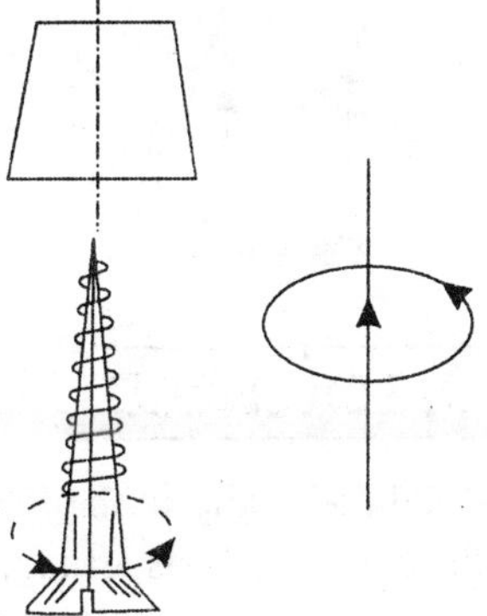

Fig. 1.19

1.16. MAGNETIC FIELD OF A CIRCULAR COIL

If a conductor is bent so as to from a circular loop and if it carries current in the clockwise direction as observed from the top as shown in Fig. 1.20, then by applying right hand rule, the lines of force are seen as concentric circles and are always at right angles to the wire. It behaves as magnet with north pole at the bottom and south pole at the top.

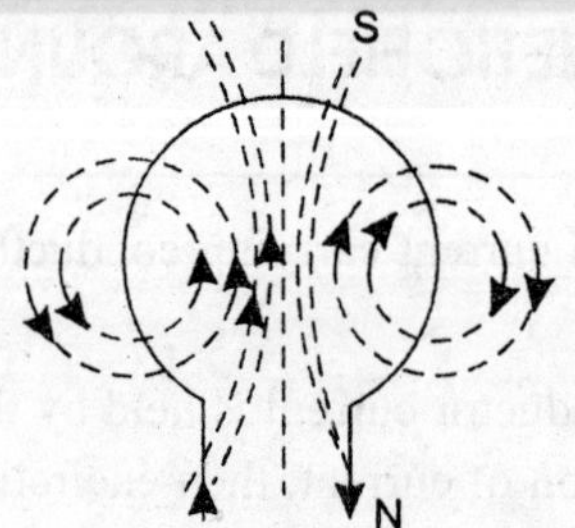

Fig. 1.20

If the direction of current is reversed, the direction of resultant field also reverses and bottom of coil behaves as south pole while the top behaves as north pole as shown in Fig. 1.21.

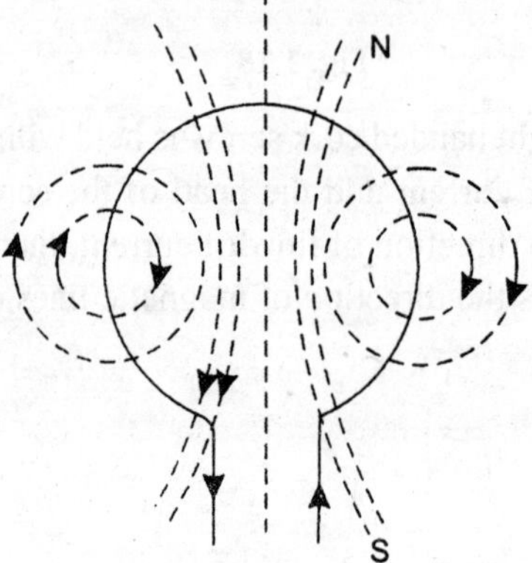

Fig. 1.21

1.17. MAGNETIC FIELD OF A SOLENOID

When a number of circular coils are arranged co-axially in the form of helix in such a way that same current flows in the same direction in all the coils, then this arrangement is called a solenoid. Magnetic field produced by the current carrying solenoid is fairly uniform over a small region in the middle of the coil and resembles the magnetic field of a har magnet having north and south pole as shown in Fig.1.22. The polarity of solenoid can be determined by right hand rule according to which if the solenoid is held in the right hand so that the fingers point in the direction of flow of current through the coils, then the thumb stretched longitudinally points towards the north pole or the direction of magnetic lines of force.

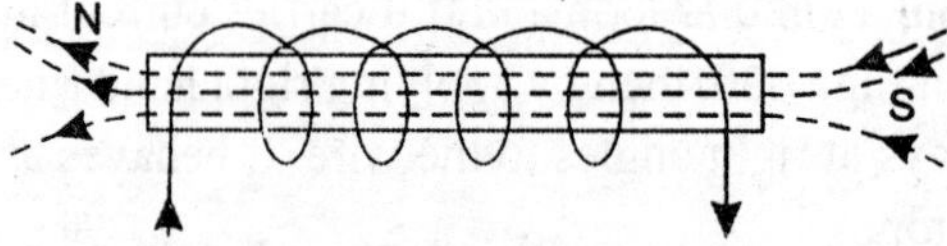

Fig. 1.22

The following important points are worth noting about the magnetic field of a solenoid.

1. Magnetic field is practically identical with that of bar magnet.

2. Inside the coil magnetic field is uniform and is represented by set of straight lines which are parallel and equally spaced.
3. Strength of magnetic field can be increased by increasing the number of turns or the current.

1.18. MAGNETIC FIELD OF A TOROID

Toroid is an endless solenoid wound on a circular soft iron core as shown in Fig. 1.23.

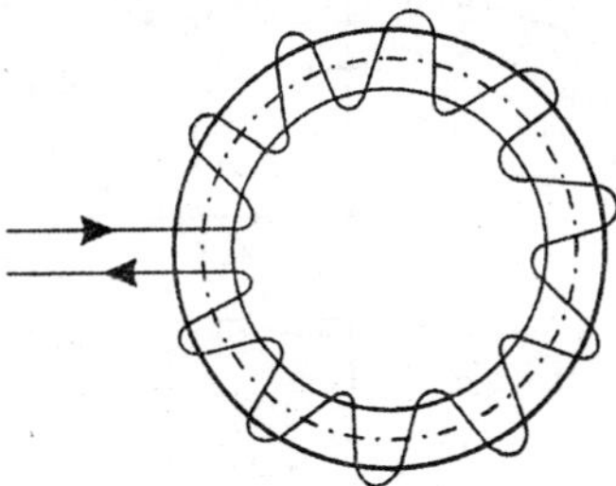

Fig. 1.23

Magnetic field of a Toroid is represented by circular lines of force and is uniform inside the toroid.

1.19. WORK LAW

If a unit north pole is placed in a magnetic field, it experiences a magnetic force. The force experienced by the unit north pole when placed in the magnetic field depends upon the magnetic field strength (H). If the pole is moved in the magnetic field opposite to the direction of lines of force, then work is done against the magnetic field.

On the other hand if the unit pole is moved in the direction of the field, then work is done by the magnetic force on whatever is restraining the movement of unit pole. According to work law. "The net work done in joules on or by a unit N pole while moving around single completed magnetic path in a magnetic field is equal to ampere-turns linked with the path".

Mathematically line integral of magnetic field intensity over a closed magnetic path is equal to ampere turns linked with the path.

i.e. $$\phi Hdr = NI$$

where H = Intensity of magnetic field at distance r

N' = Number of straight conductors or number of turns in a coil

I = Current flowing through each conductor.

1.20. STRENGTH OF MAGNETIC FIELD DUE TO CURRENT CARRYING STRAIGHT CONDUCTOR

Consider a long straight conductor carrying current I in upward direction as shown in Fig.1.24. Its magnetic field consists of circular lines of force having their plane perpendicular to the conductor with centres at the centre of the conductor.

The intensity of magnetic field (H) at point C which is at a distance r from the centre of the conductor can be found by applying work law.

Let H is the intensity of magnetic field at C. From symmetry it is clear that H is constant at all points which lie on circular path through C. If a unit northpole is moved along a line of force through. C then work done in moving the north pole around the conductor is given by

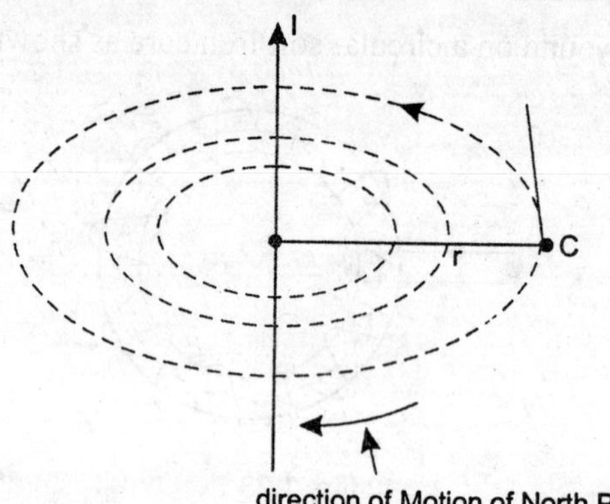

Fig. 1.24

$$W.D = \text{Force} \times \text{distance}$$

$$= H \times 2\pi r \quad ...(1)$$

By work law, this work done must be equal to ampere-turns linked with the path.

$$\text{Ampere turns linked} = \text{Number of turns} \times \text{Current}$$

$$= N.I \quad ...(2)$$

Equating Equations (1) & (2)

$$H \times 2\pi r = N \times I$$

As there is only one conductive *i.e.* $N = 1$

$$\therefore \quad H = \frac{I}{2\pi r} \text{ AT / m.}$$

Also,

$$B = \mu H$$

$$= \mu \frac{I}{2\pi r} \text{ Wb / m}^2$$

If there are N conductors, then

$$H = \frac{N.I}{2\pi r} \text{ AT / m.}$$

and

$$B = \mu \frac{N.I}{2\pi r} \text{ Web / } m^2$$

1.21. MAGNETISING FORCE OF A LONG SOLENOID

Consider a solenoid of length l having N turns. As magnetic lines of force inside the solenoid are straight lines parallel to each other, it can be assumed that intensity of magnetic field H is constant throughout the length of the solenoid. Magnetic field outside the solenoid is very weak and can be neglected. When a unit north pole is moved along a closed magnetic path in the direction opposite to the direction of magnetic field as shown in Fig.1.25. Force of H newtons acts on the unit pole only over the length of solenoid, as the intensity of magnetic field is negligible at all points outside the solenoid.

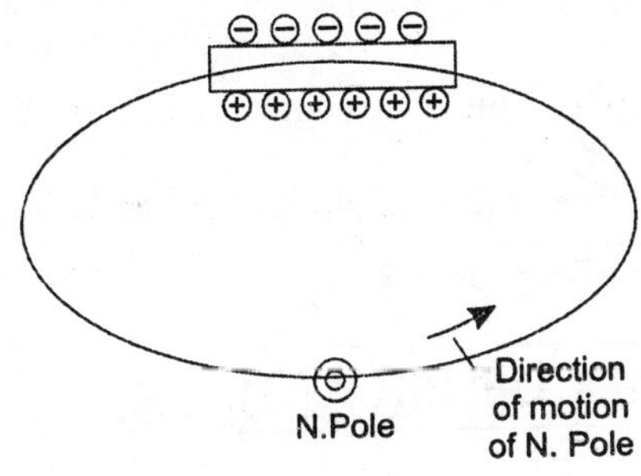

Fig. 1.25

Work done in moving the unit N-pole along the closed magnetic path around the solenoid = $H \times l$

Ampere turns linked with path = $N \times I$

By applying work law.

$$H \times l = N \times l$$

or $$H = \frac{N \times I}{l} \text{ AT / m.}$$

and $$B = \mu H$$

$$= \frac{\mu NI}{l}$$

1.22. FORCE ON A MOVING CHARGE IN MAGNETIC FIELD

When a charge is placed in a magnetic field, no force will act on it as long as it is at rest. However, when this charge is in motion, it constitutes current and will establish magnetic field just as any current does. The magnetic field due to moving charge reacts with the other field resulting in the mechanical force on the charge, the magnitude of which is given by

$$F = B I l \text{ Newtons}$$

where B = flux density in Wb/m^2 of the magnetic field in which the change moves.

I = current due to moving charge

l = length of path through which the charge moves.

1.23. MAGNETIC FLUX

Total number of lines of magnetic force contained in a magnetic field is called the magnetic flux. In S.I system a north pole of strength one weber is supposed to radiate out flux of one weber or a tube of flux. Magnetic flux is represented by symbol φ and is measured in webers. It is numerically equal to pole strength.

Therefore flux emanated from a pole of strength m weber = m Wb.

The lines of flux emanated from a pole of strength m Wb is equal to $\frac{m}{\mu}$ where μ is permeability of the space surrounding the pole.

1.24. MAGNETIC FLUX DENSITY (B)

It is defined as the flux passing per unit area through any material in a plane which is at right angles to the direction of flux.

If φ is the total flux passing through a magnetic material having cross sectional area A held normal to direction of flux, then magnetic flux density B is

$$B = \frac{\varphi}{A} \text{ Web / m}^2$$

It is found that magnetic flux density (B) is directly proportional to intensity of magnetic field (H) ie $B \alpha H$

or $$B = \mu H$$

where φ is the permeability of the magnetic material.

1.25. PERMEABILITY (μ)

It is the ability of the material to conduct magnetic lines of force. It a piece of soft iron is placed in between the poles of a magnet, it is found that the iron piece gets magnetised by induction and the lines of force get concentrated through the iron piece, indicating that it is easier for the lines of force to go through iron as compared the air. Therefore iron is the better conductor for the lines of force than air or magnetic resistance of air is more than that of iron.

Relative permeability : (μ_r)

Permeability of magnetic material as compared to that of air or free space is called relative permeability.

$$\text{Relative Permeability: } (\mu_r) = \frac{\text{Permeability of material}}{\text{Permeability of air or free space}}$$

$$= \frac{\mu}{\mu_0}$$

or $$\mu = \mu_o \mu_r$$

where μ = Absolute Permeability

$$\mu_o = \text{absolute permeability of air}$$
$$= 4\pi \times 10^{-7} \text{ H/m.}$$
$$\mu_r = \text{Relative permeability.}$$

Relative permeability of air or free space is unity.

1.26. RELUCTANCE (R)

(AMIE, May 1973 AMIE, New Scheme May 1974)

Reluctance is the resistance offered by the magnetic circuit to the flow of magnetic flux in it.

Reluctance of any part of a magnetic circuit is defined *as the ratio of the drop in magneto motive force to the flux produced in that part of the circuit.* It is measured in ampere-turn per weber and is denoted by *R*.

$$R = \frac{m.m.f.}{\phi} \text{ AT/Wb.}$$

1.27. PERMEANCE (P)

It is reciprocal of refluence and it is the readiness with which magnetic flux is developed. It is analogous to conductance in an electric circuit. Its unit is *weber per ampere turn*, and symbol is *P*. Thus

$$P = \frac{\phi}{m.m.f.} \text{ Wb/AT.}$$
$$= \frac{1}{R} \text{ Wb/AT.}$$

Magnetic Circuit

Magnetic circuit is the path following by magnetic flux. Magnetic flux follows a complete loop or circuit coming back to its starting point. In any magnet, magnetic flux leaves its north pole, passing air, enters the magnet at its south pole and finally reach the point from where it starts.

It is possible to establish magnetic flux in a definite limited path by using magnetic material of high permeability. In this manner, the magnetic flux forms a closed circuit exactly as an electric current does in an electric circuit.

The flux ϕ is produced by a source (say an electro-magnet) due to some power of force called **magneto-motive force M.M.F.)** This is comparable to E.M.F. which is the cause of an electric current.

The amount of flux produced in a magnetic circuit depends upon the property of the magnitude material opposing the production of flux and this property is called **reluctance** of the material.

Simple Magnetic Circuits

A simple magnetic circuit consisting of a closed iron ring of mean length *l m* and area of cross-section *A*,

m^2 wound with a magnetic coil of *N* turns and carrying a current of *I* amperes is shown in (Fig. 1.26). We assume that the material of the ring (iron or any other ferromagnetic material) has a high permeability and that total flux passes in the ring. Let *H* be the field strength inside the ring.

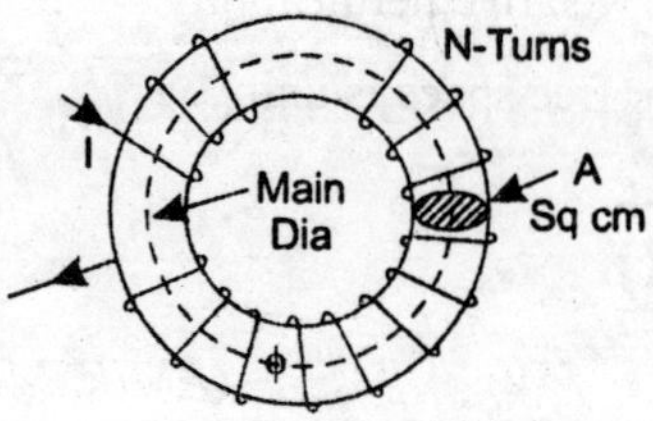

Fig. 1.26

In this case the flux ϕ is produced by the magnetising coil, which acts as the source of magneto motive force (m.m.f.) and the resistance to the flow of flux, *i.e.*, reluctance is offered by the ferromagnetic material (iron) of the ring.

Magneto-Motive Force (M.M.F.)

(*AMIE, May 1973, 74*)

Like electro-motive force in electric circuits, *magneto-motive force* (*m.m.f.*) is the force which drives or tends to drive magnetic flux through a magnetic circuit.

An m.m.f. is produced when electric current flows in a coil of several turns. This m.m.f. is measured by the product of current in amperes and the number of turns. The unit of m.m.f. is *ampere turn* and is denoted by *M* or *F*. Thus

$$M = I.N \text{ Amp Turns}$$

Magnetic Field Intensity (H)

(*AMIE New Scheme May 1974*)

Magnetic field intensity, also known as *magnetising force* is the m.m.f. per unit length along the path of magnetic flux. Its symbol is *H* and the unit is *ampere turns per metre*. Thus

$$H = \frac{m.m.f.}{l} \text{ AT/m}$$

$$= \frac{N.I}{l} \text{ AT/m.}$$

1.28. OHM'S LAW OF MAGNITUDE CIRCUITS

Consider the magnitude circuit, (Fig. 1.26). Let the magnetising coil haave *N* turns of wire and its mean length be *l*. When a current of *I* amperes flows in the coil, a flux density, *B* given by

$$B = \mu_0.\mu_r \frac{N.I}{l} \text{ Wb/m}^2$$

and this flux density B is set up along its axis. [For a non-magnetic material inside the solenoid. $\mu_r = 1$, and hence $B = \mu_0.NI/l$].

If this cross-sectional area of the coil is A, the total flux ϕ is given by

$$\phi = BA\ Wb$$

$$= \frac{\mu_0.\mu_r.N.I}{l} \times A\ Wb$$

$$= \frac{\mu_0.\mu_r.A}{l} M \qquad [\because m.m.f. = M = N.I]$$

$$= \frac{M}{\frac{l}{\mu_0.\mu_r.A}} = \frac{m.m.f.}{\text{Reluctance}}$$

where R = reluctance of the magnetic circuit and is given by $l/m_0.\mu_r.A$.

[Note that by definition, $R = \frac{m.n.f.}{\phi}$, so that $\phi = \frac{m.m.f.}{R}$ and as $\phi = \frac{m.m.f.}{l}$, therefore, $R = \frac{l}{\mu_0.\mu_r.A}$].

Thus in a magnetic circuit, the flux ϕ is directly proportional to the impressed m.m.f. M and inversely proportional to the reluctance R of the magnetic circuit, this law $\left[\phi = \frac{m.m.f.}{\text{Reluctance}}\right]$ is, therefore, similar to Ohm's law $\left[I = \frac{e.m.f.}{\text{Resistance}}\right]$. This is why it is often known as Ohm's law of the magnetic circuit.

If the coil has air or other non-magnetic material, instead of a magnetic material as its core, the magnetic field intensity H at any point on the axis of this coil would be

$$H = \frac{B}{\mu_0} = \frac{N.I}{l}\ \text{AT/m}.$$

Now, the total m.m.f. M is given by

$$M = N.I$$

$$\therefore \qquad M = H.l\ AT.$$

The flux density B with the coil is constant over the cros sectional area A, hence the total flux

$$\phi = BH \times A\ Wb$$

$$= \frac{\mu_0.N.I}{l}.A = \frac{N.I}{\frac{l}{\mu_0 A}} = \frac{m.m.f.}{R}$$

where $R = \frac{l}{\mu_0 A}$ (for non-magnetic medium).

1.29. FACTORS ON WHICH RELUCTANCE DEPENDS

The reluctance of a substance is :

1. Directly proportional to the length of the flux path (i), and
2. inversely proportional to the cross-section (A) :

i.e., $$R \propto \frac{l}{A}$$

or $$R \propto \frac{l}{\mu_0 . \mu_r . A} \text{ AT/Wb.}$$

The constant of proportionality is $\frac{1}{\mu_0 . \mu_r}$ or $\frac{1}{\mu_0}$. This shows that R is also dependent on the magnetic properties of the material of the circuit, *i.e.*, R depends *inversely* on the relative permeability μ_r.

1.30. RELUCTANCE IN SERIES

When a number of reluctances are commonly in series, then the total reluctance R is given by

$$R = R_1 + R_2 + R_3 + ...$$

$$R = \Sigma \frac{l}{\mu_0 . \mu_{r2} A} \text{ AT/Wb.}$$

1.31. RELUCTANCE IN PARALLEL

When a number of reluctance are connected in parallel, then the total reluctance R is related to the constituent reluctance as

$$\frac{1}{R} = \frac{1}{R_1} + \frac{1}{R_2} + \frac{1}{R_3} + ...$$

$$= \frac{\mu_0 \mu_{r1} . A_1}{l_1} + \frac{\mu_0 \mu_{r2} A_2}{l_2} + \frac{\mu_0 \mu_{r3} . A_3}{l_3} + ...$$

$$= \mu_0 \left[\frac{\mu_{r1} A_1}{l_1} + \frac{\mu_{r2} A_2}{l_2} + \frac{\mu_{r3} A_3}{l_3} + ... \right]$$

$$R = \Sigma \mu_0 \frac{\mu_r A}{l} \text{ AT/Wb.}$$

1.32. COMPOSITE SERIES MAGNITUDE CIRCUITS

Consider a composite magnetic circuit, consisting of three pieces of different kinds of iron (or other magnetic material) as shown in Fig. 1.27. If l_1, l_2, l_3 be the mean lengths in metres of the component pieces. A_1, A_2 and A_3 their cross-sectional areas in sq. metres and μ_{r1} + μ_{r2} and μ_{r2} their relative permeabilities, by definition.

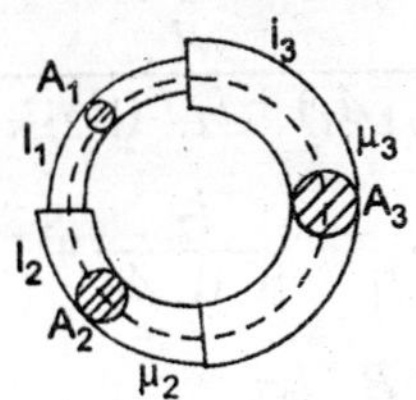

Fig. 1.27

$$R_1 = \frac{l_1}{\mu_0 \mu_{r1} . A_1}$$

$$R_1 = \frac{l_2}{\mu_0 \mu_{r2} . A_2}$$

and $$R_3 = \frac{l_3}{\mu_0 \mu_{r3} . A_3}$$

Total reluctance $= R = R_1 + R_2 + R_3$.

If a coil N turns is wound on the ring and it carries a current of I ampere, then m.m. of the coil is $N.I.$ and if ϕ is the flux, then

$$\therefore \quad \phi = \frac{m.m.f.}{\text{Total reluctance}} = \frac{N.I}{R_1 + R_2 + R_3}$$

$$= \frac{N.I}{\dfrac{l_1}{\mu_0 \mu_r A_1} + \dfrac{l_2}{\mu_0 \mu_{r2} A_2} + \dfrac{l_3}{\mu_0 \mu_{r3} A_3}}$$

or $$\phi = \frac{m.m.f.}{\sum \dfrac{l}{\mu_0 \mu_r A}}$$

1.33. AMPERE-TURNS [A.T.] FOR SINGLE MAGNETIC CIRCUIT

Usually problems necessitate determination of the number of ampere turns required to produce a given flux (ϕ) or flux density (B) in a magnetic circuit. In such cases, we see that

Flux $$\phi = \frac{m.m.f.}{\text{reluctance}} = \frac{N.I}{l / (\mu_0 \mu_r A)} \; Wb$$

i.e. $$NI = \frac{\phi.l}{\mu_0 \mu_r A} = \frac{B}{\mu_0 . \mu_r} \qquad [\because \phi = BA]$$

$$= H.l \; AT$$

1.34. AMPERE-TURNS [A.T.] FOR A COMPOSITE MAGNETIC CIRCUIT

Here $$R_{total} = \frac{l_1}{\mu_0 \mu_{r1} A_1} + \frac{l_2}{\mu_0 \mu_{r2} A_2}$$

$$\therefore \quad \phi = \frac{NI}{l_1/(\mu_0\mu_{r1}A_1) + l_2/(\mu_2\mu_{r2}A_2) + \ldots}$$

$$\therefore \quad NI = \phi\left[\frac{l_1}{\mu_0\mu_{r1}A_1} + \frac{l_2}{\mu_0\mu_r A_2} + \ldots\ldots\right]$$

$$= \frac{B_1 l_1}{\mu_0\mu_{r1}} + \frac{B_2 . l_2}{\mu_0\mu_{r2}} + \ldots\ldots. AT$$

where $B_1 = \phi/A_1$ and $B_2 = \phi/A_2$, etc.

or $N.I = H_1 l_1 + H_2 l_2 + \ldots\ldots AT.$

1.35. COMPOSITE CIRCUIT OF IRON RING AND AIR GAP

Fig. 1.28 shows an iron ring with a small radial air-gap. Practically all she flux, may be assumed to be going from the face to the other and through the air gap. In this way the length of the air gap may be assumed to be the same as that of the complete ring.

If A is the area of cross section and l_1 and l_2 are the lengths of the air gap and iron core, then

$$\text{Total reluctance} = \frac{l_1}{\mu_0\mu_{r1}A} + \frac{l_2}{\mu_0\mu_{r2}A}$$

Fig. 1.28

If a coil wound with N turns and it carries a current of I amperes, then

$$M.M.F. = N.I \text{ amperes}$$

$$\therefore \quad \phi = \frac{N.I}{l_1/(\mu_0\mu_{r1}A) + l_2/(\mu_0\mu_{r2}A)} \qquad \left(\because \phi = \frac{M.M.F.}{\text{Relcutance}}\right)$$

or

$$N.I = \frac{\phi}{\mu_0 A}\left[\frac{l_1}{\mu_{r1}} + \frac{l_2}{\mu_{r2}}\right]$$

$$= \frac{B}{\mu_0}\left[\frac{l_1}{\mu_{r1}} + \frac{l_2}{\mu_{r2}}\right] \qquad \left[\because B = \frac{\phi}{A}\right]$$

$$= \frac{B}{\mu_0\mu_{r1}} l_1 + \frac{B}{\mu_0\mu_{r2}} l_2$$

$$= H_1 l_1 + H_2 l_2 \, AT \qquad [\because H = B/\mu_0\mu_r]$$

1.36. MAGNETIC LEAKAGE

Magnetic circuits have an air path so that the magnetic flux may be utilized. This flux in the air gap is said to be useful flux. Some flux is always lost by leakage here. The flux which take the path outside the air gap, therefore, cannot be utilised, and considered as lost flux as the utility is concerned. This is called the

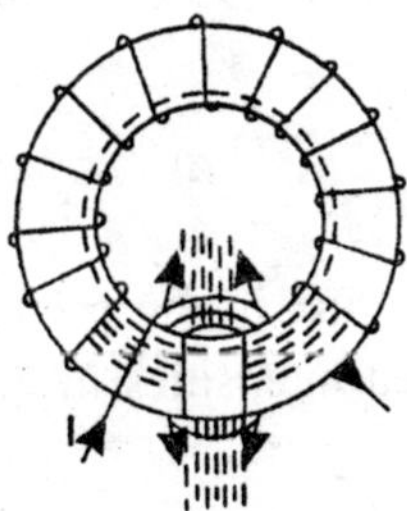

Fig. 1.29

leakage flux

Thus the total flux

$$\phi_{total} = \text{flux in the iron path } (\phi \text{ iron})$$

$$= \text{useful flux (air gap)} + \text{leakage flux } (\phi_l)$$

or

$$\phi_{iron} = \phi_{useful} + \phi_{leakage} + \phi_{total}$$

The ratio $\frac{\phi_{total}}{\phi_{useful}} = \lambda$ is called *co-efficient of magnetic leakage* or simply

Leakage factor. The value of 1 varies from 1.1 to 1.5. In other words, leakage flux may be from 10 to 50 percent of the total flux. This leakage of flux is waste of energy in electro-magnetic machines, and through it cannot be completely eliminated, it may be reduced by decreasing the air gap.

1.37. MAGNETIC CIRCUIT HAVING PARALLEL BRANCHES

Just as a single source of e.m.f. may cause the current to flow in a number of parallel circuits to which it is connected, similarly a single coil carrying current may supply m.m.f. to establish flux in several parallel branches of a magnetic circuit.

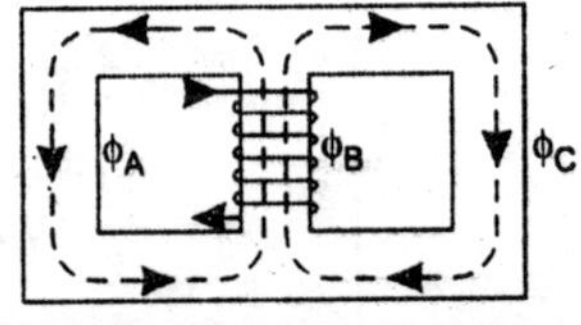

Fig. 1.30

A typical core is as shown and is used is shell type of transformers or choke coils, the winding being put on the middle portion, and the other portions serving as return paths for flux.

The flux ϕ_B must be the sum of the fluxes ϕ_A and, ϕ_C

or $$\phi_B = \phi_A + \phi_C.$$

If the two parallel branches are exactly alike, as in the above figure, a given m.m.f. produces the same flux in each circuit. If they are unlike, for example. when there lengths, their areas of cross-section of the materials of which they are made, are different, the fluxes in the branches are generally unequal.

In the two parallel branches are exactly similar then the flux ϕ_B is divided equally between them, *i.e.*,

$$\phi_A = \phi_C = \frac{1}{2}\phi_B$$

In order to establish a given amount of flux in the portion *B*, enough ampere turns have to be provided to give the required magnetic filled intensities in the central portion and in either portion according to the relations.

Total $$A.T. = H_B l_B + H_A l_A$$

or $$= H_A l_B + H_C l_C$$

1.38. COMPARISON BETWEEN ELECTRIC AND MAGNETIC CIRCUITS

Electric circuit	*Magnetic circuit*
(1)	(2)
Resistance Current Source of E M F Fig. 1.31A 1. Current $= \frac{e.m.f.}{\text{Resistance}}$ $I = \frac{E}{R}$ amperes.	Length of the magnetic path X-Section Area FLUX Fig. 1.31B 1. M.M.F. = Amp. turn Flux $= \frac{m.m.f.}{\text{Reluctance}}$ $\phi = \frac{NI}{R}$ Webers.

2. $R = \dfrac{\rho l}{\alpha}$ ohms Where ρ is the resistivity of the electric circuit	**2.** $R = \dfrac{1}{a\mu_0 . \mu_r}$ *AT*/weber or $= \dfrac{\sigma l}{a}$. where $\sigma = \dfrac{1}{\mu_0 . \mu_r}$ = reluctivity of the magnetic circuit.
3. $R \propto l$ $\propto \dfrac{1}{\alpha}$ Where a is the *X*. section of the conductor.	**3.** $R \propto i$ $\propto \dfrac{1}{a}$ *a* is the area of *X*-section of the magnetic path.
4. Greater the conductivity, *i.e.* $\dfrac{1}{\rho}$, lower is the resistance. Conductivity is the property of the conductor material to pass more current.	**4.** Higher is the permeability (relative), lower is the reluctance. Permeability is the property of the magnetic path to pass more flux.
5. $R = R_1 + R_2 + ...$ for series ckt.	**5.** $R = R_1 + R_2 + ...$
6. $\dfrac{1}{R} = \dfrac{1}{R_1} + \dfrac{1}{R_2} + ...$ for parallel ckt.	**6.** $\dfrac{1}{R} = \dfrac{1}{R_1} + \dfrac{1}{R_2} + ...$ for composite parallel circuit.
7. Current density = ampere/m^2.	**7.** Flux density $= \dfrac{\text{webers}}{\text{m}^2}$
8. Current ∝ *E.M.F.* **9.** Current $\propto \dfrac{1}{\text{Reluctance}}$.	**8.** Flux *m.m.f.* Flux $\propto \dfrac{1}{\text{Reluctance}}$.

Points of difference between the Magnetic and Electric Circuits.

Magnetic circuit		Electric circuit	
1.	**Flux** in a magnetic circuit does not actually flow.	1.	**Current** in an electric circuit does actually flow.
2.	**Permeability** does not vary greatly for different substances and there is hardly any material which can be called as an insulator to the magnetic flux	2.	**Electrical resistance** varies very largely for different materials so much so that some substances act as insulators and some as conductors.
3.	For a particular temperature the permeability (magnetic conductivity) depends upon the total flux.	3.	For a particular temperature, conductivity (resistance) is a constant and is independent of the strength of current.
4.	**Energy** is needed only to create the magnetic flux but not to maintain it.	4.	**Energy** is needed as long as the current flows.
5.	Flux can pass through air.	5.	Current would not flow through air till an air arc is struck.
6.	Residual flux persists after removal of *m.m.f.*	6.	The current is reduced to zero after removal of applied *e.m.f.*

1.39. MAGNETIC FIELD DUE TO CURRENT FLOWING IN TWO PARALLEL CONDUCTORS

Let us consider two long parallel current carrying conductors A and B, placed at a distance of 'd' metres apart in air (see Fig.1.32).

Let 'P' is the point on conductor B, the field strength, H at point 'P' due to current flowing in the conductor 'A' is given by

i.e. $$H = \frac{IA}{2\pi d} \text{ AT/m}$$

Hence flux density 'B' at point 'P' will be equal is

i.e. $$B = \mu_o \text{H} \qquad (\because \mu_r = 1 \text{ for air})$$

or $$B_B = \frac{\mu_o I_A}{2\pi d} \text{ Wb/m}^2$$

Similarly if we consider P point on conductor 'A' then flux density BA is given by :

i.e. $$B_A = \frac{\mu_o I_B}{2\pi d} \text{ Wb/m}^2$$

From the above diversion we come A know A conclusion that each current carrying conductor in lying in the magnetic field, provided by another are their when such situation arises then their exists a mutual force between them. This is because of the phenomenon that when a current carrying conductor is placed is a magnetic field, the conductor experiences a mechanical force. This force acts in a direction perpendicular to both, the direction of current f the field.

The magnitude of this mutual force between the two current carrying conductors in equal to :

i.e. $$F = B\,I\,l \text{ Newtons}$$

Hence mutual force between the two long parallel, current carrying conductor is equal to

i.e. $$F = \frac{\mu_o I_A}{2\pi d} \times I_B \times l \text{ Newtons}$$

$$= \frac{4\pi \times I_A \times I_B \times l}{2\pi d} \times 10^{-7}$$

or $$F = \frac{2 I_A I_B}{d} \times l \times 10^{-7} \text{ Newtons}$$

Therefore force per metre length is equal to,

i.e. $$\text{Force}/m = \frac{2 I_A I_B}{d} \times 10^{-7} \text{ Newtons}$$

Fig. 1.32

1.39.1. Nature of the Force

The nature of the force between two parallel conductors depends upon the direction of the current in the two conductors. The natural force between the conductors may be repulsive or attractive nature.

1.39.2. Force of Attraction

If the two parallel conductors carry currents in the same direction, then they will experience a force of attraction, see Fig. 1.33A.

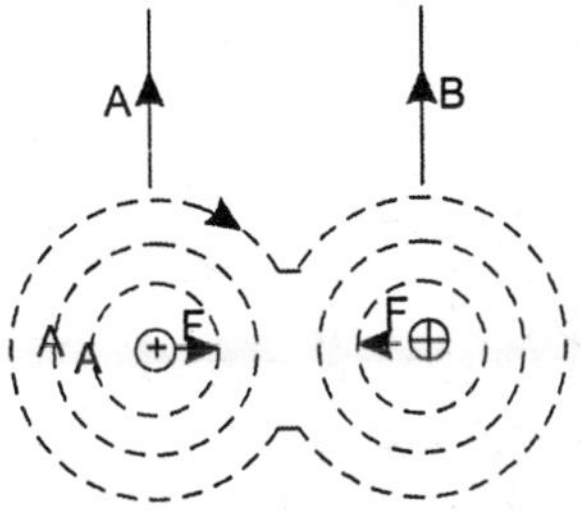

Fig. 1.33A

1.39.3. Force of Repulsion

If the two parallel conductors carry current in the opposite direction, then they will experience a force of repulsion, see Fig. 1.33B.

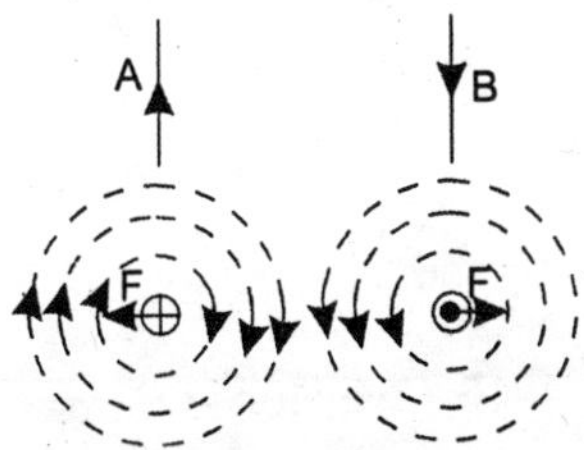

Fig. 1.33B

1.40. AMPERE'S RULE LAW AND UNIT OF CURRENT

From the earlier discussion we concluded that there exists a force between two parallel current carrying conductors, when placed in air. This is Ampere's further discovered that this force, as given in Article 1.39 is

(*i*) directly proportional to their length,

(*ii*) directly proportional to the product of the current in two conductors.

(*iii*) inversely proportional to the distance between them

so, $$F \propto \frac{I_1 I_2 l}{d}$$

or, $$F = K \frac{I_1 I_2 l}{d}$$

where I_1 and I_2 are the currents in the two conductors, in amperes,

l is the length of each conductor in metres and d is the distance between them in metres.

then, $$F = \frac{I_1 I_2 l}{d} \text{ Newtons}$$

where $$K = \frac{4\pi \times 10^{-7}}{2\pi} = 2 \times 10^{-7} \text{ H/m}$$

so $$F = \frac{2I_1 I_2 l}{d} \times 10^{-7} \text{ Newtons} \qquad \text{(as given earlier)}$$

Now, if $$I_1 = I_2 = 1 \text{ A}$$

$$l = 1 \text{ m and } d = 1 \text{ m}$$

then $$F = \frac{2 \times 1 \times 1 \times 1}{1} \times 10^{-7}$$

$$= 2 \times 10^{-7} \text{ Newtons.}$$

From this we define an Ampere, the unit of current, as follows :

"An ampere is that current which when flows through two parallel conductors, lying in air, one metre apart produces a force of 2×10^{-7} Newtons per metre length, between them".

Example 1.1. Two long straight parallel conductors have their centres, 2.5 cm apart. If each carries a current of 1000 amperes in the same direction, calculate the value of mutual force per metre run. It is one of attraction or of repulsion?

Solution. Given $d = 2.5$ cm or 2.5×10^{-2} m

$$I_A = I_B = 1000 \text{ A}$$

$$\mu_0 = 4\pi \times 10^{-7} \text{ and } \mu_r = 1$$

$$\therefore \quad \text{Force/m} = \frac{2I_A I_B}{d} \times 10^{-7} \text{ Newtons/m}$$

so force per metre

$$= \frac{2 \times 1000 \times 1000}{2.5 \times 10^{-2}} \times 10^{-7}$$

$= 8$ Newtons/m **Ans.**

It is a force of attraction, as they are carrying current in the same direction, see Fig. 1.34.

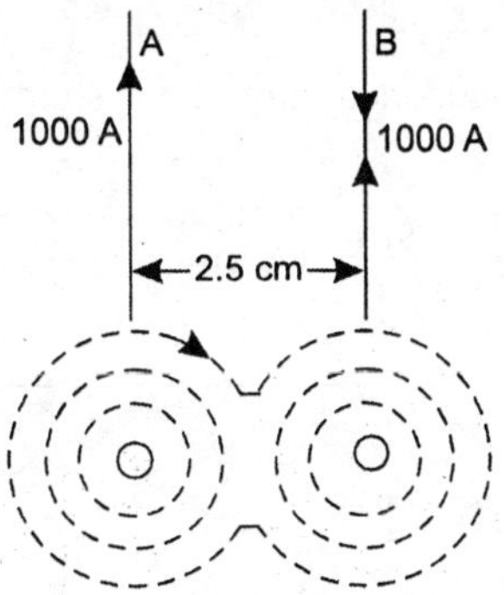

Fig. 1.34

Example 1.2. Two bus-bars each 1.5 *m* long are 0.125 *m* apart and are supported on insulators. If under short circuit conditions, current in each bus-bar becomes equal to 5000 A, then how much thrust does each insulator experiences?

Solution. Given, $l = 1.5\ m$, $d = 0.125$ m

$$I_A = I_B = 5000 \text{ A}$$

$$\mu_0 = 4\pi \times 10^{-7} \text{ and } \mu r = 1$$

Thrust or force between the two bus-bars

$$= \frac{2 I_A I_B l}{d} \times 10^{-7} \text{ Newton}$$

So thrust experienced by each bus-bar

$$= \frac{2 \times 5000 \times 5000 \times 1.5}{0.125}$$

$= 60$ Newtons

1.41. BIOT-SAVART LAW

*Biot-savart law is also known as Laplace's law of Ampere's law. This law can also be used to determine the magnetic field intensity H near a current carrying conductor. This law may be states as :

The **magnetic intensity dH** *at a point P (see Fig. 1.35) due to current I flowing through an extremely small element dl is*

(*i*) *directly proportional to current (I)*

(*ii*) *directly proportional to the length of element (dl)*

(*iii*) *directly proportional to sine of angle θ between the direction of current and the line joining the element dl to point i.e. sin θ*

(iv) *inversely proportional to the square of distance (x) of point P from the element dl.*

Mathematically ; $$dH \propto \frac{I\,dl \sin\theta}{x^2}$$

or $$dH = K\frac{I\,dl \sin\theta}{x^2}$$

where K is a constant. Its value depends upon the system of units used. In *SI* units, the value of K = $1/4\,\pi$

$$\therefore \qquad dH = \frac{I\,dl \sin\theta}{4\,\pi\,x^2} \text{ AT/m}$$

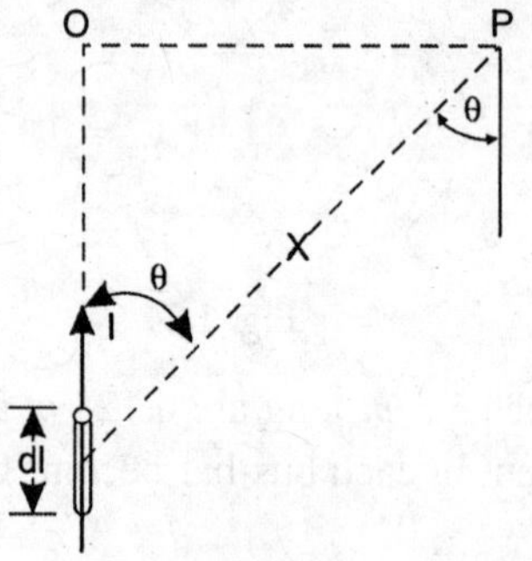

Fig. 1.35

The above expression represents the magnetic intensity produced at a given point P by an extremely small element of the conductor. The total magnetic intensity H can be integrating the above expression between the proper limits.

1.42. APPLICATION OF BIOT-SAVART SMALL LAW

In some cases where it is difficult to use simple work law, Biot-Savart law is invariably employed to determine magnetising force near a current carrying conductor arranged in different fassion. A few cases are discussed below :

1. Field strength around a long straight current carrying conductor

A small portion of a long conductor carrying current I ampere is shown in Fig. 1.36. Consider a point P at a distance of r metres from the conductor. According to Biot-Savart law, the field strength at point P due to a very small length dl of the conductor is given by the relation :

$$dH = \frac{I\,dl \sin\theta}{4\,\pi\,x^2} \qquad \text{...(i)}$$

From Fig. 1.36 ;

$$dl \sin\theta = x\,d\theta \text{ and } r = x \sin\theta$$

$$\therefore \qquad dH = \frac{I\,x\,d\theta}{4\pi x^2} = \frac{I\,d\theta}{4\pi x} = \frac{Id\theta}{4\pi r}\sin\theta$$

The field strength due to long conductor can be determined by integrating the exp. (*ii*) with in the limits 0 to π.

$$\therefore \qquad H = \int_0^\pi \frac{I \sin \theta}{4 \pi r} d\theta = \frac{1}{4 \pi r} \int_0^\pi \sin \theta \, d\theta$$

or $$H = \frac{I}{4\pi r} (-\cos \theta)_0^\pi = \frac{1}{4\pi r} \qquad [-(\cos \pi - \cos \theta)]$$

or $$= \frac{I}{2\pi r} \text{ AT/m}$$

Flux density, $$B = \mu_0 H = \frac{\mu_0 1}{2\pi r} T \qquad \text{... in air}$$

Fig. 1.36

2. Field strength at any point on the axis of a circular coil carrying current

Consider a single circular coil of radius r metres carrying current I amperes as shown in Fig. 1.37. P is a point on the axis of the coil at a distance of d metres from the centre of the coil where field strength is to be determined. Let dl_1 and dl_2 be the two extremely small lengths of coil diametrically opposite to each other. Then according to Biot-Savart law, field strength at P ;

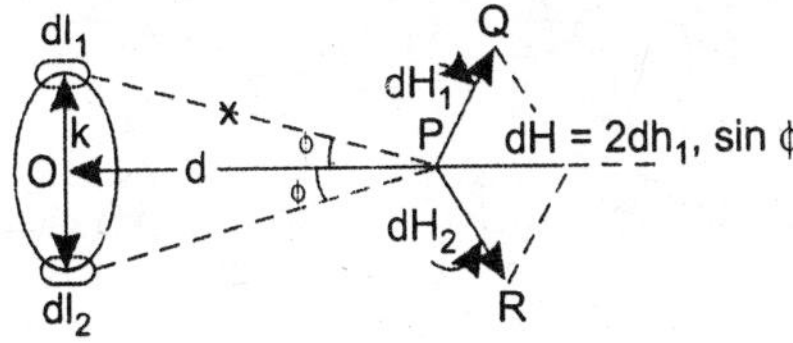

Fig. 1.37

due to $dl_1, dH_1 = I\, dl_1 / 4 \pi x^2$ (*acting along PQ*)

due to $dl_2, dH_2 = I\, dl_2 / 4 \pi x^2$ (*acting along PR*)

Their vertical components are cancelled as they are equal and opposite, whereas, their horizontal components are added to give dH as they are acting in the same direction.

$$\therefore \qquad dH = 2\, d H_1\, \phi \sin = I\, dl \sin \phi / 2 \pi x^2$$

To determine the field strength H at point P due to the whole coil, integrate exp. (*i*) in the limits from $l = 0$ to πr.

$$\therefore \quad H = \int_{l=0}^{l=\pi r} \frac{Idl \sin\phi}{2\pi x^2} = \frac{I \sin\phi}{2\pi x^2}[l]_0^{\pi r}$$

or $$H = \frac{I(r/x) \times \pi r}{2\pi x^2} = \frac{Ir^2}{2x^2} \qquad (\because \sin\phi = r/x)$$

or $$H = \frac{I r^2}{2(r^2 + d^2)^{3/2}} \qquad (\text{since } x = \sqrt{r^2 + d^2})$$

When the coil is of N turns ; $H = \dfrac{I r^2}{2(r^2 + d^2)^{3/2}}$ AT/m

When the field strength is to be determined at the centre of the coil put $d = 0$

$$\therefore \quad H = NI r^2 / 2r^3 \text{ AT/m}$$

3. Field strength at the centre of a solenoid carrying current

The cross sectional view of a current carrying solenoid is shown in Fig. 1.38. Let N be the number of turns, l the length of solenoid in metres and I amperes the current flowing through it. Considering a small length dx of the solenoid the ampere-turns of the small length will be $(NI/l)dx$.

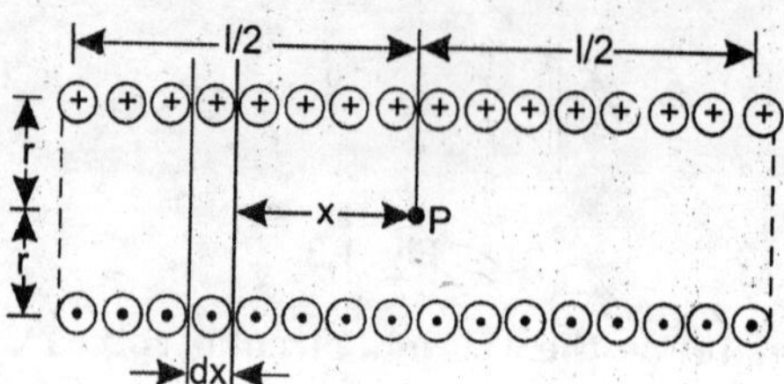

Fig. 1.38

The field strength at the centre (point P) of the solenoid due to this small length ;

$$dH = \frac{NI r^2 dx}{2(r^2 + x^2)^{3/2} \times l} \qquad ...(i)$$

(As derived earlier)

To determine the field strength at the centre of the solenoid due to whole solenoid integrate the exp. (i) in the limits $x = -l/2$ to $l/2$

$$\therefore \quad H = \int_{x=-l/2}^{x=l/2} \frac{NI r^2 dx}{2l(r^2 + x^2)^{3/2}} = \frac{NIr^2}{2l} \int_{x=-l/2}^{x=l/2} \frac{dx}{(r^2 + x^2)^{3/2}}$$

or $$H = \frac{NIr^2}{2l}\left(\frac{x}{r^2(r^2 + x^2)^{1/2}}\right)_{-l/2}^{l/2} = \frac{NIr^2}{2l} \times \frac{l}{r^2 (r^2 + l^2\, 4)\, 1/2}$$

or $$H = \frac{NI}{(4r^2 + l^2)^{1/2}} \text{ AT/m} \qquad ...(ii)$$

If the length of the solenoid is very large as compared to its radius, $4r^2$ can be neglected in the above expression.

$$\therefore \qquad H = \frac{NI}{l} \text{ AT/m}$$

Field intensity at one end of the solenoid.

$$H = NI21 \text{ AT/ht}$$

Magnetic Motive Force (m.m.f.). It is the force which produces magnetic circuit and corresponds to electro motive force (e.m.f.). It is expressed in ampere turns (A.T.).

Magnetising Force (H). Magnetising force or Magnetic field strength is defined as m.m.f. per unit length of path of the magnetic flux it measures the ability of magnetized body is produce magnetic induction. The unit of measurement is ampere turns per metre (AT/m).

EXERCISES

1. Define magnetic field. How is it represented.
   List the various properties of magnetic lines of flux.
2. Sketch the magnetic field for the following:
   (*a*) two adjacent south poles of bar magnets,
   (*b*) two adjacent north poles of bar magnets,
   (*c*) two adjacent bar magnets of opposite polarity.
3. Define the following terms along with their units:
   reluctance, permeance, mmf, magnetic field intensity.
4. (*a*) What is leakage flux? Define leakage factor.
   (*b*) Name the magnetic terms, along with their units, analogous to following electrical terms: Current, resistance, current density, resistivity.
5. Explain molecular theory of magnetism.
6. Explain (*a*) Ampere's law and (*b*) Biot-Savarat law.
7. Sketch the shape of magnetic flux lines around a current-carrying conductor. How can the direction of magnetic field be determined? Give two methods.
8. Derive expression for the magnetic field intensity and flux density due to a current-carrying straight conductor.
9. (*a*) Define the terms reluctance, mmf and flux. What are their units? How are these related?
   (*b*) What is a series magnetic circuit? If a series circuit is made up of three different magnetic materials, find the total mmf to be provided by the exciting coil. Hence, define Kirchhoff's mmf law.
10. For the magnetic circuit shown in Fig. 1.28, current 1 = 2A, number of turns N = 400, length of core l_2 = 60 cms, μ_r = 5000, flux density in core B_C = 1.2 T. For no magnetic leakage and fringing, calculate the air-gap lengths. [**Ans.** 0.718 mm]
11. Define a parallel magnetic circuit.
    Take a parallel magnetic circuit with an exciting coil. How can coil mmf be calculated for this circuit. Hence, define Kirchhoff's law.

12. Give the analogy between magnetic and electric circuits. State the units of the various terms involved.

13. Derive an expression for the field strength at the centre of a solenoid carrying current.

OBJECTIVE TYPE QUESTIONS

Tick the correct answer.

1. Unit of reluctance is
(*a*) ohm (*b*) Wb/amp (*c*) AT/Wb (*d*) Wb/AT

2. Tesla is the unit of
(*a*) flux (*b*) mmf (*c*) field strength (*d*) flux density

3. A magnet attracts
(*a*) nickel (*b*) iron
(*c*) copper (*d*) both iron and copper

4. In the figure shown here, emf induced, due to motion of the bar magnet is
(*a*) zero (*b*) cross in A, dot in B
(*c*) dot in A, cross in B (*d*) cross in both A and B

A
Motion
S N
B

5. The area of the face of a pole-shoe is 1.5 cm^2 and the total flux is 0.18 mWb. The flux density in the air gap, in Wb/m^2, is
(*a*) ohm (*b*) Wb/amp (*c*) AT/Wb (*d*) Wb/AT

6. Conductivity is analogous to
(*a*) permeability (*b*) retentivity (*c*) resistivity (*d*) reluctivity

7. In the figure shown here, emf induced, due to motion of the bar magnet is
(*a*) zero (*b*) cross in A, dot in B
(*c*) dot in A, cross in B (*d*) cross in both A and B

Motion
A B
S N

8. Two parallel conductors carry currents
(*a*) in the same direction, these repel each other,
(*b*) in the same direction, these attract each other,
(*c*) in opposite direction, these attract each other

9. Two parallel conductors carry equal current I in opposite directions. The force on each conductor is proportional to :
(*a*) I^2
(*b*) I
(*c*) distance between the conductors
(*d*) I^2 and also the distance between the two conductors.

Answers

1. (*c*)	**2.** (*d*)	**3.** (*b*)	**4.** (*b*)	**5.** (*c*)	**6.** (*a*)
7. (*a*)	**8.** (*b*)	**9.** (*a*)			

ELECTROMAGNETIC FORCE AND TORQUE

2.1. MAGNETIC HYSTERESIS

It is found that when a magnetic substances is placed in a strong magnetic field, it gets magnetised by magnetic induction. On removing the magnetic field or the magnetising force completely, considerable portion of induced magnetism is retained *i.e.* magnetic flux density does not get reduced to zero, when the magnetising force is completely removed; or, we can say that induced magnetic flux density lags behind the magnetising force. This phenomenon of retaining magnetism by the magnetic material or lagging of induced magnetic flux density behind the magnetising force is called magnetic hysteresis.

2.2. B-H CURVE

If a soft iron bar is placed within the magnetic field of a solenoid as shown in Fig. 2.1, it gets magnetised

Intensity of magnetic filed (H) produced by the solenoid, which is also called magnetising field intensity is directly proportional to current (I) through the solenoid. If it is increased gradually from zero to certain maximum value and the corresponding value of magnetic flux density induced in the soft iron bar is noted, then graph between B and H can be ploted. The graph between flux density (B) induced in the iron bar and intensity of magnetising field (H) is called B – H curve. Shape of B – H curve so obtained is shown in Fig 2.2.

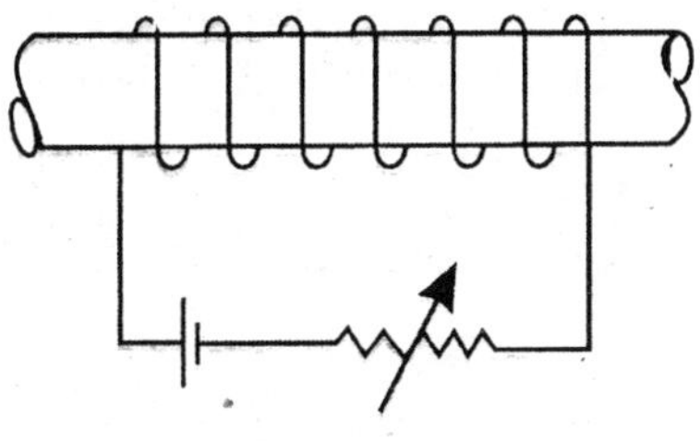

Fig. 2.1

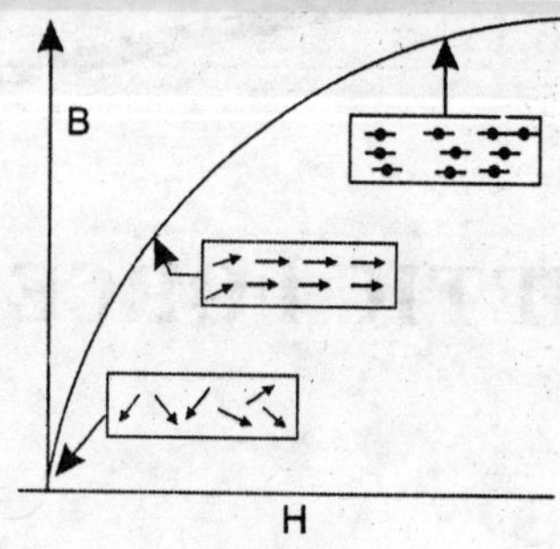

Fig. 2.2

From the shape of B-H curve, it is observed that, magnetic flux density B induced in the iron is zero when intensity of magnetising field (H) is zero. When H is increased, B increases. Flux density B does not increase linearly with H. Initially for small values of H, Flux density B increases more rapidly. Corresponding increase in B for further increments in H is less. If H is continuously increased in steps, it is found that the magnetic flux density B becomes constant at certain value of H, magnetic material is then said to be saturated.

Such behaviour of material can be explained on the basis of molecular theory of magnetism, according to which magnetic substances such as iron are composed of small paticles called moecules which themselves are small magnets. In demagnetised state these small magnets are distributed in different directions in random fashion and the resultant magnetism is zero When magnetizing force (H) is applied, these molecules orient themselves in the direction of magnetising force. When magnetising force is increased, the orientation of molecules in the direction density. At certain value of magnetising force (H), all the molecules get oriented in a particular direction, magnetic flux density then becomes constant and the magnetic material is then said to be saturated.

2.3. HYSTERESIS LOOP

Let an iron bar is magnetised by placing it in the magnetic field (H) of a solenoid. By increasing the current through the solenoid gradually, intensity of magnetising field H can be increased. If H is increased from its initial zero value gradually, to a certain maximum, till the iron bar gets saturated, the portion of magnetization curve OA is obtained as shown in Fig 2.3. If the intensity of magnetic field is now decreased gradually, it is found that the B-H curve for decreasing values of H does not follow the same path AO but follows AC. magnetic flux density B in the iron bar is not zero at zero magnetising field intensity. The value of B at zero intensity of magnetising field (= oc) measure retentionly of the material.

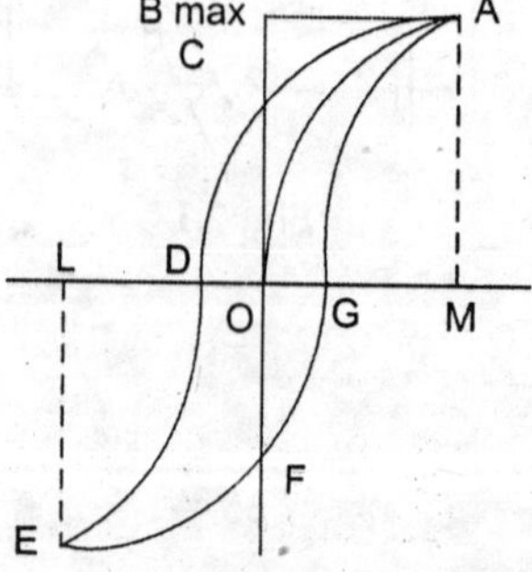

Fig. 2.3

To demagnetise the iron bar, the magnetising force in the reverse direction is to be applied. When H is reversed by reversing the current through the solenoid, the B – H curve follows the path CD and magnetic flux density B is reduced to zero at D. The value of H which is required to demagnetise the iron bar completely is called coercive force (Hc) and is a measure of coercivity of the material. If H is further increased in the negative direction, the iron bar gets magnetised in opposite direction and the B-H curve follows the path DE and again attains the state of magnetic saturation at E. By taking H back from its value corresponding to negative saturation (= OL) to its value for positive saturation (= OM), a similar curve EFGA is obtained.

It is found that magnetic flux density (B) always lag behind the intensity of magnetization (H). The two never attain zero value simultaneously. This property of lagging magnetic flux density (B) behind intensity of magnetization (H) is given the name hysteresis and the closed loop, ACDECGA obtained when the iron bar is subjected to one complete cycle of magnetization is called Hysteresis loop, An un-magnetised magnetic material if magnetised upto saturation in opposite direction, and then demagnetised again, is said to have gone through one cycle of magnetization.

2.4. HYSTERISIS LOSS

When a magnetic material is magnetised, then according to molecules theory, the molecules of the material get themselves oriented in the direction of magnetising force. An expenditure of energy is involved in this process. If the material has no retentivity, the energy spent in.

2.5. MAGNETIC HYSTERESIS

The lag or delay of a magnetic material known commonly as Magnetic Hysteresis, relates to the magnetization properties of a material by which it firstly becomes magnetised and then de-magnetised.

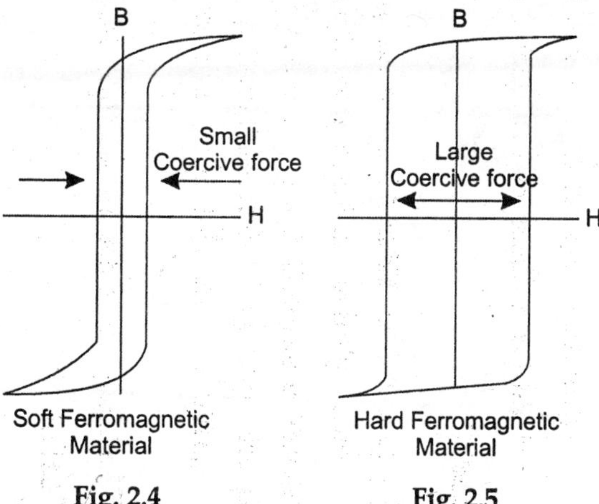

Fig. 2.4 Fig. 2.5

We know that the magnetic flux generated by an electromagnetic coil is the amount of magnetic field or lines of force produced within a given area that it is more commonly called "Flux Density". Given the symbol B with the unit of flux density being the Tesla. T.

We also know that the magnetic strength of an electromagnet depends upon the number of turns of the coil, the current flowing through the coil or the type of core material being used, and if we increase either the current or the number of turn we can increase the magnetic field strength, symbol H.

Previously, the relative permeability, symbol μ_r was defined as the ratio of the absolute permeability μ and the permeability of free space μ_0(a vacuum) and this was given as a constant. However, the relationship between the flux density, B and the magnetic field strength, H can be defined by the fact that the relative permeability, μ_r is not a constant but a function of the magnetic field intensity thereby giving magnetic flux density as: $B = \mu H$.

Then the magnetic flux density in the material will be increased by a larger factor as a result of its relative permeability for the material compared to the magnetic flux density in vacuum, μH and for an air-cored coil this relationship is given as:

$$B = \frac{\phi}{A} \text{ and } \frac{B}{H} = \mu$$

So for ferromagnetic materials the ratio of flux density to field strength (B/H) is not constant but varies with flux density. However, for air cored coils or any non-magnetic medium core such as woods or plastics, this ratio can be considered as a constant and this constant is known as μ_0 the permeability of free space, ($\mu_0 = 4.\pi.10^{-7}$ H/m).

By plotting values of flux density, (B) against the field strength, (H) we can produce a set of curves called **Magnetization Curves, Magnetic Hysteresis Curves** or more commonly **B-H Curves** for each type of core material used as shown below.

2.6. MAGNETIZATION OF B-H CURVE

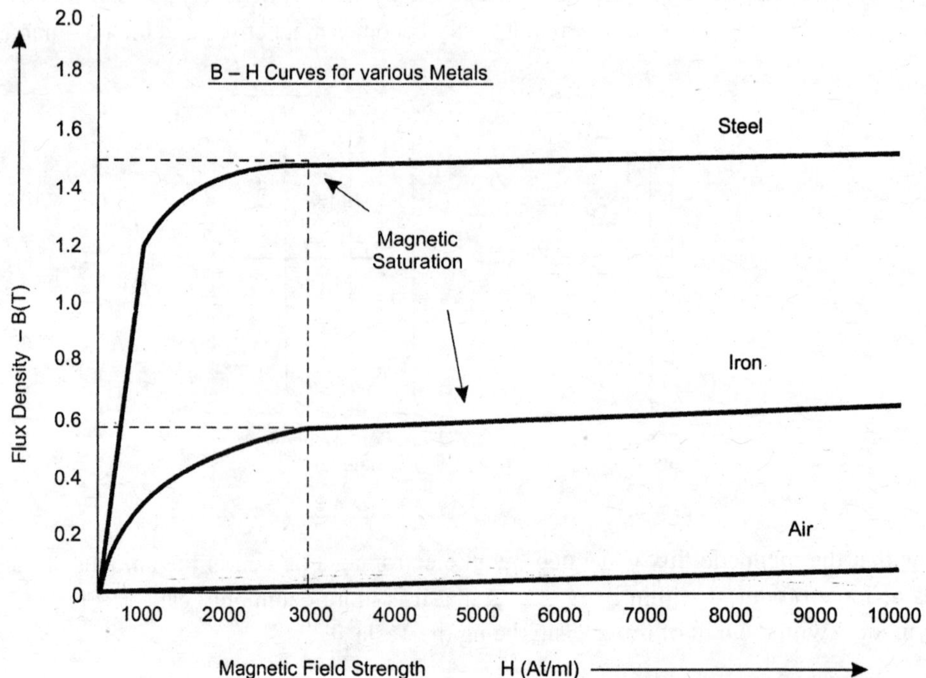

Fig. 2.6

The set of magnetization curves, M above represents an example of the relationship between B and H for soft-iron and steel cores but every type of core material will have its own set of magnetic hysteresis curves. You may notice that the flux density increases in proportion to the field strength until it reaches a certain value were it cannot increase any more becoming almost level and constant as the field strength continues to increase.

This is because there is a limit to the amount of flux density that can be generated by the core as all the domains in the iron are perfectly aligned. Any further increase will have no effect on the value of M, and the point on the graph where the flux density reaches its limit is called **Magnetic Saturation** also known as **Saturation of the Core** and in our simple example above the saturation point of the steel curve begins at about 3000 ampere-turns per metre.

Saturation occurs due to the random haphazard arrangement of the molecule structure within the core material changes as the tiny molecular magnets within the material become "lined-up". As the magnetic field strength, (H) increases these molecular magnets become more and more aligned until they reach perfect alignment producing maximum flux density and any increase in the magnetic field strength due to an increase in the electrical current flowing through the coil will have little or no effect.

Retentivity

Lets assume that we have an electromagnetic coil with a high filed strength due to the current flowing through it, and that the ferromagnetic core material has reached its saturation point, maximum flux density. If we now open a switch and remove the magnetising current flowing through the coil we would expect the magnetic field around the coil to disappear as the magnetic flux reduced to zero.

However, the magnetic flux does not completely disappear as the electromagnetic core material still retains some of its magnetism even when the current has stopped flowing in the coil. This ability for a coil to retain some of its magnetism with the core after the magnetization process has stopped is called **Retentivity** or remanence, while the amount of flux density still remaining in the core is called **Residual Magnetism,** B_R.

The reason for this that some of the tiny molecular magnets do not return to a completely random pattern and still point in the direction of the original magnetising field giving them a sort of "memory". Some ferromagnetic materials have a high retentivity (magnetically hard) making them excellent for producing permanent magnets.

While other ferromagnetic materials have low retentivity (magnetically soft) making them ideal for use in electromagnets, solenoids or relays. One way to reduce this residual flux density to zero is by reversing the direction of the current flowing through the coil, thereby making the value of H, the magnetic field strength negative. This effect is called a **Coercive Force,** H_C.

If this reverse current is increased further the flux density will also increase in the reverse direction until the ferromagnetic core reaches saturation again but in the reverse direction from before. Reducing the magnetising current, i one again to zero will produce a similar amount of residua magnetism but in the reverse direction.

Then by constantly changing the direction of the magnetising current through the coil form a positive direction to a negative direction, as would be the case in an AC supply, a Magnetic Hysteresis loop of the ferromagnetic core can be produced.

Magnetic Hysteresis Loop

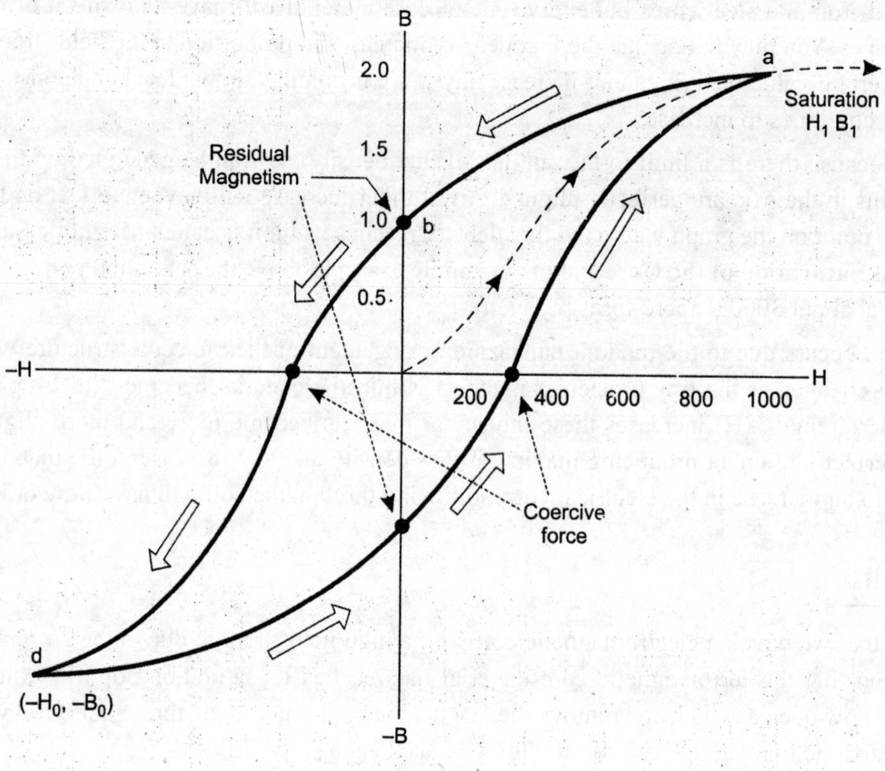

Fig. 2.6.1

The Magnetic Hysteresis loop above, shows the behaviour of a ferromagnetic core graphically as the relationship between B and H is non-linera. Starting with an unmagnetised core both B and H will be at zero, point - on the magnetization curve.

If the magnetisation current, i is increased in a positive direction to some value the magnetic field strength H increases linearly with i and the flux density B will also increase as shown by the curve from point 0 to point a as it heads towards saturation.

Now if the magnetising current in the coil is reduce to zero, the magnetic field circulating around the core also reduces to zero due to the residual magnetism present within the core and this is shown on the curve from point **a** to point **b**.

To reduce the flux density at point b to zero we need to reverse the current flowing through the coil. The magnetising force which must be applied to null the residual flux density is called a "Coercive Force". This coercive force reverses the magnetic field re-arranging the molecular magnets until the core becomes unmagnetised at point **c**.

An increase in this reverse current causes the core to be magnetised in the opposite direction and increasing the magnetization current further will caused the core to reach its saturation point but in the opposite direction, point **d** on the curve.

This point is symmetrical to point **b**. If the magnetising current is reduced again to zero the residual magnetism present in the core will be equal to the previous value but in reverse at point **e**.

Again reversing the magnetising current flowing through the coil this time into a positive direction will cause the magnetic flux to reach zero, point f on the curve and as before increasing the magnetization current further in a positive direction will cause the core the reach saturation at point **a**.

Then the B-H curve follows the path of **a-b-c-d-e-f-a** as the magnetising current flowing through the coil alternates between a positive and negative value such as the cycle of an AC voltage. This path is called a **Magnetic Hysteresis Loop.**

The effect of magnetic hysteresis shows that the magnetization process of a ferromagnetic cor and therefore the flux density depends on which part of the curve the ferromagnetic core is magnetised on as this depends upon the circuits past history giving the core a form of "memory". Then ferromagnetic materials have memory because they remain magnetised after the external magnetic field has been removed.

However, soft ferromagnetic materials such as iron or silicon steel have very narrow magnetic hysteresis loops resulting in very small amounts of residual magnetism making them ideal for use in relays, solenoids and transformers as they can be easily magnetised and demagnetised.

Since a coercive force must be applied to overcome this residual magnetism, work must be done in closing the hysteresis loop with the energy being used being dissipated as heat in the magnetic material. This heat is known as hysteresis loss, the amount of loss depends on the material's value of coercive force.

By adding additive's to the iron metal such as silicon, materials with a very small coercive force can be made that have a very narrow hysteresis loop. Materials with narrow hysteresis loop are easily magnetised and demagnetised and known as soft magnetic materials.

Magnetic Hysteresis Loops for Soft and Hard Materials

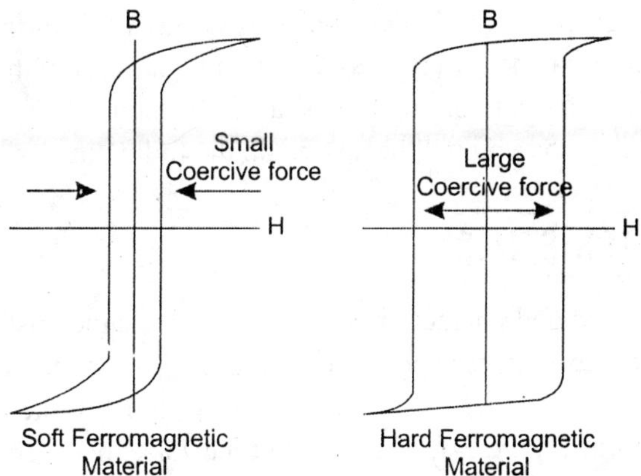

Fig. 2.6.2

Magnetic Hysteresis results in the dissipation of wasted energy in the form of heat with the energy wasted being in proportion to the area of the magnetic hysteresis loop. Hysteresis losses will always be a problem in AC transformers where the current is constantly changing direction and this the magnetic poles in the core will cause losses because they constantly reverse direction.

Rotating coils in DC machines will also incur hysteresis losses as they are alternately passing north the south magnetic poles. As said previously, the shape of the hysteresis loop depends upon the nature of the iron or steel sued and in the case of iron which is subjected to massive reversals of magnetism, for example transformer cores, it is important that the B-H hysteresis loop is as small as possible.

2.7. LINEAR AND NON LINEAR MAGNETIC CIRCUITS

Introduction

Before really starting, let us look at some magnetic circuits shown in the following figures.

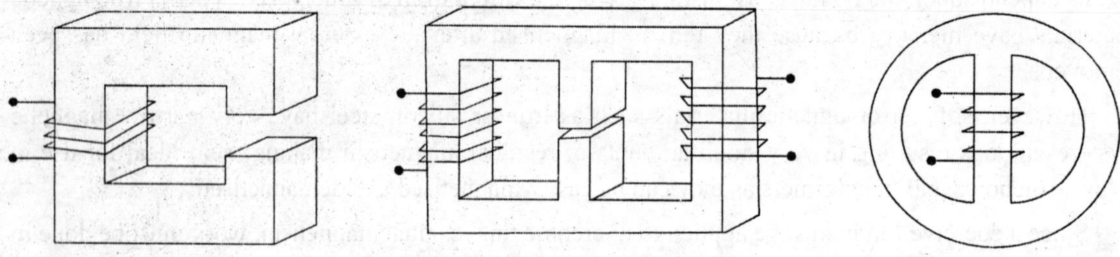

Fig. 2.7

All of them have a magnetic material of regular geometric shape called *core*. A coil having a number of turns (= *N*) of conducting material (say copper) are wound over the core. This coil is called the *exciting coil.* When no current flow through the coil, we don't expect any magnetic field or lines of forces to be present inside the core. However in presence of current in the coil, magnetic flux ϕ will be produced within the core. Is it not somewhat similar to an *electrical circuit* problem where a voltage (emp) is used in relation to producing flux in the core by applying mmf (= *Ni*). We shall see more similarities between an *electrical circuit* and a *magnetic circuit* in due course as we go along further. At this point you may just note that a magnetic circuit may be as simple as shown in figure 21.1 with a single core and a single core or as complex as having different core materials, air gap and multiple exciting coils as in figure 21.2. After going through this lesson you will be able to do the following.

2.8. B-H CHARACTERISTICS

A magnetic material is identified and characterized by its $B - H$ characteristic. In free space or in air the relationship between the two is linear and the constant of proportionality is the permeability μ_0. If *B* is plotted against *H*, it will be straight a line. However, for most of the materials the relationship is not linear and is as shown in Figure 2.7.1. A brief outline for experimental determination of B-H characteristic of a given material si given now. First of all a simple magnetic circuit (with the give material) is fabricated with known dimensions and number of turns. Make a circuit arrangement such as shown in Figure 2.7.1, to increase the current from 0 to some safe maximum value. Apart from ammeter reading one should record the amount of flux produced in the core by using a flux meter-let us not bother how this meter works!

Let,

Number of turns = N

Mean length of the flux path $= l$ in m.

Cross sectional area $=$ a in m^2

Reading of the ammeter $= I$ in A

Reading of the flux meter $= \phi$ in Wb

Now corresponding to this current, calculate $H = \frac{NI}{l}$ and $B = \frac{\phi}{\alpha}$ and tabulate them. Thus we have several pair of H & B values for different values of currents. Now by choosing H to be the x axis B to be the y axis and plotting the above values one gets a typical B-H curve as shown in Figure 21.7 below.

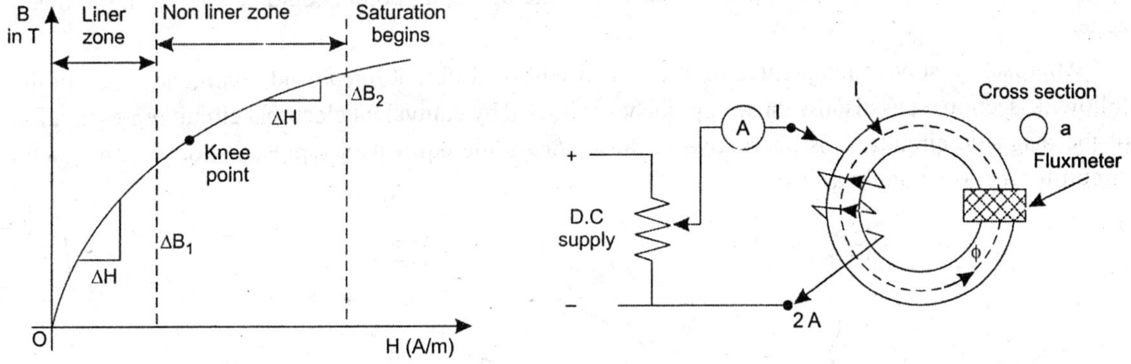

Fig. 2.7.1

2.8.1. Different Zones of B-H Characteristic

The initial portion of the B-H curve is nearly a straight lien and called *linear zone*. After this zone the curve gradually starts deviating from a straight line and enter into the nonlinear zone.

The slope of the curve $\frac{dB}{dH}$ starts gradually decreasing after the linear zone. A time comes when there is practically no increase in B in spite of the fact that H is further increased. The material is then said to be saturated. The rise i the value of B in the linear zone is much more than in the nonlinear or saturation zone for some ΔH. This can be ascertained for the B-H curve by noting $\Delta B_1 > \Delta B_2$ for same ΔH.

For this lesson, a brief qualitative explanation for the typical nature of the B-H curve is given. In a ferromagnetic material, very large number of tine magnets (*magnetic dipoles*) are present at the atomic/molecular level. The material however does not show any net magnetic property at macroscopic level due to random distribution of the dipoles and eventual cancellation of there effects. In presence of an external field *H*, these dipoles get aligned (resulting into more B) as the H *i.e.*, current in the exciting coil is increased. At the initial phases, increase in B is practically proportional to H. However rat of this alignment gets reduced after a definite value of H as number of randomly distributed dipoles decreases. This is reflected in the nonlinear zone of the Figure 2.7.1. Obviously if we further increases H, a time will come when almost all the dipoles will get aligned. Under such circumstanced we should not expect any rise in B even if H is increased and the core is said to be saturated. At the saturation zone, the characteristic becomes almost parallel to the H axis.

Different materials will have different B-H curves and if the characteristics are plotted on same graph paper, one can readily decides which of them is better than the other. Referring to Figure 2.8.1, one can easily conclude that material-3 is better over two as flux produced in material-3 is the highest for same applied field H.

From the above discussion it can be said that there is no point in operating a magnetic circuit deep into saturation zone as because large exciting current will put extra a overhead on the sources supplying power to the coil. Also any desire to increase B by even a small amount in this zone will call for large increase in the value of the current. In case of transformers and rotating machines operating point is chosen close to the *knee point* of the B-H characteristic in order to use the magnetic material to its true potential. To design a constant value of *inductance*, the operating point should be chosen in the linear zone.

Approach to solve a magnetic circuit problem will be different *linear* and *nonlinear* cases. In the following section let us discuss those approaches followed by equivalent electrical circuit representation of the magnetic circuits. It is instructive to draw *always* the equivalent representation of a magnetic circuit for the following reasons:

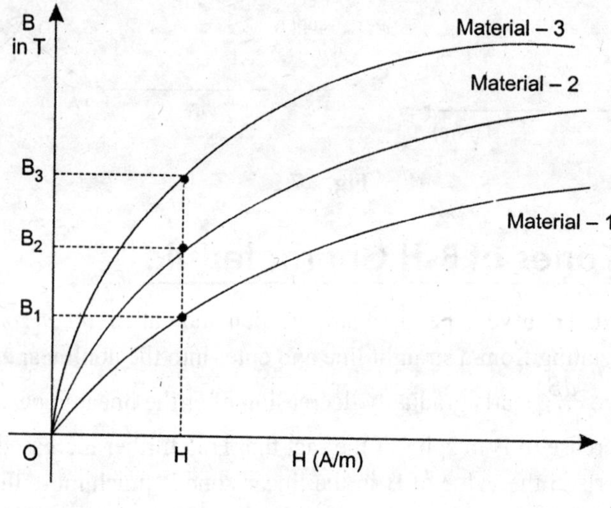

Fig. 2.8.1

(*a*) It helps us to visualize the problem in term of more familiar series and series and series parallel

(*b*) We can apply with ease KFL (Kirchhoff 's flux law) at the junctions in the same manner as we apply KCL in circuit analysis.

(*c*) Similar to KVL equations, we can apply *mmf* balance equations in different closed paths of the magnetic circuit.

(*d*) Above all, with this circuit before hand, one can decide upon the strategy of solving the problem.

2.9. ANALYSIS OF SERIES MAGNETIC CIRCUIT

Consider first a simple magnetic circuit, shown in Figure 2.9 with a single core material having uniform cross sectional area A and mean length of flux path l. Reluctance offered to the flow of flux is R . The corresponding electrical representation is rather simple. Due to the fact that $NI = \phi R = Hl$, the equivalent electrical circuit is also drawn beside the magnetic circuit. Polarity of mmf is decided on the basis of the direction of the flux which is clockwise inside the core in this case. Although in the actual magnetic circuit there is no physical connection of the winding and the core, in the electrical circuit representation mmf and reluctance are shown to be connected. One should not feel disturbed by this as because the relationship between mmf and flux prompted us to draw an electrical equivalent to facilitate easier calculation and meat visualization of the actual problem.

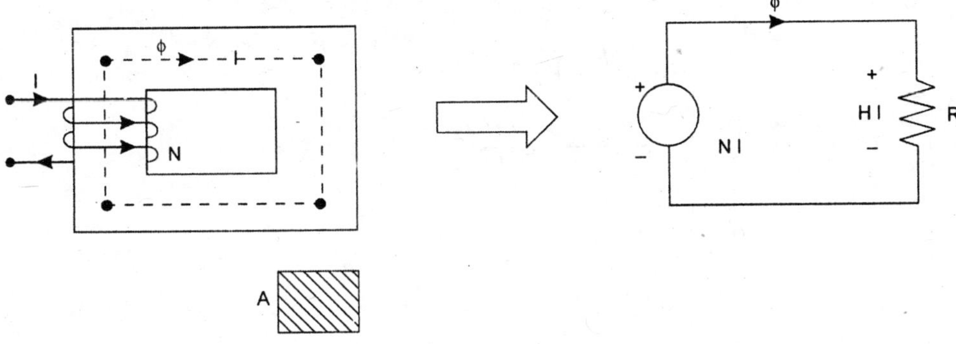

Fig. 2.9

Let us now consider another magnetic circuit which is similar to the earlier one but has a *small air* gap of length l_g as shown in Figure 2.9.1 and not that it is a series circuit involving tow medius, namely (i) iron and (ii) air. It is a series circuit because same flux () has to flow through the mediums. Hence total reluctance will be the sum of reluctances of iron and air (R = Ri + Rair).

For this circuit basic equations can be developed as follows:

Let,

Number of turns = N

Exciting current i = I in A

Mean length of the flux path through iron = l_i in m

Lenth of the flux path through air = l_g in m

Cross sectional area = A in m^2

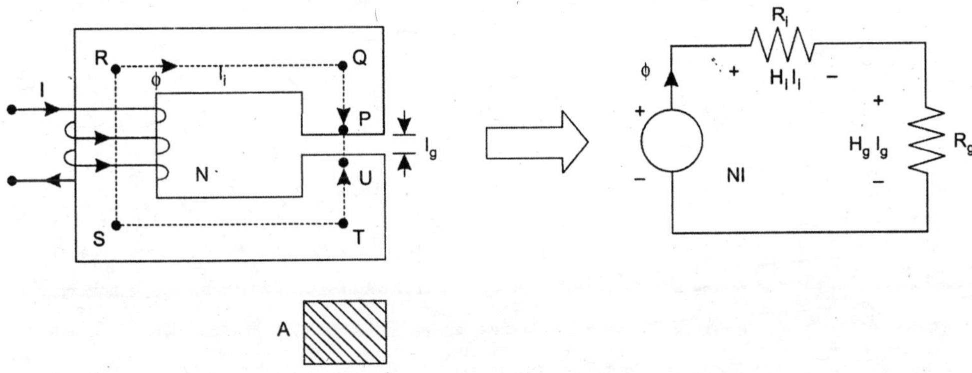

Fig. 2.9.1

H required for iron, Hi $= \frac{B}{\mu_o \mu_i} \Re$

H required for air, Hg $= \frac{B}{\mu o}$

$\because$ Ampere circuital law gives NI = Hili + Hglg

$$= \frac{B}{\mu_o \mu_i} li + \frac{B}{\mu_o} lg$$

$$= \frac{\frac{\phi}{A}}{\mu_o \mu_i} l_i + \frac{\frac{\phi}{A}}{\mu_o} l_g$$

$$= \phi \frac{I}{\mu_o \mu_i} \frac{l_i}{A} + \phi \frac{I}{\mu_o} \frac{l_g}{A}$$

$$NI = \phi \Re_i + \phi \Re_g$$

$$NI = \phi (\Re_i + \Re_g)$$

$$\text{or, } \phi = \frac{NI}{(\Re_i + \Re_g)}$$

So as expected these two reluctances are connected in series. In fact, for series magnetic circuit having different reluctance segments, total reluctance will be the sum of individual reluctances.

2.10. ANALYSIS OF SERIES-PARALLEL MAGNETIC CIRCUIT

We now take up the following magnetic circuit (Figure 2.10) which appears to be not so straight forward as the previous cases. As a first step to solve this circuit, we would like to draw its equivalent electrical representation. Vertical links of the core are called *limbs* and the horizontal links are called *yoke* of the magnetic circuit. In the figure PU, QT and RS are the limbs whereas PQ, QR, UT and TS are the yokes. It is customary to fix up the corner points P, Q, R etc. from the given physical dimensions, joining of which will give you the mean length of the flux paths.

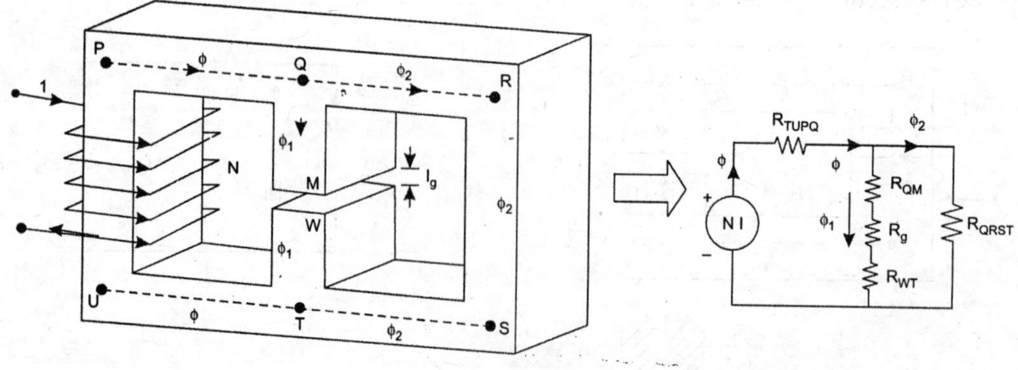

Fig. 2.10

If the coil carries a current I in the direction shown, flux , produced in the first limb will be in the upward direction. Same ϕ is constrained to move along the yoke PQ. At point Q, two parallel paths are available to ϕ for its onwards journey namely (*i*) the central limb QT and (*ii*) the yoke QR. In other words, ϕ will be divided into two components ϕ_1 and ϕ_2 as shown with the obvious condition $\phi = \phi_1 + \phi_2$. The relative values of these components will be decided by respective reluctances of the paths. ϕ_1 and ϕ_2 once again recombine at point T and completes the path. Now in the path TUPQ flux ϕ is same, it is made of same , material and has same cross sectional area A, Then its reluctance $\Re_{TU\,PQ} \propto \frac{l_{TU\,PQ}}{A}$. In the central limb, flux is same (ϕ_1), however it encounters two materials, one is iron (QM and WT) and the other is a small air gap (MW). The reluctance of the air gap $\Re g = \frac{l_g}{\mu_0 A}$. The two reluctances $\Re_{QM}$ and $\Re_{WT}$ of the magnetic material may however be combined into a single reluctance as $\Re_1 = \Re_{QM} + R_{WT}$. The portion of the magnetic circuit which caries flux $\phi 2$ can be represented by a single reluctance $\Re_{QRST}$ $\propto \frac{l_{QRST}}{A}$. Instead of carrying on with long suffixes let us call $\Re_{QRST}$ to be $\Re_2$. To write down the basic equations let us redraw the electrical equivalence of the above magnetic circuit below (Figure 2.10.1):

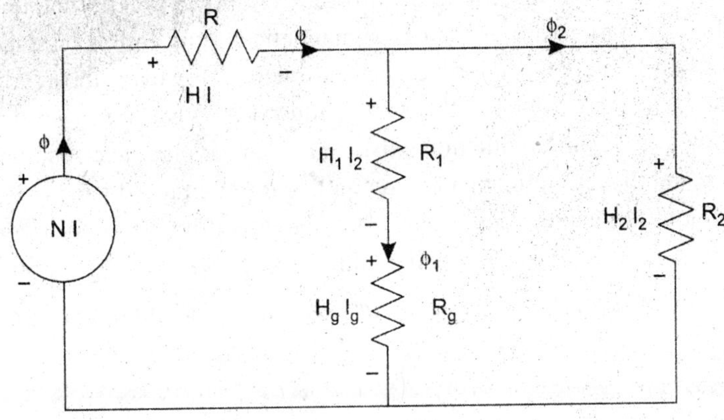

Fig. 2.10.1

2.10.1. Important equations

The various equations which will hold good are written below:

$$\begin{aligned} \phi &= \phi_1 + \phi_2 \\ NI &= Hl + H_1 l_1 + H_g l_g = \Re\phi + (\Re_1 + \Re_g)\phi_1 \text{ balance in loop 1} \\ (\Re_1 + \Re_g)\phi_1 &= \Re_2\phi_2 \text{ mmf balance in loop 2} \\ \mathrm{H}_1 l_1 + \mathrm{H}_g l_g &= \mathrm{H}_2 l_2 \text{ mmf balance in loop 2} \\ NI &= \mathrm{H}l + H_2 l_2 \text{ mmf balance in the outer loop.} \end{aligned}$$

2.11. GENERAL DISCUSSION ON SOLVING PROBLEMS

As pointed out earlier, the approach to solve a magnetic circuit problem is primarily guided by the fact that whether the magnetic circuit is *linear* or *non linear*. If it is linear then the material is fully characterized by its relative permeability μ_r and the reluctance which remains constant (independent of the operating point) can be easily calculated and shown in the equivalent circuit. In other words, for liner electric circuits. Depending on situation, one can invoke any convenient method of solving electrical circuit problem here as well.

Let us go through the following solved linear magnetic circuit numerical problem to understand the steps involved.

However, in case of non linearity (which is more common in practice), one has no other alternative but to refer to *graphical solution involving* B-H characteristic of them material or materials. The reason being, the material can not be characterized by a unique μ_r of different operating points as $\frac{dB}{dH}$ is a function of the operating point. The values of B's (B, B_1, B_2) in the three limbs are expected to be different in the magnetic circuit of Figure 2.10.1 Instead of looking for relative permeabilities, it will be much easier to read the corresponding H value (H, H_1, H_2) from the B-H curve of the material and calculate the respective mmf drops as Hl, Hl_1 and Hl_2. Generally the pair of B-H values are given in tabular form for some fixed number of points. One has to plot these points on a simple graph paper and join them by a smooth curve to get the characteristic and use it for problem solving.

In practical situations we would like to know how much mmf (NI) is needed in order to establish a definite amount of flux at a particular portion of the magnetic circuit. In this lesson, we have primarily discussed the methods to be adopted to solve such problems. However, the reverse problem *i.e.*, if the mmf (NI) is known how to calculate the flux produced at a particular portion of the magnetic circuit is somewhat involved. Similar situation exists in non linear electric circuit analysis as well with supply voltage known and the circuit elements are non linear in nature. In such cases, one has to either adopt *numerical* techniques or solve the problem graphically by drawing appropriate load lines. In this introductory lesson of magnetic circuit, we shall confine ourselves in solving problem of the first kind.

Let us go through the following solved non *linear magnetic circuit* numerical problem to understand the steps involved.

2.11.1. Example

Example 2.1: In the magnetic circuit detailed in Figure 2.11.1 with all dimensions in mm, calculate the required current to be passed in the coil having 200 turns in order to establish a flux of 1.28 mWb in the *air gap*. Neglect fringing effect and leakage flux. The B-H curve of the material is given in Figure 2.11.2. Permeability of air may be takne as, $\mu_0 = 4\pi \times 10^{-7}$ H/m

Solution:

Step 1 First draw the simplified diagram of the given magnetic circuit along with the equivalent circuit as shown in Figure 2.11.3.

Step 2 To calculate *mean lengths* of various parts, mark the centre points of various limbs and yokes with small bullets.

Step 3 Name the different portions which will carry same flux as 1, 2 and 3. For example, the path CFED is in fact path 1 where flux ϕ_1 will remain. Similarly the path DC (path 2) will carry same flux ϕ_2 and path CBAD (path 3) will carry same flux ϕ_3.

Step 4 Calculation of mmf required for the path 2:

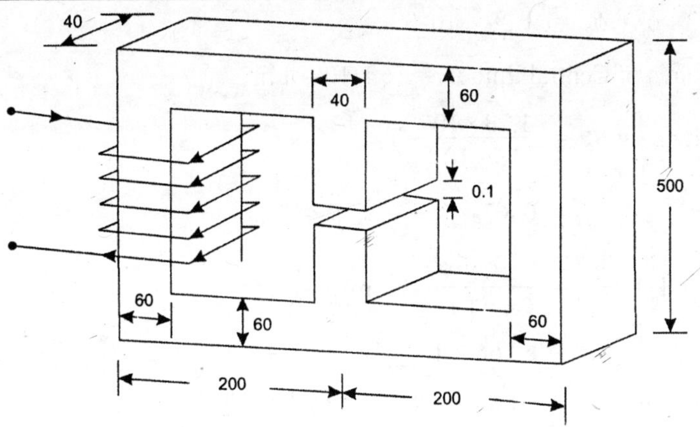

Fig. 2.11.1

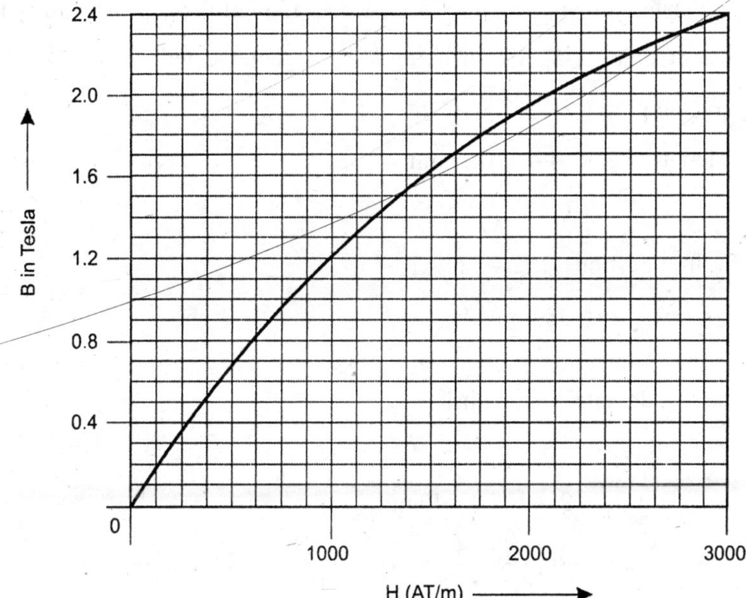

Fig. 2.11.2

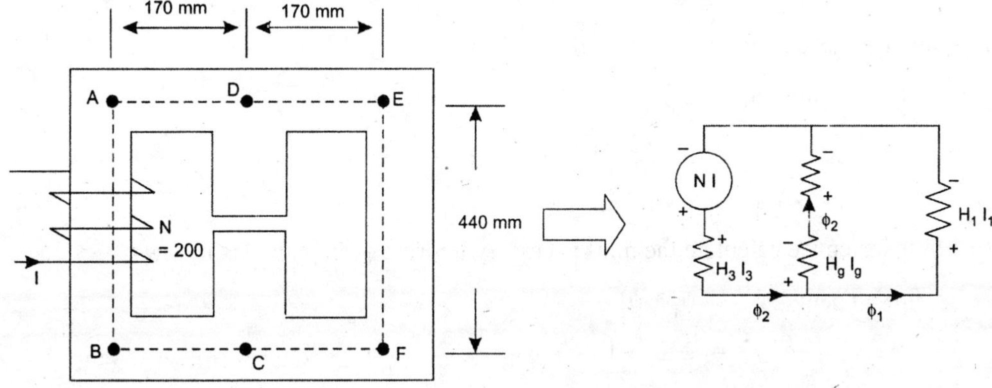

Fig. 2.11.3

$$\phi_g = \phi_2 = 1.28 \times 10–3$$

Cross sectional area of Central limb $A_2 = 16 \times 10 - 4\ m^2$

$$\text{Flux density } B_g = B_2 = \frac{1.28 \times 10^{-3}}{16 \times 10^{-4}}\ T$$

$$= 0.8\ T$$

$$\therefore \quad H_g = \frac{B_g}{\mu_0} = \frac{0.8}{4\pi \times 10^{-7}}\ AT/m$$

$$= 63.66 \times 10^4\ AT/m$$

mmf required for gap $H_g l_g = 63.66 \times 10^4 \times 1 \times 10^{-4}$ AT

$$= 63.66\ AT$$

Now we must calculate the mmf required in the iron potion of the central limb as follows:

flux density, $B_2 = 0.8$ T $\because$ fringing & leakage neglected

corresponding H from graph, $H_2 \approx 500$ AT/m

Mean iron length, $l_2 = (440 - 0.1)$ mm

$$\approx 0.44\ m$$

mmf required for iron portion, $H_2 l_2 = 220$ AT

$$mmf_{CD} = 283.66\ AT.$$

Step 5 Due to parallel connection, mmf acting across path 1 is same as mmf acting across path 2 Our intention here, will be to calculate ϕ_1 in path 1

mean length of the path, $l_1 = l_{DE} + l_{EF} + l_{FC}$

$$= 2 \times 170 + 440\ mm$$

$$= 0.78\ m$$

$$\because \quad H1 = \frac{283.66}{0.78}$$

$$= 363.67\ AT/m$$

corresponding flux density from graph, $B_1 \approx 0.39$ T

$$\therefore \quad \text{flux, } \phi_1 = B_1 A_1$$

$$= 0.39 \times 24 \times 10^{-4}\ Wb$$

$$\therefore \quad \phi_1 = 0.94 \times 10^{-3}\ Wb$$

Step 6 In this step we calculate the mmf necessary to drive ϕ_3 in path 3 as follows.

flux in path 3, $\phi_3 = \phi_1 + \phi_2$

$$= 2.22 \times 10^{-3}\ Wb$$

$$\text{flux density, } B_3 = \frac{\phi_3}{A_3}$$

$$= \frac{2.22 \times 10^{-3}}{24 \times 10^{-4}}$$

$$\therefore B_3 = 0.925 \text{ T}$$

Corresponding H from graph, $H_3 \approx 562.5$ AT/m

$$\text{mean length of path3, } l_3 = 2 \times 170 + 440 \text{ mm}$$

$$= 0.78 \text{ m}$$

$$\text{total mmf required for path 3} = H_3 l_3$$

$$= 562.5 \times 0.78 \text{ AT}$$

$$= 438.7 \text{ AT}$$

$\therefore$ mmf to be supplied by the coil, $NI = 283.66 + 438.7$ AT

$$\text{or } 200I = 722.36 \text{ AT}$$

$$\therefore \text{exciting current needed, } I = \frac{722.36}{200} \text{ A}$$

$$= 3.61 \text{ A}$$

Straightening the molecules can be recovered by reducing the magnetising force (H) to zero, just as the energy stored up in a spring, can be recovered by allowing the spring to release it energy by driving some kind of load. If the magnetic material has high retentivity, all the energy expended originally for straightening the molecules can be not be recovered when the magnetising force H is reduced to zero.

If a specimen of magnetic material is subjected to alternate magnetic field, the molecules of the specimen orient themselves in one direction and then in other direction. In this process continuous expenditure of energy is involved which appear in the form of heat and sound. The noise produced is called the hysteresis noise and the energy spent when a piece of magnetic material is subjected to alternate magnetic field is called the hysteresis loss.

Hysteresis loss per cycle of magnetization is proportional to area of the hysterisis loop. Hysterisis loss is common in all electrical machine which are taken through rapid magnetic cycle. Therefore it is necessary to calculate this loss in these machines. Hysterisis loss can be calculated by using steinmetz formula given by

$$W = n\, B_{max} \text{ joules / m}^3 \text{ / cycle}$$

Where n is a constant depending upon the type of material used and is called steinmez hysteresis co-efficient. Approximate value of steinmetz hysteresis coefficient for some magnetic materials is given below.

soft Iron	502
cast steal	753
cast Iron	2763
silicon steal	191

Hysterisis loss in electrical machines should be kept minimum. Therefore materials having low area of hysterisis loop and high permeability are used in these machines. Most of machines use silicon steel.

Magnetic materials having high retentivity or high hystrisis loss also find applications in certain machines, such.as hysterisis motors.

2.12. ENERGY STORED IN MAGNETIC FIELD

In an electric circuit, energy is required to maintain the flow of current through it but in magnetic circuit, energy is required only to create magnetic flux in it. No energy is required to maintain it. For example when energy is supplied to exciting coils of an electromagnet, a part of it si utilized to create flux and is stored in the magnetic field created by it, which can be recovered later on. Some of the energy suppled is wasted in the from of heat in the resistance of the coil.

To find out expression for energy stored in the magnetic field, consider an inductive coil of inductance L. When current through this inductive coil is changed gradually from zero to certain maximum value I, then every change of current through coil is opposed by the self induced emf produced due to this change of current. Therefore work is to be done in order to overcome this opposition which is stored in the magnetic field of the coil and can be recovered later on when the field collapse.

if at any instant

$$i = \text{Current through coil}$$

$$e = \text{Induced emf in the coil} = L\frac{di}{dt}$$

$$dw = \text{Work done in order to overcome this opposition in time dt}$$

$$= e\,i\,dt$$

$$= i\,.\,L\frac{di}{dt}\,.\,dt$$

$$= L\,i\,di$$

$$W = \text{Total work done in establishing the steady current I}$$

$$= \int_0^w dw$$

$$= \int_0^I L\,i\,di$$

$$= L\left|\frac{i^2}{2}\right|_0^I$$

$$= \frac{1}{2}LI^2$$

This work done is stored in the magnetic field of the coil as electromagnetic energy.

$$\therefore \text{Energy stored} = \frac{1}{2}LI^2$$

The expression for energy stored in the magnetic field can also be obtained in terms of magnetic flux density B and intensity of magnetic field or magnetization force H. To get such an expression consider a solenoid of cross sectional area A square meters and of length l meters having N turns. If whole of the energy supplied is stored in the magnetic field, then intensity of magnetic field inside the solenoid is

$$H = \frac{N.I}{l}$$

$$\text{And Flux } \varphi = \frac{mmf}{\text{Reluctance}}$$

$$= \frac{N.I}{t/\mu A}$$

2.13. ENERGY STORED IN MAGNETIC FIELD

Co-energy

Co-energy is a non-physical quantity useful for theoretical analysis of system storing and transforming energy. Co-energy is expressed in the same units as energy and is especially useful for calculations of magnetic forces and torque in rotating machines.

The co-energy E (or W) is zero for systems incapable of storing energy. All energy delivered to such system is dissipated or used otherwise - for instance energy of electric current dissipated in an ideal resistor. But in systems storing energy it is also possible to define the co-energy.

In electromagnetic systems the concept of co-energy arises from mathematical analysis of the given circuit, from the viewpoint of thermodynamics and statistical mechanics. It can be mathematically shown that the co-energy for a system containing magnetic and/or dielectric materials. [8)] This is because energy can be stored in magnetic or electrostatic field.

Co-energy can be used for computation of mechanical forces in electromagnetic systems with current-carrying coils or permanent magnets.

Mechanical analogy

Similar energy-co-energy analysis can be carried out for other systems capable of storing energy, for instance in elastic deformation of a mechanical spring. In a mechanical system it is not possible to apply a force instantaneously to a spring, because this would required an instantaneous deformation of such spring, which in turn would require infinite velocity which is not possible.

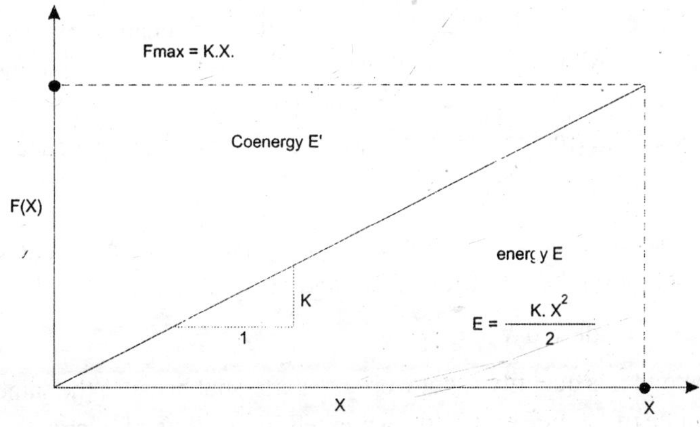

Fig. 2.13

Fig. 2.13. is illustration of the concept of co-energy in a mechanical liner spring.

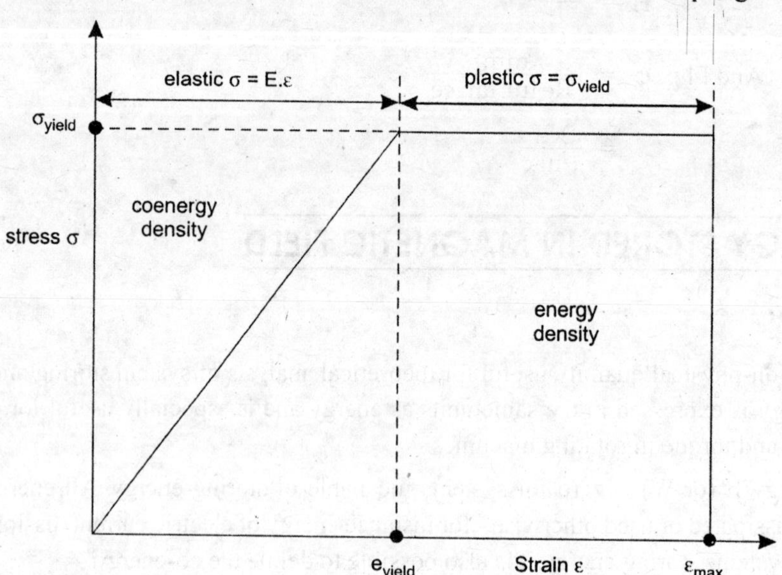

Fig. 2.13.1

Fig. 2.13.1. is illustration of the concept of co-energy in a mechanical liner spring.

Work W hence also energy E stored in the spring is defined as the product of force F and displacement x of the spring (X - total deflection of the spring):

$$\text{Espring} = \int_0^X F(x).dx \qquad ...(2.1)$$

However, for an ideal linear springs the force F is directly proportional to the displacement XX through the spring constant K, so that:

$$\text{Espring}(x) = k.x \ \ N-2)$$

Therefore, eqn 2.1 can be rewritten as:

$$\text{Espring} = \int_0^x F(x)\,dx = \frac{k.x^2}{2} \qquad ...(2.2)$$

The meaning of the integral eqn (2.1) is that for infinitesimal change of displacement the force can be assumed constant. According to the SI definition, "the joule is the work done when the point of application of 1 newton moves a distance of 1 meter in the direction of the force". Therefore, a product of constant force and some displacement is some amount of work or energy, hence:

$$F.dx = dW = dE \qquad ...(2.3)$$

However, similar calculation can be performed by fixing the displacement and changing the force. But according to the SI definition the product of force and no displacement is not work:

$$x.dF \neq dW \qquad ...(2.4)$$

From physical viewpoint this quantity is not work or energy, but because the same units are involved in the calculations the value of **co-energy** is also expressed in the units of energy.

The concept of co-energy is also useful for non-linear systems, but in such case the energy and co-energy can be different. However, knowing one allows calculation of the other one by subtraction of the value from the rectangular area.

Fig. 2.13.1 illustrates a stress-strain curve for a non-linear material approximated with an ideal elastic and ideal plastic behaviour. The density of co-energy is proportional to the energy which is stored and can be returned from the system. The values of stress and strain (maximum and yield points) can be measured. In the linear part the co-energy is equal to the stored energy and can be used for estimation of a "spring back".

Electromagnetic co-energy

Fig. 2.13.2. is illustration of electromechanical system with co-energy.

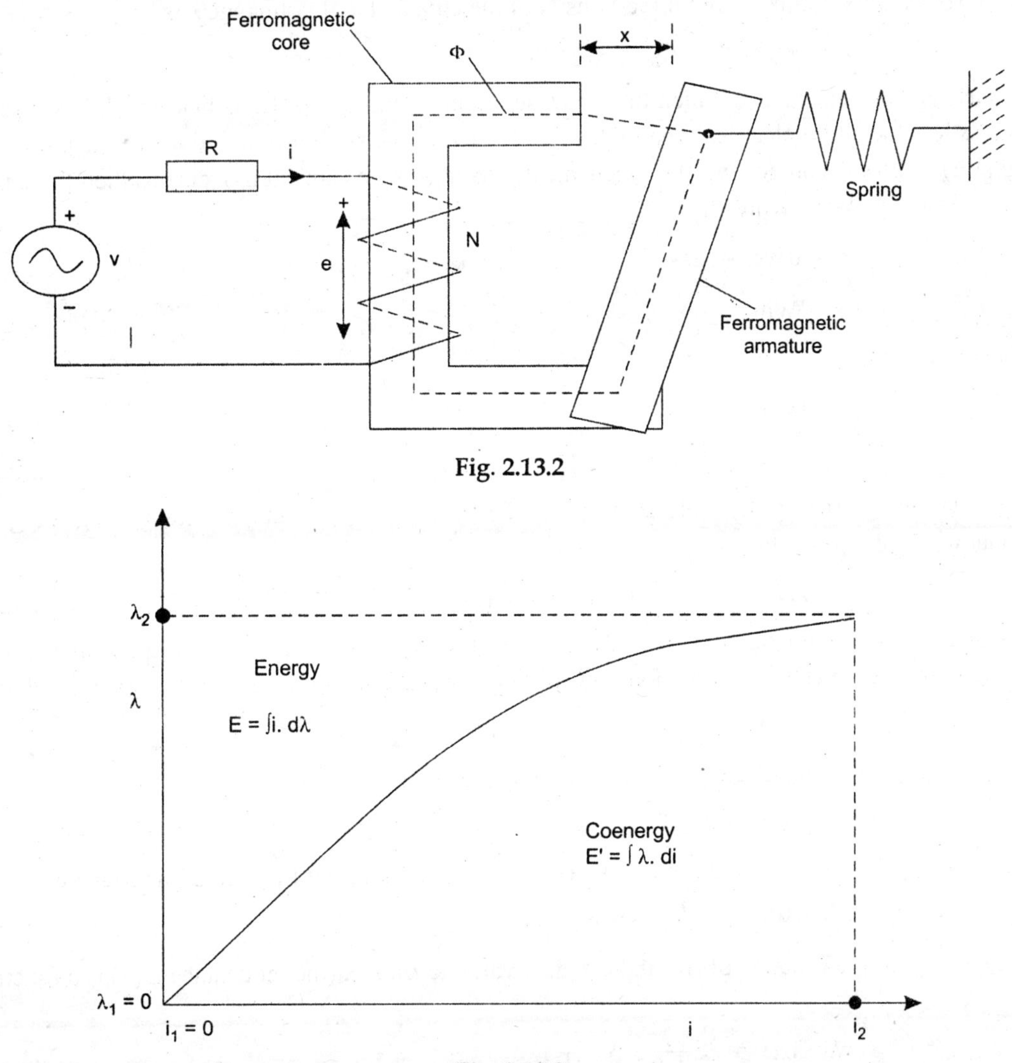

Fig. 2.13.2

Fig. 2.13.3

Fig. 2.13.3 is illustration of electromechanical system with co-energy.

In an electromagnetic system the energy can be stored in the electric field of capacitance or magnetic field of inductance.

The explanation and derivation of co-energy equations is usually illustrated in textbooks by an arrangement of an electromagnet coupled with mechanical spring as shown in Fig. 2.13.2.

A few assumptions re made for performing the analysis:

- The resistance R of the coil is represented as a lumped value outside of the coil. Thus the coil itself is losses.
- The leakage flux is negligibly small and does not take part in the energy conversion. Therefore the leakage inductance is also negligible. This can be assumed if the air gap in the system is small.
- The ferromagnetic core and armature are loss less and their reluctances are negligible.
- All the flux Φ links with all the turns N of the coil, so the flux linkage λ is:

$$\lambda = N.\Phi \quad \text{(Wb)} \qquad ...(2.5)$$

Let us consider the case in which the movable armature in Fig. 2.13.2 is held fixed. Because the coil is loss less the entire electrical energy (We) delivered to the system is stored as the magnetic field energy (Wf). If all the components are mechanically fixed (no mechanical movement) then there is no mechanical energy (Wm involved:

$$dWe = dWf \qquad ...(2.6)$$

$$dWm = 0d \qquad ...(2.7)$$

Where:

$$dWm = e.i.dt \quad \text{(J)} \qquad ...(2.8a)$$

$$dWe = i.d\lambda = N.i.d\Phi \quad \text{(J)} \qquad ...(2.8b)$$

The total energy (orange triangle area in Fig. 2.13.3) can be calculated by integrating the given functional with appropriate limits:

$$\Delta Wf = \int_{\lambda_1}^{\lambda^2} 1\,(\lambda).d\lambda \quad \text{(J)} \qquad ...(2.9)$$

However, instead of the flux linkage λ also the the current ii can be used as the independent variable, and therefore the complementary are of **co-energy** (blue triangle in Fig. 2.13.3) can be calculated as:

$$\Delta W'f = \int_{i_1}^{i^2} \lambda\,(i).di \quad \text{(J)} \qquad ...(2.10)$$

The total area of the rectangle is the sum of the tow triangles so that:

$$\Delta Wf + \Delta W'f = \lambda.i \quad \text{(J)} \qquad ...(2.11)$$

and hence the energy stored (and the co-energy) are equal to half of the area of the triangle:

$$\Delta Wf = \frac{\lambda.i}{2} \quad \text{(J)} \qquad ...(2.12)$$

The energy Wf is a function of two independent variable λ and x (the inductance L (x) is a function of x

$$Wf\,(i,x) = \frac{1}{2}\frac{\lambda^2}{L(x)} \quad \text{(J)} \qquad ...(2.13)$$

The co-energy W'f is also a function of two independent variable: i and x:

$$W'f(i,x) = \frac{1}{2}.L(x).i^2 \qquad ...(2.14)$$

Equation (13) and (14) are general expressions for energy and co-energy in a magnetostatic system (with the assumptions as given above).

Direction of the mechanical force developed in such system is always such as to increase the co-energy and reduce the store field energy. Force is a gradient of the co-energy (taken with the negative sign).

Fig. 2.13.4 Co-energy in a non-linear electromagnetic

The energy and co-energy are equal only in a completely linear and loss less system. In reality the systems are non-linear, especially if magnetic saturation takes place

Because of the non-linearity, the values of energy and co-energy must be calculated by appropriate integrals (equation (2.9) and (2.10)), as illustrated in Fig. 6. The energy no longer equals co-energy, so $W \neq W'$ or $E \neq E'$

However, it is always true, for both linear or non-linear systems that the sum of co-energy and energy is equal to the area of the shaded rectangle so that:

$$E + E' = \lambda.i \quad J \qquad ...(2.15)$$

As shown in Fig. 6, with the onset of saturation the energy will also stop increasing (the orange area) whereas the con-energy will grow as long as the current increases.

The generalised force and co-energy equations should not be used. Such equations should be derived for each case to make sure that fundamental physical laws like energy conservation are satisfied.

Rotating and multiple-excited systems

The force or torque can be calculated also for systems with multiple sources of excitation, as it is the case for instance for three-phase machines. The analysis and relationships can be extended to such multiply excited systems (that is systems with any number of terminal pairs). [35)36)]

The force or torque T becomes then a function of all the exciting currents and angular position or angle θθ, for example:

$$T = \frac{\partial W'(i_1, i_2 ... in, \theta)}{\partial \theta} \quad (N - m) \qquad ...(2.16)$$

Electrostatic co-energy

Electrostatic systems are capable of storing in electric field. Therefore, the co-energy analysis can be carried out in a similar way, also including materials exhibiting nonlinearity. 42)

Examples of applications

Finite - element Modelling (FEM)

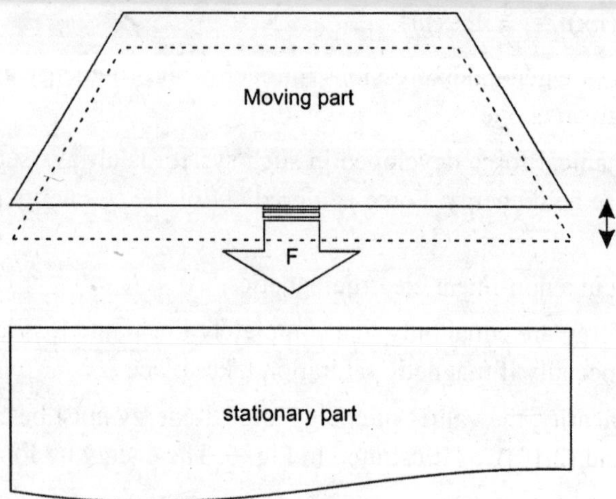

Fig. 2.13.4

Fig. 2.13.4 is illustration of the virtual displacement.

In electric machines (motors, generators) and other devices (actuators, relays) it is important to calculate the relationship between the mechanical force and electric current (or magnetic field of a permanent magnet).

Such calculations are more complex if the stored energy is used as a basis. Inversion of the relation between flux linkage and current is required which might be mathematically cumbersome, especially that for real devices there might be no simple algebraic from. However, by using the co-energy approach it is sufficient to apply partial differentiation with respect to displacement to obtain the force function.

The property can be used for instance in finite-element modelling (FEM) for finding the force and torque acting on a given component. Many other such methods exists (Maxwell stress tensor, Lorentz force equation, rate of change of field energy), but co-energy method can be also used. One of the advantages of using the co-energy method can be also used. One of the advantages of using the co-energy method is that it allows calculation of forces for elements which are connected to other magnetic parts (rather than being separated from them by some sort of air gap). For a given volume the magnetic field the co-energy can be calculated as:

$$W' = \int v \left(\int_0^H B(H)\, dH\right) dv \quad J \qquad \text{...(2.17)}$$

To compute force from co-energy, the currents are held constant and the position of the object for which the acting force is to be calculated is perturbed slightly, for instance by distorting the mesh locally.

The force can be estimated by performing partial differential of co-energy with respect to displacement δδ (relative to the original position pp):

$$F = W'(p + \delta) - W'(p) \quad (N) \qquad \text{...(2.18)}$$

The component of force is evaluated for the direction in which the perturbations was applied. Therefore, the calculation is performed twice for 2D problems (*e.g.* in *x* and *y* directions) or three times for 3D problems (*x*, *y* and *z*). The direction of the displacement can be arbitrary, but displacement along the main reference axes is often used.

The technique of force calculation is often referred to as the virtual displacement method.

The method can be implemented automatically in the FEM software, or it can also be executed manually by solving the problem with small displacement of the part in question. and direct application of equation (2.18).

Singly excited rotating system

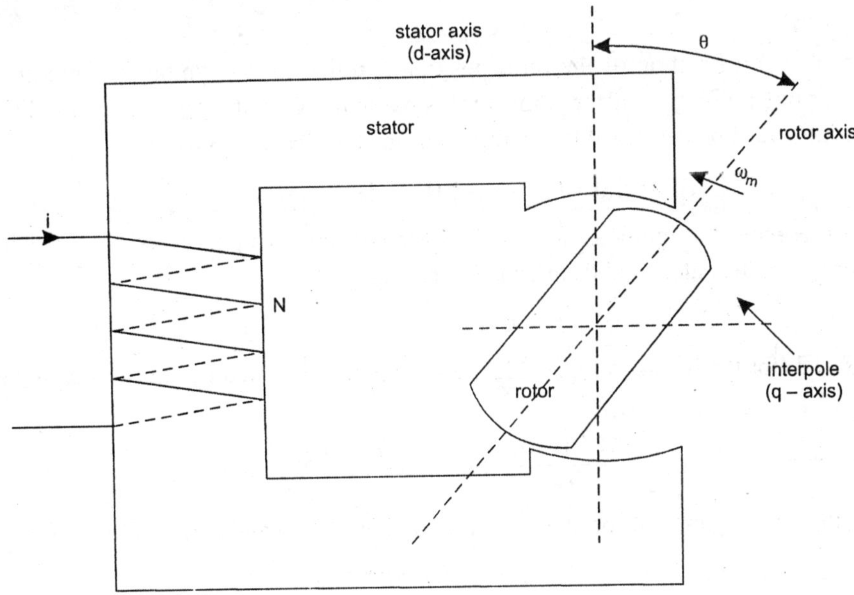

Fig. 2.13.5

Fig. 2.13.5 is Singly excited rotating system.

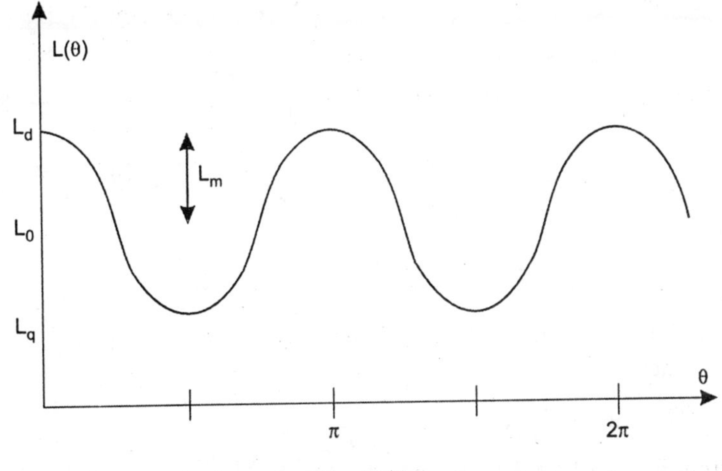

Fig. 2.13.6

Fig. 2.13.6. is variation of inductance with the position of rotor.

A simple singly excited rotating system is shown in Fig. 2.13.5. A sinusoidal current is applied to the stator winding and there rotor is free rotated on its shaft. The developed torque T can be calculated from the variables of i and θ, according to according to equation (2.16).

The sinusoidal current can be expressed as:

$$i(t) = I \cdot \sin(\omega.t)\, i \quad (A) \qquad ...(2.19)$$

(it should be noted that the stator current frequency ω is different from the mechanical rotation frequency ωm.

The reluctance is a function of the rotor position and due to the symmetry there are two cycles of reluctance per one revolution of the rotor. In this particular case the reluctance, and hence also the inductance variation can be described by a simplified function (Fig. 2.13.6):

$$L(\theta) = L0 + L_m \cdot \cos(2.\theta) \quad H \qquad ...(2.20)$$

Due to the presence of a significant air gap the system is linear and the co-energy (which in this case equals the energy) can be calculated from equation (2.14) as:

$$W' = \frac{1}{2} L(\theta) \cdot i^2 \quad (J) \qquad ...(2.21)$$

The torque Td (for the d axis in Fig. 2.13.5) can be then calculated by substituting equation (2.21) into (2.16):

$$Td = \frac{\partial W'(L,\theta)}{\partial \theta} = \frac{1}{2} \cdot i^2 \cdot \frac{\partial L(\theta)}{\partial \theta} \; N-m \qquad ...(2.22)$$

and using the known function for inductance (equation (2.20)) and current (equation (2.19)):

$$Td = \cdot I^2 \cdot I_m \cdot \sin(2 \cdot \theta) \cdot \sin^2(\omega.t) \; Nm \qquad ...(2.23)$$

The assumption is that the rotor rotates at an angular velocity $\omega_m \omega_m$ (Fig. 2.13.5). so that:

$$\theta = \omega_m \cdot t - \delta \quad rad \qquad ...(2.24a)$$

At the instant of t = 0t by definition of equation (2.19) it is i = 0i , so the rotor position is:

$$\theta = \delta\theta \quad (rad) \qquad ...(2.24b)$$

Equation (2.23) can be therefore rewritten by using trigonometric identities for sin2 (x) and sin (y). sin (z) as:

$$Td = \frac{I^2 L_m}{2} \cdot (\sin\{2.(\omega_m \cdot t - \delta)\} - \frac{\sin\{2.[(\omega m + \omega).t - \delta]\}}{2} -$$

$$t \frac{\sin\{2.[(\omega_m - \omega).t - \delta]\}}{2} \; N-m$$

An average value of a sine function is zero. The only case in which the average torque Td,avg is not zero is if the two frequencies are equal that is $\omega_m = \omega$, so that:

$$Td,avg = \frac{-I^2 L_m}{4} \cdot \sin(2.\delta) \; Nm \qquad ...(2.25)$$

It can be seen from Fig. 2.13.6 than LmLm is the amplitude of the the inductance variation which in this case can be described as:

$$L_m = \frac{Ld - Iq}{2} \quad H \qquad ...(2.26)$$

Therefore, the average developed torque for this particular case is given as:

$$Td,avg = -\frac{I2\,(Id - Iq)}{8}\,.\,\sin(2.\delta)\ N - m \quad ...(2.27)$$

Permanent magnet system

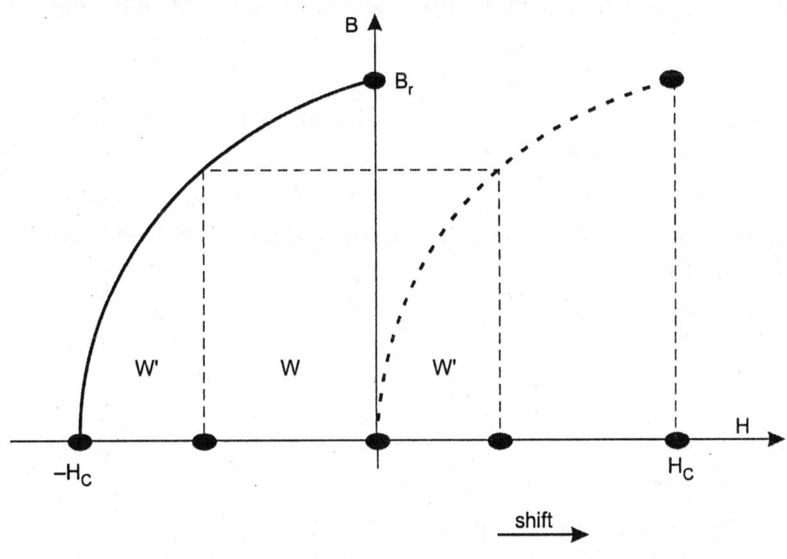

Fig. 2.13.7

Fig. 2.13.7. is second quadrant demagnetization curve shifted to first quadrant.

The energy/co-energy values in systems with permanent magnets cannot be attributed just to the currents, because some energy is stored in the magnets. The forces still can be computed using the co-energy method, but the mathematical models must be modified to include the information about flux linkages due to the presence of the permanent magnets.

A permanent magnet can be represented by an equivalent winding with current (*e.g.* current sheet).

With this method the corresponding demagnetization curve can be shifted from the second quadrant to the first quadrant and the co-energy density (or energy density) can be calculated accordingly. This sift is executed by applying an offset to all corresponding values of HH.

B-H loop modelling

Hysteresis loop of ferromagnetic materials can be approximated by jiles-Atherton model (J-A model). The energy loss of material is proportional to the are of the B-H loop. The area contained between the B-H curve and the BB axis is energy (similar as in Fig. 6), whereas area between the B-H curve and the HH axis is co-energy. The J-A model is based on an entity resembling co-energy calculation.

The area of the B-H loop in both cases (calculated from energy or co-energy) is the same. However, the instantaneous values of integrals are not equal which might lead to small errors in prediction of the shape of the loop even through the total area is predicted with better accuracy.

2.14. ENERGY STORED IN MAGNETIC HELD CONSERVATION OF ENERGY

A method of calculating electromagnetic fore based on the lorentz force is given by Eqn. However this method is applicable only when the flux density is known and the system is simple. Generally energy method is used to determine electromagnetic force. This energy method is based on the principal of conservation of energy.

Energy can be neither created nor destroyed. It is converted from one form to another form only. Hence the total energy in a system is always constant.

This energy conversion process involves interchange between electrical and mechanical energy via the stored energy in the magnetic field. Thus, the energy method is a powerful tool for determining the coupling force of electro-mechanics.

In a energy conversion device the total input energy is equal to the sum of the following three components.

1. Energy dissipated.
2. Energy stored.
3. Useful output energy.

Hence, energy balance equation for motor action can be written as under where electrical energy input and mechanical energy output are treated as positive.

Electrical energy as input	=	Total energy stored in system	+	Total energy Loss	+	Electrical energy as input

For generator action, the energy balance equation is written as under

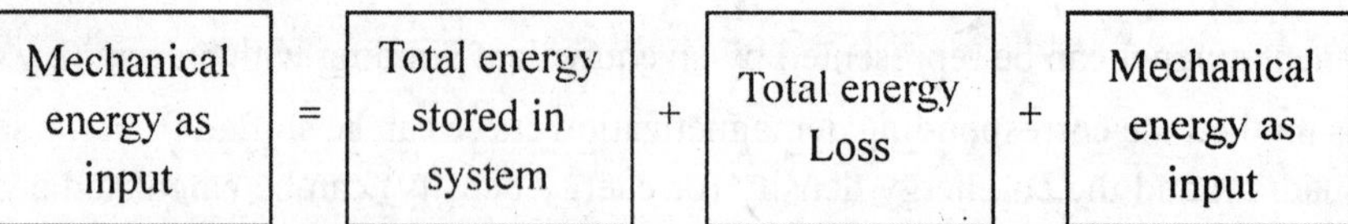

Following are the various forms of energy for motor and generator equations:

(1) Total electrical energy input from the main supply in case of generator and mechanical energy in case of motor.

(2) Total energy stored in system includes energy stored in magnetic field and energy stored in electrical system or mechanical system.

(3) Total energy dissipated = (Electrical loss *i.e.*, ohmic loss + Magnetic loss, *i.e.*, eddy current and hysteresis + Mechanical loss, *i.e.*, friction and windage loss).

2.14.1. Energy Stored in a Magnetic Field

Suppose a coil of N turns is mounted on a magnetic core and is connected to voltage source By applying KVL, the voltage applied is given as

$$v = iR + e \qquad ...(2.27.1)$$

where e is the voltage induced in the coil or back emf of the coil which opposes the applied voltage and R is the resistance of the coil. The instantaneous power input to the system is given by

$$P = vi = i^2 R + ei \qquad ...(2.27.2)$$

Now suppose DC voltage is applied tot he circuit at timer r = 0 and at end of the T seconds the current has attained a value of I amperes. The energy input tot eh system during this interval is

$$W = \int_{o}^{T} P\,dt = \int_{o}^{T} i^2 Rdt + \int_{o}^{T} eidt \qquad ...(2.27.3)$$

Equation 2.27.3 shows that the input energy consists of two parts. The first part is energy dissipated in the ohmic loss while the second part is the energy stored in the magnetic field.

By using Faraday's law, as per Eqn. 1.6.3

$$e = \frac{d\lambda}{dt} = -N\frac{d\phi}{dt},$$ where λ is the magnetic flux linkage given by $N\phi$

Field energy is given by $$W_{\text{Field}} = \int_0^T \frac{d\lambda}{dt}\, i\,dt = \int_0^{\lambda} i\,d\lambda \qquad ...(2.27.4)$$

or $$W_{\text{Field}} = \int_0^T N\frac{d\phi}{dt}\, i\,dt = \int_0^{\phi} Ni\,d\phi = \int_0^{\phi} F d\phi \qquad ...(2.27.5)$$

where $F = Ni$ is the mmf

Energy stored in the a magnetic field, is called field energy; it is given by Eqn. 2.27.4 and 2.27.5 and is shown in Figs. 2.14(a) and (b), respectively.

The electrical energy which is converted into magnetic energy is called co-energy. From Fig. 2.14 (a), the area above the magnetization curve (or $\lambda - i$) gives the field energy while the area below the magnetization curve gives the co-energy which is denoted by W'_{FIELD}. However, co-energy has no physical significance but it is used in finite element systems to find mechanical force between magnetized parts. Co-energy is also shown in Figs. 2.14.

2.15. FIELD ENERGY IN A MAGNETICALLY LINEAR SYSTEM

For a liner system, the field energy is given by:

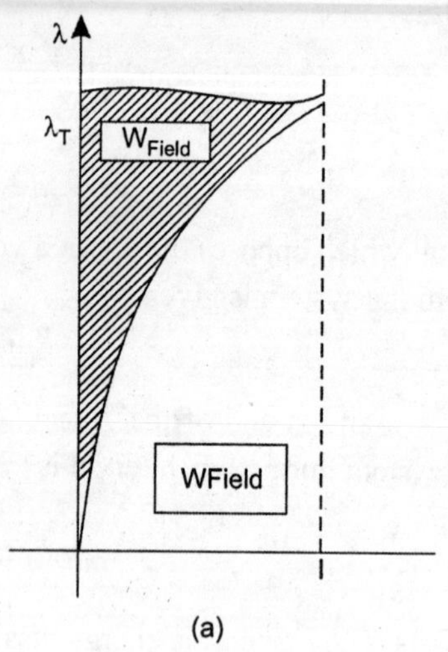

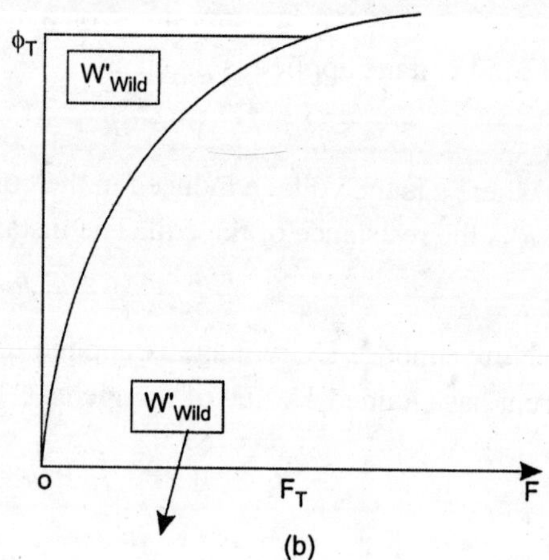

Fig. 2.14

Fig. 2.14 is graphical representation of energy and co-energy

$$W_{FIELD} = \int_0^{\lambda} i d\lambda = \int_0^{\lambda} \frac{\lambda}{L} d\lambda = \frac{\lambda^2}{2L} \quad \text{...(2.28.1)}$$

Now $\lambda = Li$

$$W_{FIELD} = \frac{(Li)^2}{2L} = \frac{1}{2} Li^2 \quad \text{...(2.28.2)}$$

Co-energy is given by

$$W'_{FIELD} = \int_0^{i} \lambda\, di = \int_0^{i} Li\, di = \frac{1}{2} Li^2 \quad \text{...(2.28.3)}$$

Thus, for a linear system, the field energy and co-energy, both are equal.

Thus, for a linear system, Total energy = Co-energy + Field energy.

2.16. SINGLY EXCITED SYSTEMS

A simple, singly excited system is shown in Fig. 2.15. A coil is wound round a magnetic core and is connected to a voltage Source. The rotor will experience a torque where the magnetic field is strong. So, the rotor will try to take a position where the reluctance of the magnetic path is the minimum. This reluctance is dependent on the rotor angle. This torque is called reluctance torque or saliency torque due to saliency of the rotor.

We have made the following assumptions in this discussion:

(1) The relationship between flux-linkage and current for any rotor position is linear, *i.e.*, $\lambda = L(\theta)\, i$

(2) The magnetic field is stronger than electric field hence electric field has been neglected.

(3) Iron losses, *i.e.*, eddy current and hysteresis losses have been totally neglected.

(4) All the fluxes are useful, no leakage flux has been considered.

Now, suppose R is the resistance of the coil. We apply KVL to get the instances stage as under.

$$v = Ri + \frac{d\lambda}{dt} \quad \text{...(2.29.1)}$$

Multiplying the above equation with current i, we get

$$vi = Ri^2\,dt + i\,\frac{d\lambda}{dt} \quad \text{...(2.29.2)}$$

Integrating both sides with respect to time from $t = 0$ to $t = t$, assuming that flux linkage and current to be initially zero.

$$\int_0^t vi\,dt = \int_0^t Ri^2\,dt + \int_0^\lambda i d\lambda \quad \text{...(2.29.3)}$$

We can write the above equation as under

Total electrical input energy = (Electrical energy losses) + (Useful electrical energy) ...(2.29.4)

or $$W_{EI} = W_{ELOSS} + (W_{EFIELD} + \mu_{MECH}) \quad \text{...(2.29.5)}$$

and $$\int_D^\lambda i d\lambda = W_{EFIELD} + W_{MECH} = W_{FIELD} \quad \text{...(2.29.6)}$$

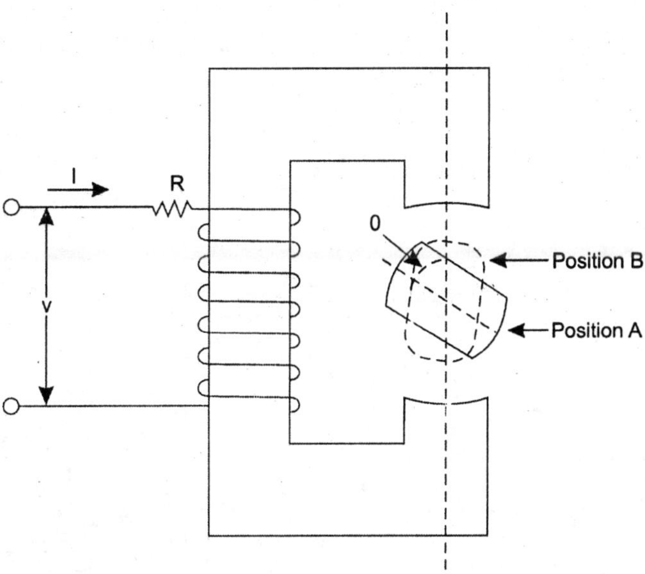

Fig. 2.15

2.16.1. Equation for Static Energization

A curve between flux linkage and current i can be drawn as in Fig. 1.20 for any position of the rotor For stationary position for the rotor, the mechanical output will be zero and all the useful energy is connected to field energy.

$$W_{FIELD} = \int_0^{\lambda} = i\, d\lambda = \int_0^{\lambda} \frac{\lambda}{L}\, d\lambda = \frac{\lambda^2}{2L}$$

Now $\lambda = Li$ $\quad\therefore W_{FIELD} = \frac{(Li)^2}{2L} = \frac{1}{2} Li^2$

Areas OPQ and ORS represent the stored energy for position *A* and *B*, respectively.

Know that mechanical work is obtained only in moving state. The moving state can be understood by three different conditions which are:

(*a*) Very slow movement of the rotor.

(*b*) Instantaneous or sudden movement of the rotor.

(*c*) Transient movement (neither too slow not too fast)

(a) Slow Movement

AS the rotor moves, it may move either slow or fast from position *A* to position *B*. For a slow movement, the current is λ_1 and the operating point is *P* for position *A*. For slow movement of the rotor, the counter emf $\left(\frac{d\lambda}{dt}\right)$ is very small. Hence, current i_1 remain almost constant. The flux linkage

may be increased from λ_1 to λ_2 at constant current i_1. Hence, the operating point *P* moves to the new position at *R* along the vertical line *PR* as shown in Fig. 2.15.2. Change in stored energy of magnetic field is given by

W_{FIELD} = (Magnetic energy Mored in position *B*) – (Magnetic energy stored in position *A*)

W_{FIELD} = Area OP′RSQO – Area OPP′QO ...(2.29.7)

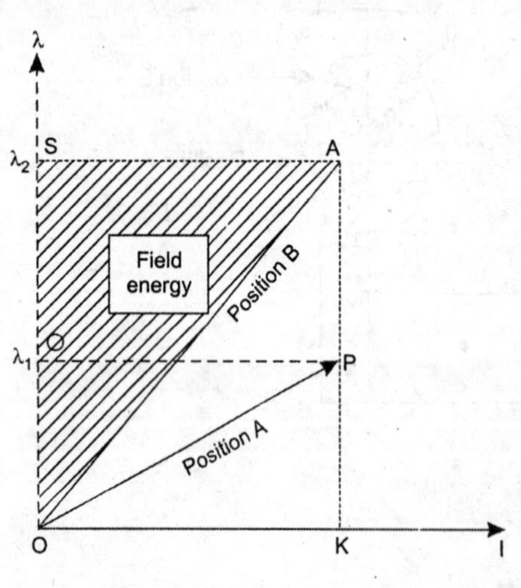

Fig. 2.15.1

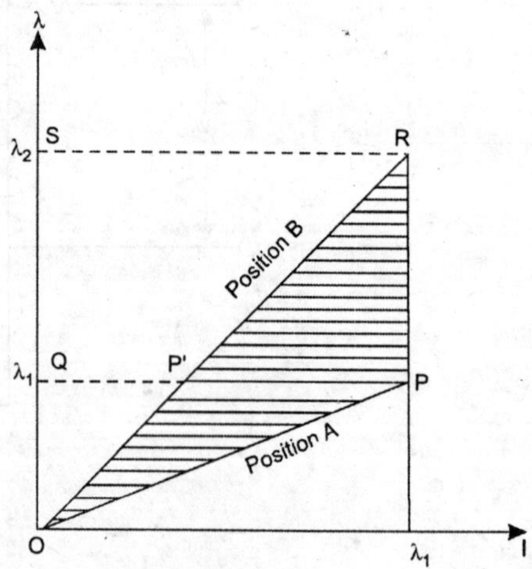

Fig. 2.15.2

Electrical energy input during this change.

$$W_{EI} = \int_{\lambda_1}^{\lambda_0} i_1\, d\lambda = i_1(\lambda_2 - \lambda_2) = \text{Area PRSQP'P} \qquad ...(2.29.8)$$

But $\qquad W_{EI} = W_{FIELD} + W_{MECH}$

$\therefore \qquad \text{Area PRSQP'P} = (\text{Area OP'RSQO} - \text{Area OPP'QO}) + W_{MECH}$

$$\therefore \qquad W_{MECH} = \text{Area OPRSQO} - \text{Area OP'RSQO} = \text{Area OPRP'O} \qquad \text{...(2.29.9)}$$

From the Eqn. 2.29.9. it can be said that hte mechanical work done is given by the area covered between tow $\lambda - i$ characteristics in positions A and B and the vertical $\lambda - i$ locus during the slow movement.

Moreover, it can be seen that for a linear system, half of the useful electrical input energy stored in the magnetic field and the other half is obtained as mechanical energy output during the slow movement of the rotor

Now, electromagnetic torque is given by

$$Te = \lim_{\Delta\theta_{.} \to 0} \left\{\frac{\Delta W'E_{FIELD}}{\Delta\theta_m}\right\}_{\text{constant } i} \qquad \text{...(2.29.10)}$$

$$Te = \left\{\frac{\partial W'_{EFIELD}}{\partial\theta_m}\right\}_{\text{constant } i}$$

$$Te = \left\{\frac{\partial}{\partial\theta_m}\left(\frac{1}{2}Li^2\right)\right\}_{\text{constant } i} \quad or \quad \frac{i^2}{2}\frac{\partial L}{\partial\theta_m} \qquad \text{...(2.29.11)}$$

For a linear system, L is not a function of i

$$Te = \frac{i^2}{2}\frac{dL}{d\theta_m} \qquad \text{...(2.29.12)}$$

(b) Instantaneous Movement

In this case the rotor moves very fast from position A to B. According to the constant flux linkage theorem, in an inductive circuit the flux linkage cannot change suddenly. Thus, during the instantaneous movement of the rotor, the flux linkage remains constant at λ_1. Hence, the operating point shifts horizontally from P to P' as in Fig. 2.15.3.

Both λ and i increase slowly and reach their steady state values. The final operating point is R.

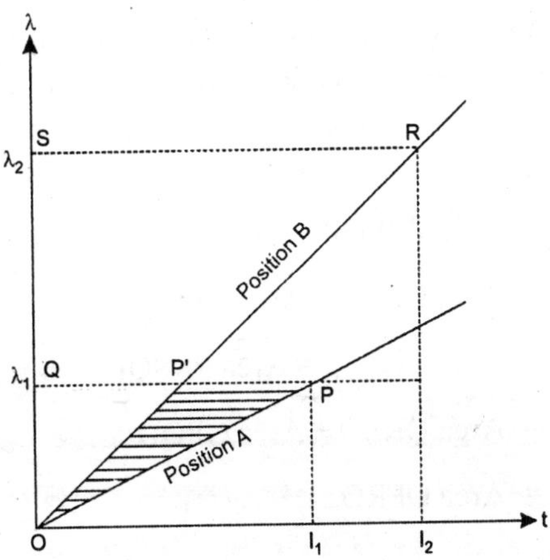

Fig 2.15.3

Since, $$W_{EI} = \int_{\lambda_1}^{\lambda_2} i d\lambda$$

And $\lambda 1 = \lambda 2$ during the fast movement of the rotor.

hence

$$W_{EI} = \int_{\lambda_1}^{\lambda_2} i d\lambda = 0$$

From the above equation we can say that during fast movement of the rotor, no energy is drawn from the supply and mechanical energy output is obtained from the stored magnetic field energy which reduce by an equal amount.

For the movement of the rotor angle θ_m. the mechanical work corresponds to the loss in the stored magnetic field energy

Electromagnetic torque is given by.

$$Te = \lim \left\{ -\frac{\Delta W_{EFIELD}}{\Delta \theta_m} \right\}$$

$$\Delta \theta_m \to 0$$

$$\left\{ \frac{\partial W_{EFIELD}}{\partial \theta_m} \right\} \text{constant } \lambda = \left\{ -\frac{\partial}{\partial \theta_m} \frac{\lambda^2}{2L} \right\} \text{constant } \lambda$$

$$Te = \frac{\lambda^2}{2} \frac{1}{t^2} \frac{\partial L}{\partial \theta_m} \quad ...(2.29.13)$$

$$Te = \frac{i^2}{2} \frac{\partial L}{\partial \theta_m} \quad ...(2.29.14)$$

For a linear system

$$Te = \frac{i^2}{2} \frac{dL}{d\theta_m} \quad ...(2.29.15)$$

(c) Transient Movement

We have discussed two cases—too slow and too fast = but the actual rotor movement is never too slow or too fast, it lies between the tow extremes. Generally, both the current and flux linkages change during the movement of the rotor. The corresponding $\lambda - i$ characteristic is shown in Fig. 2.15.4 it is path from *P* to *R*.

Here $$W_{EI} = \text{Area PRSQP}$$

$$W_{FIELD} = \text{Area ORSO} - \text{Area PRSQP}$$

But $$W_{MECH} = W_{EI} - W_{FIELD} = \text{Area PRSQP}$$

$$- \text{Area ORSO} + \text{Area OPQO}$$

$$= \text{Area OPRO}$$

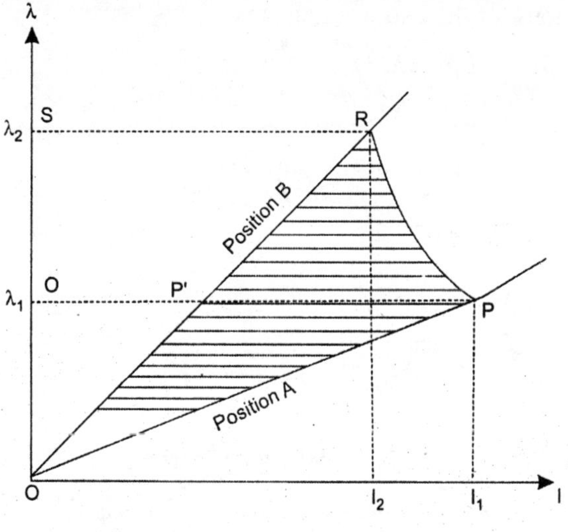

Fig. 2.15.4

Hence, the mechanical output is given by the shaded area in Fig. 2.15.4. Since *PR* is a general movement, this area is to be computed graphically or numerically.

From the above discussion following conclusion can be made:

(1) Two fluxes are required to produce mechanical energy—one produced from the stationary system and the second is produced by the moving system.

(2) The magnetism produced in the system by using the electrical energy is called as excitation.

(3) The electrical energy suppled to the system is called as co-energy.

2.17. DOUBLY EXCITED SYSTEMS

A doubly excited system is shown in Fig. 2.16. In this case, there are two independent sources of excitation such as DC separately excited generator, synchronous motor, loud speakers, tachometers, etc. Consider that both the stator and the rotor have saliency. Assumptions are same as for singly excited system.

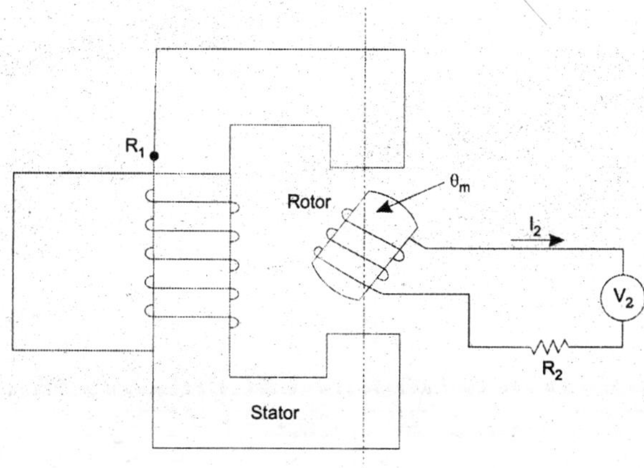

Fig. 2.16

The flux linkage equations for the two winding are:

$$\lambda_1 = L_1 i_1 + M i_2 \quad \text{...(2.30.1)}$$

$$\lambda_2 = L_2 i_2 + M i_1 \quad \text{...(2.30.2)}$$

The instantaneous voltage equations for two coils are:

$$v_1 = R_1 i_1 + \frac{d\lambda_1}{dt} \quad \text{...(2.30.3)}$$

$$v_2 = R_2 i_2 + \frac{d\lambda_2}{dt} \quad \text{...(2.30.4)}$$

Hence,

$$v_1 = R_1 i_1 + \frac{d}{dt}(L_1 i_1) + \frac{d}{dt}(M i_2) \quad \text{...(2.30.5)}$$

$$v_2 = R_2 i_2 + \frac{d}{dt}(L_2 i_2) + \frac{d}{dt}(M i_1) \quad \text{...(2.30.6)}$$

Now, inductances of the coils do not depend on current flowing through them but they depend on the position of the rotor angle θ_m and θ_m is a function of the time. Similarly, currents are time-dependent and they are not functions of inductances. Hence, Eqn. (2.30.5) and can be given as:

$$v_1 = R_1 i_1 + L_1 \frac{di_1}{dt} + i_1 \frac{dL_1}{dt} + M \frac{di_2}{dt} + i_2 \frac{dM}{dt} \quad \text{...(2.30.7)}$$

$$v_2 = R_2 i_2 + L_2 \frac{di_2}{dt} + i_2 \frac{dL_2}{dt} + M \frac{di_1}{dt} + i_1 \frac{dM}{dt} \quad \text{...(2.30.8)}$$

Multiplying Eqn. (2.30.7) with i_1 and Eqn. (2.30.8) by i_2 we get

$$v_1 i_1 = R_1 i_1^2 + L_1 i_1 \frac{di_1}{dt} + i_1^2 \frac{dL_1}{dt} + i_1 \text{M} \frac{di_2}{dt} + i_2 i_2 \frac{dM}{dt} \quad \text{...(2.30.9)}$$

$$v_2 i_2 = R_2 i_2^2 + L_2 i_2 \frac{di_2}{dt} + i_2^2 \frac{dL_2}{dt} + i_2 \text{M} \frac{di_1}{dt} + i_2 i_2 \frac{dM}{dt} \quad \text{...(2.30.10)}$$

Equations (2.30.9) and (2.30.10) are the power equations for the coils. Integrating these equations with respect to time and adding, we get

$$\int (v_1 i_1 + v_2 i_2)\, dt = \int (R_1 i_1^2 + R_2 i_2^2)\, dt +$$

$$\int (L_1 i_1 d_{i1}^0 + L_2 i_2 d_{i2} + i_1 M\, di_2 + 2 i_1 i_2 dM + i_1^2\, dL_1 + i_2^2 dL_2 + M di_1) \quad \text{...(2.30.11)}$$

Also, [Useful electric input energy] $= \iint (v_1 i_1 + v_2 i_2)\, dt - \iint (R_1 i_1^2 + R_2 i_2^2)\, dt$

...(2.30.12)

(Energy to field storage in the electric system) + (electrical to mechanical energy or energy transferred between rotor and stator)

$$= \int (L_1 i_1 d_{i1} + L_2 i_2 d_{i2} + i_1 M\, di_2 + 2 i_1 i_2 dM + i_2^2\, dL_2 + i_2 M\, di_1)$$

...(2.30.13)

2.17.1. Energy Stored in a Doubly Excited System

The instantaneous value of the energy stored in the magnetic field depends on two things—the inductance and the current at that instant. This energy may be obtained by considering the transducer to be stationary and the coils to be energized from zero current to the required instantaneous value of current. There is no mechanical output, *i.e.*, W_{EM} is zero. The inductance values are constant. Hence, the terms dL_1, dL_2 and dM become zero.

From Eqn. 2.30.13.

$$\int dW_{FIELDE} = \int_0^{i_1} L_1 i_1 d_{i1} + \int_0^{i_2} L_2 i_2 d_{i2} + \int_0^{i_1 . i_2} (i_1 M\, di_2 + i_2 M\, di_1)$$

$$W_{FIELDE} = \frac{1}{2} L1 i_2^2 + Mi_1 i_2 \quad ...(2.30.14)$$

2.17.2. Electromagnetic Torque in a Doubly Excited System

Equation 2.30.14 holds good for any transducer position. If the transducer is rotating, the rate of change of field energy with respect to time is given by differentiating Eqn. 2.30.14.

$$\frac{dW_{FIELDE}}{dt} = \frac{1}{2} L_1 \frac{d}{dt} i_1^2 + \frac{1}{2} i_1^2 \frac{dL1}{I} + \frac{1}{2} L_2 \frac{di_2^2}{dt} + \frac{1}{2} i_1^2 \frac{dL_2}{dt} + i_1 i_2 \frac{dM}{dt} + i_1 M \frac{di_2}{dt} + i_2 M \frac{di_1}{dt}$$

$$\frac{dW_{FIELDE}}{dt} = L_1 i_1 L_1 \frac{di_1}{dt} + \frac{1}{2} i_1^2 \frac{dL1}{I} + \frac{1}{2} L_2 i_2 \frac{di_2}{dt} + \frac{1}{2} i_1^2 \frac{dL_2}{dt} + i_1 i_2 \frac{dM}{dt} + i_1 M \frac{di_2}{dt} + i_2 M \frac{di_1}{dt} \quad ...(2.30.15)$$

Integrating above equation with respect to time, we get

$$\int dW_{FIELDE} = W_{FIELDE} = \int \left(L_1 i_1 di_1 + \frac{1}{2} i_1^2 dL_1 + L_2 i_2 di_2 + \frac{1}{2} i_2^2 dL_2\right)$$

$$+ \; i_1 i_2 dM + i_1 M di_2 + i_2 M\, di_1 \quad ...(2.30.16)$$

This is the general equation for a rotating transducer. Here L_1, L_2, M, i_1 and i_2 all vary with position and time. Comparing Eqn. 2.30.16 with Eqn. 2.30.13, we get

$$\text{WMECH (electrical to mechanical)} = \int \left(\frac{1}{2} i_1^2 dL_1 + \frac{1}{2} i_2^2 dL_2 + i_1 i_2 dM\right) \quad ...(2.30.17)$$

Differentiating Eqn. (2.30.17) with respect to θ_m

$$\frac{dW_{MECH}}{d\theta_m} = \frac{1}{2} i_1^2 \frac{dL_1}{d\theta_m} + \frac{1}{2} i_2^2 \frac{dL_2}{d\theta_m} + i_1 i_2 \frac{dM}{d\theta_m}$$

as only L_1, L_2, and M are dependent on θ_m.

In Eqn. 1.10.18 singly excited system is also included when one of the two currents is zero so that the torque is given by.

$$Te = \frac{i^2}{2} \frac{dL}{d\theta_m}$$

The first two terms of Eqn. 1.10.18 give the reluctance torques or saliency torque while the last term $i_1 i_2 \frac{dM}{d\theta_m}$ is called co-alignment torque, that is, two superimposed fields trying to align with each other.

It should be noted that in machines having a uniform air-gap, reluctance torque is to produced.

2.18. FORCE AND TORQUE AS A PARTIAL DERIVATIVE OF STORED ENERGY

Before deriving equations for force and torque as a partial derivative of stored energy let us discuss same basic features and properties of inductance.

2.18.1. Self-Inductance

The voltage impressed on a series inductive circuit in which the capacitance effects are negligible and in which there are no thermal or electrolytic sources of emf, is expressed by

$$v = Ri + \frac{d\lambda}{dt}$$

Where

v = the applied voltage in volts

i = the current in amperes

R = the resistance in ohms

A = the magnetic flux linkage in weber turns

t = time in seconds

The flux linkage λ may be due only to the current i in the circuit itself; in addition it may be due to current in other circuits that are coupled magnetically with the circuit under discussion. For that matter a **permanent magnet** in the vicinity of the circuit may contribute flux linkage also.

If, however, the flux linkage λ is produced solely by the current i in the circuit itself and if the relationship between λ. and i is a linear fiction, then the expression for the applied voltage becomes

$$v = Ri + L\frac{di}{dt} \quad \text{...[2.31.1]}$$

where L = self-inductance in henries. Figure 2.17.1 shows a schematic diagram of an inductive circuit. The dotted lines indicate the **magnetic flux**.

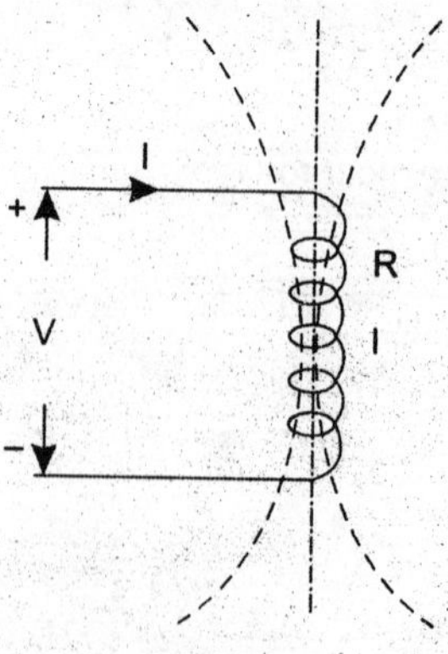

Fig. 2.17.1

The voltage that is induced by the time variations in the current of a circuit is called the electromotive force of self - Induction, or simply the emf of self-induction, and is expressed in terms of the self-inductance by

$$e = L\frac{di}{dt} \quad ...[2.31.2]$$

The flux linkage λ can be a linear function of the current i only if the self-inductance L is constant. In circuits where the self-inductance is a variable, as for example in the case of electromagnets with variable length of air gaps as well as in some generators, the time variation of the self-inductance will affect the voltage and must be taken it account. Circuits with variable inductance will be discussed later in this chapter.

The emf induced in a circuit can always be expressed by

$$e = \frac{d\lambda}{dt} \quad ...[2.31.3]$$

This is true whether L is a constant or a variable, or whether the flux linkage λ is produced solely by the current in that circuit or whether current in other circuits contribute to the flux linkage as well.

However, if the self -inductance is constant and the only flux linkage is the one resulting from the current i in the circuit itself, then Eq. 2.31.2 can be equated to Eq. 2.31.3 with the result that

$$L\frac{di}{dt} = \frac{d\lambda}{dt} \quad ...[2.31.4]$$

from which

$$L = \frac{d\lambda}{dt} \quad ...[2.31.5]$$

and

$$L = \frac{\lambda}{i} \quad ...[2.31.6]$$

Equation 2.31.6 defines inductance as the flux linkage per ampere. Consider the toroid shown in Fig. 2.17.1 and assume the thickness R_2 - R_1 to be small compared with R_1. Then the expression for the flux produced by current i in the winding is

$$\phi = \frac{Ni\mu w}{\pi}\frac{R_2 - R_1}{R_2 + R_1} \quad ...[2.31.7]$$

which can be reduced to the more general form

$$\phi = \frac{\mu NiA}{l} = Ni\Pi \quad ...[2.31.8]$$

where A is the cross - sectional area of the flux path and I is the length of the flux path. When all of the flux ϕ links all the turns N the flux linkage is

$$\lambda = N\phi$$

The flux ϕ in the toroid links all N turns, so that on the basis of Eqs. 2.31.6 and 2.31.8. the self-inductance is

$$L = \frac{\mu N^2 A}{l} = N^2\Pi \quad ...[2.31.9]$$

$$L_{11}\int_0^{i_1} i_1\, di_1 + M\int_{0.0}^{i_1 i_2} d(i_1 i_2) + L_{22}\int_0^{i_2} i_2\, di_2$$

The permeability for an air core is $\mu = \mu_0 = 4\pi \times 10^{-7}$ h per m, and the expression for self-inductance if the core has a uniform cross-sectional area becomes

$$L = 4\pi \times 10^{-7} \frac{N^2 A}{l} \text{ h} \qquad ...[2.31.10]$$

If the core material has constant relative permeability of μ_r then the self - inductance is given by

$$L = 4\pi \times 10^{-7} \mu_r \frac{N^2 A}{l} \qquad ...[2.31.11]$$

When both sides of Eq. 2.31.9 are multiplied by $i^2/2$ the result expresses the energy stored in the filed thus

$$W_\phi = L\frac{i^2}{2} = \mu \frac{(Ni)^2 A}{2l} \qquad ...[2.31.12]$$

Where

$$\frac{(Ni)^2}{l} = H^2 l \qquad ...[2.31.13]$$

Substitution of Eq. 2.31.13 in Eq. 2.31.12 yields

$$W_\phi = \frac{Li^2}{2} = \frac{\mu H(HlA)}{2} = \text{Vol}\,\frac{HB}{2} \qquad ...[2.31.14]$$

This term Vol HB/2 is the value of the energy stored magnetically in volume Vol. When Eq. 2.31.6 is substituted in Eq. 4-14 the energy that is stored magnetically can be expressed in terms of flux linkage and current as follows

$$W_\phi = \frac{\lambda i}{2} \qquad ...[2.31.15]$$

Equations 2.31.14 and 2.31.15 apply only tot he case of core materials that have constant permeability. There is the further restriction on Eq. 2.31.14 that the flux density B is practically uniform throughout the core.

2.18.2. Variable Self-Inductance

There are electric circuits in which the self-inductance is not constant but in which it varies as a result of relative linear motion or rotary motion between portions of the magnetic circuit. Relays, solenoids, and some types of electric motors and generators are examples of variable self-inductance due to one member moving with respect to another.

When the self-inductance L is a variable Eq. 2.31.2 does not express the induced emf because it does not take into account the time variation of L. According to Eq. 2.31.6 the flux linkage is expressed in terms of self-inductance and the current by

$$\lambda = Li \qquad ...[2.31.16]$$

A time variation of flux linkage inducing the voltage

$$e = \frac{d\lambda}{dt} = L\frac{di}{dt} + i\frac{dL}{dt} \qquad ...[2.31.17]$$

Equation 2.31.17 shows that there are generally two components in the emf of self-induction. One of these is L di/dt and is due to the time variation in the current, and the other, i dL/dt is due to the time variation of the self-inductance. It is important to note that emf can be induced in an inductive circuit even when the current is constant if the inductance undergoes a variation with time.

2.19. FORCE AND TORQUE IN A CIRCUIT OF VARIABLE SELF-INDUCTANCE

The energy stored in and inductance, the magnetic circuit of which has constant permeability, is expressed by

$$W_\phi = \frac{Li^2}{2} \quad \text{...[2.32.1]}$$

which is true regardless of whether the inductance is constant or varies with time.

The power required to change the energy stored in the field is related to the inductance and current as follows

$$P_\phi = \frac{dW_\phi}{dt} = \frac{d}{dt}\frac{(Li^2)}{2} = Li\frac{di}{dt} + \frac{i^2}{2}\frac{dL}{dt} \quad \text{...[2.32.2]}$$

It follows from Eq. 2.32.2 that the differential gain in reversible energy is

$$dW\phi = P_\phi\, dt = Li\, di + \frac{i^2}{2}dL \quad \text{...[2.32.3]}$$

The expression for the electrical power input to the circuit during this change in the stored energy is

$$P_e = vi = \left(Ri + L\frac{di}{dt} + i\frac{dL}{dt}\right)i = Ri^2 + Li\frac{di}{dt} + i^2\frac{dL}{dt} \quad \text{...[2.32.4]}$$

and the differential electrical energy input therefore must be

$$dW_e = P_e\, dt = Ri^2\, dt + Li\, di + i^2\, dL \quad \text{...[2.32.5]}$$

Equation 2.32.3 expresses the part of the electrical energy input that is stored in the magnetic field. In addition there is the energy that is converted directly into heat, namely Ri^2 dt and that which is converted into mechanical energy. The mechanical energy output then is, as in the electromagnet of Fig. 3.25, f dx. The electrical differential energy input must therefore satisfy the following relationship

$$dW_e = Ri^2\, dt + dW_\phi + f\, dx = Ri^2\, dt + Li\, di + \frac{i^2}{2}dL + f\, dx \quad \text{...[2.32.6]}$$

Equations 2.32.5 and 2.32.6 express the same amount of differential energy, and when equated to each other yield the following results

$$f\, dx = \frac{i^2}{2}dL \quad \text{...[2.32.7]}$$

from which the expression for the force becomes

$$f = \frac{i^2}{2}\frac{dL}{dx} \quad \text{...[2.32.8]}$$

In Eq. 2.32.8 f is the force produced by the system. This means that when dL/dx is positive, *i.e.*, if the inductance increases with displacement, motor action results. On the other hand, a decrease in the inductance with displacement makes dL/dx negative and an external force is required resulting in generator action. If the length of the air gap in the electromagnet shown in Figure 2.18 is increased, it is necessary to apply a positive external force. An increase in the length of air gap corresponds to a decrease in the inductance, and dl/dx is then negative.

Torque

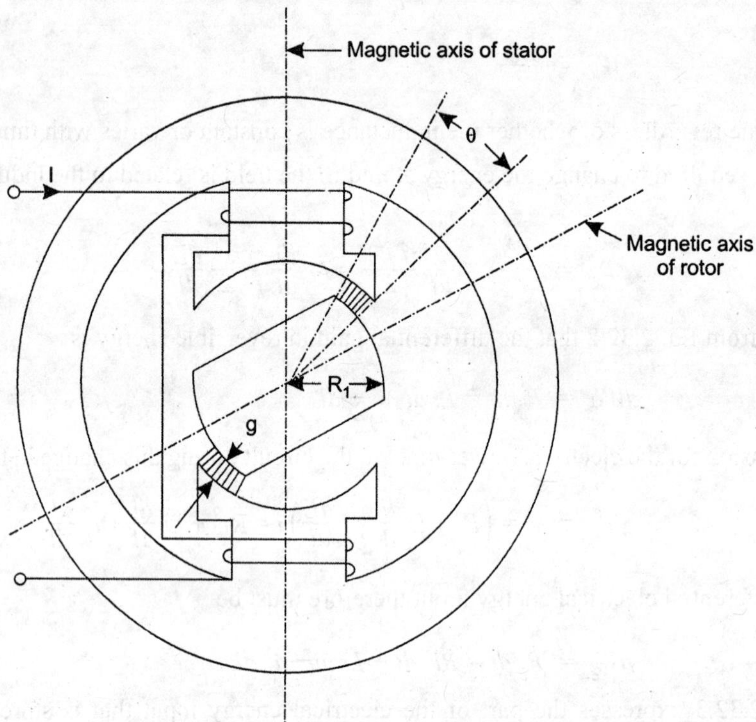

Fig. 2.18. Rotary electromagnet

In the case o rotary motion the mechanical energy is given by the product of torque and angular displacement as compared with that offeree and linear displacement for linear motion. Figure 2.18 shows a schematic diagram of a magnetic circuit with a winding on the stator, and with the magnetic axis of the rotor displaced from that of the stator by an angle Θ. The developed torque can therefore be related to the current and self-inductance by replacing the quantity f dx in Eq. 2.32.7 with TdΘ,

Where

T = torque in newton meters

Θ = angular displacement in radians

This results in

$$T = \frac{i^2}{2}\frac{dL}{d\theta} \qquad ...[2.32.9]$$

2.20. INDUCTANCE IN TERMS OF MAGNETIC RELUCTANCE AND MAGNETIC PERMEANCE

As mentioned previously, the magnetic circuit is similar in some respects to the electric circuit. In the case of the simple d - c circuit current, voltage and resistance are related to each other, under steady - state conditions, in accordance with Ohm's Law. The same kind of relationship is sometimes applied to magnetic circuits as follows

$$F = \phi R \qquad \text{...[2.33.1]}$$

$$\phi = \lambda / N \qquad \text{...[2.33.2]}$$

Where

F = magneto motive force (mmf) in ampere turns (Ni)

Φ = the equivalent flux linking all N turns of the exciting winding

R = magnetic reluctance in ampere turns per weber

The relationship expressed by Eq. 2.33.1 can be stated in terms of the magnetic permeance as follows

$$\phi = FP \qquad \text{...[2.33.3]}$$

where

$$P = \frac{1}{R} \qquad \text{...[2.33.4]}$$

In the case of magnetic circuits in which there is no leakage, all the flux serves to link each turn of the winding and Φ represents the total flux. The magnetic circuit practically satisfies that condition. However, in magnetic circuits where there is magnetic leakage and the flux follows paths such that different amounts of flux link different numbers of turns in the exciting winding, the value of Φ in Eqs. 2.33.1 to 2.33.3 is less than the total flux. Such situations exist in air-core solenoids as well as in many circuits having ferromagnetic cores. Figure 2.18.1 shows a coil in which the current produces complete and partial flux linkages.

The symbol $\underline{P}$ stands for permeance, which is the reciprocal of reluctance. Magnetic reluctance in these relationship corresponds to resistance in the electric circuit; permeance corresponds to conductance. Both these quantities, reluctance and permeance, are functions of the magnetic permeabilities of the different parts of the magnetic circuit as well as the configurations of these parts.

Substitution of Eq. 2.33.2 in Eq. 2.33.1 yields

$$F = \frac{\lambda}{N} R \qquad \text{...[2.33.5]}$$

but F = Ni and λ/i = L, hence

$$Ni = \frac{\lambda R}{N}$$

from which

$$L = \frac{\lambda}{i} = \frac{N^2}{R} = N^2 P \qquad \text{...[2.33.6]}$$

For the special case in which all the flux is confined to a path of constant cross-sectional area A and the mean length of flux path is l the expression for the reluctance is reduced to

$$R = \frac{l}{\mu A} \qquad ...[2.33.7]$$

Magnetic pull and magnetic torques can also be expressed as function of permeance and reluctance from Eq. 2.33.6

$$\frac{Li^2}{2} = \frac{R(Ni)^2}{2} \qquad ...[2.33.8]$$

and the developed force can be written as

$$f = +\frac{i^2}{2}\frac{dL}{dx} = +\frac{(Ni)^2}{2}\frac{dP}{dx} = \frac{F^2}{2}\frac{dP}{dx} \qquad ...[2.33.9]$$

and the developed torque as

$$T = \frac{i^2}{2}\frac{dL}{d\theta} = \frac{(Ni)^2}{2}\frac{dP}{d\theta} = \frac{F^2}{2}\frac{dP}{d\theta} \qquad ...[2.33.10]$$

The force and torque can be expressed in terms of reluctance by replacing P with $1/R$ in Eq. 2.33.10, thus

$$f = \frac{F^2}{2}\frac{dP}{dx} = \frac{F^2}{2}\frac{d}{dx}\left(\frac{l}{R}\right) = -\frac{F^2}{2R^2}\frac{dR}{dx} = -\frac{\phi^2}{2}\frac{dR}{dx} \qquad ...[2.33.11]$$

and

$$T = -\frac{\phi^2}{2}\frac{dR}{d\theta} \qquad ...[2.33.12]$$

In Eqs. 2.33.9 to 2.33.12 the expressions for force and torque are those developed by the electromagnetic structure, in other words, motor action is involved when there is motion of translation or rotation in the direction of the developed forces.

Example 2.2: The rotary electromagnetic device shown in Fig. 2.18 has 1,560 turns on each stator pole. The magnetic structure is of cast steel. The dissensions are as follows

R1 = 0.75 in. radius of rounded part of rotor

W = 1.00 in. width of rotor - and stator-pole face at right angles to page

g = 0.05 in. length of single air gap

Θ = angle between stator-pole tip and adjacent rotor-pole tip

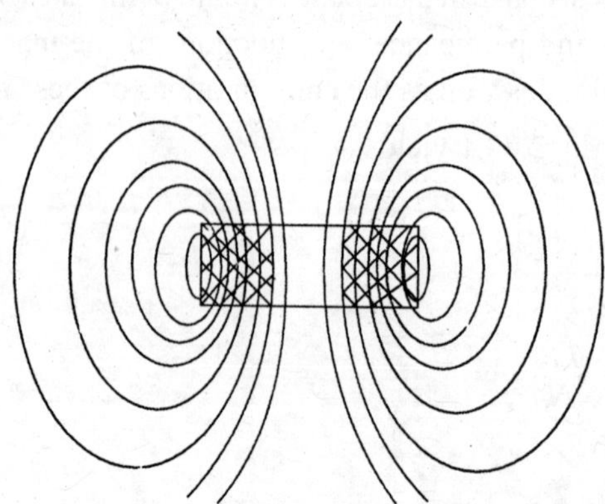

Fig. 2.18.1

(*a*) Neglect the effect of the iron and of flux fringing and determine the self inductance in terms of Θ assuming a linear relationship between the area of the air gap and Θ[(1)]

(*b*) Determine the maximum torque for a current of 1.2 amp.

(*c*) Express the permeance as a function of the angle Θ.

(*d*) Express the reluctance as a function of the angle Θ.

(*e*) Express the energy stored in the air gap as a function of the angle Θ fro a current of 1.2 amp.

Solution: (a)
$$L = \frac{\mu N^2 A}{l}$$

$$A = w\left(R_1 + \frac{g}{2}\right)\theta \text{ area of air gap in square meters}$$

$$l = 2g \text{ length of double air gap in meters}$$

$$\mu = 4\mu \times 10^{-7}$$

$$N = 1,560 \times 2 = 3,120$$

$$L = \frac{4\pi \times 10^{-7}(3,120)^2\, 1.00\,(0.75 + 0.025) \times 2.54 \times 10^{-2}\theta}{0.10}$$

$$= 2.505\theta \text{ h}$$

(*b*)
$$T = \frac{i^2}{2}\frac{dL}{d\theta} = \frac{(1.2)^2}{2} \times 2.405$$

$$= 1.73 \text{ newton m}$$

(*c*)
$$P = \frac{\mu A}{1} = \frac{4\pi \times 10^{-7} \times 1.00 \times 0.775 \times 2.54 \times 10^{-2}\theta}{0.10}$$

$$= 2.475 \times 10^{-7}\theta \text{ Webers per amp turn}$$

(*d*)
$$R = \frac{1}{P} = \frac{4.04 \times 10^6}{\theta} \text{ amp turns per weber}$$

(*e*)
$$W_\phi = \frac{Li^2}{2} = 1.73\theta \text{ j}$$

Example 2.3: Describe mutual inductance as a parameter that is associated with the flux linkage produced in one circuit by the current in another circuit.

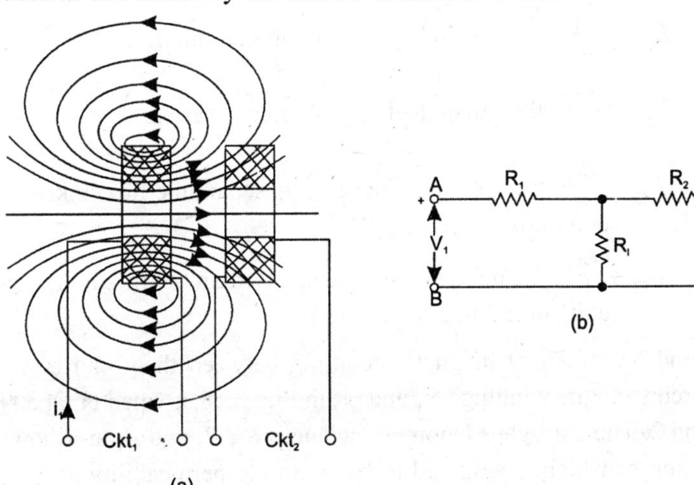

Fig. 2.18.2

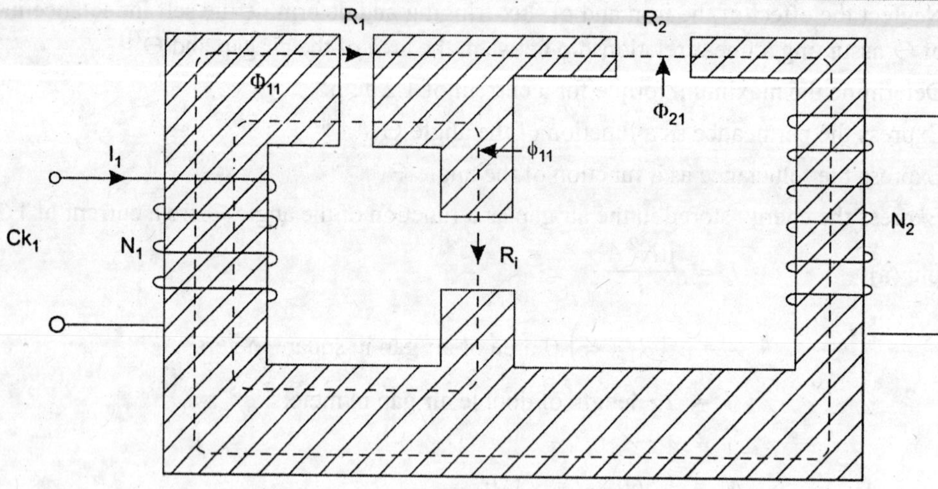

Fig. 2.18.3

Quantitatively, the mutual inductance between two circuits may be defined as the flux linkage produced in one circuit by a current of one ampere in the other circuit. In this discussion a circuit is considered as having one or more turns. Figure 2.18.2 shows a schematic diagram of circuits that are coupled inductively, *i.e.*, **magnetic flux** from one circuit links the other circuit. A current i_1 in circuit 1 produces magnetic flux, some of which links some of the turns of circuit 2 and thus induces a voltage in circuit 2 when i_1 changes.

Let

λ_{11} = Flux linkage of circuit 1 produced by its won current i_1

λ_{21} = Flux linkage of circuit 2 produced by the current i_1 in curcuit 1

λ_{22} = Flux linkage of circuit 1 produced by its current i_2

λ_{12} = Flux linkage of circuit 1 produced by the current i_2 in curcuit 2

The unit of flux linkage is the weber turn and that of inductance is the henry, which can be expressed as a weber turn per ampere. Hence

$$L_{11} = \frac{\lambda_{11}}{i_1}, \text{ the self-inductance of circuit 1 alone}$$

$$L_{22} = \frac{\lambda_{22}}{i2}, \text{ the self-inductance of circuit 2 alone}$$

$L_{12} = \frac{\lambda_{11}}{i_1}$, the mutual inductance, based on the flux linkage with circuit 1 for unit current in circuit 2

$L_{12} = \frac{\lambda_{11}}{i_1}$, the mutual inductance, based on the flux linkage with circuit 1 for unit current in circuit 2

The two circuits and the effect of magnetic coupling between them can be represented by the equivalent magnetic circuit and the windings N_1 and N_2 in Fig. 2.18.3, when N_1 and N_2 are the number of turn sin circuits 1 and 2. Three air gaps having reluctances R_1, R_2 and R_1 are shown in the magnetic circuit, the shaded portion of which is assumed to have infinite permeability and, consequently, zero reluctance. The resistivity of the material in the shaded portions is considered infinite so that no eddy currents can flow.

Assume a current of i_1 to flow in circuit 1 while the current in circuit 2 is zero. Let Φ_{11} be an equivalent flux, which, in linkage all N_1 turns of circuit 1, produces the flux linkage λ_{11}. Then

$$\phi_{11} \equiv \frac{\lambda_{11}}{N_1} \qquad \text{...[2.33.13]}$$

In Fig. 2.18.3 (b) the equivalent flux Φ_{11} is shown as having two components, Φ_{21} and Φ_{11}, in which Φ_{21} is the equivalent flux, in linking all N_2 turns of circuit 2, produces the flux linkage λ_{21}. Therefore

$$\phi_{21} \equiv \frac{\lambda_{21}}{N_2} \qquad \text{...[2.33.14]}$$

The remaining component Φ_{11} is the equivalent leakage flux of circuit 1 linking all N_1 turns without linking all N_1 turns without linking any of the N_2 turns of circuit 2. This means that

$$\phi_{11} = \phi_{11} - \phi_{21} \qquad \text{...[2.33.15]}$$

The magnetic circuit of Fig. 2.18.3. is comparable to the electric circuit of Fig. 2.18.2 (b), which is the equivalent T-Circuit for any 3 - terminal arrangement of pure resistances. The resistances R_1, R_2, and R_1 correspond to the reluctances V_1, is analogous to the mmf $N_1 i_1$ produced by the N_1 - turn winding. Therefore, it is evident, on the basis of elementary electric circuit theory, that

$$\phi_{21} = \frac{R_l}{R_1 R_2 + R_1 R_l + R_2 R_l} N_1 i_1 \qquad \text{...[2.33.16]}$$

and the resulting flux linkage produced in circuit 2 by i_1 is

$$\lambda_{21} = \frac{R_1 N_1 N_2 i_1}{R_1 R_2 + R_1 R_l + R_2 R_l} N_1 i_1$$

The mutual inductance based on the flux linkage with circuit 2 due the current in circuit 1 is therefore

$$L_{21} = \frac{\lambda_{21}}{i_1} = \frac{R_1 N_1 N_2}{R_1 R_2 + R_1 R_l + R_2 R_l} \qquad \text{...[2.33.17]}$$

The mutual inductance L_{12}, based on the flux linkage with circuit 1 due the current in circuit 2, can be found by considering a current i_2 in circuit 2 while the current i_1 in circuit 1 is zero, and then going through the process used previously, or simply by interchanging the subscripts 1 and in Eq, 2.33.17. This results in

$$L_{21} = \frac{\lambda_{21}}{i_1} = \frac{R_l N_2 N_2}{R_2 R_1 + R_2 R \ + R_1 R_l} \qquad \text{...[2.33.18]}$$

Equations 2.33.17 and 2.33.18 show the mutual inductance between two electric circuits to be reciprocal when the circuits are coupled by a homogeneous magnetic medium of constant permeability, *i.e.*

$$L_{12} = L_{21} \qquad \text{...[2.33.19]}$$

In cases where there are only two magnetically coupled circuits, the letter M is used to represent mutual inductance, *i.e.*

$$M = L_{12} = L_{21}$$

Coefficient of coupling

The mutual inductance between two circuits can be expressed in terms of their self-inductances L_{11}, L_{22} and their coefficient of coupling k, which is a function f the reluctance of the leakage flux path. It can be seen from Eq. 2.33.18 that for given values or R_1 and R_2 the mutual inductance increases with the reluctance R_l of the leakage path, becoming a maximum when R_l approaches infinity, the condition for perfect magnetic coupling between the two circuits. Let

$$k = \frac{\phi_{21}}{\phi_{22}} = \frac{R_l}{R_2 + R_l} \qquad \text{...[2.33.20]}$$

and

$$k_2 = \frac{\phi_{21}}{\phi_{22}} = \frac{R_l}{R_1 + R_l} \qquad \text{...[2.33.21]}$$

from which the coefficient of coupling is, by definition

$$k \equiv \sqrt{k_1 k_2} = \frac{R_l}{\sqrt{(R_1 + R_l)(R_2 + R_l)}} \qquad \text{...[2.33.22]}$$

The self-inductance of circuit 1 is

$$L_{11} = \frac{\lambda_{11}}{i_1} = \frac{N_1 \phi_1}{i_1} = \frac{(R_2 + R_l)N_1^2}{R_1 R_2 + R_1 R_l + R_2 R_l} \qquad \text{...[2.33.23]}$$

and that of circuit 2 is

$$L_{22} = \frac{\lambda_{22}}{i_2} = \frac{N_2 \phi_2}{i_2} = \frac{(R_1 + R_l)N_2^2}{R_1 R_2 + R_1 R_l + R_2 R_l} \qquad \text{...[2.33.24]}$$

$$\frac{L_{12}}{\sqrt{L_{11} L_{22}}} = \frac{R_l}{\sqrt{(R_1 + R_l)(R_2 + R_l)}} \qquad \text{...[2.33.25]}$$

A comparison of Eqs. 2.33.22 and 2.33.25 shows the mutual inductance to be

$$M = L_{12} = L_{21} = v3\sqrt{L_{11} L_{22}} \qquad \text{...[2.33.26]}$$

The coefficient of coupling k cannot exceed unity, although values as high as 0.998 are not unusual in iron-core transformers, whereas k in air-core transformers is generally smaller than 0.5.

2.21. ENERGY IN THE FIELD OF COUPLED CIRCUITS

The electromagnetic differential energy supplied to an electric circuit carrying a current i si given by

$$dW_{em} = i\, d\lambda \qquad \text{[2.34.1]}$$

It should be remembered that electric energy over and above that required to supply the irreversible energy over the above that required to supply the irreversible energy dissipated in the form of heat is required to maintain current in a circuit that is subjected to a variation of flux linkage. This is true whether the flux linkage λ is produced only by the current i in the circuit itself, or whether it is produced only by magnetic fields from other sources, or by fields from its own current in combination with those from other sources. The electromagnetic differential energy input to two magnetically coupled circuits is

$$dW_{em} = dW_{em_1} + dW_{em_2} \qquad ...[2.34.2]$$

$$= i_1\, d\lambda_1 + i_2\, d\lambda_2$$

where

$$\lambda_1 = L_{11}i_1 + Mi_2 \qquad \lambda_2 = Mi_1 + L_{22}i_2 \qquad ...[2.34.3]$$

from which

$$dW_{em} = i_1\, d(L_{11}i_1 + Mi_2) + i_2\, d(Mi_1 + L_{22}i_2) \qquad ...[2.34.4]$$

If there is no motion of one circuit relative to the other, and if there is no change in the configuration of the magnetic circuit, the self-inductances L_{11} and L_{22} as well as the mutual inductance M are constant, and no mechanical energy is supplied to or abstracted from the field. It is assumed, of course, that the inductances are independent of the current i_1 and i_2 *i.e.*, that the magnetic circuit is linear. Equation 2.34.4 can, therefore, be reduced to the form

$$dW_{em} = L_{11}i_1\, di_1 + M(i_1\, di_2 + i_2\, di_1) + L_{22}i_2\, di_2 \qquad ...[2.34.5]$$

$$= L_{11}i_1\, di_1 + M\, d(i_1\, i_2) + L_{22}i_2\, di_2$$

and the energy present in the field due to the currents i_1 and i_2 is

$$W\phi = \frac{1}{2}L_{11}i_1^2 + Mi_1 i_2 + \frac{1}{2}L_{22}i_2^2 \qquad ...[2.34.6]$$

Although the inductances were assumed constant while the currents were increased from zero to i_1 and i_2 in cicuits 1 and 2. Eq. 2.34.6 expresses the energy stored in the field for the particular values of L_{11}, L_{22}, M, i_1 and i_2 whether the inductances are constant or variable. This means that the energy stored in the field, for given values of L_{11}, L_{22}, M, i_1 and i_2, is unaffected by previous values these inductances might have had.

The development that led to Eq. 2.34.6 can be generalized to include n instead of two magnetically coupled circuits expressing the energy stored in the field by

$$W\phi = \sum_{j=1}^{n}\sum_{k=1}^{n}\frac{1}{2}L_{jk}i_j i_k \qquad ...[2.34.7]$$

2.22. TORQUE AND FORCE IN INDUCTIVELY COUPLED CIRCUITS

It is evident from Eqs. 2.34.6 and 2.34.7 that the energy stored in the magnetic field associated with two or more magnetically coupled circuits can be varied by changing the current in one or more of the circuits, or by changing the current in one or more of the circuits, or by changing one or more of the self-inductances or mutual inductances. If all currents are held constant, mechanical work is involved in changing the stored energy; this necessitates a change in one or more of the inductances. The rotary electromagnet in Fig. 2.19 illustrates two inductively or magnetically coupled circuits and in which the reluctance of the iron is considered negligible in comparison with that of the air gaps between the stator and the rotor. When the currents i_1 adn i_2 are flowing in circuits 1 and 2 in the directions shown, and with the angle θ smaller than 90°, the magnetic forces develop torque in the counterclockwise. If the angle θ is increased by the differential amount dθ, and the applied torque is dθ, then the mechanical differential energy input is

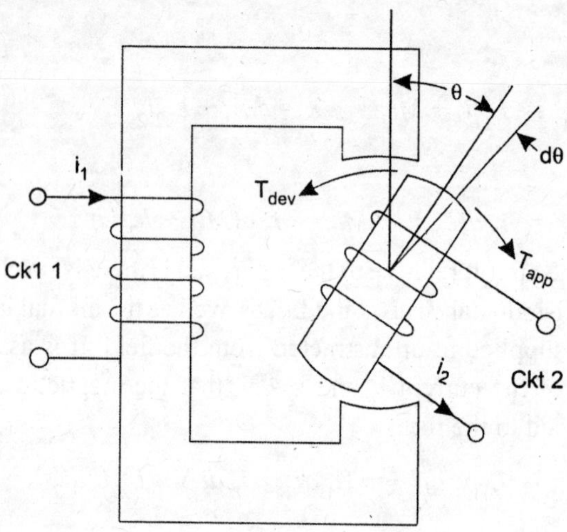

Fig. 2.19

$$dW_{mech} = T\,d\theta \quad \text{...[2.35.1]}$$

If, at the same time, there is an electromagnetic differential energy input dW_{em}, the energy stored in the field will be increased by the differential amount

$$dW_{\phi} = dW_{em} + dW_{mech} \quad \text{...[2.35.2]}$$

When the differentiation in Eq. 2.34.4 is performed, the expression for the electromechanical differential energy becomes

$$dW_{em} = L_{11}i_1\,di_1 + M(i_1\,di_2 + i_2\,di_1) + L_{22}i_2\,di_2 + i_1^2\,dL_{11} + 2i_1i_2\,dM + i_2^2 \quad \text{...[2.35.3]}$$

It should be noted that the inductances L_{11}, L_{22}, and M are not constant but are functions of the angle θ.

The energy stored in the field is given by Eq. 2.34.6 and it will be remembered that the energy stored in the field can be changed by a change in one or both of the currents as well as by a change in one or all of the inductances, so that the differential energy input to the magnetic field can be written as

$$dW_{\phi} = L_{11}i_1\,di_1 + M\,d(i_1\,i_2) + L_{22}i_2\,di_2 + \frac{1}{2}i_1^2\,L_{11} + i_1 i_2\,dM + \frac{1}{2}i_2^2 \quad \text{...[2.35.4]}$$

When Eq. 2.35.4 is subtracted from 2.35.3, then, on the basis of Eq. 2.35.5, the mechanical differential energy stored in the field is found to be

$$dW_{mech} = -\left(\frac{1}{2}i_1^2\,L_{11} + i_1 i_2\,dM + \frac{1}{2}i_2^2 dL_{22}\right) \qquad ...[2.35.5]$$

and, according to Eq. 2.35.1, the applied torque must be

$$T_{app} = -\left(\frac{1}{2}i_1^2\frac{dL_{11}}{d\theta} + i_1 i_2\frac{dM}{d\theta} + \frac{1}{2}i_2^2\frac{dL_{22}}{d\theta}\right) \qquad ...[2.35.6]$$

The magnet develops a torque equal and opposite to the applied torque, that is

$$T_{dev} = -T_{app} = \frac{1}{2}i_1^2\frac{dL_{11}}{d\theta} + i_1 i_2\frac{dM}{d\theta} + \frac{1}{2}i_2^2\frac{dL_{22}}{d\theta}$$

Similarly the developed force for a linear displacement is given by

$$T_{dev} = -T_{app} = \frac{1}{2}i_1^2\frac{dL_{11}}{dx} + i_1 i_2\frac{dM}{dx} + \frac{1}{2}i_2^2\frac{dL_{22}}{dx} \qquad ...[2.35.7]$$

When there are n-coupled circuits instead of 2-coupled circuits, and there is only one movable member in the electromagnet, as in the case of conventional motors and generators, the torque is found on the basis of Eq. 2.34.7 to be

$$T_{dev} = \sum_{j=1}^{n}\sum_{k=1}^{n}\frac{1}{2}i_j i_k\frac{dL_{jk}}{d\theta} \qquad ...[2.35.8]$$

If the change in inductance takes place while the currents are held constant, one-half of the electromagnetic energy input is stored in the magnetic field, whereas the other half is converted into mechanical energy. This is evident from Eqs. 2.35.4 and 2.35.5 because for constant currents, di_1 and di_2 must be zero. This equal division of stored energy and mechanical energy with constant currents is true only for linear circuits and does not hold for nonlinear magnetic circuits, *i.e.*, where there is appreciable saturation.

On the other hand, if the flux linkages are held constant while there is a change of inductance, the electromagnetic energy input must equal zero as is shown by Eq. 2.34.2 for $d\lambda_1$ and $d\lambda_2 = 0$. In that case energy stored in the field is given up to be converted into mechanical energy, *i.e.*, the mechanical energy is abstracted from the energy absorbed in the field.

2.23. FORCES IN NONLINEAR MAGNETIC CIRCUITS

The equations of force and torque which have been derived in the foregoing pages are based largely on the concept of inductance, and therefore apply strictly only to magnetic circuits that are linear. However, they may yield values saturated. Graphical analysis may be used to yield more accurate results and more valid relationships than those that make use of inductance. To keep the discussion simple, we shall consider only magnetic circuits that are excited from one winding, *i.e.*, magnetic circuits that are singly excited. Certain conclusions, however, can be drawn from the study of singly excited circuits that apply also to multiply excited circuits.

2.24. INDUCTANCE OF MAGNETIC CIRCUITS CONTAINING IRON

The concept of inductance when applied to nonlinear magnetic circuits leads to inconsistencies, depending upon how inductance is defined. The self-inductance of a circuit is defined in several ways, all of which are consistent in the case of air-core circuits. These are first

$$L = \frac{\lambda}{i} \quad ...[2.36.1]$$

Second

$$L = e\Big/\frac{di}{dt} \quad ...[2.36.2]$$

and third

$$L = \frac{2W\Phi}{i^2} \quad ...[2.36.3]$$

In Equation 2.36.3, Wϕ is the energy stored in the magnetic field

The emf of self-induction is also expressed by

$$e - \frac{d\lambda}{dt} \quad ...[2.36.4]$$

Another expression for self-inductance is obtained when Eq. 2.36.4 is substituted in Eq. 2.36.2, namely

$$L = \frac{d\lambda}{di} \quad ...[2.36.5]$$

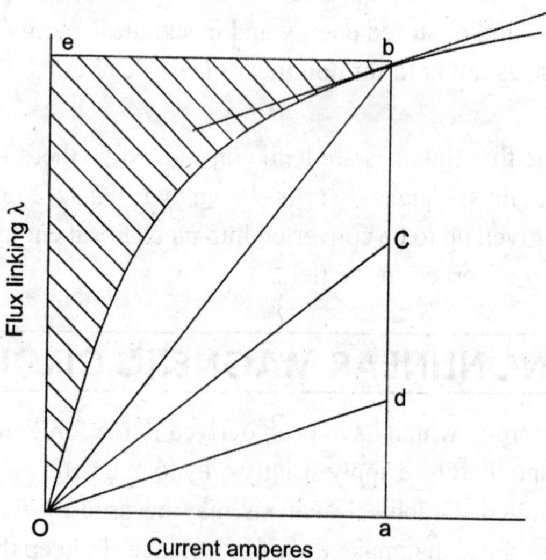

Fig. 2.19.1 Magnetzation curve

Equations 2.36.1, 2.36.3, and 2.36.5 do not yield the same values of inductance in a magnetic circuit containing iron or other ferromagnetic materials. This is particularly evident when there is appreciable saturation of the magnetic material.

Figure 2.19.1 shows the magnetization curve of a magnetic circuits containing iron. Such a curve is typical of a - c and d - c rotating machines, chokes, transformers, and other electromagnetic devices. Let the self-inductance be evaluated on the basis of Eqs. 2.36.1, 2.36.3, and 2.36.5 for this magnetic circuit when the flux linkage is oa amp.

Then, on the basis of Eq. 2.36.1, the apparent self-inductance is

$$L_a = \frac{\lambda}{i} = \frac{ab}{oa} \quad \text{...[2.36.6]}$$

and, on the basis of Eqn. 2.36.3, the effective self-inductance is

$$L_e = \frac{2W_\phi}{i^2} \quad \text{...[2.36.7]}$$

The shaded are in Figure 2.19.1 corresponds to Wϕ in Eq. 2.36.3. The line oc is constructed so that the area of the triangle oac equals this shaded area. Hence.

$$L_e = \frac{2W_\phi}{i^2} = \frac{ac}{oa} \quad \text{...[2.36.8]}$$

Finally, on the basis of Eq. 4 - 72, the differential self-inductance is

$$L_d = \frac{d\lambda}{di} = \frac{ad}{oa} \quad \text{...[2.36.9]}$$

The line od is drawn parallel to the tangent at the point b and has a slope of dλ/di.

It is apparent, from Eqs. 2.36.6 and 2.36.8, that three different values of inductance are obtained in the same non-linear circuit for a given current when three basic definitions of self-inductance are applied, although all three definitions lead to the same value for linear magnetic circuits. In spite of these inconsistencies, Eqs. 2.36.6, and 2.36.8 lead to adequate approximations in many cases. Certain analyses fo the steady-statet performance of synchronous machines make use of the relationship expressed by Eq. 2.36.6, whereas in the cases of chokes and transformers, in which small amounts of a - c flux are superimposed on a relatively large value of d-c flux, the differential inductance in Eq. 2.36.9 is useful. Equation 2.36.8 leads to a value of inductance that is convenient, for example, as a guide for evaluating the duty imposed upon contacts in switches or circuit breakers that interrupt the current in inductive circuits. Generally, however, the problem of the nonlinear magnetic circuit is approached from standpoints that avoid the use of inductance in the analysis and instead make use of the magnetization curve. The analysis of forces and torques in nonlinear magnetic circuits is a case in point that makes use of the magnetization curve.

2.25. FORCE AND ENERGY RELATIONSHIP BASED ON THE MAGNETIZATION CURVE

The energy stored in the magnetic field of the circuit, which has the magnetization curve shown in Fig. 2.19.1, is represented by the shaded are, *i.e.*

$$W_\phi = \int_0^\lambda i\, d\lambda = \text{area } oeb \quad \text{...[2.37.1]}$$

The area oba under the magnetization curve is also a product of flux linkage and current and represents the coenergy, *i.e.*

$$W_\phi = \int_0 i\,d\lambda = \text{area } oba \qquad \text{...[2.37.2]}$$

In linear magnetic circuits the energy stored in the field and the coenergy are equal, whereas in nonlinear magnetic circuits the coenergy is greater than the stored energy, as can be seen from Fig. 4-6.

Consider the rotary electromagnet shown in Fig. 2.19.2 (*a*). Since there is only one winding (that on the stator), the flux linkage can be plotted against the current in that winding as in Figs. 2.19.2 (*b*) and 2.19.2 (*c*).

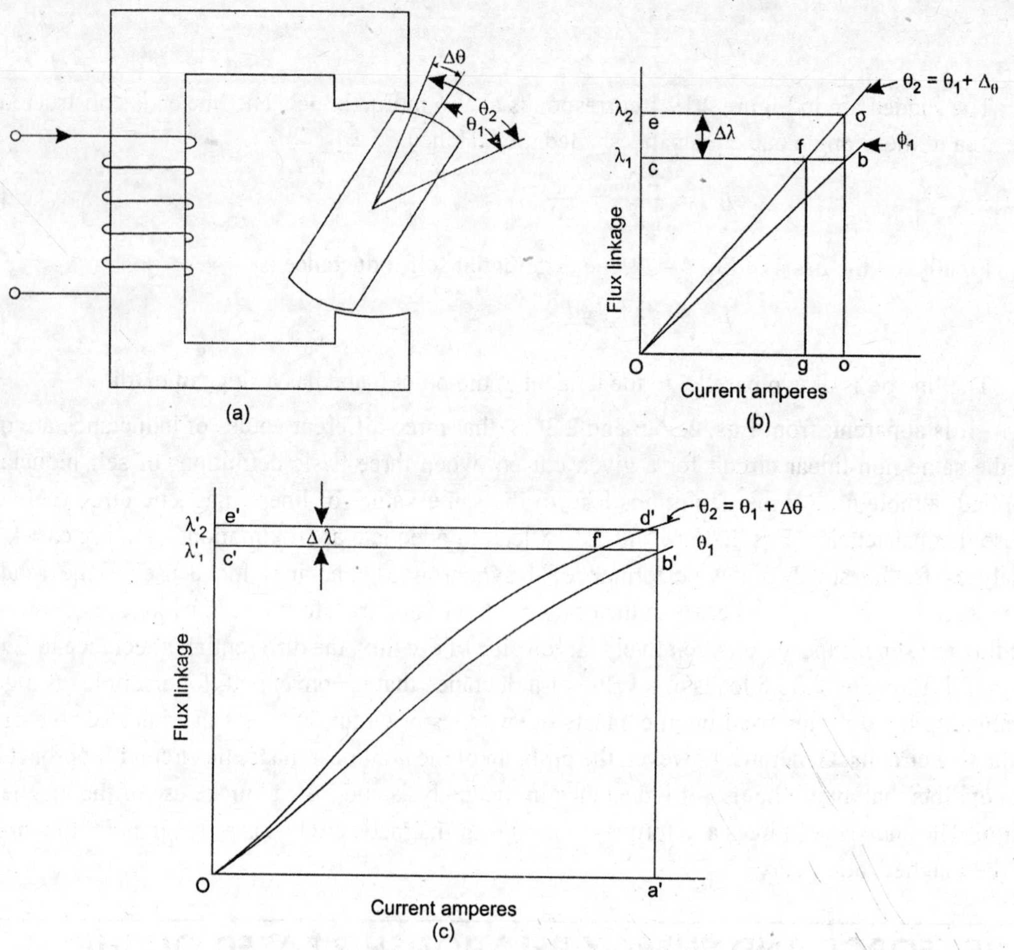

Fig. 2.19.2 (*a*) Single-exicited electromagnet; (*b*) magnetization curves iron unsaturated: (*c*) magnetization curves iron saturated

Linear Operation (Unsaturated Region). Suppose that the excitation of the electromagnet is held to values low enough so that the iron remains unsaturated so that the reluctance of the iron is negligible in comparison with that of the air gap. Then, for the angle Θ_1 between the magnetic axis of the rotor and an arbitrary reference line through the centre of the rotor, the magnetization curve is represented to a good degree of approximation by the straight line ob in Fig. 2.19.2 (b).

If the angle is increased from Θ_1 to $\Theta_2 = \Theta_1 + \Delta\Theta$, the reluctance of the air gap is decreased and the magnetization curve is then represented by the straight line od. Now if the current i is held constant at the value oa in Fig. 2.19.2 (*b*) while the displacement angle is increased from θ_1 to θ_2, the flux linkage increases from 1 to $\lambda_2 = \lambda_1 + \Delta_\lambda$ and the electromagnetic energy input is

$$W_{em} = \int_{\lambda_1}^{\lambda_2} i\, d\lambda \qquad \text{...[2.37.3]}$$

and is represented by the are of the rectangle bced. The energy originally stored in the field, *i.e.*, for the angle Θ_1, is represented by the area of the triangle obc, and when the area of the rectangle bced is added, the area obdeo is obtained. The final energy stored in the field, *i.e.*, for the angle Θ_2, is represented by the area of triangle obd, which must represent the mechanical energy. The area of triangle obd is one-half that of rectangle cbde, which shows that, for constant current in a linear magnetic circuit, the mechanical energy output equals one-half the electromagnetic energy input, as shown in the derivations making use of variation in inductance with displacement.

If the flux linkage is held constant while the rotor is advanced through the angle $\Delta\theta$, the current I decreases for oa to og in Fig. 2.19.2 (*b*). Furthermore, the the electromagnetic energy input is zero whne the flux linkage is constant. The energy stored in the field, when the angle is θ_2, is represented by the area of the triangle ofc and the mechanical energy output by the triangle obf. The mechanical energy when the flux linkage is constant is therefore abstracted from the energy stored in the field.

The average torque that is developed when the current is constant while the displacement $\Delta\theta$ occurs is

$$T_{av} = \frac{\text{Area of trinagle } obd}{\Delta\theta} \qquad \text{...[2.37.4]}$$

And for the case of constant flux linkage

$$T_{av} = \frac{\text{Area of trinagle } obf}{\Delta\theta} \qquad \text{...[2.37.5]}$$

The same considerations, as far as force is concerned,. apply to electromagnets in which the displacement is linear, say Δx, in that case Δx is substituted for $\Delta\theta$ in Eqs. 2.37.4 and 2.37.5.

The areas of the triangles must, of course, be in terms of flux linkage and current, thus, the area of triangle obd would be one half the product of $\Delta\lambda$ or $\lambda_2 - \lambda_1$ and oa in amperes.

Nonlinear Operation (Saturated Region). If the current in the exciting winding is increased to a value represented by oa' so that the iron becomes saturated as shown in Fig. 2.19.2 (*c*), the magnetization curves for the rotor positions at Θ_1 to Θ_2 are no longer linear. The graphical analysis, nevertheless, may be applied just as in the case of linear operation.

If the current is held constant while the rotor undergoes a change in angular displacement of $\Delta\Theta = \Theta_2 - \Theta_1$ the flux linkage increases from λ'_1 to λ'_2 ob by an amount $\Delta\lambda'$ and the electromagnetic input is

$$\Delta Wem = i\,\Delta\lambda \qquad \text{...[2.37.6]}$$

Which is represented by the area of the rectangle c'b'd'e'. The energy stored in the field changes by an amount corresponding to the difference between the areas od'e'o for Θ_2 and ob'c'o for Θ_1 The mechanical energy output is then represented by the area. Similarly, if the flux linkage is held constant during the rotor displacement $\Delta\Theta$, the mechanical energy output is represented by the area of ob'f'o since there is no electromagnetic energy input, and we have

$$\Delta W_{mech} = W_{\phi 1} - W_{\phi 2} = \Delta W\phi \quad ...[2.37.7]$$

where $W_{\phi 1}$ and $W_{\phi 2}$ is the energy stored in the field at Θ_1 and Θ_2 for λ' constant λ'_1. the average developed torque when the flux linkage is held constant must therefore be

$$T_{av} = \frac{\Delta W_{mech}}{\Delta\theta} = -\left.\frac{\Delta W_\phi}{\Delta\theta}\right|_{\lambda = constant}$$

On the other hand, when the current is held constant, the mechanical energy output equals the increase in the coenergy (area ob'd'o), and for constant current the average torque is

$$T_{av} = +\left.\frac{\Delta W_\phi}{\Delta\theta}\right|_{\lambda = constant} \quad ...[2.37.8]$$

The difference between the areas ob'd'o for constant current and ob'f'o is the area f'b'd', which becomes smaller and smaller as $\Delta\Theta$ is made smaller, vanishing as $\Delta\Theta \to 0$ so that torque is expressed by

$$T = -\frac{\partial W_\phi}{\partial\theta}(\lambda, \theta) = +\frac{\partial W_\phi}{\partial\theta}(i, \theta) \quad ...[2.37.9]$$

It is important to note that when the energy W_ϕ can be expressed analytically it must be explicitly in terms of the flux linkage λ and the angular position Θ, whereas the coenergy W'_Θ must be expressed explicitly in terms of the current i and the angular position Θ. This follows from the fact that the energy stored in the field is given by

$$W\phi = \int_0^{\lambda} i\, d\lambda$$

and the current to produce a given value of flux linkage λ is determined not only by the value of λ, but also by that of the parameter Θ, so that the current is expressed implicitly by

$$i = f(\lambda, \theta)$$

Also, the coenergy is obtained as follows

$$W'\phi = \int_0^{i} \lambda\, di$$

in which the flux linkage is a function of the current and Θ, or

$$\lambda = \phi(i, \theta)$$

It should be carefully noted that Eq, 2.37.9 expresses the developed torque, the direction being such as to decrease the stored energy for a given value of λ, as indicated by the minus sign, or such as to increase the coenergy for given value of i

In system where translational rather than totary displacement occurs, the developed force is

$$f = \frac{\partial W_\phi}{\partial x}(\lambda, x) = +\frac{\partial W'_\phi}{\partial x}(i, x) \quad ...[2.37.10]$$

As mentioned previously, the stored energy and the coenergy are equal in linear systems. Then, on basis of Eqs, 2.37.4, the torque, as $\Delta\Theta \to 0$ is expressed by

$$T = \frac{\partial W_\phi}{\partial\theta}(i, \theta) = +\frac{\partial W'_\phi}{\partial\theta}(i, \theta) \quad ...[2.37.11]$$

Or in translational systems

$$f = +\frac{\partial W_\phi(i,x)}{\partial x} = +\frac{\partial W'_\phi(i,x)}{\partial x} \quad ...[2.37.12]$$

Various torque and force relationships can be derived for linear systems on the basis of Eqs. 2.37.11 and 2.37.12 since the energy stored in the field, whether the system is linear or not, is determined from the integral

$$W_\phi = \int_0^\lambda i\,d\lambda = \int^\phi i\,d(N\phi) = \int_0^\phi Ni\,d\phi = \int_0^\phi F\,d\phi$$

The following relationships obtain for linear system

$$\lambda = Li, \quad F = \phi \quad \phi = FP$$

So that the energy stored in the field can be written as

$$W_\phi = \frac{1}{2}Li^2 = \frac{1}{2}F^2P = \frac{1}{2}\frac{F^2}{R}$$

and the force can be written as

$$T = \frac{\partial W\phi(i,\theta)}{\partial\theta} = \frac{1}{2}i^2\frac{dL}{d\theta} = \frac{1}{2}F^2\frac{dP}{d\theta} = -\frac{1}{2}\frac{F^2}{R^2}\frac{dR}{d\theta} = -\frac{\phi^2}{2}\frac{dR}{d\theta} \quad ...[2.37.13]$$

and the toque can be expressed as

$$f = \frac{1}{2}i^2\frac{dL}{d\theta} = \frac{1}{2}F^2\frac{dP}{d\theta} = -\frac{1}{2}\frac{F^2}{R^2}\frac{dR}{d\theta} = -\frac{\phi^2}{2}\frac{dR}{d\theta} \quad ...[2.37.14]$$

Various relationships for torque and force can be derived for linear systems on the basis of Eqs. 2.37.11 and 2.37.12 since the energy stored in the field (whether the system is linear or nonlinear) is given by

$$W_\phi = \int_0^\lambda i\,d\lambda = \int_0^\phi F\,d\phi \quad ...[2.37.15]$$

Where φ is the equivalent flux linking all N turns and F = Ni. However for linear

$$\lambda = \mathrm{Li} \quad \phi = \mathrm{FP}, = \frac{F}{\mathrm{R}} \quad ...[2.37.16]$$

and when eq 2.37.16 is substituted in 4-90 the result

$$W_\phi = \frac{1}{2}Li^2 = \frac{1}{2}F^2P = \frac{1}{2}\frac{F^2}{R} \quad ...[2.37.17]$$

Then from eqs. 2.37.11 and 2.37.12 the torque and force are

$$T = \frac{\partial W\phi}{\partial\theta}(i,\theta) = \frac{1}{2}i^2\frac{dL}{d\theta} = \frac{1}{2}F^2\frac{dP}{d\theta} = -\frac{1}{2}\frac{F^2}{R^2}\frac{dR}{d\theta} = -\frac{\phi^2}{2}\frac{dR}{d\theta} \quad ...[2.37.18]$$

and

$$f = \frac{\partial W\phi}{\partial x}(i,x) = \frac{1}{2}i^2\frac{dL}{dx} = \frac{1}{2}F^2\frac{dP}{dx} = -\frac{1}{2}\frac{F^2}{R^2}\frac{dR}{d\theta} = -\frac{1}{2}\phi^2\frac{d\theta}{d\theta} \quad ...[2.37.19]$$

Equations 2.37.18 and 2.37.19 show that the developed torque and developed force are in a direction such as to increase the energy stored in the field if the current is held constant. In other words, the forces on the members of the system are such as to increase the flux linkage if the current remains constant. In the case of a solenoid, the force is such as the shorten the length of the air gap, *i.e.*, dP/dx is positive and dR/dx is negative since the permeance is inversely proportional to the length of the air gap and the reluctance is directly proportional to the gap length.

It is necessary when performing the partial differentiation of Eqs. 4-93 and 4-94 to express the stored energy W_ϕ in terms of the current i or the mmf F rather than the flux Φ. For example, since F = ΦR the energy stored in the field is

$$W_\phi(\phi, \theta) = \frac{1}{2}\phi^2 R$$

and if the partial derivative is taken of W_ϕ the result is

$$\frac{\partial W_\phi(\phi, \theta)}{\partial \theta} = \frac{1}{2}\phi^2 \frac{dR}{d\theta} = \frac{1}{2}\frac{F^2}{R}\frac{dR}{d\theta} \qquad ...[2.37.20]$$

When this result is compared with that in Eq. 4-94, it will be found that the sign are opposite. This is to be expected since, in taking the partial derivative of the stored energy with respect to Θ, the flux Φ is a parameter assumed constant. Also, a decrease in the reluctance is accompanied by a decrease in the energy stored on the field, whereas, for constant current, a decrease in the reluctance is accompanied by an increase in the stored energy.

2.26. LIFTING POWER OF A MAGNET

Consider two opposite poles, each of area '*a*' square metres are facing each other as shown in Fig. 2.20 (*a*). Let the force of attraction acting between the two poles be *P* newtons. If one of the poles (say S-pole) is pulled apart through a small distance *dx*, then work will be done against the force of altraction ;

$$\text{Work done} = P \times dx \text{ joules} \qquad ...(i)$$

By pulling one of the pole apart an additional volume ($a \times dx\ m^3$) of magnetic field will be created between the poles. The above work done will be stored in this additional volume ;

$$\text{Energy stored in the additional volume} = \frac{B^2}{2\mu_0} \times adx \text{ joules} \qquad ...(ii)$$

Equating eq. (*i*) and (*ii*), we get,

$$P \times dx = \frac{B^2}{2\mu_0} \times a \times dx \text{ (here B is the flux density in wb/m}^2\text{)}$$

or

$$P = \frac{B^2 a}{2\mu_0} \text{ newtons}$$

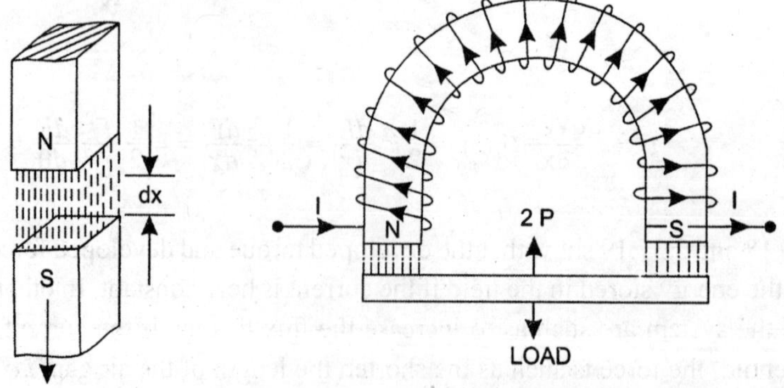

(*a*) (*b*)

Fig. 2.20

Note : P is the force of attraction at each pole. In practice, U-shaped two-pole magnets are used, as shown in Fig. 2.20 (b), in such magnets, the total pulling force will be 2 P. Electromagnets are widely used for commercial lifting jobs such as lifting of iron scrap by electromagnetic jaws of cranes and loading it into the truck ; lifting of heavy iron machine parts in the industries etc.

Example 2.4 : The inductance of a coil is 0.15 H. The coil has 100 turns. Find (i) total magnetic flux through the coil when the current is 4 A ; (ii) energy stored in the magnetic field ; (iii) voltage induced in the coil, when current is reduced to zero in 0.01 second.

Solution : Inductance of the coil, $L = \frac{N\phi}{I}$

where $N = 100$ turns ; $L = 0.15$; $I = 4A$;

∴ Flux, $\phi = \frac{0.15 \times 4}{100} = 6$ m Wb (*Ans.*)

Energy stored $= LI^2/2 = 0.15 \times (4)2/2 = \mathbf{1.2\ J}$ (*Ans.*)

Voltage induced, $e = L\frac{di}{dt} = 0.15 \times \frac{4}{0.01} = \mathbf{60\ V}$ (*Ans.*)

EXERCISES

1. Draw B-H curve for a ferromagnetic material. Explain why the curve is non-linear. Discuss what saturation means.
2. Draw hysteresis loops for; soft-magnetic material, hard-magnetic material. Discuss the applications of these materials on the basis of size of the loops.
3. Sketch a typical magnetic hysteresis loop and indicate the following on this loop.

   Retentivity, residual magnetism, coercive force, saturation. Give the significance of these terms.
4. What is a series magnetic circuit? If a series circuit is made up of three different magnetic materials, find the total mmf to be provided by the exciting coil. Hence, define Kirchhoff's mmf law.
5. For a linear magnetic circuit, derive the following relations for the energy stored in magnetic field W_{fld} and co-energy W'_{fld}.

$$W_{fld} = W'_{fld} = \frac{1}{2} F\phi = \frac{1}{2} \psi.i = \frac{1}{2} \phi^2.Rl = \frac{1}{2} . \frac{F^2}{Rl} = \frac{1}{2} LI^2$$

   Hence show that the magnetic stored energy density is given by $\frac{1}{2}\frac{B^2}{\mu}$ Joules/m^3.
6. A simplified reluctance motor is shown in Fig. 2.13.5. Sinusoidal inductance variation is shown in Fig. 2.13.6, where

L_d = maximum inductance when rotor axis is along direct axis. *i.e*., when 0 = 0 and π

L_q = minimum inductance when rotor axis is in the quadrature axis, *i.e.* when $\theta = \frac{\pi}{2}$ and $\frac{3\pi}{2}$

(*a*) Find an expression for the instantaneous torque on the rotating element. Assume $\theta = \omega_{mt} - \delta$ and $i = I_m \sin \omega t$

(*b*) In case rotor speed ω_m is made equal to time angular velocity ω, show that the average torque is

$$\frac{1}{8} I_m^2 (L_d - L_q) \sin 2\delta$$

7. (*a*) Distinguish between singly and doubly-excited magnetic systems.

(*b*) In a doubly-excited rotary machine, the inductance co-efficients are

$$L_{11} = (1.1 + 0.4 \cos 2\,\theta),$$

$$L_{22} = (0.03 + 0.005 \cos 2\,\theta),$$

$$L_{12} = 0.2 \cos \theta$$

The exciting currents are i_1 = 8A and i_2 = 5A

Obtain the torque/angular displacement relation. Derive the expression used, if any.

[Ans. (*b*) (–38.1 sin 2θ – 80 sin θ) Nm.]

8. Define a parallel magnetic circuit.

Take a parallel magnetic circuit with an exciting coil. How can coil mmf be calculated for this circuit. Hence, define Kirchhoff's flux law.

9. Show that energy stored in the field of coupled circuits is given by

$$\frac{1}{2} L_{11} \,.\, i_1^2 + \frac{1}{2} L_{22} \,.\, i_2^2 + M\, i_1\, i_2$$

10. Derive an expression for the lifting power of a magnet.

11. In the electromagnet shown in Fig. 2.20 (*b*), area of each pole is 25 cm^2. Flux crossing each pole is 125 μWb. Calculate the weight that can be lifted by the magnet. **[Ans.** 0.507 kg]

12. Lifting magnet shown in Fig. 2.20 (*b*) has per pole area of 30 cm^2. A soft-iron plate is being lifted by the magnet. If total flux around the magnetic circuit is 6×10^{-4} Wb, then calculate the weight of the iron plate being lifted. **[Ans.** 9.73 kg]

OBJECTIVE TYPE QUESTIONS

Tick the correct answer.

1. For a linear magnetic circuit, stored magnetic energy is

(*a*) $F\phi$ (*b*) $\frac{1}{2}\frac{\Psi^2}{L}$ (*c*) $\frac{F^2}{Rl}$ (*d*) $\psi . i$

2. Magnetic stored-energy density in iron is given by

(*a*) $\frac{1}{2}\phi^2 Rl$ (*b*) $\frac{1}{2} . B^2 \mu$ (*c*) $\frac{1}{2}\frac{B^2}{\mu}$ (*d*) $\frac{1}{2}\frac{B}{\mu}$

3. A linear magnetic circuit has flux-linkages of 1.2 Wb turns when a current of 15 A flows through its coil. Energy stored in the magnetic field of this coil, in Joules, is

(*a*) 18 (*b*) 36 (*c*) 9 (*d*) 3.6

4. The electromagnetic force, developed in any physical system, acts in such a direction as to tend to

(*a*) decrease the co-energy at constant mmf
(*b*) increase the co-energy at constant flux
(*c*) decrease the co-energy at constant flux
(*d*) increase the co-energy at constant mmf.

5. Lifting power of a magnet is given by

(*a*) $\frac{1}{2} \cdot \frac{B^2}{\mu_0} \cdot a$ (*b*) $\frac{B^2}{\mu_0} \cdot a$ (*c*) $2\frac{B^2}{\mu_0} a$ (*d*) $\frac{1}{2}\frac{B}{\mu_0} \cdot a$

6. The developed electromagnetic force and/or torque in an electromechanical energy conversion system act in such a direction that tends.

(*a*) to increase the stored energy at constant mmf
(*b*) to decrease the stored energy at constant flux
(*c*) to decrease the coenergy at constant mmf
(*d*) to decrease the stored energy at constant mmf

7. A magnetic relay has linear magnetization curve at its open and closed positions. If the armature moves slowly from open to closed position, then electrical energy input to the relay

(*a*) gets stored in the magnetic field
(*b*) gets converted into mechanical work
(*c*) gets divided equally between the magnetic and electric fields
(*d*) gets divided equally between magnetic field and mechanical work.

8. The inductance of a coil is 0.2 H. The coil has 100 turns. For a coil current of 5A, the magnetic flux through the coil is

(*a*) 4 mWb (*b*) 1 mWb (*c*) 10 mWb (*d*) 100 mWb

Answers

1. (*b*) 2. (*c*) 3. (*c*) 4. (*d*) 5. (*a*) 6. (*b*)
7. (*d*) 8. (*c*)

THE DIRECT CURRENT MACHINES

3.1. INTRODUCTION

All the Direct Current Machines work on the **Principle of Electro magnetic induction** and may be regarded as energy converters, either converting electrical into mechanical energy (motors), or mechanical into electrical energy (Generators), or electrical energy at one voltage into electrical energy at another voltage (Transformers). The operation of all the rotating electromagnetic machines depends on two fundamental principles, *i.e.*

(*a*) The induction of e.m.f. in a circuit undergoing a change of flux linkages, and

(*b*) The force or torque imposed on a current-carrying circuit situated in a magnetic field.

The numerical value of such an induced e.m.f. in a complete circuit is given by the equation,

$$e = \frac{d}{dt}(N\phi) \text{ volts} \quad ...(i)$$

and the numerical value of the torque is given by,

$$T = I.\frac{d}{d\theta}(N.\phi) \text{ Newton–metres} \quad ...(ii)$$

NOTE: It should be clearly understood that both of the basic actions referred to above apply equally to generators and motors.

3.2. BASIC PRINCIPLE OF GENERATOR

A generator is a machine which converts mechanical energy (or Power) into electrical energy (or Power) as shown in power flow Fig. 3.1. This energy conversion is based on the principle that whenever a conductor or coil rotates in a stationary magnetic field (or flux), an e.m.f. is induced in the conductor or coil by cutting the magnetic flux. This e.m.f. is known as dynamically (or motionally) induced e.m.f. and causes a current to flow if the conductor or coil circuit is closed.

The magnitude of the induced e.m.f. in the conductor depends on the rate at which the lines of force are cut. The direction of the e.m.f. induced can be found out from the Fleming's right hand Rule.

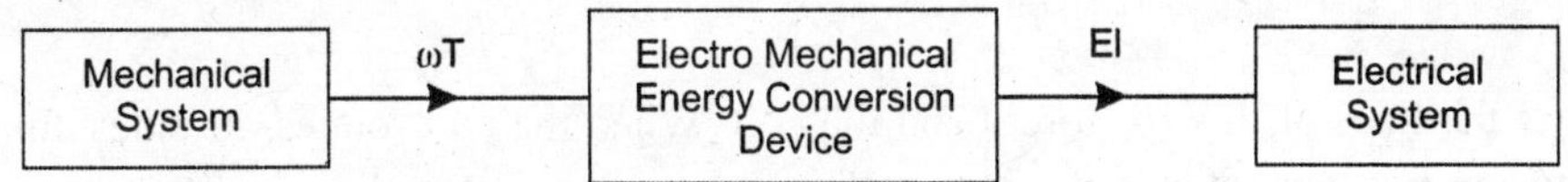

Fig. 3.1. Power flow diagram

(It should be kept in mind that in D.C. generators the magnetic field is stationary and the conductors move, where as in A.C. generators, *i.e.* alternators the conductors are stationary and the magnetic field moves).

3.3. ESSENTIAL PARTS OF A D.C. GENERATOR

There are two basic essential Parts of a D.C. generator

1. **Armature,** *i.e.* system of conductors which cuts the flux when moved.
2. **Magnetic field,** *i.e.* field system which produces the magnetic field and is stationary.

3.4. SIMPLE A.C. GENERATOR (ALTERNATOR) CONSTRUCTION

The simplest generator shown in Fig. 3.2 consists of;

(*a*) A uniform magnetic field provided by the north and south poles ;

(*b*) A shaft upon which is mounted a single loop of copper wire or coil;

(*c*) Some means of driving the shaft at constant speed (*e.g.* engine).

The two ends of the loop are connected to two brass collars called slip rings *A* and *B*, which are fixed to shaft and insulated from it and each other. Two collecting brushes (of carbon or copper) which rub constantly against slip rings. Their function is to collect the current induced in the coil and supply it to the external load resistance *R*.

The rotating coil may be named as 'armature' and the magnets as 'field magnets'.

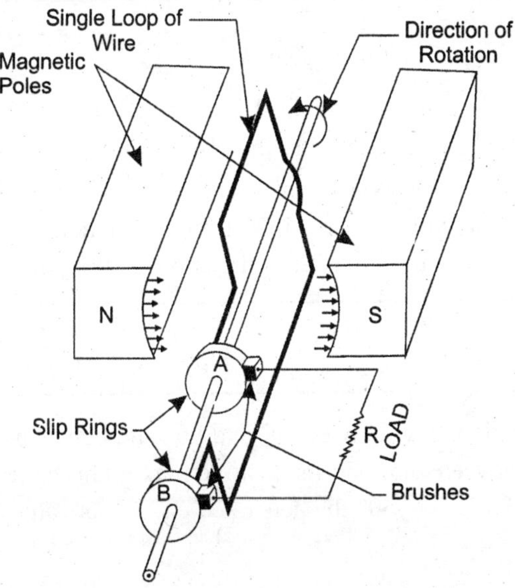

Fig. 3.2. The simple generator

Working

Fig. 3.3 shows the lines of flux (or force) and the coil. When the coil rotates, its sides cut the lines of flux and some e.m.f. is generated in it. This e.m.f. is not constant but is changing its value and direction as the coil rotates inside the magnetic field or flux. The graph shown in Fig. 3.4 shows how the value and direction of the generated e.m.f. changes with the position of the coil. From the graph the following points should be noted:

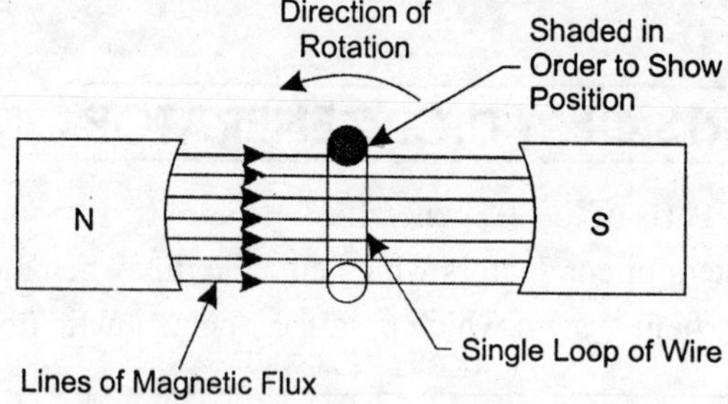

Fig. 3.3. Front view of simple generator showing magnetic field and loop of wire

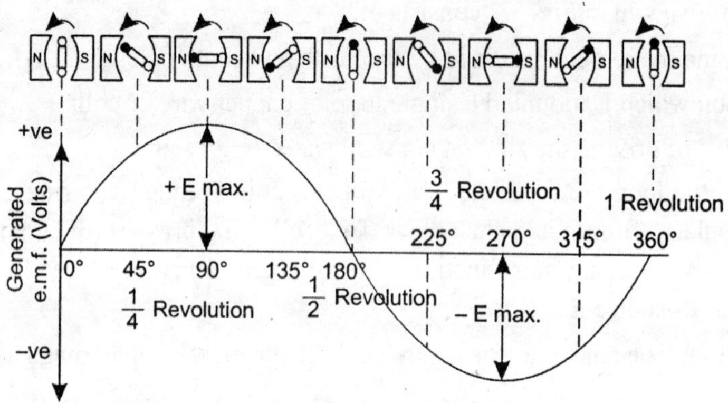

Fig. 3.4

1. When the coil is at right-angles to the direction of the flux no e.m.f. is generated, *i.e.* the e.m.f. is zero at 0°, 180° and 360°, because at these positions the coil is moving along the lines of flux and, therefore, not cutting across them.
2. When the coil is in line with the direction of flux the generated e.m.f. is at a maximum, this occurs at 90° and 270°. At these positions the coil is cutting maximum lines of flux.

Note. These two maximum values are opposite in sign, one positive and the other negative. This is because the coil, though being in line, has undergone a rotation of 180°.

3. At intermediate positions (*i.e.* between 0° and 90° and between 90° and 180°) the generated e.m.f. has values between zero and its positive maximum value. Whilest between 180° and 270° and between 270° and 360° the generated e.m.f. has values between zero and negative maximum value.

The shape of the graph as shown in Fig. 2.5, which results for one revolution of the coil, is called the waveform. Further rotation would produce identical patterns.

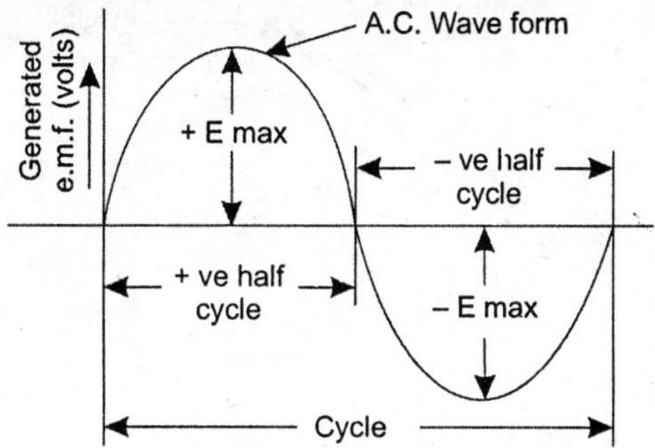

Fig. 3.5. Alternating voltage (Sine–wave)

The parts of the waveform which corresponds to half a revolution are called half cycles.

Since the waveform has positive and negative half cycles it is said to be alternating and the output is an alternating voltage. This machine is, therefore, called an a.c. generator or alternator. The waveform of this alternating voltage is called a sine wave. The value of the voltage at any position of the coil (called the instantaneous value) is given by the equation

$$\text{Instantaneous value} = \text{Maximum value of e.m.f. x } \sin\theta$$

or

$$e = E_{max} \cdot \sin\theta$$

where θ is the angle moved through measured from the vertical.

3.4.1. Factors on which the E.m.f of a Generator Depends

The magnitude of the generator e.m.f depends upon the rate of cutting of flux by various conductors. It will, therefore, depend upon:

(*i*) The number of conductors

(*ii*) The speed of rotation

(*iii*) The flux density and

(*iv*) The nature of the armature winding.

3.5. SIMPLE D.C. GENERATOR

We have seen that when a single loop of wire is rotated inside a magnetic field an alternating voltage is produced. This happened because the coil was connected to slip rings. The only function of the slip rings is to collect the current from the coil and give to the outer circuit. But to obtain a unidirectional current or direct current from the coil the slip rings would have to be replaced by a two part commutator or split ring.

This is shown in Fig. 3.6. The function of the split ring or the commutator is to reverse the connections to the rotating coil through fixed brushes and to collect the e.m.f. in one direction. Thus the resultant current in the external circuit becomes unidirectional.

The commutator or split ring is made of copper segments, which are insulated from the shaft and each other, as shown in Fig. 3.7. Each end of the coil is connected to a segment.

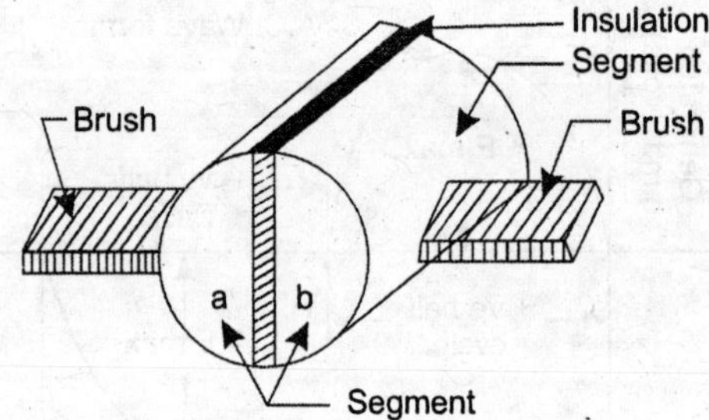

Fig. 3.6. Two part commutator or split ring

Two brushes make alternate contact with each part of the commutator as it rotates.

Fig. 3.8 illustrates the way in which the commutator works. The commutator rotates with the coil so that the segments continually interchange with the two stationary brushes.

The generated e.m.f. in the coil alternates as before but the output voltage at the brushes retains the same polarity. This is because after a half revolution (180° rotation) the segments interchange their brushes so that as the voltage begins to increase again in the opposite direction the polarity of the output voltage remains the same. The output waveform is as shown in the Fig. 3.9. Its maximum value is the same as that of the simple alternator, if generated under the same conditions. The output voltage fluctuates but does not alternate.

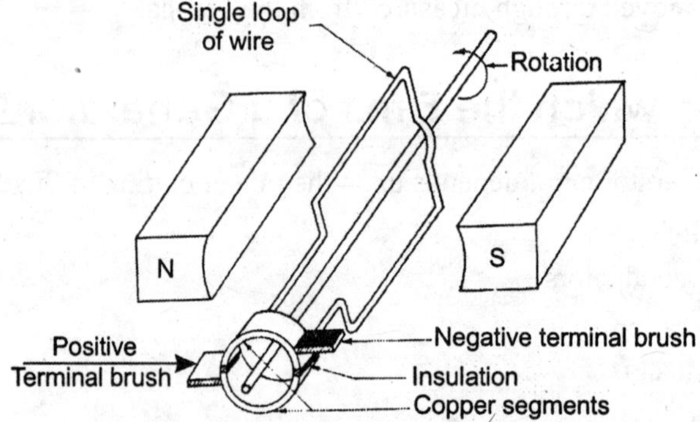

Fig. 3.7. Simple D.C. Generator

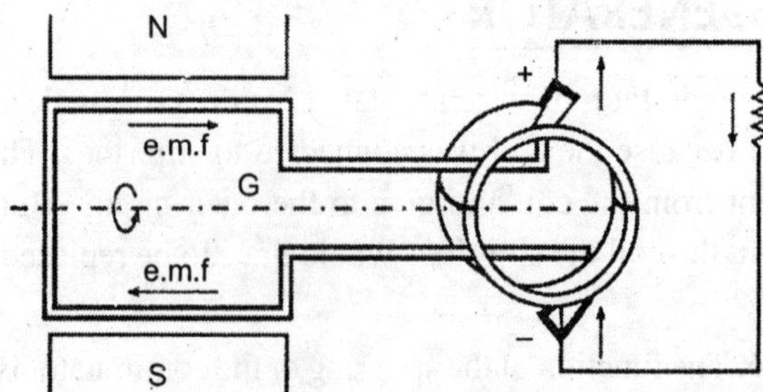

Fig. 3.8. Operation of a two part commutator

The arrows in the Fig. 3.8 indicate the direction of current flow. Although the direction of the current in the rotating coil reverses each half revolution, the direction of the current through the load remains unaltered. However, though the current is unidirectional, it is not steady but fluctuates in value as the coil rotates.

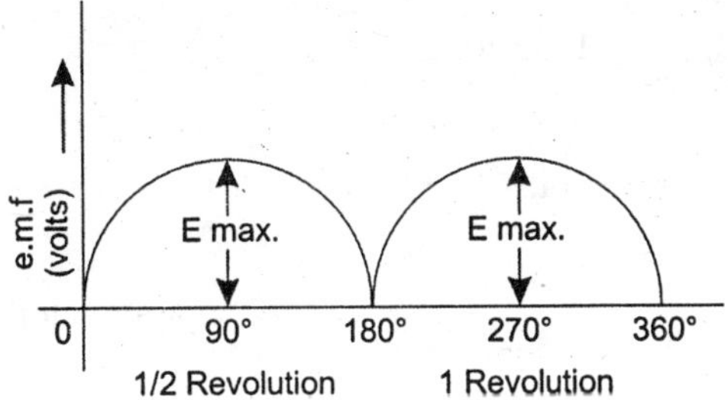

Fig. 3.9. Output voltage waveform

As seen, the current to the external circuit is uni-directional, but rising and falling between zero and maximum for each 180° of rotation. One step to over come this defect of big variation in the magnitude of e.m.f. to use two coils instead of one coil at rt. angles to each other connected in series with their two ends connected to the two segments of the commutator then since the two coils have 90° phase difference, their individual outputs will be as shown in Fig. 3.10 and the resultant will be of much smaller ripple than that of Fig. 3.9 where only one coil was used. It should be noted that the voltage between the brushes is never zero in this case.

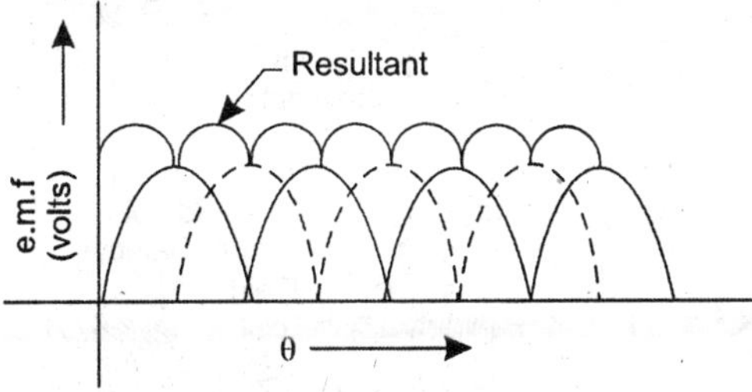

Fig. 3.10

In actual practice a generator has a number of coils with ends connected to a number of segments of the commutator, so that the ripple of the resultant e.m.f. is so much reduced that it can be taken as a direct current of constant value.

3.6. BASIC CONSTRUCTION OF D.C. MACHINES

The simple loop generator has been discussed in detail merely to understand the basic principle underlying the construction and working of an actual generator. From our study so far we have seen that a D.C. Machine consists essentially of a stationary magnet assembly called a stator and a rotating armature carrying properly wound conductors connected to the commutator, mounted on the same shaft as the armature. There is an air gap between the poles and the armature. The other parts of the machine are the brushgear, the bearings and the end shields. Fig. 3.11 shows the various parts of a disassembled medium size machine. Basically there is no difference between generator and motor. Any direct current generator can be run as a motor *i.e.* converts electrical energy into mechanical energy if its field and armature are connected to a suitable electric supply. So, the D.C. Machine whether generator or motor has the following main parts which are discussed in details:

(*a*) **Stator**

(*i*) Yoke or Frame

(*ii*) Main poles → Pole cores; → Pole shoes

(*iii*) Field or Magnetising coils

(*b*) **Rotor**

(*i*) Armature (*ii*) Commutator

(*c*) **Brushes**

(*d*) **End Plates**

(*e*) **Bearings.**

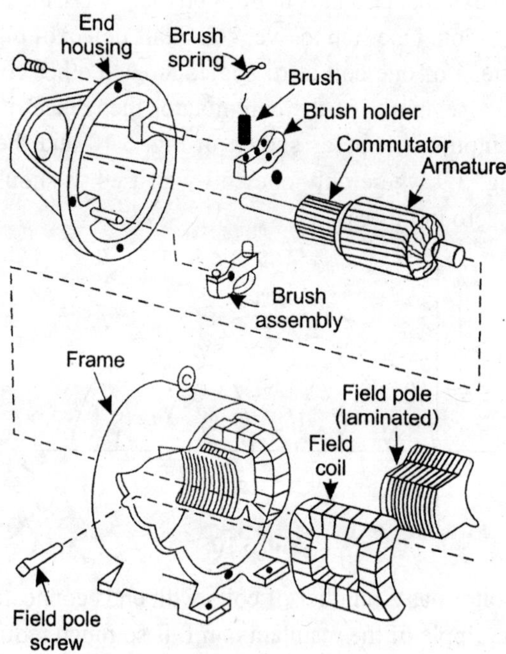

Fig. 3.11. Disassembled parts of D.C. machine

(*i*) **Yoke or Frame:** The yoke as shown in Fig. 3.12 is the outermost cylindrical part of a D.C. Machine and is usually made of cast or wrought iron or from cast steel or rolled steel. The yoke or frame may have its inside face machined to receive the poles and inter-poles which are secured by bolts. Yokes of small machines are made of cast iron with cast feet for supports. But for large machines rolled steel frames of rectangular cross-section are used because this material is more economical and also reduces the weight of the frame. Such frames possess greater mechanical strength and have high permeability. The yoke does not carry any winding and there is no principal part outside the yoke so the outer dimensions of the yoke do not affect any other part. As the yoke carries one half of the pole flux so, the cross-section of the yoke has to be selected accordingly. Thus yoke or frame serves the following two important functions:

(*a*) It carries the main field flux produced by the poles and ;

(*b*) It provides the protection for whole machine.

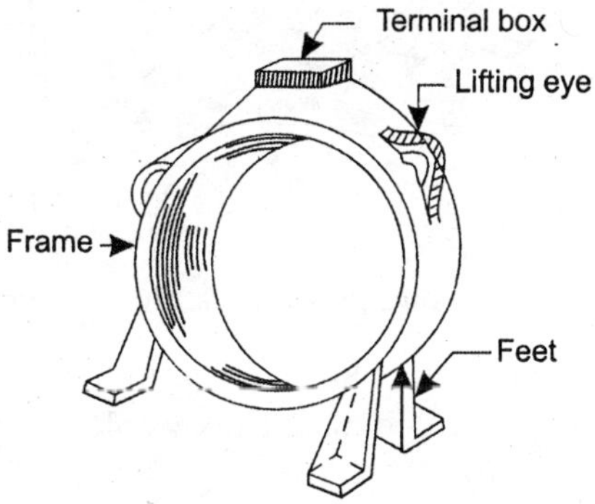

Fig. 3.12. Yoke or Frame

(*ii*) **Main poles:** Poles of large machines are made from sheet steel laminations which are rivetted together under hydraulic pressure. The poles of such type of machines are usually fastened inside the yoke or frame with the help of bolts or screws. But for small machines the poles are casted with the frame and both are of cast iron. The pole carries a field coil or the exciting coil which on passing current through it, magnetises the pole. The poles are alternatively north and south making the flux in armature and yoke half of that in the poles. Every machine has an even number of poles or pole pairs or a whole number. As a winding has to be there on the poles; a large pole cross-section also means larger coil turn or more cost of the field coil. The pole consists of the following two parts namely.

(*a*) the pole core

(*b*) the pole shoe.

The pole shoe serves two purposes *viz*: it spreads out the flux over a greater armature periphery than that represented by the pole core width in the air gap and also, being of larger cross-section, reduces the reluctance of the magnetic path.

Secondly it supports the exciting coil or field coil.

In small machines the pole core is often cast solid with the yoke, while in larger machines the poles may be constructed separately then placed in the correct position in the mould and the metal for the yoke then poured in. In this way yoke and poles are finished in one piece. More generally the poles are separate and there are two possible constructions. Firstly the pole core may be solid, of either cast steel or mild steel, and the pole shoe, which is almost invariably laminated, fastened to the pole face by means of screws. The pole core itself, which may be of either circular or rectangular section is, fastened to the yoke with bolts. This construction is shown in Fig. 3.13. Secondly, the pole core may be built up of laminations, the stamping of which can be of such shape as to include the pole shoe.

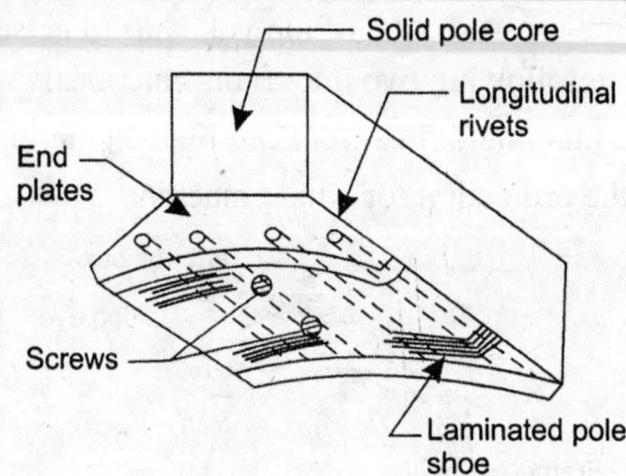

Fig. 3.13. Solid pole and laminated shoe

The section of the completed pole core is of necessity rectangular. The laminations are assembled between thicker end plates, the whole being secured by rivets as shown in Fig. 3.14.

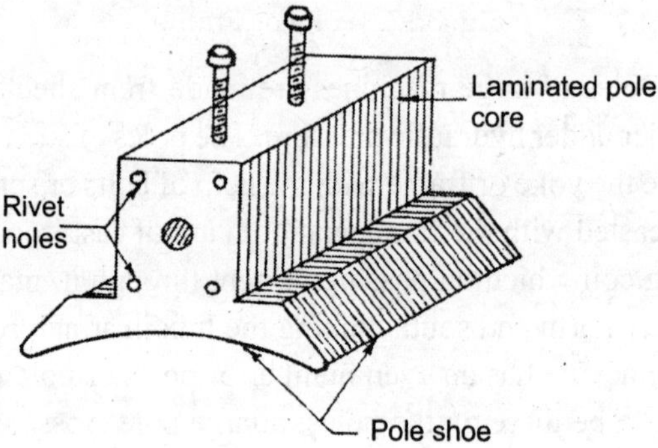

Fig. 3.14. Unit construction pole and shoe

It is possible to fasten such a pole to the yoke by means of bolts screwed directly in to the laminated pole body, similar to the construction for solid pole cores, but a better construction is to insert a steel bar through the pole across the plane of the laminations, and to screw the bolts into this. This construction is shown in Fig. 3.15

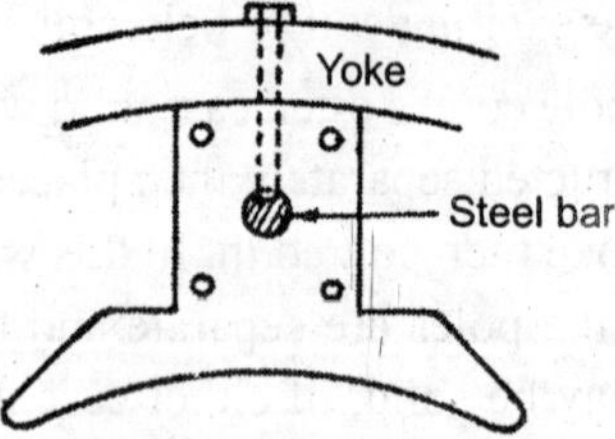

Fig. 3.15. Pole mounting

(iii) **Field or Magnetising Coils.** The field coils are of two types, namely shunt coils which consist of a large number of turns of comparatively small conductor and series coils which consist of few turns of large *x*-section conductor. Series coils derive their name from the fact that they are connected electrically in series with the main circuit and thus

carry the total current generated. For a given field system and armature the necessary flux will be set up when each exciting coil has the necessary ampere turns.

The field coils or pole coils which consist of copper wire or strip are former wound for the correct dimensions as shown in Fig. 3.16. Then the former is removed and the wound coil is put into place over the core.

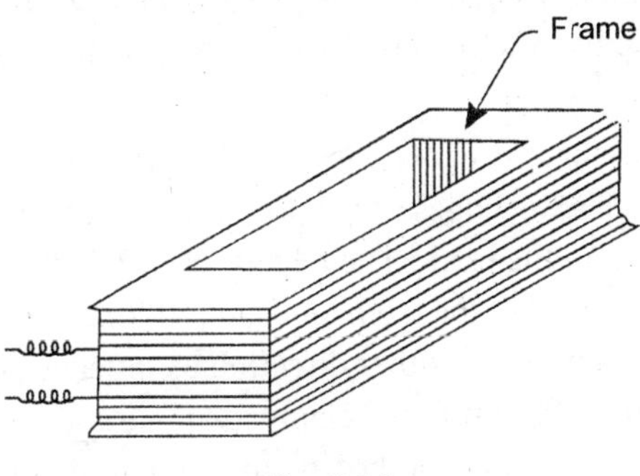

Fig. 3.16

For shunt machines the field coils consist of many turns insulated wire wound on suitable frames of insulated material. Vacuum dried coils are used, after which they are impregnated with insulating compound and baked. The series windings are usually of strap copper, wound on edge to secure better radiation. In the compound machines, over the shunt windings series winding is placed but is blocked away from it to facilitate ventilation. The coils on the poles are connected in such a manner, that adjacent poles are made of opposite polarity. When the current is passed through these windings, they magnetise the poles, which produces the necessary flux.

(*b*) (*i*) **Armature.** This is the rotating part of the machine and is often called the part of rotor.

When the armature rotates it is subjected to an alternating flux varying a frequency, $f = \frac{PN}{120}$ c/s.

This alternating flux would give rise to eddy current and hysteresis loss. To reduce eddy currents the armature core is made up of thin annealed sheet steel laminations about 0.4 to 0.5 mm. thick. The armature core is supported with a key on a cast iron or fabricated spider. The spider is itself is keyed to the shaft. The laminations are insulated from each other by light coat of varnish or rarely by

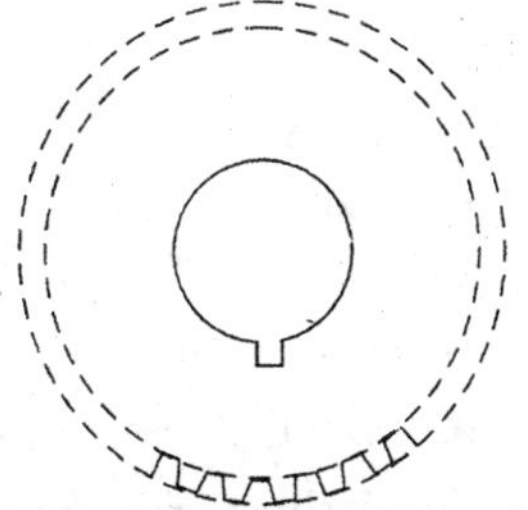

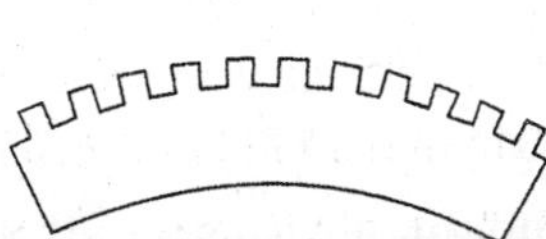

Fig. 3.17. Core punchings of small machine **Fig. 3.18.** Core punchings of large machine

thin paper. The core punchings up to a diameter of about 75 cm. are normally blanked out in one piece as shown in Fig. 3.17. The slots are then punched with the help of indexing punch press. Small punchings of this type are directly keyed to the shaft and are usually provided with holes to form longitudinal ventilating passages. The larger punchings are dovetailed on to a spider which is keyed to the shaft, thus affecting ventilation, cost of the core and reduction in weight. The cores which are having diameter greater than 75 cm are built up of segments as shown in Fig. 3.18 which are attached to the spider by means of dovetail joints.

The core laminations are stacked in such a manner that the slots become parallel to the shaft, so also to the axial edges of the pole shoes. Objectionable noise may result because of vibration set up in the teeth. The tension along the lines of magnetic force that passes between the pole face and the teeth tends to pull the teeth in one direction when the tooth approaches a pole and in the other direction as in leaves it. The tooth, therefore, tends to vibrate in a manner of a short reed clamped at one end and this is accentuated as the teeth are narrower at the base than at the tip. For preventing this effect the slots are sometimes skewed by a slight angular displacement of successive laminate or else the axial edge of the pole face is slightly off parallelism with the shaft. Also some times the semiclosed slots may be used. Open slots with parallel walls are generally used in almost all sizes of d.c. machines. Typical shapes of teeth and slot are shown in Fig. 3.19. The coils are held in the slot against centrifugal force by wooden or fibre wedges driven from the side. The coils which form the armature winding are usually made of double-cotton covered copper wire ; enamed wire is often used in small machines. If the coil consists of two or more turns these are held together with a cotton tape and two or more such coils may then be taped together so that they will form a unit adapted to slip in to the open slot. Coils thus formed are usually dipped in to insulating compound and then baked to give them firmness and increased dielectric strength. In case of semi-closed slots, the taped coil can not be used and each individual conductor is slipped in.

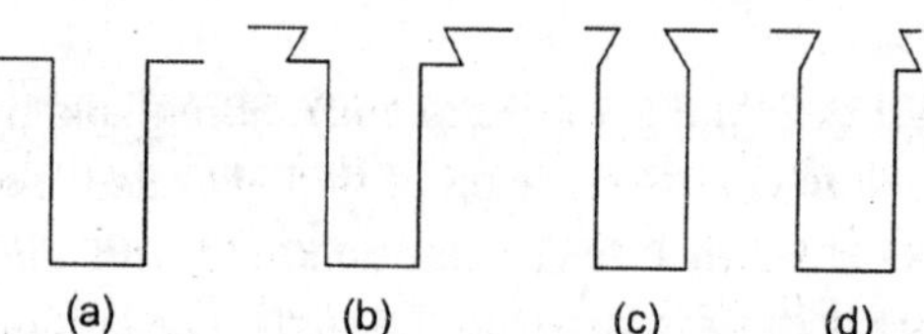

Fig. 3.19. Different shapes of teeth and slots

These of the slots are always filled to remove burrs and then given a coating of varnish. A slot liner must be used to protect the coils from mechanical injury while they are being inserted and to guard against chafing under operating conditions. The slot liner is normally made of fish paper, Press board, fibre or mica cloth that is itself lined with empire cloth or Varnished Cambric. The winding of most d.c. machines have two layers. A strip of hard fibre or leatheroid paper is inserted between the layers as separator.

(*ii*) **Commutator.** This is truly the heart of the d.c. machine. It must operate with temperature variations of at least 55°C and with peripheral speeds that may reach 7000 ft/min.

The commutator is really an extension of the armature windings, and is arranged so that the current from the armature can be collected by means of the brushes pressing on it. The commutator together with brushes rectifies the alternating current or e.m.f. induced in the armature coils or another words converts alternating current or e.m.f. induced in armature coils or windings in to direct current in the external load circuit. It is constructed of copper segments arranged to form a cylinder, each segment being connected to an armature coil by means of a lug (for small diameter armatures) or a strap (for large diameter armatures). Both types of segments are shown in Fig. 3.20.

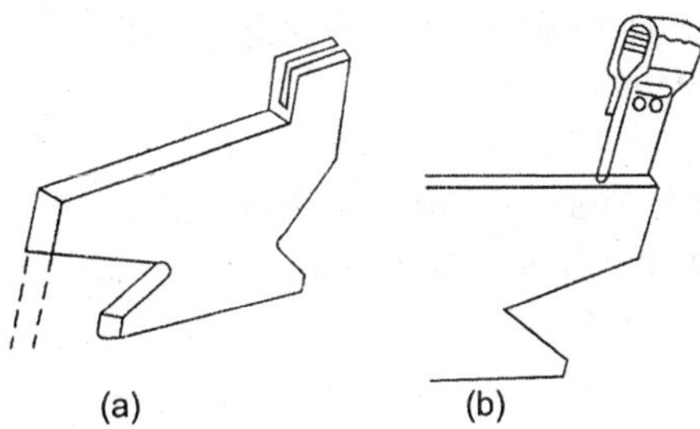

Fig. 3.20. Commutator segments

Owing to the centrifugal force which acts on each segment it is necessary to make provision against the commutator flying apart, and this is done by cutting Vee-shaped pieces from the ends and assembling them between vee rings. This construction is shown in Fig. 3.21.

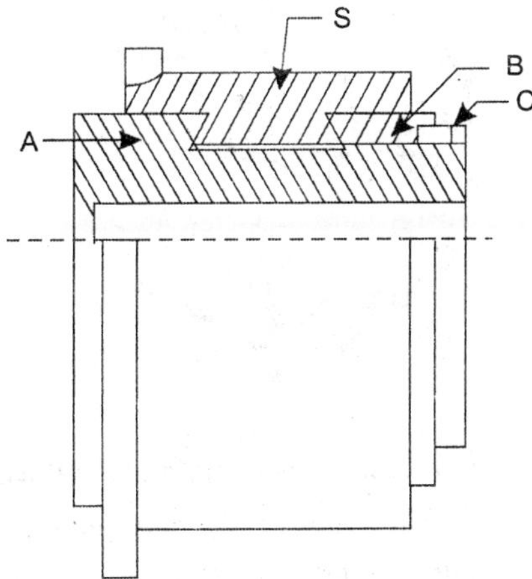

Fig. 3.21. Part sectional view of commutator for small machine

"*A*" hub having a Vee–shaped extension is keyed to the shaft and the segment "*S*", held between this and the Vee–ring, "*B*" by means of the securing ring "*C*".

The insulation consists of micanite between segments and two conical micanite rings, one at each end as shown. The lug is integral with the segment and is slotted at the end so as to facilitate in soldering of the coil ends.

This simple construction is suitable for small machines only. But for a bigger machine, *i.e.* 3 B.H.P., 300 R.P.M., Machine, it will be seen that the foundation is a cast iron hub pressed on the shaft. The segments are held between the coned collars, the pressure being retained by means of the end ring. In this case the lug is of the same diameter as the segment of which it forms a part, and the conductors from the armature coils, round wire in this case, are brought down to it.

Now a days normally the mica in solution is cut away between the bars to a depth of about 1.5 mm with the aid of a special slotting tool. This process is called "Under cutting the mica".

After the armature is wound, the ends of the armature coils are connected to the commutator copper strips called necks or risers. In fact, the ends of the armature coils are laid in slots in the necks or risers. When the winding is complete the ends of the coil are finally soldered to the risers.

(*c*) **Brushes and brush gear.** The brushes which are made of high grade of carbon or graphite ride on the commutator bars and carry the load current from the rotor coils to the external circuit. For low voltage machines, the copper or other low resistance brushes may be used. The precise composition of brushes depends on the machine on which they are to be used, and is chosen to give desired values of contact resistance, specific resistance and co-efficient of friction. To ensure that there is no sparking at the commutat or the resistance must be suitable, and the manufacturers supply a wide range of brushes from which suitable types can be chosen. In addition to these electrical requirements the physical characteristics must also be taken in to account ; these include hardness, tensile strength, specific gravity and homogeneity. Four main grades of Brush are in common use. These are carbon, electrographite, natural graphite and copper graphite. The arrangement of brush in a brush holder is shown in Fig. 3.22.

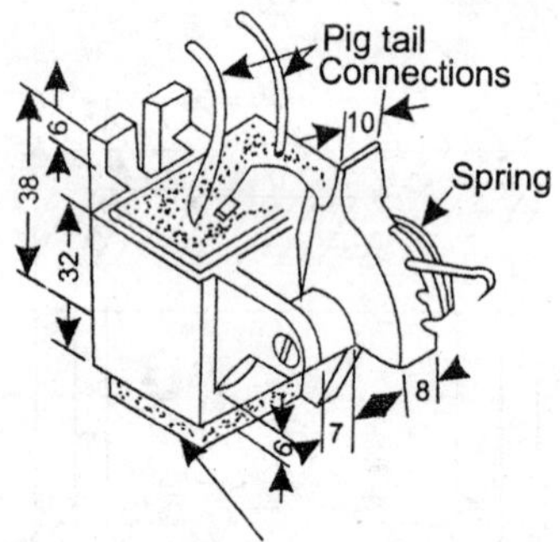

Fig. 3.22. Brush and brush holder

The brush holders hold the brushes against the commutator surface by springs to maintain a fairly constant pressure and smooth riding. The tension of the spring may be adjusted by means of rachet. The brush holders are fixed to the rocker arm. The whole assembly is mounted on a ring, named as Rocker. The brush stud is insulated from the rocker arm by means of an insulating brushing and washer. The brush should be free to slide on its holder so that it may easily follow any irregularities on the surface of the commutator.

To ensure satisfactory commutation the correct pressure of the order of 0.1 kg/cm^2 to 0.25 kg/cm^2 of contact area should be applied to the brushes. The current density at the brush contact is normally kept between 4 and 8 Amps. per sq cm. The width of the brush in tangential direction is generally 3 to 5 times the width of a commutator segment, so that several armature coils are simultaneously short circuited. In a large machine a brush arm may have several brush holders. The brush holders serve as a guide for the brushes and should allow for any radial movement of the brushes resulting from vibration or eccentricity of the commutator. The area of an individual brush should be small as compared to the total brush area provided per set as otherwise slight disturbance in the contact of one brush will overload the set very much. The connection between the brush and the brush holder is made through a flexible lead of braided copper wire called the pig tail. In case of small machines the spring and the sliding contact between the brush and sleeve serve the purpose.

The current collected by the brush is led to the terminal by means of a copper flexible (Pig tail). It will be obvious that this pig tail must be a very securely fixed to the carbon brush.

(*d*) **End Plates or Housings.** These are attached to the both ends of the frame or yoke of the d.c. machine with the help of bolts and contain the bearings for the armature. The rear housing usually supports the bearing only in which shaft of the armature revolves. While the front housing supports the brush assemblies.

(*e*) **Bearings.** The bearings are the very important part of all types of rotating machines. Their function is to support the rotating part and to allow a smooth motion with little friction. Generally two types of bearings are used. The large machines have pedestal bearings and the others have bearings housed in the end shield. Small machines are generally fitted with gun-metal bush bearings. Ball or roller bearings are used in the medium size machines, while Babit-metalbushes made in two halves are fitted in very large machines.

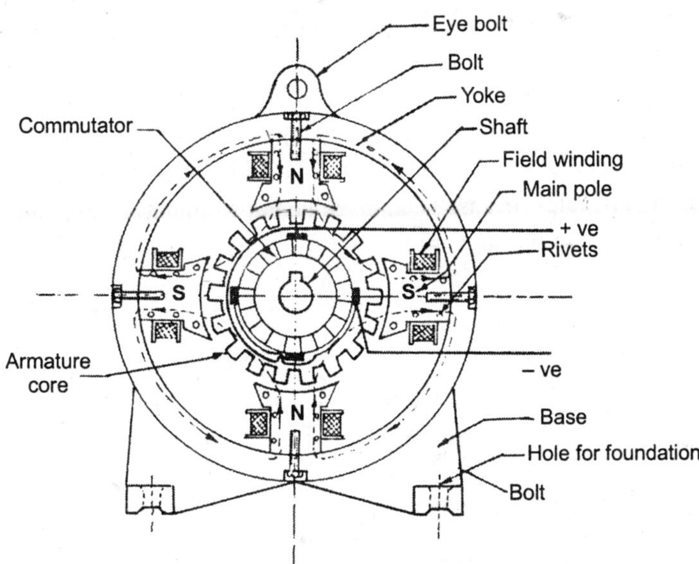

Fig. 3.23. Dynamo having 4-poles

The d.c. machine whether a motor or generator having 4 poles as shown in Fig. 3.23. In this, field system consists of:

(*i*) a cylindrical *yoke* which carries the main magnetic flux and called as the frame of the machine.

(*ii*) the poles with pole cores and pole shoes, and

(*iii*) the field or exciting coils which carry a current called the exciting current.

3.6.1. M.M.F. and Flux Density Waveforms in D.C. Machines

It has been shows in Art. 4.1 that the current distribution under each pole of a D.C. machine is uniform and is equivalent to a constant current sheet of proper polarity. The space distribution of m.m.f. produced by the armature winding is triangular, with its peak value along the quadrature or brush axis (or 90° away from the main field axis) as shown in Fig. 3.35. The effect of armature m.m.f. on the main-field flux distribution in the air gap is called armature reaction. In this article, armature reaction and its effects are dealt with in detail.

3.6.2. Armature Reaction

The armature m.m.f. produces two undesirable effects on the main field flu and these are:

(*i*) net reduction in the main field flux per pole and

(*ii*) distortion of the main field flux wave along the air-gap periphery.

Reduction in the main flux per pole reduces the generated voltage and torque, whereas the distortion of the main-field flux influences the limits of successful commutation in D.C. machines. The purpose of this article is to investigate these effects and to discuss the methods of minimising the problems arising from armature reaction effects.

Fig. 3.6 (*a*) shows the flux path for the main poles of a 2-pole D.C. machine at no-load, *i.e.* with no armature currents. This main field flux, produced by field m.m.f. $I_f N_f$ is shown by horizontal phasor $OA = \phi_f$ on the right hand side of Fig. 3.16 (*a*). When the D.C. machine is loaded, currents flow in the armature winding. These currents are shown in Fig. 3.16 (*b*), by dots under main *S* pole and by crosses under main *N*-pole. These armature currents set up armature flux shown by vertical flux lines in Fig. 4.16 (*b*), with field winding un-excited. In this figure is also shown armature flux ϕ_a by s vertical phasor *OB*. Flux ϕ_a is produced armature m.m.f. $I_a N_a$. If the D.C. machine of Fig. 3.16 is working as a motor, then its armature must rotate anti-clockwise, because of the fact that *N*, *S* poles of the main field must attract armature produced *S*, *N* poles. In case D.C. machine is working as a generator, then its armature must be driven clockwise by the prime-mover.

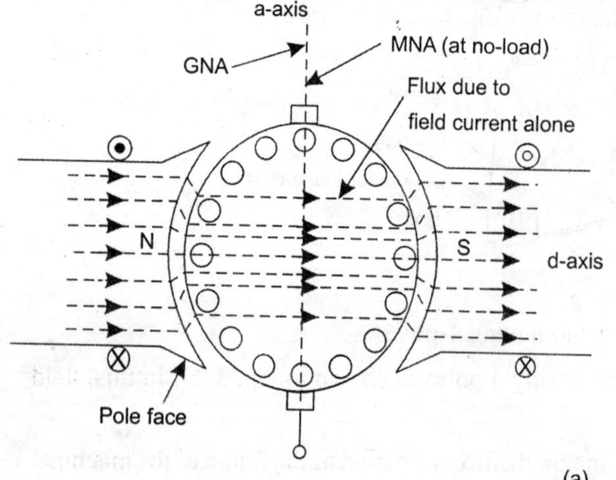

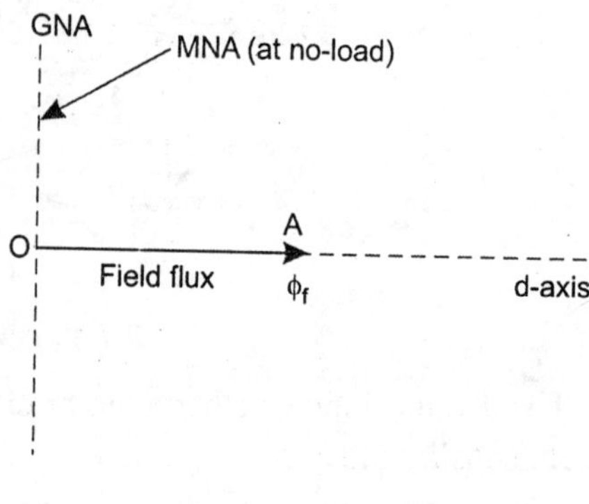

(a)

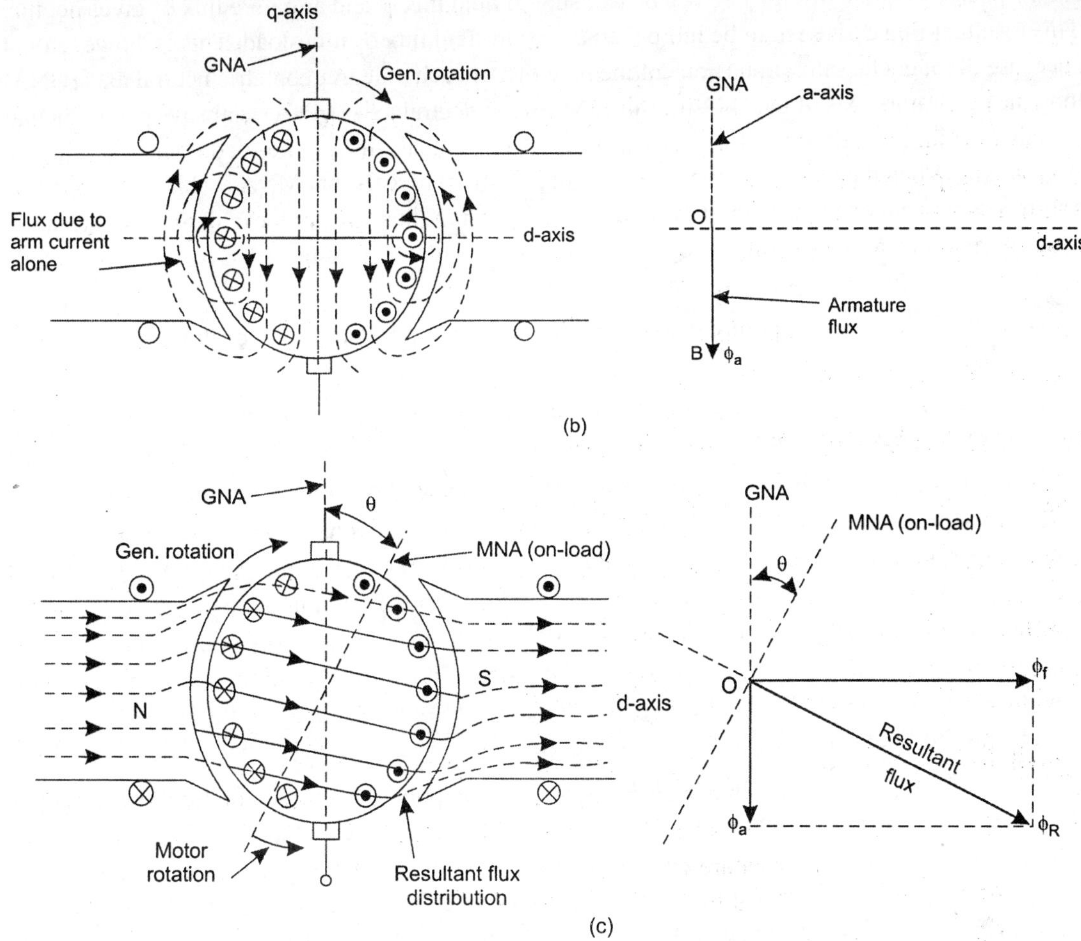

Fig. 3.6.1. Illustrating the space distribution of (*a*) main-pole flux (*b*) armature flux and (*c*) resultant of both main-field and armature fluxes

An examination of Fig. 3.16 (*a*) and (*b*) reveals that the path of armature flux ϕ_a is perpendicular to the main flux path ϕ_f. In other words, the path of the armature flux *crosses* the path of the main-field flux. Thus the effect of armature flux on the main field is entirely *cross-magnetizing* and it is for this reason that the flux created by the armature m.m.f. is called *cross-flux*.

When current flows in both the armature and field windings, the resultant flux distribution is obtained by superimposing the two fluxes of Fig. 3.16 (*a*) and (*b*). This is illustrated on left-hand side of Fig. 3.16 (*c*). It is seen that armature flux aids the main field flux at upper end of *N*-pole and at the lower end of *S*-pole, therefore, at these two pole ends (or tips), the armature flux strengthens the main field flux. Likewise, the armature flux weakens the main field flux at lower end of *N*-pole and at upper end of *S*-pole. If there is no magnetic saturation, then the amount of strengthening and weakening of the main field flux are equal and the resultant flux per pole remains unaltered from its no-load value. Actually, magnetic saturation does occur and as a consequence, the strengthening effect is less as compared to the weakening effect and the resultant flux is decreased from its no-load value. This is called *demagnetizing effect* of armature flux.

In the phasor diagram of Fig. 3.16 (c), phasor sum of field flux ϕ_f and armature flux ϕ_a gives net flux ϕ_R. This resultant flux ϕ_R is seen to be more than the main-field flux ϕ_f at no-load. This is, however, not true because of magnetic saturation is one of the pole tips of each pole. A geometric neutral axis (GNA) is along the quadrature axis of the D.C. machine. Magnetic neutral axis (MNA) is always perpendicular to the axis of resultant field flux. It is seen from Fig. 3.16 (a) that MNA at no-load coincides with the GNA or q-axis. When the D.C. machine is loaded, Fig. 3.16 (c) reveals that MNA is shifted from GNA. This shift is dependent upon the magnitude of armature current. Thus, greater the magnitude of armature (or load) current, greater is the shift of MNA from GNA. It may therefore be stated from above that net effect of armature flux on the main-field flux is

(*i*) to distort the main-field flux thereby causing non-uniform distribution of flux under the main poles,

(*ii*) *to shift the* MNA *in the direction of the rotation for a generator and against the direction of rotation for a motor*, and

(*iii*) to reduce the main-field flux from its no-load value due to magnetic saturation.

Graphical picture of armature reaction. For better understanding of the interaction between main-field flux and armature flux, it is preferable and convenient to draw the developed diagram of armature conductors and poles. The developed view of Fig. 3.16 (a), with no armature currents under each pole, is shown in Fig. 3.17 (a). The brushes are along the interpolar axes midway between the main-pole axes. Dotted lines in Fig. 3.17 (a) show the distribution of main-field flux in the air gap with no armature currents. In Fig. 3.17 (b), the variation of main field-flux density along the air-gap periphery is shown by a solid line.

In Fig. 3.17 (c), currents are indicated by dots under S pole and crosses under N pole. These armature currents, with field winding unexcited, produce magnetic flux as shown in Fig. 3.17 (c). As the armature flux produced by armature currents alone is normal to the main-field flux, as before, it is called *cross-flux*. The m.m.f. created by armature currents in a D.C. machine, as per Fig. 3.35 (d), is triangular in nature and is depicted accordingly by a solid line in Fig. 3.17 (d). The air-gap flux due to armature m.m.f. is given by $\dfrac{\text{armature m.m.f.}}{\text{air - gap reductance}}$. Under the poles, the air gap is uniform, thereby, the air-gap flux variation under the poles is proportional to armature m.m.f. and is shown in Fig. 3.17 (d). In between the poles, *i.e.*, in the interpolar region, the long air gap reluctance, consequently the armature flux is much smaller in this region, in spite of a large value of m.m.f. The armature flux density waveform created by armature currents is, therefore, saddle-shaped* as depicted by dotted curve in Fig. 3.17 (d). It is observed from this figure that armature flux-density waveform has (*i*) zero value at the centre of the pole (*ii*) increases from zero to maximum value at the pole tips and then (*iii*) decreases rapidly to a minimum value at the middle of main poles.

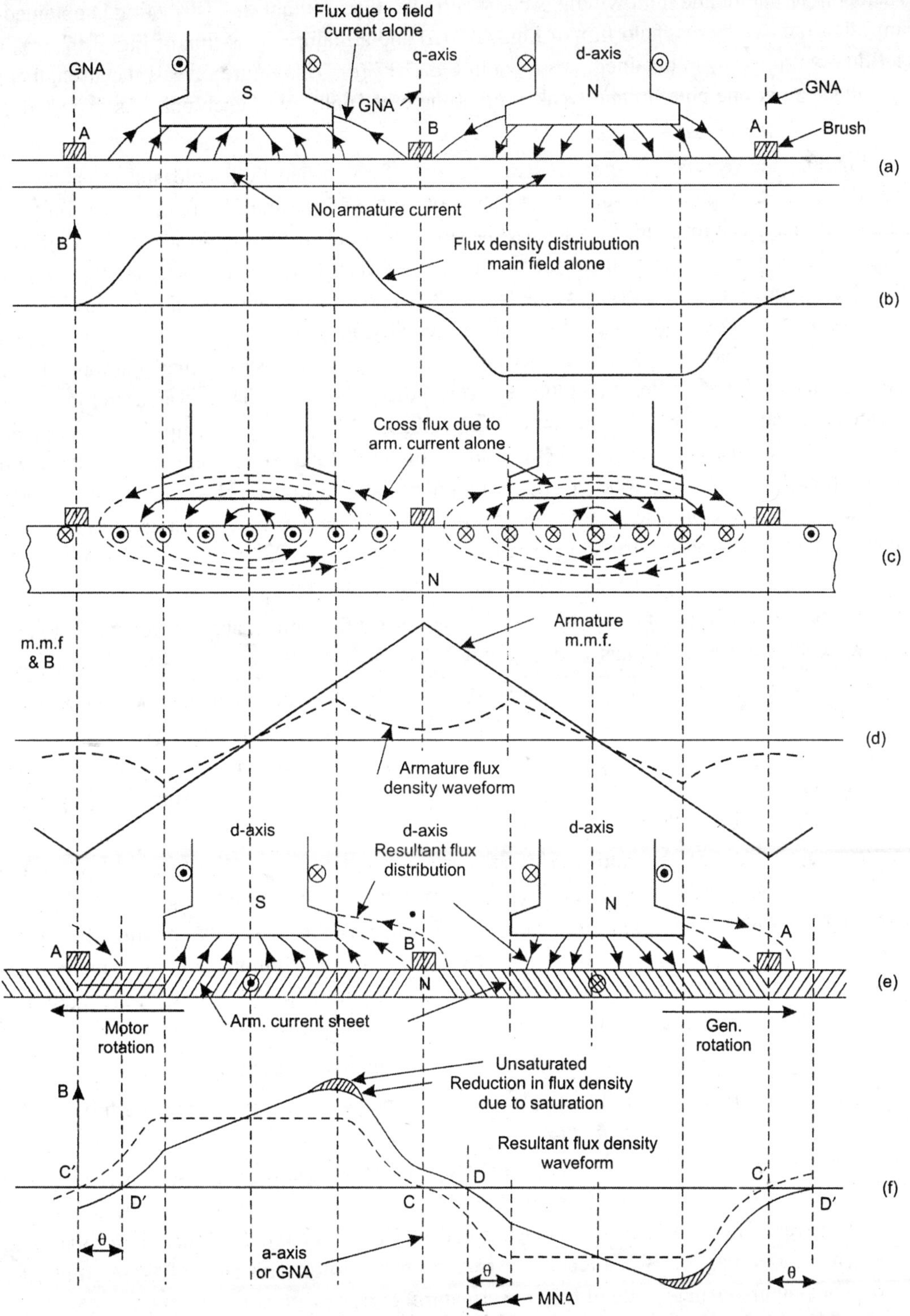

Fig. 4.17. Flux distribution and flux-density waveforms respectively due to (a), (b) field current alone (c), (d) armature current alone and (e), (f) both field and armature currents

When both armature and field windings carry currents, the resultant flu distribution is obtained by superimposing the two fluxes, field flux of Fig. 3.17 (*a*) and armature cross-flux of Fig. 3.17. (*c*). The resultant flux distribution, so obtained, is shown in Fig. 3.17 (*e*). This figure reveals the strengthening of the resultant flu at one pole tip and weakening at the other pole tip of each pole. As expected, this agrees with Fig. 3.16 (*c*).

For obtaining the resultant air-gap flux density waveform, when both field and armature carry currents, add the corresponding flux-density ordinates of Figs. 3.17 (*b*) and 3.17 (*d*) at every point along the air-gap periphery. The resultant flux-density distribution in the air gaps is shown by the solid curve in Fig. 3.17 (*f*). It may be seen from the resultant flux-density distribution curve that the effect of cross-magnetizing armature m.m.f. is to decrease the flux density under the leading pole tips** and to increase it under the trailing pole tips for generator operation. Actually, the magnetic saturation in the iron does occur and its effect is to increase the flux density under the trailing pole tips by a smaller amount than the decrease under the leading pole tips. Saturation effect is indicated by cross-hatched areas in Fig. 3.17 (*f*). Thus, under saturated conditions, the amount of flux increase under trailing pole tips is almost equal to the decrease under leading pole tips and the total flux per pole on load remains almost unchanged from its no-load value. Under saturated conditions, the amount of increase in flux is less than the decrease and therefore total flux per pole on load is less than its no-load value. Hence, under saturated conditions, the effect of cross-magnetizing effect armature m.m.f., *i.e.* cross-flux, is to demagnetize the main field. But note that the demagnetizing effect of cros-flux is due to saturation only.

Fig. 3.17 (*f*) reveals that point of zero flu density has shifted through an angle θ from C, C′ to D, D′ respectively. In other words, MNA has shifted from GNA by an angle θ.

For a motor, a dot under such pole and a cross under north pole results in a anticlockswise rotation in Fig. 3.16. Therefore, above results are also applicable to D.C. motor. Since the direction of rotation is reversed, the leading pole tips for a motor are the trailing pole tips for a generator. Hence for a motor, the effect of cross-magnetizing armature m.m.f. is to decrease the flux under the trailing pole tips and to increase it under the leading pole tips.

Note from above that for a generator, the effect of armature reaction is to distort the flux and shift the zero crossing of the flux density wave in the direction of rotation. In the case of motor, the distortion of the flux and zero crossing of the flux-density wave is shifted against the direction of rotation. In constant flux D.C. machines, such as shunt machines, the flux distortion is much more prominent under heavy loads. In series and compound machines, the flux distortion is minimum, because with the increase of armature m.m.f. there is a corresponding increase in the field m.m.f.

The effects of armature m.m.f. described above, may be summarised as follows:

(*i*) Armature flux path is normal to flux path of main poles. That is why armature flux is called *cross-flux* or *cross-magnetizing flux*.

(*ii*) The armature section distorts the main-field flux distribution along the air-gap periphery. This distortion is in the direction of rotation for a D.C. generator and opposite to the direction of rotation for a D.C. motor. This also means that MNA is shifted in the direction of rotation for a generator and against the direction of rotation for a motor. This shift of MNA from GNA depends upon the magnitude of load (or armature) current.

(*iii*) The demagnetizing effect of armature m.m.f. reduces the total flux per pole. This reduction has been found to be 1 to 5% from no-load to full-load.

Example 3.1. *Explain how the demagnetizing effect of armature m.m.f. on the main-field flux can be investigated through the use of magnetization curve of a D.C. machine.*

Solution. The effect of magnetic saturation on the reduction of main-field flux caused by armature reaction can be visualized with the help of Fig. 3.18. In this figure, magnetization curve, triangular armature m.m.f. variation and *S* pole of a D.C. machine are shown. The brushes are in the GNA. For field current I_f, the field m.m.f. is AT_f. At no-load, the flux density B_0, under the entire pole shoe is *ab* for a field m.m.f. *AT*. For armature current I_a, armature m.m.f. is $+AT_a$ under pole tip *Q* and $-AT_a$ under pole tip *P*. The net m.m.f. under pole tip *Q* is $(AT_f + AT_a)$ and that under pole tip *P* is $(AT_f - AT_a)$ as shown. The m.m.f. $(AT_f + AT_a)$ under pole tip *Q* corresponds to a flux density B_1. Under pole tip *P*, net m.m.f. $(AT_f - AT_a)$ corresponds to a flux density B_2. It is observed from Fig. 3.18 that increase in flux at pole tip *Q*, proportional to $(B_1 - B_0)$ is less than the decrease in flux under pole *P*, proportional to $(B_0 - B_2)$. This shows that under saturated conditions, the resultant flux per pole is reduced from its no-load value. Therefore, the field excitation has to be increased under loaded conditions if the field flux is to be kept constant as its no-load value.

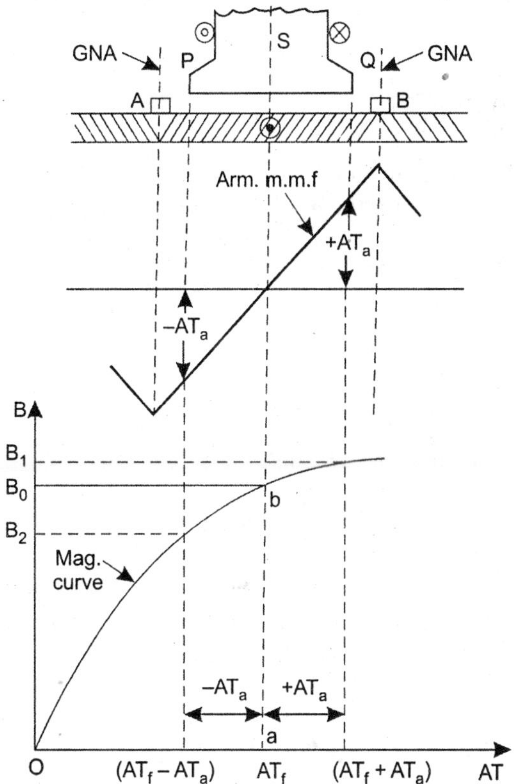

Fig. 3.18. Demagnetizing effect of armature m.m.f. on the main-field flux

Note that the flux density at the middle of pole face is not effected by armature m.m.f.

3.7. COOLING OF D.C. MACHINES

The losses in a machine appear in the form of heat and raise its temperature. This heat must be dissipated without undue temperature rise. In small machines it is done naturally by the convection of the surrounding air and radiation. But in case of large machines some artificial means have to be provided. The radial and axial ventilating ducts provide a means of cooling. The armature end plates are fitted with fans which also serve to circulate air round the machine. Some times, the machines are fitted with external cooling fans,

3.8. PROTECTION OF D.C. MACHINES

All electrical machines must be protected for the safety of the operator as also against the damage by external agencies to the machine itself.

Care and Maintenance. Whenever a d.c. machine is to be used, guidance from technical leaflet of the manufacture should always be taken. The preventive maintenance and care should be done as far as possible as per instructions from the manufacturer. In case, such information is not available, lubrication should be done periodically and care should be taken to clean the motor every day and put in a cover when not in use.

3.9. ARMATURE WINDINGS

Introduction. A single conductor in a machine when rotated has very small induced e.m.f. This e.m.f. or voltage can not be usefully employed for the big jobs as the electric machines and

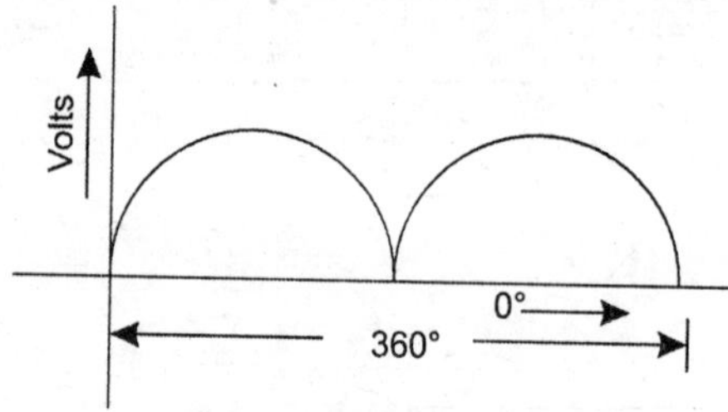

Fig. 3.24

other appliances are doing at present. Also with a single coil, the voltage supplied will of course not remain steady, but will pulsate as shown in Fig. 3.24. A pulsating voltage would be undesirable commercially, and furthermore, a single coil would utilise very little of the space available on the cylindrical iron core.

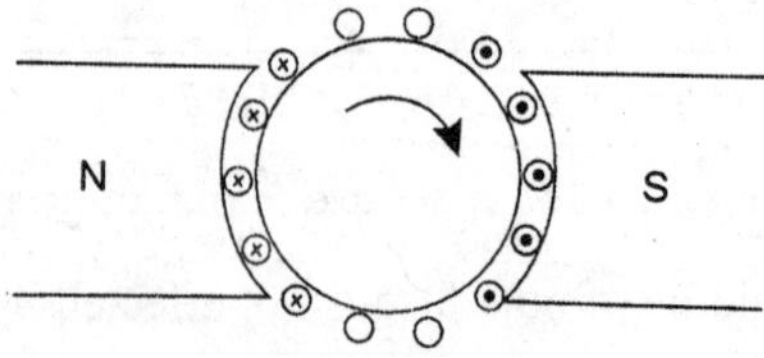

Fig. 3.25

The undesirable features of a single coil may be eliminated by placing a number of such coils on a cylindrical iron core as shown in Fig. 3.25. If we can connect these conductors or a coil sides in series in a way that their e.m.f.'s add as we travel along the circuit, substantially larger e.m.f. can be made available. As the conductors can be connected at ends only so it becomes essential that the two e.m.f.s be in opposite directions so that they add in a coil. Thus a conductor under *N*-pole has to be connected to a conductor under *S*-pole. To make all the coils identical it is most convenient and practical to connect conductors which are placed in slots one pole pitch apart. Fig. 3.26 shows the connections of conductors to make coils. Here if one considers the conductors, it can be seen that if one conductor under *N*-pole is connected to another under *S*-pole on the right side the next conductor shall be connected to the conductor under *S*-pole on the other side. In case, there are two poles only one connection is made while going clock-wise and other in the other direction so as to facilitate the use of formed coils. The coils also have to be connected in series and the end of a coil is connected to the start of another coil so that their e.m.f.'s are adding. If the connection is made to a coil under the same pair of poles the winding is called lap winding and if it goes for a coil under the next pole pair we call it a wave winding.

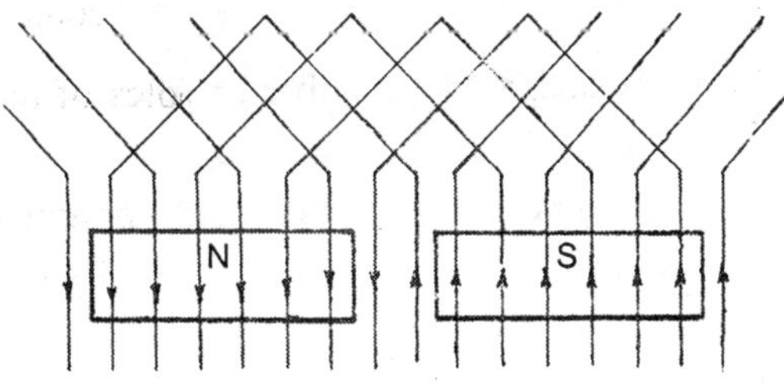

Fig. 3.26

Before discussing the wave and lap windings we will first discuss the following various terms used in connection with Armature Windings:

Conductor. Every individual length of wire lying in a magnetic field and in which e.m.f. is induced is known as a conductor as shown in Fig. 3.27. It is also referred to as winding element.

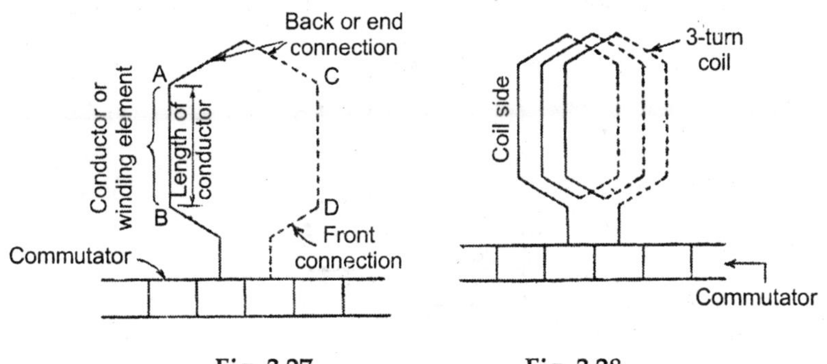

Fig. 3.27 **Fig. 3.28**

Turn. When the two conductors which are lying in a magnetic field are connected in series so that the e.m.f. which is induced in them help each other or the resultant e.m.f. induced becomes double (considering full pitch coil) of that due to one conductor, is called as turn.

Coil. The two wires or conductors *AB* and *CD* along with their end connections termed as one coil as shown in Fig. 3.27. The coil may be single turn coil (Fig. 3.27) or multi-turn coil (Fig. 3.28).

In Fig. 3.28, each coil side is having 3-conductors. The group of conductors or wires constituting a coil side of a multi-turn coil is wrapped with a tape as a unit as shown in Fig. 3.29 and is placed in the armature slot. These coils are used when total number of armature conductors are excessive and it is not feasible to use single turn coils due to the reason that it will require large number of commutator segments and if used it will not give sparkless commutation and it will not be economical due to use of more copper in end connections.

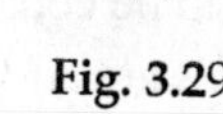

Fig. 3.29

Coil side. Each coil, single turn or multi turn has two sides known as coil sides. The coil sides are placed in the different armature slots nearly a pole pitch apart.

Coil Group. In a coil group there may be one or more single coils.

Winding. The number of coils arranged in coil groups is known as winding.

Pole-Pitch. It may be defined as:

(*i*) The number of armature conductors (or Armature slots) per pole. If there are 54 conductors and 6 poles, then, Pole pitch is $\frac{54}{6} = 9$ conductors per pole.

(*ii*) The armature periphery divided by the number of poles of the generator, *i.e.* the distance between two adjacent poles.

Coil span or coil pitch. It is the distance, measured in terms of armature conductors (or armature slots, between the two sides of a coil). In fact, it is the periphery of the armature spanned by the two sides of the coil.

If a coil spans from the centre of one pole to the centre of an adjacent pole, it has a full pitch. Full pitched coils have an advantage of giving maximum e.m.f. induced in the coil. If the coil spans less than full pitch, it has a fractional pitch, which should not be less than 0.9 full pitch. In Fig. 3.30, coils 1, 2 and 3 are short pitched, full pitched and over-pitched coils respectively.

If the pitch is too small, an appreciable reduction in generated e.m.f. results. The fractional pitch type of winding is in general use, because it produces less sparking and it requires less copper, which means lower armature resistance. Fractional pitch windings also improve commutation.

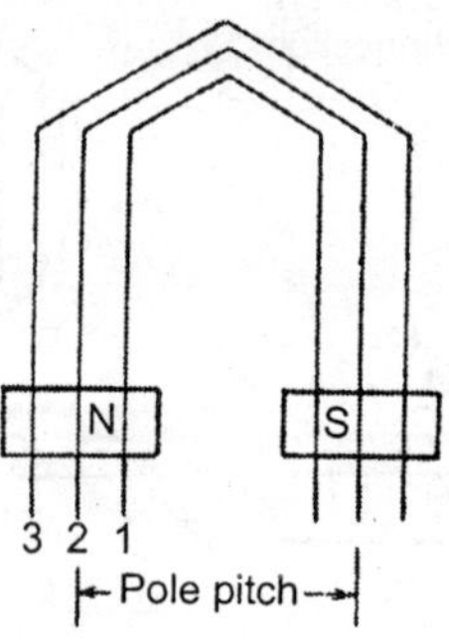

Fig. 3.30

The most convenient way of expressing the span of a coil is in terms of the slots. To span from the centre of one pole to nearly the centre of an adjacent pole, a coil must have span nearly half the distance around the armature in a 2-pole winding, $^1/_4$ the distance in a 4-pole winding, $\frac{1}{6}$ the distance in a 6-pole winding etc. Then for any number of slots "*S*" and poles "*P*", the slot span is

$$Y_S = \frac{S}{P} \text{ (Preferably slightly less.)}$$

Winding Pitch. The distance (in terms of coil sides) between the start of two consecutive coils is called the winding pitch and is denoted by *Y*. Actually, it consists of two parts:

(i) Back pitch, *i.e.* the width or span of the coil and

(ii) Front pitch, *i.e.* the distance between the two sides which are connected together at the commutator

$$Y = Y_f + Y_b$$

Front Pitch (Y_F). The front pitch is defined as the distance (in terms of armature conductors) between the second conductor of one coil and the first conductor of the next coil which are connected together at the front, *i.e.* Commutator end of the armature.

Or

The number of armature conductors or elements spanned by a coil on the front (or commutator end of the armature) is called the front pitch and is denoted by Y_F.

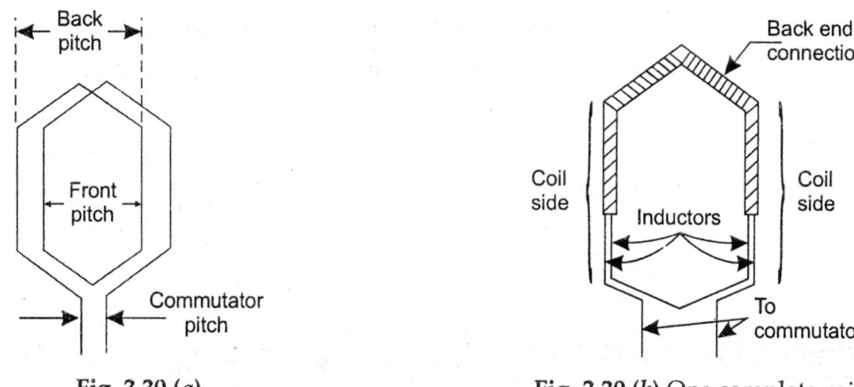

Fig. 3.30 (a) **Fig. 3.30 (b)** One complete coil

Inductor. One of the wires making up the coil side. A voltage is induced in the inductor.

Front End Connection. A wire that connects the end of a coil to a commutator segment. This wire is located at that part of the coil that is nearest to the commutator.

Back End Connection. A wire or conductor that connects an inductor or one side of the coil to an inductor on the other side of the coil. It is on the end opposite to the commutator

or

It is the number difference of the conductors connected together at the back end of the armature. In Figs. 3.31 and 3.32 front pitch for lap and wave wound is shown.

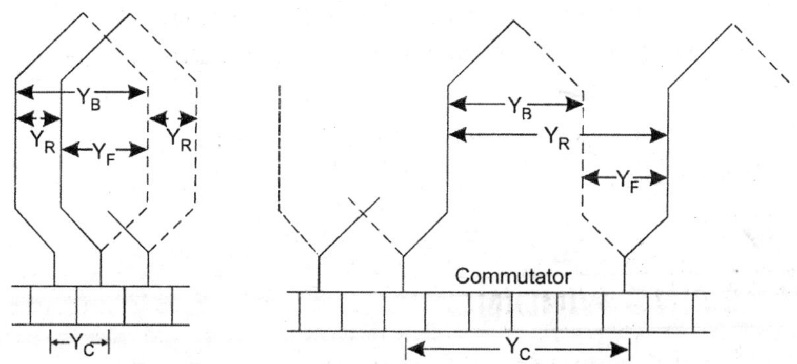

Fig. 3.31. Lap windings **Fig. 3.32.** Wave windings

Back Pitch (Y_B). It is defined as the distance, measured in terms of the armature conductors, which a coil advances on the back of the armature.

Or

It is equal to the number difference of the conductors connected to a given segment of the commutator. In Figs. 3.31 & 3.32 Back pitch for lap and wave wound is shown.

Resultant Pitch (Y_R). It is defined as the distance between the beginning of one coil and beginning of the next coil to which it is connected as shown in Figs. 3.31 & 3.32.

As a precautionary measure, it should be noted that all these pitches, though normally stated in terms of armature conductors, are also sometimes given in terms of armature slots or commutator bars.

Commutator Pitch (Y_C). It is the distance (measured in commutator segments or bars) between the segments to which the two ends of a coil are connected. From Figs. 3.31 & 3.32 it is clear that for wave winding it is the sum of Y_B & Y_F whereas for lap winding it is the difference of Y_B & Y_F.

If a coil covers a span of 180 electrical degrees, it is called a full pitch coil, whereas one that spans less than 180° is called a fractional pitch coil.

The armature wound with a fractional pitch is called a 'Chorded' winding. In chorded winding less copper is required than full pitch coils, but they have approximately the same characteristics because shorter front-end back-end spans are inactive. A coil which spans at 160 electrical degree will have a pitch factor $\frac{160}{180} = 0.9$ (90 %). In general pitch factor less than 80% is avoided.

3.10. OPEN COIL AND CLOSED COIL WINDINGS

According to the degree of closure produced by the winding, the armature windings are of two types namely:

(*i*) Open coil winding

(*ii*) Closed coil winding.

Open coil winding is that winding which does not close on itself, *i.e.* Where will not be formed close circuit until some external connection is made to source or load. This type of winding is always employed in a.c. machines and is never employed in d.c. machines.

Closed coiled winding is that winding which closes on itself. In this winding, if one starts tracing through it, one will come back to the starting point without passing through any external connection. In D.C. Machines only closed coil windings are employed in order to provide for the commutation of the coils. Though closed type winding can be used in A.C. machines also, but normally open coil type windings are mostly used.

The closed or continuous armature windings are also of two types.

(*a*) Gramme Ring Winding,

(*b*) Drum Winding.

3.11. GRAMME RING WINDING

The gramme ring winding or simply called as ring winding was suggested by Pacinotti in 1864 for D.C.

Machines (usually associated with Gramme in English literature). In this winding the e.m.f. induced in a coil always contributes to the total e.m.f. at the terminals. The core of a ring wound armature may be either a ring built of sheet iron rings or laminations insulated from one another or a hollow cylinder of steel supported by cast spider keyed to the shaft. In each case the core is without the teeth and the slots.

A 2-pole ring winding with 16 single turn coils is represented by Fig. 3.33. The core is wound with number of coils, each of these coils may consist of any desired number of turns, *i.e.* may be either a single turn or a multi-turn coils. The coils are joined consecutively as it were in series so as to form a closed circuit. The finish of the one coil is connected to the start of the second coil and the finish of the second coil is connected to start of the third coil and so on, until the finish of the last coil is connected to the start of the first coil. The junction neighbouring coils are connected to the commutator segments so that any particular commutator segment is connected to the finish of one coil and the start of the next coil.

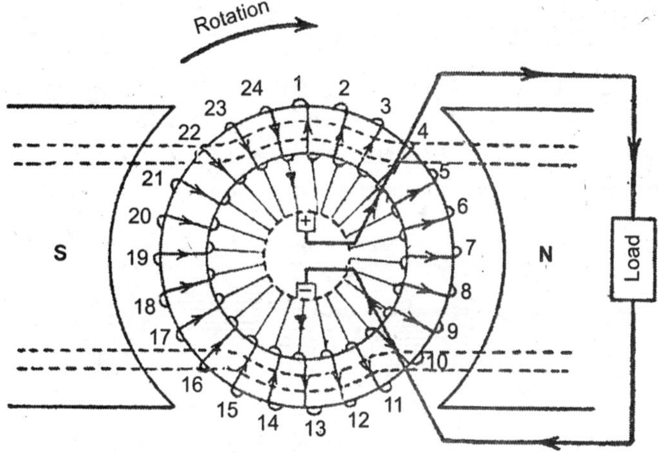

Fig. 3.33. 2-Pole Gramme ring armature winding

When such a closed winding is rotated inside the poles, the direction of the induced e.m.f. in the coils is found by applying Fleming's Right Hand Rule. According to this rule the induced e.m.f.'s are inward under the north pole and outward under the south pole so that in the complete winding the e.m.f.'s in the halves of the winding are in opposition. The total value of the e.m.f. acting around the closed armature winding is thus zero. However, when brushes are placed on the commutator there will always be two circuits in parallel between them. Maximum e.m.f. will be induced between brushes, when they are placed so as to devide the winding into two equal sections one of which is entirely under south-pole. The brushes must be placed one pole pitch or 180° electrical degrees apart and in the neutral position.

An advantage of the Gramme Ring Winding is that theoretically the same winding is adopted to any number of poles.

This types of armature winding is an early form of armature winding which has been replaced by the more efficient drum type of winding. The reasons which have made this winding obsolete are given below.

(*i*) It is difficult to insulate the winding.

(*ii*) It is difficult to repair with these windings.

(*iii*) As each turn is to pass through the central opening in the core, its winding becomes difficult and laborious hence is costlier.

(*iv*) The winding conductors which lie inside the core cut practically no flux and hence act merely as connectors for the active conductors, hence there is wastage of copper.

(*v*) The construction requires such a large air gap between the pole faces and the surface of the armature core that the field excitation to maintain the required flux is unduly large.

(*vi*) Cooling of the machine is difficult.

(*vii*) For the same pole flux and armature velocity the e.m.f. induced in ring winding is half of that induced in the drum winding having same number of coils.

3.12. DRUM WINDING

Due to the various disadvantages of Gramme ring type winding led to the development of the *Drum winding* in which each turn instead of returning inside the armature, is brought back on the surface one pole pitch away. Both sides of the turn are, therefore, active; and since they lie under the poles of opposite polarity, the induced e.m.f.s are opposite in direction but assist each other round the turn so

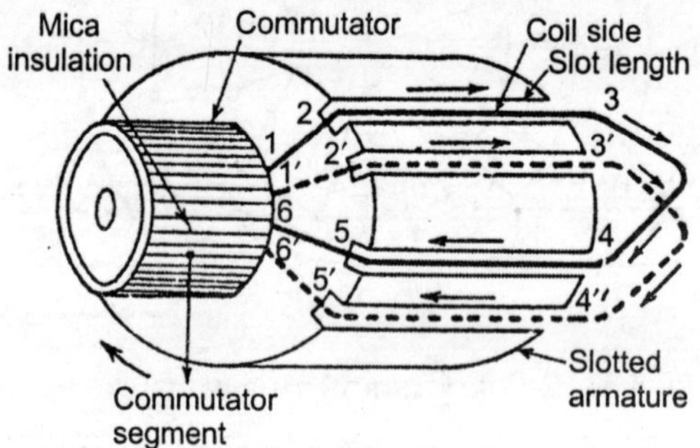

Fig. 3.34. Slotted armature with commutator (Drum winding)

that the resultant e.m.f. is the sum of the two. A further advantage is that all coils are similar and can be wound on a former and fully insulated before being placed in the slots.

The Fig. 3.34 shows drum wound armature in which the conductors or coil sides (2-3 or 2′-3′) all lie in slots in the surface of the armature and are connected to one another by front and back connectors. The front connection is on the commutator side and the back-connection is on the back of the commutator. In Fig. 3.34, 3-4 is the back connector and 2-1 and 5-6 are the front connectors which end at the commutator. In this type of winding excepting the end connections, all the armature copper is active *i.e.* two sides of the coils *viz.* 2-3 and 4-5 both of their cut the flux so is active in generating e.m.f. The requirements which a winding should meet are that the winding be closed or continuous, *i.e.* is that it be a closed coil winding in order that all the coil shall be active except during a period of commutation. The portions 3-4, 1-2 and 5-6 are simply end connectors. The coil sides 2-3 and 4-5 must approximately be in the centre of the two adjacent poles, *i.e.* N and S poles so that when the e.m.f. in the coil side 2-3 is in the direction as shown by an arrow, the e.m.f. induced in coil side 4-5 must be in opposite direction so that the total e.m.f. induced in the two sides of any coil must be additive. In order to obtain economy in winding the coil should be *pre-formed* and insulated before being placed on the armature.

To obtain a satisfactory arrangement of the end connections d.c. armature windings are universally of the two layer type. Each coil thus consists of an upper side placed at the top of one slot and a lower side situated at the bottom of another slot normally distant by one pole pitch from the upper side as shown in Fig. 3.35. Generally the complete coil is made out of one length of conductor, so that there are

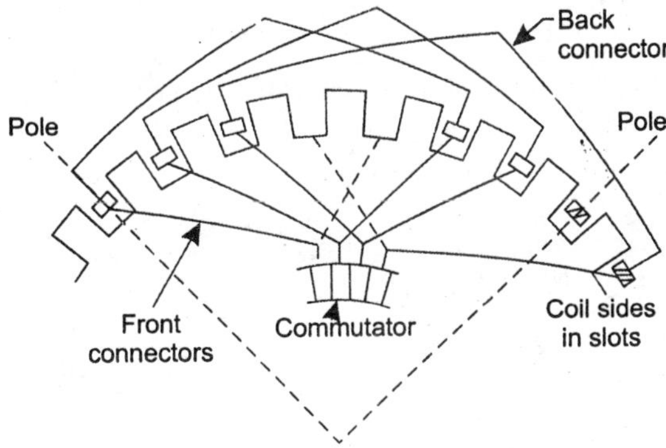

Fig. 3.35. Slots for double layer winding

no joints at the back end of the machine, the change from the upper to the lower portion of the coil being affected by a bend introduced at the back end of the coil.

It should be noted that the upper conductor in a slot does not form part of the same coil as the lower conductors.

If each slot contains only one upper coil side and one lower coil side, the number of slots required would be equal to the number of coils.

Also this process is advantageous in assuring both strength against centrifugal forces and nearly perfect equality in size, shape and weight of all coils.

Frequently however two or more coils are lapped together to form a multiple coil in which the several coil sides occupy the top of one slot and other sides occupy the bottom of some other slot at a distance of approximately one pole pitch apart.

In order that the e.m.f. induced in the coil be a maximum, other conditions being fixed, the span of the coil, *i.e.* span should be equal to pole pitch. For a smaller span, the coil will not embrace a maximum flux so the induced e.m.f. will be somewhat reduced when the coil span is less than the pole pitch, the winding is called a *Fractional pitch* one or its winding is said to be chorded.

This type of winding (Fractional pitch winding) effect substantial saving in the copper of the end connections and improves connection owing to the lesser mutual inductance between coils.

3.13. TYPES OF ARMATURE WINDINGS

It has been seen that the most important part of direct current machines is the armature winding. The reason being that it is the seat of the generated output of the machine and in addition the generated power is delivered by it to the out side circuit without any increase in its temperature and without any excessive sparking at the brushes. This armature winding is supposed to have quite a long life as it is difficult to replace it, unlike the wearing parts like brushes, or bearings etc. whose replacement is quite easy. In an alternator, the armature windings can be housed in the stationary part of the machine *i.e.* in stator but in case of D.C. generator, the windings are essentially to be housed in the rotating part. This is required because conversion of alternating voltage which is the one always generated in all types of generating machines is required to be converted to D.C. with the help of commutator fixed along with the armature. Conversion is possible when commutator revolves and when commutator revolves, the armature shall also revolve.

Armature conductors are housed in slots in the armature periphery. The simplest type of armature winding is thus a single conductor winding as shown in Fig. 3.36. For the type of field polarity and the direction of rotation of armature, the e.m.f. in the conductor is induced from left to right as shown in Fig. 3.36.

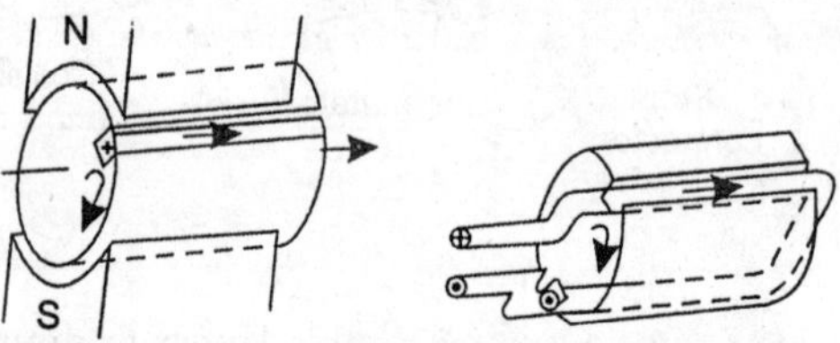

Fig. 3.36

If there is another conductor, placed diametrically opposite to the first, the e.m.f. induced in this conductor shall act from right to left, *i.e.* in the direction opposite to that in the first conductor. If these two conductors are joined at one end, of the armature, a single coil winding is obtained which has the pitch around the armature circumference the same as the pole pitch. The e.m.f.s in these two conductors thus become additive. The single coil of the pitch equal to or nearly equal to the pole pitch is the unit from which the armature windings of all direct current generators are derived.

In order to get current from the armature coil for feeding it to the outside circuit, the two ends of the coil (unconnected ends of the two conductors) are connected to two insulated metal slip rings against which two fixed brushes remain pressed from which connections can be given to the external circuit. Fig. 3.37 shows the whole arrangement.

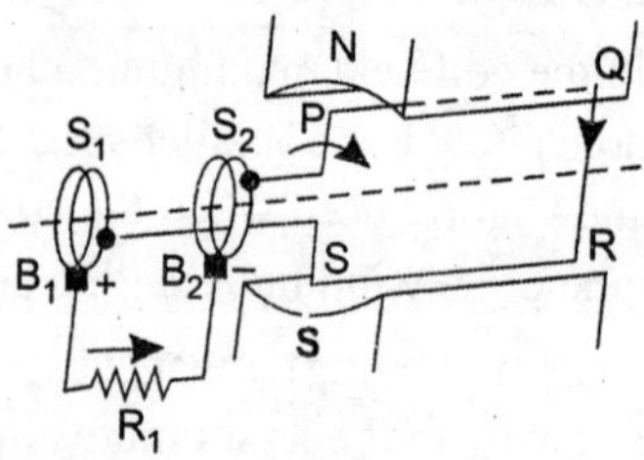

Fig. 3.37

Thus it can be concluded that since e.m.f. induced in each conductor is very small and if large e.m.f. is to be developed in the armature, these e.m.fs. should get added and for that it is essential that conductor under one pole should be connected with another conductor, occupying the similar or nearly similar position under the next pole of opposite polarity. Mainly there are two types of windings used in D.C. generators depending upon the manner in which conductors are joined to the commutator, namely.

(*i*) Lap or parallel winding

(*ii*) Wave or series winding

3.14. LAP WINDING

In a simple lap winding (drum type), the connections are made from one segment, through the two sides of a coil and hence back to the next adjacent segment, from which similar connection is made to the next coil as shown in fig 3.38 (a).

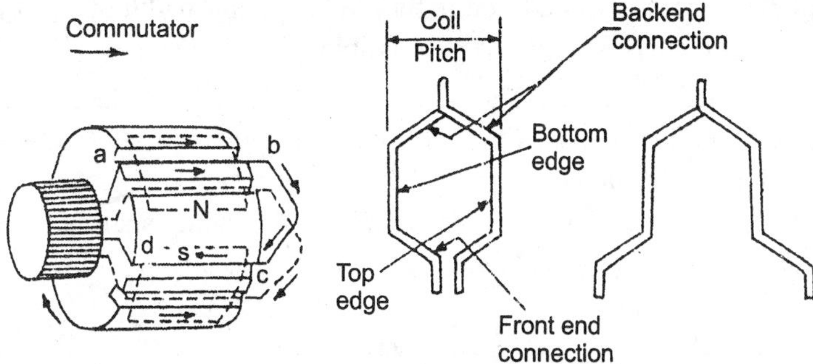

Fig. 3.38 (*a*) Lap winding view on armature and doubled to the commutator

Fig. 3.38 (*b*) End connections of coils

When the various armature coils are connected together to form a winding the end of a given coil must be connected to the beginning of another, the generated e.m.f of which adds to its own. A winding, connected as shown in fig. 3.38 (*b*) is called a lap winding because it alternately progresses forward and then laps back upon itself.

In lap windings, the two ends of any one coil are taken to adjacent segments of the commutator. The winding is known as lap winding because the sides of successive coils overlap each other. This can be explained better by taking an example.

Let there be a machine with 4 number of poles and having 28 number of conductors. The number of conductors per pole becomes $\frac{28}{4} = 7$. Conductors under the north pole have the e.m.fs. induced in one direction, *i.e.* from top to bottom as shown in Fig. 3.38, whereas that under the south poles have the e.m.fs induced in the opposite direction, *i.e.* from bottom to top.

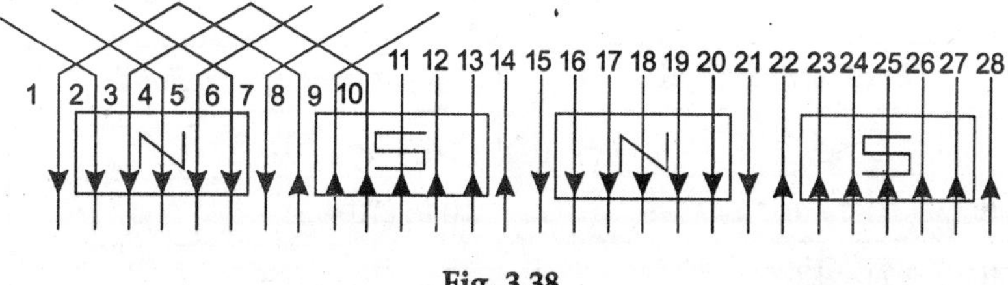

Fig. 3.38

If conductor 3 is taken under the first north pole, this is to be connected to another conductor further on so that e.m.fs. in both sides of the coil so formed will act in the same sense round the coil.

For this, conductor number 3 could be connected to any of the conductors under the next south pole but as mentioned already conductor under one pole is got to be connected to another conductor occupying similar position under the next opposite pole. For this reason, the width of the coil must be equal to or nearly equal to pole pitch. In this example pole pitch = $\frac{28}{4}$ = 7 conductors. Thus conductor 3 shall be connected to conductor number 3 + 7 = 10. The connections being made by triangular connection as shown in Fig. 3.38. These end connectors are sometimes called winding overhang.

Assuming the top of the diagram as the back of the winding, it can be decided as to how the end connection is to be made in case of lap winding. The backward connection is made as shown in Fig. 2.39 to form a closed coil. It can be seen from Fig. 3.39 that the width of the coil must be an odd number when seen in terms of armature conductors since the end connections have to bend alternatively to the right and to the left. The necessary condition is fulfilled by a coil width of 7 but a width of 6 or 8 although very close to the pole pitch shall not be permissible.

Thus as already mentioned conductor 3 shall be connected with conductor 10, then conductor 10 shall be connected to a conductor which is with in 2 conductors of starting conductor 3. When conductor 10 is connected to conductor 5 (3 + 2 = 5), the winding will be progressive. On the other hand, if conductor 10 is connected to conductor 1(3 – 2 = 1), then the winding shall be retrogressive. On its way it must be connected to commutator segment as shown in Fig. 3.39.

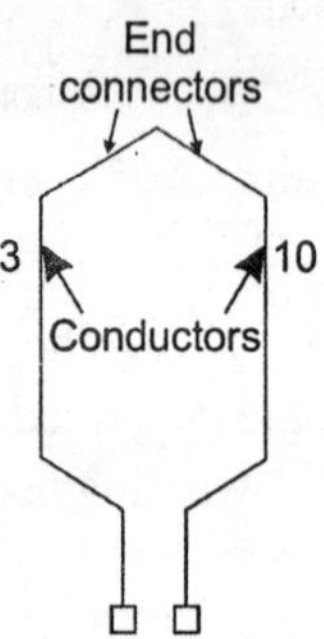

Fig. 3.39. Lap winding

Assuming the lap winding to be progressive, the front connection will be from conductor 10 to conductor 5. Conductor 5 shall be connected to conductor 12 (5 + 7 = 12), by means of another end connector at the back conductor 12 shall be connected to conductor 7 (12 – 5 = 7) by means of a front connector via a commutator segment and so on.

Thus for this winding of Fig. 3.38, the rule is to go forward 7 at the back and to come backward 5 via a commutator segment at the front. Thus simple table of the winding is given below.

Back connections	***Front connections***
1 to (1 + 7) = 8	8 to (8 – 5) = 3
3 to (3 + 7) = 10	10 to (10 – 5) = 5
5 to (5 + 7) = 12	12 to (12 – 5) = 7
7 to (7 + 7) = 14	14 to (14 – 5) = 9

9 to (9 + 7) = 16	16 to (16 – 5) = 11
11 to (11 + 7) = 18	18 to (18 – 5) = 13
13 to (13 + 7) = 20	20 to (20 – 5) = 15
15 to (15 + 7) = 22	22 to (22 – 5) = 17
17 to (17 + 7) = 24	24 to (24 – 5) = 19
19 to (19 + 7) = 26	26 to (26 – 5) = 21
21 to (21 + 7) = 28	28 to (28 – 5) = 23
23 to (23 + 7) = 30 = (30 – 28) = 2	2 to (30 – 5) = 25
25 to (25 + 7) = 32 = (32 – 28) = 4	4 to (32 – 5) = 27
27 to (27 + 7) = 34 = (34 – 28) = 6	6 to (34 – 5) = 29
	= (29 – 28) = 1

Thus this table is continued until the starting point in 2nd column comes as conductor 1. The complete winding diagram is shown in Fig. 3.40. Because each front connection is made with one

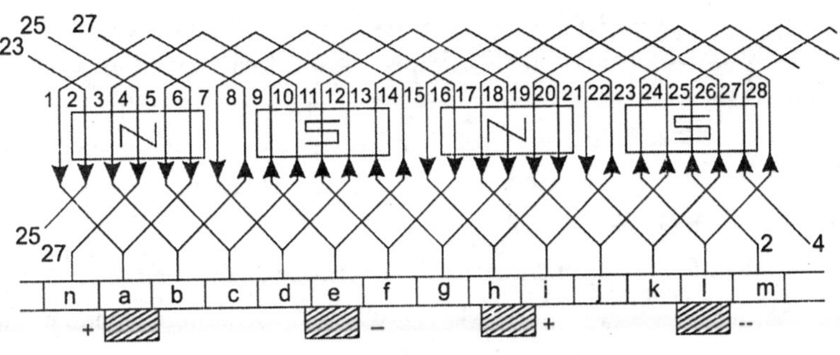

Fig. 3.40

commutator segment thus there are 14 number of coils $\left(\frac{28}{2}=14\right)$ of one turn only connected with 14 number of commutator segments named from *a* to *n*.

Now in order to find out the exact number of brushes and their actual location, the rule is that a brush is to be placed at each meeting point and also at each separating point. The brushes placed at the meeting point are of positive polarity while those at separating points are of negative polarity.

If the arrows of the e.m.f.s in various conductors which determine the direction of e.m.f.s in Fig. 2.40 are examined, it shall be observed that commutator bars *a* and *h* are meeting points and, therefore, they determine the position of + ve brushes whereas commutator bars *e* and *l* are separating points and they determine the position of negative brushes.

In Fig. 3.40 it has been shown that the brushes are equally spaced and are located directly opposite the pole centres. This shows that in certain positions of commutator, the brushes will actually short circuit the coils connected to the segments with which they are in contact. It can be seen from the Fig. that there are four number of coils which are getting shorted. These short circuits continue to take place because of the larger brush width as compared to thickness of mica insulation between two commutator segments. The short circuiting of these coils does not materially make much difference as both the conductors of the coil are situated in inter polar gaps where the e.m.f.s induced are very small.

Thus brush when coming in contact with segment *a* and *b* of commutator, short circuits the winding consisting of conductors 1 and 8 as shown in Fig. 3.40 but as already explained that these two conductors are in interpolar position when flux is very small and hence very small e.m.f.s are induced and thus short circuit of these e.m.f.s is of much little effect than might have been supposed.

The two positive brushes are joined together and then connected to the + ve terminal of the machine. Similarly two negative brushes are joined together and then connected to the negative terminal of the machine.

These four meeting and separating points divide the winding in four identical sections and connections to the machine terminals via the brushes place these sections in parallel. Hence there are four parallel paths for the current through the 4 pole lap wound armature as shown in Fig. 2.40. Thus a lap winding has:

(*i*) As many parallel paths as the number of poles of the machine.

(*ii*) The number of brush sets is equal to the number of poles.

In lap wound armatures, number of parallel paths is more than the number of parallel paths in wave wound armatures. Thus for the same number of total conductors, conductors in each parallel path of lap wound armature shall be lesser than that in wave wound armature. Lesser conductors in each parallel path of lap wound generator accounts for lesser e.m.f. of each parallel path and since voltage developed in a generator is the same as the one developed in each parallel path, so voltage developed in the generator having lap wound armature is lesser than in one having wave wound armature provided all other conditions remain same. On the same analogy it can be seen that current in the lap wound generators is more than in the wave wound generators.

Thus when lower voltages are to be generated at higher currents, lap winding is made in the armature and if higher voltages are to be developed at lower currents, wave winding is made in the armature.

Thus in lap winding, the coil pitch or the back pitch Y_b must approximately be equal to pole pitch

i.e. $$Y_b \doteq \frac{Z}{P}$$

where Z = total no. of armature conductors or coil sides

and P = number of poles

in the example that has been taken

$$Y_b = \frac{28}{4} = 7$$

front pitch Y_f is either 2 more or 2 less than the back pitch.

i.e., $$Y_f = Y_b \pm 2.$$

If the front pitch is 2 more than the back pitch, the winding is known as *retrogressive* and if it is 2 less, then it is known as progressive.

Thus for retrogressive lap winding, $Y_f = Y_b + 2$

and for progressive lap winding, $Y_f = Y_b - 2$

In the example that has been taken above, $Y_f = Y_b - 2 = 7 - 2 = 5$, thus the winding is progressive lap winding.

Hence from here we can conclude that "In a simple lap-winding, front and back pitches are always odd and differ by 2; while the average pitch is an even number".

As from the above discussion

$$\text{Back Pitch } (Y_b) = 7 \text{ (Odd number)}$$

$$\text{Front Pitch } (Y_f) = 5 \text{ (Odd number)}$$

$$\text{Average Pitch} \Rightarrow \frac{\textit{Back Pitch } (Y_b) + \textit{Front Pitch } (Y_f)}{2}$$

$$\Rightarrow \frac{7+5}{2} \Rightarrow 6 \text{ (Even Number)}$$

Commutator Pitch. As each commutator segment is connected to two conductors, the total number of commutator segments is one-half the number of conductors on the armature in a single turn coil. Thus number of commutator segments N_c is equal to the number of coils N or half the number of conductors. Mathematically

$$N_c = N = \frac{Z}{2}$$

The winding advances by one commutator segment for each complete turn. Thus commutator pitch $Y_c = 1$.

Fundamental conditions of Lap windings: There are three main conditions to be fulfilled by a lap winding, namely;

(*i*) The pitch must be such that the opposite sides of a coil lie under unlike poles.

(*ii*) The winding must include each element once and only once.

(*iii*) The winding must close on itself *i.e.*, must be re-entrant.

Example 3.2. Develop a lap winding for a 6 pole armature having 24 conductors.

Solution. Pole Pitch $= \frac{Z}{P} = \frac{24}{6} = 4$

Front Pitch, $Y_f = \frac{Z}{P} - 1 = 4 - 1 = 3$

Back Pitch, $Y_b = \frac{Z}{P} + 1 = 4 + 1 = 5$

Now if starting of winding is done from conductor 1, then conductor 1 shall be connected with conductor 6 on the back side and conductor 6 shall be connected with conductor 3.

The sample table of winding connection is as given below:

Back connections	*Front connections*
1 to 1 + 5 = 6	6 to 6 − 3 = 3
3 to 3 + 5 = 8	8 to 8 − 3 = 5

5 to 5 + 5 = 10	10 to 10 – 3 = 7
7 to 7 + 5 = 12	12 to 12 – 3 = 9
9 to 9 + 5 = 14	14 to 14 – 3 = 11
11 to 11 + 5 = 16	16 to 16 – 3 = 13
13 to 13 + 5 = 18	18 to 18 – 3 = 15
15 to 15 + 5 = 20	20 to 20 – 3 = 17
17 to 17 + 5 = 22	22 to 22 – 3 = 19
19 to 19 + 5 = 24	24 to 24 – 3 = 21
21 to 21 + 5 = 26, *i.e.* 26 – 24 = 2	26 to 26 – 3 = 23
23 to 23 + 5 = 28, *i.e.* 28 – 24 = 4	4 to 4 – 3 = 1

at this stage the winding gets closed.

The sequence of connections of these windings is as shown below in Fig. 3.41.

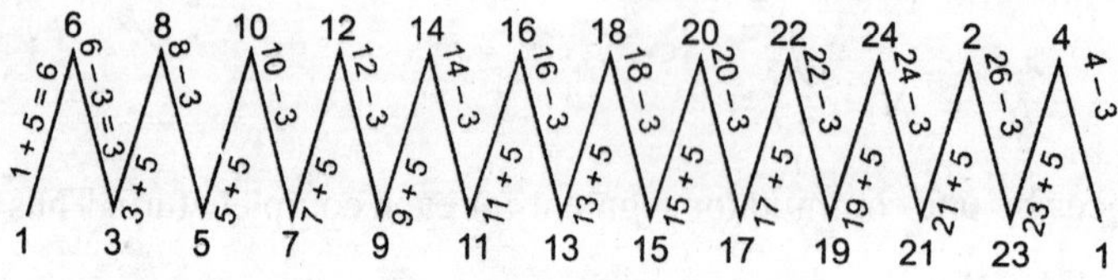

Fig. 3.41

The complete winding diagram can be had in a similar way as shown in Fig. 3.40.

3.14.1. General Rules for D.C. Armature Windings

The following rules should be followed in the design of d.c. Armature windings (Lap or wave):-

(*i*) The back pitch (Y_B) as well as front pitch (Y_F) should be nearly equal to pole pitch. This will result in increased e.m.f. in the coils.

(*ii*) Both pitches (Y_B and Y_F) should be odd. This will permit all end connections (back as well as front connection) between a conductor at the top of a slot and one at the bottom of a slot.

(*iii*) The number of commutator segments is equal to the number of slots or coils (or half the number of conductors).

No. of commutator segments = No. of slots = No. of coils

It is because each coil has two ends and two coil connections are joined at each commutator segment.

(*iv*) The winding must close upon itself *i.e.*, it should be a closed circuit winding.

3.14.2. Relations between Pitches for Simplex Lap Winding

In a simplex lap winding, the various pitches should have the relation given below:

(*i*) The back and front pitches are odd and are of opposite signs. They differ numerically by 2,

$$Y_B = Y_F \pm 2$$

$$Y_B = Y_F + 2 \quad \text{... for progressive winding}$$

$$Y_B = Y_F - 2 \quad \text{...for retrogressive winding}$$

(*ii*) Both Y_B and Y_F should be nearly equal to pole pitch.

(*iii*) Average pitch = $\frac{Y_B + Y_F}{2}$. It equals pole pitch (= Z/P).

(*iv*) Commutator pitch, $Y_C = \pm 1$

$Y_C = +1$ for progressive winding

$Y_C = -1$ for retrogressive winding

(*v*) The resultant pitch (Y_R) is even, being the arithmetical difference of two odd numbers *viz.*, Y_B and Y_F.

(*vi*) If Z = number of armature conductors and P = number of poles, then,

$$\text{Pole-pitch} = \frac{Z}{P}$$

Since Y_B and Y_F both must be about one pole pitch and differ numerically by 2,

$$\left.\begin{aligned} Y_B &= \frac{Z}{P} + 1 \\ Y_F &= \frac{Z}{P} - 1 \end{aligned}\right\} \text{For progressive winding}$$

$$\left.\begin{aligned} Y_B &= \frac{Z}{P} - 1 \\ Y_F &= \frac{Z}{P} + 1 \end{aligned}\right\} \text{For retrogressive winding}$$

It is clear that Z/P must be an even number to make the winding possible.

Example 3.3: With a lap winding having 40 conductors and 4 poles, write down the winding table.

Solution. With a lap-winding.

Pole pitch, $\quad Y_A = \frac{\textit{number of conductors}}{\textit{number of poles}} = \frac{40}{4} = 10.$

suppose if $\quad Y_B = 10 + 1 = 11.$

then $\quad Y_F = 10 - 1 = 9.$

Starting from number 1 (Fig. 2.41 (*a*)) the winding table progresses as:

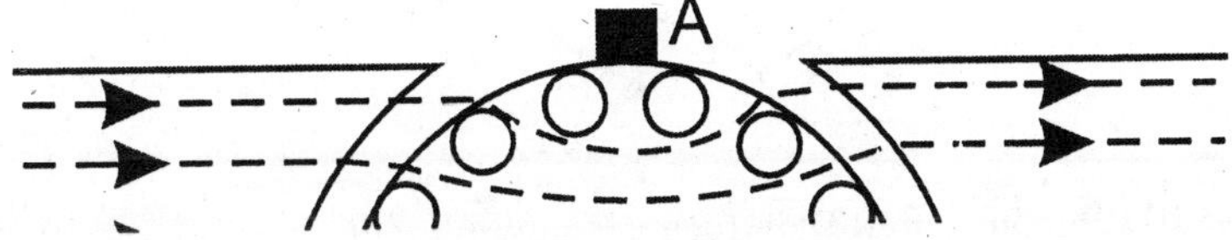

Fig. 3.41 (*a*) Lap winding table

Conductor number 1 is connected to 1 + 11 = No. 12 at the rear end stepping forward. No. 12 is connected to 12 – 9 = No. 3 at the front end stepping backward, and so on.

The winding is then complete. The winding is shown in Fig. 3.41(*b*)

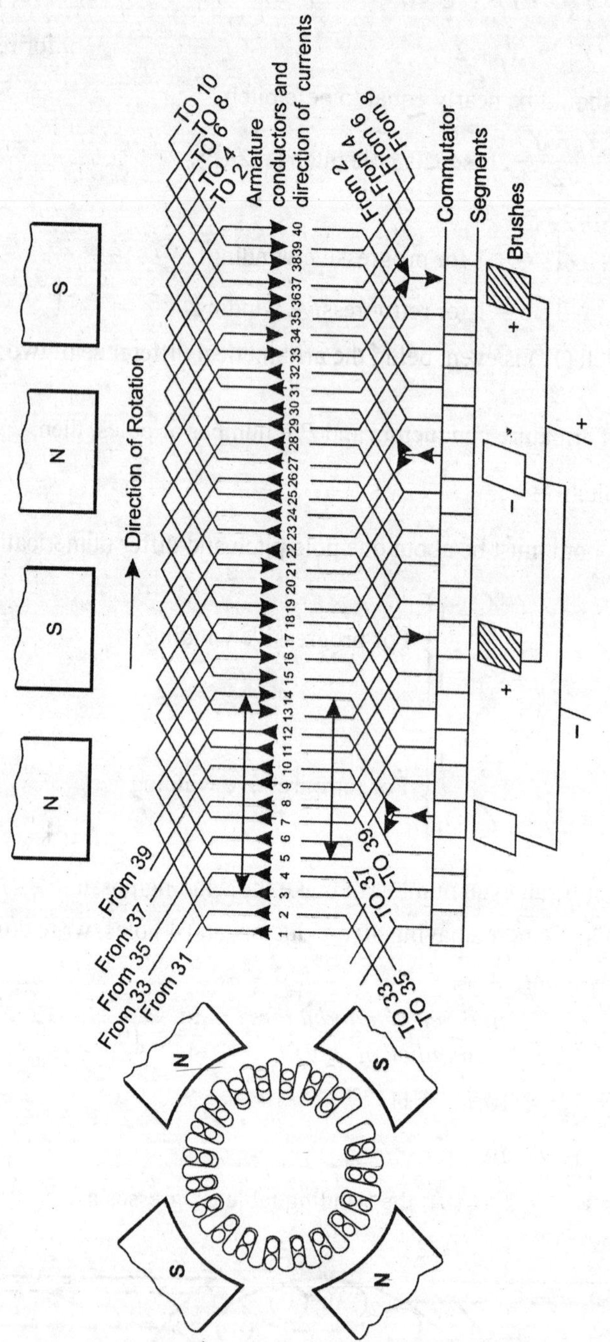

Fig. 3.41. (b) Four pole 40 conductor lap winding of a D.C. machine

Example 3.4: Give the winding table for an armature having 36 conductors. The machine has 4 poles and is lap wound.

Solution. Since there are 36 conductors and 4 poles, therefore the average pitch should be

$$Y_A = \frac{36}{4} = 9.$$

If the back pitch is made equal to 9

i.e. $Y_B = 9$

Then the front pitch is

$$Y_F = 7.$$

If we start from 1, the winding will be progressing as in Fig. 3.41 (*c*)

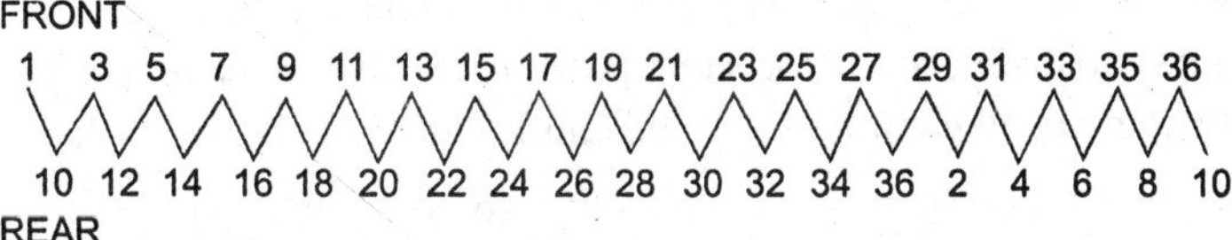

Fig. 3.41. (*c*)

3.15. EQUALISER CONNECTIONS IN LAP WINDINGS

In lap winding all the conductors in any parallel path lie under one pair of poles. If flux from all the poles is exactly the same the induced e.m.f. in each path hence; current carried by each path will be equal. But inspite of best efforts this condition is not practicable either due to variation in gap length or due to different magnetic properties of steel. The currents flowing in various paths may also differ due to difference in their resistances. Hence; there is always slight difference in generated voltage in the various parallel paths and as a result, large circulating currents flow in the armature winding. These circulating currents not only tend to heat the armature above the temperature caused by the normal load current, but also cause an undue amount of sparking at the brushes. Since, such currents must circulate from one path to another through the contacts between brushes and commutator, sparking should, of course, be avoided, because it causes undue burning and wear of the commutator and brushes and if carried too far, may result in flash over from + ve to – ve brushes, a condition representing a short circuit across the supply lines.

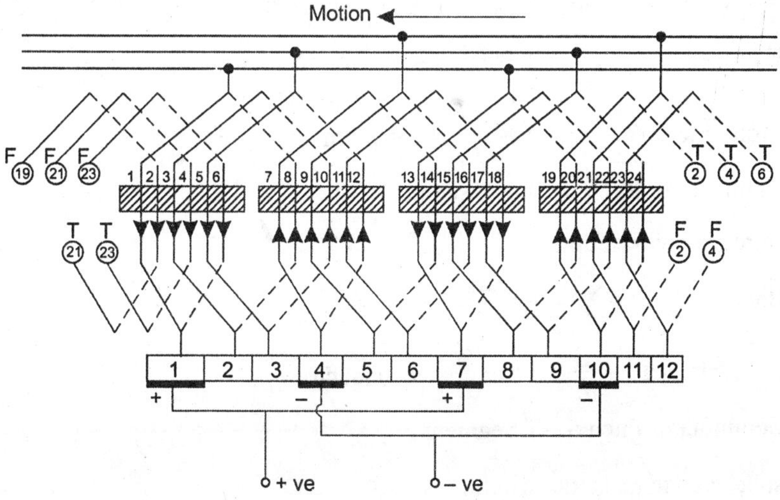

Fig. 3.42. Simplex lap windings with equaliser connections

To overcome the detrimental effects resulting from the circulating currents, it is customary to employ equaliser connections in all lap wound armatures. These are low resistance copper wires that connect together points in the armature winding which should, under ideal conditions be at exactly the same potential all times but which because of mechanical and electrical differences, are not. Thus the equaliser rings relieve the brushes to the circulating current load by causing the later to be by-passed.

To make these equalizer connections, the no. of coils should be multiples of the no. of poles and the no. of coils per pole should be divisible by a small no. 2 or 3. As an example assume a 4 - pole generator having 24 coil sides. The no. of coil sides per pole will be six. The winding with equaliser connections is as shown in Fig. 3.42.1. Note that every 3rd coil is connected to an equaliser. The coils that are connected to the same equaliser occupy the same position relative to the poles. This is necessary as such coils at any instant should be generating the same e.m.f. Note in Fig. 3.42.1 that

(*i*) One equaliser ring is connected to coil side two pole pitch apart.

(*ii*) No. of connections to one equalising ring is equal to the pair of poles and

(*iii*) No. of rings is equal to the no. of coils under one pair of poles *i.e.* equal to $\frac{No.\ of\ coils}{No.\ of\ Pair\ of\ Poles}$ in case every coil is connected to an equaliser.

Theoretically, every coil should be connected to an equaliser but as this would require an undue no. of equalisers, it is sufficient, practically, to connect every 3rd or 4th coil. This is the reason why the no. of coils per pole should be divisible by a small no. as 2, 3 or 4. In Fig. 3.42.1 alternate coil has been connected to the equaliser ring and in such a case the winding is to be 50% equalised. If all the coils were connected to the equalising then the winding would have been 100% equalised.

Example 3.5: A 6–Pole simplex lap wound armature contains 24 slots and has 2 coil sides per slot. Find out (*i*) Back pitch (*ii*) Front pitch (*iii*) Commutator pitch in case of (*a*) progressive winding (*b*) Retrogressive winding.,

Solution: No of poles, $P = 6$

No. of conductors, $Z = 24 \times 2 = 48$

$$\therefore \quad \text{pole pitch} = \frac{Z}{P} = \frac{48}{6} = 8$$

(*a*) For progressive winding

(*i*) Back pitch, $Y_B = \frac{Z}{P} + 1 = \frac{48}{6} + 1 = 9$ conductors

(*ii*) Front pitch, $Y_F = \frac{Z}{P} - 1 = \frac{48}{6} - 1 = 7$ conductors

(*iii*) Commutator Pitch, $Y_C = +1$ Segment

(*b*) For Retrogressive winding

(*i*) Back pitch, $Y_B = \frac{Z}{P} - 1 = \frac{48}{6} - 1 = 7$ conductors

(*ii*) Front pitch, $Y_F = \frac{Z}{P} + 1 = \frac{48}{6} = 9$ conductors

(*iii*) Commutator Pitch $= -1$ Segment

So, $\frac{Z}{P}$ must be even to make the winding possible.

3.13.1. Fundamental Conditions of Lap Windings

There are three basic conditions to be fulfilled by a lap winding namely:

(*i*) The winding must include each element once and only once

(*ii*) The winding must close on itself *i.e.* must be re-entrant.

(*iii*) The pitch must be such that the opposite sides of a coil lie under unlike poles.

3.13.2. Progressive Winding

When the armature winding viewed from the commutator end is such that the winding is in position *a'b'*, *i.e.*, after passing once round the armature, falls in a slot to the right of its starting position, then it is said to be a Progressive winding as shown in Fig 3.42.1 (*a*)

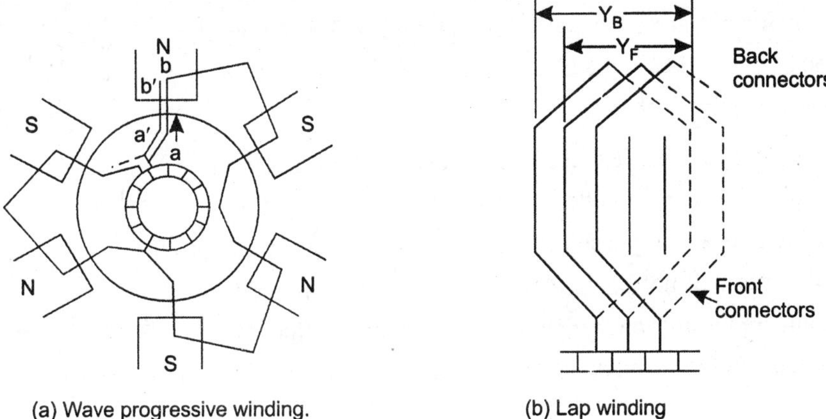

(a) Wave progressive winding.

(b) Lap winding

Fig. 3.42.1. (*a*) wave, (*b*) Lap winding

Also progressive Lap winding is one in which, as one traces through the winding, the connections to the commutator will progress around the machine in the same direction as is being traced along the path of each individual coil. In Fig. 3.42.1 (*b*) $Y_B > Y_F$ and $Y_C = +1$.

Retrogressive Winding

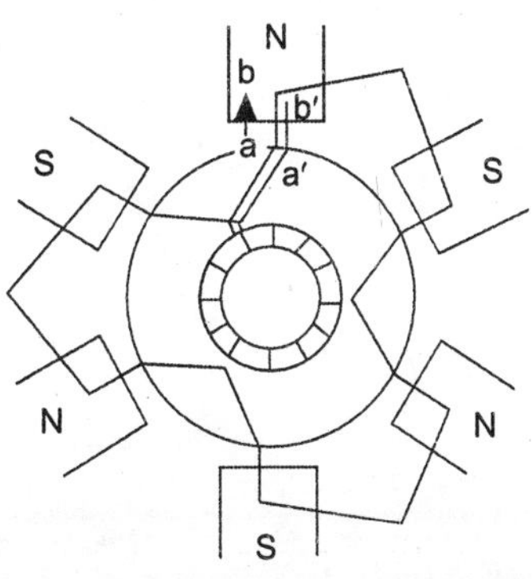

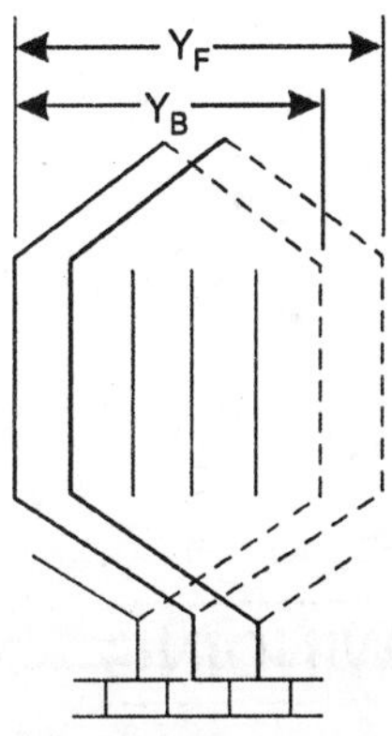

(a) Retrogressive wave winding

(b) Retrogressive Lap winding

Fig. 3.42.2

When $a'b'$ falls in a slot on the left of the starting slot, it is said to be retrogressive wave winding as shown in fig 3.42.2 (*a*).

A Retrogressive lap winding is one in which, as one traces through the winding, the connections to the commutator will progress around the machine in the opposite direction to that which is being traced along the path of each individual coil. Fig 3.42.2 (*b*) shows the retrogressive lap winding. It should be noted here that $Y_F > Y_B$ and $Y_C = -1$. This winding is rarely used because more copper is required.

Full - pitched coil:

If the coil-span or coil pitch is equal to pole pitch, it is called *full-pitched coil* (as shown in fig. 3.42.3) In this case, the e.m.f.s in the coil sides are additive and have a phase difference of 0°. Therefore, e.m.f induced in the coil is maximum. If e.m.f. induced in one coil side is 2.5 V, then e.m.f across the coil terminals = 2 × 2·5 = 5 V. Therefore, coil span should always be one pole pitch unless there is a good reason for making it shorter.

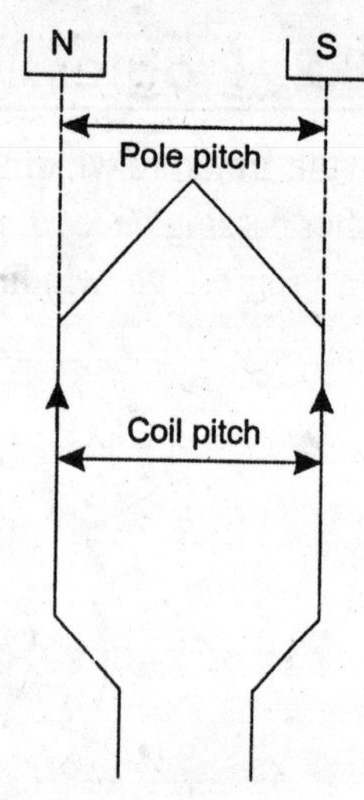

Fig. 3.42.3. Full-pitched coil

Fractional pitched coil. If the coil span or coil pitch is less than the pole pitch, then it is called fractional pitched coil (See Fig. 3.42.4) In this case, the phase difference between the e.m.f.s in the two coil sides will not be zero so that the e.m.f of the coil will be less compared to full-pitched coil. Fractional pitch winding requires less copper but if the pitch is too small, an appreciable reduction in the generated e.m.f. results.

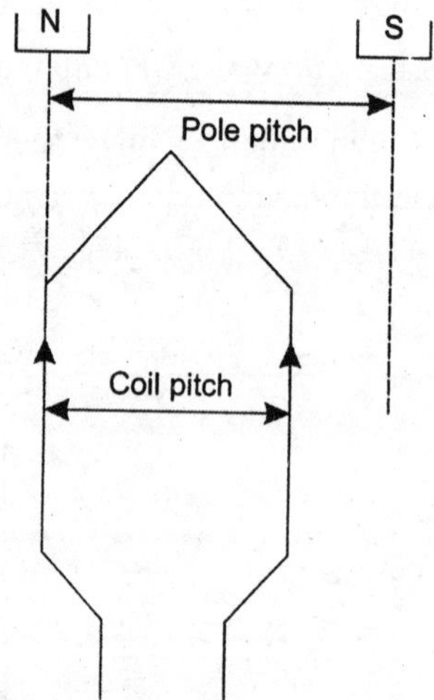

Fig 3.42.4. Fractional Pitched coil

3.16. WAVE WINDING

In case of wave winding a conductor *AB* under the north pole *N* is connected with another conductor *CD*, occupying similar position under the south pole *S*. The conductor *CD* is further connected with conductor *EF* under the next north pole *N* or other than returning to same north pole as in case of lap winding. This process goes on and the winding goes on moving forward to successive north pole and south pole before it comes to original north pole from which the winding was started and it joins conductor A_1 B_1.

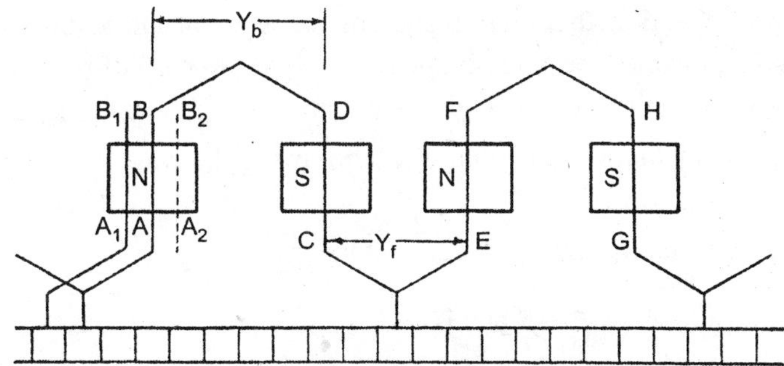

Fig. 3.43. Wave Winding

The winding is known as wave winding as it has the appearance of a wave.

Approximate value of Average pitch of the coil $= \dfrac{Z}{P}$

where Z = no. of conductors P = no. of poles.

The number of conductors spanned by the end connections on the back of the armature is called the back pitch Y_b shown in Fig. 3.43 and similarly number of conductors spanned by end connections on the commutator end of the armature is known as front pitch Y_f.

Average pitch $$Y = \frac{Y_f + Y_b}{2}$$

As in case of lap winding Y_b and Y_f, the back and front pitches in case of wave winding should also be odd but unlike lap winding, Y_b and Y_f may differ from each other by two or more or can be equal.

The average pitch can be odd or even also.

Average pitch $Y = \dfrac{Z \pm 2}{P}$ which should be a whole number.

In order that the wave winding may close finally, the average pitch must agree to the formula given above. In this formula ± 2 has been taken because of the reason that after one tour of the armature, the winding falls short of two coil sides from the point from which the winding was started or two coil sides part from the starting coil side. In Fig. 3.43 the winding has fallen short by two coil sides as shown in Fig. 3.43.

If average pitch is taken as $\dfrac{Z}{P}$ and not as $\dfrac{Z+2}{P}$, then the winding will again come back to the original coil side from which the winding was started after one tour of the armature, so the winding shall close upon itself without using all the coil sides.

If positive sign is taken in the formula, then the winding end falls two coil sides part the starting coil side after one clockwise tour of the armature and is connected to the adjacent segment to the first but part from the starting segment. In the 2nd tour of the armature, winding end will go to the adjoining segment in the clockwise direction.

Thus the winding progresses in the clockwise direction and is known as progressive wave winding. In progressive wave winding after one tour of the armature in the clockwise direction, the winding end is connected to coil side A_2B_2 as shown in Fig. 3.43. When negative sign is used, after one tour of the armature in a clockwise direction, the winding ends two coil sides short of the starting point and is connected to the segment adjacent to the first in the direction left to it. Thus after each tour of the armature in the clockwise direction, the coil falls short of one segment and so the winding progresses left. Such type of winding is known as retrogressive wave winding. In case of retrogressive wave winding after one tour, of the armature, the winding ends are connected as shown in Fig. 3.43 to coil side A_1B_1.

Further details of wave winding can be known by drawing the wave winding by taking a suitable example

Let, there be a 4-pole machine having 28 conductors.

The pole pitch $= \dfrac{28}{4} = 7$ and is odd.

This number, being odd could be used for end connections at both, back and front. Thus assuming both back pitch Y_b and front pitch Y_f to be 7 each

$$\therefore \quad Y_b = Y_f = 7$$

Thus if conductor 1 is connected to 8

Conductor 8 is connected to 8 + 7 = 15

Conductor 15 is connected to 15 + 7 = 22

Conductor 22 is connected to 22 + 7 = 29.

Since conductor 29 is no longer existing and there are only 28 conductors, therefore, 29 conductors means conductor 29 – 28 = 1. Thus starting of winding was made from conductors no 1 and it ended at conductor 1 in one tour of the armature and conductors included for connection are 1, 8, 15 and 22, *i.e.* only four. Remaining 24 conductors are not included. Thus such type of winding is not desirable.

$$\text{Thus Average pitch} = \frac{Y_b + Y_f}{2} = \frac{Z \pm 2}{P}$$

$$Y_b + Y_f = \frac{2\,(28 \pm 2)}{4} = \frac{2 \times 30}{4} \; or \; \frac{2 \times 26}{4}$$

$$Y_b + Y_f = 15 \text{ or } 13, \text{ both being odd.}$$

When $Y_b + Y_f$ is odd, either Y_b or Y_f shall be even.

But for proper wave winding it has already been established that both Y_b and Y_f ought to be odd. Thus winding, wave type is not possible with 28 number of conductors.

Thus let the number of conductors be 26, in that case

$$\frac{Y_b + Y_f}{2} = \frac{z \pm 2}{P} \; or \; \frac{Y_b + Y_f}{2} = \frac{26 \pm 2}{4}$$

$$\text{or} \qquad Y_b + Y_f = \frac{26 \pm 2}{2} = 14 \; or \; 12.$$

Now sum of two pitches is even which means each could be odd as sum of two odd numbers is always even.

Thus assuming, $Y_b = Y_f = 7$ $Y_b + y_f = 7 + 7 = 14$

The winding table is as given below

Back connections	***Front connections***
1 to 1 + 7 = 8	8 to 8 + 7 = 15
15 to 15 + 7 = 22	22 to 22 + 7 = 29, *i.e.* 29 – 26 = 3
3 to 3 + 7 = 10	10 to 10 + 7 = 17
17 to 17 + 7 = 24	24 to 24 + 7 = 31 *i.e.* 31 – 26 = 5
5 to 5 + 7 = 12	12 to 12 + 7 = 19
19 to 19 + 7 = 26	26 to 26 + 7 = 33
7 to 7 + 7 = 14	14 to 14 + 7 = 21
21 to 21 + 7 = 28,	
i.e. 28 – 26 = 2	2 to 2 + 7 = 9
9 to 9 + 7 = 16	16 to 16 + 7 = 23
23 to 23 + 7 = 30,	4 to 4 + 7 =11
i.e. 30 – 26 = 4	
11 to 11 + 7 = 18	18 to 18 + 7 = 25
25 to 25 + 7 = 32,	6 to 6 + 7 =13
i.e. 32 – 26 = 6	
13 to 13 + 7 = 20	20 to 20 + 7 = 27, *i.e.* 27 – 26 = 1

The complete winding is shown drawn in Fig. 3.44. The direction of the induced e.m.f.s is also shown by the arrows. In order to find out the position of the brushes, the melting and separating points of two e.m.f.s must be traced. There is one separating point at commutator segment a so that one negative brush could be fixed up with this segment. Now since the brushes are equally spaced, three other positions are found out which are not opposite to the poles.

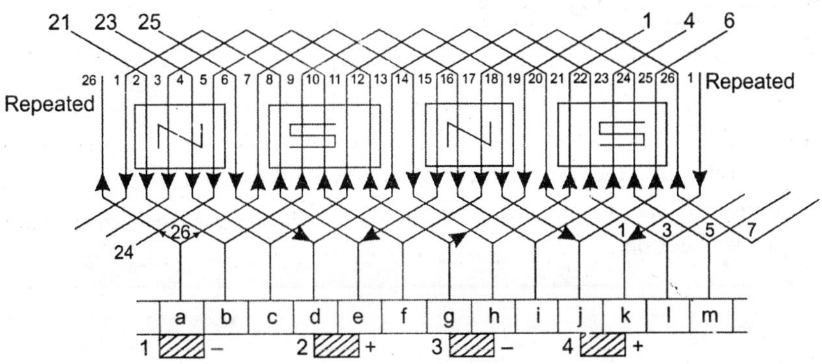

Fig. 3.44 Developed winding scheme for 4 pole wave wound armature

The other three brush positions occur at consecutive meeting and separating points, although they involve simultaneous contact with two segments.

Thus it can be seen that even in four pole wave windings also, four brush positions could be had but still it differs from lap winding in a way that in lap winding, exactly one quarter of the winding is included between two consecutive brushes due to which the winding gets divided into four identical parallel paths.

But in case of wave winding as drawn and shown in Fig. 3.44 the portion of the winding between the two negative brushes is that portion which includes conductors 7 and 14 only and as both of these are in the inter polar gaps, the e.m.fs in them are negligibly small. Similarly between two + ve brushes, there is a portion made up of conductors 13 and 20 only, these are also in inter polar gaps. It shows that the portions mentioned do not contribute to the e.m.f. of the machine but merely serve to bridge brushes virtually at the same potential. Hence two brushes say 3 and 4 could be easily omitted leaving only brushes 1 and 2.

It can be concluded that since there are only two brushes, one positive and one negative, so there are only two parallel paths for the flow of current through the armature irrespective of number of poles the machine has.

Even if the number of brushes used are 4, the number of parallel paths still remains 2. In that case the coils in the interpolar gaps then merely serve as connectors between the brushes of the same polarity.

Thus a wave wound armature has:

1. Two number of parallel paths irrespective of any number of poles.
2. The brush sets could be either two or as many as the number of poles are there.

In fact if the machine is a large machine having large current flow, and only two brushes are used, one positive and one negative, then the whole current is carried by one brush set, and axial length of all brushes per set and also through commutator. Thus all these three must be accordingly designed for higher value of current which shall make all these three quite expensive.

If the number of brush sets is increased, the current per set is decreased. For example a 6 - pole machine with 6 brush sets will have only $\frac{1}{3}$ rd of the total current carried by any one set. Thus the axial length of the commutator and therefore, its cost is tremendously reduced.

Due to this reason, large wave wound machines, usually have as many brush sets as there are poles.

3.16.1 Simplex Wave winding

In simplex wave winding, the commutator pitch, $Y_c \simeq 2$ pole pitches and coil span $\simeq$ pole pitch. The result is that the coils under consecutive pole pairs will be joined together in series thereby adding together their e.m.f.s [See Fig. 3.44.0]. After passing once around the armature, the winding falls in a slot to the left or right of the starting point and thus connecting up another circuit. Continuing in this way, all the conductors will be connected in a single closed winding. This winding is called wave winding from the appearance of the end connections.

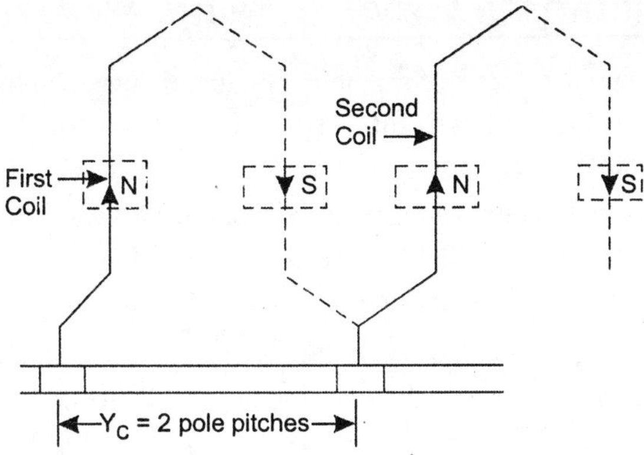

Fig. 3.44

Simplex wave winding is sometimes also called as **series winding.** The main difference between simplex lap winding and a simplex wave winding is in the commutator connections. In simplex lap winding, the coils which are approximately pole pitch apart are connected in series and the Commutator pitch, $Y_C = \pm 1$ Segment. As a result the coil voltage add as shown in Fig. 3.44 (*a*). But in a simplex wave winding the coils approximately pole pitch apart are connected in series and the commutator pitch $Y_C \simeq 2$ pole pitches (segments) as shown in Fig below:

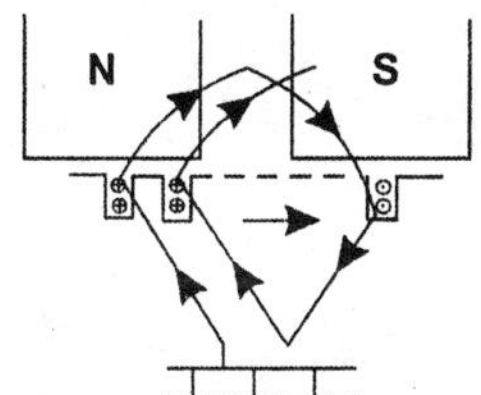

Fig. 3.44 (a) Lap winding

The wave winding must not close after it passes once around the armature but it must connect to a commutator segment adjacent to the first and the next coil must be adjacent to the first as indicated in Fig. 3.44 (*b*). This is repeated each time around until connections are made to all commutator segments and all the slots are occupied after which the winding automatically returns to the starting point.

If after passing one round the armature, the winding connects to a segment to the left of the starting point, the winding is said to be retrogressive. If however, it connects to a segment to the right of the starting point, it is **progressive.**

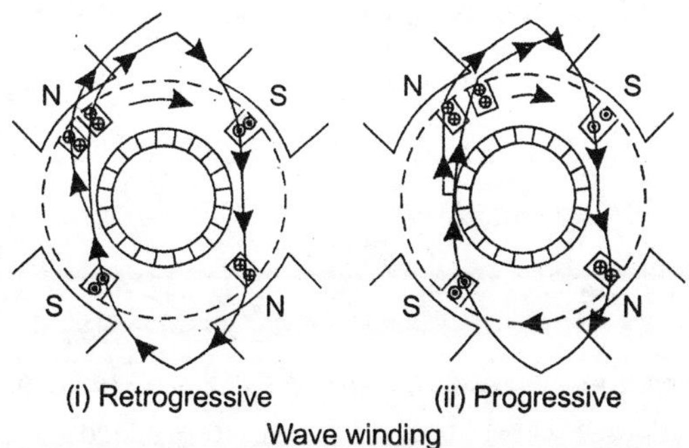

Fig. 3.44 (b)

3.16.2. Various Pitches in Wave Winding

(*i*) The distance measured in terms of armature conductors between the two sides of a coil at the back of the armature is called **back pitch Y_B** (See Fig. 3.44 (c)). *The Y_B must be an odd integer so that a top conductor and a bottom conductor will be joined.*

(*ii*) The distance measured in terms of armature conductors between the coil sides attached to any one commutator segment is called **front pitch Y_F** (See Fig. 2.44(c)). *The Y_F must be an odd integer so that a top conductor and a bottom conductor will be joined.*

(*iii*) Resultant pitch, $Y_R = Y_B + Y_F$ (See Fig 3.44(c))

The resultant pitch must be an even integer since Y_B and Y_F are odd. Further Y_R is approximately two pole pitches because Y_B as well as Y_F is approximately one pole pitch.

(*iv*) Average pitch, $Y_A = \dfrac{Y_B + Y_F}{2}$

When one tour of armature has been completed, the winding should connect to the next top conductor (progressive) or to the preceding top conductor (retrogressive). In either case, the difference will be of 2 conductors or one slot. If P is the number of poles and Z is the total number of armature conductors, then,

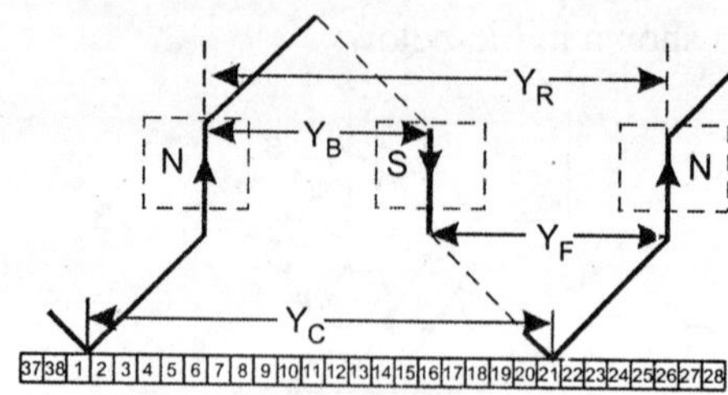

Fig. 3.44 (c)

$$P \times Y_A = Z \pm 2$$

or $$Y_A = \frac{Z \pm 2}{P} \qquad \text{...}(i)$$

Since P is always even and $Z = PY_A \pm 2$, Z must be even. It means that $Z \pm 2/P$ must be an integer. In eq. (*i*), plus sign will give progressive winding and the negative sign retrogressive winding.

(*v*) The number of commutator segments spanned by a coil is called **commutator pitch (Y_C)** (See Fig. 2.44 (c)). Suppose in a simplex wave winding.

P = Number of poles;

N_C = Number of commutator segments;

Y_C = Commutator pitch.

$\therefore$ Number of pair of poles = $P/2$

If $Y_C \times P/2 = N_C$ then the winding will close on itself in passing once around the armature. In order to connect to the adjacent conductor and permit the winding to proceed,

$$Y_C \times \frac{P}{2} = N_C \pm 1$$

or
$$Y_C = \frac{2N_C \pm 2}{P}$$

$$= \frac{N_C \pm 1}{P/2} = \frac{\textit{No. of commutator seg.} \pm 1}{\textit{Number of pair of poles}}$$

Now $Y_C = \frac{2N_C \pm 2}{P} = \frac{Z \pm 2}{P} = Y_A$ $\qquad (\because 2N_C = Z)$

$\therefore$ Commutator pitch, $Y_C = Y_A = \frac{Y_B + Y_F}{2}$

In a simplex wave winding Y_B, Y_F and Y_C may be equal. Note that Y_B, Y_F and Y_A are in terms of armature conductors whereas Y_C is in terms of commutator segments.

3.16.3. Design of Simplex Wave Winding

While designing simplex wave winding, the following points may be kept in mind:

(*i*) Both pitches Y_B and Y_F are odd and are of the same sign.

(*ii*) Average pitch, $Y_A = \frac{Z \pm 2}{P}$ ...(*i*)

(*iii*) Both Y_B and Y_F are nearly equal to pole pitch and *may be equal or differ by* 2. If they differ by 2, they are one more and one less than Y_A.

(*iv*) Commutator pitch is given by;

$$Y_C = Y_A = \frac{\textit{Number of commutator segments} \pm 1}{\textit{Number of pair of poles}}$$

The plus sign for progressive winding and negative for retrogressive winding.

(*v*)
$$Y_A = \frac{Z \pm 2}{P}$$

Since Y_A must be a whole number, there is a restriction on the value of Z. With $Z = 180$, this winding is impossible for a 4-pole machine because Y_A is not a whole number.

(*vi*)
$$Z = PY_A \pm 2$$

$\therefore$ Number of coils $= \frac{Z}{2} = \frac{PY_A \pm 2}{2}$

Example 3.6: A 4-pole armature has 42 armature conductors. The armature is to be simple wave-wound with single-turn coils. Determine for a retrogressive winding (*i*) back pitch (*ii*) front pitch (*iii*) commutator pitch.

Solution. Number of poles, $P = 4$, Number of Armature conductors, $z = 42$

(*i*) Average pitch, $Y_A = \frac{Z \pm 2}{P}$

For a retrogressive winding,

$$Y_A = \frac{Z-2}{P} = \frac{42-2}{4} = 10 \text{ conductors}$$

$\therefore$ $\quad$ $\mathbf{Y_B = 10}$ **conductors** **Ans.**

(*ii*) Average pitch, $\quad Y_A = \frac{Y_B + Y_F}{2}$

or $\quad 10 = \frac{10 + Y_F}{2}$ $\quad \therefore Y_F = 10$ **conductors**

(*iii*) $\quad Y_C = Y_A = 10$ **commutator segments** **Ans.**

Alternatively, for a retrogressive winding,

$$Y_C = \frac{\textit{No. of commutator segments} - 1}{\textit{No. of pair of poles}}$$

$$= \frac{21-1}{2} = 10 \text{ commutator segments}$$ **Ans.**

Example 3.7: A 4-pole, simplex wave-wound armature has 21 slots and 21 segments. Find The Commutator pitch.

Solution. Commutator pitch,

$$Y_C = \frac{2N_c \pm 2}{P}$$

$$= \frac{2 \times 21 \pm 2}{4} = 10 \text{ or } 11$$ **commutator-segments Ans.**

Example 3.8: Design a 4-pole wave winding for an armature with 21 slots. Assume single turn coils and two conductors per slot.

Solution. Average pitch, $Y_A = \frac{Z+2}{2} = \frac{42+2}{4} = 11$ conductors. We have taken + 2 on the assumption that progressive winding is desired. Since Y_A is a whole number, the wave winding is possible. Taking $Y_B = 11$ conductors,

we have $Y_F = 11$ conductors.

commutator pitch, $\quad Y_C = Y_A = 11$ segments.

Winding Table: the winding table for the winding is given below:-

Back connections	***Front connections***
1 to (1 + 11) = 12	12 to (12 + 11) = 23
23 to (23 + 11) = 34	34 to (34 + 11) = 45 – 42 = 3
3 to (3 + 11) = 14	14 to (14 + 11) = 25
25 to (25 + 11) = 36	36 to (36 + 11) = 47 – 42 = 5
5 to (5 + 11) = 16	16 to (16 + 11) = 27

27 to (27 + 11) = 38	38 to (38 + 11) = 49 – 42 = 7
7 to (7 + 11) = 18	18 to (18 + 11) = 29
29 to (29 + 11) = 40	40 to (40 + 11) = 51 – 42 = 9
9 to (9 + 11) = 20	20 to (20 + 11) = 31
31 to (31 + 11) = 42	42 to (42 + 11) = 53 – 42 = 11
11 to (11 + 11) = 22	22 to (22 + 11) = 33
33 to (33 + 11) = 44 – 42 = 2	2 to (2 + 11) = 13
13 to (13 + 11) = 24	24 to (24 + 11) = 35
35 to (35 + 11) = 46–42 = 4	4 to (4 + 11) = 15
15 to (15 + 11) = 26	26 to (26 + 11) = 37
37 to (37 + 11) = 48 – 42 = 6	6 to (6 + 11) = 17
17 to (17 + 11) = 28	28 to (28 + 11) = 39
39 to (39 + 11) = 50 – 42 = 8	8 to (8 + 11) = 19
19 to (19 + 11) = 30	30 to (30 + 11) = 41
41 to (41 + 11) = 52 – 42 = 10	10 to (10 + 11) = 21
21 to (21 + 11) = 32	32 to (32 + 11) = 43 – 42 = 1

Since we have come back to conductor No. 1 from where we started, the winding gets closed at this stage.

Developed diagram. Fig. 3.44 (*d*) shows the developed diagram for the winding. Note that full lines represent the top coil sides (or conductors) and dotted lines represent the bottom coil sides (or conductors). The two conductors which lie in the same slot are drawn nearer to each other than to those in the other slots.

Referring to Fig. 3.44 (*d*), conductor 1 connects at the back to conductor 12 (1 + 11) which in turn connects at the front to conductor 23 (12 + 11) and so on round the armature until the winding is complete. Note that the commutator pitch $Y_C = 11$ segments. This means that the number of commutator segments spanned between the start end and finish end of any coil is 11 segments.

Position and number of brushes. We now turn to find the position and the number of brushes. The arrowhead marked "rotation" in Fig. 3.44 (*d*) shows the direction of motion of the conductors. By right hand rule, the direction of e.m.f. in each conductor will be as shown.

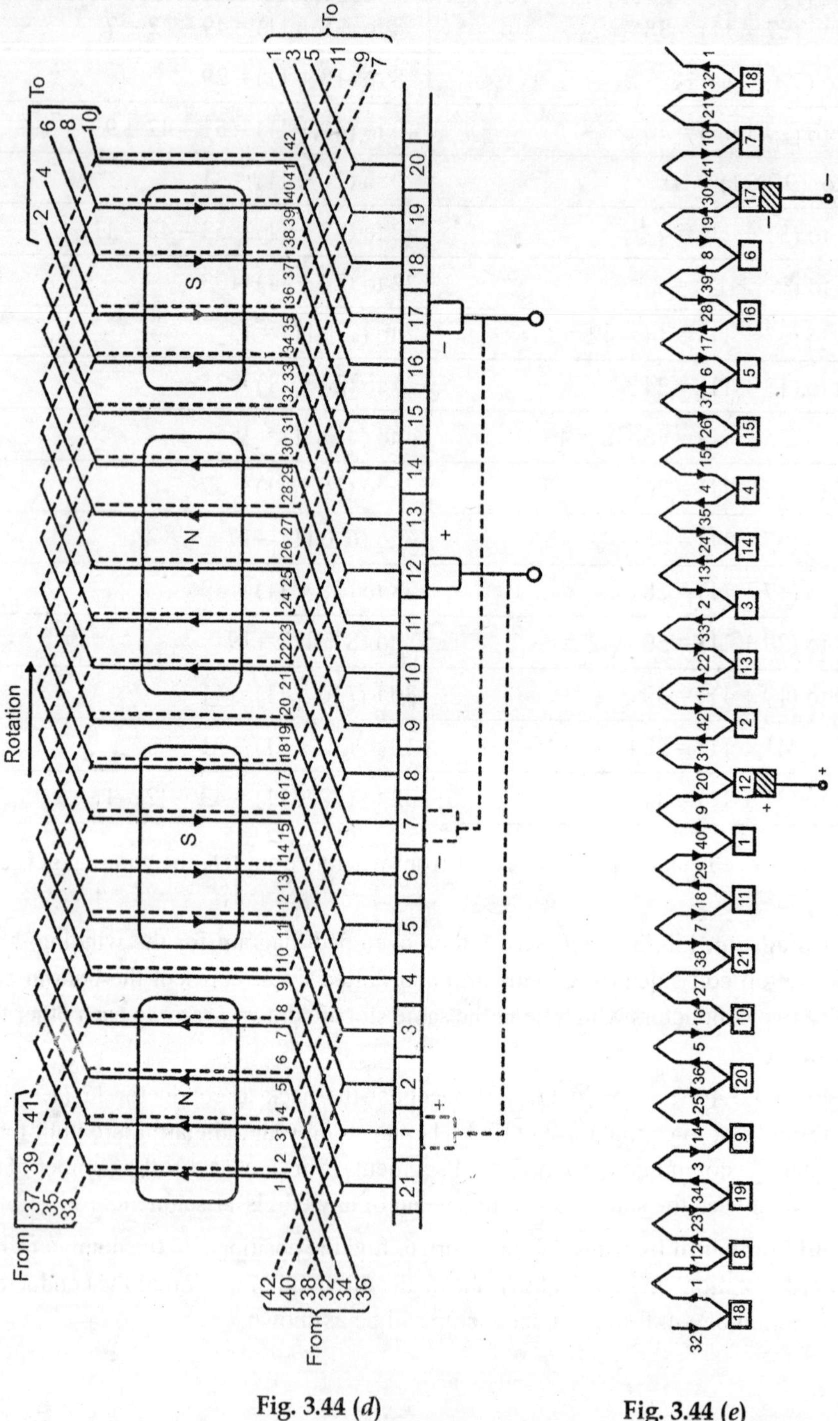

Fig. 3.44 (*d*)

Fig. 3.44 (*e*)

In order to find the position of brushes, the ring diagram shown in Fig. 3.44 (*e*) is quite helpful. It is clear that only two brushes – one positive and one negative—are required (though two positive and two negative brushes can also be used). We find that there are two parallel paths between the positive brush and the negative brush. Thus is illustrated in Fig. 3.44 (*f*)

Therefore, we arrive at a very important conclusion that *in a simplex wave winding, the number of parallel paths is two irrespective of the number of poles*. Note that the first parallel path has 11 coils (or 22 conductors) while the second parallel path has 10 coils (or 20 conductors). This fact is not important as it may appear at first glance. The coils in the smaller group should supply less current to the external circuit. But the identity of the coils in either parallel path is rapidly changing from moment to moment. Therefore, the average value of current through any particular coil is the same.

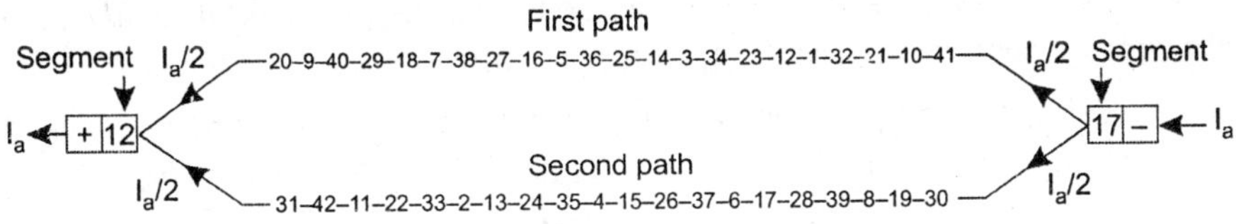

Fig. 3.44 (*f*)

Conclusions. From the above discussion, the following conclusions can be drawn:

(*i*) Only two brushes are necessary but as many brushes as there are poles may be used.

(*ii*) *The armature winding is divided into two parallel paths irrespective of the number of poles.* If the total number of armature conductors is Z and P is the number of poles, then,

$$\text{Number of conductors/path} = \frac{Z}{2}$$

(*iii*) E.M.F. generated = E.M.F. per parallel path

$$= \text{Average e.m.f. per conductor} \times \frac{Z}{2}$$

(*iv*) Total armature current, $I_a = 2 \times$ current per parallel path

(*v*) The armature can be wave-wound if Y_A or Y_C is a whole number.

3.16.4. Dummy Coils

In a simplex wave winding, the average pitch Y_A (or commutator pitch Y_C) should be a whole number. Sometimes the standard armature punchings available in the market have slots that do not satisfy the above requirement so that more coils (usually only one more) are provided than can be utilised. These extra coils are *called dummy or dead coils*. The dummy coil is inserted into the slots in the same way as the others to make the armature *dynamically balanced but it is not a part of the armature winding.

Let us illustrate the use of dummy coils with a numerical example. Suppose the number of slots is 22 and each slot contains 2 conductors. The number of poles is 4. For simplex wave wound armature,

$$Y_A = \frac{Z \pm 2}{P} = \frac{2 \times 22 \pm 2}{4} = \frac{44 \pm 2}{4} = 11\frac{1}{2} \text{ or } 10\frac{1}{2}$$

Since the results are not whole numbers, the number of coils (and hence segments) must be reduced. If we make one coil dummy, we have 42 conductors and

$$Y_A = \frac{42 \pm 2}{4} = 11 \text{ or } 10$$

This means that armature can be wound only if we use 21 coils and 21 segments. The extra coil or dummy coil is put in the slot. One end of this coil is taped and the other end connected to the unused commutator segment (segment 22) for the sake of appearance. Since only 21 segments are required the two (21 and 22 segments) are connected together and considered as one.

3.16.5 Use of Lap and Wave Windings

A lap winding, because of the large number of parallel paths is more suitable for generating large currents. To obtain high voltage in a lap winding it is necessary to have a large number of small conductors and it means a higher winding cost and lower efficiency for the utilization of the space in the slots.

For a certain fixed number of poles and armature conductors, a wave winding gives higher e.m.f. Hence the wave-winding is very useful for small generators, say upto about 660 volts. Wave windings also have the advantage that due to unbalancing of magnetic reluctances or flux densities, no circulatory currents are produced like lap windings. This is so because each conductor is series connected in a wave winding and has to pass under all the north and south poles, and the corresponding conductors of each path of the armature move under the same poles, thus producing a similar and equal unbalancing effect in each path.

3.17. COMPARISON BETWEEN LAP AND WAVE WINDINGS

Let there be a machine whose armature winding has 648 conductors. Let the average e.m.f. induced in each conductor is 2 volts and let each conductor be of such cross section that its normal current is 50 A having number of parallel paths *i.e.* 6 numbers

(a) *When the machine is lap wound machine*:

Equivalent circuit of the armature is shown in Fig. 3.45.

Total No. of conductors = 648

No. of parallel paths = 6

Conductors per parallel path

$$\frac{648}{6} = 108$$

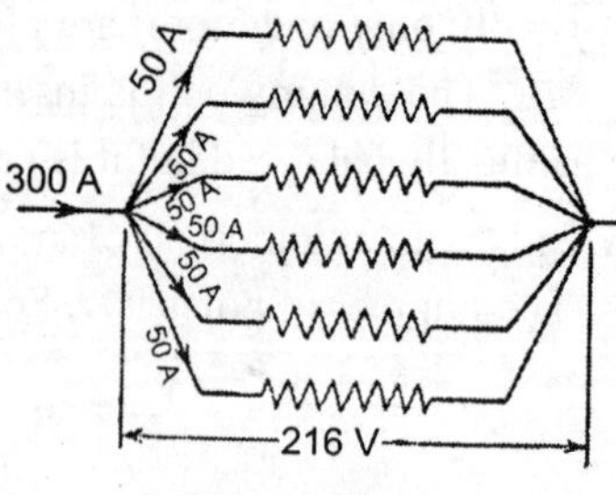

Fig. 3.45

E.m.f. per parallel path

$$= 108 \times 2 = 216 \text{ V}$$

Current per path $= 50$ A

Total current in the armature

$$= 50 \times 6 = 300 \text{ A.}$$

$\therefore$ Output of the generator

$$= 216 \times 300$$

$$= 64,800 \text{ W} = 64.8 \text{ kW.}$$

(b) *When the machine is wave wound.*

Equivalent circuit of the machine is shown in Fig. 3.46.

Total No. of conductors

$$= 648$$

$$\text{No. of parallel path} = 2$$

$$\text{Current per parallel path} = \frac{648}{2} = 324$$

$$\text{emf per parallel path} = 324 \times 2 = 648 \text{ V}$$

Current per parallel path

$$= 50 \text{ A}$$

Total current in the armature

$$= 50 \times 2 = 100 \text{ A}$$

Output of the generator

$$= 648 \times 100 = 64,800 \text{ W} = 64.8 \text{ kW.}$$

It can thus be concluded that whether the winding is lap or wave connected, as far as the output in kW is concerned, that remains the same but output voltage and current are definitely affected.

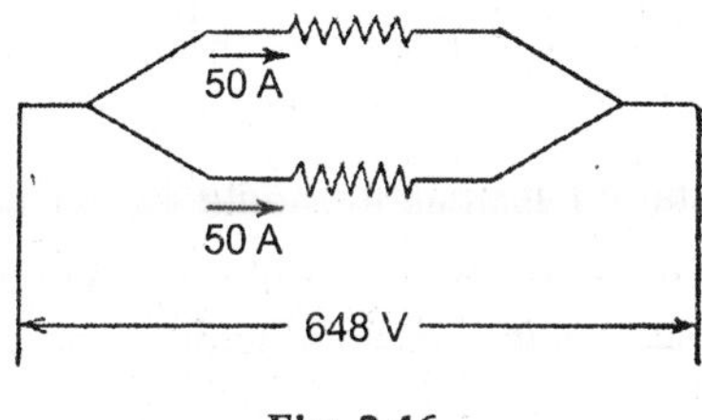

Fig. 3.46

The lap winding gives greater current at lower voltage while wave winding gives lower current at higher voltage.

3.17.1. Multiplex Windings

A simplex lap–wound armature has as many parallel paths as the number of poles. A simplex wave-wound armature has two parallel paths irrespective of the number of poles. In case of a 10-pole machine, using simplex windings, the designer is restricted to either two parallel circuits (wave) or ten parallel circuits (lap). Sometimes it is desirable to increase the number of parallel paths. For this purpose, *multiplex windings* are used. The sole purpose of multiplex windings is to increase the number of parallel paths enabling the armature to carry a large total current. The degree of multiplicity or plex determines the number of parallel paths in the following manner:

(*i*) A lap winding has pole times the degree of plex parallel paths.

Number of parallel paths, $A = P \times$ plex

Thus a *duplex lap winding* has $2P$ parallel paths, *triplex lap winding* has $3P$ parallel paths and so on. If an armature is changed from simplex lap to duplex lap without making any other change, the number of parallel paths is doubled and each path has half as many coils. The armature will then supply twice as much current at half the voltage.

(*ii*) A wave winding has two times the degree of plex parallel paths.

Number of parallel paths, $A = 2 \times$ plex

Note that the number of parallel paths in a multiplex wave winding depends upon the degree of plex and not on the number of poles. Thus a *duplex wave winding* has 4 parallel paths, *triplex wave winding* has 6 parallel paths and so on.

3.17.2. Function of Commutator and Brushes

The e.m.f. generated in the armature winding of a d.c. generator is alternating one. The commutator and brushes cause the alternating e.m.f. of the armature conductors to produce a p.d. always in the same direction between the terminals of the generator. In lap as well as wave winding, it will be observed that currents in the coils to a brush are either all directed towards the brush (positive brush) or all directed away from the brush (negative brush). Further, the direction of current in coil reverses as it passes the brush. Thus when the coil approaches the contact with the brush, the current through the coil is in one direction; when the coil leaves the contact with the brush, the current has been reversed. *This reversal of current in the coil as the coil passes a brush is called* **commutation** *and takes place while the coil is short-circuited by the brush.* These changes occur in every coil in turn. If, at the instant when the brush breaks contact with the commutator segment connected to the coil undergoing commutation, the current in the coil has not been reversed, the result will be sparking between the commutator segments and the brush.

The criterion of good commutation is that it should be sparkless. In order to have sparkless commutation, the brushes on the commutator should be placed at points known as *neutral points* where no voltage exists between adjacent segments. The conductors connected to these segments lie between the poles in position of zero magnetic flux which is termed as *magnetic neutral axis* (M.N. A.).

Magnetic Circuit

Fig 3.46 (*a*) illustrates schematically a part of a four–pole D.C. machine and pictures the magnetic flux created by the main poles.

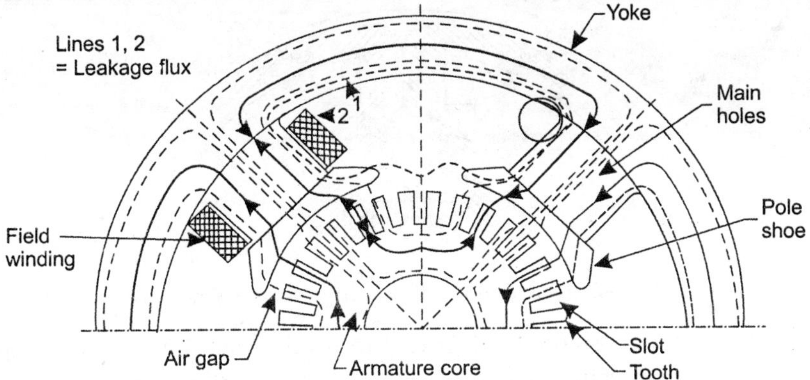

Fig. 3.46 (a) Magnetic circuit of the main poles of a four pole D.C. machine

- Due to complete symmetry of the machine, the flux induced by each of the poles is divided with respect to the pole centre line into two parts forming two identical magnetic circuits symmetrically disposed on both sides of the centre line of the given pole. *The number of such circuits is equal to the number of field poles.*
- That part of the main flux which corresponds to one-half of a pole is arbitrarily depicted in Fig. 3.46(*a*) by two heavy dotted lines showing the external and internal boundaries of the circuit, and by one solid line passing through the middle of the circuit.
- The main flux is only part of the total flux induced by a pole. The other part of the flux, called the *leakage flux*, branches off into the space between the poles, and therefore, does not penetrate into the armature core and takes part in the creation of e.m.f. The two thin dotted lines 1 and 2 depict the leakage flux in Fig. 3.46 (*a*)

3.18. E.M.F EQUATION

Let ϕ = Flux per pole in webers

Z = Total number of armature conductors in the slots or coil sides on armature.

P = Number of poles = $2p$, where p is equal to number of pairs of poles.

N = Armature rotational speed in r.p.m.

$= \frac{N}{60}$ rev./sec.

A = Number of parallel paths through the armature

A = 2 for wave wound armature and

A = P, for lap wound armature.

Consider one pole of a D.C. machine as shown in Fig. 3.47. Planes P and Q are situated in between the middle of the poles and are ‿ ·eutral planes where the flux distribution in the air gap is almost zero.

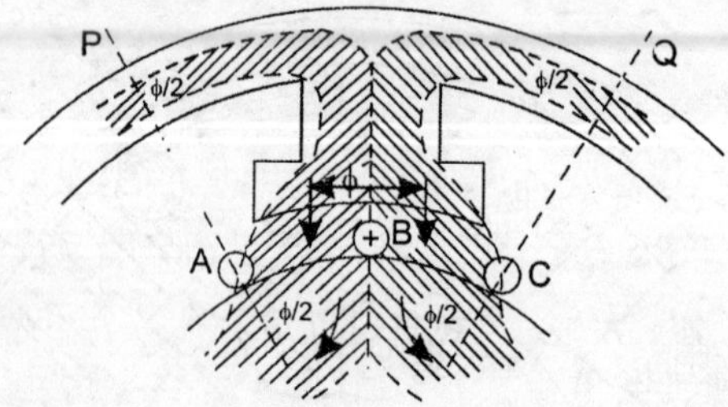

Fig. 3.47. Distribution of flux in pole and armature

An armature conductor in position A will have zero e.m.f. induced in it. In position B its induced e.m.f. will have the maximum value, while in position C, the e.m.f. will again be zero. Hence e.m.f. induced in one particular conductor or an armature of a D.C. Machine goes through considerable variations in magnitude so that the e.m.f. induced during one rotation of the conductor is decided by the average value of the e.m.f.

Hence for a single conductor average induced e.m.f. during path A to C

i.e. $$E_{av} = \frac{\textit{Flux cut}}{\textit{Time taken}} \text{ volts}$$

The time taken is the time in seconds required to move from A to C.

Then time taken for one revolution

$$= \frac{1}{N} \text{ minute}$$

$$= \frac{1}{N} \times 60 \text{ seconds.}$$

Now in moving from A to C, The distance is one pole pitch, *i.e.* $\frac{1}{P}$ of the periphery or circumference.

∴ The time taken to move the conductor under one pole, *i.e.* from A to C (pole pitch) during which the flux ϕ is cut is:

$$t = \frac{1}{P} \times \frac{60}{N} = \frac{60}{PN} \text{ sec.}$$

Hence average value of induced e.m.f. per conductor

$$E_{av} = \frac{\phi}{t} = \frac{\phi}{\frac{60}{PN}} \text{ volts}$$

$$= \frac{\phi . PN}{60} \text{ volts}$$

Now if there are Z number of armature conductors connected in series with each other then the total e.m.f. generated for the whole winding is

$$E = \frac{\phi PN}{60} \times Z \text{ volts}$$

Re-arranging the equation we can write

$$E = \frac{P\phi ZN}{60} \text{ volts.}$$

In actual practice all the conductors are not in series, but instead, the winding may have, A, parallel paths. The. e.m.f. per path may then be written as

$$E = \frac{P\phi ZN}{60\,A} \text{ volts.}$$

where A = 2 (for wave winding)

= P (for lap winding).

OR

E.M.F. EQUATION (Second method):

Let P = Number of poles

ϕ = Flux per pole in wbs.

Z = Total number of armature-conductors

N = Speed of armature in R.p.m.

A = Number of parallel paths in armature winding.

$$\begin{bmatrix} A = 2 \textit{ for wave winding and} \\ A = P \textit{ for lap winding} \end{bmatrix}$$

Generated E.m.f, E_g = E.m.f of the generator per parallel path

In one revolution of the armature,

Flux cut by one conductor,

$$d\phi = P\phi \text{ webers}$$

Time taken to complete one revolution,

$$dt = \frac{60}{N} \text{ seconds.}$$

e.m.f. generated per conductor

$$= \frac{d\phi}{dt} = \frac{P\phi}{60/N} = \frac{P\phi N}{60} \text{ volts}$$

$\therefore$ e.m.f of generator, E_g = e.m.f per parallel path

= e.m.f per conductor × No. of conductors in series per parallel path,

$$= \frac{P\phi N}{60} \times \frac{Z}{A}$$

$$\therefore \quad E_g = \frac{P\phi ZN}{60A} \text{ volts.}$$

For a given machine, the no. of poles and no. of armature conductors per parallel path (Z_A) are constant.

Example 3.9. Calculate the e.m.f. generated by a 4 pole wave wound armature having 45 slots with 18 conductors per slot driven at 1200 r.p.m. The flux per pole is 0.016 wb.

(A.M.*I.e.* Nov. 1992)

Solution. Given,

$$P = 4, A = 2 \qquad [\because \text{ in wave winding, } A = 2]$$

$$Z = 45 \times 18 = 810 \text{ conductors}$$

$$\phi = 0.016 \text{ Wb, and } N = 1200 \text{ r.p.m.}$$

Now formula used is, *i.e.*

$$E = \frac{P\phi ZN}{60A} \text{ volts}$$

$$= \frac{4 \times 0.016 \times 810 \times 1200}{60 \times 2} \text{ volts}$$

$$= \mathbf{518.4 \text{ volts}}$$

Ans.

Example 3.10: What e.m.f. will be generated in an 8 pole, lap wound generator if it is rotated at 200 r.p.m.? The flux per pole is 0.05 Wb and the number of armature conductors are 960.

Solution. Formula used is,

i.e. $$E = \frac{P\phi NZ}{60A} \text{ volts}$$

where $$\phi = 0.05 \text{ Wb}$$

$$Z = 960 \text{ conductors}$$

$$N = 200 \text{ r.p.m}$$

$$P = 8$$

$$A = 8 \text{ (lap winding)}$$

$$E = \frac{8 \times 0.05 \times 960 \times 200}{60 \times 8} \text{ volts}$$

$$= \mathbf{160 \text{ volts.}}$$

Ans.

Example 3.11: The armature of a 4 pole wave wound d.c. generator has 144 slots and 3 conductors per slot. If armature is rotated with a speed of 1200 r.p.m. and the flux per pole is 0.025 Wb. Calculate the e.m.f. generated.

Solution.

Formula used is, $$E = \frac{P\phi ZN}{60A} \text{ volts.}$$

$$P \Rightarrow 4$$

$$\phi \Rightarrow 0.025 \text{ Wb.}$$

$$N \Rightarrow 1200 \text{ r.p.m.}$$

No. of slots = 144

Conductors per slot = 3

Total number of conductor,

$$Z \Rightarrow 144 \times 3 \Rightarrow 432$$

As we know that in a wave wound generator there are only two numbers of parallel paths irrespective of the number of poles.

Hence $$A \Rightarrow 2$$

$$E \Rightarrow \frac{4 \times 0.025 \times 432 \times 1200}{60 \times 2} \Rightarrow 432 \text{ volts}$$ **Ans.**

Example 3.12: The Armature of a 4 pole D.C. generator is required to generate an e.m.f of 520 V on open ckt when revolving at a speed of 660 r.p.m. Calculate the magnetic flux per pole required if the armature has 144 slots with two coil sides per slot, each coil consisting of three turns. The armature is wave wound.

Solution: Formula used

$$E_g = \frac{\phi ZN}{60} \times \left(\frac{P}{A}\right) \text{ volt}$$

Here $E_g = 520\ V, N = 660$ r.p.m.

$$Z = 144 \times 2 \times 3 = 864, \quad P = 4, \quad A = 2 \text{ (Due to wave winding)}$$

$$\therefore \quad 520 = \frac{\phi \times 864 \times 660}{60} \times \frac{4}{2}$$

$$\therefore \quad \phi = \frac{60 \times 520}{2 \times 864 \times 660} = 0.0274 \text{ wb.}$$ **Ans.**

3.19. RELATIONSHIP BETWEEN INDUCED E.M.F. AND TERMINAL VOLTAGE

As is clear that in case of a d.c. generator mechanical energy is converted into electrical energy. This electrical energy is utilised in supplying to the d.c. loads.

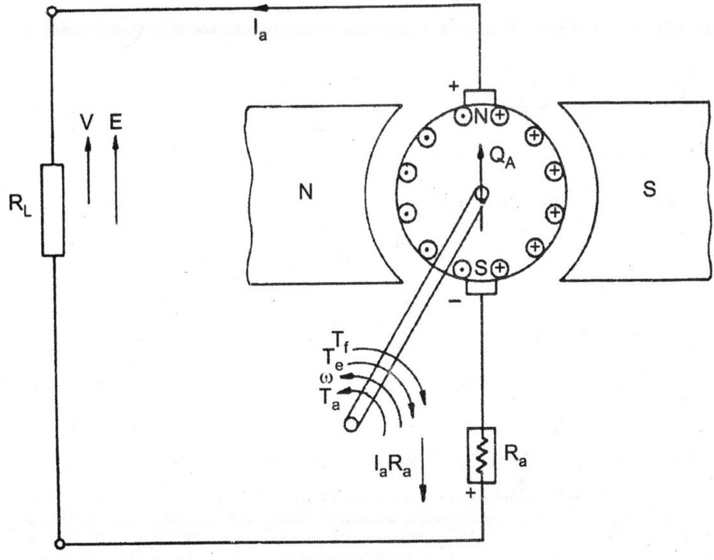

Fig. 3.48

Let

$E \Rightarrow$ Induced E.M.F.

$V \Rightarrow$ Terminal Voltage

$I_a \Rightarrow$ Armature Current.

$R_a \Rightarrow$ Armature Resistance.

$T_a \Rightarrow$ Applied Mechanical Torque.

$T_e \Rightarrow$ Electromagnetic Torque.

$T_f \Rightarrow$ Frictional Torque.

$\omega \Rightarrow$ Angular velocity.

From the Fig. 3.48

$$E = V + I_a R_a. \qquad \text{...}(i)$$

i.e. E.M.F. induced in the armature winding

= Terminal Voltage + Resistance drop of the armature.

In this case 'E' is always greater than 'V'

Multiplying equation (*i*) by I_a

$$E \cdot I_a \Rightarrow VI_a + I_a^2 R_a \qquad \text{...}(ii)$$

Also $\omega T_e \Rightarrow E \cdot I_a$

So, equation (*ii*) can be modified as

$$\omega T_e \Rightarrow VI_a + I_a^2 R_a \qquad \text{...}(iii)$$

Hence from equation (*iii*) it is clear.

That,

Input Mechanical Power $\Rightarrow$ Output Electrical power + Electrical power lost in the armature.

Now from mechanical power point of view

$$\omega T_a \Rightarrow \omega T_e + \omega T_f \qquad \text{...}(iv)$$

'ωT_f' *i.e.* frictional power loss is very much low as compared to 'ωT_e' so neglecting 'ωT_f' the equation (*iv*) becomes

$$\omega T_a = \omega T_e \qquad \text{...}(v)$$

It is obviously clear from the said discussion that if the load on the alternator is increased, the current I_a increases. From eq. (*iii*) ωT_e also increases. Due to the increase in 'ωT_e', ωT_a should be increased for keeping the balance. [From equation (*V*)]. So we can say that if the load on the generator is increased the applied mechanical torque should also be increased.

SHORT ANSWER TYPE QUESTIONS

Q.1. Why the armature core of a d.c. generator is laminated?

Ans. To reduce eddy current losses.

Q.2. What are the different types of armature winding commonly used in d.c. machines?

Ans. Lap and wave winding

Q.3. What is the best suited material for commutator segments?

Ans. Silvered copper which should contain about 0.05% silver

Q.4. What is the necessity to use a large number of coils and Commutator segments with the coils evenly distributed around the surface of the armature of a d.c machine ?

Ans. It is done to have practically constant unidirectional voltage at the brushes.

Q.5. What is the function of commutator in a d.c machine?

(*i*) in motoring action **(*ii*) in generating action**

Ans. (*i*) To convert D.C. into A.C.

(*ii*) To convert A.C. into D.C

Q.6. An electric motor or generator is also called electro-mechanical energy conversion device? Why? **[Tech. Edu. May 2005]**

Ans. The electric motor or generator is also called electro-mechanical conversion device because these are used to convert the form of energy. An electric motor converts electrical energy into mechanical energy where as a generator converts mechanical energy into Electrical energy.

Q.7. Armature core of d.c. machine is always laminated. Why ?

Ans. The armature core of a d.c. machine is always laminated to reduce the eddy current losses.

Q.8. Which law is more suitable to determine the direction of induced *e.m.f.* in a coil ? **[Tech. Edu. May 2005]**

Ans. The more suitable law to determine the direction of induced *e.m.f.* in a coil is Fleming's Right hand Rule. (F.R.H.R)

Q.9. Can we use wood for the construction of yoke of a d.c. machine? State why? **[Tech. Edu. Dec. 2004]**

Ans. No, we cannot use wood for the construction of yoke because wood is a non-magnetic material and therefore the path of the magnetic field produced by the field coils will not pass through the yoke and the magnetic circuit will not complete. So the D.C. machine will not work.

Q.10. No residual flux, no building up of voltage in d.c. shunt generators. State, why ? **[T.Edu. Dec. 2004]**

Ans. One of the reasons of not building up the voltage by the self excited d.c. generator is stated below:

To build up the voltage in the start, some residual magnetism is required. If there is little or no residual magnetism, then no voltage will be induced and this can further produce field current.

Q.11. State the Faraday's Laws of Electro-magnetic Induction. **[T.Edu. Dec. 2004]**

Ans. Faraday formulated two laws which are as under:

Faraday's First Law: This law states that when a conductor cuts across the magnetic field, an *e.m.f.* is induced in the conductor.

Faraday's Second Law: The magnitude of the induced *e.m.f.* in the coil is directly proportional to the rate of change of flux linkages.

Mathematically, $e = -N.\dfrac{d\phi}{dt}$

Q. 12. What are the different type of excitations employed for d.c generators? (Imp)

Ans. The D.C. generators are classified according to their methods of excitation. On this basis, d.c. generators are divided into two types as stated below:

(*i*) Self excited d.c. generators

(*ii*) Separately excited d.c. generators

Self excited generators are further classified as follows:

(*a*) D.C. series generator.

(*b*) D.C. shunt generators.

(*c*) D.C. Compound generators.

Q.13. A particular application employing a d.c. generator requires high voltage and low currents. Should the machine be wave wound or lap wound connected. ?

Ans. Wave wound connected.

Q.14. Interpole winding is always connected in series with the armature. Why?

[Tech. Edu. May 2005, 2007]

Ans. The interpole winding consists of few turns of heavy gauge copper wire and are connected in series with the armature, so it carries the full armature current. The polarity (in case of generator) is the same as that of the main poles ahead in the direction of rotation. Since the polarity is the same as that of the main, an e.m.f is induced in the coil under commutation. This induced e.m.f in the coil neutralizes the reactance e.m.f thus making commutation sparkless.

Q.15. Shunt field resistance should not be more than critical resistance. Why? (V.V. Imp)

Ans. If the shunt field circuit resistance is increased more than the critical resistance, then the generator will not excite and will not build up the voltage. Therefore, it should be noted that shunt generator will build up the voltage, only if the shunt field circuit resistance is less than the *critical field resistance*. Due to this reason the shunt field resistance should not be more than the critical resistance.

Q.16. Briefly describe the function of interpoles in a d.c. machine. (Tech. Edu. Dec. 2004)

Ans. The functions of interpoles are as mentioned below:

1. To counter the effect of armature reaction, usually a set of interpoles are placed in between the main poles of a d.c. machine. It induces e.m.f. in the coil under commutation and thus help in reversal of current. This is known as commutating e.m.f. The commutating e.m.f. neutralizes the reactance e.m.f. and makes commutation sparkless,
2. Interpoles carry armature current, therefore commutating *e.m.f.* is proportional to armature current. Thus the reactance voltage is automatically neutralized which is due to armature current.

The cross magnetising effect is also neutralized by interpoles or commutating poles. For this reason, we no longer have to shift the brushes from their original positions.

Q.17. Why are the brushes staggered?

Ans. The brushes are staggered in order to prevent ridge formation on the surface of the commutator.

OBJECTIVE TYPE QUESTIONS

Tick the correct answer.

1. The segments of the commutator of dc machine are made of
   (*a*) Carbon (*b*) Copper
   (*c*) Brass (*d*) Silicon steel
2. The segments of the commutator of a d.c. machine are insulated from each other by
   (*a*) Rubber (*b*) Porcelain
   (*c*) Mica (*d*) Varnish
3. The armature of D.C. generator is made of laminated sheets to
   (*a*) Reduce armature copper losses.
   (*b*) Increase dissipation of heat from armature surface
   (*c*) Insulate the core
   (*d*) Reduce eddy current losses.
4. The yoke of dc machine is made of
   (*a*) Steel (*b*) Plastic
   (*c*) Cast iron (*d*) Copper
5. The resistance of the armature winding of d.c. machine is dependent upon
   (*a*) Length of the conductor (*b*) Number of conductor
   (*c*) Cross sectional ores of the conductor (*d*) All the above.
6. The electromagnetic-torque developed in a d.c. machine is dependent upon
   (*a*) Armature current (*b*) Magnetic field.
   (*c*) *a* & *b* both. (*d*) Motion.
7. The function of interpoles in a d.c. machine are to
   (*a*) Neutralize the effect of armature reaction in the interpolar region.
   (*b*) Provide more magnetic effect
   (*c*) Generate more e.m.f. .
   (*d*) Minimise the demagnetisation effect.
8. The induced e.m.f. in a coil will be maximum if
   (*a*) The rate of change of flux linkages is maximum.
   (*b*) The flux linkage is maximum.
   (*c*) The flux linkage is minimum.
   (*d*) The rate of change of flux linkages is minimum.

9. The number of parallel paths in wave wound armature of dc generator are equal to:
(*a*) The number of armature slots. (*b*) Two.
(*c*) The number of poles (*d*) The number of commutator segments.

10. The commutator segments are connected to the armature conductors by
(*a*) Copper lugs (*b*) Soldering
(*c*) Brazing (*d*) Aluminium conductors.

11. The number of parallel paths in the armature winding of a Four-pole Lap connected d.c. machine of 24 coil sides is
(*a*) 2 (*b*) 4
(*c*) 12 (*d*) 24.

12. The relation between induced e.m.f. 'E' and terminal voltage 'V' of a d.c. generator is
(*a*) $E > V$ (*b*) $E = V$
(*c*) $E < V$ (*d*) $E - V = 1$.

13. The polarity of induced e.m.f. of generator action can be reversed by
(*a*) Reversing the direction of rotation of the rotor.
(*b*) Reversing the polarity of magnetic flux of the field.
(*c*) Reversing the direction of rotation of rotor and field flux both.
(*d*) Either reversing the direction of rotation or field flux.

14. The e.m.f. induced in a conductor rotating in a bipolar field is (a) d.c. (b) a.c.
(*a*) *d.c.* (*b*) *a.c*
(*c*) d.c. & a.c. both (*d*) None of the above

(*A.M.I.e. 'W'93*) (Section *B* Elect.)

15. The field coils of a dynamo have an inductance of 8 H and have a resistance of 60 ohms and are connected to 120 V d.c. source. The steady state current in the field coils is
(*a*) 15 amp (*b*) 2 amp
(*c*) Zero amp (*d*) None of the above.

(*A.M.I.e. 'W'93*) (Section *B* Elect.)

16. Approximately physical size of the 50 kW, 1800 r.p.m. dynamo as a fraction of a 25 kW, 900 r.p.m. dynamo will be (A.M.*I.e.* 'W' 93)
(*a*) 1 (*b*) $^1/_2$
(*c*) $^1/_4$ (*d*) None of the above.

17. The number of brushes provided in a lap winding are always
(*a*) 'Two' in numbers (*b*) Equal to the number of poles.
(*c*) Equal to half number of poles. (*d*) Equal to double the number of poles.

18. If number of armature conductors and number of poles are fixed for a D.C. generator, then which type of the winding should be used for inducing high voltage
(*a*) Wave winding (*b*) Lap winding.
(*c*) Either wave winding or lap winding. (*d*) None of the above.

19. The insulating material used between the commutator segments is generally

(*a*) Graphite (*b*) Paper

(*c*) Mica (*d*) Rubber.

20. The cause of rapid brush wear is due to:

(*a*) Loose contacts. (*b*) Sparking

(*c*) Rough surface of commutator (*d*) Any of the above.

21. For generating higher currents irrespective of the induced e.m.f. the winding used is

(*a*) Wave winding. (*b*) Lap winding.

(*c*) Either wave winding or lap winding. (*d*) None of the above.

22. The armature of d.c. machines is usually supported in

(*a*) Ball or Roller Bearings (*b*) Magnetic Bearing

(*c*) Bush Bearings

23. The thickness of laminations used for armature core of d.c. machines is of the order of.

(*a*) ·05 mm (*b*) 0·5 mm

(*c*) 5 mm

24. Which generator is preferred for charging automobile batteries?

(*a*) Series generators (*b*) Shunt generators

(*c*) Compound generators

25. For a fixed number of poles and armature conductors, which winding will give higher e.m.f

(*a*) Lap winding (*b*) Wave winding

(*c*) Any of the above

26. Hysteresis loss in a d.c. machine depends upon

(*a*) Frequency of magnetic reversal (*b*) Volume and grade of iron

(*c*) Maximum value of flux density (*d*) All of the above

27. Out of the following losses in d.c. machines, which one has the highest proportions?

(*a*) Armature copper loss (*b*) Field copper loss

(*c*) Hysteresis loss (*d*) Eddy current loss.

28. Interpoles are usually wound with;

(*a*) Very fine gauge copper wire (*b*) Heavy gauge copper wire

(*c*) Insulating material

29. In d.c. generators, interpole field coils are connected,

(*a*) in series with armature winding. (*b*) in series with the load

(*c*) in series with the shunt field winding (*d*) None of these.

30. In d.c. generators, the brushes remain in contact with conductors which lie,

(*a*) in the interpole gaps (*b*) under north pole

(*c*) under south pole

31. An exciter for alternator is a

(*a*) Compound generator (*b*) Shunt generator

(*c*) Series generator (*d*) None of these

32. The voltage at the terminals of a d.c. series generator running at rated r.p.m. and no load will be

(*a*) Zero (*b*) Very small voltage

(*c*) Full rated voltage

33. D.C. machines are generally designed for maximum efficiency at

(*a*) 25% of full load (*b*) 75% of full load

(*c*) around full load (*d*) 100% of full load

Answers

1. (*b*)	**2.** (*c*)	**3.** (*d*)	**4.** (*c*)	**5.** (*d*)	**6.** (*c*)	**7.** (*a*)
8. (*a*)	**9.** (*b*)	**10.** (*a*)	**11.** (*b*)	**12.** (*a*)	**13.** (*d*)	**14.** (*b*)
15. (*b*)	**16.** (*d*)	**17.** (*b*)	**18.** (*a*)	**19.** (*c*)	**20.** (*d*)	**21.** (*b*)
22. (*a*)	**23.** (*b*)	**24.** (*b*)	**25.** (*b*)	**26.** (d)	**27.** (*a*)	**28.** (*b*)
29. (*a*)	**30.** (*a*)	**31.** (*b*)	**32.** (*b*)	**33.** (*c*)		

True or false Questions

1. The yoke of a d.c. machine is made of laminations.
2. Pole shoes are never laminated.
3. Armature winding in located is the armature.
4. Interpoles are never made of laminated construction.
5. The commutator is made of brass.
6. The commutator segments are made of copper.
7. The generated e.m.f. and current are in the same direction in case of d.c. generator.
8. The polarity of a d.c. generator can be reversed by reversing field current.
9. Lap winding is preferred for welding generators.
10. A series generator develops voltage at no load.
11. Eddy current is a part of copper losses.
12. The condition for maximum efficiency in case of d.c. generator is
    Variable loss = 2 × constant loss.
13. Hysteresis loss in a d.c. shunt generator depends only on the lamination thickness.
14. In a d.c. generator sparking between brushes and commutator surface may be due to under commutation.
15. In series field, many turns of fine wire are used whereas in shunt field few turns of thick wire are used.
16. Iron losses in d.c. machines take place in commutator.

Answers

1. False	**2.** False	**3.** False	**4.** False
5. False	**6.** True	**7.** True	**8.** True

9. True	**10.** False	**11.** False	**12.** False
13. True	**14.** True	**15.** False	**16.** False

Fill in the Blanks with appropriate words

1. The polarity of a d.c generator can be reversed by reversing the .... **Tech. Edu. Dec. 2004**
2. Maximum efficiency occurs when variable losses are .... to constant losses.
3. In the d.c. machine, iron losses occur in.......... **Tech. Edu. May 2005**
4. A 4 pole d.c lap winding will have .... parallel paths. **Tech. Edu. Dec. 2005**
5. A 4 pole d.c. wave winding machine will have .... parallel paths. **Tech. Edu Dec. 2004**
6. The number of parallel paths in wave wound armature is .... **Tech. Edu. May. 2003**
7. The number of parallel paths in lap wound armature is equal to .... **Tech. Edu. Dec. 2002**
8. In generating action, armature rotates in the same direction as that of .... torque.
9. In. d.c machines, brushes are placed on .... **Tech. Edu. May. 2003**
10. The amount of e.m.f induced in the d.c. generator is given by ....
11. For ordinary lighting .... (shunt/series/compound) generators are used.
12. If shunt field is connected across armature the Compound generator is said to have .... connections.
13. If the back pitch is less than front pitch the winding is said to be ....
14. The armature of a high voltage low current armature is .... wound.
15. Eddy current loss is a part of .... losses.
16. Both front and back pitches in a d.c. armature are always ....
17. .... is used as insulating material between the Commutator segments.
18. The copper loss of a d.c. generator is dissipated in the form of ....
19. .... generator is normally preferred for charging automobile batteries.
20. The polarity of a d.c. generator can be reversed by ....
21. If there is no residual magnetism a .... excited generator cannot Build up its e.m.f.
22. Laminations in the armature core reduces the .... loss.
23. The yoke of a d.c. machine is made of ....
24. The armature of d.c. machine is made of ....
25. In lap winding, the number of parallel paths is .... to number of poles.
26. Field coils are made of ....
27. Pole shoes of a d.c. machine are fastened to the pole core by ....
28. Laminations are used in armature of d.c. machine to reduce ....
29. The brushes for commutator are made of ....
30. Copper losses vary considerably when ....
31. The effect of iron losses on d.c. generator is ....
32. The .... winding on d.c. generators is preferred for generating large currents.

33. The conductors of a d.c. machine armature are .... to armature.
34. Each commutator segment is connected to the armature conductor by means of ....
35. The residual magnetism of a d.c. shunt generator can be regained by connecting the shunt field to a ....

Answers

1. Field current	2. equal	3. Iron parts	4. 4
5. 2	6. 2	7. Number of poles	8. Driving
9. Commutator surface	10. $\frac{\phi ZN}{60} \times \frac{P}{A}$ Volts	11. shunt	12. short shunt
13. Retrogressive	14. wave	15. Iron	16. odd
17. Mica	18. Heat	19. Shunt	20. Reversing field current
21. Self	22. Eddy current	23. Cast iron	24. Silicon steel
25. Equal	26. Copper	27. Counter sunk screw	28. Iron
29. Carbon	30. Load changes	31. Loss of efficiency and excessive healing of core	
32. Lap	33. Soldered	34. Copper lug	35. Battery

EXERCISES

1. Explain the constructional features and the principle of working of a D.C. generator.
2. Name the different parts of a D.C. Generator and give their constructional details.
3. Explain the function of commutator in a simple D.C. generator.
4. Explain the following terms as applied to D.C. armature windings:
   (*i*) Back pitch
   (*ii*) Front pitch
   (*iii*) Commutator pitch
   (*iv*) Coil pitch
   (*v*) Pole pitch.
5. Derive an expression for e.m.f. generated in a D.C. machine.
6. What are the different types of D.C. generators ?
7. Write down the various applications of the following:
   (*a*) Series generator
   (*b*) Shunt generator
   (*c*) Compound generator.
8. What is the condition of maximum efficiency of a D.C. generator ?
9. What are the different losses occur in a D.C. generator ?
10. How the Hysteresis losses and Eddy current losses are reduced ?
11. Define the following:
    (*a*) Armature reaction
    (*b*) Commutation

12. Why carbon brushes are generally used for collection of current in D.C. machines ? Can we use copper brushes?
13. A 4-pole, 1200 r.p.m. generator with a lap wound armature has 65 slots and 12 conductors per slot, the flux per pole is 0.02 weber. Determine the e.m.f. induced in the armature. (A.M.I.E)

[**Ans.** 312 V.]

14. Sketch and explain the load characteristics of each of the following types of D.C. generators:

    (*i*) Shunt (*ii*) Series

    (*iii*) Compound.

    State with reasons where each type is used. (*A.M.I.e. Winter 1974*)
15. Describe how a self excited D.C. generator build up its terminal voltage as it is run by a prime mover and clearly bring out the importance of

    (*i*) Residual magnetism in field core

    (*ii*) The value of shunt field resistance,

    (*iii*) Speed of the armature in the process of building up the terminal voltages in the generator. (*A.M.I.e. Dec. 1975*)
16. Draw developed winding diagrams to distinguish between lap winding and wave winding of a 4 pole D.C. generator indicating the poles, the conductors, brush polarities and their positions on the commutator. (*A.M.I.e. Summer 1976*)
17. Distinguish between

    (*i*) a D.C. shunt generator, and

    (*ii*) a D.C. compound generator. Show and explain the nature of the external characteristics of each of them. (*A.M.I.e. Winter, 1976*)
18. Sketch and explain the load characteristics of the following types of D.C. generators:—

    (*i*) Shunt, (*ii*) Series,

    (*iii*) Commutatively compounded, (*iv*) Differentially compounded

    (A.M.*I.e.* Summer, 1977)
19. Explain clearly the process of building of voltage in a D.C. shunt generator. A shunt generator when driven at its normal speed fails to excite. Discuss briefly the most likely reasons for it and state how would you move to remedy the fault. (*A.M.I.e. Winter, 1977*)
20. A short shunt compound generator has armature, shunt field and series field resistance of 0.8 Ω, 45 Ω and 0.6 ohm respectively and supplies a load of 5 kW at 250 V. Calculate the e.m.f. generated in the armature. [*Ans. 282.66 V*]
21. The following table relates to the open circuit curve of a shunt generator running at 750 RPM.

Generated voltage (*V*)	10	172	300	360	85	395
Field current (*A*)	0	1	2	3	4	5

Determine the no load terminal voltage if field circuit resistance is 125 Ω

If the speed is now halved, what is the resultant terminal voltage. At the reduced speed, what value of field circuit resistance will give a no load terminal voltage of 175 V.

[**Ans.** 354 V; 5 V; 64.5 Ohm]

22. The open circuit characteristics of a certain D.C. generator when running at 500 RPM is given below:

Field current (A)	2	4	6	8	10
Generated e.m.f. (V)	71	135	179	202	214

The generator is now shunt connected and run at 600 RPM, the resistance of the field circuit being 25 Ω. What e.m.f. will it generate ?

If the generator is placed on load and terminal p.d. becomes 230 V, what is the load current? The armature resistance is 0.2Ω and armature reaction is to be neglected.

[Ans. 258 V; 100 A]

23. Calculate the number of series turns per pole required on a compound generator to enable it to maintain the voltage constant at 460 V between no load and full load of 100 kW. Without any series winding it is found that shunt current has to be 2 A on no load and 2.65 A at full load to maintain the voltage constant at 460 V. Number of turns on shunt winding = 2000. If the series coils were wound with 8 turns per pole and had a total resistance of 0.01 Ω, what value of divertor resistance would be required to give level compounding. **[Ans.** 6, 0.0296Ω]

24. A 250 V, 50 kW shunt generator has 1000 turns on each pole of its field winding. On no load a current of 3.5 A in the field winding produces a terminal voltage of 250 V, but on full load, the shunt current has to be increased to 5 A for the same terminal voltage at the same speed. Calculate the number of series field turns per pole required for level compounding. **[Ans.** 7.5]

D.C. MACHINE: MOTORING AND GENERATION

4

4.0. INTRODUCTION

To meet the demand (of power) all the times the electricity must be generated continuously. An efficient and convenient way to generate electric power is by conversion of mechanical power into electrical power in a rotating device called a generated. In this process a small part of power is lost in the generator itself (efficiencies in bigger generators are above 90%). So far mechanical power is concerned it is itself obtained from heat power by thermodynamical means in a steam turbine (whose efficiency is in the range of 40–50% as the present upper limit) or by the conversion of potential energy of water in a hydraulic turbine with very little loss. The basic source of mechanical power–hydraulic/steam turbine is called the prime mover. The electromechanical process of electric power generation is schematically shown in Fig 4.0. (*a*) under steady conversion conditions.

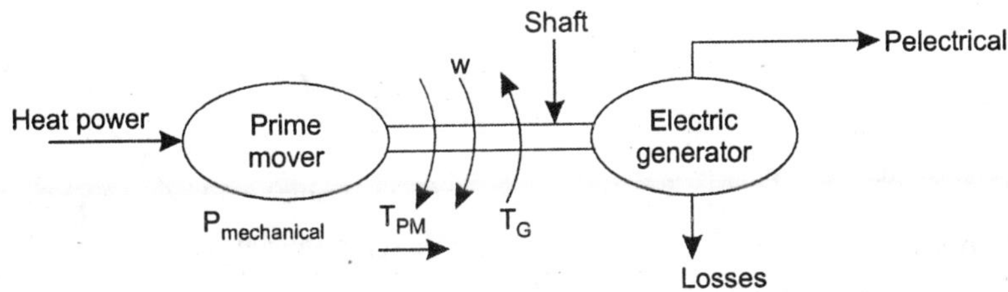

Fig. 4.0. (*a*) Schematic diagram of Electric Generator

T_{PM} (Prime Mover) = T_G (Generator). The turbine and Generator run at steady speed. Other than lighting and heating, (keep in mind it is expensive to use electricity for heating purposes except in special processes, *e.g.* electric arc furnaces and where highly accurate controlled heating is required *i.e.* induction heating), the major use of electric energy is made by converting it back to the mechanical form to run the wheels of industry as well as small household appliances. The intermediate, the electric power, permits the use of Big efficient Central generating stations, while it is easily transported to the myriads of use points. The electro-mechanical energy conversion process in reversible one and simple adjustment of mechanical shaft and electrical conditions reverses the flow of power as shown in Fig. 4.0 (b).

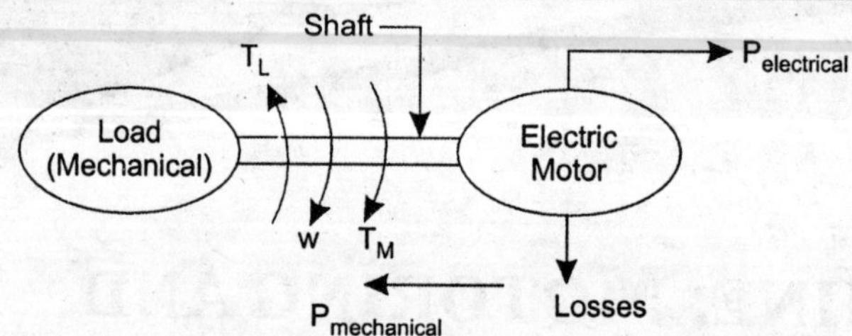

Fig. 4.0. (*b*) Motor mode of operation of an electric machine

In this mode of operation, the electro-mechanical device, in general called the electric machine, which is known as the motor and the machine is said to be in the motoring mode. Under steady speed operation, again T_M (motor) = T_L (load). Both in generating and motoring modes. Losses occur in the electric machine but the overall conversion efficiencies are very high (above 90%).

Electric machines are employed in almost every industrial and manufacturing. process. Papers can be filled in listing the applications of electric machines right from 500 MW and above generators, industrial motors ranging up to a very few maga-watts to fractional-kw domestic appliances and aerospace applications requiring stringent reliability in operation.

4.1. CIRCUIT MODEL OF D.C. MACHINES

In D.C. Machines all the parallel paths in the armature are symmetrical and each has an induced e.m.f. or generated e.m.f., E_a and a resistance R_p as shown in Fig. 4.1 (a). The armature can be represented by the circuit-model with voltage E_a and a series resistance, $R_a = R_p/A$ where 'A' is the number of parallel paths.

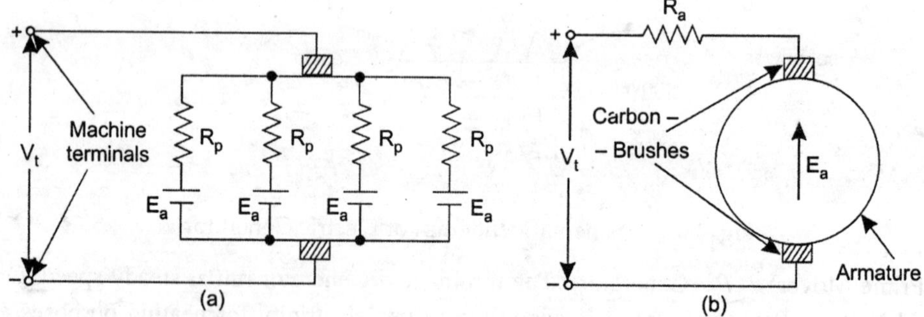

Fig. 4.1. Relating to the armature circuit of a D.C. machine

D.C. machine field winding must also be represented in the circuit model. Now, the schematic representation, or circuit model of D.C. Machine is as shown in Fig. 4.1. (a) for a D.C. Generator and in Fig. 4.1 (*b*) for a D.C. Motor. It is observed from this figure that for a generator, electromagnetic Torque T_e is opposite to the rotor rotation *i.e.* T_e opposes the prime-mover torque. This is required for the conversion of energy from Mechanical to Electrical. This torque, t_e may be, therefore, called Counter-torque in a D.C. generator. The Magnitude of this Counter torque is given by *i.e.* $T_e = K_a \phi I_a$ where $K = \frac{PZ}{2\pi A}$. For a motor, the electromagnetic torque T_e is in the direction of rotor direction.

4.2. GENERATING MODE

When armature current I_a is in the direction of generated e.m.f. E_a, D.C. machine operates in the generating mode. Electromagnetic power is $E_a I_a$ watts and the electrical power output or load power is equal to terminal power $V_t I_a$ watts, Fig. 4.2 (a).

For a D.C. generator, shaft power input = $E_a I_a$ + no-load rotational loss

and $$V_t = E_a - I_a R_a \quad \text{...(4.1)}$$

where V_t = armature terminal voltage, V

I_a = armature current, A

R_a = armature circuit resistance, in ohm

Brush contact drop is usually takens as constant at 1 or 2 V. This drop is independent of armature current as the conduction process is primarily through numerous short arcs. Taking this drop as 2 V, Eq. (4.9) can be written as

$$V_t = E_a - I_a R_a - 2$$

or $$V_t I_a = E_a I_a - I_a^2 R_a - 2I_a$$

or Electrical power output = Electromagnetic power – Ohmic losses – Brush contact loss ....(4.2)

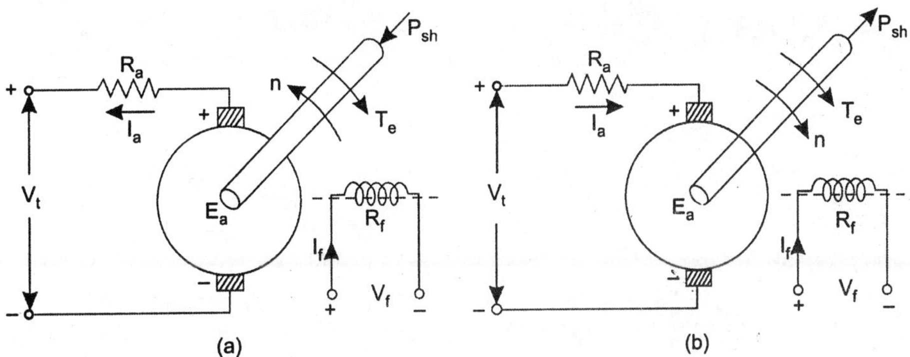

Fig. 4.2. Circuit model of a D.C. machine for (a) generating mode and (b) motoring mode

4.3. MOTORING MODE

When armature current I_a flows in opposition to generated e.m.f. E_a as in Fig. 4.2 (*b*), D.C. machine operates in motoring mode.

For a D.C. motor, shaft power output = $E_a I_a$ – no-load rotational loss

and $$V_t = E_a + I_a R_a + 2 \quad \text{...(4.3)}$$

or $$V_t I_a = E_a I_a + I_a^2 R_a + 2I_a$$

or Electrical power input = Electromagnetic power + Ohmic losses + Brush contact loss ...(4.4)

It is stated above that for generator operations, the e.m.f. and current in a conductor are in the same direction. This is shown in a 2-pole D.C. generator of Fig. 4.3. (*a*). In this figure, for anti-clockwise rotation of armature, generated e.m.fs. are indicated by crosses and dots below the circles in the shots (use right-hand rule). For assumed anticlockwise rotation, *S* and *N* poles indicated on the rotor in Fig. 4.3 (*a*) must be created by armature currents. This magnetic polarity demands the current directions in the conductors to be indicated by crosses under *S* pole and by dots under *N* pole. Current directions in slots are indicated by crosses and dots within the circles in Fig. 4.3 (*a*). This shows that generated e.m.fs. and currents in a conductor are in the same direction for a D.C. machine working as a generator.

Fig. 4.3 (*b*) shows motoring-mode operation of a D.C. machine. Direction of currents in the armature conductors is indicated by crosses and dots within the circles in the slots. These currents establish *N* and *S* poles on the rotor and their interaction with the stator N and S poles results in clockwise rotation of armature. With the armature rotation, the conductors cut the same flux that gives rise to motor torque. This flux cutting action thus causes the generation of e.m.f. in the very same conductors that experience motor action. The generated e.m.fs. in Fig. 4.3 (*b*) are indicated by crosses and dots below the circles in the slots (use right hand rule). It is seen that generated e.m.fs. are in directions opposite to the flow of conductor current. Since this generated e.m.f. opposes the flow of current, it is called counter electromotive force of **counter e.m.f.** Note that counter e.m.f. E_a can never be equal to applied voltage V_t. E.m.f. E_a must always be less than V_t because direction of current, as per Eq. (4.3), first determines the direction of rotation and then the direction of counter e.m.f. The magnitude of counter e.m.f. is governed by *Eq.*, $E_a = P_n \phi \left(\frac{z}{a}\right) = \frac{P\phi Zn}{a}$

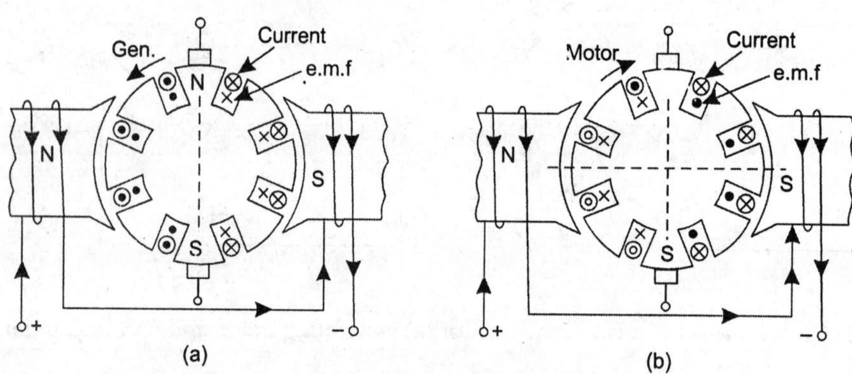

Fig. 4.3. (*a*) Generating mode and (*b*) motoring mode

Summarising the above, e.m.f. E_a in Eqs. (4.1) and (4.3) is the generated e.m.f. In a generator, $E_a > V_t$ and in a motor, $E_a < V_t$. When D.C. machine is working as a motor, the generated e.m.f. E_a is often called the *counter e.m.f.* or *back e.m.f.* As stated above, the word *counter* is used because E_a opposes the flow of current I_a. The word *back* is used because E_a is the voltage at the back of R_a when viewed from the armature terminals. Therefore, the generated e.m.f. E_a for a motor may also be called *voltage behind armature circuit resistance.*

Example 4.1: A D.C. generator having a voltage of 220 V supplies 4 K W at a terminal voltage of 220 V, the armature resistance being 0.4 Ω. If the machine is now operated as a motor at the same terminal voltage with same armature current. Calculate the ratio of a generator speed at the motor speed.

Assume the flux/pole is made to increase by 10% as the operation is changed over from generator to motor.

Solution. We know

$$n \propto \frac{E_a}{\phi} \quad ...(i)$$

For a generator $\quad I_a = \frac{4 \times 1000}{220} = 18.19$ Amp.

$$E_{ag} = 220 + 0.4 \times 18.19 = 227.4 \text{ Volt} \quad ...(ii)$$

For a Motor $\quad E_{am} = 220 - 0.4 \times 18.19 = 212.8$ Volt $\quad ...(iii)$

Also $\quad \phi = 1.1\ \phi_g \quad ...(iv)$

Substituting in eq. (*i*)

$$\frac{n_g}{n_m} = \frac{227.4}{212.7} \times \frac{\phi_m}{\phi_g} = \frac{227.4}{212.7} \times 1.1$$

$$= 1.177 \text{ Ans.}$$

Example 4.2: A D.C. shunt generator driven by a belt from an engine which runs at 750 R.p.m. during feeding 100 kW of electric power into 230 volts mains. When the belt breaks, it continues to run as a motor drawing 9 kW from the mains. At what speed would it run? Given armature resistance 0.08Ω and field resistance 115 Ω.

Solution. The operation of D.C. shunt generator/Motor is indicated in the circuit models of Figs 4.4. (*a*) and (*b*).

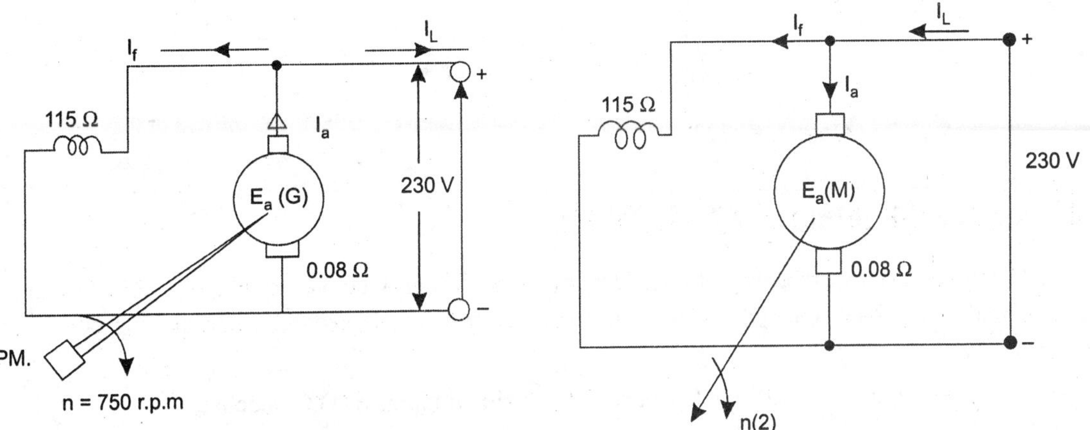

Fig. 4.4. (*a*) Generating; (*b*) Motoring (Prime Mover-disconnected)

Note. In a shunt Machine the field is connected across the armature and therefore it is connected directly to the 230 V mains. The field excitation therefore remains constant as the machine operation changes as mentioned above.

The operation of a D.C. shunt generator/motor is indicated in the circuit models of Figs 4.4 (a) and (b) above

Field Current, $I_f = \frac{230}{115} = 2$ Amp. remains constant in operation change-over. Running as generator (feeding power to mains).

Line current, $I_L = \frac{100 \times 1000}{230} = 434.8$ A

$$I_f = 2 \text{ Amp}$$

$$I_a = I_L + I_f = 434.8 + 2$$

$$= 436.8 \text{ Amp.}$$

$$E_a(G) = 230 + 0.08 \times 436.8 = 237.8\ V$$

$$n(G) = 750 \text{ r.p.m. (given)}$$

Running as motor(drawing power from mains)

$$I_L = \frac{9 \times 1000}{230} = 39.13$$

$$I_f = 2 \text{ Amp.}$$

$$I_a = I_L - I_f = 39.13 - 2 = 37.13 \text{ A}$$

$$E_a(M) = 230 - 0.08 \times 37.13 = 229.3 \text{ volt.}$$

As field current (*i.e.* flux/pole) do not change during the two kinds of operation, the induced e.m.f. (E_a) is proportional to armature speed. Hence

$$\frac{n\,(\text{Motor})}{n\,(\text{Generator})} = \frac{n\,(\text{Motor})}{750}$$

$$= \frac{229.3}{237.3}$$

$$n\,(\text{Motor}) = 723.2 \text{ r.p.m.}$$

4.4. TYPES OF FIELD EXCITATIONS

The D.C. machine can work only as the electro-mechanical energy converter when its field winding is excited by the Direct-current (D.C.). For small D.C. machines it is excited by employing permanent magnets only.

Normally there are two methods for exciting the field windings of D.C. machines.

(*i*) Separately excited and

(*ii*) Self-excitation.

D.C. machines can have one or more field windings and their method of excitation, determines the performance characteristics of the D.C. machines. In Fig. 4.5 (*a*), the diagram which is on the left hand side give the physical details of the internal connection for a 2-pole machine, whereas the right hand side diagram give the schematic representation of D.C. machine with the method of excitation *i.e.* separately excitation.

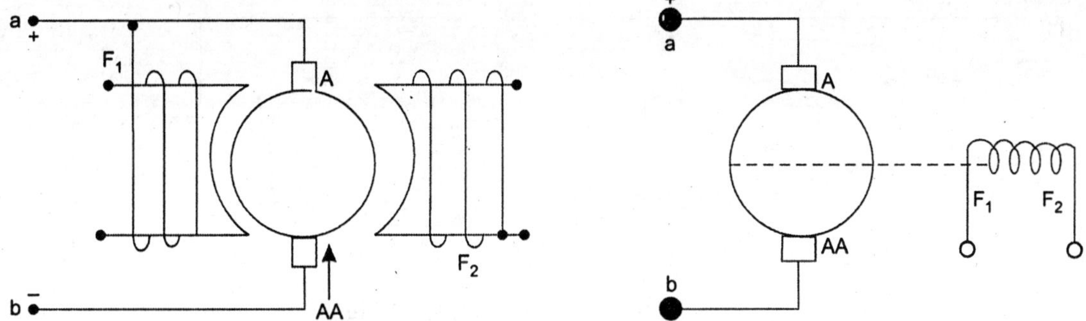

Fig. 4.5. (*a*) Separately excited D.C. Machine

(*i*) **Separately excitation.** The separately excited field winding consists of several hundred turns of fine wire and is connected to a separate or externally D.C. source as shown in fig. 4.5. (a). The voltage of the external D.C. source has no relation with the armature voltage *i.e.* field winding energised from a separate supply can the designed for any convenient voltage.

(*ii*) **Self-excitation.** When the field winding is excited by its own armature, the machine is said to be a *self-excited D.C, machine.* In these machines, the field poles must have a residual magnetism, so that when the armature rotates, a residual voltage appears across the brushes. This residual voltage should establish a current in the field winding so as to reinforce the residual flux.

A self-excited D.C. machine can be sub-divided as follows:

(*a*) **Series excitation.** The field winding consists of a few turns of thick wire and is connected in series with the armature, Fig. 4.5 (*b*). In other words, the series field current depends on the armature current and in view of this, a series field may be called a *current-operated field.*

(*b*) **Shunt excitation.** The field winding consists of a large number of turns of fine wire and is connected in parallel (or in shunt) with the armature, Fig. 4.5 (*c*). Therefore, the voltage across the armature terminals and the shunt field is the same and it is for this reason that a shunt field may be called a *voltage-operated field.*

Remember that series and shunt field windings are characterised by low and high resistances respectively.

(*c*) **Compound excitation**. A compound excitation involves both the series excited winding and the shunt-excited winding. In some applications, a shunt-excited winding may be replaced by a separately-excited winding. Here a D.C. compound machine, with series and shunt field windings will be discussed.

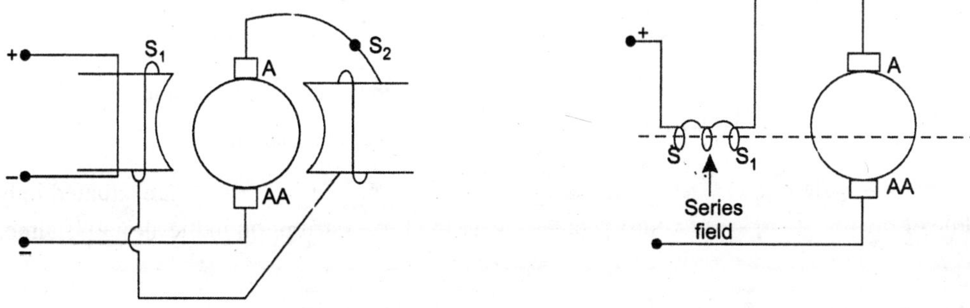

Fig. 4.5. (*b*) Series excited D.C. Motor

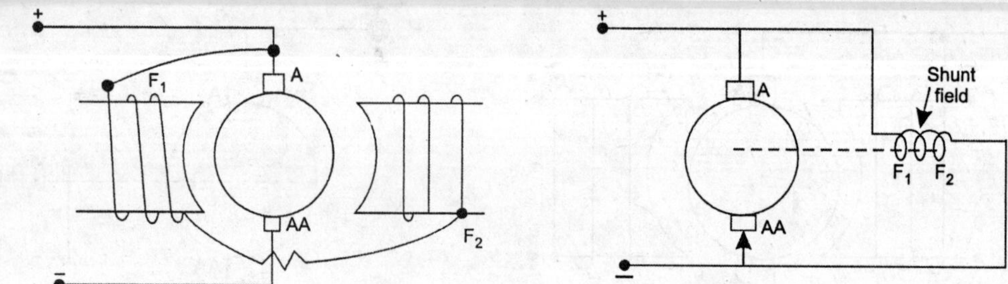

Fig. 4.5. (*c*) Shunt-excited D.C. Machine

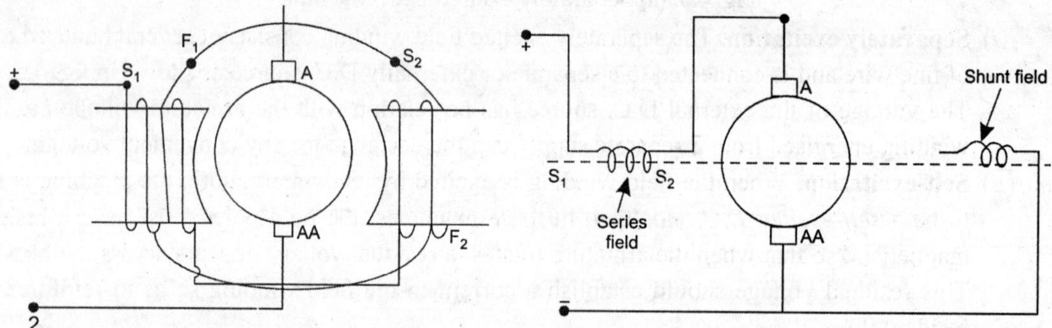

Fig. 4.5. (*d*) Methods of Excitation of D.C. Machines

4.5. E.M.F EQUATION

Let ϕ = Flux per pole in webers

Z = Total number of armature conductors in the slots or coil sides on armature.

P = Number of poles = $2p$, where p is equal to number of pairs of poles.

N = Armature rotational speed in r.p.m.

$= \frac{N}{60}$ rev./sec.

A = Number of parallel paths through the armature

A = 2 for wave wound armature and

A = P, for lap wound armature.

Consider one pole of a D.C. machine as shown in Fig. 4.6. Planes P and Q are situated in between the middle of the poles and are at neutral planes where the flux distribution in the air gap is almost zero.

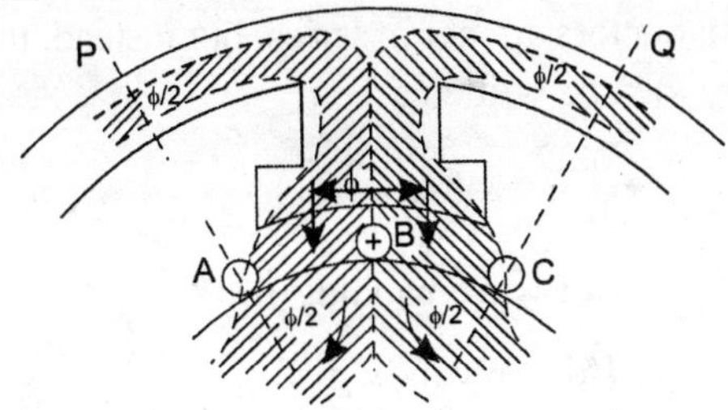

Fig. 4.6. Distribution of flux in pole and armature

An armature conductor in position A will have zero e.m.f. induced in it. In position B its induced e.m.f. will have the maximum value, while in position C, the e.m.f. will again be zero. Hence e.m.f. induced in one particular conductor or an armature of a D.C. Machine goes through considerable variations in magnitude so that the e.m.f. induced during one rotation of the conductor is decided by the average value of the e.m.f.

Hence for a single conductor average induced e.m.f. during path A to C

i.e.
$$E_{av} = \frac{\textit{Flux cut}}{\textit{Time taken}} \text{ volts}$$

The time taken is the time in seconds required to move from A to C.

Then time taken for one revolution

$$= \frac{1}{N} \text{ minute}$$

$$= \frac{1}{N} \times 60 \text{ seconds.}$$

Now in moving from A to C, The distance is one pole pitch, *i.e.* $\frac{1}{P}$ of the periphery or circumference.

$\therefore$ The time taken to move the conductor under one pole, *i.e.* from A to C (pole pitch) during which the flux ϕ is cut is:

$$t = \frac{1}{P} \times \frac{60}{N} = \frac{60}{PN} \text{ sec.}$$

Hence average value of induced e.m.f. per conductor

$$E_{av} = \frac{\phi}{t} = \frac{\phi}{\frac{60}{PN}} \text{ volts}$$

$$= \frac{\phi.PN}{60} \text{ volts}$$

Now if there are Z number of armature conductors connected in series with each other then the total e.m.f. generated for the whole winding is

$$E = \frac{\phi PN}{60} \times Z \text{ volts}$$

Re-arranging the equation we can write

$$E = \frac{P\phi ZN}{60} \text{ volts.}$$

In actual practice all the conductors are not in series, but instead, the winding may have, *A*, parallel paths. The. e.m.f. per path may then be written as

$$E = \frac{P\phi ZN}{60\,A} \text{ volts.}$$

where $A = 2$ (for wave winding)

$= P$ (for lap winding).

OR

E.M.F. EQUATION (Second method):

Let P = Number of poles

ϕ = Flux per pole in wbs.

Z = Total number of armature-conductors

N = Speed of armature in r.p.m.

A = Number of parallel paths in armature winding.

$$\begin{bmatrix} A = 2 \textit{ for wave winding and} \\ A = P \textit{ for lap winding} \end{bmatrix}$$

Generated E.m.f, E_g = E.m.f of the generator per parallel path

In one revolution of the armature,

Flux cut by one conductor,

$$d\phi = P\phi \text{ webers}$$

Time taken to complete one revolution,

$$dt = \frac{60}{N} \text{ seconds.}$$

e.m.f. generated per conductor

$$= \frac{d\phi}{dt} = \frac{P\phi}{60/N} = \frac{P\phi N}{60} \text{ volts}$$

$\therefore$ e.m.f of generator, E_g = e.m.f per parallel path

= e.m.f per conductor × No. of conductors in series per parallel path,

$$= \frac{P\phi N}{60} \times \frac{Z}{A}$$

$$\therefore \quad E_g = \frac{P\phi ZN}{60A} \text{ volts.}$$

where A = 2 for ware winding and

$A = P$ for lap winding

For a given machine, the no. of poles and no. of armature conductors per parallel path (Z_A) are constant.

Example 4.3. Calculate the e.m.f. generated by a 4 pole wave wound armature having 45 slots with 18 conductors per slot driven at 1200 r.p.m. The flux per pole is 0.016 wb.

(A.M.*I.e.*)

Solution. Given,

$$P = 4, A = 2 \qquad [\because \text{ in wave winding, } A = 2]$$

$$Z = 45 \times 18 = 810 \text{ conductors}$$

$$\phi = 0.016 \text{ Wb, and } N = 1200 \text{ r.p.m.}$$

Now formula used is, *i.e.*

$$E = \frac{P\phi ZN}{60A} \text{ volts}$$

$$= \frac{4 \times 0.016 \times 810 \times 1200}{60 \times 2} \text{ volts}$$

$$= \textbf{518.4 volts Ans.}$$

Example 4.4. What e.m.f. will be generated in an 8 pole, lap wound generator if it is rotated at 200 r.p.m.? The flux per pole is 0.05 Wb, and the number of armature conductors are 960.

Solution. Formula used is,

i.e. $$E = \frac{P\phi NZ}{60A} \text{ volts}$$

where $$\phi = 0.05 \text{ Wb}$$

$$Z = 960 \text{ conductors}$$

$$N = 200 \text{ r.p.m}$$

$$P = 8$$

$$A = 8 \text{ (lap winding)}$$

$$E = \frac{8 \times 0.05 \times 960 \times 200}{60 \times 8} \text{ volts}$$

$$= \textbf{160 volts. Ans.}$$

Example 4.5. The armature of a 4 pole wave wound d.c. generator has 144 slots and 3 conductors per slot. If armature is rotated with a speed of 1200 r.p.m. and the flux per pole is 0.025 Wb. Calculate the e.m.f. generated.

Solution.

Formula used is, $$E = \frac{P\phi ZN}{60A} \text{ volts.}$$

$$P \Rightarrow 4$$

$$\phi \Rightarrow 0.025 \text{ Wb.}$$

$$N \Rightarrow 1200 \text{ r.p.m.}$$

$$\text{No. of slots} = 144$$

$$\text{Conductors per slot} = 3$$

Total number of conductor,

$$Z \Rightarrow 144 \times 3 \Rightarrow 432$$

As we know that in a wave wound generator there are only two numbers of parallel paths irrespective of the number of poles.

Hence $A \Rightarrow 2$

$$E \Rightarrow \frac{4 \times 0.025 \times 432 \times 1200}{60 \times 2} \Rightarrow 432 \text{ volts } \textbf{Ans.}$$

Example 4.6. The Armature of a 4 pole D.C. generator is required to generate an e.m.f of 520 V on open ckt when revolving at a speed of 660 r.p.m. Calculate the magnetic flux per pole required if the armature has 144 slots with two coil sides per slot, each coil consisting of three turns. The armature is wave wound.

Solution: Formula used

$$E_g = \frac{\phi Z N}{60} \times \left(\frac{P}{A}\right) \text{ volt}$$

Here $E_g = 520\ V, N = 660$ r.p.m.

$$Z = 144 \times 2 \times 3 = 864, \quad P = 4, \quad A = 2 \text{ (Due to wave winding)}$$

$$\therefore \quad 520 = \frac{\phi \times 864 \times 660}{60} \times \frac{4}{2}$$

$$\therefore \quad \phi = \frac{60 \times 520}{2 \times 864 \times 660} = 0.0274 \text{ wb. } \textbf{Ans.}$$

4.6. RELATIONSHIP BETWEEN INDUCED E.M.F. AND TERMINAL VOLTAGE

As is clear that in case of a d.c. generator mechanical energy is converted into electrical energy. This electrical energy is utilised in supplying to the d.c. loads.

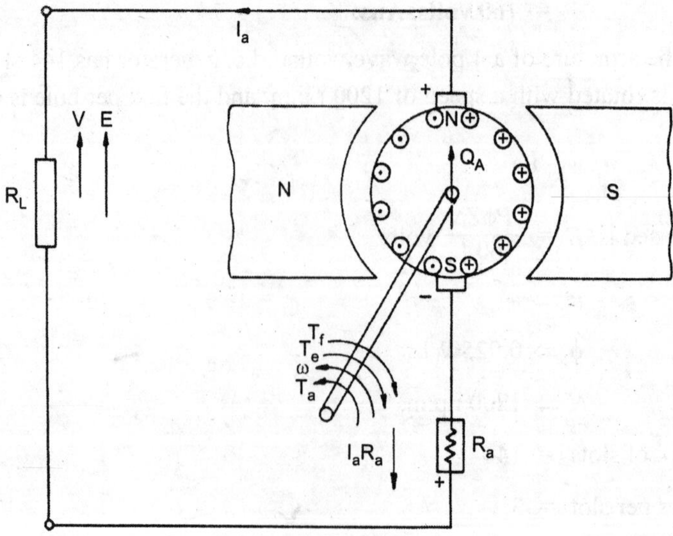

Fig. 4.7

Let,

$E \Rightarrow$ Induced E.M.F.

$V \Rightarrow$ Terminal Voltage

$I_a \Rightarrow$ Armature Current.

$R_a \Rightarrow$ Armature Resistance.

$T_a \Rightarrow$ Applied Mechanical Torque.

$T_e \Rightarrow$ Electromagnetic Torque.

$T_f \Rightarrow$ Frictional Torque.

$\omega \Rightarrow$ Angular velocity.

From the Fig. 4.7

$$E = V + I_a R_a. \quad ...(i)$$

i.e. E.M.F. induced in the armature winding

= Terminal Voltage + Resistance drop of the armature.

In this case 'E' is always greater than 'V'

Multiplying equation (*i*) by I_a

$$E I_a \Rightarrow VI_a + I_a^2 R_a \quad ...(ii)$$

Also $\omega T_e \Rightarrow EI_a$

So, equation (*ii*) can be modified as

$$\omega T_e \Rightarrow VI_a + I_a^2 R_a \quad ...(iii)$$

Hence from equation (*iii*) it is clear.

That,

Input Mechanical Power $\Rightarrow$ Output Electrical power + Electrical power lost in the armature.

Now from mechanical power point of view

$$\omega T_a \Rightarrow \omega T_e + \omega T_f \quad ...(iv)$$

'ωT_f' *i.e.* frictional power loss is very much low as compared to 'ωT_e' so neglecting 'ωT_f' the equation (*iv*) becomes

$$\omega T_a = \omega T_e \quad ...(v)$$

It is obviously clear from the said discussion that if the load on the alternator is increased, the current I_a increases. From eq. (*iii*) ωT_e also increases. Due to the increase in 'ωT_e', ωT_a should be increased for keeping the balance. [From equation (*v*)]. So we can say that if the load on the generator is increased the applied mechanical torque should also be increased.

4.7. TYPES OF GENERATORS

Generators are normally classified according to the method of their field excitation*. On this basis, generator can be mainly classified into following two types:

(*i*) Separately Excited D.C. Generators.

(*ii*) Self-excited D.C. Generators.

1. **Separately Excited D.C. Generators.** A D.C. Generator whose field winding is supplied exciting current from some external source, the machine is said to be separately excited as shown in Fig. 4.8 (*i*) and (*ii*). The field current of this type of machine is supplied by another generator called excitor or a battery. Examples of such machines are low voltage heavy current generators used in electroplating and electrorefining of metals ; main generators in D.C. ship propulsion.

Simple relation

(*i*) Armature current,

$$I_a = I_L \text{ Amps.}$$

(*ii*) Terminal voltage, $V = E - I_a R_a$ volts

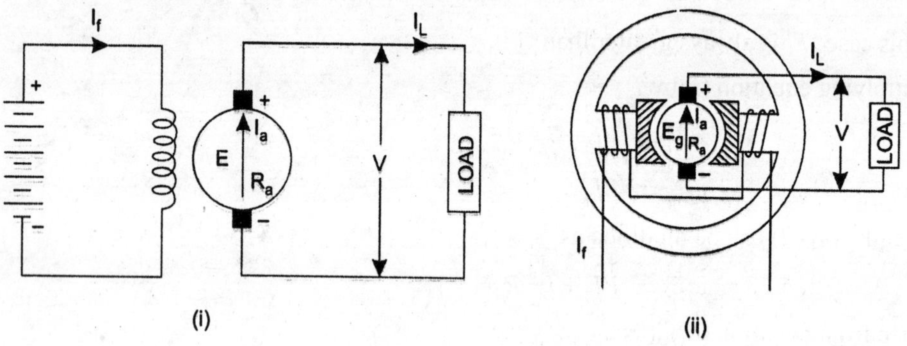

Fig. 4.8. Separately Excited Generator

(*iii*) Power developed

$$P = E I_a \text{ watts}$$

(*iv*) Power delivered to load $= VI_L$

$$= EI_a - I_a^2 R_a = I_a (E - I_a R_a)$$

$$= VI_a \text{ watts.}$$

$$= VI_L \text{ watts.}$$

2. **Self-excited Generator.** When the field coils are excited by the exciting current supplied by the generator itself, it is said to be self-excited generator.

In a self-excited generator, the field coils may be connected in series with the armature coils

* Permanent magnets are used as field poles for some very small generators called magnetos; all other machines are supplied with electromagnets, the strength of which can readily be controlled by varying the exciting current through the field coil.

(series) or in parallel with the armature coils (shunt) or partly in series and partly in parallel with armature coils (compound). According to the type of connections of the field coils with the armature coils the self-excited generators may be classified into:

(*i*) Series wound generator.

(*ii*) Shunt wound generator.

(*iii*) Compound wound generator.

(*i*) **Series Wound Generator.** Fig. 4.9 shows a series excited generator in which the field coils are in series with the armature and carry the total current of the generator. Fig. 4.9 (*i*) shows the connections of a series wound generator whereas Fig. 4.9 (*ii*) shows its conventional diagram. Since the field coils carries the full load current therefore, it has a few turns of wire of large cross-sectional area having low resistance. Before the machine will excite, the external circuit must be closed. Series generators are scarcely ever used except for special purposes *e.g.*, boosters.

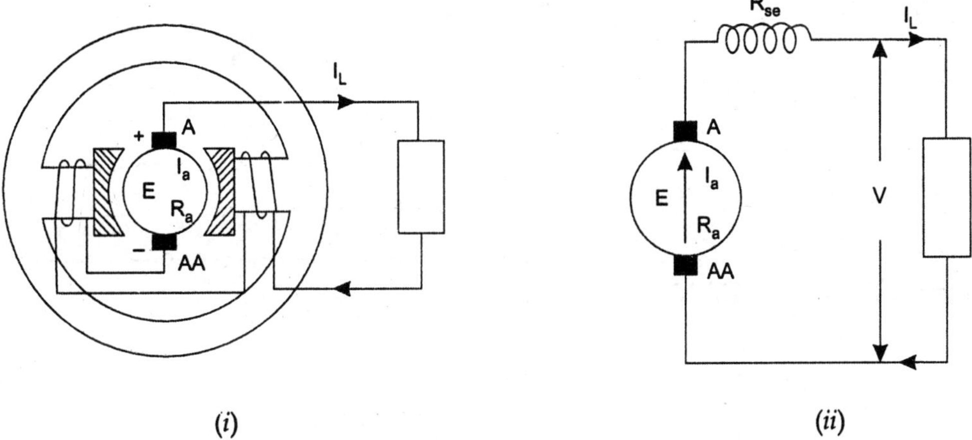

Fig. 4.9. Series Excited Generator

Simple relations

(*i*) $I_a = I_{se} = I_L = I \text{ (say)}$

(*ii*) $V = E_g - I(R_a + R_{se})$

(*iii*) Power developed, $P = E_g I_a$

(*iv*) Power delivered to load $= E_g I_a - I(R_a + R_{se})$

$= I_a[E_g - I(R_a + R_{se})] = VI_a \text{ or } = VI_L$

(*ii*) **Shunt Wound Generator.** In a shunt wound generator the field coils are connected in parallel (or shunt) across the armature teminals as shown in Fig. 4.10 (*i*) & (*ii*). These coils have many turns of relatively small wire having high resistance and carry a current I_f or $I_{sh} = \frac{V}{Rsh}$, the terminal voltage divided by the resistance of the field coil circuit. This exciting current varies from about 0·5 percent of the full load current of the machine to about 5 percent, depending chiefly on the size of the machine, the larger proportion of current being taken by the smaller machines. Fig. 4.10 (*i*) & (*ii*) shows the connections and conventional diagrams of a shunt wound generator.

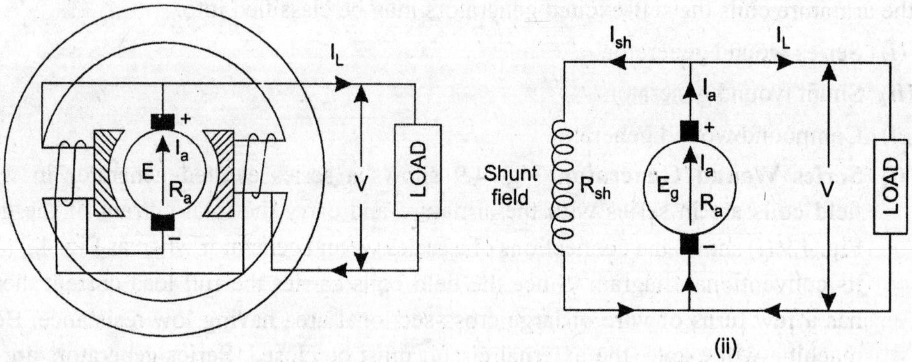

Fig. 4.10. Shunt Wound Generator

Simple relations

(*i*) Shunt field current, $I_{sh} = \frac{V}{R_{sh}}$

(*ii*) Armature current, $I_a = I_{sh} + I_L$

(*iii*) Terminal voltage, $V = E_g - I_a R_a$

(*iv*) Power developed, $P = E_g I_a$

(*v*) Power delivered to load $= VI_L$

Uses – Main generators on board ship.
– Charging accumulators,
– Small installations,

(*iii*) **Compound Wound Generators.** Figs. 4.11 (*i*) & (*ii*) shows compound wound generators in which there are both shunt and series field coils on each pole–One is in series and the other in parallel with the armature; thus the compound wound generator may be:

(*a*) **Short shunt.** In which the shunt coils are connected inside the series coils or in which the shunt field coils are only in parallel with armature, the connection is said to be short shunt as shown in Fig. 4.11 (*i*).

(*b*) **Long shunt.** When the shunt coils are connected outside the series coils, the machine is said to have a long-shunt connection as shown in Fig. 4.11 (*ii*).

It makes no appreciable difference in the operating characteristics which way the shunt is connected and the choice is determined by mechanical considerations of connections or reversing switches.

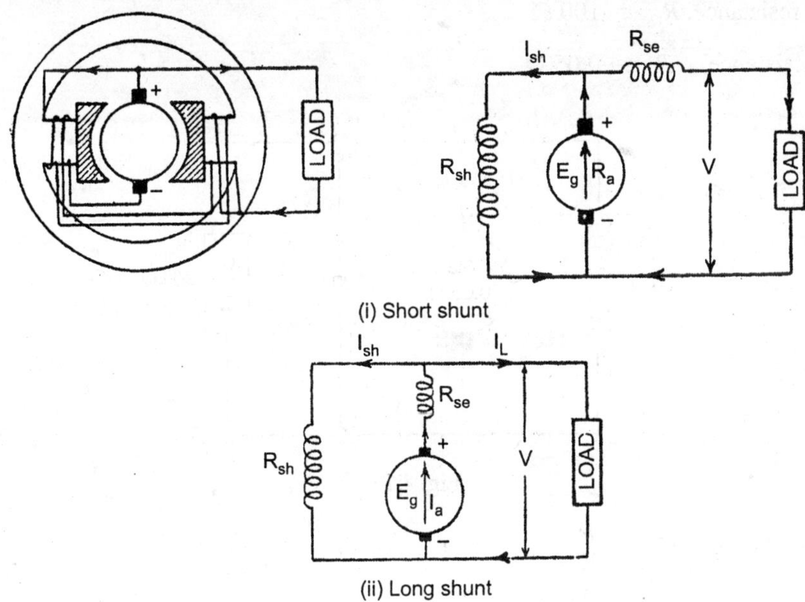

Fig. 4.11. Compound Generators

Simple relations

(a) Short shunt compound generator:

(*i*) Series field current, $I_{se} = I_L$

(*ii*) Shunt field current, $I_{sh} = \frac{V + I_{se} R_{se}}{R_{sh}}$

(*iii*) Terminal voltage, $V = E_g - I_a R_a - I_{se} R_{se}$

(*iv*) Power developed, $P = E_g \cdot I_a$ watts

(*v*) Power delivered to load $= V \cdot I_L$ watts

(b) Long shunt compound generator:

(*i*) Series field current, $I_{se} = I_a = I_L + I_{sh}$

(*ii*) Shunt field current, $I_{sh} = \frac{V}{R_{sh}}$

(*iii*) Terminal voltage, $V = E_g - I_a(R_a + R_{se})$

(*iv*) Power developed, $P = E_g . I_a$ watts

(*v*) Power delivered to load $= V. I_L$ watts

Example 4.7. A 30 KW, 300 V, d.c. shunt generator has armature and field resistances of 0.05 ohm and 100 ohms respectively. Calculate the total power delivered by the armature when it delivers full load output. [A.M.*I.e.* Elect. M/cs. Summer 1995, 2003]

Solution. Output of Generator,

$$P = 30 \text{ kW (given)} = 30 \times 10^3 \text{ Watt}$$

Terminal voltage, $V = 300$ volts

Shunt field resistance, R_{sh} = 100 Ω

Armature resistance, R_a = 0.05 Ω

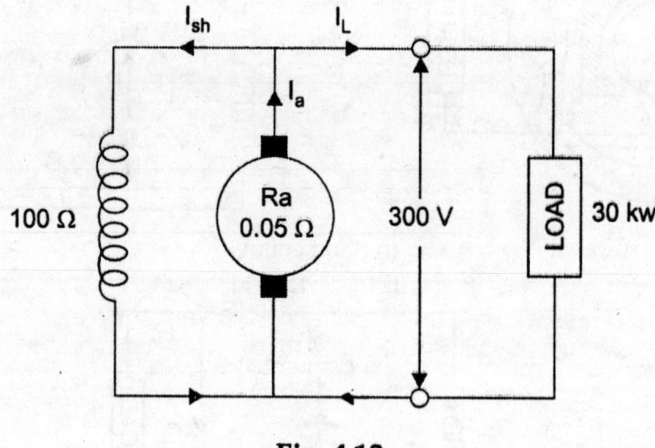

Fig. 4.12

∴ Load current, $I_L = \frac{P}{V}$

$= \frac{30 \times 10^3}{300} = 100$ amp.

Shunt field current, $I_{sh} = \frac{V}{R_{sh}} = \frac{300}{100} = 3$ amp.

∴ Armature current, $I_a = I_L + I_{sh} = 100 + 3 = 103$ amp.

Generated e.m.f., $E_g = V + I_a R_a = 300 \times 103 \times 0.05$

$= 305.15$ volts

∴ Power developed by the armature = $E_g I_a$

$= 305.\ 15 \times 10^3$

= 31.43 × 10³ watts

= 31.43 kW. Ans.

Example 4.8. A shunt dynamo supplies a load of 15 kilowatts at 200 volts through feeders of resistance 0.08 ohm. Resistance of shunt field winding 80 ohm, resistance of armature 0.04 ohm, find the terminal voltage and the e.m.f generated.

Solution. 15 kW = 15,000 W (given)

Load current, $I_L = \frac{15{,}000}{200} = 75$ amp.

Volt drop in feeders = 75 × 0.08 = 6 volts

∴ Terminal voltage, V_T = 200 + 6 = **206 volts. Ans.**

Now field current,

I_f or $I_{sh} = \frac{V_T}{R_{sh}} = \frac{206}{80} = 2.575$ amps.

$\therefore$ Armature current, $I_a = 75 + 2.575 = 77.575$ amps.

Volt drop in armature $= 77{\cdot}575 \times 0.04 = 3.1$ volts

e.m.f. generated $= 206 + 3.1 =$ **209.1 volts. Ans.**

Example 4.9. A short shunt compound dynamo supplies 100 amperes at 110 volts. Shunt field resistance 50 ohms ; series resistance 0.015 ohm and armature resistance 0.02 ohm. Find the e.m.f generated.

Solution. Voltage drop in series winding

$$= I_{se} \times R_{se} = 100 \times 0.015$$

$$= 1.5 \text{ Volts}$$

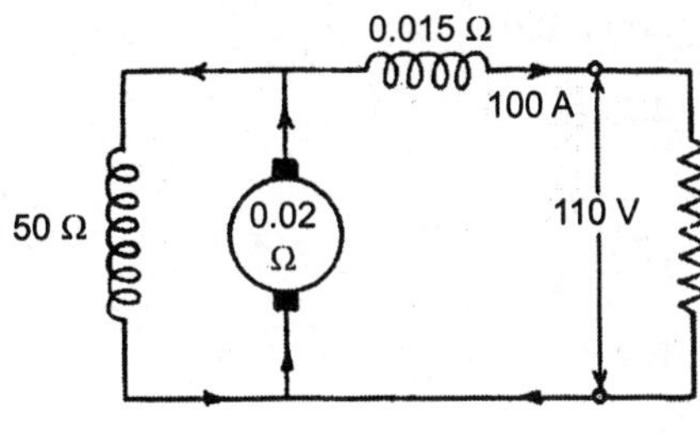

Fig. 4.13

Voltage drop at brushes

$$V_b = 110 + 1.5 = 111.5 \text{ volts}$$

Field current,

$$I_{sh} = \frac{111.5}{50} = 2.23 \text{ amps.}$$

Armature current, $I_a = I_{sh} + I_L$

$$= 2.23 + 100 = 102.23 \text{ amps.}$$

Voltage drop in armature $= 102.23 \times 0.02 = 2.044$ volts

$\therefore$ E.m.f. generated $= 111.\,5 + 2.04 =$ **113.5 volts. Ans.**

Example 4.10. A compound generator is to supply a load of 250 amps, each rated at 100 watts, 250 volts. The armature, series and shunt windings have resistances of 0.06 ohm, 0.04 ohm and 50 ohms respectively. Find the e.m.f. generated in the armature when the machine is connected:

(*i*) Short shunt

(*ii*) Long shunt.

Take drop per brush as 1 volt. (A.M.*I.e.*, Section B. Elect. 1992)

Solution. Generator power output,

$$P = 250 \times 100$$

$$= 25 \times 10^3 \text{ Watts}$$

Terminal Voltage, V_T = 250 volts

Armature resistance, R_a = 0.06 Ω

Series field resistance, R_{se} = 0.04 Ω

Shunt field resistance, R_{sh} = 50 Ω

Volt drop per brush = 1 volt

∴ Load current, $I_L = \frac{P}{V} = \frac{25 \times 10^3}{250} = 100$ A.

***(i)* short shunt**

Voltage drop in series resistance $= I_L \times R_{se}$

$= 100 \times 0.04$

$= 4\ V$

∴ Voltage at the brushes

= Voltage across R_{sh}

$= V + I_L \times R_{se}$

$= 250 + 4$

$= 254$ V

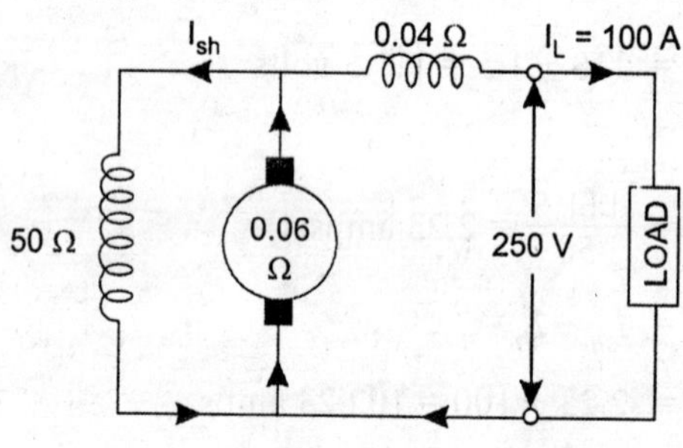

Fig. 4.14

∴ Shunt field current, $I_{sh} = \frac{254}{50} = 5.08$ A

Now armature current, $I_a = I_L + I_{sh}$

$= 100 + 5.08 = 105.08$ A

∴ E.m.f. generated, $E_g = V + I_L R_{se} + I_a R_a$ + Total brush drop

$= 250 + 100 \times 0.04 + 105.08 \times 0.06 + 2 \times 1$

$= 250 + 4 + 6.3 + 2 = 262.3$ V. Ans.

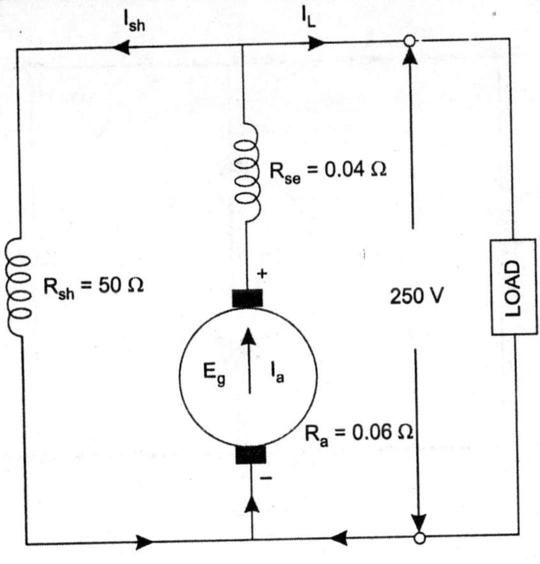

Fig. 4.15

(*ii*) Long shunt

Here shunt Current $I_{sh} = \dfrac{V}{R_{sh}}$

$$= \frac{250}{50} = 5 \text{ Amp}$$

Armature current, $I_a \Rightarrow I_{sh} + I_L$

$$\Rightarrow 5 + 100 \Rightarrow 105. \text{ Amp.}$$

Voltage drop in between Armature Resistance & Series Resistance

$$\Rightarrow I_a (R_a + R_{se})$$

$$\Rightarrow 105\ (0.06 + 0.04) \Rightarrow 105\ (0.1)$$

$$\Rightarrow 10.5 \text{ Volts}$$

∴ E.m.f. generated, $E_g = V + I_a (R_a + R_{se})$ + Total Brush drops

$$\Rightarrow 250 + 10.5 + (2 \times 1)$$

$\Rightarrow$ 262.5 Volts **Ans.**

Example 4.11. A 4 pole lap wound 11.5 kW, 230 V d.c. shunt generator has armature resistance of 0.2 Ω. and shunt field resistance 100 Ω. Calculate:

(*i*) The e.m.f generated if the brush contact drop = 1 V/brush

(*ii*) The magnetic flux per pole if the m/c is run at 1000 r.p.m. and there are 1200 conductors in the armature slots.

Solution.

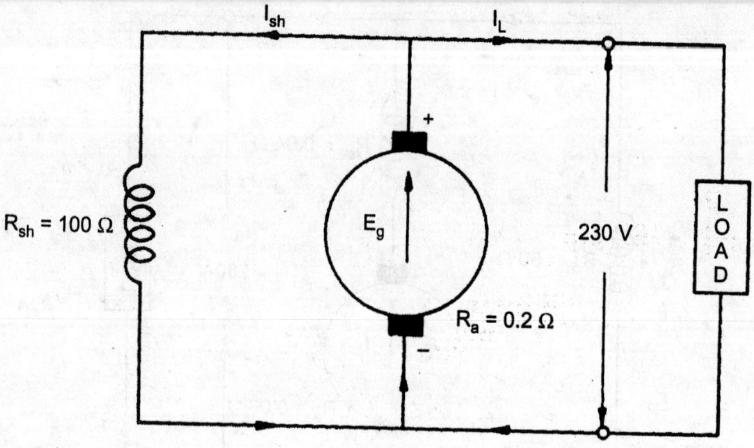

Fig. 4.16

Generator Power Output,

$$P = 11.5 \text{ kW.}$$
$$= 11500 \text{ Watts.}$$

Terminal Voltage, $V_T = 230$ V

Shunt field current $I_{sh} = \frac{V_T}{R_{sh}} \Rightarrow \frac{230}{100} = 2.3$ Amp.

Load current $I_L \Rightarrow \frac{P}{V} = \frac{11500}{230} = 50$ Amp.

Armature Current, $I_a = I_L + I_{sh}$

$$= 50 + 2.3. \Rightarrow 52.3 \text{ Amps.}$$

$E_g \Rightarrow$ Terminal Voltage + Armature Voltage drop + Total brush drop

$$= 230 + (52.3 \times 0.2) + (2 \times 1)$$
$$\Rightarrow 230 + 10.46 + 2 \Rightarrow 242.46 \text{ volts}$$ **Ans.**

(*ii*) We know that

$$E_g = \frac{P\phi NZ}{60\,A}$$

$$242.46 = \frac{4 \times \phi \times 1000 \times 1200}{60 \times 4}$$

or

$$\phi \Rightarrow \frac{242 \times 60 \times 4}{4 \times 1000 \times 1200} \Rightarrow 12.123 \text{ mWb.}$$ **Ans.**

4.8. LOSSES IN A D.C. GENERATOR

A dynamo or generator is a machine which converts mechanical energy into electrical energy. When such a conversion takes place, certain losses occur inside the machine which are dissipated in the form of heat. These losses are of greater importance as they result in waste of power and rise in temperature of the machine. A reduction in these losses leads to an increased rating as well as higher efficiency. Due to this reason, the main objective in the design and construction of a dynamo is the reduction of losses.

The various losses which occur in a D.C. generator may be grouped under three headings namely,

1. Copper Losses,
2. Iron Losses, and
3. Mechanical Losses.

1. **Copper Losses.** (Sometimes called electrical losses). The reason of occurring these losses is the current flowing in the various windings of the D.C. machine. This loss is about 30 to 40% of full load losses.

   (*i*) **Armature Copper Loss = $I_a^2 R_a$ watts**

   (*ii*) **Field Copper Loss in Shunt Winding**

   $$= I_{sh}^2 R_{sh} \text{ watts}$$

   In series winding $= I_{se}^2 R_{sh}$ watts

   In interpole winding $= I_i^2 R_i$ watts

   (*iii*) **Brush contact loss.** This loss is due to brush contact resistance (between surface of brush and surface of commutator). Usually taken into account by including brush contact resistance with armature resistance. This loss is about 20 to 50% of F.L.

2. **Iron Losses.** These are sometimes called magnetic or Core losses which include:

   (*i*) Hysteresis loss in armature

   (*ii*) Eddy current loss in armature and pole shoes.

   (*i*) **Hysteresis loss** is due to the reversal of magnetism of the armature core. It is found that when a magnetic material is taken through a cycle of magnetisation, some energy is wasted in this process, which goes to rise the temperature of the specimen. This loss is named as hysteresis loss. The hysteresis loss per unit volume is given by the area of the hysteresis Loop.

   The hysteresis loss per unit volume per cycle of magnetisation of a magnetic material depends on:

   (*i*) The maximum flux density in webers per m^2, *i.e.*, B_{max}

   (*ii*) The magnetic property of the material.

The hysteresis loss is determined separately for teeth and core. For core Steinmetz' formula can be used according to which the hysteresis loss W_h can be given as:

$$W_h = \eta B_{max}^{1.6} f. V. \text{ joules/sec or watt.}$$

where f is the frequency in cycles/sec.

V is the volume of the material in m^3

η is a constant, depending upon the type of steel used for stamping and varies from 191 for silicon steel to 753.5 for cast steel.

In the case of magnetic materials used for building electrical apparatus, such materials are used which have low hysteresis coefficient. Silicon steel is often used for this purpose. It has a low Steinmetz' co-efficient.

For finding the hysteresis loss for teeth this formula cannot be used due to the reason that the flux density in the teeth is very high and Steinmetz' formula does not hold good for such high densities. The hysteresis loss for teeth is usually determined from curves which are drawn for loss against average flux densities. The average flux density for the teeth is taken half way down the teeth.

(ii) **Eddy Current Loss.** If a loop of material, Fig. 4.17 (*a*) or a block of material, Fig. 4.17(*b*) is linked by a changing flux, ϕ, then an e.m.f. will be induced in the loop or block. If the loop or block happens to be a conducting material then the e.m.f. will give rise to currents circulating round the loop or block. Such currents are called *Eddy currents*. These eddy currents will give rise to a power loss in the resistance of the conducting material. This loss is called the *Eddy current* loss.

The eddy currents will always be in such a direction as to oppose the flux changes occurring and it is found that at higher frequencies the eddy currents may greatly alter the magnitude and distribution of the flux over the cross-section of the loop or block. For thin sheets at low frequencies (50 c/s) it is possible to assume that the flux magnitude and distribution are undisturbed by the eddy currents produced.

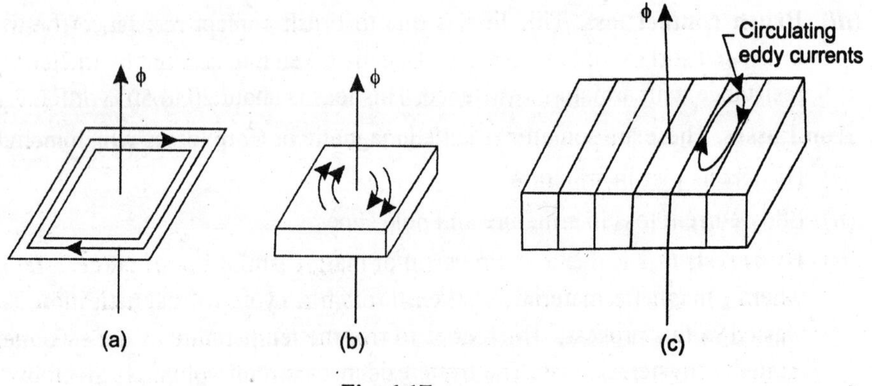

Fig. 4.17

The eddy e.m.f. depends upon the speed of rotation or frequency '*f*' and the flux density *B*. The eddy e.m.f. causes eddy currents. The loss due to this eddy current is known as eddy current loss given as $\frac{E^2}{R}$, where *E* is eddy e.m.f. and *R* is the resistance of stamping.

The eddy current loss is also given as,

$$W_e = K_e \times (\text{r.p.m})^2 \times (B_{max})^2 \times t^2 \times V \text{ watt}$$

or

$$= k_e f^2 B^2_{\max} t^2 V \text{ watt.}$$

where K_e = constant.

B_{max} = Max. flux density in Wb/m^2.

t = Thickness of each lamination.

V = Volume of armature core in m^3.

In many pieces of apparatus it is necessary to have a magnetic materials carrying a varying flux. Since magnetic materials are conductors there will be eddy currents in these materials and in general there would be a quite excessive eddy current power loss if a solid block of the material were used. To reduce the power loss to a reasonable value the apparatus is usually constructed of a number of sheets called laminations, which are 'Lightly' insulated from one another by an oxide or a varnish layer. Dividing the block in this manner reduces the flux linking any given eddy current path and greatly increases the resistance of such a path Fig. 4.17 (*c*). It is also useful to have an iron with as high a resistivity as possible provided its magnetic properties are satisfactory. The eddy current power loss is also inversely proportional to the resistivity of the material.

3. **Mechanical Losses.** These losses comprise of:
   (*i*) Friction loss at bearings and commutator, and
   (*ii*) Air friction or windage loss of rotating armature.

   These losses are 10 to 20% of the total losses. These losses depend upon the speed of the machine but for a given speed, they are practically constant.

   Stray Losses: Usually the magnetic or iron losses and mechanical losses are combined together and are called the stray losses.

   i.e. Stray losses = Iron losses + Mechanical losses.

   The total losses in a D.C. generator are summarized as below.

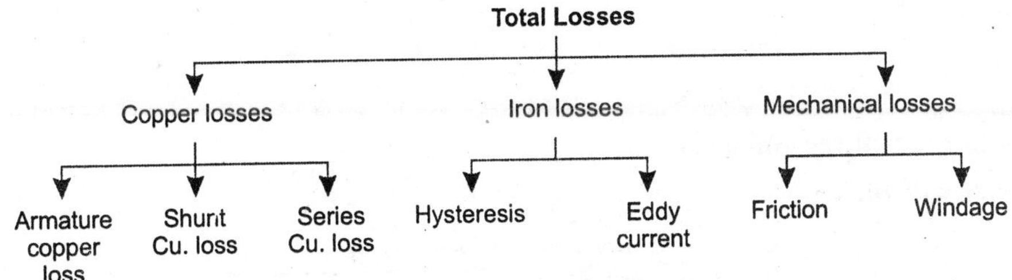

4.9. CONSTANT AND VARIABLE LOSSES

In a D.C. generator the losses may also be sub-divided into:

1. Constant losses
2. Variable losses.

1. **Constant Losses.** The losses which remain constant at all loads in a D.C. generator are known as constant losses. These include
   (*a*) Iron losses
   (*b*) Mechanical losses
   (*c*) Shunt field Cu. losses.

The iron losses depend upon flux density and speed whereas mechanical losses depend upon speed only. Iron and mechanical losses are very small as compared to input of the machine and can be practically considered constant. As the shunt field current is constant at all loads, due to this reason the shunt field copper loss is also constant.

Variable losses. The losses which vary with load in a D.C. generator are called variable losses. These losses include:

(*i*) Copper loss in series field winding,

(*ii*) Copper loss in armature winding, and

(*iii*) Copper loss in interpole and compensating winding.

∴ Total losses = Constant losses + Variable losses.

4.10. EFFICIENCY OF THE GENERATOR

The various power stages in case of a D.C. generator are given below:

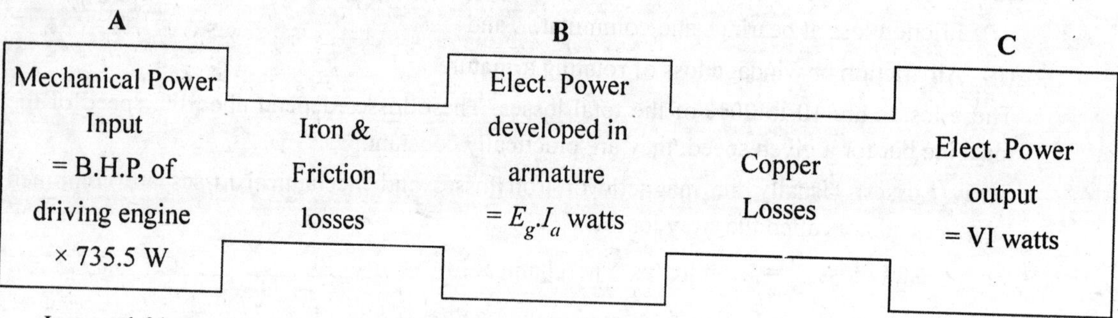

Iron and friction losses

$$= A - B$$

$$\text{Copper losses} = B - C$$

Following are the three efficiencies:

1. Electrical efficiency.

$$\eta_e = \frac{\textit{Generator output in watts}}{\textit{Elect. power developed in armature}}$$

$$= \frac{C}{B} = \frac{VI_L}{E_g I_a}$$

2. Mechanical efficiency,

$$\eta_m = \frac{\textit{Elect. power developed in armature in watts}}{\textit{Mechanical power input}}$$

$$= \frac{B}{A}$$

$$= \frac{E_g I_a}{B.H.P \times 735.5}$$

3. Overall or commercial efficiency,

$$\eta_c = \frac{\textit{Generator out put}}{\textit{Mech. power input}}$$

$$= \frac{C}{A} = \frac{VI_L}{B.H.P. \times 735.5}$$

Unless otherwise told, commercial efficiency is always understood.

4.11. CONDITION FOR MAXIMUM EFFICIENCY

Let V is the output voltage, I_L is the load current of the generator, then its

$$\text{Output} = V \times I_L \text{ watts.}$$

and

$$[I_a = I_L + I_{sh}$$

$$= I_L \text{ (As } I_{sh} \text{ is very small)}].$$

$\therefore$

$$\text{Generator Input} = \text{Output} + \text{Losses}$$

$$= VI_L = I_a^2 R_a + \text{Constant losses.}$$

$$= VI_L + (I_L + I_{sh})^2 R_a + W_c$$

$$= VI_L + I_L^2 R_a + W_c \qquad [\because I_{sh} \text{ is small hence neglected}]$$

$$\text{Efficiency} = \frac{\textit{Output}}{\textit{Input}} = \frac{VI_L}{VI_L + I_L^2 R_a + W_c}$$

$$= \frac{1}{1 + \left(\frac{I_L R_a}{V} + \frac{Wc}{VI_L}\right)} \qquad ...(i)$$

Now for maximum efficiency the terms in brackets of the denominator should be minimum *i.e.*

$$\frac{d}{dI}\left(\frac{I_L R_a}{V} + \frac{W_c}{VI_L}\right) = 0.$$

or

$$\frac{R_a}{V} - \frac{W_c}{VI_L} = 0$$

or

$$\frac{R_a}{V} = \frac{W_c}{VI_L^2}$$

or

$$I_L^2 R_e = W_c$$

i.e.

$$\text{Variable loss} = \text{Constant loss.}$$

Hence, the condition for maximum efficiency is that copper losses must be equal to constant losses

or

$$I_L = \sqrt{\frac{W_c}{R_a}}$$

which is the another condition for the efficiency to be maximum.

4.12. EFFICIENCY CURVE

The curve which is drawn between load current and efficiency of the generator is known as efficiency curve as shown in Fig. 4.18. The following points are to be noted from this curve:

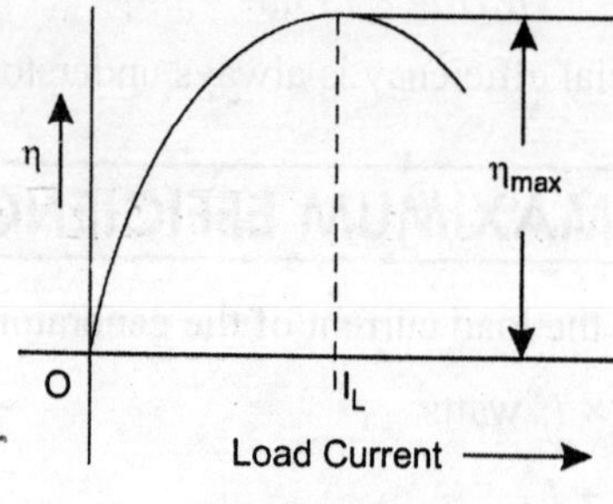

Fig. 4.18

(*i*) At low values of load currents, the efficiency is small because of the presence of constant losses.

(*ii*) The generator efficiency varies with the load current.

(*iii*) At some fixed load current (I_L as shown in the Fig. 4.18) the variable loss is equal to constant loss and hence the generator efficiency is maximum.

4.12.1. Ratings of Electrical Machines

The *rated duty* of an electrical machine is its duty in the conditions for which it has been designed by the manufacturer. The rated duty is characterised by values given on the machine's rating plate, and termed rated values, as, for instance:

– *rated output,*

– *rated voltage,*

– *rated current,*

– *rated speed, etc.*

The '*rated*', however, may also be applied to the values not inscribed on the rating plate, but *relating* to the rated duty, as, for example:

– *rated torque*

– *rated efficiency, etc.*

The rated output of a D.C. machine:

(*i*) **When Operating as a "Generator"**–The *electrical power* delivered into the external circuit, expressed in watts (W) or in kilowatts (kW).

(*ii*) **When Operating as a 'Motor'**–The useful mechanical power at the shaft expressed in watts (W) or kilowatts (kW).

It may be noted that rated values should not be confused with normal values. If, for example, the rated voltage of motor is 220 V, in actual working conditions, the voltage may fluctuate and be more or less than the rated value. If we take the average value of voltage for a long period, it may be arbitrarily called the *normal or operating voltage* of the machine. Hence in the *general case normal* (operating) *values are not equal to rated values.*

— According to rated output the D.C. machines (which are produced in very wide range of rated quantities) may be conditionally divided as follows

	Machines	*Rated output*
1.	Midget	Less than 40 W
2.	Fractional horse power	From 40 to 745 W
3.	Low power	From 745 W to 10 KW
4.	Medium power	From 10 to 100 kW
5.	High power	From 100 to 1000 kW
6.	Very high power	Over 1000 kW

— According to the magnitude of the rated voltage the machines are generally classified as follows:

	Machines	*Rated voltage*
1.	Low voltage	Below 100 V
2.	Medium voltage	From 100 to 1000 V
3.	High voltage	Above 1,000 V

— According to their *speed* the machines are most frequently distinguished as follows:

	Machines	*Rated speed*
1.	Low-speed	Below 250 r.p.m.
2.	Medium-speed	From 250 to 1,000 r.p.m.
3.	High-speed	From 1,000 to 3,000 r.p.m.
4.	Super-high-speed	Over 3,000 r.p.m.

— When a large D.C. power (in some cases) is required, it is good practice to mount on one shaft two D.C. machines instead of one, joining their armatures electrically in series or in parallel.

Example 4.12. A shunt dynamo supplies 100 amperes at a terminal voltage of 200 volts. The Prime mover is developing 32 B.H.P Shunt field resistance 50 ohms, armature resistance 0.1 ohm. Find (a) the copper losses, (b) iron and friction losses (c) the commercial efficiency.

Solution.

$$I_{sh} = \frac{200}{50}$$

$$= 4\text{ A.}$$

$$\therefore \quad I_a = I_L + I_{sh}$$

$= 100 + 4 = 104$ A.

Voltage drop in armature

$= 104 \times 0.1 = 10.4$ V.

$\therefore$ e.m.f. generated

$= 200 + 10.4$

$= 210.4$ V

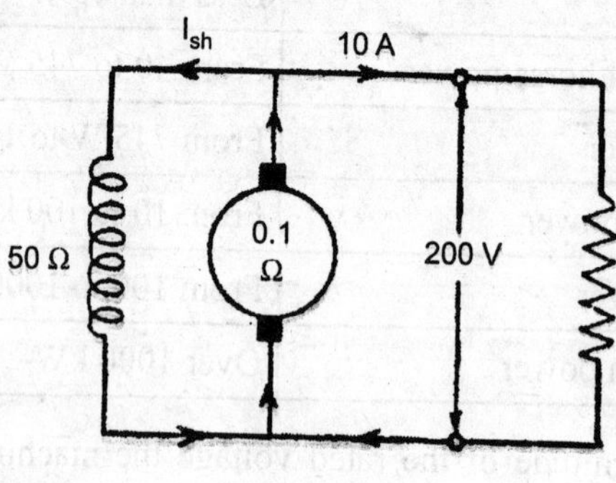

Fig. 4.19

Mechanical power input (A)

$= 32 \times 746 = 23,872$ watts.

[Or it could be taken 32×735.5 W]

Elect. power developed in armature (B)

$= E_g I_a = 210.4 \times 104$

$= 21,882$ watts.

$\therefore$ (*ii*) Iron and friction losses

$= (A - B) = 23,872 - 21,882$

$=$ **1,990 watts. Ans.**

Elect. power output, $(C) = VI_L$

$= 200 \times 100$

$= 20,000$ watts.

$\therefore$ (*i*) Copper losses $= (B) - (C)$

$= 21,882 - 20,000$

$=$ **1,882 watts. Ans**

(*ii*) Commercial efficiency

$$\eta_c = \frac{Output}{Input} = \frac{20,000}{23,872} \times \frac{100}{1}\%$$

$=$ **83. 8 % Ans.**

Example 4.13. A short shunt compound generator supplies a current of 100 amps, at 220 volts. The resistance of the shunt field is 50 ohms, the series winding is 0.025 ohm and of the armature 0.05 ohm. Iron and friction losses amount to be 1 kW. Find (*i*) the e.m.f. generated (*ii*) the copper losses (*iii*) the B.H.P. of the prime-mover (*iv*) the commercial efficiency.

Solution. Voltage drop in series winding = 100 × 0.025 = 2.5 volts

$$\therefore \quad V_b = 220 + 2.5$$

$$= 222.5 \text{ volts at brushes}$$

$$I_{sh} = \frac{222.5}{50} = 4.45 \text{ A}$$

$$\therefore \quad I_a = I_L + I_{sh} = 100 + 4.45$$

$$= 104.45 \text{ amp.}$$

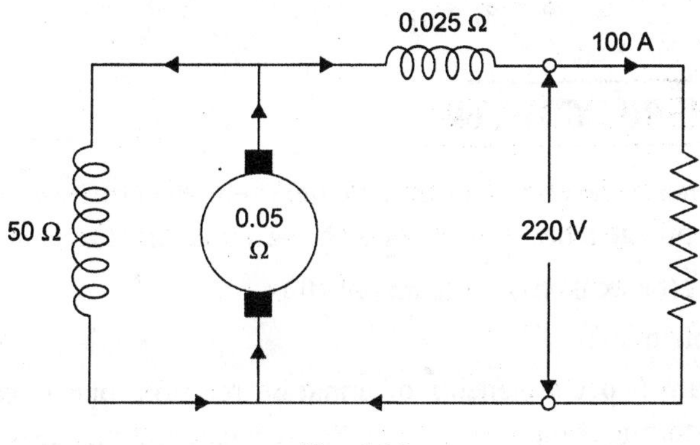

Fig. 4.20

Voltage drop in armature = 104·45 × 0·05 = 5·22 volts.

∴ (*i*) E.M.F. generated

$$= 222.5 + 5.22 = \mathbf{227.72 \text{ volts.}} \textbf{ Ans.}$$

Elect. power output (C)

$$= V \times I_L = 220 \times 100$$

$$= 22,000 \text{ watts. } \textbf{Ans.}$$

Elect. power developed in armature (B)

$$= E_g \cdot I_a.$$

$$= 227.72 \times 104{\cdot}45 = 23,790 \text{ watts}$$

∴ (*ii*) Copper losses $= (B - C)$

$$= 23,790 - 22,000$$

$$= \mathbf{1790 \text{ watts.}} \textbf{ Ans.}$$

Iron and friction losses

$$= 1000 \text{ watts (given).}$$

∴ Mechanical power input (A)

$$= \text{Output} + \text{Losses}$$

$$= 23,790 + 1000$$

$$= 24,790 \text{ watts.}$$

∴ (*iii*) B.H.P. of prime mover

$$= \frac{24,790}{746} = \mathbf{33.24\ H.P.\ Ans.}$$

(*iv*) Commercial efficiency,

$$\eta_c = \frac{22,000}{24,790} \times 100\%$$

$$= \mathbf{88.74\%\ Ans.}$$

4.13. ARMATURE REACTION

By armature reaction is meant the effect of magnetic field setup by armature current on the distribution of flux under main poles of a generator (or motor). This armature field has two effects:

1. It demagnetises (or weakens) the main pole flux
2. It distorts the main flux.

Accordingly, there are two components of armature reaction, one is called the demagnetising component and other 'distorting component'. Both these components increase with increase in armature current, that is with increase in the load on the generator. Under severe overloads or short circuit, the demagnetising component of armature reaction may become so strong as to reverse the polarity of the main poles. In general when the main flux ϕ is decreased due to armature reaction, the e.m.f. induced in the armature of a D.C generator is also decreased because $E \propto \theta$ (Fig. 4.21).

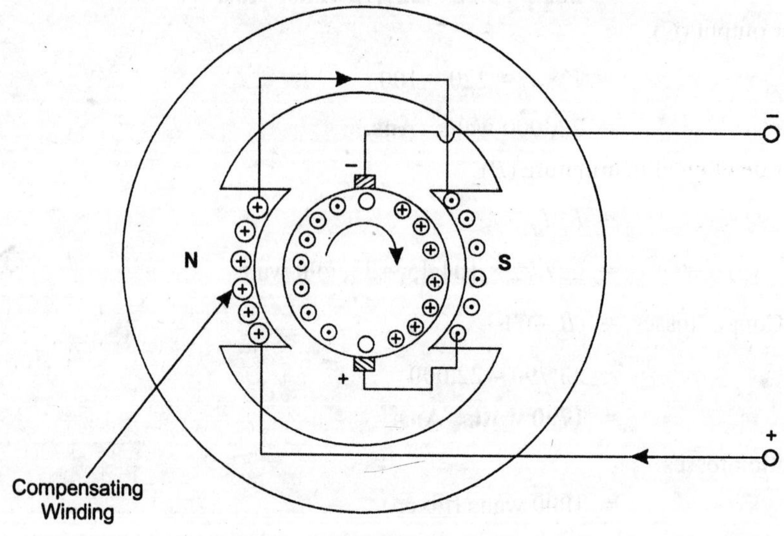

Fig. 4.21

The demagnetising effect of armature reaction is neutralized by adding a few extra ampere-turns to the main field wdg. The distorting effect is neutralized by using 'compensating windings'. These windings are embedded in slots in the pole shoes and are connected in series with armature in such a way that current in them flows in a direction opposite to that of the armature current flowing in the armature conductors directly below the pole shoes.

Armature reaction is defined as the effect of magnetic flux produced as a result of currents flowing in the armature of a machine on the main flux of the field system.

Consider a two pole machine having an armature with 16 conductors.

Fig. 4.21 (a) shows the distribution of flux when the current in the armature is not flowing. The flux in the gap is practically radial and uniformly distributed and is on account of the field magnets only. Since armature current is zero, so no flux is developed on this account.

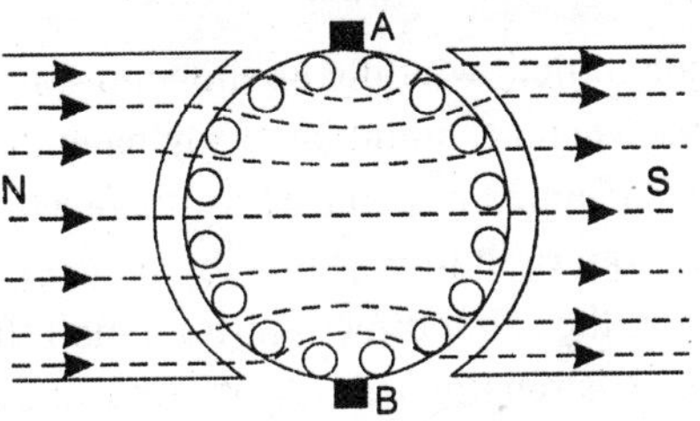

Fig. 4.21 (*a*)

Now if the armature is driven in the anticlockwise, the direction of e.m.f.s induced in as shown in Fig. 4.21 (*b*). If the direction of these e.m.f.s are followed, it is found that brush A is + ve and brush B is –ve. It is usual to show the brushes mid way between the poles because it is at these places that e.m.f. induced in the conductor is zero and is on the point of reversing its direction. The e.m.f.s induced at such point, is zero, because flux at such point is zero, being at neutral plan. Thus, the brushes are placed in the plan which is called the geometrical neutral plane (GNP).

In Fig. 4.21 (*b*) the direction of e.m.f. induced in the conductors under north pole is outward as shown by dot (•) sign while that induced in the conductors under south pole is inward as shown by plus (+) sign.

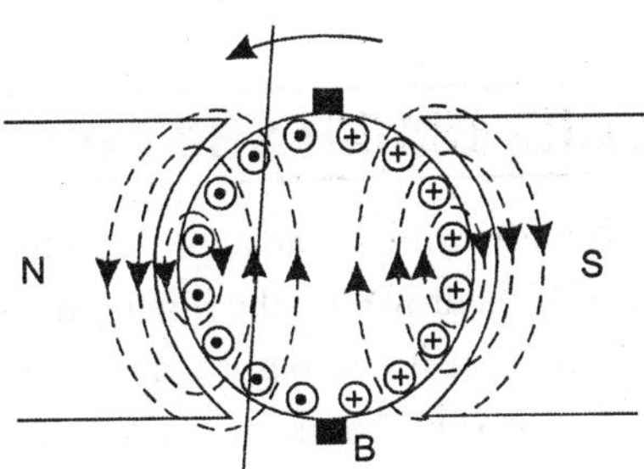

Fig. 4.21 (*b*)

When the generator is loaded currents start flowing in the conductors in the direction of e.m.f.s as already seen *i.e.* inward in the conductors under south pole and outwards in the conductors under north pole. These currents develop flux, the distribution of which is as shown in Fig. 4.21 (*b*) and the direction of flux distribution is as shown by the arrows obtained by Cork Screw rule.

It can be seen that the direction of this flux at the centre of the core of the armature and in the pole shoes is at right angles to that due to field winding. This is the reason why the flux due to armature current is termed as cross flux.

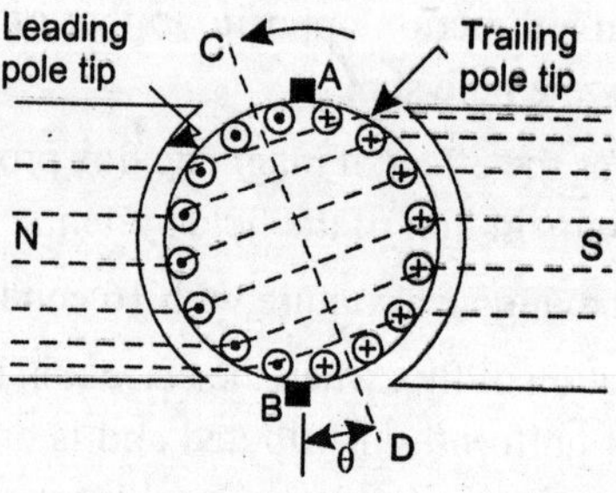

Fig. 4.21 (*c*)

Now these two fluxes, that due to field winding as shown in Fig. 4.21 (*a*) and that due to armature currents as shown in Fig. 4.21 (*b*), when act simultaneously have then their resultant as shown in Fig. 4.21 (*c*) over the leading halves of the pole faces, the cross flux is in opposition to main flux, (main flux is from left to right and cross flux from right to left) thereby reducing the flux density whereas over the trailing halves, the two fluxes are in the same direction (both main flux and cross flux are in the same direction), so that the flux density is strengthened. Apart from the effect of magnetic saturation, the increase of flux over one half of the pole face is the same as decrease over the other half, the total flux per pole remaining unaltered.

Hence in a generator, the effect of the armature reaction is to twist or distort the flux in the direction of rotation.

One important result of the distortion of this flux is that magnetic neutral axis is shifted through an angle θ *i.e.* from AB to CD as shown in Fig. 4.21 (*c*).

When the machine is on no load, magnetic neutral axis is AB. Thus conductors passing through this axis do not have any e.m.f. induced in them as they are moving parallel to the magnetic flux, whereas when the machine is loaded as generator and flux distorted as shown in Fig. 4.21 (*c*) no e.m.f. is induced in the conductors when passing through axis CD as the conductors are moving parallel to the magnetic flux.

4.14. EFFECT OF FORWARD BRUSH SHIFT (OR LEAD)

Suppose now that the brushes are shifted forward by an angle θ from axis *AB* to axis *CD* as already told and as shown in Fig. 4.22. If now line *EF* is drawn on the other side of *AB* which makes the same angle θ with it, then with anticlockwise rotation of the armature, all conductors on the left hand side of *CD* carry current outwards and all these on the right hand side carry current towards the paper.

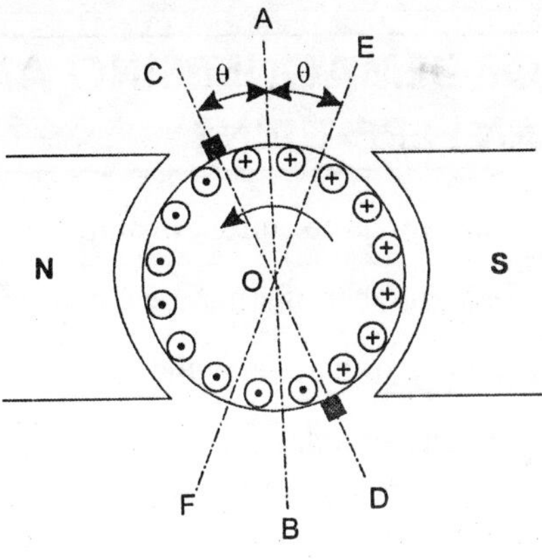

Fig. 4.22

The armature ampere turns can now be divided in two groups.

(*i*) Those ampere turns due to conductors in angle *COE* and *FOD* as shown separately in Fig. 4.23 (*a*). From Fig. 4.23 (*a*) it is clear that these armature conductors between *COE* and *FOD* are carrying current in such a direction that they set up a flux opposite in direction to that produced by the field winding. Hence ampere-turns due to these conductors are known as demagnetising ampere-turns.

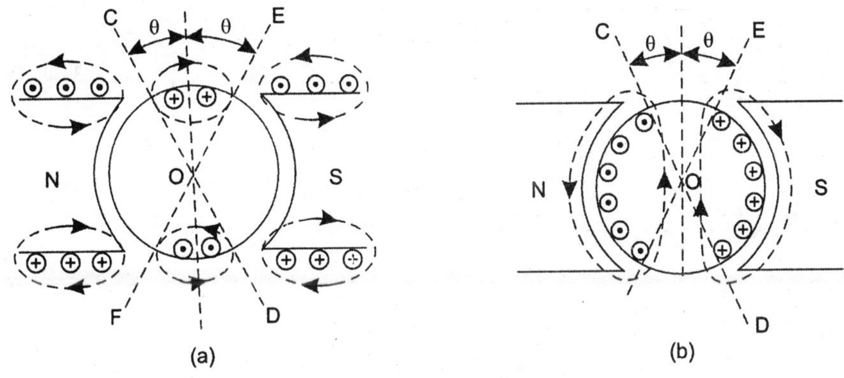

Fig. 4.23

(*ii*) Those ampere-turns due to conductors in angles *CO* and *EOD* are shown separately in Fig. 4.23 (*b*).

The flux produced as a result of current flowing in these conductors is in such a direction that it becomes perpendicular to the flux due to the main field winding. Thus the flux of the main field winding gets distorted.

Ampere-turns due to these conductors between angles *COF* and *EOD* are known as distorting or cross-magnetising ampere-turns.

4.15. CALCULATION OF DEMAGNETISING AND CROSS-MAGNETISING AMPERE-TURNS

I = Total armature current in amperes.

Z = Total number of armature conductors.

A = Number of parallel paths.

P = Number of poles.

∴ Current per conductor

$$= \frac{I}{A}$$

$$\text{Conductors per pole} = \frac{Z}{P}$$

Ampere conductors per pole

$$= \frac{I}{A} \cdot \frac{Z}{P}$$

Since two armature conductors form one turn,

∴ Ampere-turns per pole

$$= \frac{ZI}{2AP}$$

If θ is the brush shift in electrical degree,

$$1 \text{ electrical degree} = \frac{P}{2} \times (\text{Mechanical degrees})$$

∴ θ electrical degree

$$= \frac{P}{2} \times (\text{Brush shift in mech. degree})$$

If all the conductors are distributed in 360 elect-degress (between two poles), them number of conductors in $\angle COE$ and $\angle FOD$ *i.e.* in 4θ electrical degrees = $\frac{Z}{360} \times 4\theta$ = conductors × $\frac{4\theta}{360}$. The conductors between $\angle COE$ and $\angle FOD$ as already mentioned form demagnetising amp-turns.

Total of number demagnetising ampere-turns per pole,

$$= \text{Total ampere-turns per pole} \times \frac{4\theta}{360}$$

$$= \frac{ZI}{2AP} \times \frac{4\theta}{360}$$

Total ampere turns per pole

$$= \frac{ZI}{2AP}$$

∴ Distorting ampere-turns per pole

= (Total amp-turns per pole) – (Demagnetising amper turns per pole)

$$= \frac{ZI}{2AP} - \frac{ZI}{2AP} \times \frac{4\theta}{360}$$

$$= \frac{ZI}{2AP}\left(1 - \frac{4\theta}{360}\right)$$

4.16. METHODS OF IMPROVING ARMATURE REACTION

There are three methods for improving armature reaction.

(*i*) By providing compensating winding.

(*ii*) By increasing the length of Air Gap.

(*iii*) By decreasing the cross section of pole pieces.

(*i*) **By providing compensating Winding:** The compensating winding is placed in slots cut in pole faces and the winding is connected in series with the armature winding. The connections are made so that the direction of flow of current in compensating winding is opposite to that of armature winding.

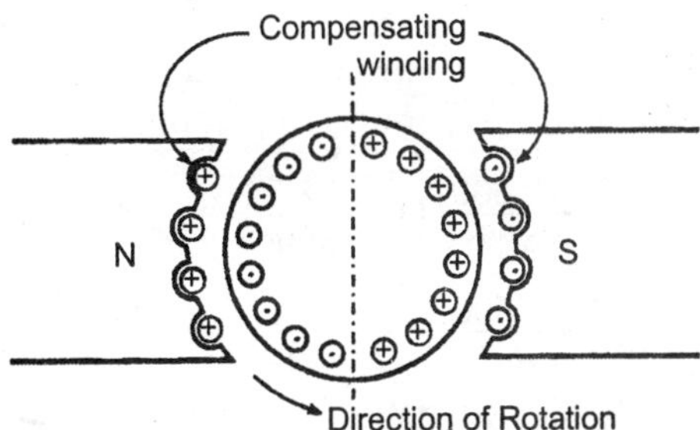

Fig. 4.24

This process of improving armature reaction is only used for some special purposes such as rolling mill motors and tourbo generators etc. because this method is very expensive as the compensating winding adds considerable to the winding cost and also copper losses are increased highly.

(*ii*) **By increasing the Length of Air Gap.** A considerable higher air gap is made under the poles. By increasing the air gap, the reluctance is increased which requires higher m.m.f. to pass the magnetic flux through the air gap. So by virtue of it the effect of armature ampere-turns on main field flux is minimised considerably as the field is not much influenced by the armature reaction.

(*iii*) **By Decreasing the Cross Section of Pole-pieces.** Highly reluctance is offered due to the saturation, if the cross section of pole pieces is decreased.

Example 4.14. A 300 KW, 500 V, eight pole d.c. generator has 768 armature conductors, lap connected. Calculate the number of demagnetising and cross amp. turns per pole, when the brushes are given a lead of 5 elect. degrees from the geometric neutral axis. Neglect the effect of shunt current.

Solution.

$$\text{Total arm. Current} = \frac{300 \times 1000}{500} = 600 \text{ A}$$

Thus

$$I = 600\text{A}$$

$$\theta = 5° \text{ elect.}$$

$$Z = 768$$

$$A = 8 \text{ being lap connected}$$

$$= \text{No. of poles.}$$

Demagnetising amp-turns per pole

$$= \frac{ZI}{2\,PA} \times \frac{4\theta}{360}$$

$$= \frac{768 \times 600}{2 \times 8 \times 8} \times \frac{4 \times 5}{360}$$

$$= 200 \text{ AT} \quad \textbf{Ans.}$$

Cross amp-turns per pole,

$$= \frac{ZI}{2AP}\left(1 - \frac{4\theta}{360}\right)$$

$$= \frac{768 \times 600}{2 \times 8 \times 8}\left(1 - \frac{4 \times 5}{360}\right)$$

$$= \frac{768 \times 600}{128} \times \frac{17}{18}$$

$$= \textbf{3400 AT Ans.}$$

4.17. COMMUTATION

The induced current in the armature conductors of a d.c. generator are alternating currents *i.e.* these currents flow in one direction when conductors are under N-Pole and in exactly opposite direction when they are under S-Pole. As conductors Pass out of the influence of a N-Pole and enter that of a S-Pole, the current in them is reversed. This reversal of current takes place along magnetic neutral axis (M.N.A) or brush axis *i.e.* when the brush spans and hence short-circuits the particular coil undergoing reversal of current through it.

This process by which current in the short circuited armature coil is reversed while it crosses the M.N.A is called **commutation.**

The brief period during which coil remains short-circuited is known as **commutation period** T_C.

If current reversal is completed within the time T_C, then commutation is ideal. If not then sparking is produced between the brush and the commutator which damages both.

The main factor which does not allow the armature current to completely reverse its direction within the specified period T_C is the production of the self induced e.m.f called reactance voltage in the conductors through which the current is reversing. If the current changes from +1 to –1 in Time T_C then reactance voltage is $L\ 2I/T_C$ where L is the inductance of the armature conductors.

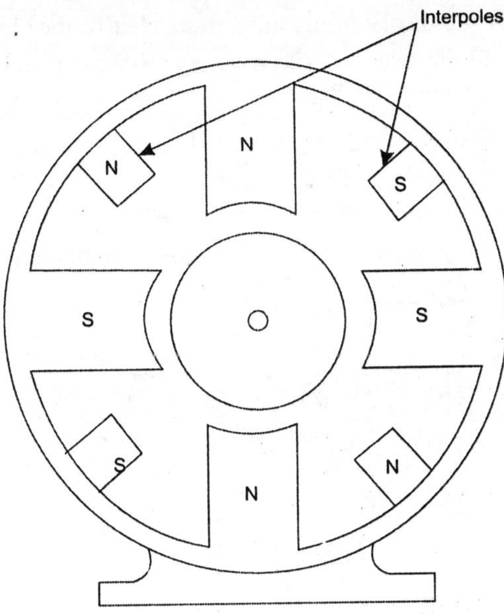

Fig. 4.25

Commutation can be improved *i.e.* current reversal can be made sparkless by using inter poles. These are small poles fixed to the yoke and spaced in between the main pole as shown in Fig. 4.25. They are wound with a few thick copper wire turns and are connected in series with armature so that they carry full armature current. Their polarity is the same as that of the main pole ahead in the direction of rotation.

The e.m.f. generated in the conductor of a d.c. machine is always alternating. The direction of the current in the conductors moving under the effect of north pole is on one side while that of the conductors moving under the effect of south poles in the opposite direction. This has been shown in Fig. 4.26. This reversal of current in a coil has to take place while the two commutator segments to which the coil is connected are being shorted by a brush and the process as a whole is termed as commutation. The time for which the segments remain shorted is quite small may be of the order of about $\frac{1}{500}$ seconds.

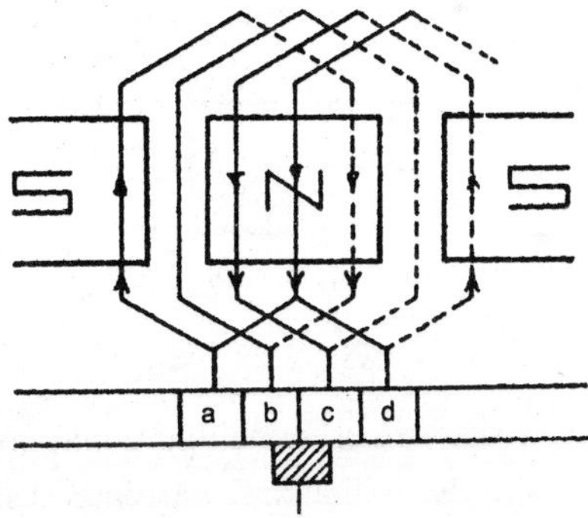

Fig. 4.26. Brush shorting the two commutator segments to which two ends of the coil are connected

If about 100 ampere of the current is to get reversed in an inductive circuit in such a small time, this might cause same difficulties including the sparking at the brushes.

In order to understand the process of commutation more clearly, the coils and commutation segments are shown as in Fig. 4.27 where the two ends of any one coil are connected to adjacent segments as in lap winding.

If it is assumed that the armature is moving from right to left and that the current per conductor is I amps, and assuming the brush to be + ve, then coil C is carrying current from right to left and coil A is carrying current from left to right. Coil B which lies in between coil A and C is connected to commutator segments 1 and 2. The variation of current in coil B is required to be seen.

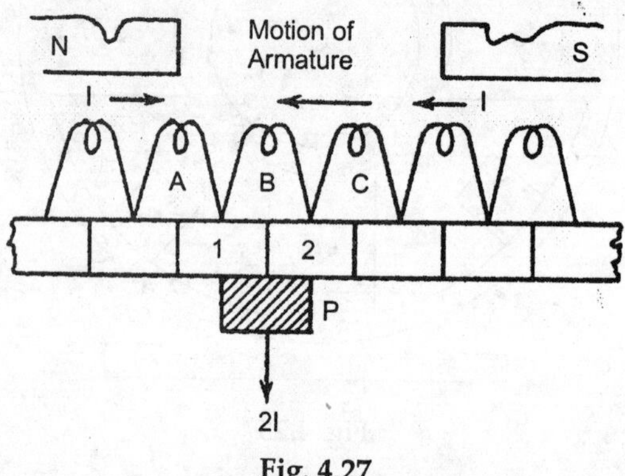

Fig. 4.27

The current in coil B remains at its full value from Right (R) to Left (L) until brush P begins to make contact with segment 2 of the commutator. This is shown in Fig. 4.28 when brush P makes contact with segment 2, part of the current i_1, of coil B flows out to the brush through segment 2 and remaining current ($I - i_1$), flows through coil B. The magnitude of this current i_1 goes on increasing as the contact area of the brush P with segment 2 increases and accordingly the current $(I - i_1)$ through the coil B goes on decreasing.

If current distribution between segments 1 and 2 were determined by the areas of contacts of these segments with brushes only, then as the movement of armature or commutator takes place, the current through coil B decreases linearly as is shown in Fig. 4.29.

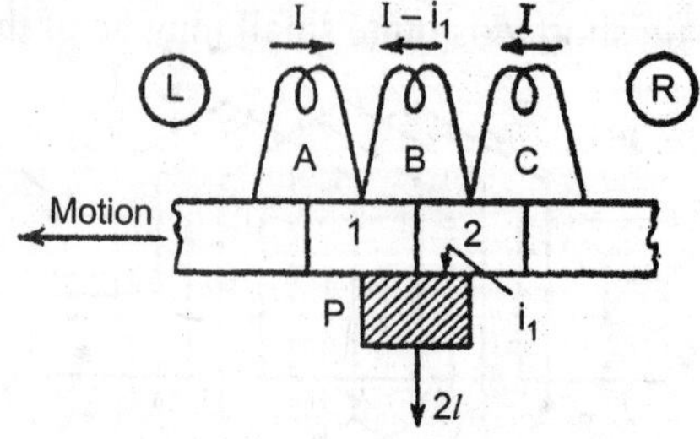

Fig. 4.28

It is evident from Fig. 4.29 that when brush is making equal contact with segments 1 and 2 the current through coil B becomes zero because in that case current I is supplied by coil A and I by coil C, so that total current through brush P still remains = 2 I. If the armature moves further, the current in coil B gets reversed. This is shown in Fig. 4.30.

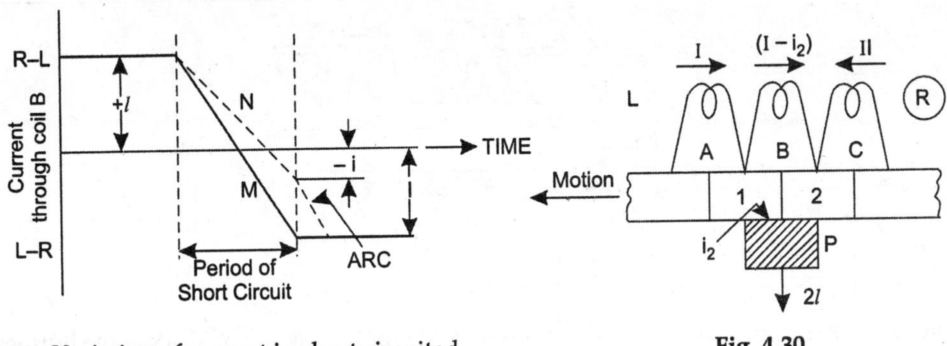

Fig. 4.29. Variation of current in short circuited coil.

Fig. 4.30

Fig. 4.30 represents the position of the coils near the end of short circuit because a little movement of the armature further would just put the brush in contact with segment 2 only.

Now since a small area of segment 1 is coming in contact with brush *P*, therefore the current delivered by segment 1 to brush *P* is small equal to i_2. Thus the remaining current $(I - i_2)$ flows through the coil *B* from left to right. As soon as the contact of segment with the brush gets broken, current i_2 becomes zero and in that case the current through coil *B* attains full value of *I* from left to right. Under these conditions, there should not be any sparking at the brush.

This linear variation of the current in short-circuited coil is referred to as straight line or linear commutation.

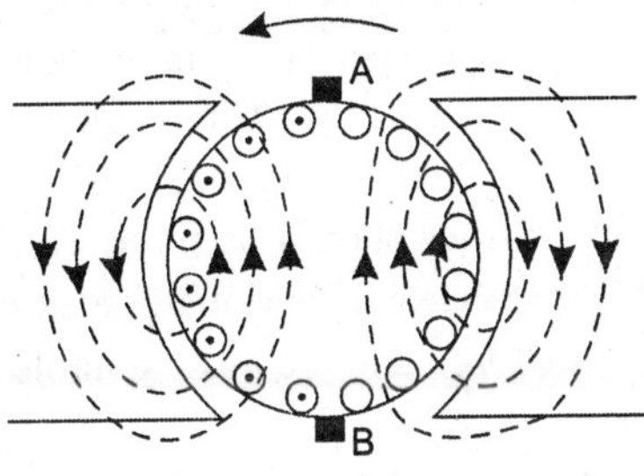

Fig. 4.31

It has already been explained in armature reaction that armature currents have their own magnetic field produced. The diagram has been reproduced as shown in Fig. 4.31 which shows the direction of magnetic field set up by armature currents which is in the cross to actual magnetic field of the main poles from the direction of magnetic field (cross) set up by the armature currents and assuming the director of rotation of the clockwise, it can be found out that additional e.m.f. is generated in a conductor moving near the brush A and the direction of this e.m.f. would be towards the paper. This direction is the same as the direction in which the current was flowing in the conductor before the latter was short circuited by the brush. This generated voltage is known as reactance voltage and is responsible for delaying the reversal of current in the short circuited coil. This delay is shown by curve N in Fig. 4.29. Due to this reactance voltage developed, the current in coil *B* grows to same value *i* at the time when segment 1 is due to break contact with the brush as shown in Fig. 4.32. the remainder current $(I - i)$ has to pass between segment 1 and the brush in the form of the arc. This arc rapidly gets extinguished and the current through coil *B* grows quickly from *i* to *I*.

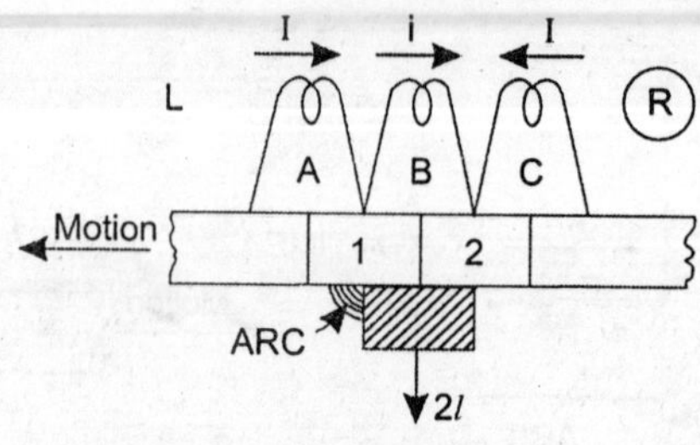

Fig. 4.32

It is in fact this reactance voltage which is responsible for production of spark at the brushes in d.c. machine and most of the methods of reducing sparking are aimed at reduction or neutralisation of this reactance voltage.

4.18. METHODS OF IMPROVING COMMUTATION

There are three methods of improving commutation.

(*i*) By increasing the brush contact resistance.

(*ii*) By shifting the position of brushes.

(*iii*) By using commutating poles.

(*i*) By increasing the brush conduct resistance

If the brush contact resistance is made very low, a large current shall continue to flow from leading segment to the brush even when the area of contact has decreased to a very small value, making the current density very high. This high current density leads to the formation of an arc when the commutator segment leaves the brush. Thus if the sparking is to be avoided, the contact resistance of the brushes should be made considerably high. This shall improve the commutation to quite a great extent. Various grades of carbon brushes having different contact resistances are manufactured and the most suitable grade for a particular machine can be determined by experience.

(*ii*) By shifting the position of brushes

If the brushes of a generator are moved forward to the magnetic neutral zone *C.D.* as already shown in armature reaction and reproduced in Fig. 4.33, the short circuited coils would not be generating any e.m.f. and the reversal of the current in short circuited coil in that case shall depend upon the relative resistance of the coil and the area of contact between the brush and the segment as explained in method 1.

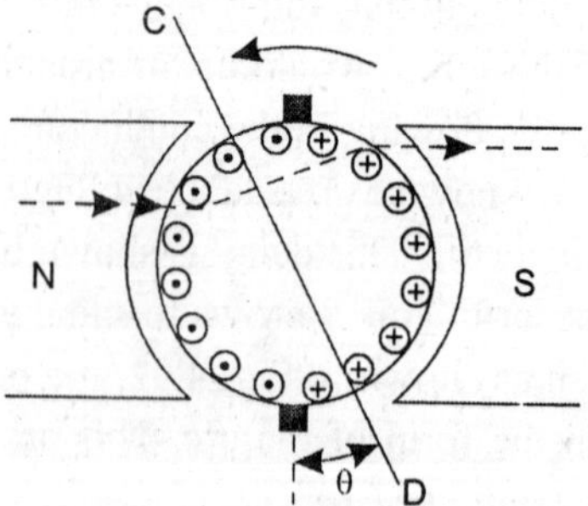

Fig. 4.33

It is however preferred to shift the brushes further a little ahead of the magnetic neutral zone so that the short circuited coil cuts the fringing flux of the main pole immediately in front as shown in Fig. 4.34. E.m.f. (e_g) generated in the coil *B* then helps in forcing the reversal of the current in the coil more hastily. This particular method suffers from a disadvantage that since for every load, position of magnetic neutral axis changes, so the brush position has also got to be shifted. In addition, larger the forward shift in case of generators and a backward shift in case of motors is made in brush position, more shall be demagnetising amp-turns produced.

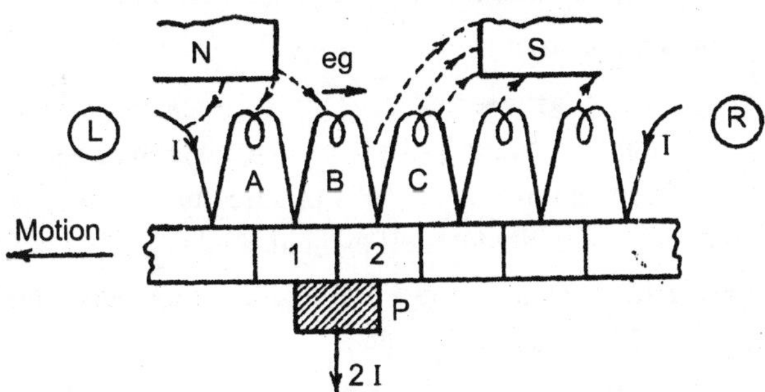

Fig. 4.34

(*iii*) By using Commutating Poles

Instead of shifting the position of brushes beyond the magnetic neutral zone every time, the load changes so as to produce requisite amount of e.m.f. in the short circuited coil which may help in reversal of current, the same effect can be produced by inserting auxiliary poles between the two main poles. The polarity of these poles must be the same as that of the main pole immediately ahead. These poles are known as commutating poles or inter poles. In that case the position of brushes always remains fixed on the geometric neutral axis. The exciting winding of the commutating poles is connected in series with the armature winding so that the flux set up by these poles is proportional to the armature current.

The idea of all this is that the e.m.f. (e_g) generated in that part of the short circuited coil which is opposite to the face of inter pole is sufficient to produce neutralising effect of e.m.f. generated in the same coil by the cross flux due to armature reaction and in addition produce a little more e.m.f. which should help the reversal of current more quickly. This is shown in Fig. 4.35.

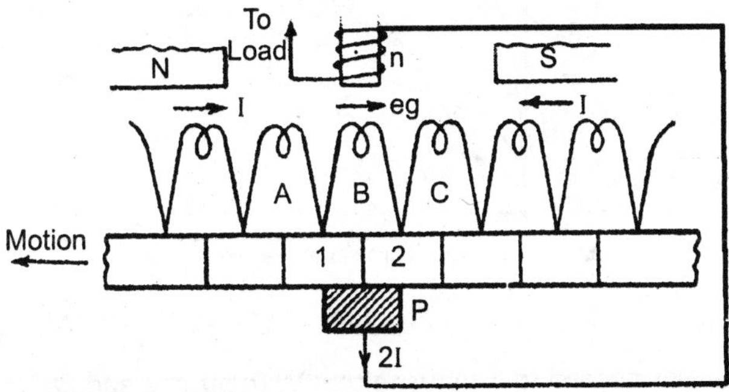

Fig. 4.35

Since the value of e_g is proportional to the armature current and the flux in the inter poles is proportional to the armature current, it is calculated that if value of e_g produced is satisfactory on full load, it is automatically satisfactory on all loads, between no load to full load.

In practice the number of amper-turns per inter-pole is about 1·2 to 1·3 times the number of armature amp turns per pole.

4.19. CHARACTERISTICS AND APPLICATIONS OF D.C. GENERATORS

There are three most important characteristics of D.C. generators.

(1) **Magnetic or open ckt characteristics:** This characteristic is also known as no load characteristic and represents the relation between the generated e.m.f (E_g) and field current (I_f) at a constant speed. The shape of the curve is practically the same for all types of generators whether they are separately excited or self excited.

(2) **External characteristics:** This is the curve which represents the relation between The terminal voltage (V) and the load current (I_L)

(3) **Internal or Total characteristics:** This is the curve which represents the relation between the generated emf (E_g) and armature current (I_a).

Before the characteristics of various types of D.C. generators are studied, it shall be advisable if the relationship between the magnetic flux and the exciting ampere-turns of a generator on no load is considered. It has been observed that ampere-turns of one field coil have to maintain the flux through (*i*) air gap, (*ii*) a pole core, (*iii*) part of yoke (*iv*) one set of armature teeth and part of armature core. As far as air gap is concerned, flux in it is directly proportional to ampere turns as air gap does not get saturated. This is shown by straight line *OA* in Fig. 4.36. For low values of flux, the number of Amp turns needed to send the flux through the iron portion of the magnetic circuit is very small as the iron portion has not got saturated and therefore curve is a straight line. This is shown by the portion *OF* of the curve *OFB* in Fig. 4.36. But when flux becomes more than a certain value, the iron portion, specially the teeth start getting saturated and in that case the increase in amp-turns is far more rapid than the flux as shown by the portion of the flux FB in curve OFB.

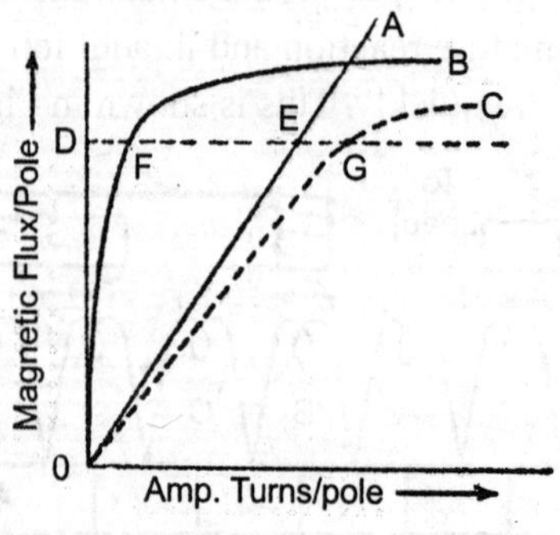

Fig. 4.36

Now *DE* is the Amp. turns needed to establish flux *OD* in air gap and *DF* is the amp. turns needed to establish flux *OD* in iron portion. Then total amp turns per pole needed to establish the flux, *OD* in air gap and iron portion = $DE + DF = DG$ [$\because EG = DF$]. By taking different values of fluxes for different values of amp. turns, the magnetisation curve *OGC* could be established which would give relationship between the useful magnetic flux per pole and the total amp-turns per pole.

4.20. SEPARATELY EXCITED D.C. GENERATORS

Open circuit characteristics (O.C.C.) Open circuit characteristic also sometimes called no-load characteristic, is a graph showing the relation between induced e.m.f. of a generator on no-load and the field current. The e.m.f. E_o of the generator at no-load is given by the formula.

$$E_o = \frac{\phi ZNP}{60\,A}$$

Z, P and *A* being constant

$$\therefore \qquad E_o \propto \phi N.$$

If the speed be kept constant while this characteristic is being drawn, in that case E_o becomes proportional to flux ϕ, but flux is proportional to field current.

Thus E_o becomes proportional to field current I_f. The curve between ϕ and I_f is known as magnetisation characteristic while between E_o and I_f is known as open circuit characteristic. Thus the open circuit characteristic of a generator is identical in shape with its magnetisation characteristic.

The same graph will therefore serve to relate both e.m.f. and field current and also effective magnetic flux and field current.

In order to determine the open circuit characteristic of a machine, it is made to run at normal speed, exciting current is increased from zero to the full value by varying the resistance in the field circuit as shown in Fig. 4.37 and terminal voltage read for each value of exciting current. On open circuit, the terminal voltage is the same as the induced e.m.f. Thus when the graph is plotted between this voltage and field current, it comes out to be curve *OCP* as shown in Fig. 4.37.

If it is assumed that machine has no initial magnetisation, there shall be zero voltage for zero field current and the graph shall pass through origin *O* as shown in Fig. 4.37.

If now the excitation is decreased slowly and for each value of field current, the terminal voltage noted again, the graph does not retrace but it takes the shape *PCS*. Thus even at zero field current also, some voltage is still induced which is given by *OS*. This is due to the fact that the field system has the residual magnetism in the poles. If now the test is repeated, the curve shall retrace the path SCP.

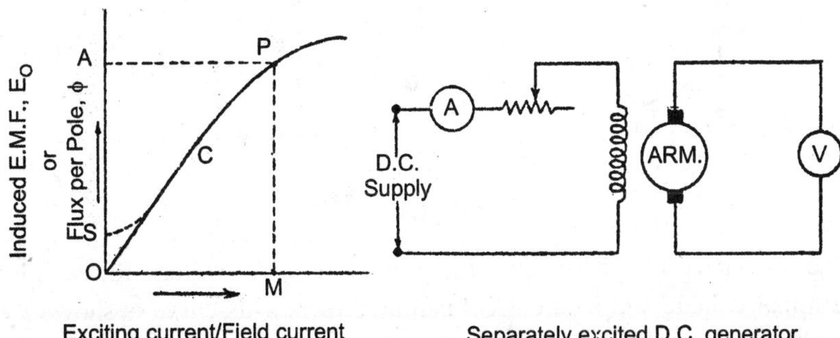

Fig. 4.37. Open circuit characteristics or Magnetisation characteristics

Such curves are termed as open circuit characteristics of the machine.

The curve is almost a straight line up to point P but after that is starts bending. This is due to the fact that field system has started getting saturated *i.e.* flux remains constant even after the value of field current gets increased. Thus voltage also remains constant. This results in portion of curve getting parallel to field current axis. If the speed of the generator is now increased from N to N1 and kept constant at N1 and process repeated, a similar type of curve shall be obtained passing through point S but above the curve *S'CP*. Both these characteristics are shown in Fig. 4.38

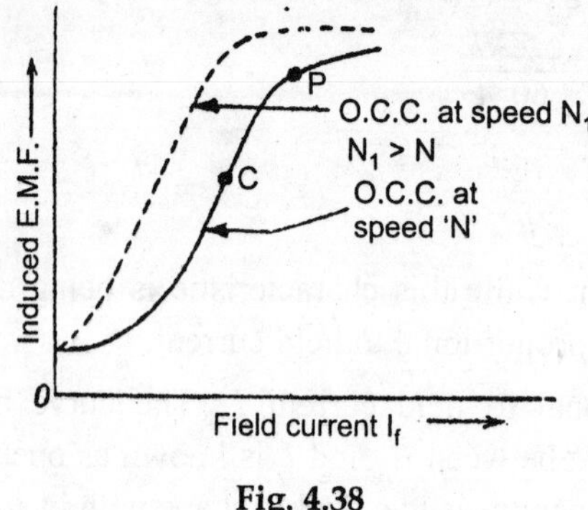

Fig. 4.38

4.21. EXTERNAL CHARACTERISTICS

The curve between terminal voltage V and load current I_L of a D.C. generator is known as external characteristic. It is known as external characteristic because terminal voltage V and current I_L are considered as the external circuit value. This characteristic is considered as quite important as through this it is known as to whether a given generator is suitable for a particular purpose or not. So long as the switch S remains opened in Fig. 4.39, the armature circuit also remains opened and therefore terminal voltage V is the same as the e.m.f. E_o induced in the armature. When switch S is closed, Armature current I_a starts flowing in the circuit. The magnitude of this current shall depend upon the resistance R_L in the circuit.

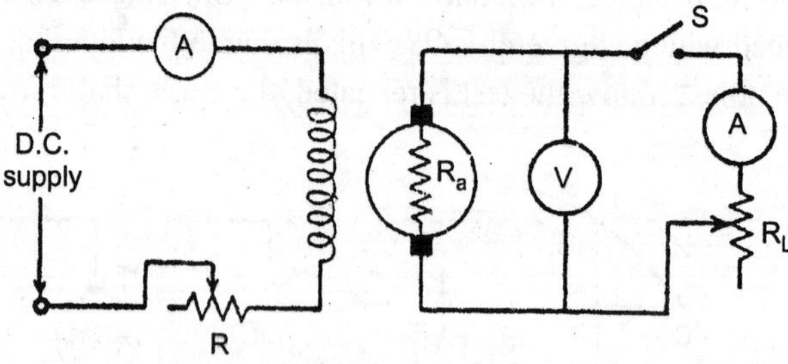

Fig. 4.39

By varying the resistance of resistor R_L and noting the terminal voltage for each load current, the curve between terminal voltage and load current can be drawn. This curve is shown by M in the Fig. 4.40. This is termed as load or external characteristics of the generator. The decrease in terminal voltage with increase of load current is mainly due to resistance drop in the armature circuit.

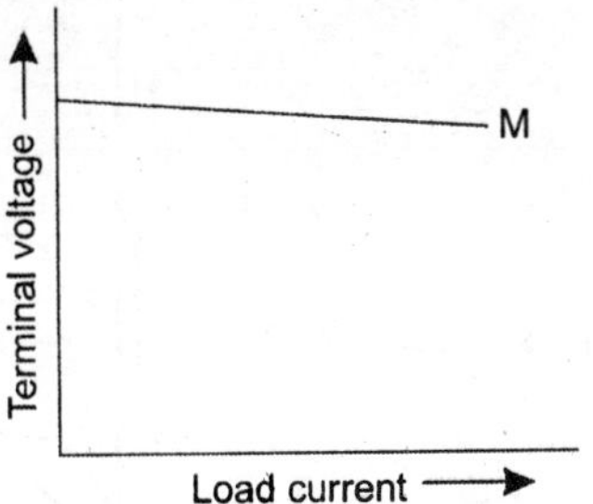

Fig. 4.40. Load characteristics of separately excited generator

Terminal voltage,

$$V = E_o - I_a R_a$$

where V = Terminal voltage

E_o = Generated e.m.f.

I_a = Armature current

R_a = Resistance of the armature circuit.

Thus if the load current is 50 A and the resistance of armature circuit is 0.06 ohm, the voltage drop in the armature circuit is $0.06 \times 50 = 3$ *V*. Thus if the generated voltage is 240 *V* the terminal voltage

$$= 240 - 3 = 237 \text{ V}.$$

Another factor that may cause the decrease in terminal voltage is the decrease of the flux. This is due to:

(*i*) Demagnetising ampere turns of the armature

(*ii*) Magnetic saturation in the armature teeth.

Due to decrease in flux on account of above two factors, induced e.m.f. gets reduced which results in reduction of terminal voltage.

Separately excited has the disadvantage of requiring a separate source of direct current for excitation and is therefore employed in special cases, for instance when a wide range of terminal voltage is required.

4.22. BUILDING UP OF E.M.F. IN SHUNT WOUND GENERATORS

In case of shunt wound generators, field winding is in parallel with the armature and also with the load. Shunt field winding consists of large number of turns of comparatively thin wire which makes its resistance sufficiently high and as a result power absorbed by shunt circuit is 2 to 3% of its rated output. Self-excited generators are supplied field current from the generated e.m.f. in the armature. To start with, there shall be no e.m.f. induced in the armature and therefore no current shall flow in the field winding. If no current flows in the field, no flux is developed and therefore e.m.f. cannot be generated. How is then voltage built up in the armature of D.C. shunt generator?

A shunt generator can excite only if the Poles have some residual magnetism and also resistance of shunt circuit is less than some critical value. The actual value depending upon the machine and also the speed at which it is driven.

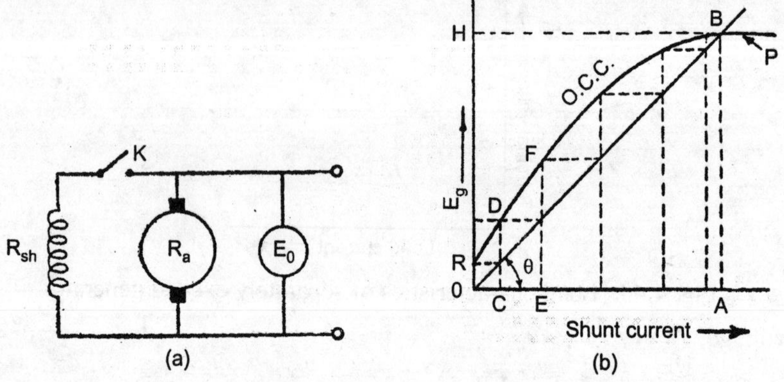

Fig. 4.41. O.C.C. Characteristics

The open circuit characteristics of shunt generator is shown in Fig. 4.41 (*b*) by the curve *P*. For *OA* value of shunt current, the generated voltage is *AB* and therefore corresponding resistance of

$$\text{shunt circuit} = \frac{\textit{Terminal voltage}}{\textit{shunt current}}$$

$$= \frac{AB}{OA}$$

$$= \text{Tan}\,(\angle BOA) = \tan\theta$$

$$= \text{Slope of } OB.$$

When the machine is running at its rated speed with the shunt circuit disconnected by opening of key *K* as shown in Fig. 4.41 (*a*), current in shunt field is zero, but still e.m.f. *OR* is being generated as shown in Fig. 4.41 (*b*). This is on account of the fact that poles do have some residual magnetism.

Now if the shunt field circuit is closed by closing the key "*K*" then e.m.f. *OR* circulates a current *OC* through the shunt field winding. Magnetic flux produced as a result of shunt field current *OC*, generates e.m.f. *CD* in the armature which in turn circulates a larger shunt current *OE*. As a result of this large shunt current *OE*, more e.m.f. is generated. This is shown by *EF* in Fig. 4.41 (*b*). The building up process continues till the e.m.f. generated equals *AB*. During this continuous process of building up the excitation, the e.m.f. generated by the given shunt current (shown by *O.C.C.*) is greater than that required to send the current through the resistance of the shunt circuit (given by line *OB*).

The building up action comes to an end at point *B* where the *O.C.C.* intersects the shunt field resistance line *OB*, the reason being that beyond this point *B*, the voltage generated is less than that is needed to maintain the corresponding field current. Thus for a given *O. C. C.* the maximum voltage built up by the generator is *AB* or *OH* for the maximum field current of *OA*.

It is therefore inferred that the max. voltage built up by a shunt generator is given by *B*, the point of intersection of *O.C.C.* and R_{sh} line *OB*. The position of point *B* depends upon the slope of R_{sh} line which further depends upon the value of shunt field resistance.

4.23. CRITICAL FIELD RESISTANCE OF A SHUNT GENERATOR

Fig. 4.42 shows *O.C.C.* and also the effect of varying the resistance of shunt circuit. Four differed shunt field resistance lines *OB, OC, OE* and *OH* have been drawn (Fig. 4.42).

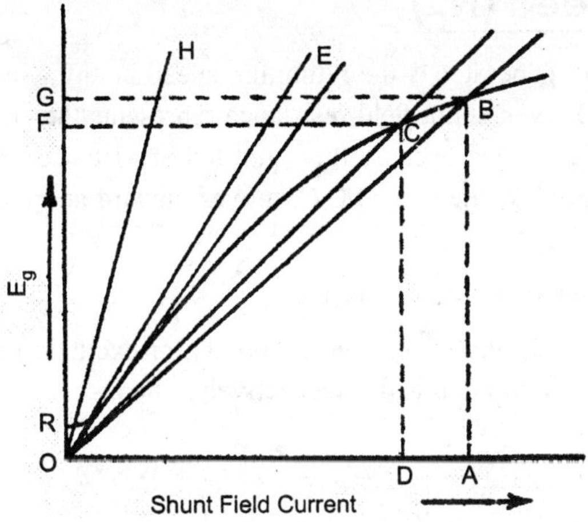

Fig. 4.42

The maximum voltage built up due to shunt field line OC, corresponding to point of intersection C is OF. $\left(\textit{Shunt field resistance being } \frac{OF}{OD}\right)$.

The resistance line OB represents smaller shunt field resistance $\left(\textit{shunt field resistance being } \frac{OG}{OA}\right)$.

There being very small difference between *OG* and *OF*, but there is comparatively large difference between *OA* and *OD*, and therefore e.m.f. induced *OG* is little more than *OF*. Thus as the resistance of the shunt field circuit is decreased, voltage generated increases and as the resistance of shunt field circuit is increased, the slope of resistance line increases and accordingly the maximum voltage generated by the generator decreases.

If the value of shunt resistance is such that the shunt resistance line just touches the *O.C.C. i.e.* it is tangential to *OCC*, in that case the generator will just excite. At this value of the field current, the e.m.f. induced in the generator is extremely sensitive to variation of shunt field resistance *i.e.* a very slight reduction in the value of shunt resistance is accompanied by relatively large increase in the value of e.m.f. and a slight increase in the value of shunt field resistance from this point shall not excite the generator at all and the generator shall not build up any voltage.

This value of shunt field resistance given by the tan ($\angle EOA$) is known as critical resistance of shunt field circuit. This is the maximum value of shunt field resistance at which the generator just excites.

Thus if the resistance of the field circuit is given by resistance line *OH* which does not cut *O.C.C*, the slope of this line is more than the critical resistance line *i.e.* shunt field resistance is more than the critical resistance, in that case the generator shall not build up any voltage.

When the shunt field circuit is broken, the resistance of the field circuit becomes infinite which is more than the critical resistance, and therefore no e.m.f. is generated. The e.m.f. —*OR*— which is generated when the field circuit is broken is on account of residual magnetism in the poles and not on any other account.

4.23.1. Critical Speed (N_C)

The critical speed of a shunt generator is the minimum speed below which it fails to excite. Clearly, it is the speed for which the given shunt field resistance represents the critical resistance. In Fig. 4.43 curve 2 corresponds to critical speed because the shunt field resistance (R_{sh}) line is tangential to it. If the generator runs at full speed *N*, the new O.C.C. moves upward and the R'_{sh} line represents critical resistance for this speed.

$$\therefore \qquad \text{Speed} \propto \text{Critical resistance}$$

In order to find critical speed, take any convenient point *C* on excitation axis and erect a perpendicular so as to cut R_{sh} and R'_{sh} lines at points *B* and *A* respectively. Then,

$$\frac{BC}{AC} = \frac{N_C}{N}$$

$$N_C = N \times \frac{BC}{AC}$$

Fig. 4.33

4.24. CHARACTERISTICS OF A SHUNT GENERATOR

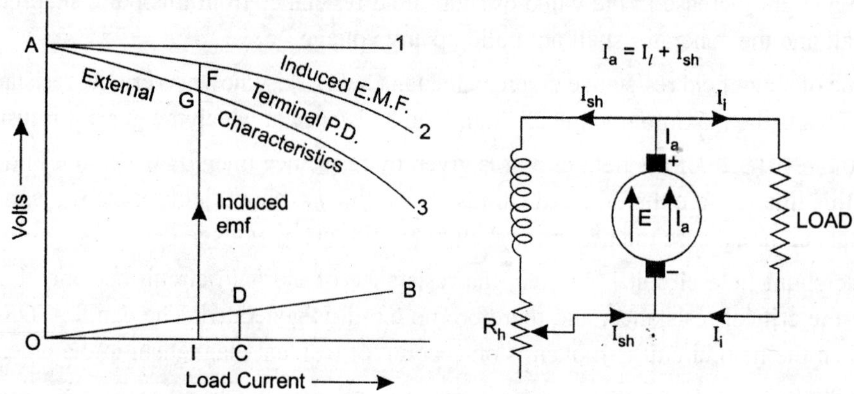

Fig. 4.44. Load characteristics of shunt generator

The simple circuit for drawing characteristics of shunt generator is given in Fig. 4.44.

The machine will generate an e.m.f. whose value is decided by the setting of the regulator resistance R_h, before any load is applied. The no-load voltage shall be given by *OA* on the vertical axis. If there is no armature reaction effect and no internal drop in volts because of armature resistance, the internal characteristics would be the horizontal line shown by graph 1 through A.

But actually when load current is there, current also flows through the armature and this armature current produces a flux which has demagnetising effect (Armature reaction) and as a result, flux per pole falls off as the current increases and therefore the induced e.m.f. also decreases. This is shown by slightly drooping curve 2. From the circuit diagram of Fig. 4.44, it is clear that armature current $I_a = I_l + I_{sh}$. The effect of current I_{sh} is taken into account as follows. A resistance line *OB* is drawn to represent the armature resistance plus the resistance of interpoles *i.e.* total series resistance. The slope of this resistance line *OB* is small because the resistance of the series circuit is small.

In any load current *OI*, the appropriate shunt current *IC* is added to get the length *OC* which gives the total armature current. The perpendicular *DC* thus represents the voltage drop in the series circuit (product of series resistance and armature current).

For the load current *OI*, the induced e.m.f. is given by the ordinate *FI* and therefore if $FG = DC$ is marked off from *FI*, the remainder *GI* will give the terminal potential difference and *G* shall be a point on the external characteristics.

Similarly other points can be obtained and the graph of terminal potential difference drawn which shall come out to be similar to that of curve 3.

Thus curve 3 represents the external characteristics of shunt generator. It can be seen from the shape of the curve that highest voltage is at no load, the voltage falling off some what as the out put current is increased. In fact the fall from no load to normal full load is so small that this fall can always be compensated by suitable adjustment of shunt regulator R_h and full voltage maintained. For this reason, the shunt generators are termed as constant voltage machines.

In fact external characteristics can be obtained experimentally by running the machine to its normal speed and then loading it by a variable load. The reading of the terminal voltage obtained for each value of load current and graph plotted. This gives the external characteristics as shown in Fig. 2.84 by curve 1. Internal characteristics can be deduced in the following way. A shunt field resistance line *OC* is drawnand another line *OB* representing resistance of series circuit (*i.e.* resistance of armature plus interpoles) is also drawn. Any horizontal distance measured from *OA* on to shunt resistance line will give the shunt current in relation to corresponding terminal voltage. For example for a terminal voltage, *OF*, the shunt current is *FG*. By producing *FG* horizontally and marking of *HK* equal to *FG*, the armature current *FK* can be obtained for a terminal voltage of *OF* the armature current.

$$FH = \text{Load current,}$$

$$FG = HK = \text{shunt current}$$

$$FK = FH + HK = I + I_{sh} = I_a,$$

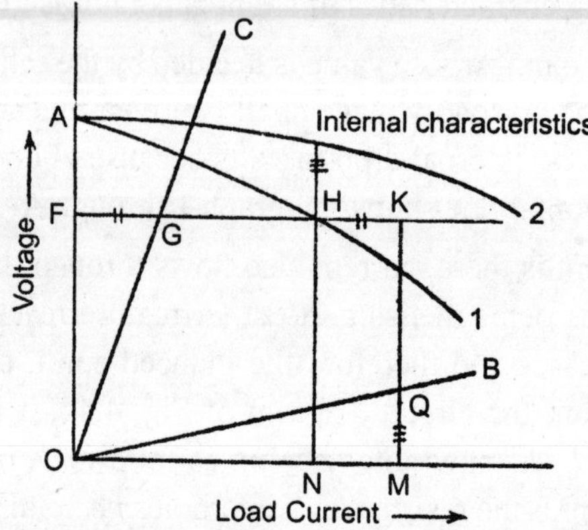

Fig. 4.45. Total characteristics of shunt generator

By drawing the ordinate through *K*, the internal voltage drop *QM* can be obtained. The line current (load current) corresponding to the drop *QM* is *ON* or *FH*. Hence if *HP* = *QM* is marked off, then total e.m.f. *PN* is obtained. Thus point *P* is obtained on the internal *characteristics*. Similarly number of such points are obtained and curve 2 is obtained which represents the total characteristics or internal characteristics of shunt generator. External or internal characteristics of shunt wound generator are as per Fig. 4.45 where the terminal voltage falls as the load current is increased by decreasing the load resistance.

The decrease in terminal voltage with load current is only up to point *S* as shown in Fig. 4.46. If the load resistance is decreased after this, the increase in load current does not take place. The reason is that at this value of load current, the demagnetising effect due to armature reaction is so high, that over all flux gets reduced tremendously which reduces the e.m.f. induced in the generator which in turn reduces the terminal voltage, thus reducing the load current to a value below to its previous value.

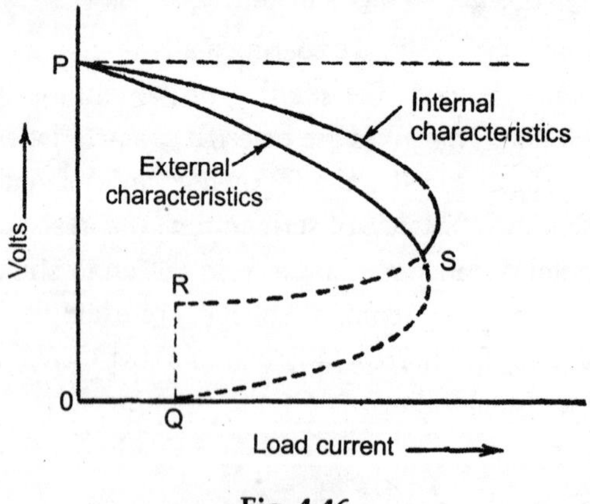

Fig. 4.46

When the load resistance becomes so small that virtually the terminals could be assumed to be short circuited, in that case the terminal voltage should be zero and hence excitation also becomes zero, under these conditions, the only current that flows in the circuit is that produced by voltage *QR* due to residual magnetism. Thus when shunt generators get connected to a low resistance or get short circuited, a very high value of current shall not flow as terminal voltage falls down as shown above and accordingly current gets reduced and thus shunt generator gets protected against short circuits automatically.

4.25. APPLICATIONS

Since the variation in terminal voltage of D.C. Shunt generator with load current is not much, as is seen from the load characteristics. So shunt generators are used where approximately constant voltage is required to be generated and which should not change much with the variation of load current.

4.26. CAUSES OF FAILURE OF VOLTAGE BUILD-UP IN D.C. SHUNT GENERATORS

There are certain reasons due to which a d.c. shunt generator fails to build up the voltage. These are given as follows:

1. **Failure due to residual-magnetism**

   The starting of d.c. generator depends upon the residual magnetism in the field, (as explained earlier). At the Ist moment of starting the d.c. generator, the residual magnetism in the field comes into picture, by virtue of which some e.m.f. is generated in the armature winding and due to this e.m.f., field current 'I_f' starts flowing in the field winding, hence strengthening the magnetic field. But if due to some reasons the residual magnetism vanishes, the generator will fail to build up the voltage because the magnetic field shall not be sufficient at the starting time of the d.c. generator.

   To overcome this a separate source of d.c. voltage is applied across the shunt field. Due to this, current flows in the shunt winding, which results in production of the magnetic field and now this magnetic field is sufficient to build up the voltage. The separate source of dc 'current' is connected for a very short time and the process is called the "Flashing of the field".

2. **Failure due to "Reversal of Field Connections"**

   At start the e.m.f. generated in the armature is due to the residual magnetism of the field. Due to this e.m.f., the current flows in the field winding and this current should produce the magnetic flux in the same direction as that of the residual magnetism. If the connections of the field are reversed due to some reason, the direction of the magnetic field produced by the current flowing through the field winding will be opposite to that of the direction of the residual magnetism, the result of which will be neutralising the effect of magnetic field rather strengthening it. Hence the generator will fail to build up the voltage. This can be avoided by reversing the connections of field winding.

3. **Failure due to "Open Field-Connections"**

   As discussed in *O.C.C.* in Fig. 2·82, regarding critical resistance, if field connections of dc generator are opened due to some reasons the resistance offered by the field winding will be infinite *i.e.* much greater than the critical value of the resistance, hence the generator will not be able to build up the voltage.

4.27. D.C. SERIES GENERATOR

In case of series generators, the armature, field and load are all connected in series with each other and therefore carry the same current. This is shown in Fig. 4.47. Let us assume the load to be of a variable resistance, which can be adjusted to any desired value. Assuming this load resistance to be quite high to start with, the small e.m.f. induced because of residual magnetism shall be able to send a very small current in the series circuit. This small current shall not be able to develop more e.m.f. in the generator. This can be seen from the curves of Fig. 4.47. The magnetisation characteristics of the generator drawnfrom a separate excitation is shown in Fig. 4.47. For any point B on this curve, BM represents the voltage and OM as current.

$$\therefore \quad \frac{BM}{OM} = \frac{Voltage}{Current} = \text{Resistance}$$

$$= \text{Slope of the line } OA.$$

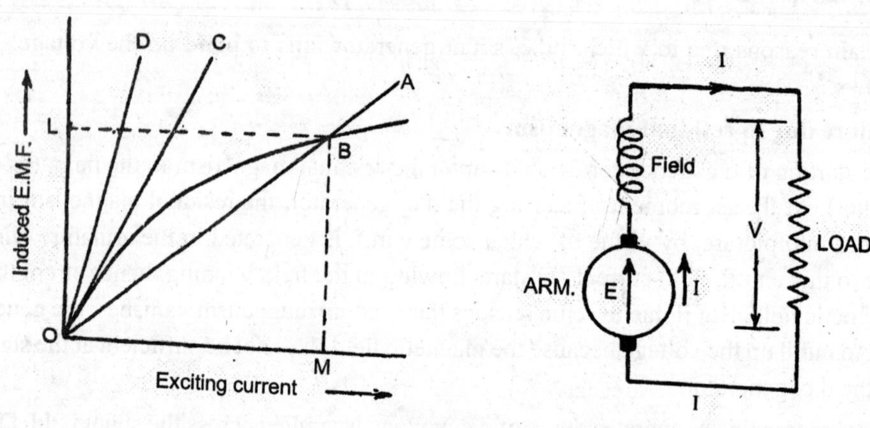

Fig. 4.47

Thus it can be seen that if number of lines are drawn through O, the slope of each line shall represent the resistance. If such a line cuts the magnetisation curve at point B, then BM represents the voltage and OM represents the current of the machine having a resistance equal to slope of the line OA. If this resistance line does not cut the characteristics, there cannot be any voltage developed. Thus the slope of the line OC represents the maximum resistance which a generator can have so that it is able to generate e.m.f. in a machine running at a particular speed.

This resistance is known as the critical resistance. If the resistance of the machine is more than this critical value represented by the slope of the line OD, then the machine shall not generate any voltage. Thus *for the generator to develop any voltage, the resistance of the machine should be lesser than the critical resistance defined above.*

If the resistance of the machine is lesser than the critical value, the machine develops a small voltage on account of its residual magetism, which sends a small current in the series circuit, increasing the field Amp-turns which further increase the flux. This increased flux develops more e.m.f. which sends more current through the field circuit. This process of increase of flux and then increase of e.m.f. goes on till the flux and e.m.f. settle down to a value determined by the resistance.

4.28. CHARACTERISTICS OF D.C. SERIES GENERATOR

The curve shows the relation between no-load generated e.m.f. E_0 and field current I_f ($I_f = I_a = I_l$ in case of D.C. series generator) when the generator is made to run at a constant speed. When no load is there across the generator, field current shall also become zero in this case, therefore no voltage shall be developed. For this reason, this curve is obtained by exciting the series field coils separately. Since no current shall flow in the armature, the terminal voltage shall be no load generated e.m.f. E_0. The generated e.m.f. increases with the load current because the load current is also field current and with the increase in field current the voltage generated also gets increased. Thus curve 1 in Fig. 4.48 represents *O.C.C.* or open circuit characteristics.

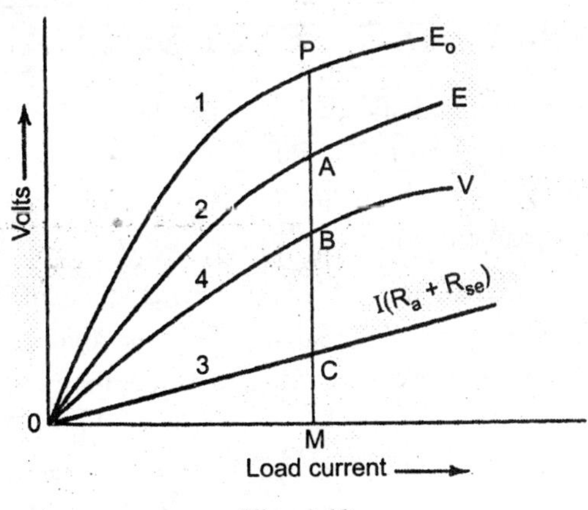

Fig. 4.48

In fact when the generator is supplying some load to the external circuit, the current flowing in the armature produces flux which has demagnetising effect on the main field, thus reducing the total flux set up by the generator and also reducing the voltage induced in the machine. Thus voltage E developed in the machine at load is lesser than the one developed at no load. This is shown by the curve 2 in Fig. 4.48 and is known as *Internal Characteristics of the Machine*.

Thus the curve representing the internal characteristics of the machine shall always lie below the *O.C.C.*

In fact terminal voltage of the Machine is always lesser than the induced voltage by an amount equal to voltage drop across the combined resistance of the armature and series field.

Thus terminal voltage,

$$V = E - I(R_a + R_{se})$$

where

V = Terminal voltage

E = E.m.f induced

R_a = Resistance of the armature.

R_{se} = Resistance of the series field.

and $I(R_a + R_{se})$ is the total internal drop which is represented by the straight line 3 through the origin in Fig. 2.87. If for any point P on curve 1, an ordinate *PM* is drawn cutting curves 2 and 3 at points *A* and *C* respectively,

then

AM = The induced e.m.f.E,

CM = internal voltage drop for current OM.

If distance $AB = CM$ is marked off on the line PM then point B shall lie on the curve of terminal potential difference against load current. By taking various points such as P on curve 1 and drawing ordinates such as PM, and marking off distances such as CM on lines such as AM, a series of points can be obtained and curve drawn. The curve such as shown by 4 is obtained and is known as External characteristic. From the curve of external characteristic, it can be seen that as the load current increases, the terminal voltage increases, reaches a maximum and then decreases.

4.29. APPLICATIONS OF D.C. SERIES GENERATOR

It can be seen from the load characteristic of Fig. 4.48 that as load current increases, voltage also increases. This is shown by the portion OB of curve 4 which is almost a straight line. Thus a series wound generator is quite unsuitable when the voltage is to be maintained constant or even approximately constant over a wide range of load current.

However this property of the *D.C.* series generator is made use of in a booster which a *D.C.* series generator used to boost up the voltage of the supply. Suppose that at the far end of the transmission line, there is an appreciable voltage drop due to line resistance, then this drop is proportional to the line current (drop being equal to IR). If a booster is inserted in the line and adjusted to give an additional voltage equal to the line drop at all currents, the voltage at the far end can be maintained constant.

4.30. COMPOUND GENERATORS

In this type of generator, a series field is connected in series with the armature in addition to the shunt field. It has already been observed that the terminal voltage of shunt generator falls with the load. This fall can be compensated by increasing the field excitation with the help of hand regulators. Sometimes when there are large variations in load currents, compensation by hand regulators is not possible and in that case series field winding is provided along with shunt field winding which provides to some extent automatic compensation.

One such compound generator with C as shunt field coils and S as series field coils is shown in Fig. 4.49 (*a*). Shunt field windings and series field windings are so connected that their Ampere-turns help each other. Thus larger the load current, the greater shall be the series field Amp. Turns to help shunt field amp. Turns and thus greater shall be the flux to generate higher e.m.f.

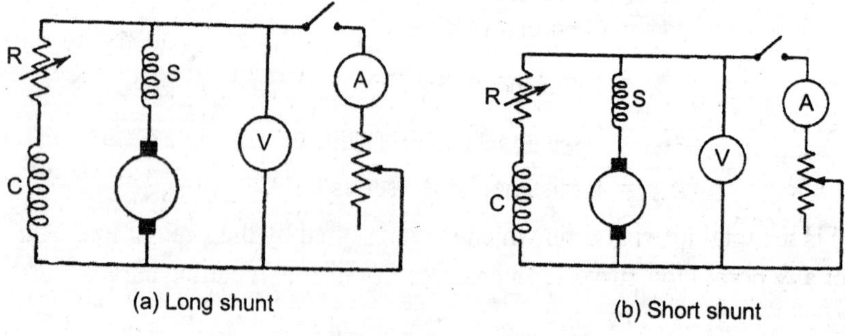

Fig. 4.49. Compound wound generator

It makes very little difference whether shunt winding is connected with long shunt as shown in Fig. 4.49 (*a*) or short shunt as shown in Fig. 4.49 (*b*) in which shunt field winding is connected directly across the armature. Shunt field winding has large number of turns with very small current in them whereas series field winding has few turns with large current (load current) flowing through it. Curve *S* in Fig. 4.50 shows the load characteristic of the machine when only shunt winding is connected in the circuit.

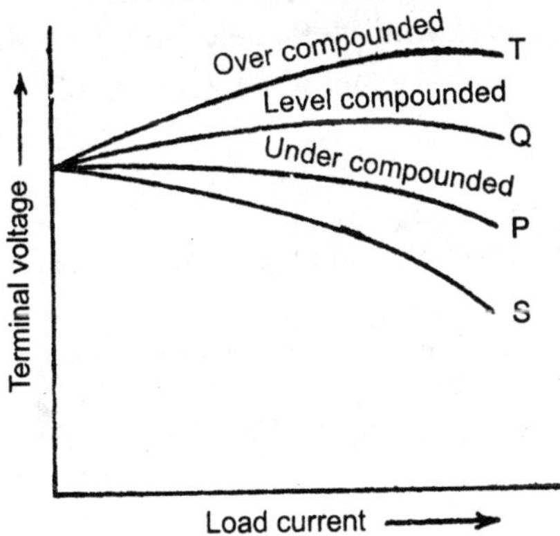

Fig. 4.50. Load characteristics of compound wound generator

Now if the series field is also connected in the circuit, the total flux gets increased due to increase in the ampere-turns which produces more induced e.m.f. and thus fall in terminal voltage with increase in load is reduced as indicated by curve *P* in Fig. 4.50. Such a compound machine is known as under compounded.

If the series turn are increased little more, the amp. turns further increase which results in more amount of total flux developed thus generating more voltage and this increase thus compensating almost completely the otherwise voltage drop because of load current at all currents.

Thus the terminal voltage remains practically constant between full load to no-load. Such type of compound generator is known as *level compounded generator* and the load characteristic of this generator is shown by curve *Q* in Fig. 4.50.

If the series turns are further increased, by the same argument, the terminal voltage now increases with the load current.

Such type of compound generator is known as *over compounded generator*. The load characteristics of over compounded generator are shown by curve *T* in Fig. 4.50.

4.31. APPLICATIONS

An over compounded generator may be used to compensate for the voltage drop in a feeder system. For example if the voltage to be maintained at the far end of the feeder is say 430 V and if the total resistance of the feeder is 0.1 Ω, the voltage drop due to a current of 200 *A* is 20 V. Thus voltage at the sending end of the feeder must be (430 + 20) = 450 V. When there is no load on the feeder, the voltage at the sending end is the same as at the far end say 430 V, thus a generator, over compounded to give 430 V on no load and 450 V with 200 A maintains the voltage at the far end of the feeder approx. constant over this range of load.

Example 4.15. The open circuit characteristics of DC generator when separately excited and driven at 1100 R.P.M. is given by:

Field, Amps	0.5	1.0	1.5	2.0	2.5	3.0	3.5
O.C. Voltage	61.5	123	165	198	220	238	253

If the generator is shunt connected with a total field circuit resistance of 80 Ω., determine (i) The no load e.m.f and (*ii*) the out put current when terminal voltage is 200 V, if the armature resistance is 0.1 ohm.

[AMIE Elect. M/cs. (New scheme) Nov. 94]

Solution.

(*i*) The open circuit characteristics of shunt generator with the given data has been shown drawn by the curve *OABD* in Fig. 4.51.

Field resistance = 80 Ω

If field current is assumed to be 2 *A*, then voltage across the field = 80 × 2 = 160 *V* which is also the voltage generated on open circuit.

Thus (2A, 160 V) should be a point on the resistance line and is represented by point *P*.

O and *P* are joined together and the line is extended to meet the *O.C.C.* at point *C*. Thus line *OPC* represents the resistance line. Thus corresponding to 80 ohms resistance of shunt field winding, the voltage generated is 237.5 V. This can be seen by the ordinate of point *C*, the point of intersection of resistance line and *O.C.C.*

∴ No load e.m.f. = 237.5V **Ans.**

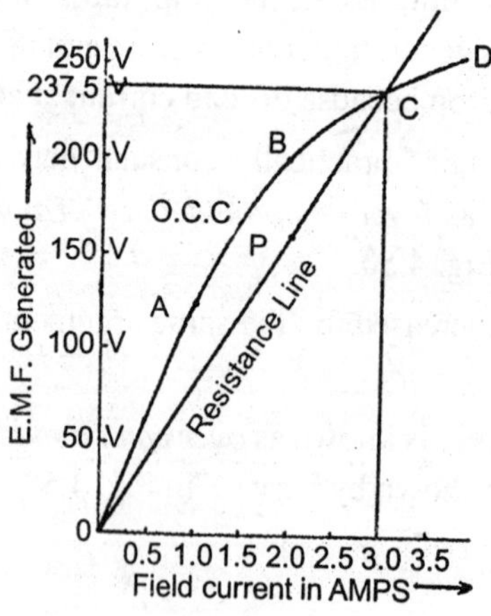

Fig. 4.51

(*ii*) Terminal voltage $V = 200\ V$

Shunt field resistance = 80 Ω

∴ Field current $= \frac{200}{80} = 2.5$ A.

Corresponding to field current of 2.5 A, the e.m.f. induced in the armature is 220 V (from the given data of *O.C.C.* and also from the graph drawn for *O. C. C.*)

Thus $E = 220$ V

$$V = E - I_a R_a$$

or $$I_a R_a = E - V$$

$\therefore$ $$I_a = \frac{E - V}{R_a}$$

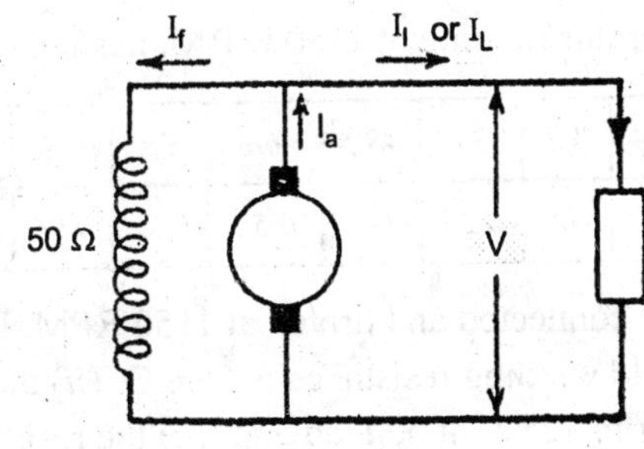

Fig. 4.52

Armature current, $I_a = \frac{220 - 200}{0.1} = \frac{20}{0.1} = 200\ A$

The output current = Load current.

$= I_l = I_a - I_f = 200 - 2{\cdot}5$

= **197.5 A Ans.**

Example 4.16. A short shunt compound generator supplies a load current of 100 A at 250 V. The generator has the following winding resistances: Shunt field 130 ohms, armature 0.1 ohms and series field 0.1 ohm. Find the e.m.f generated if the brush drop is 1 volt per brush.

(AMIE Elect. M/cs. May, 1997)

Solution. Short shunt compound generator is shown connected in Fig. 4.53 current in the series field = 100 A.

$\therefore$ Voltage across the armature = 250 + 100 × 0.1 = 260 V

Voltage across shunt field = voltage across the armature = 260 V

Current through shunt field

$$\frac{260}{130} = 2\text{ A}$$

$\therefore$ I_a = current through armature

= 100 + 2 = 102 A

voltage drop across the armature

$= I_a R_a = 102 \times 0.1 = 10.2$ volts.

$\therefore$ Induced e.m.f. in the generator,

= 260 + 10.2

= 270.2 V

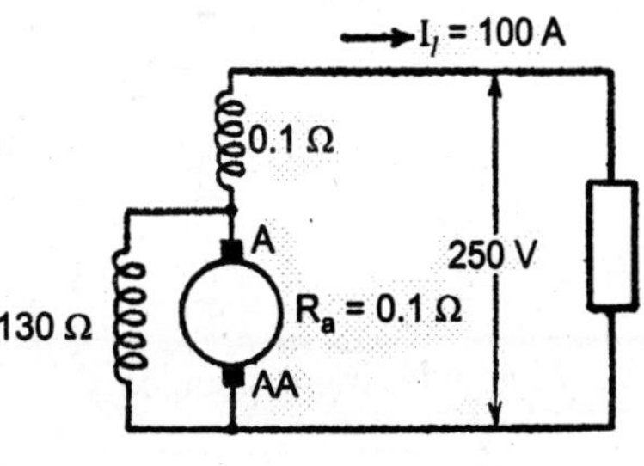

Fig. 4.53

Total voltage drop across two brushes,

$$= 2 \text{ V.}$$

∴ E.m.f. generated in the armature

$$= 270.2 + 2$$

$$= \mathbf{272.2 \text{ V Ans.}}$$

Example 4.17. A D.C. generator running at 1150 R.P.M. has the magnetisation curve as follows:

O.C voltage (in volts)	5.2	30	48.5	60	78	98	115	125	140	150
Field current (in amp)	0	0.22	0.4	0.52	0.72	0.96	1.18	1.33	1.59	1.82

When the generator is shunt connected and driven at 1150 RPM, Find (*i*) no load voltage to which the generator shall build if its field winding resistance is 66.6 Ω. (*ii*) the resistance that must be inserted in the field to bring the generator to 125 V at no load and (*iii*) the resistance that must be inserted in the field to prevent the generator from building up to more than 50 V at no load.

(*AMIE Elect. M/cs. May,* 75)

Solution.

(*i*) Open circuit characteristics of shunt generator with the given data is shown drawn by curve *OA BC* which is further extended upto point *D* as shown in Fig. 4.54.

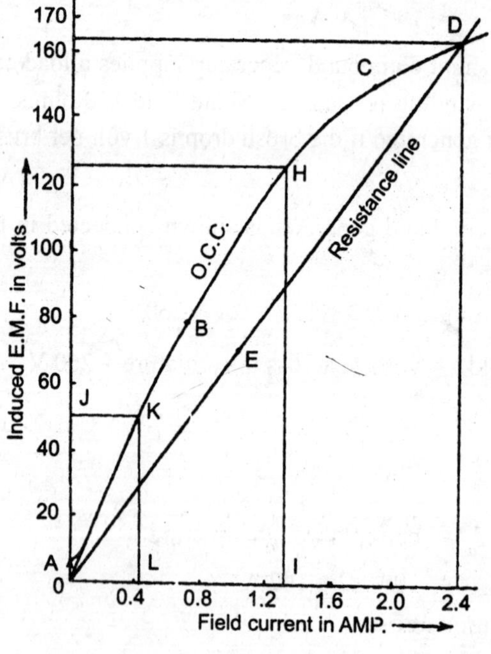

Fig. 4.54

Field winding resistance

$$= 66.6 \ \Omega$$

Assuming the field current to be

$$= 1 \text{ A}$$

Voltage across field winding on open circuit.

$$= 66.6 \times 1 = 66.6 \text{ V.}$$

Thus we have a point E (1, 66.6) on the resistance line. Join OE and extend it further so that it cuts the $O.C.C.$ at point D. The OD is the resistance line.

The ordinate of point D is OF

$$= 163\ V$$

Thus max. no-load voltage for shunt field winding of 66.6 Ω

$$= \mathbf{163\ V\ Ans.}$$

(*ii*) G is the point on the voltage axis which represents a voltage of 125 V at no load. Corresponding to this voltage of 125 V, the field current is as given by OI

$$= 1.32 \text{ A}$$

∴ Total resistance of field circuit

$$= \frac{\textit{Open circuit voltage}}{\textit{Corresponding field current}}$$

$$= \frac{125}{1.32} = 94.7\ \Omega$$

Resistance of field winding

$$= 66.6\ \Omega$$

Additional resistance to be added in the field circuit

$$= 94.7 - 66.6 = \mathbf{28.1\ \Omega\ Ans.}$$

(*iii*) J is the point on the voltage axis which represents a voltage of 50 V at no-load. Corresponding to this voltage of 50 V, the field current is as given by $OL = 0.44\ A$.

∴ Total resistance of field circuit when 50 V is to be generated on no-load,

$$= \frac{50}{0.44} = 113.6\ \Omega$$

∴ Additional resistance to be added in the field circuit for generating voltage not more than 50 V is

$$= 113.6 - 66.6 = 47\ \Omega \text{ Ans.}$$

Example 4.18. An 8-pole lap connected armature has 960 conductors, a flux of 4 mega lines (40 m wb) per pole and a speed of 400 R.P.M. Calculate the e.m.f generated on open circuit. If the armature were wave connected, at what speed it must be driven to generate 400 V.

(AMIE Elect M/cs, May, 1976)

Solution.

E.M.F. developed in a generator is given by,

$$E = \frac{\phi ZNP}{60A}$$

(i) $P = 8$

$Z = 960$

$\phi = 40 \text{ m-wb} = 40 \times 10^{-3} = 0.04 \text{ wb}$

$N = 400 \text{ RPM.}$

It is lap connected, therefore, A

= number of parallel paths

= number of poles = 8

$$\therefore \quad E = \frac{0.04 \times 960 \times 400 \times 8}{60 \times 8}$$

= 256 V Ans.

(*ii*) $E = 400 \text{ V}$

When armature is wave connected, $A = 2$

$$\therefore \quad 400 = \frac{0.04 \times 960 \times N \times 8}{60 \times 2}$$

$$\text{or} \quad N = \frac{400 \times 120}{0.04 \times 960 \times 8}$$

= 156. 25 RPM Ans.

Example 4.19. In a 50 KW 230/250 V (230 V on no-load and 250 V on load) over compounded d.c. generator (long shunt), the flux per pole required to produce 230 V on no-load at 1050 RPM is 0.06 wb. The resistance of the armature and series field are 0.04 Ω and 0.01 Ω. respectively and the shunt field resistance is 100 ohm. Calculate the value of flux per pole at full load, 1000 RPM. Neglect brush drop.

(AMIE, Winter 1977)

Solution.

At no load, e.m.f. induced,

$E = 230 \text{ V}$

$\phi = 0.06 \text{ Wb.}$

$N = 1050 \text{ RPM.}$

$$\therefore \quad E = \frac{\phi ZNP}{60A}$$

$$\text{or} \quad 230 = \frac{0.06\, ZP \times 1050}{60A}$$

$$= \frac{ZP \times 1050}{1000A}$$

$$\therefore \quad \frac{ZP}{A} = \frac{230 \times 1000}{1050}$$

$$\text{Output on full load} = 50 \text{ kW.}$$

$$\text{Output voltage} = 250\ V$$

$$\text{Load current} = \frac{50 \times 1000}{250} = 200 \text{ A}$$

$$\text{Shunt field current} = \frac{250}{100} = 2.5 \text{ A}$$

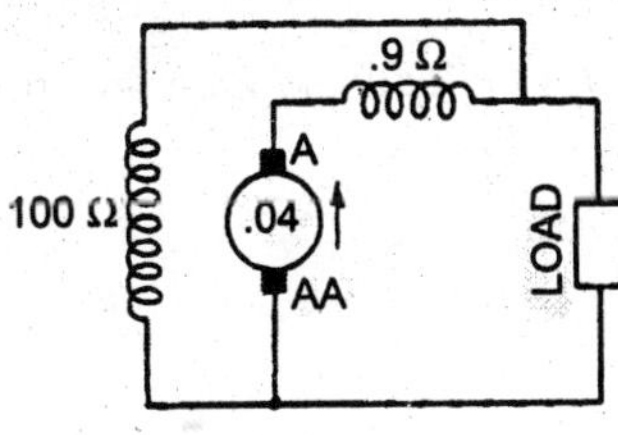

Fig. 4.55

Current in series field winding

$$= 200 + 2.5 = 202.5 \text{ A}$$

Voltage drop across series field winding

$$= 202.5 \times 0.01$$

$$= 2.025 \text{ V.}$$

$$\text{Voltage across A–} \quad \text{AA} = 250 + 2.025$$

$$= 252.025\ V$$

Voltage drop across armature

$$= 202.5 \times 0.04 = 8.100 \text{ V}$$

$$= 8.1 \text{ V}$$

$$\text{Voltage developed} = 252.025 \times 8.1$$

$$= 260.125 \text{ V}$$

Now $$E = \frac{\phi ZNP}{60A}$$

$$\text{but now speed in R.P.M} = 1000$$

and $$\frac{ZP}{A} = \frac{230 \times 1000}{1050}$$

$$\therefore \quad 260.125 = \frac{\phi}{60} \times \frac{1000}{1} \times \frac{230 \times 1000}{1050}$$

$$\phi = \frac{260.125 \times 60 \times 1050}{230 \times 10^6}$$

$$= \mathbf{0.07125 \text{ wb}} \quad \textbf{Ans.}$$

Example 4.20. A 6 Pole generator has 1000 shunt field turns and 12 series field turns per pole. The shunt field takes a current of 2 A for a terminal voltage of 220 V on no load. When supplying 300 A at 240 V, the amp-turns have to be 2.5 times the amp-turns on no-load. Find the resistance of the series field divertor when the generator supplies this load as a compound generator. The series field winding has a resistance of 0.005 Ω.

(AMIE Elect. M/cs. Winter, 1976)

Solution. On no-load, current does not flow through the series field but it flows through shunt field.

Current through shunt field on no-load = 2 A

$\therefore$ Resistance of shunt field $= \dfrac{220}{2} = 110\ \Omega$

Let I_d be the current in the field divertor on load and I_s be the current in the series field, on load such that

$$I_d + I_s = 300\ A \qquad ...(i)$$

On no load, total amp-turns are

$$= 1000 \times 2 + 0 \times 12$$

$$= 2000 \text{ AT}$$

On full load amp-turns are

$$= 2000 \times 2.5 = 5000 \text{ AT}$$

E.m.f. induced when full load is being supplied

$$= 240 + 0.005\ I_s$$

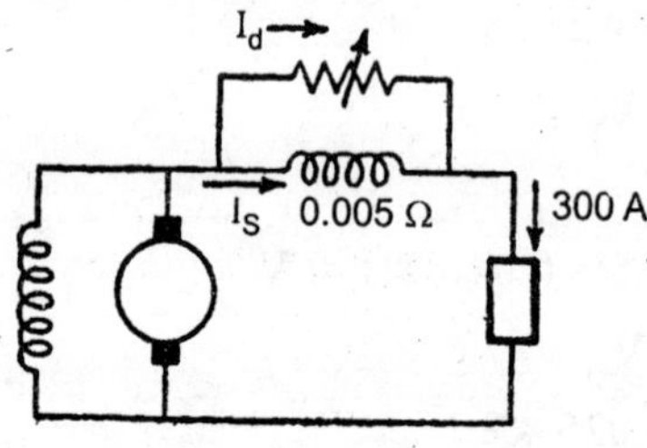

Fig. 4.56

$\therefore$ Current through shunt field

$$= \frac{240 + 0.005\ I_s}{110}$$

Amp-turns of shunt field and series field on load

$$= \left(\frac{240 + 0.005\ I_s}{110}\right) \times 1000 + I_s \times 12$$

$$= 5000$$

from equation (i) $I_s = 300 - I_d$ ...(ii)

$$\therefore \left\{\frac{240 + 0.005\,(300 - I_d)}{110}\right\} 1000 + 12\ I_s = 5000$$

or $\dfrac{24000 + 150 - 0.5\, I_d}{11} + 12\,(300 - I_d) = 5000$

or $24150 - 0.5\, I_d + 39000 - 132\, I_d = 55000$

or $\quad 132.5\, I_d = 8750$

or $\quad I_d = 66.037$ A

Now from equation (*ii*) $I_s = 300 - 66.037 = 234\,A$

Voltage across divertor $= 234 \times 0.005 = 1.17$V

Current through divertor $= 66.037$ A

∴ Resistance of the divertor

$$= \frac{1.17}{66.037} = 0.017\ \Omega \textbf{ Ans.}$$

Example 4.21. The armature of a dynamo having 8 Poles and revolving at 600 r.p.m. has a volume of 10,000 c.c. of iron lamination. If the flux density in the core is 1.0 weber per sq. m., calculate the hysteresis loss in watts assuming the hysteresis constant for the iron to be 25.12.

(*A.M.I.e. Elect.*)

Solution.

The hysteresis constant $= 25.12$

Volume $= 10{,}000$ c.c.

$= 10{,}000 \times 10^{-6}$

$= 0.01$ cubic metres

$B = 1.0\ \text{wb/m}^2$

$$f = \frac{PN}{120}$$

$$= \frac{8 \times 600}{120} = 40 \text{ cycles per second.}$$

Hysteresis loss, $\quad W_h = \eta\, B_{max}^{\ 1.6} \times f \times V$ Watts.

$= 25.12 \times 1.0^{1.6} \times 40 \times 0.01$

$=$ **10.048 Watts Ans.**

Example 4.22. A 4-pole, wave wound generator delivers 40 KW at 200 volts. Its armature has 151 turns and a resistance of 0.01 ohm. Air gap flux per pole is 0.02 weber. Calculate the speed of the machine, neglecting any voltage drop at the brushes, and taking the shunt field resistance as 50 ohms.

Solution.

Load current, $\quad I_L = \dfrac{40{,}000}{200} = 200$ amps

Field current, $\quad I_{sh} = \dfrac{200}{50} = 4$ amps

Hence Armature Current,

$$I_a = I_L + I_{sh} = 200 + 4 = 204 \text{ amp.}$$

Voltage drop in armature resistance,

$$= 204 \times 0.01$$

$$= 2.04 \text{ volts}$$

$$\text{Generated e.m.f} = \text{Terminal P.D.} + \text{Voltage drop}$$

$$= 200 + 2.04 = 202.04 \text{ V}$$

Expression for generated e.m.f is:

$$E = \frac{P\phi ZN}{60A} \text{ V}$$

Putting the values,

$$202.04 = \frac{4 \times 0.02 \times 151 \times 2 \times N}{60 \times 2} \qquad \left[\begin{array}{l}\because 1 \; turn = 2 \; conductors \\ \therefore 151 \; turns = 302 \; conductors\end{array}\right]$$

Also as the generator is wave wound

$$\therefore \qquad A = \frac{P}{2}$$

or

$$N = \frac{202.04 \times 60 \times 2}{0.02 \times 151 \times 2}$$

$$= \textbf{10003 R.P.M Ans.}$$

Example 4.23. A shunt dynamo is used to charge a battery of cells with a current of 10 amps. The cells have an e.m.f. of 150 volts and an internal resistance of 0.5 ohm. The dynamo resistances are 160 ohms for the shunt and 0.5 ohm for the armature, the leads connecting the machine to the cells have a total resistance of 0.6 ohm.

Calculate the e.m.f. of the dynamo. If during charging the e.m.f. of the cells rises by 10 per cent and the current is kept constant, calculate approximately the percentage change of speed of the dynamo needed if the shunt resistance is kept constant, and also the percentage change needed in the shunt resistance if the speed is kept constant. It may be assumed that for small changes the percentage increase of field strength is half that of the field current. [*I.e.E. May,* 1957]

Solution.

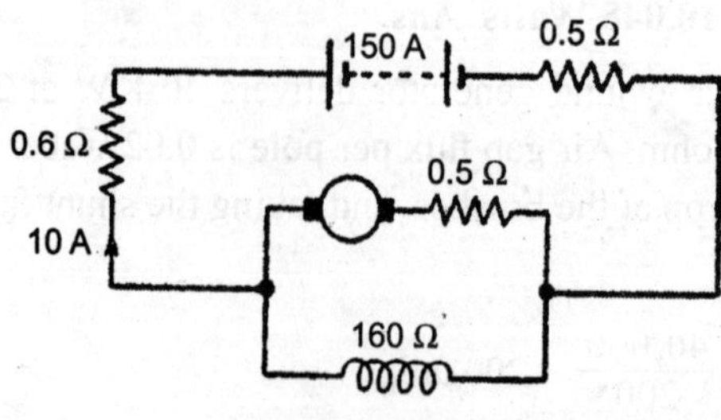

Fig. 4.57

Terminal voltage of a dynamo

$$= \text{E.m.f. of battery}$$

$$+ \text{ voltage drop in leads and battery resistance.}$$

$$= 150 + 10\,(0.5 + 0.6)$$

$$= 161 \text{ volts.}$$

Field current, $I_{sh} = \dfrac{161}{160} = 1.006$ amps.

Armature current, $I_a = I_L + I_{sh} = 10 + 1.006 = 11.006$ amps.

Voltage drop in armature resistance

$$= 11.006 \times 0.5 = 5.503 \text{ V.}$$

Dynamo e.m.f. = Terminal voltage + Voltage drop

$$= 161 + 5.5 = 166.5 \text{ V.}$$

If the battery e.m.f rises by 10 %, new e.m.f of the battery,

$$150 + \frac{10}{100} \times 150 = 165 \text{ volts.}$$

New terminal voltage

$$= 165 + 10\,(0.6 + 0.5)$$

$$= 176 \text{ volts.}$$

New field current, $= \dfrac{176}{160} = 1.1$ amps.

New armature current

$$= 10 + 1.1 = 11.1 \text{ amps.}$$

New voltage drop in armature resistance

$$= 11.\,1 \times 0.5 = 5.55 \text{ V.}$$

New dynamo e.m.f.

$$= 176 + 5.55 = 181.55 \text{ V.}$$

Increase in field current

$$= \frac{1.1 - 1.006}{1.006} \times 100 \text{ per cent}$$

$$= 9.346\ \%$$

Hence increase in field strengths

$$= 4\,.673\ \%$$

i.e. Ratio of field strength

$$\frac{\phi_2}{\phi_1} = 1.0467$$

Dynamo e.m.f is proportional to (Speed × Field strength)

$$\frac{E_1}{E_2} = \frac{\phi_1 N_1}{\phi_2 N_2}$$

or
$$\frac{N_2}{N_1} = \frac{E_2 \phi_1}{E_1 \phi_2}$$

$$= \frac{181.55 \times 1}{166.5 \times 1.0467}$$

$$= 1.0417.$$

Therefore the speed must be increased by 4.17%.

If the speed is kept constant

$$\frac{\phi_2}{\phi_1} = \frac{E_2}{E_1} = \frac{181.55}{166.5} = 1.090$$

i.e. there must be a 9.0% increase in field strength and therefore an 18.0 per cent increase in the field current.

Hence the ratio of field current,

$$= \frac{I_2}{I_1} = \frac{1.180}{1}$$

Ratio of shunt resistances

$$= \frac{R_2}{R_1} = \frac{1}{1.180} = 0.848.$$

Therefore the *resistance must be reduced by* (100–84.8) per cent *i.e.* by **15.2 per cent. Ans.**

Example 4.24. An 8-pole armature is wound with 480 conductors. The magnetic flux and the speed are such that the average e.m.f. generated in each conductor is 2.2V and each conductor is capable of carrying a full load current of 100 A . Calculate the terminal voltage on no load, the output current on full load and the total power generated on full load when the armature is (a) lap connected and (b) wave connected.

Solution. (*a*) When the armature is lap connected,

No. of parallel paths in the armature winding

$$= \text{Number of poles}$$

$$= 8.$$

∴ No. of conductors/path

$$= \frac{480}{8} = 60.$$

Terminal voltage on no load

$$= (\text{E.m.f/conductor}) \times (\text{No. of conductors/path.})$$

$$= 2.2 \times 60 = 132 \text{ V}.$$

Output current on full load

$$= \text{(Full load current per conductor)} \times \text{(No. of parallel paths)}.$$

$$= 100 \times 8 = 800 \text{ A}.$$

Total power generated on full load

$$= \text{Output current} \times \text{Generated e.m.f}$$

$$= 800 \times 132 = 105{,}600 \text{ W}.$$

$$= 105.6 \text{ kW}$$

(*b*) *With the armature wave connected,*

No. of parallel paths $= 2$

$\therefore$ No. of conductors/path

$$= 480/2 = 240.$$

Terminal voltage on no load

$$= 2.2 \times 240 = 528 \text{ V}.$$

Output current on full load

$$= 100 \times 2 = 200 \text{ A}.$$

Total power generated on full load

$$= 200 \times 528 = 105{,}600 \text{ W}.$$

$$= 105.6 \text{ kW}.$$

It will be seen from the above example that the total power generated by a given machine is the same whether the armature winding is lap or wave connected.

4.32. TYPES OF D.C. MOTORS

Just as D.C. generators, D.C. motors are characterized by the connection of field winding in relation to the armature are of three main types:

(*i*) **The shunt wound motors:** As shown in Fig. 4.58, it may be observed that field winding is connected in parallel with the armature winding and only it is the characteristic of shunt wound motors. It is also clear from here that field current remains constant as field is directly connected to supply which is assumed to be at constant voltage. As current is approximately constant (may be just varied by varying the variable resistance). So magnetic flux of field will also be constant and also the back e.m.f. is almost constant under normal conditions. Hence the speed is approximately constant. This is not strictly true but it is usual for all practical purposes as regard the shunt motor as a constant speed motor. Therefore this motor is applicable where constant speed is required. But however if necessary, speed may be varied by varying the value of variable resistance which may be connected in series with the field winding as shown in Fig. 4.58. This can be done up to certain extent only.

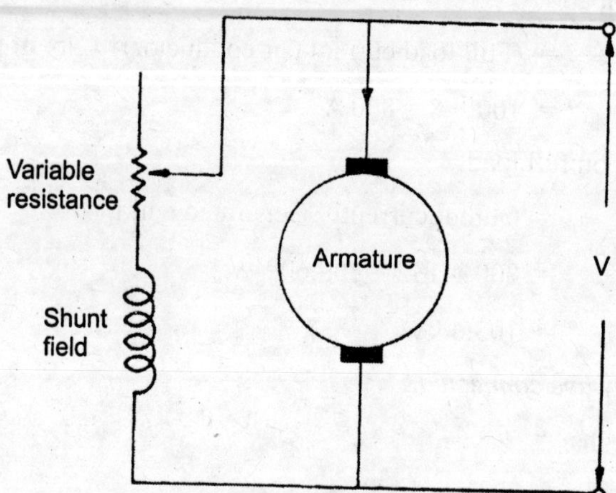

Fig. 4.58. D.C. Shunt Motor

(ii) **The series wound motors:** The field winding is connected in series with the armature winding, as shown in Fig. 4.59. So from here it is clear that whatever current flows through the armature winding, that is passed through field winding also.

Now let's suppose that load on motor-armature is increased, armature will take more current and all this current would pass through the field winding, resulting in increasing the magnetic

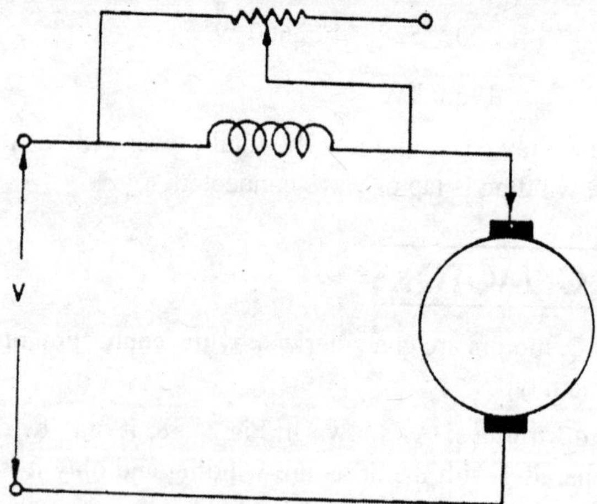

Fig. 4.59. DC. Series-Motor

flux of the field, which in turn will reduce the speed of the motor. This can be shown with the expression that,

$$E_b = \frac{P\phi NZ}{60A} \qquad ...(i)$$

$$E_b = K\phi N \qquad ...(ii) \left[K = \frac{PZ}{60A}, Constant\right]$$

From equation (*ii*)

$$N = \frac{E_b}{K\phi} \quad ...(iii)$$

or

$$N \propto \frac{E_b}{\phi} \quad ...(iv)$$

From equation (*iv*) it may be clearly understood that speed is inversely proportional to magnetic flux. As flux is directly proportional to the current flowing through the field, so we can say that when current of the motor is low, speed is high and vice-versa.

(*iii*) **Compound wound motor**

Compound motor is that motor in which both shunt field winding and series field windings are used. These again are of two types *viz.* Cumulative compound motors & Differential compound motors. The magnetic flux produced by both the windings, depends upon the flux direction of the shunt coil in relation to that of the series coil. When these two magnetic fluxes assist each other the machine is a cumulative compound motor as shown in Fig. 4.60. On the other hand if these two magnetic fluxes oppose each other, the machine is said to be differential compound motor as shown in Fig. 4.61.

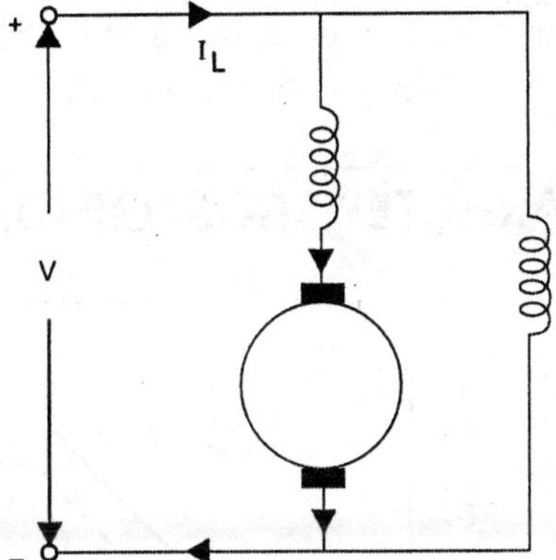

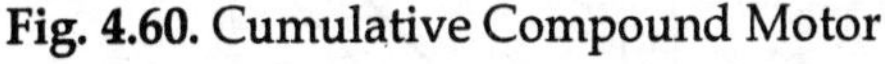

Fig. 4.60. Cumulative Compound Motor

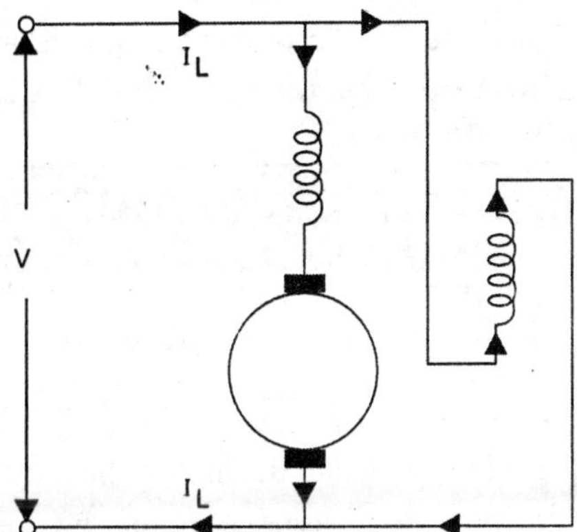

Fig. 4.61. Differential Compound Motor

4.33. CHARACTERISTICS OF D.C. MOTORS

The performance of a machine is judged from its performance or characteristic curves or simply, motor characteristics. The below given are the important typical characteristics of a d.c. motor.

(*i*) **Torque and armature current characteristics:** T_a/I_a It is a curve for armature torque, T_a versus armature current, I_a of the d.c. motor. It is the electrical characteristics of the d.c. motor.

(*ii*) **Speed torque characteristics:** N v/s T_a. It is a curve between speed, N and armature torque, T_a, of the motor. It is a mechanical characteristics of the d.c. motor.

(*iii*) **Speed-armature current characteristics:** Nv/s I_a. It is a curve between speed N and armature current, I_a, of the motor. This characteristics, being very important, decides the selection of a d.c. motor for a particular application.

4.34. CHARACTERISTICS OF THE SHUNT-WOUND OR SEPARATELY EXCITED D.C. MOTORS

In both the cases of shunt separately and sparely exited d.c. motors the field is supplied from a constant voltage so that the filed current is constant. The two motors therefore have similar characteristics.

As already explained in section 4.32 and shown in Fig. 4.62, the shunt-wound motor has the field winding connected in parallel with the armature. Line current, I_L is divided into two paths, one I_{sh} flows through shunt winding and the other I_a armature current flows in the armature circuit. The field current is constant as it depends upon the field (shunt) winding resistance, R_{sh} and the supply voltage, V, which is assumed to be constant.

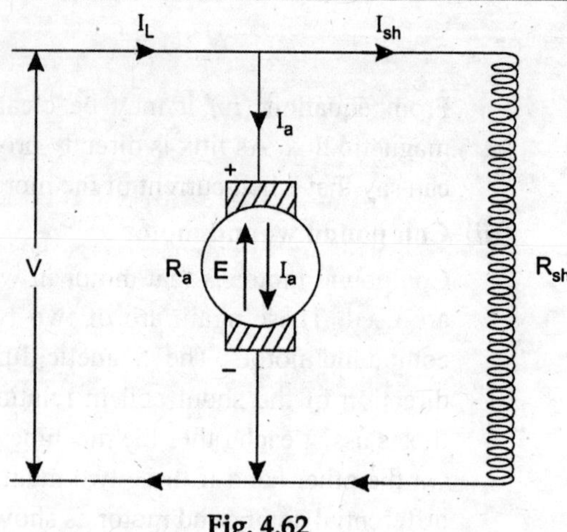

Fig. 4.62

Hence the flux in a shunt motor is approximately constant. (The flux decreases a little due to armature reaction but the decrease in flux is usually found negligible under normal conditions).

4.35. TORQUE-ARMATURE CURRENT CHARACTERISTICS OF D.C. SHUNT WOUND MOTOR

(T_d/I_a *characteristics*). As already explained for a d.c. motor,

$$T_a \propto \phi I_a$$

If load is applied to the motor, the motor immediately tends to slow down. With this type of motor, the flux remains substantially constant and the decrease of speed decreases the counter e.m.f. E_b. If the counter e.m.f. decreases, the armature current increases. This continues until the increased armature current produces sufficient torque to meet requirements of increased load. Therefore, *the shunt-wound motor is always in a condition of stable equilibrium and the flux is substantially constant*. Therefore,

Fig. 4.63

$$T_a \propto I_a$$

or $$T_a = KI_a$$

where K is the slope of T_a vs. I_a curve which is a straight line (OA) represents slope of the straight line in Fig. 4.63.

The shaft torque versus armature current has also been shown dotted OA' in Fig. 4.63. It can be seen that a larger armature current is required to start a heavy load. Therefore, *shunt motors should not be started on heavy load.*

4.36. SPEED-ARMATURE CURRENT CHARACTERISTICS (N/I_a CHARACTERISTICS)

As already explained the Speed of a d.c. motor is directly proportional to its back e.m.f. and inversely proportional to excitation, ϕ (ϕ = flux per pole).

Thus, $$N \propto \frac{E_b}{\phi} \propto \frac{V - I_a R_a}{\phi}$$

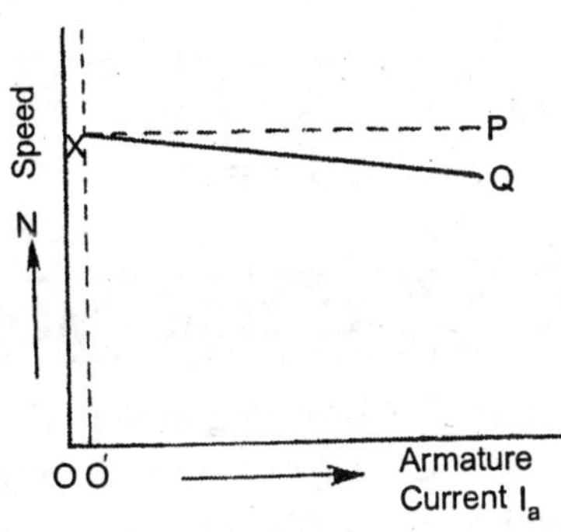

Fig. 4.64

Under normal conditions, the back e.m.f., E_b and the flux per pole, ϕ in a d.c. shunt motor are almost constant and therefore, speed will remain constant as the armature current varies.

This is shown as *XP*, a dotted straight line in Fig. 4.64. But at no load, the no load speed, N_0 is $N_0 \propto \frac{V - I_o R_a}{\phi}$ where I_o is no load armature current.

Since I_o is small, the drop of speed of a shunt motor from load to any other load is proportional to the drop of volts in the armature at that load. Here zero armature reaction in the motor is assumed; actually since the armature exerts a demagnetising action, ϕ will decrease as I_a increases, the E_b, decreases slightly more than ϕ and therefore fall in speed will not be so great as indicated by the above expression.

Since the full-load drop in the armature is small compared with applied voltage, V, it can be seen that the speed-current curve of a shunt motor is a slightly droping curve, *XQ*, as shown in Fig. 4.64.

Shunt motors being constant speed motors are best suited for driving of line shafts, machine lathes. Milling machines, conyeyors, fans and for all purpose where constant speed is required. It is not suitable for use with flywheel or with fluctuating loads or for parallel operation due to its constant speed characteristics.

4.37. SPEED-TORQUE CHARACTERISTICS (N/T_A CHARACTERISTICS)

This curve is plotted from curves shown in Figs. 4.63 and 4.64. *i.e.* by plotting the values of N and T_a for various armature currents I_a. From the curve of Fig. 4.65 it can be seen that the speed falls slightly, if the torque of load increases. From this curve, we can determine which type of motor is most suited to drive a given load.

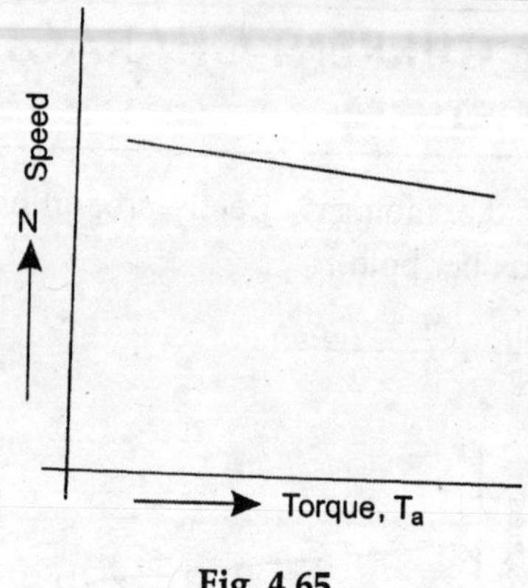

Fig. 4.65

4.38. CHARACTERISTICS OF D.C. SERIES MOTOR

Fig. 4.66. represents d.c. series motor. The field winding having winding resistance R_{se} is connected in series with the armature. The field winding is always of low resistance in a d.c. series motor. Here, same current passes through the field winding as well as the armature. With the increase in load of d.c. series motor, the armature current also increases and thus the flux increases and *vice-versa.*

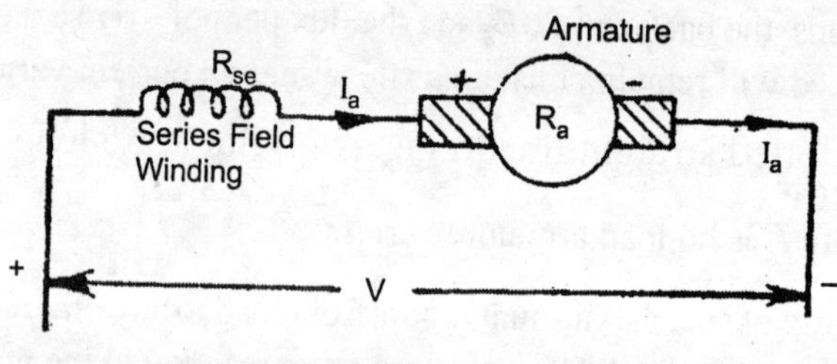

Fig. 4.66

4.39. TORQUE/ARMATURE CURRENT (T_A/I_A) CHARACTERISTICS

$$\text{Torque} \propto \text{flux} \times \text{Armature current}$$

Therefore, $T_a \propto \phi I_a$

Since the field winding is in series with the armature therefore, the flux has linear relation with armature current, I_a, until the saturation of flux ϕ occurs.

i.e. $\phi \propto I_a$

Hence, $T_a \propto I_a^2$

It shows that the armature torque is proportional to the square of the armature current, upto the magnetic saturation. It means that if I_a is doubled, the armature torque developed is almost four times.

On light loads the torque-current curve is therefore a parabola, but when I_a is so great that ϕ becomes nearly constant, as saturation of magnetic field will occur, T_a becomes proportional to I_a and has straight line relationship as represented by straight line *ab*. The characteristics has been shown in Fig. 4.67.

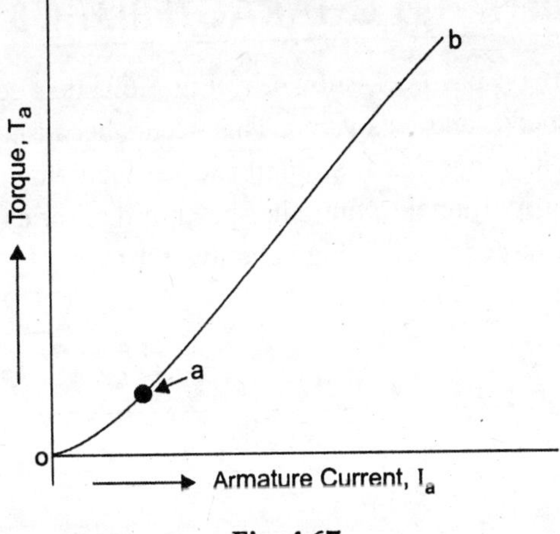

Fig. 4.67

4.40. SPEED-ARMATURE CURRENT (N/I_A) CHARACTERISTICS

The speed-current characteristic of a d.c. series motor has been shown in Fig. 4.68.

As explained in para section 4.39. the flux is proportional to current I_a in d.c. series motor.

Therefore, $$N \propto \frac{1}{\phi}$$

$$\propto \frac{1}{I_a}$$

Thus, the curve N/I_a follows the hyperbolic path. When the saturation of field occurs, the flux becomes constant and so does the speed

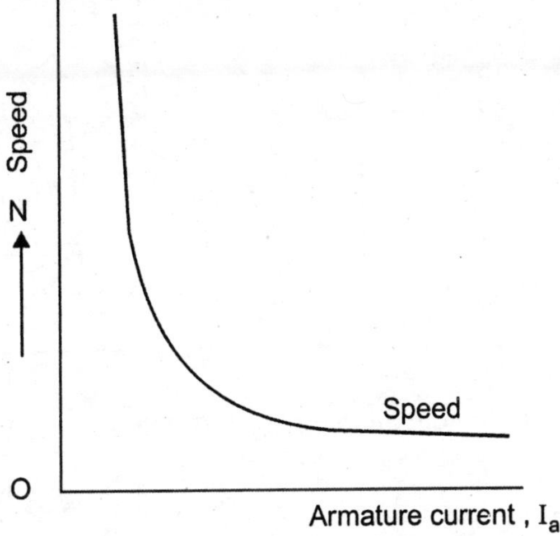

Fig. 4.68

4.41. SPEED-TORQUE (N/T_A) CHARACTERISTICS

The speed *vs* Torque characteristic has been shown by Fig 4.69. It is seen that the d.c. series motor develops heavy torque at low speeds and *vice-versa.* This occurs because an increase in torque requires an increase in armature current and thus flux is strengthened as the field current is the same in armature current. As speed is inversely proportional to flux, the speed of d.c. series motor drops with increase in armature current. Similarly, the motor speed is high at a low torque.

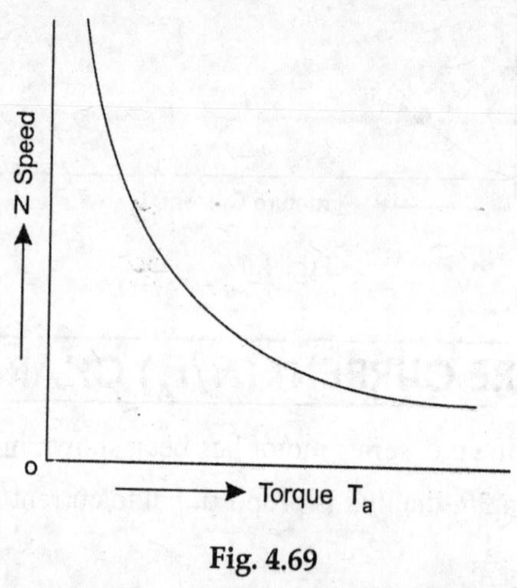

Fig. 4.69

4.42. CHARACTERISTICS OF COMPOUND WOUND MOTORS

A compound motor as the name speaks, is a combination of and compromise between the shunt and the series motors. It has two field windings, one in series and the other in parallel with the armature.

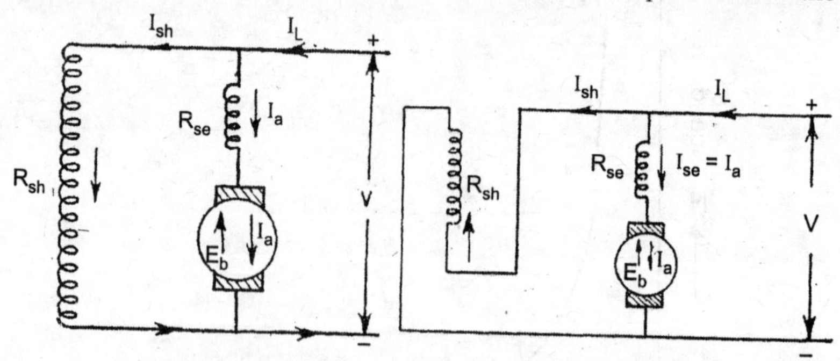

Fig. 4.70. Cumulative compound motor **Fig. 4.71. Differential compound motor**

Depending upon the direction of magnetising effect of shunt and series field windings, these motors are classified in the following two types:

(*i*) Cumulative compound motor (Fig. 4.70)

(*ii*) Differential compound motor (Fig. 4.71)

4.43. CHARACTERISTICS OF CUMULATIVE COMPOUND MOTORS

The field windings are so connected that the field due to series field winding is in the same direction as the field due to the shunt field winding. Thus the total flux, for any load, is the sum of both the fluxes, *i.e.*

$$\phi_t = \phi_{sh} + \phi_{se}$$

The resultant flux of machine, thus depends upon currents in the series and shunt field windings.

The cumulative compound motor is shown in Fig. 4.70.

4.44. TORQUE V/S. CURRENT (T_A/I_A) CHARACTERISTIC

We have

Torque ∝ flux × Armature current

i.e., $T_a \propto \phi \times I_a$

In this case, $\phi_t = \phi_{sh} + 1\phi_{se}$

Thus the total flux is strengthened and consequently torque is increased. The increase in torque, T_a with increase in I_a is greater than that in shunt motor. The T_a/I_a characteristic has been shown in Fig. 4.72.

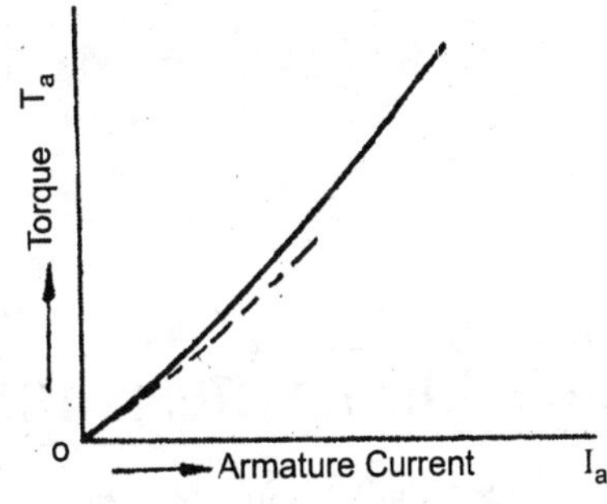

Fig. 4.72

4.45. SPEED ARMATURE CURRENT (N/IA) CHARACTERISTIC

We have already deduced

$$N \propto \frac{E_b}{\phi}$$

Here, $\phi = \phi_{sh} + \phi_{se}$

The total flux increases with the increase in load and hence the speed of this type of motor falls as in a series motor, but not so rapidly as in the case of the plain series motor, because of the constant flux produced by shunt field. The N/I_a characteristic has been shown in Fig. 4.73. The characteristics is between those of the series and shunt motors, its nearness to one or the other depending upon the number of series turns.

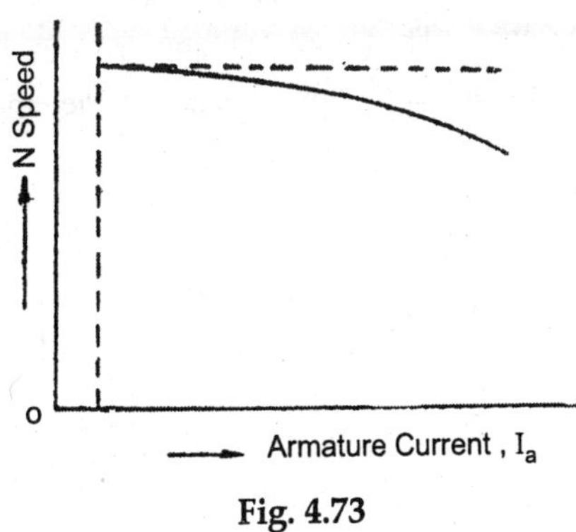

Fig. 4.73

It may be noted that:

(*i*) The speed of cumulative compound motor reduces at heavy loads as it is in case of d.c. series motor.

(*ii*) The speed of motor, at no load, is within safe limits. It is because of this reason that shunt field winding produces flux even on no load.

4.46. SPEED V/S ARMATURE TORQUE (N/Ta) CHARACTERISTICS

This characteristics is shown in Fig. 4.79. The curve lies in between those of a shunt motor and of a series motor. The falling off in speed affords relief to the motor if sudden load comes on. This motor is largely used for driving heavy machine tools where sudden deep cuts may be taken. Examples are punching, shearing and coal cutting machines.

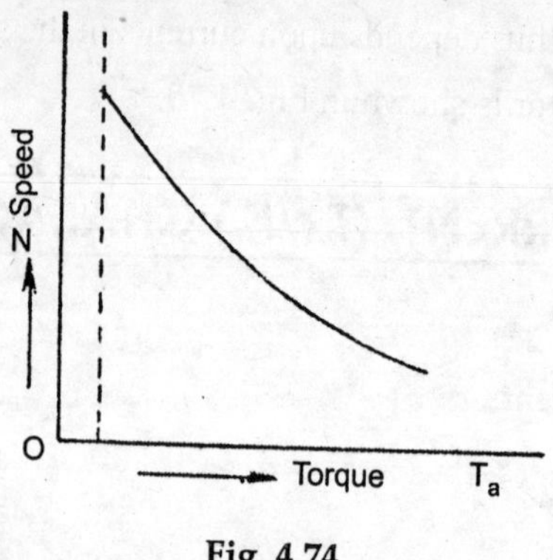

Fig. 4.74

4.47. CHARACTERISTICS OF DIFFERENTIAL COMPOUND MOTORS

The differentially compounded motor has been shown in Fig. 4.71. In this type of motor, the flux due to series field winding is in opposite direction to the flux due to shunt field winding. Thus, for any load, the total flux is the difference of the shunt and series field fluxes *i.e.* $\phi_t = \phi_{sh} - \phi_{se}$.

4.48. TORQUE V/S. ARMATURE CURRENT (TA/IA) CHARACTERISTICS

The characteristics has been shown in Fig. 4.75. With the increase in armature current the resultant flux decreases. Thus, torque being product of flux and armature current, does increase with armature current but not so rapidly as in case of series motor.

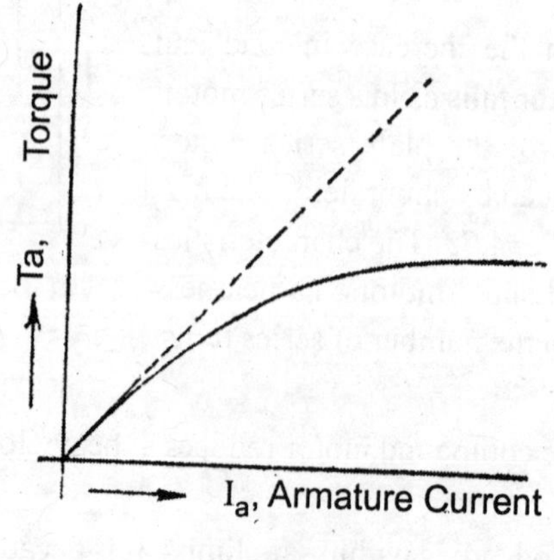

Fig. 4.75

4.49. SPEED V/S ARMATURE CURRENT (N/I_A) CHARACTERISTICS

In d.c. motors speed,

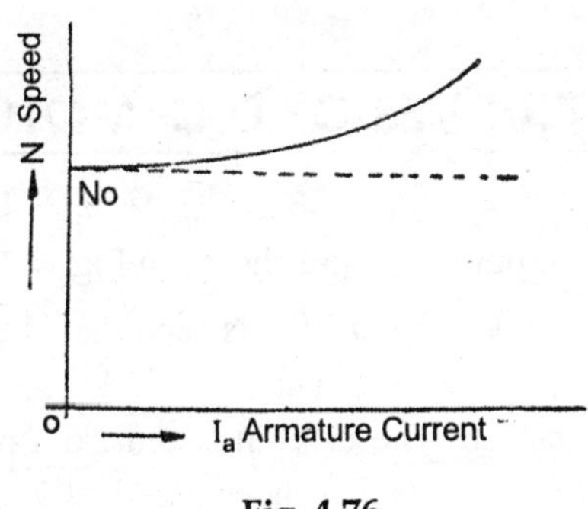

Fig. 4.76

$$N \propto \frac{E_b}{\phi}$$

With increase in armature current (*i.e.* load) the flux in this type of motor decreases and hence the motor speeds up. Greater the load on the motor, faster would the motor tend to run and at such a high speed may burst under the centrifugal forces.

Therefore, care should be taken while connecting compound motors, so as to avoid differential connection.

4.50. SPEED VS TORQUE (N/T_A) CHARACTERISTICS

If the series field of this type of motor is so adjusted that the full load decrease in flux produced by it is just sufficient to make the full-load speed equal to the speed on no-load, then, for any other load within this range its speed will be approximately constant. The mechanical (N/T_a) characteristics has been shown in Fig. 4.77. At first sight, this appears to be an advantage, but there are two disadvantages:

(*i*) When the motor is being started, the shunt field will take some time to build up, and therefore, the series field will be established first, owing to the initial rush of current through the armature and the series field. The motor will therefore tend to start up the wrong way. When the shunt field is fully established the total field will be so small that there may not be sufficient torque to run the motor, and the armature will take much current from the supply. This difficulty can be overcome by short-circuiting the series field during starting, and only putting it in circuit when the motor is under way.

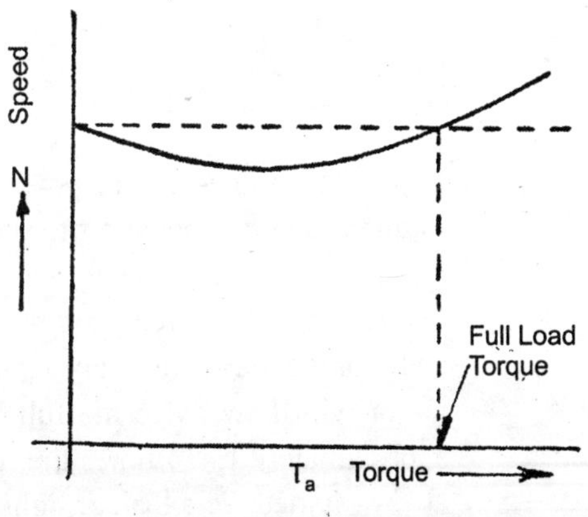

Fig. 4.77

(*ii*) If the motor becomes overloaded, the resulting decrease in flux will tend to force up the speed so that the motor will be very seriously overloaded. In fact when the current attains a certain value, the motor becomes unstable, and it begins to race like a series motor on no load. The motor is thus dangerous to use unless there is no possibility of the load exceeding the normal full load.

4.51. PERFORMANCE CURVES OF D.C. MOTORS

The four most important characteristics of a d.c. shunt motor, namely, torque, speed, armature current and efficiency, plotted against the output power are shown in Fig. 4.78.

(*i*) *From the speed and output power curve*, it is seen that shunt motor has definite speed at no load. This motor does not "*run away*" when the load is suddenly removed provided, its field winding circuit remains closed. The drop in speed from no load to full load is very small. Hence these motors are most suitable where practically constant speed is required as in a machine shop, electric drives etc.

(*ii*) *From the efficiency output power curve*, it is seen that the efficiency of a shunt motor increases rapidly in the very begining, reaches maximum value and then falls. The efficiency of shunt motor becomes maximum when variable loss is equal to the constant loss. After reaching to maximum value, it drops. At this stage, losses are increased and therefore, the efficiency falls.

(*iii*) *From Armature current-output power curve*, it is noted that a small amount of current is required even when the motor is running at no load. This current is known as "no load current" (I_0). When the motor is loaded, its armature current as well as output power is also increased as shown in Fig. 4.78.

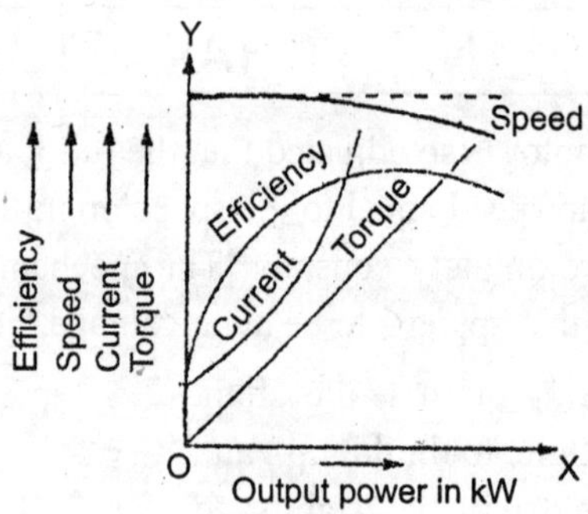

Fig. 4.78

(*iv*) From the Torque-out put power curve, a shunt wound motor is said to be a low starting torque motor as compared to other motors. But is does not mean that a shunt motor is not capable of Starting a heavy load. D.C shunt motor can start heavy load but it would require excess armature current to carry the heavy load as compared to normal values than the series and compound motors. For example, if twice full load torque is required at start, the shunt motor will draw twice the full load current, ($T_a \alpha I_a$) but a series wound motor will draw approximately 1.414 times the full load current (Ta α I_a^2). For this reason, shunt motors are always started at no load or light load. After starting, the load is applied to the motor. When a motor is required to start heavy load, then series motors or compound motors are suitable.

4.52. PERFORMANCE CURVES OF A D.C. SERIES MOTOR

The four important characteristics of a d.c. series motor namely torque, speed current and efficiency, each poltted against output power are shown in Fig. 4.79.

(i) *From torque-output power curve*, it is seen that series motor develops a starting torque comparatively greater than that developed by a shunt motor for a given current *i.e.*, why these motors are most suitable where large starting torque is required. These motors are used in cranes, hoists and electric locomotives.

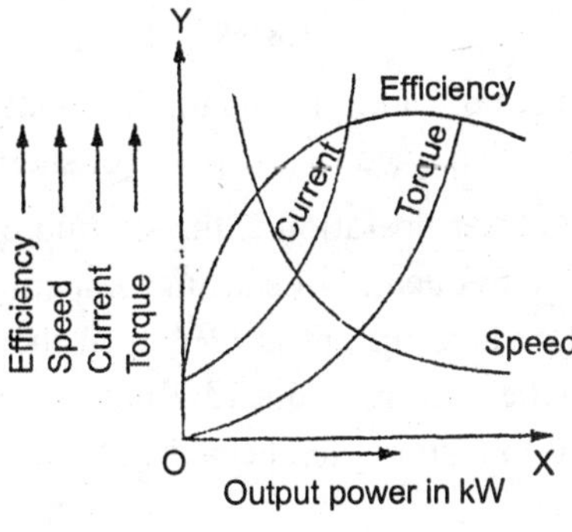

Fig. 4.79

(ii) *From Speed-output power characteristics*, the speed of series motor falls rapidly with the increase in load and vice versa. Therefore, these motors are known as variable speed motors. These motors are not suitable for services requiring substantially constant speed.

(iii) *From the armature current-output power curve*, it is seen that when the motor is started on load, the armature draws a definite amount of armature current and when the load is further increased, the current as well as out put power increases, but on the other hand, the speed of the motor falls.

(iv) *From efficiency-output power characteristics*, it is seen that the efficiency increases rapidly in the beginning, reaches its maximum value, and then decreases. This is due to the fact, that at light loads the friction and iron losses are more comparatively copper loss. The effect of these losses becomes less with the increase in load. Since the field winding is in series with the armature, therefore armature and field losses vary as the square of the current. So these losses increase rapidly with the increase in load. The efficiency of the motor will be maximum when friction and iron losses are equal to copper Iosses.

4.53. COMPARISON OF THREE TYPES OF MOTORS

Let us consider the three motors, a series, a shunt and a cumulatively compound one, ail giving the same torque and speed at normal full-load. The characteristics of all will intersect at the full-load armature current I_a, *i.e.*, point *A*, and a comparison is provided by the characteristic curves. (Fig. 4.80).

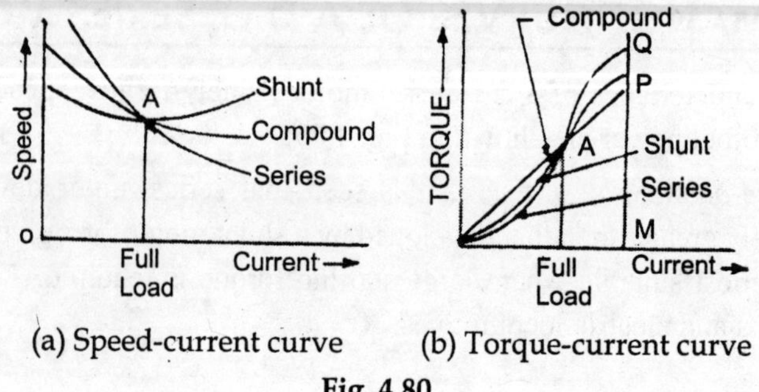

(a) Speed-current curve (b) Torque-current curve

Fig. 4.80

If we were to consider the range no load to full-load, the shunt motors have the advantage over the other two types because of their practically constant speed (or small speed change).

A very important point in the motor operation is the starting of the motor, especially if the load is such that the starts and the stops are frequent. For starting, sometimes the current exceeds the full-load value by 50%. Suppose that the starting current is *OM*, then the starting torque (*MQ*) for the series motor, is considerably higher than the starting torque (*MP*) for the shunt motor. Hence series motors are best suited for electric traction and in cranes, etc., because of their utility to accelerate the heavy loads from rest.

4.54. APPLICATIONS OF D.C. MOTORS

(*a*) **Shunt wound motors.** The speed of the motor is approximately constant and is suitable for industrial application in cases:

(*i*) where there is requirement of almost constant speed from no load to full load on the motor;

(*ii*) where many speeds are required to be attained and any one of which is required to remain almost constant.

Such cases are light machine tools *i.e.* lathes, drills, boring mills, shapers, grinders, spinning and weaving machines etc.

(*b*) **Series motors.** As can be seen from speed-torque characteristics of the motor, it is a variable speed motor *i.e.* the speed is low at high torque and vice-versa. At no load or light load the motor attains dangerously high speed. Therefore, the motor is never run without some mechanical load. It is, therefore, used in such cases:

(*i*) Where large starting torque is required for accelerating quickly heavy masses such as for electric traction and for hoist work; cranes, elevators, vacuum cleaners, sewing machines, hair driers, air compressors and fans etc. Here the load is subjected to heavy fluctuations and speed automatically reduces at high torques.

Example 4.25. A series motor rated at 50 Amps has a total resistance between terminals of 0.16 Ω and operates from a 220 volt source. Data for the magnetisation curve was taken in terms of field amperes and generated volts when the speed was 1000 r.p.m as follows.

I	0	5	10	15	20	25	30	35	40	45	50	55	57.5
E	10	45	79	112	141	165	185	201	211	219	224	228	230

Calculate the speed and the torque at 50 amperes load.

Solution: Supplied voltage $V = 220$ volts

Total resistance between motor terminals,

$$R_m = 0.16\ \Omega$$

Field current = Line current $I_1 = 50A$

Back e.m.f developed

$$Eb_1 = V - I_a R_a \Rightarrow 220 - 50 \times 0.16 = 212\ \text{V}$$

Let speed be $= N_1$

From given datas for the magnetisation curve when field current = 50 A

E.M.F developed, $Eb_2 = 224\ V$

Speed $N_2 = 1{,}000$ r.p.m.

Since $N \propto \dfrac{E_b}{\phi}$

$$\therefore \quad \frac{N_1}{N_2} = \frac{Eb_1}{Eb_2} \times \frac{\phi_2}{\phi_1}$$

or $N_1 = N_2 \times \dfrac{E_{b1}}{E_{b2}}$ since $\phi_2 = \phi_1$ field current remaining the same

$$= 1000 \times \frac{212}{224} = 946 \text{ r.p.m } \textbf{Ans.}$$

Torque developed, $T = \dfrac{Eb_1\ Ia_2}{2\pi N_1/60} = \dfrac{212 \times 50}{2\pi \times 946/60} = 107$ N-M **Ans.**

(c) Compound wound motors

(i) ***Cumulative compound motors.*** These motors attain increase in flux with increase in load with the result that the speed falls but not as rapidly as in case of the plain series motors. This is because there is a constant flux produced by the shunt field. The falling off in speed relieves the motor if a sudden load comes on it. These motors are used where huge starting torque is required, where series motors could not be used in the event when the load may fall so low and where the load is subjected to heavy fluctuations and the motor is coupled to a heavy fly wheel. The examples are steel rolling mills, punching and shearing machines pumps and power fans, large printing presses, lifts and mine hoists etc.

(ii) ***Differential compound motors.*** As in the cumulative compound motor, where there are light loads on the motor, the speed is limited to safe value. However, at heavy loads, the speed may be arranged so as to remain constant. Therefore the use of the differential compound motors is restricted to the cases which require constant speed *e.g.*, battery boosters.

4.55. SPEED CONTROL OF D.C. MOTORS

The speed of a d.c. motor is given by the relation $N = \frac{E_b}{\phi}$

Where $E_b = V - I_a R_a$

$$\therefore \quad N \propto \frac{V - I_a R_a}{\phi} \quad ...(3.1)$$

or $N = K \frac{V - I_a R_a}{\phi}$, (where, $V - I_a R_a = E_b$)

From equation (3.1) it is concluded that speed of the motor can be controlled thus:

(*a*) By varying the flux per pole ϕ. This method is known as flux control method.

(*b*) By varying the resistance in the armature circuit. This method is known as armature resistance control method.

(*c*) By varying the applied voltage. This is known as voltage control method.

4.56. SPEED CONTROL OF D.C. SHUNT MOTORS

As already explained in previous sections that a shunt motor is approximately a constant speed motor because its speed changes very slightly with load. However a fine speed control over a wide range can be obtained with a suitable arrangement for speed control.

(*a*) Armature control or Armature resistance control method.

Since $N \propto \frac{V - I_a R_a}{\phi}$

where ϕ is almost constant. Hence in case of shunt motors.

$$N \propto (V - I_a R_a)$$

Hence N can be varied by varying the supply voltage V or by inserting a resistance (rheostat) in series with it as shown in Fig. 4.81. Since ϕ is almost constant in case of shunt motors. Therefore,

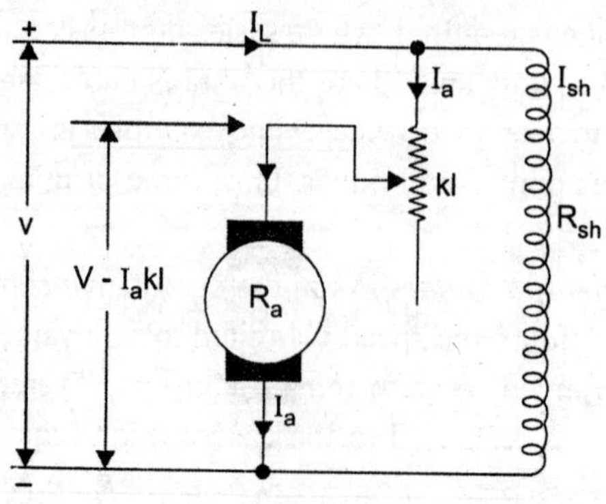

Fig. 4.81

$$N \propto (V - I_a R_a)$$

Hence speed control of the motor is shown affected through a resistance inserted in the armature circuit as shown in Fig. 4.81. A rheostat having k ohms per unit length has been placed in series with the armature. The effective voltage at any time across the armature will be $(V - I_a Kl)$. As this series resistance is increased, the voltage drop in the series resistance increases and that on the armature decreases and hence the speed falls. The speed goes on decreasing with increase in series resistance until the back e.m.f. has decreased so much that it does not produce any torque and then the motor comes to a standstill.

Because this method involves voltage drop in the series resistance (or controller resistance) or rheostat, the armature does not receive full supply voltage and consequently the back e.m.f. will be less than when the armature is subjected to full voltage. Hence the speed is reduced. By this way on changing the value of controller resistance, different motor speeds can be obtained, but the speed in any case will be lower than the normal.

This method is not very useful because of the large amount of losses in the rheostat and also the efficiency of the motor is reduced. This method of speed control is uneconomical. Since a large amount of heat is developed in the series resistance, dissipation of heat may be a very expensive problem. This method is, therefore, very useful where low speeds are required for a short period. The examples are the experimental work in the laboratories and for initial starting of the motors.

(*b*) ***Field or flux control method.*** If the supply voltage is kept constant, the speed of *d.c.* motor is inversely proportional to the flux per pole *i.e.* $N \propto \frac{1}{\phi}$. This method is based on varying the flux ϕ and hence the name field or flux control method. A variable resistance (or rheostat) as shown in Fig. 4.82. is connected in series with the shunt field. The resistance in the shunt field can be increased or decreased. The current, I_{sh} at any time will be

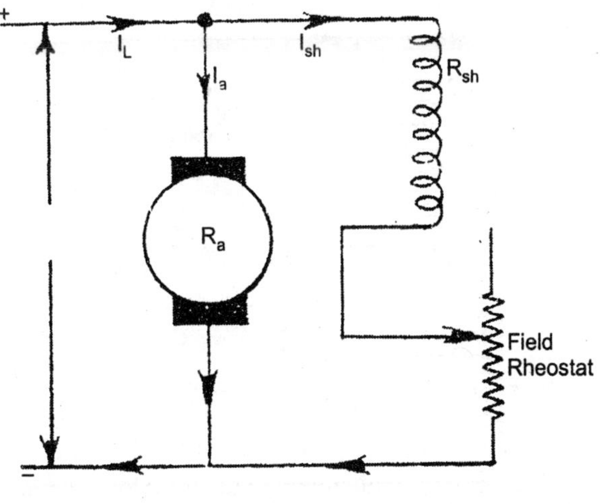

Fig. 4.82

$$I_{sh} = \frac{V}{R_{sh} + R}$$

Where R is the resistance of the variable resistance (field rheostat).

By increasing the resistance, the field current is decreased and thus the field flux weakens, and the speed increases.

In this method the shunt field rheostat reduces the field current I_{sh}, and hence the flux ϕ. Consequently, the motor runs at a speed higher than normal speed, the value of speed increase depends upon the value of resistance added through field rheostat.

The advantages of this method are:

(*i*) This is a convenient and easy method:

(*ii*) Because the shunt field current I_{sh} is always of small amount, hence very little power is wasted as heat in shunt field rheostat and thus easy to dissipate heat by usual inexpensive methods.

(*iii*) The speed control obtained is independent of load on the motor.

The disadvantages of this method are:

(*i*) Only speeds higher than the normal speed can be obtained since R_{sh} can not be decreased in this case and the total shunt field resistance at any time, shall be more than R_{sh}, the shunt field resistance of the motor.

(*ii*) There is a maximum limit of speed that can be obtained with this method. It is because of the fact that if the flux per pole is too much weakened, commutation becomes poorer.

(*c*) ***Ward-Leonard method of speed control.*** In this system variable voltage supply is given to the motor. This system is used for controlling the speed of separately excited motors only. As shown in Fig. 4.83. a generator '*G*' is mechanically coupled with a prime mover 'PM' which

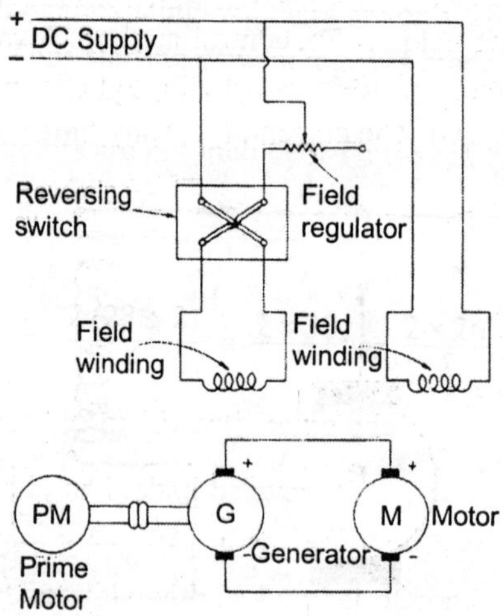

Fig. 4.83. Ward Leonard System

rotates the generator shaft at a constant speed. Field winding of dc generator is connected to a constant voltage dc supply through a field regulator and reversing switch. The dc motor '*M*' is fed from the generator '*G*' and its field winding is directly connected to a dc supply. The voltage of the generator fed to the motor can be varied from zero to maximum by the help of field regulator. By reversing the connections of field with the help of Reversing Switch the direction of field current of generator can be reversed, the polarity of generated voltage can be reversed and hence the direction of rotation of the motor can be reversed.

So from this method speed of the motor 'M' can be varied as well as direction of rotation can be changed.

Advantages

(*i*) Smooth control of speed over a wide range in both directions is possible.

(*ii*) The system is more efficient at low speeds as there are no resistors connected in series with the armature circuit.

Disadvantage

The only disadvantage of this system is that a separate 'Motor-Generator' set is required which is more expensive than the other systems.

(*d*) **Voltage control method.** In this method, the voltage source supplying the field current is different from that which supplies the armature. This method avoids the disadvantages of poor speed regulation and low efficiency as in armature control method. However, it is quite expansive. Therefore, this method of speed control is employed for large size motors where efficiency is of great importance.

(*i*) **Multiple voltage control.** In this method, the shunt field of the motor is connected permanently across (*a*) fixed voltage source. The armature can be connected across several different voltages through a suitable switch gear. In this way, voltage applied across the armature can be changed. The speed will be approximately proportional to the voltage applied across the armature. Internal speeds can be obtained by means of a shunt field regulator.

Example 4.26. A 250 volt d.c. shunt motor having an armature resistance of 0.25 ohm carries an armature current of 50 amperes and runs at 750 r.p.m. If the flux is reduced by 10%, find the speed. Assume load torque remains the same.

Solution.

Initial conditions:

Supply voltage across the motor terminals, V

$$= 250 \text{ Volts}$$

Armature current $I_{a_1} = 50$ Amps,

Armature resistance, R_a

$$= 0.25 \text{ ohms.}$$

Speed of motor, $N_1 = 750$ r.p.m

Therefore, back e.m.f., E_{b1}

$$= V - I_{a1}R_a$$

$$= 250 - 50 \times 0.25$$

$$= 237.5 \text{ volts}$$

Then, $$N_1 \propto \frac{E_{b1}}{\phi_1} \quad ...(i)$$

and $$T_1 \propto \phi_1 I_{a1} \quad ...(ii)$$

Here, ϕ_1 and T_1 are flux per pole and load torque initially before the weakening of the shunt field flux.

After weakening of field flux:

Field flux $\phi_2 = 0.9\,\phi_1,$

Thereby, $\frac{\phi_2}{\phi_1} = 0.9$ ...(*iii*)

Speed $N_2 \propto \frac{E_{b2}}{\phi_2}$ ...(*iv*)

and load torque $T_2 \propto \phi_2 I_{a2}$ ...(*v*)

But load torque remains the same,

Therefore, $T_1 = T_2$

and Thus, $\phi_1 I_{a1} = \phi_2 I_{a2}$

or $\frac{\phi_2}{\phi_1} = \frac{I_{a1}}{I_{a2}} = 0.9$ (from *iii*)

or $\frac{I_{a1}}{I_{a2}} = 0.9$

$$I_{a2} = \frac{I_{a1}}{0.9} = \frac{50}{0.9}$$

$$= 55.6 \text{ amps.}$$

Therefore, back e.m.f.

$$E_{b2} = V - I_{a2}R_a$$

$$= 250 - 55.6 \times 0.25$$

$$= 250 - 13.9 = 236.1 \text{ volts}$$

Dividing (*iv*) by (*i*)

$$\frac{N_2}{N_1} = \frac{E_{b2}}{E_{b1}} \times \frac{\phi_1}{\phi_2}$$

$$N_2 = N_1 \times \frac{E_{b2}}{E_{b1}} \times \frac{1}{\phi_2/\phi_1}$$

$$= 750 \times \frac{236.1}{237.5} \times \frac{1}{0.9}$$

$$= \mathbf{828.4 \text{ r.p.m Ans.}}$$

Example 4.27. A 220 volts D.C shunt motor having armature resistance of 0.5Ω and shunt field resistance of 110 Ω drives a load of 500 r.p.m., taking 25 amperes. It is desired to run the motor at 600 r.p.m. Assuming the load torque to be constant, find the value of resistance to be used in the field as field regulator. Neglect saturation effect.

Solution.

Initial conditions:

Speed $N_1 = 500$ r.p.m

Supply voltage across the motor,

$$V = 220 \text{ Volts.}$$

Shunt field resistance,

$$R_{sh} = 110 \text{ ohm.}$$

Shunt field resistance, $R_a = 0.5\ \Omega.$

Line current, $I_L = 25$ amperes

Field current, $I_{sh} = \dfrac{V}{R_{sh}} = \dfrac{220}{110}$ Where is (*i*)

$$= 2.0 \text{ amperes.}$$

Therefore, armature current

$$I_{a1} = 25 - 2 = 23 \text{ amperes.}$$

Back e.m.f., $E_{b1} = V - I_{a1}R_a.$

$$= 220 - 23 \times 0.5$$

$$= 208.5 \text{ volts.}$$

Now, load torque,

$$T_1 \propto \phi_1 I_{a1}$$

or $T_1 \propto I_{sh1} I_{a1}$ $\left[\because \text{neglecting saturation effect, } \phi \propto I_{sh}.\right]$

Also $N_1 \propto \dfrac{E_{b1}}{\phi_1} \propto \dfrac{E_{b1}}{I_{sh1}}$ ...(*ii*)

After weakening of field due to insertion of variable resistance in series with the shunt field to obtain speed.

$$N_2 = 600 \text{ r.p.m}$$

Let $R_{sh2} = R_{sh1} + R$ (resistance inserted) be the new shunt field resistance and I_{a2} be the new armature current.

$$E_{b2} = V - I_{a2} R_a = (220 - I_{a2} \times 0.5) \text{ volts}$$

Now, torque $T_2 \propto \phi_2 I_{a2}$

or $T_2 \propto I_{sh2} I_{a2}$ ...(*iii*)

Also, $N_2 \propto \dfrac{E_{b2}}{I_{sh2}}$ ...(*iv*)

Since load torque is same, therefore,

$$T_1 = T_2$$

or $$I_{sh1} I_{a1} = I_{sh2} I_{a2}$$ [from (*i*) and (*iii*) equations]

$$2 \times 23 = I_{sh2} I_{a2}$$

$$\therefore \quad I_{sh2} = \frac{46}{I_{a2}}$$

and $$E_{b2} = (220 - I_{a2} \times 0.5)$$ (already found)

Dividing (*ii*) by (*iv*) we have

$$\frac{N_1}{N_2} = \frac{E_{b1}}{E_{b2}} \times \frac{I_{sh2}}{Is_{h1}}$$

$$\frac{500}{600} = \frac{208.5}{(220 - 0.5\, I_{a2})} \times \frac{46/I_{a2}}{2}$$

$$5(220 - I_{a2})\, I_{a2} = 6 \times 23 \times 208.5$$

$$I_{a2}^2 - 440\, I_{a2} + 11509 = 0$$

Solving for this quadratic equation

$$I_{a2} = 28 \text{ amperes.}$$

and $$I_{sh2} = \frac{46}{I_{a2}} = \frac{46}{28}$$

$$= 1.65 \text{ amperes}$$

Therefore, $$R_{sh2} = \frac{V}{I_{sh2}} = \frac{220}{1.65}$$

$$= 133.33 \text{ ohms.}$$

Hence resistance of field rheostat or speed controller to be inserted in field of D.C shunt motor,

$$R = R_{sh2} - R_{sh1}$$

$$= 133.33 - 100 \text{ ohms} = 33.33 \text{ ohms.}$$ **Ans.**

Example 4.28. A shunt wound motor has an armature resistance of 1.0 ohm. It is connected across 220 volt supply. The armature current taken by the motor is 20 amperes and the motor runs at 800 r.p.m. Calculate the additional resistance to be inserted in series with the armature to reduce the speed to 520 r.p.m. Assume that there is no change in armature current.

Solution.

Initially when no additional resistance is inserted:

Back e.m.f., $$E_{b1} = V - I_{a1} R_a$$

$$\therefore \quad E_{b1} = 220 - 20 \times 1.0$$

$$= 200 \text{ volts.}$$

Speed of motor, $N_1 = 800$ r.p.m.

Since the excitation remains the same, there is no change in flux so long as V and R_{sh} are the same.

or $E_{b1} \propto N_1$

After insertion of resistance in the shunt field:

$$N_2 = 520 \text{ r.p.m.}$$

Let the back e.m.f. be E_{b2}.

Then $E_{b2} \propto N_2$

or $$\frac{E_{b2}}{E_{b1}} = \frac{N_2}{N_1}$$

or $$E_{b2} = E_{b1} \times \frac{N_2}{N_1}$$

$$= 200 \times \frac{520}{800} = 130 \text{ volts}$$

Voltage drop in the armature circuit

$$= 220 - 130 = 90 \text{ volts.}$$

The armature circuit current is the same as 20 amperes.

Therefore, total resistance of armature circuit

$$= \frac{90}{20} = 4.5 \text{ ohms}$$

Hence additional series resistance required

$$= 4.5 - 1.0 = \mathbf{3.5 \text{ ohms.}}$$

4.57. SPEED CONTROL OF D.C SERIES MOTORS

Speed of series motors can be controlled in one of the following methods:

(*i*) ***Flux or Field control method.*** In this method the flux produced by the D.C. series motor varies and hence the speed control is achieved. This can be brought about in the following ways:

(*a*) ***By field divertors.*** A variable resistance called the field divertor is inverted in parallel with the series field winding having resistance R_{se} as shown in Fig. 4.84. Some of the field current is shunted through this field divertor, thus decreasing the current in the series field winding R_{se}. Thus the field is weakened and speed $\left(N \propto \frac{1}{\phi}\right)$ is in creased. On the other hand, if divertor resistance is reduced, the current through series field winding decreases and hence flux is decreased. Consequently the speed of the motor is increased. Through this method only speed more than the normal speed of the motor can be achieved.

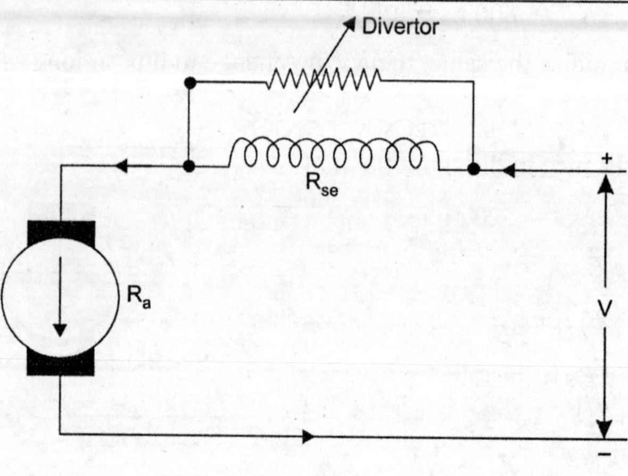

Fig. 4.84

(*b*) ***By Armature divertors.*** A variable resistance shown in Fig. 4.85 is connected across the armature circuit. The motor works as a compound wound motor with facility of shunt field control. The speeds below the normal speed can be achieved through this method. The divertor shunts some of the armature current. Thus for the same load torque and with the decreased armature current, the flux ϕ must increase according to the formula

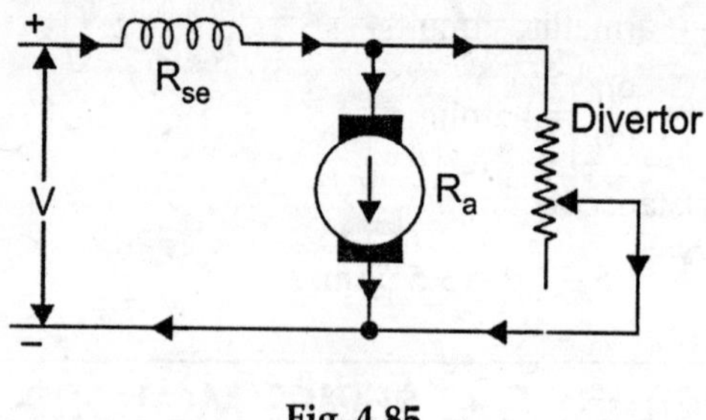

Fig. 4.85

$$T \propto \phi I_a.$$

This results in increase in line current of the motor and hence the field increases. Since the speed is inversely proportional to the field flux, therefore, motor speed is decreased. Hence by this method, any speed lower than the normal speed can be obtained. This method of speed control is usually employed for traction and crane hoist motors.

(*c*) ***By tapping the field of D.C. series motor by splitting the field coils.*** The number of turns of the series field winding can be varied by closing the switch *X* as shown in Fig. 3.37, thus short circuiting some of the turns of the field winding. Thus by segregating the field winding into 3 or 4 sections, and controlled through switches, 3 or 4 speeds can be obtained.

When the switch *X* is closed, some part of the field winding is short circuited. This decreases the flux and consequently speed increases. In this way, speeds more than normal are achieved.

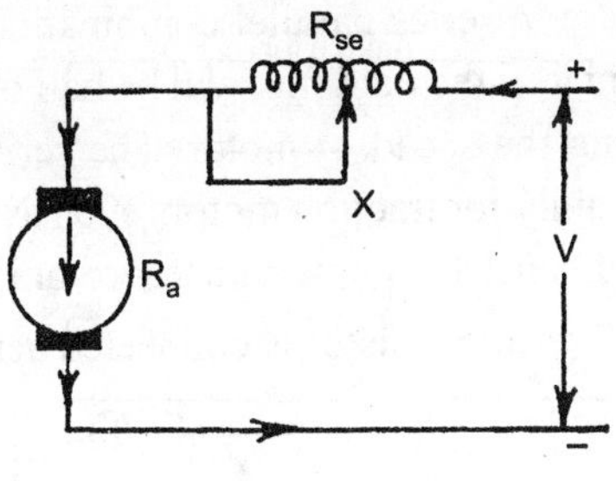

Fig. 4.86

(*ii*) ***Variable resistance in series with the armature.*** As shown in Fig. 4.87, a variable resistance is connected in series with the armature. This additional resistance causes additional voltage drop in the armature circuit and the voltage across the armature is reduced thus back e.m.f. and hence speed of the motor falls. By changing the resistance R, any speed below the normal speed can be obtained. This is a wasteful and uneconomical method because there is a considerable wastage of energy in the resistance R because of full current flowing through it.

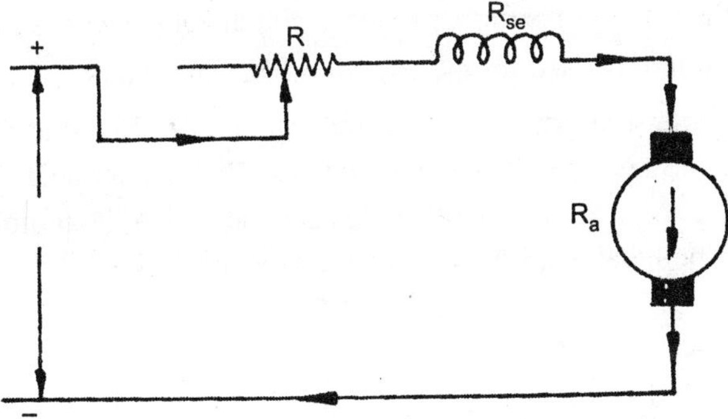

Fig. 4.87

(*iii*) In multipolar machines, low or high speeds are obtained by connecting the field coils either in series or in parallel as shown in Fig. 4.88. (*a*) & (*b*) respectively.

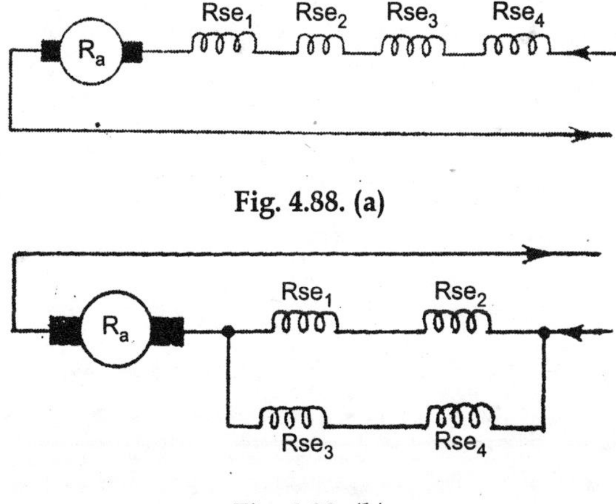

Fig. 4.88. (a)

Fig. 4.88. (b)

In Fig. 4.88 (*b*) the coils are in series parallel combination. In each coil half of the armature current will be flowing, and thus the field flux will be half of that in case of combination in Fig. 4.81 (*a*), thereby increasing the speed of motor. The series-parallel combination method of speed control is utilised mainly for traction motors such as those used in electric locomotives, trolley, cars, buses etc. and consists in normal use two or three motors mechanically coupled.

(*iv*) As shown in Fig. 4.89, a diverting resistor is connected across the field coils.

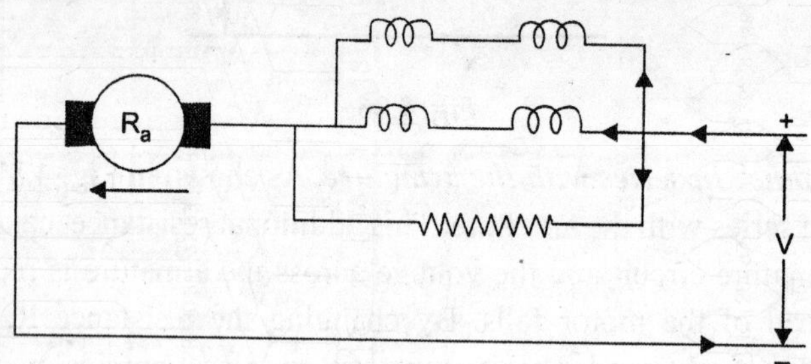

Fig. 4.89

In this case, the field strength is further reduced and thereby occurs a further increase of speed. This method is very commonly used for the control of the fan motors.

Example 4.29. A two pole series motor runs at 600 r.p.m. at full load at 500 volts when taking a current of 10 amperes. If the armature has 500 conductors and the flux per pole is expressed by $\phi = 0.03.\ I^{1/2}$ webers, whose I is the motor current, calculate the speed at which the motor will run, if the supply voltage and load torque are both halved. Ignore iron and windage losses.

[AMIE Nov. 1996]

Solution.

Since torque, $T \propto \phi I$

Then, $T \propto 0.03 I^{1/2}.I$

$$\propto 0.03 I^{3/2} \quad ...(i)$$

where, $I = 10$ amperes (Given)

Let the new load current be I_1 When T_1 is the new torque

$$\left(T_1 = \frac{T}{2}\right)$$

Therefore, $T_1 \propto 0.03 I_1^{3/2}$ ... (*ii*)

Dividing (*i*) by (*ii*),

$$\frac{T}{T_1} = \frac{I^{3/2}}{I_1^{3/2}}$$

Substituting the values,

$$2 = \frac{10^{3/2}}{I_1^{3/2}}$$

or $$I_1^{3/2} = \frac{10^{3/2}}{2}$$

or $$I_1 = \frac{10}{2^{2/3}} = 6.3 \text{ amperes.}$$

For the calculation of speed we need to know the back e.m.f.,

$$E_b = \frac{P\phi ZN}{60A} \text{ volts.}$$

where $Z = 500$ conductors,

$P = 2, A = 2,$

$N = 600$ r.p.m.

and $$\phi = 0.03I^{1/2}$$

$$= 0.03 \times 10^{1/2} = 0.0948 \text{ wb.}$$

Therefore, $$E_b = \frac{2 \times 0.0948 \times 500 \times 600}{60 \times 2}$$

$$= 474 \text{ volts.}$$

$$E_b = V - I(R_a + R_{se}) \text{ (In case of series motor)}$$

$$474 = 500 - 10\,(R_a + R_{se})$$

or $$(R_a + R_{se}) = \mathbf{2.6\ ohms.}$$

Now, when the supply voltage is reduced to half value, *i.e* $\frac{500}{2} = 250$ volts, then back e.m.f at this value of voltage

$$E_{b1} = V - I(R_a + R_{se})$$

or $$E_{b1} = 250 - 6.3\,(2.6) = 233.6 \text{ volts.}$$

and $$\phi_1 = 0.03 \times (6.3)^{1/2} = 0.03 \times 2.51$$

$$= 0.0753 \text{ wb.}$$

Now $$N_1 \propto \frac{E_{b1}}{\phi_1}$$

or $$\frac{N_1}{N} = \frac{E_{b1}}{E_b} \times \frac{\phi}{\phi_1}$$

or $$N_1 = 600 \times \frac{233.6}{474} \times \frac{0.0948}{0.0753}$$

$$= \mathbf{372\ r.p.m}$$

4.58. LOSSES IN A D.C MOTOR

The losses which occur in a d.c. motor are exactly the same as the case of a d.c. generator which are as under:–

(*i*) Copper losses.

(*ii*) Iron losses.

(*iii*) Frictional and windage loss (Mechanical losses).

As in the case of d.c. generator these losses cause (*i*) an increase of temperature (*ii*) reduce in life and efficiency of the d.c. motor.

Efficiency of a D.C. Motor: The efficiency of a d.c. motor is defined as *the ratio of out put power to the input power i.e.*

$$\% \eta = \frac{Power\ output}{Power\ input} \times 100$$

$$= \frac{Power\ output}{Power\ output + Total\ losses} \times 100$$

The condition for maximum efficiency is the same as in the case of a d.c. generator *i.e.* variable losses = constant losses.

Power Stages in a D.C. Motor: The power stages in a d.c. motor are given diagrammatically in the 4.90.

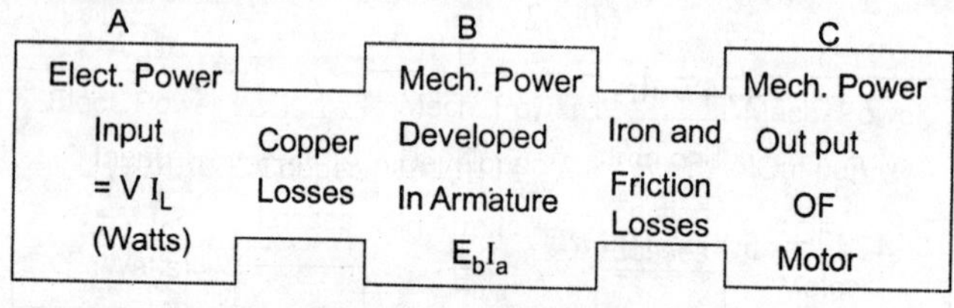

Fig. 4.90

From the block diagram:–

$$A - B = \text{Copper losses}$$

$$B - C = \text{Friction and iron losses}$$

$$\text{Electrical efficiency} = \frac{B}{A} = \frac{Mech.\ power\ developed}{Power\ input}$$

$$\text{Mechanical efficiency} = \frac{C}{B} = \frac{Power\ output}{Mech.\ power\ developed}$$

$$\text{Overall efficiency or commercial efficiency} = \frac{C}{A} = \frac{Power\ output}{Power\ input}$$

Example 4.30. A 220 V shunt motor is taking a current 30 A. Armature and shunt field resistances are 0.2 Ω and 100 Ω respectively. Iron and friction losses amount to 500 watts. Find the efficiency of the motor.

Sol. Supply voltage, $V = 220\ volts$

Line current, $I_L = 30\ A$

Armature resistance, $R_a = 0.2\ \Omega.$

Shunt field resistance, $R_{sh} = 100\ \Omega$

Iron and frictional loss,

$$W_i = 500 \text{ watts.}$$

Shunt field current, $I_{sh} = \frac{220}{100} = 2.2A$

$\therefore$ Armature current, $I_a = 30 - 2.2 = 27.8$ A

Armature copper loss $= I_a^2 . R_a = (27.8)^2 \times 0.2 = 154.57$ watts

Shunt field copper loss $= I_{sh}^2 . R_{sh} = (2.2)^2 \times 100 = 484$ watts

Total copper losses $= 154.57 + 484 = 638.57$ watts

Total losses $= 638.57 + 500 = 1138.57$ watts

Power input $= V \times I_L = 220 \times 30 = 6600$ watts

Power output $=$ Input – T. losses $= 6600 - 1138.57 = 5461.43$

$$\% \eta = \frac{Output}{Input} \times 100 = \frac{5461.43}{6600} \times 100 = 82.74\% \textbf{ (Ans.)}$$

Example 4.32. A 200 volt d.c. series motor takes 60 A. Armature resistance is 0.08 Ω, series field resistance 0.05 Ω. If iron and frictional losses are twice to copper losses of this load, find the B.H.P. and efficiency.

Sol. Supply voltage, $V = 200$ *volts*

Line current, $I_L = 60\ A$

Armature resistance, $R_a = 0.08\ \Omega$

Series field resistance, $R_{se} = 0.05\ \Omega$

$\therefore$ Copper losses $= I_a^2 (R_a + R_{se}) = (60)^2 (0.08 + 0.05)$

$= 468$ watts

Since iron and frictional losses

$= 2 \times$ copper loss

$\therefore$ Iron and friction losses $= 2 \times 468 = 936$ *watts*

and Total losses $= 468 + 936 = 1404$ *watts.*

we know that, Power output = Input – T. losses.

$\therefore$ Power Input $= V.I_L = 200 \times 60 = 12000$ *watts.*

Power output $= 12000 - 1404 = 10596$ watts.

$$\text{B.H.P} = \frac{10596}{735.5} = 14.406 \textbf{ (Ans.)}$$

$$\%\text{Efficiency of the motor} = \frac{Output}{Input} \times 100$$

$$\% \eta = \frac{10596}{12000} \times 100 = 88.3\% \textbf{ (Ans.)}$$

Example 4.33. A 230 V–shunt motor takes 5 A at no load. The resistance of the armature and field circuit are 0.25 Ω and 115 Ω respectively. If the motor is loaded so as to carry 40 A, determine (i) Iron and frictional losses and (*ii*) efficiency.

Sol. Supply voltage, $V = 230$ volts

No load line current, $I_o = 5\ A$

Armature resistance, $R_a = 0.25\ \Omega$

Shunt field resistance, $R_{sh} = 115\ \Omega$

Loaded line current, $I_L = 40\ A$

When the motor is on No load

Power Input to Motor $= V.I_o = 230 \times 5 = 1150$ watts.

At no load the power supplied to the motor is used in overcoming the following losses:- (*a*) No load armature copper loss (*b*) Shunt field copper loss. (*c*) Iron and Mechanical losses.

Shunt field current, $I_{sh} = \dfrac{V}{R_{sh}} = \dfrac{230}{115} = 2\ A$

No load armature current,

$$I_{ao} = I_o - I_{sh} = 5 - 2 = 3\ A$$

Armature copper losses $= I_{ao}^2 . R_a = (3)^2 \times 0.25 = 2.25$ watts **(Ans.)**

Shunt field copper loss $= I_{sh}^2 . R_{sh} = (2)^2 \times 115 = 460$ watts. **(Ans.)**

Total copper loss $= 2.25 + 460 = 462.25$ watts.

Iron and frictional losses $=$ Input – Total Copper loss

$= 1150 - 462.25 = 687.75$ watts. **(Ans.)**

When the motor is loaded:

Line current, $I_L = 40$ A

$\therefore$ Armature current, $I_a = 40 - 2 = 38$ A

Armature copper loss $= I_a^2 . R_a = (38)^2 \times 0.25 = 361$ watts.

Constant losses $=$ Iron and Friction loss + Shunt field loss

$= 687.75 + 460 = 1147.25$ watts

Total losses $= 1147.25 + 361 = 1508.75$ watts

Power Input $V.I_L = 230 \times 40 = 9200$ watts.

Power output $=$ Input – *T*. losses $= 9200 - 1508.75 = 7691.25$ *watts*

$\therefore$ % efficiency $= \dfrac{Output}{Input} \times 100 = \dfrac{7691.25}{9200} \times 100 = 83.6\%$ **(Ans.)**

Example 3.33. A long shunt compound generator running at 1000 r.p.m delivers 22 kW at terminal voltage of 220 V. The resistance of armature, shunt field and series field are 0.05, 110 and 0.06 Ω respectively. The overall efficiency at above load is 88%. Find (*i*) copper loss (*ii*) iron and friction losses.

Solution. Power delivered by the generator,

$$P = 22000 \text{ Watts}$$

Terminal voltage, $V = 220\ V$

Speed of the generator, $N = 1000\ r.p.m.$

Output load current, $I_L = \frac{P}{V} = \frac{22000}{220} = 100\ A$

Shunt field current, $I_{sh} = \frac{V}{R_{sh}} = \frac{220}{110} = 2\text{ A}$

Armature current, $I_a = I_L + I_{sh}$

$= 100 + 2 = 102\ A$

Armature copper loss $= I_a^2 . R_a$

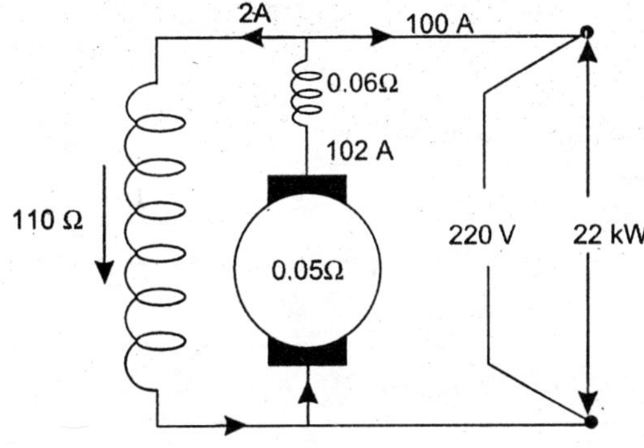

Fig. 4.91

$= (102)^2 \times .05 = 520.2W$

Series field copper loss $= I_{se}^2 . R_{se} = (102)^2 \times 0.06 = 624.24W$

Shunt field copper loss $= I_{sh}^2 . R_{sh} = (2)^2 \times 110 = 440\ W$

Total copper loss $= 520.2 + 624.4 + 440 = 1584.44\ W$

Power input to generator $= \frac{22000}{0.88} = 25000W$

Total losses = Power input–power output

$\therefore$ Total losses $= 25000 - 22000 = 3000\ W$

Iron and frictional losses,

P_i = Total losses – Total copper losses

i.e. $P_i = 3000 - 1584.44 = 1415.56\ W$ **(Ans.)**

4.59. EFFICIENCY OF A D.C. MACHINE

The ratio of output power to the input power of a d.c. machine is called its efficiency.

$$\text{Efficiency } \eta = \frac{Output}{Input}$$

(*i*) **When machine is working as a generator:**

$$\text{Power output} = VI \textit{ watts}$$

$$\text{Power input} = \text{Power output} + \text{Variable losses} + \text{Constant losses.}$$

Since the shunt field current I_{sh} is very small as compared to line current, therefore,

$$I \approx I_a \text{ (neglecting } I_{sh})$$

$$\therefore \quad \text{Variable losses} = I^2 R_a$$

$$\text{Constant losses} = P_c \text{ (say)}$$

$$\text{Then, power output} = VI + I^2 R_a + \text{Pc}$$

$$\therefore \quad \eta = \frac{VI}{VI + I^2 R_a + P_c}$$

(*ii*) When machine is working as a motor:

$$\text{Power input} = \text{VI watts}$$

$$\text{Power output} = \text{Power input} - \text{Variable losses} - \text{constant losses}$$

$$= VI - I^2 R_a - P_c$$

$$\therefore \quad \eta = \frac{VI - I^2 R_a - P_c}{VI}.$$

4.60. CONDITION FOR MAXIMUM EFFICIENCY

Let us consider that the d.c machine is working as a generator. Then,

$$\text{Efficiency,} \quad \eta = \frac{output}{output + variable\ losses + constant\ \ losses}$$

$$= \frac{VI}{VI + I^2 R_a + P_c}$$

$$= \frac{I}{1 + \frac{IR_a}{V} + \frac{P_c}{VI}} \quad \text{...(}i\text{)}$$

Now, efficiency will be maximum when the denominator of eq. (*i*) is minimum *i.e.*

$$\frac{d}{dI}\left(1 + \frac{IR_a}{V} + \frac{P_c}{VI}\right) = 0$$

or

$$\frac{R_a}{V} - \frac{P_c}{VI^2} = 0$$

or

$$\frac{R_a}{V} = \frac{P_c}{VI^2}$$

or

$$I^2 R_a = P_c$$

i.e. Variable losses = Constant losses.

The same condition will arrive when the d.c. machine works as a motor.

Hence, The efficiency of a d.c. machine will be maximum when the line current is such that constant loss is equal to the variable loss.

The line current at which the efficiency of d.c. machine is maximum,

$$I = \sqrt{\frac{P_c}{R_a}}.$$

Efficiency of D.C Machines. To find the efficiency of d.c. machines the following tests are to be carried out on a d.c. machine:

I. Direct Testing. The direct load test is carried out on a d.c. machine by putting the direct load on the d c. machine. The power output is wasted across the load. Usually a pulley brake system is used as load on the machine. The pulley brakes are adjusted till full load current flows. The readings on the voltmeter, ammeter and spring balances connected to the two sides of the pulley are noted.

V = Reading of voltmeter in volts

I = Reading of a meter in amps

T_1 = Reading of spring balance of tight side of the belt in kg

T_2 = Reading of spring balance on slick side of the belt in kg

R = Radius of the pulley in metres.

Torque acting on the pulley

$$= (T_1 - T_2)\ R.\ \text{kg.M.}$$

$$= 9.81\ (T_1 - T_2)\ \text{R.N.M.}$$

$$\text{Output} = \frac{2\pi N\ [9.81\ (T_1 - T_2) R]}{60} \text{ Joules/sec or watts}$$

$$= \frac{2\pi\ N\ 9.81\ (T_1 - T_2) R}{60} \text{ Joules/sec or watts sec}$$

$$\text{Input} = V \times I \text{ watts}$$

$$\%\ \text{Eff.} = \frac{Output}{Input} \times 100.$$

This is simple method, but at the same time is wasteful.

II. Indirect Testing. These tests are performed without actually loading the machines. The most important indirect test is Swinburne's Test. This is also called no load running test.

4.61. SWINBURNE'S TEST

This is the simple and indirect method, in which the losses are measured separately and efficiency at any desired load is pre-determined in advance. The machine is run as a motor at no load. The field current is adjusted to give the normal speed, whereas normal (*rated*) voltage is applied across the motor terminals. This test is applicable to those machines in which flux is practically constant *i.e.*, shunt and compound machines. The connection diagram for determining the no load losses of a d.c. shunt machine is shown in Fig. 4.92.

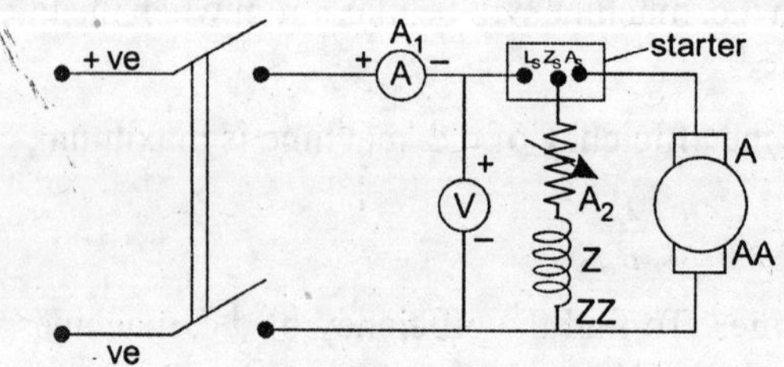

Fig. 4.92

The resistances of the field winding and armature are measured using a battery, voltmeter and an ammeter. Since these resistances are measured when the machine is cold, so they should be converted to the values corresponding to the temperature at which the machine would work on full load. Generally, these values are measured for a temperature rise of 40°C above the room temperature.

Let the value of armature resistance is R_a and shunt field resistance is R_{sh}.

The no load current I_o is measured by the ammeter A_1 whereas shunt field current I_{sh} is given by ammeter A_2. The no load armature current I_{ao} is $(I_o - I_{sh})$

Let the supply voltage $= V$

No load power input $= V.I_o.$ *watts*

Power input to the armature $= V.I_{ao} = V(I_o - I_{sh})$ *watts*

Shunt field copper loss $= V.I_{sh}$ *watts*

Armature copper loss at no load

$$= I_{ao}^2 . R_a = (I_o - I_{sh})^2 . R_a \text{ watts}$$

Stray losses, P_s = Input at no load – Shunt field loss – Armature loss

$$= V.I_o - VI_{sh} - I_{ao}^2 R_a$$

Constant losses = Stray loss + Shunt field copper loss

or $$P_c = P_s + VI_{sh}$$

or $$P_c = VI_o - VI_{sh} - I_{ao}^2 R_a + VI_{sh}$$

or $$P_c = VI_o - I_{ao}^2 . R_a$$

Efficiency of the machine running as a motor:

Let the line current of the motor $= I_L$ *amp.*

Power input to the motor $= V.I_L.$ *Watts*

Armature copper loss $= (I_L - I_{sh})^2 . R_a$

Total losses, $P_T = (I_L - I_{sh})^2 . R_a + P_c$

Power output $= [VI_L - (I_L - I_{sh})^2 . R_a + P_c]$

$$\% \text{ Efficiency of the motor} = \frac{Output}{Input} \times 100$$

Efficiency of machine running as a generator:

Let the load current I_L be supplied by the Generator at a terminal voltage of V volts

$$\text{Generator output} = V.I_L. \text{ watts}$$

$$\text{Armature copper loss} = I_a^2.R_a = (I_L + I_{sh})^2.\ R_a$$

$$\text{Total loss} = \text{Armature copper loss} + \text{Constant losses}$$

i.e.

$$P_T = (I_L + I_{sh})^2 .\ R_a + P_c$$

$$\text{Generator input} = \text{Generator output} + \text{Total losses}$$

$$= V.\ I_L + \{(I_L + I_{sh})^2.\ R_a + P_c\}$$

$$\% \quad \text{Generator efficiency} = \frac{Generator\ output}{Generator\ input} = \frac{V.\ I_L}{VI_L + P_T} \times 100ssssss$$

4.61.1. Advantages And Disadvantages of Swinburn's Test

Following are the major advantages of Swinburn's test for D.C. motors.

1. It is convenient and economical because power required to test a large machine is small *i.e.*, only no load input power.
2. The efficiency can be predetermined at any load because constant losses are known.

Following are the few disadvantages of Swinburn's test for which this test is considered to be unfit for accuracy requirements.

1. It does not take into consideration of stray losses, when the machine is loaded.
2. This test does not enable us to check the performance of the machine on full load. It is impossible to know about the commutation, would be satisfactory at full load and whether the temperature rise is within the specified limits.
3. This test does not give accurate results because iron losses under actual load are more than those measured. It is mainly due to armature reaction distorting the field.

4.62. BACK TO BACK TESTING OR HOPKINSON'S TEST OF D.C. MACHINES

In this test, full-load test can be carried out on two identical shunt machines without wasting their outputs. Figure 4.93. shows the connection diagram for this test on a pair of shunt machines.

Figure 4.93. shows two machines which are mechanically coupled. Their fields are adjusted in such a way that one runs as a generator and the other as a motor. The power produced by the generator is utilised by the motor driving the generator. The power taken from the supply is used to supply losses only. Two identical machines of any size can be tested under full-load conditions. This method is very useful to determine the efficiency as well as for a heat run test for determining the temperature rise. The following procedures are followed:

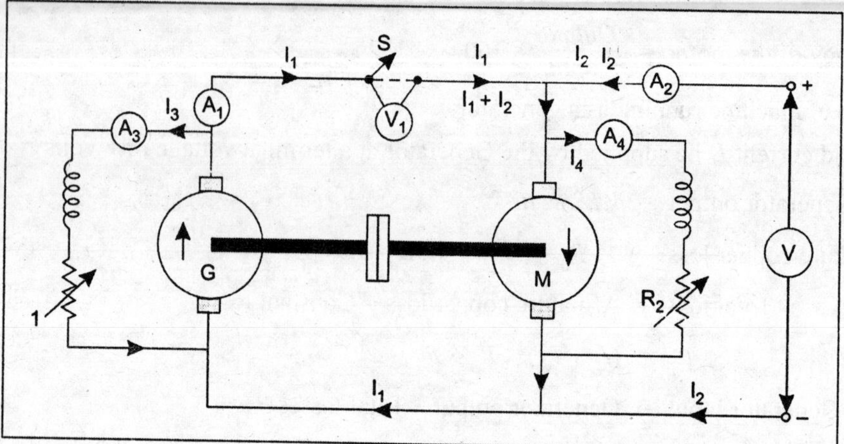

Fig. 4.93. Back to Back Testing (Hopkinson's Test)

- The machine M in Figure 4.93 is started through a starter. Its field excitation is adjusted to take it to normal speed. The machine *M* drives the machine *G*. The switch *S* is kept open.
- The excitation of machine *G* is gradually increased so that the reading of the voltmeter becomes zero. The switch *S* is closed, and the machine *G* is at the floating stage. The shunt regulators are adjusted to put any desired load.

The input power is used to meet losses only.

Let

V_t be the supply voltage

I_1 be the output current of generator

I_2 be the current taken from the supply

I_3 be the exciting current of the generator

I_4 be the exciting current of the motor

R_a be the armature resistance of each machine

$$\text{Motor input} = V_t(I_1 + I_2)$$

$$\text{Generator input} = V_t I_1$$

If the efficiency of both the machines be η, we have

$$\text{output of the motor} = \eta \times \text{Input}$$

$$\text{output of the generator} = \eta \times \text{Input} = \eta \times \eta\, V_t(I_1 + I_2) = \eta^2\, V_t\,(I_1 + I_2)$$

$$\eta^2 V_t(I_1 + I_2) = V_t I_1$$

$$\therefore \qquad \eta = \sqrt{\frac{I_1}{I_1 + I_2}}$$

In practice it is very difficult to get two machines having identical efficiency.

Armature Cu-loss in generator = $(I_1 + I_2)^2 R_a$

Shunt Cu-loss in generator = VI_3

Armature Cu-loss in motor = $(I_1 + I_2 - I_4)^2 R_a$

Shunt Cu-loss in generator = $V_t I_4$

The overall motor and generator losses are equal to the power supplied by the mains.

Power taken from supply = $V_t I_2$

Therefore, stray losses for the set

$$= V_t I_2 - [(I_1 + I_2)^2 R_a + (I_1 + I_2 - I_4)^2 R_a + V_t I_3 + V_t I_4] = P_{stray}$$

If the stray losses are equally divided between the two machines

$$\text{Stray loss per machine} = \frac{P_{stray}}{2}$$

For generator:

$$\text{Total losses} = (I_1 + I_2)^2 R_a + V_t I_3 + \frac{P_{stray}}{2}$$

$$\text{Output} = VI_1$$

$$\therefore \text{ efficiency of generator } (\eta_g) = \frac{\text{Output}}{\text{Output} + \text{Losses}}$$

$$= \frac{V_t I_1}{V_t I_1 + (I_1 + I_2)^2 R_a + V_t I_3 + \dfrac{P_{stray}}{2}}$$

$$\text{Efficiency of generator } (\eta_m) = \frac{\text{Input} - \text{Losses}}{\text{Input}}$$

$$= \frac{V_t(I_1 + I_2) - \left[(I_1 + I_2 - I_4)^2 R_a + V_t I_4 + \dfrac{P_{stray}}{2}\right]}{V_t(I_1 + I_2)}$$

This test has the following advantages:

- This test is very economical since power required in small.
- Commutation and temperature rise to the machine can be studied property.
- Since the test is conducted at full-load, any change in iron losses due to flux distortion at full-load is taken into account.

The main disadvantages of this test is that two identical machines cannot be obtained very easily.

Example 4.34. Hopkinson's test on two identical shunt machines gave the following readings:

Supply voltage = 240 V, field currents = 6 A and 5A, line current = 40 A, armature current of motor = 240 A, armature resistance of each machine = 0.014 Ω, voltage drop/brush = 1 V.

Find the efficiency of each machine.

Solution.

V_t = 240 V, I_{sh1} (field current of generator) = 6A, I_{sh2} (field current of motor) = 5A, supply current = 40 A, armature current of motor = 240A, armature resistance of each machine = 0.014Ω, voltage drop per brush = 1 V.

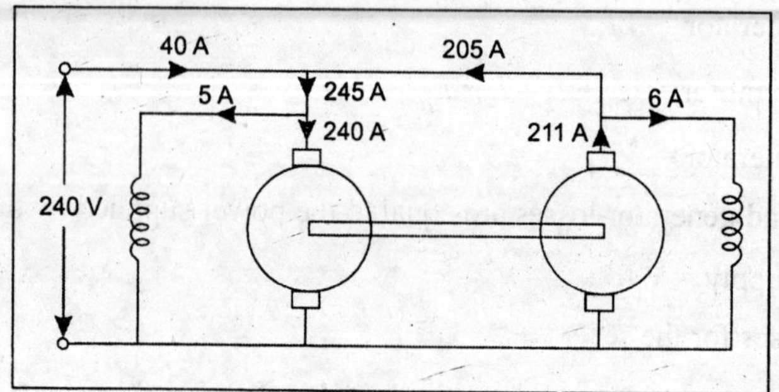

Fig. 4.94

From Figure 4.94. we get the following:

Motor:

$$\text{Motor input current} = 245 \text{ A}$$

$$\text{Armature Cu-loss} = 245^2 \times 0.014 = 840.35 \text{ W}$$

$$\text{Shunt field Cu-loss} = 240 \times 5 = 1200 \text{ W}$$

$$\text{Brush contact loss} = 240 \times 1 \times 2 = 480 \text{ W}$$

$$\text{Total Cu-loss} = 840.35 + 1200 + 480 = 2520.35 \text{ W}$$

Generator:

$$\text{Generator output current} = 205 \text{ A}$$

$$\text{Generator input current} = 211 \text{ A}$$

$$\text{Armature Cu-loss} = 211^2 \times 0.014 = 623.3 \text{ W}$$

$$\text{Shunt field Cu-loss} = 240 \times 6 = 1440 \text{ W}$$

$$\text{Brush contact loss} = 211 \times 1 \times 2 = 422 \text{ W}$$

$$\text{Total Cu-loss} = 623.3 + 1440 + 422 = 2458.3 \text{ W}$$

Total power input from supply = total losses in the set

or, $$240 \times 40 = 2458.3 + 2520.35 + \text{Stray load losses}$$

so, $$\text{Stray load losses} = 4594.35 \text{ W}$$

Therefore, stray losses per machines = 2297.17 W

More efficiency:

$$\text{Total losses} = 2520.35 + 2297.17 = 4817.52 \text{ W}$$

$$\text{Generator input} = 240 \times 245 = 58800 \text{ W}$$

$$\text{Generator output} = 58800 - 4817.52 = 53982.48 \text{ W}$$

Therefore, generator efficiency $(\eta_g) = \dfrac{\text{Output}}{\text{Input}}$

$$= \frac{53982.48}{58800} = 0.9180 \text{ pu} = 91.80\%$$

Generator efficiency:

$$\text{Total losses} = 2458.3 + 2297.17 = 4782.47 \text{ W}$$

$$\text{Motor output} = 240 \times 205 = 49200 \text{ W}$$

$$\text{Motor output} = 49200 + 4782.47 = 53982.47 \text{ W}$$

$$\text{Therefore, motor efficiency } (\eta_m) = \frac{\text{Output}}{\text{Input}}$$

$$= \frac{49200}{53982.47} = 0.9914 \text{ pu} = 91.14\% \textbf{ Ans.}$$

4.63. BRAKE OR LOAD TEST

It is a direct method and consists of applying a brake to a water-cooled pulley mounted on the motor shaft as shown in Fig. 4.95. (*a*) One end of the rope is fixed to the floor via a spring balance '*S*' and the other is connected to a known mass W_1 suspended at the other end. The motor is running and the load on the motor is adjusted till it carries its W_2 full load current.

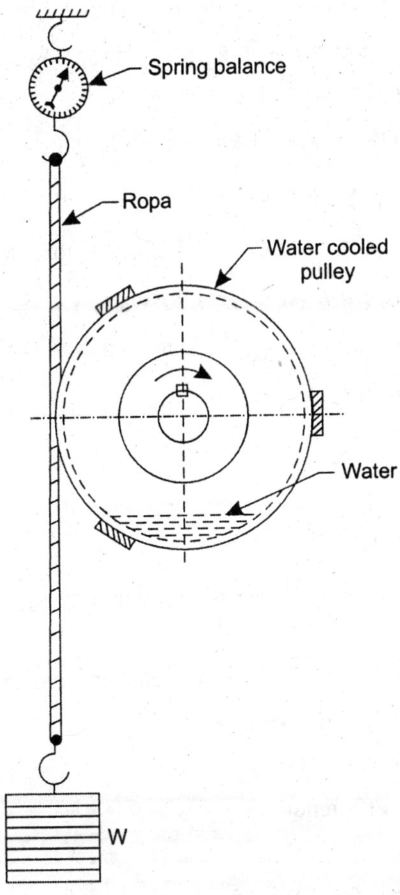

Fig. 4.95. (*a*)

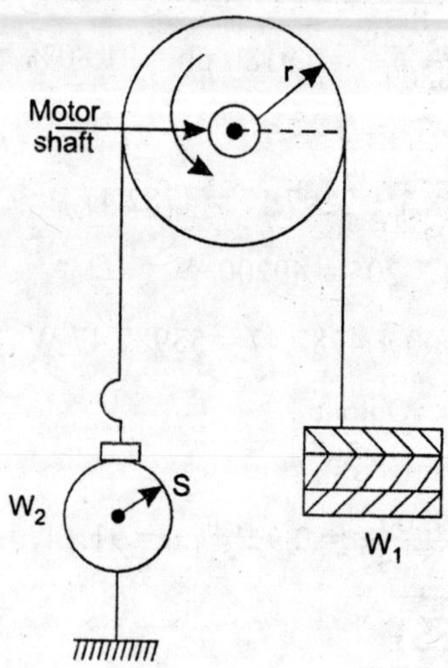

Fig. 4.95. (*b*)

Let

W_1 = Weight in kg which is suspended

W_2 = Reading on spring to balance in kg–wt.

Net pull on the rope = $(W_1 - W_2)$ kg wt or 9.81 $(W_1 - W_2)$ Newtons. If r is the radius of pulley in metres, then the shaft torque T_{sh} developed by the motor

$$= (W_1 - W_2) \times r \text{ kg} - \text{m} = 9.81\,(W_1 - W_2) \times r \text{ N} - \text{m}.$$

Motor output power $= T_{sh} \times 2\,\pi\,N$ watts (Where N = motor or pulley speed in r.p.s.)

$$= 2\,\pi \times 9.81 \text{ N}\,(W_1 - W_2) \times r \text{ watts}$$

$$= 61.70\,N\,(W_1 - W_2) \times r \text{ watts}$$

Let V = Supply voltage in volts

I = Full load current in amps taken by the motor.

∴ Input to motor = VI watts

Then Efficiency, $$\eta = \frac{\text{output}}{\text{Input}} = \frac{61.70\,N\,(W_1 - W_2)\,r}{VI}$$

Example 4.35. The following readings are obtained when doing a load test on a d.c. shunt motor using a brake drum.

Reading on spring balance = 10 kg and 35 kg; Diameter of the drum = 40 cm

Motor speed. = 950 r.p.m. Applied = voltage 200 V

Line current = 30 A

Calculate the output power and efficiency. (Madras univ. 1986 Elec. Eng.)

Solution.

On the drum surface Force, $F = (35 - 10) = 25$ kg wt.

$= 25 \times 9.8$ Newton

Drum Radius, $r = 20 \text{ cm} = 0.2 \text{ m}$

$\therefore$ Torque $= F \times r = 25 \times 9.8 \times 0.2$

$= 49$ Newton

Speed, $N = \frac{950}{60} = \frac{95}{6}$ r.p.s

$\therefore$ $\omega = 2\pi N = 2\pi \times \frac{95}{6}$

$= 99.6$ rad./sec.

Motor Output $= T_{sh} \times \omega$ watt

$= 49 \times 99.6 = 4{,}876$ watts

Motor Input $= 240 \times 30 = 6000$ watts

$\therefore$ η (Efficiency) $= \frac{4876}{6000} = 0.812$ or 81.2% Ans.

Example. 4.36. In a brake test on a small motor, the speed was 1500 r.p.m., the load on one side of the brake band was 28.9 Newton and on the other side 1.67 Newton. The diameter of the brake pulley was 15.2 cm. If the input current was 2 Amp. At 250 volts. Calculate (*i*) The Torque (*ii*) Brake horse power and (*iii*) Efficiency.

Solution. (*i*) Torque, $T_{sh} = (W - S) \times r$

$= (28.9 - 1.67) \times \frac{0.152}{2}$

$= 2.07 \; N-m$

(*ii*) Output Power $= \frac{2\pi N T_{sh}}{60}$

$= \frac{2\pi \times 1500 \times 2.07}{60}$

$= 325$ walts

Brake horse power $= \frac{325}{746} = 0.436 \; H.l.$

(*iii*) Input to motor $= VI = 250 \times 2 = 500$ watts

Efficiency $= \frac{\text{Output}}{\text{Input}} \times 100$

$= \frac{325}{500} \times 100 = 65\%$

Example 4.37. The below given readings were obtained when doing a load test on a d.c. shunt motor while using a Brake drum:–

Spring balance readings = 10 kg and 35 kg

Diameter of drum = 40 cm.

Speed of the motor = 950 r.p.m; Applied voltage = 220 V; Line current = 30 A.

Calculate: (*i*) Output Power

(*ii*) Efficiency of the motor

Solution.

Force on the Drum, $F = 35 - 10 = 25$ kg – wt.

$= 25 \times 9.81$ Newton

Shaft Torque, $T_{sh} = F \times r = 25 \times 9.81 \times 0.2$

$= 49$ Newton-metre

(*i*) Motor output $= \dfrac{2\pi N T_{sh}}{60} = \dfrac{2\pi \times 950 \times 49}{60}$

$= 4877$ walts

(*ii*) Motor input $= VI = 200 \times 30 = 6000$ watts

Efficiency $= \dfrac{\text{output}}{\text{Input}} \times 100 = \dfrac{4877}{6000} \times 100$

$= 81.4\%$

Examination Problems

1. A shunt generator supplies 195 A at 220 V. Armature resistance = 0.02 Ω: shunt field resistance = 44 Ω. If the iron and frictional losses amount to 1600 W, find (*i*) e.m.f. generated (*ii*) Cu losses (*iii*) B.H.P. of the engine (*iv*) electrical and commercial efficiencies.

   [(*i*) 224 V (*ii*) 1900 W (*iii*) 62.25 H.P. (*iv*) 95.8% ; 92.5%]

2. The output of a shunt generator is 23kW at a terminal voltage of 200 V. Armature resistance = 0.05 Ω and shunt field resistance = 40 Ω. If the iron frictional losses equal the copper losses at this load, find (*i*) B.H.P. of the engine (*ii*) overall efficiency. **[(*i*) 36.9 H.P. (*ii*) 87.1 %]**

3. A shunt generator has a full-load current of 196 A at 220 V. The stray losses are 720 W and the shunt field coil resistance is 55 Ω. If it has a F.L. efficiency of 88%, find the armature resistance. Also find the load current corresponding to maximum efficiency.

   [0.107 Ω ; 122.3 A]

4. The output of a shunt generator of 66 A at 100 V. Armature resistance = 0.04 Ω, shunt field resistance 25 Ω. If the overall efficiency at this load is 88%, find (*i*) Cu losses (*ii*) iron and frictional losses (*iii*) B.H.P. of te driving engine. **[(*i*) 596 W (*ii*) 304 W (*iii*) 10 H.P.]**

5. A 4-pole d.c. shunt generator is delivering 20 A to a load to 10 Ω. If the armature resistance = 0.5 Ω and the shunt field resistance = 50 Ω, find the induced e.m.f. and efficiency of the machine. Allow a drop of IV per brush. **[214 V ; 77.9%]**

6. A short-shunt compound generator supplies a load of 10 kW at 200 V through a pair of feeders of total resistance 0.1 Ω. Armature resistance = 0.01 Ω; shunt field resistance = 52.5 W; series

field resistance = 0.1. Ω. Iron frictional losses amount to 631 W. Find (*i*) terminal p.d. (*ii*) e.m.f generated (*iii*) Cu losses (*iv*) B.H.P. of the driving engine (*v*) commercial efficiency.

[(*i*) 205 V (*ii*) 210.5 V (*iii*) 1119 W (*iv*) 16.1 H.P. (*v*) 85.4%]

7. In a determinate, the total iron loss is 8 kW at its rated speed and excitation. If excitation remains the same but speed is reduced by 25%, the total iron loss is found to be 5 kW. Calculate the hysteresis and eddy current losses at (*i*) full speed (*ii*) half the rate speed.

[(*i*) P_h = 2.67 m kW ; P_e = 5.33 kW (*ii*) P_h = 1.335 kW ; P_e 1.332 kW]

8. A short-shunt compound generator supplies 100 A at 110 V. Armature resistance = 0.05 Ω. shunt field resistance = 57 Ω; series field resistance = 0.04 Ω. Iron and frictional losses amount to 852 W. Find (*i*) generated e.m.f. (*ii*) total Cu losses (*iii*) overall efficiency.

[(*i*) 119.1 V (*ii*) 1148.1 W (*iii*) 84.7%]

Short Answer Questions

1. What is the important of d.c. machines?

Ans. D.C. generators are not as common as they used to be, because direct current when required is mainly products by electronic rectifiers. However d.c. motors are widely used in industry due to the following reasons:

(*i*) Speed of d.c. motor can be changed easily over easily over a wide range.

(*ii*) Speed regulation of d.c. motors is very good.

(*iii*) The torque-speed characteristics of d.c. motors can be varied over a wide range while retaining high efficiency.

Due to above reasons. d.c. motors are used to drive such devices as hoists, fans, pumps, punch-presses etc.

2. What purpose is served by the pole shoe in a d.c. machine?

Ans. The pole shoes serve the following purpose:

(*i*) They spread out the flux in the air gaps.

(*ii*) Since they are of large cross-sections, the reluctance of the magnetic path is reduced.

(*iii*) They support the field coils.

3. What are the advantages and disadvantages of carbon brushed ?

Ans. Advantages:

(*i*) They lubricate and polish the commutator.

(*ii*) If sparking occurs, they damage the commutator less then than with the copper brushes.

(*iii*) They provide good commutation.

Disadvantages:

(*i*) The contact resistance is high and causes a loss of about 2V. Hence they are unsuited for low voltage machine in which this forms a large percentage loss.

(*ii*) Due to high voltage drop, the commutator must be made larger than for copper brushes.

(*iii*) Their low current density necessitates large brush holders ?

4. Why is the armature of d.c. machine made of silicon steel ?

Ans. The most important function of an armature is to provide a low reluctance path for the flux through the armature from N-pole shoes to the S ones. It is, therefore, made of material having permeability *e.g.*, silicon steel. An additional advantages of silicon steel is that it has low hysteresis loss.

5. Why do we slotted armature in a d.c. machine ?

Ans. The slotted armature has the following advantages:

(*i*) The air-gap can be reduced to a value required for mechanical clearance. This reduces the reluctance of the magnetic circuit.

(*ii*) The conductors can be properly placed so that there is little fear of them being displaced.

(*iii*) The drag on the conductors is greatly reduced so that insulation is in no danger of damage by pressure.

6. What is armature winding placed on the rotor of a d.c. machine ?

Ans. The armature winding of a d.c. machine is placed on the rotor to facilitate commutation *i.e.*, to convert the alternating voltage produced in the winding into direct voltage at the brushes.

7. What factors determine the number of poles in a d.c. machine ?

Ans. The number of poles in a d.c. machine is governed by:

(*i*) frequency (*ii*) current per brush arm

The upper limit to the number of poles is imposed by frequency which is of the order 20-30 Hz for large machines and not exceeding 50 Hz for small machines. The lower limit is due to current per brush arm which should not exceed 400 A otherwise an excessively long commutator will be necessary.

8. What is armature winding of a d.c. machine always double layer winding ?

Ans. When the coil sides are placed in one layer, it is difficult to arrange their ends so that will pass other. In other to avoid this difficult, the coils are generally arranged in two layers. Each coil has one of its sides at the top of the slot and the other at the bottom of some other slot. The coil ends will then lie side by side.

9. What is the essential difference between lap and wave winding ?

Ans. The essential difference between a lap winding and a wave winding is in the commutator connections. In a lap winding, the commutator pitch is 1 whereas for a wave winding it is about twice the pole pitch.

10. The armature winding of a d.c. machine is a single closed loop. How do we parallel paths?

Ans. Whether the winding be lap or wave, when the brushes are lifted, the armature circuit is a single closed loop. However, when brushes are lowered on to the commutator, two or more parallel paths are formed depending upon the types of winding. Each parallel path consists of same number of coils in series.

(*i*) With a lap winding, the number of parallel paths formed is equal to the number of poles.

(*ii*) With a wave winding, the number of parallel paths formed is 2 irrespective of the number of poles.

11. Why is lap winding used in large multipolar d.c. generators ?

Ans. For a given number of armature conductors, a lap winding can carry a heavier current than a wave winding because it has more parallel paths. Therefore, lap winding is used in large multipolar d.c. generator to avoid having conductor of large cross-section.

12. Why are "*equalisers*" not used in wave winding ?

Ans. There is no need for "*equalisers*" in a wave-wound machine because conductors in each of the two parallel path under all the N and S pole successively.

13. What is the need to multiplex winding ?

Ans. With a simplex wave winding, there are only 2 parallel paths whereas for a lap winding, the number of parallel paths is equal to the number of poles. Thus is case of a 10-pole machine, using simples winding, the designer is restricted to either two parallel circuits (wave) or ten parallel circuits (lap). However, sometimes, it is desired to increase the number of parallel paths, enabling the armature to carry large current and at the same time reducing the conductor current, For this purpose, multiplex windings are used. Thus with duplex wave winding, the above 10-pole machine will have 4 parallel paths. Likewise, with duplex lap winding, the machine will have 20 parallel paths.

14. Discuss the nomenclature of multiplex winding.

Ans. The nomenclature of multiplex winding is according to the number of parallel paths formed.

(*i*) The number of parallel paths in a multiplex lap winding is given by:

No. of parallel paths = No. of poles (P) × Degree of plex

Thus, a duplex lap winding is one in which number of parallel paths is 2P. The triplex lap winding is one in which number of parallel paths is 3P.

(*ii*) The number of parallel paths in a multiple wave winding is given by:

No. of parallel paths = 2 × Degree of plex

Thus, a duplex wave winding is one in which the number of parallel path = 2 × 2 4. A triplex wave winding will have 2 × 2 = 6 parallel paths.

15. What are the advantages of using a large number of poles in d.c. machine ?

Ans. The advantages of using a large number of poles in a d.c. machine are:

(*i*) The flux per pole is reduced. This reduces the thickness of armature core and yoke and hence the weight of machine.

(*ii*) The length of the magnetic circuit is reduced, resulting in the reduction of field ampere turns.

(*iii*) The length of the armature end connections is reduced.

(*iv*) The current per brush arm is reduced. This reduces the length of the commutator.

(*v*) Too small a number of poles reaction a large number of armature ampere-turns per pole and a high value of armature reactions, which requires a longer air-gap.

16. What are the disadvantages of using a large number of poles in a d.c. machine ?

Ans. The disadvantages of a large number of poles in d.c. machine are:

(*i*) More commutator segments are needed or alternatively there must be more volts per segment for a given commutator diameter and thickness of segment.

(*ii*) The brush arms are closer together, increasing the danger of flash-over.

(*iii*) Frequency is proportional to number of poles and core loss depends upon frequency.

(*iv*) The armature diameter is increased.

17. What decides the upper and lower limit to the number of poles in d.c. machine ?

Ans. The upper limit to the number of poles is imposed by frequency which is of the order 20-30 Hz for large machines and not exceeding 50 Hz for small ones. The lower limit is decided by the current per brush arm which should not exceed 400 A otherwise excessively long commutator will be necessary. These limits usually restrict the choice to about two alternatives.

18. What are the advantages and disadvantages of a separately excited generator over a self-exicted generator ?

Ans. The advantages of a separately excitedly generator over a self-excited generator are:

(*i*) The field ampere-turns can be independently controlled.

(*ii*) It will operate in a stable condition with any field excitation.

(*iii*) We can have a wide range of output voltage.

The disadvantages of a separately excited generator as compared to a self-excited generator are:

(*i*) A separate d.c. source is required.

(*ii*) It is an incontinent arrangement.

Note: D.C. generators are rarely separately excited. But practically all a.c. generator are separately excited.

19. Upon what factors the armature resistance (R_a) of a d.c. machine depends ?

Ans. The armature resistance of d.c. machine depends upon:

(*i*) number, size and connection of armature coils.

(*ii*) Contact resistance between the carbon brush and the copper commutator.

20. What does the name plate of d.c. generator indicate ?

Ans. The name plate of a d.c. generator generally indicates:

(*i*) output in kW (*ii*) output voltage

(*iii*) speed (*iv*) permissible temperature rise.

Multiple-Choice Questions

1. The armature of d.c. machine is made of ....

(*i*) silicon steel (*ii*) wrought iron

(*iii*) cast steel (*iv*) soft iron

2. A 4-pole d.c. machine has .... magnetic circuits.

(*i*) 2 (*ii*) 8

(*iii*) 4 (*iv*) none of the above

3. The greatest eddy current loss occurs in the .... of d.c. machine.

(*i*) field poles (*ii*) yoke

(*iii*) commutating poles (*iv*) armature

4. The commutator pitch for a simplex lap winding is equal to ....

(*i*) number of poles of the machine (*ii*) pole paris

(*iii*) 1 (*iv*) none of the above

5. In a d.c. machine, the number of commutator segments is equal to ....

(*i*) number of conductors (*ii*) twice the number of poles

(*iii*) number of coils (*iv*) none of the above

6. The nature of armature winding of a d.c. machine is decided by ....

(*i*) front pitch (*ii*) commutator pitch

(*iii*) back pitch (*iv*) none of the above

7. An 8-pole duplex lap winding will have ....

(*i*) 8 (*ii*) 4

(*iii*) 32 (*iv*) 16

8. A triplex wave winding will have .... parallel paths.

(*i*) 6 (*ii*) 2

(*iii*) 4 (*iv*) none of the above

9. A 6-pole lap-wound generator has 300 conductors; the e.m.f. induced per conductor being 5 V. The generated voltage of the generator is ....

(*i*) 60 V (*ii*) 1500 V

(*iii*) 360 V (*iv*) 250 V

10. The armature of d.c. machine having 10 poles is rotating at a speed of 10 revolutions per second. The number of hysteresis loops formed per second is ....

(*i*) 10 (*ii*) 10

(*iii*) 150 (*iv*) 50

11. The greatest percentage of heat loss in a d.c. machine is due to ....

(*i*) eddy current loss (*ii*) hysteresis loss

(*iii*) copper loss (*iv*) frictioal loss

12. A shunt generator delivers 195 A at a terminal p.d. of 250 V. The armature resistance and shunt field resistance are 0.02 Ω and 50 Ω respectively. What is the value of generated e.m.f. ?

(*i*) 246 V (*ii*) 270 V

(*iii*) 254 V (*iv*) 282 V

13. In the above questions, what is the value of copper losses ?

(*i*) 825 W (*ii*) 2050 W

(*iii*) 1025 W (*iv*) 282 W

14. In W_c is the constant loss and R_a is the armature resistance of a d.c. generator, then load current I_L corresponding to maximum efficiency is

(*i*) $IL = \sqrt{\frac{R_a}{W_c}}$ (*ii*) $I_L = \frac{W_c}{\sqrt{R_a}}$

(*iii*) $I_L = \frac{R_a}{\sqrt{W_c}}$ (*iv*) $I_L = \sqrt{\frac{W_c}{R_a}}$

15. Stray losses consist of

(i) magnetic and mechanical losses

(ii) magnetic and copper losses

(iii) mechanical and copper losses

16. A 30 kW, 300 V d.c. shunt generator has armature and field resistance of 0.05 Ω and 100 Ω respectively. What is the generated e.m.f ?

(i) 295.25 V (ii) 311.25 V

(iii) 305.15 V (iv) none of the above

17. In the above question, what is the total power developed when the generator delivers full outpout power ?

(i) 16.34 kW (ii) 20.62 kW

(iii) 12.46 kW (iv) 31.43 kW

18. In Fig. 4.96 the electrical efficiency is

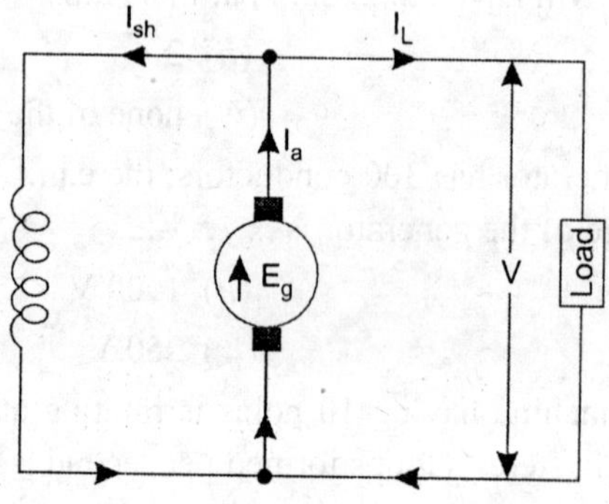

Fig. 4.96

(i) $\frac{VI_a}{E_g I_a}$ (ii) $\frac{VI_L}{E_g I_a}$

(iii) $\frac{E_g I_a}{V I_a}$ (iv) none of the above

19. The efficiency of a d.c. generator means its

(i) electrical efficiency (ii) overall efficiency

(iii) mechanical efficiency (iv) none of the above

20. A 4-pole, lap-wound d.c. shunt generator has an armature winding consisting of 220 turns each of 0.004 Ω. The armature resistance is

(i) 0.5 Ω (ii) 1 Ω

(iii) 0.025 Ω (iv) 0.055 Ω

Answers to Multiple Questions

1.	(i)	2.	(iii)	3.	(iv)	4.	(v)	5.	(iii)
6.	(ii)	7.	(iv)	8.	(i)	9.	(iv)	10.	(iv)

11. (iii)	12.	(iii)	13.	(ii)	14.	(iv)	15.	(i)
16. (iii)	17.	(iv)	18.	(ii)	19.	(ii)	20.	(iv)

Hints to Multiple-Choice Questions

1. It is desired that armature should provide a path of low reluctance for the flux. For this reason, armature is made of material having high permeability *e.g.*, silicon steel.
2. In a d.c. machine, there are as many magnetic circuits as there are poles. Thus, a 4-pole d.c. machine will have 4 magnetic circuits. However, m.m.f. acting in each circuit is due to the ampere-turns of a pair of poles.
3. Since every part of the armature sees cyclic reversals in magnetic flux direction, it is potentially subjected to more severe eddy current-losses than the field pole shoes. Hence armature is invariably laminated to reduce the eddy current loss.
4. The commutator pitch for a simplex lap winding is given by ;

$$Y_c = \pm 1$$

The plus sing applies if, as is usual, the winding is progressive; the minus sing, if it is retrogressive.
5. In a d.c. armature winding, the two ends of coil are connected to two different commutator segments and two coils are connected to each segment so that number of commutator segments is equal to the number of coils.
6. It is commutator pitch that determines the grouping of the series and parallel. In other words, it is commutator pitch that determines as to how many parallel paths, each consisting of equal number of coils in series, will be formed. Hence the nature of winding is determined by the commutator pitch.
7. With a n-plex lap winding, the number of parallel paths is $P\,n$ where

P = number of poles

n = 2, 3 etc and stands for duplex, triplex etc.

Hence 8-pole duplex lap winding will have $8 \times 2 = 16$ parallel paths.
8. With a n-plex wave winding, the number of parallel paths is $2n$ where $n = 2, 3$ etc. and stands for duplex, triplex etc.

Hence a triplex wave winding will have $2 \times 3 = 6$ parallel paths.
9. Number of conductors per parallel path = 300/6 = 50. Hence the generator voltage = 50×5 = 250 V.
10. Once hysteresis current is formed as the armature traverses a pair of poles. Hence number of loops formed = $5 \times 10 = 50$ loops per seconds.
11. The armature current of a d.c. machine is very large. Since copper loss is proportional to the square of current, hence a greater part of power loss occurs in the armature.
12. $I_{sh} = 250/50 = 5\text{A} \quad \therefore \quad I_a = I_{sh} + I_L = 5 + 195 = 200$ A

$$\text{Armature drop} = I_a R_a = 200 \times 0.2 = 4 \text{ V}$$

$$\therefore \quad \text{Generated e.m.f} = V + I_a R_a = 250 + 4 = 254 \text{ V}$$

13. Armature Cu loss $= I_a^2 R_a = (200)^2 \times 0.02 = 800$ W

Shunt Cu loss $= V I_{Sh} = 250 \times 5 = 1250$ W

Total Cu loss $= 1250 + 800 = 2050$ W

14. The efficiency of a d.c. generator is maximum when

Variable loss = Constat loss

Or $I_L^2 R_a = W_c$ or $I_L = \sqrt{\dfrac{W_c}{R_a}}$

15. Usually magnetic and mechanical losses are collectively called stray losses.

16. $$I_L = \frac{30 \times 10^3}{300} = 100 \text{ A} ; I_{sh} = \frac{V}{R_{sh}} = \frac{300}{100} = 3\text{A}$$

$$\therefore \quad I_a = I_L + I_{sh} = 100 + 3 = 103 \text{ A} = 103 \text{ A}$$

Generated e.m.f $E_g = V + I_a R_a = 300 + 103 \times 0.05 = 300 + 5.15 = 305.15$ V

17. Power developed in armature $= E_g I_a = \dfrac{305.15 \times 103}{1000} = 31.43$ kW

18. Electrical efficiency, $\eta_e = \dfrac{\text{Power in load}}{\text{Total power generated}} = \dfrac{V I_L}{Eg\, I_a}$

19. Unless stated otherwise, efficiency of a d.c. generator means its overall commercial efficiency.

20. Total resistance of 220 turns $= 200 \times 0.004 = 0.88\ \Omega$

Since there are 4 parallel paths in armature,

Resistance of each path $= 0.884/4 = 0.22\ \Omega$

Now, there are four such resistances in parallel each of value $0.22\ \Omega$.

$\therefore$ Armature resistance, $R_a = 0.22/4 = 0.055\ \Omega$.

Short Answer type Questions

1. What is the principle of DC motor ? [*SBTE June* 2005]

Ans. When a current carrying conductor is placed in a magnetic field, it experiences a force which pushes the conductor out of the field. Direction of force is given by Fleming's left hand rule. Magnitude of force is given by

$$F = \text{B I L Sin } \theta$$

Where B = Magnetic flux density in web/m^2

I = Current through the conductor in Amps

L = Length of conductor

θ = Angle which the conductor makes with direction of field.

2. What is Fleming's left hand rule ? [*SBTE June* 2006]

Ans. If the left hand is stretched in such a way that the thumb, fore finger and central finger are mutually perpendicular to each other. Then if fore finger points in the direction of field] central finger points in the direction of current, then thumb points in the direction of motion (Force) as shown in fig. 4.97.

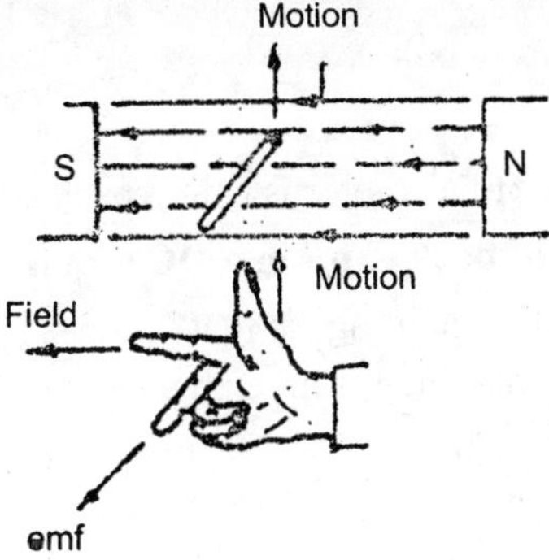

Fig. 4.97

3. What are the two main parts of a d.c motor ?

Ans. The two main parts of DC motor are

(*i*) Stator (*ii*) Rotor

4. Rotor in a DC motor is also known as............. ? [SBTE *June* 2006]

Ans. Armature.

5. In a DC motor, DC supply is given to...........through commutator and brush assembly ?

Ans. Armature.

6. Commutator of DC motor is............. ? (Stationary / Rotating)

Ans. Rotating.

7. What is the fuction of commutator in a DC motor ? *V. Imp*

Ans. It reverses the current in each conductor as it passes from one pole to another pole to develop continuous and unidirectional torque.

8. Commutator of a DC motor is made of.......... ?

Ans. Hard drawn copper.

9. Brushes of DC motor are made of...........? [*SBTE June* 2007]

Ans. Graphite.

10. In DC motor carbon brushes are............. ? (stationary / rotating)

Ans. Stationary.

11. Name the stationary parts in a DC motor ?

Ans. (*i*) Yoke (*ii*) Pole core (*iii*) Pole shoes (*iv*) Carbon brushes

12. Name the rotating parts in a DC motor ?

Ans. (*i*) Armataure (*ii*) Commutator

13. Give expression for e.m.f induced in the armature of a DC motor ? [SBTE, 2007]

Ans. $$E_b = \frac{\phi ZN}{60} \times \frac{P}{A}$$

where ϕ = flux/pole in webers

Z = Total number of armature conductors

N = Speed of rotor in r.p.m.

A = Number of parallel paths

P = No of poles

14. What is back e.m.f ? **[SBTE June 2008]**

Ans. E.M.F induced in the armature of DC motor is called back e.m.f.

15. What is the significance of back e.m.f in a DC motor ?

Ans. Back e.m.f makes the motor self regulating, so that it draws as much current as is just necessary. It controls the armature current which is given by

$$I_a = \frac{V - E_b}{R_a}$$

Where V = applied voltage

E_b = Back e.m.f

R_a = Armature Resistance

16. Why DC motor draws high current at the time of starting ?

Ans. We know that armature current $I_a = \frac{V - E_b}{R_a}$. When the motor is just switched on, $E_b = 0$

$$\therefore \quad I_a = \frac{V}{R_a}$$

As armature resistance is very small, the motor draws high current at the time of starting.

17. Why starter is necessary for a DC motor ? *V. Imp*

Ans. Starter is needed for the proctection of motor against excessive currents at the time of starting.

18. What is a self excited motor ?

Ans. The motor which does not require any external excitation. The same supply is given to armature as well as field winding. The armature and field windings are either connected in series or parallel.

19. What is a compound motor ?

Ans. The compound motor is one in which a part of field winding is connected in series with armature and the other part is connected in parallel as shown in Fig. 4.98.

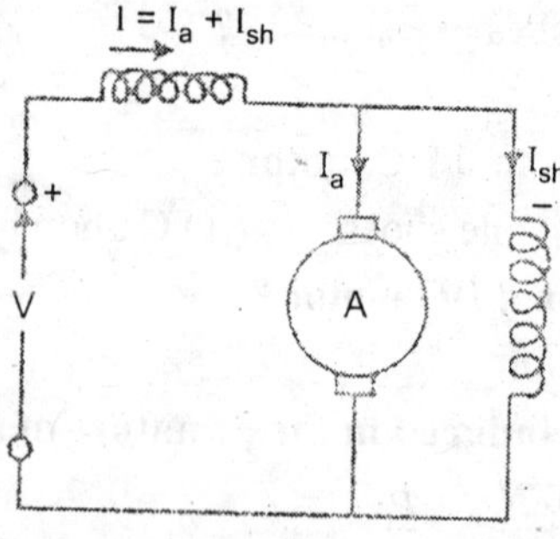

Fig. 4.98

20. How speed of a DC motor can be controlled?

Ans. Speed of DC motor is given by

$$N = \frac{V - I_a R_a}{\phi}$$

i.e. speed of DC motor depends upon supply voltage armature resistance and field flux. Therefore speed of motor can be varied by controlling any of these factors.

21. Why DC series motor should not be run without load ? ***V. Imp***

Ans.A DC series motor can not be run without load as it acquires dangerously high speed at no load.

22. Why speed of DC series motor is dangerously high at no load ?

Ans. In series motor armature and field windings are connected in series. At no load armature current is zero, hence there is no flux in the field winding. As the speed of motor is inversely proportional to field flux, motor acquires dangerously high speed.

23. DC shunt motor is a ....speed motor ?

Ans. Constant.

24. What is the effect of connecting additional resistance in series with armature of DC motor ?

Ans. Speed decreases.

25. Write down power equation for DC motor ?

Ans. $P_m = E_b I_a = VI_a - I_a^2 R_a$

26. What is the condition for maximum power developed by a motor ?

Ans. $E_b = \frac{V}{2}$

27. Name the two most commonly methods for windings of armature in DC machines ? .

Ans. Armature of DC motor is wound in two ways

(*i*) Lap winding (*ii*) Wave winding

28. What is the difference between lap winding and wave winding ?

Ans. In lap winding no. of parallel paths in the armature is equal to the number of poles. Whereas in wave winding, the number of parallel path is always two. High voltage low current machines are wave wound but low voltage, high current machines are lap wound.

29. Give any one application of DC series motor ?

Ans.DC series motor is used in traction.

30. Name the factors on which torque produced in a DC motor depends.

Ans. Torque produced in a DC motor is given by T = Kϕ.I_a

Where K = constant.

I_a = Armature current

A = Number of parallel paths.

Therefore torque produced in a DC motor is directly proportional to product of armature current and field flux/pole.

31. Three point starter is used for the starting of DC shunt motor? State T/F

Ans. True.

Medium/Long Answer type Questions

1. Give emf equation of DC machine. How the e.m.f generated and currents are affected when DC machine is changed from lap to wave winding and vice versa.

[SBTE June 2005]

Ans. EMF equation of DC machine is given by

$$E = \frac{\phi ZN}{60} \times \frac{P}{A}$$

Where

ϕ = flux/pole in webers

Z = Total number of armature conductors

N = Speed of rotor in r.p.m

A = Number of parallel paths

P = number of poles

= 2 for wave wound machine

= P for lap wound machine

Effect of changing connections of windings from Lap wound to wave wound and vice versa:-

In lap wound machine, there are as many parallel paths as there are number of poles. As in a parallel circuit, e.m.f remains the same but total current is the sum of currents in the individual paths. Therefore when connections are changed from wave winding to lap winding, total output current will Increase but e.m.f will come down. In a wave wound machine there are only two parallel paths. Therefore a number of conductors are connected in series, so that e.m.f induced in the individual conductors add up but the current in them remains the same. Therefore when connections are changed from lap winding to wave winding, output e.m.f will increase but the current will come down.

2. Derive expression for torque developed in a DC motor. ***[SBTE Dec 2005]***

Ans. Mechanical power developed in the armature of a DC motor.

$$P_m = E_b I_a$$

Where

E_b = back emf

I_a = Armature current

If ω = angular velocity in rpm and T is the electromagnetic torque in N-m, then work done per sec is equal to the mechanical power developed in the armature.

$\therefore$ Work done (ωT) = Mechanical power developed in Armature

$$= I_a E_b$$

$$\therefore \quad T = I_a \frac{E_b}{\omega}$$

If N = Speed in rpm

$$\omega = \frac{2\pi N}{60} = \text{angular distance travelled in one sec.}$$

$$\therefore \quad T = \frac{E_b I_a}{2\pi N} \times 60 \text{ N-m}$$

but
$$E_b = \frac{\phi Z N}{60} \times \frac{P}{A}$$

$$\therefore \quad T = I_a \frac{\phi Z N I_a \times 60}{2\pi N \times 60} \times \frac{P}{A}$$

$$= \frac{1}{2\pi} \times \frac{\phi Z P}{A} \times I_a$$

$$= \mathrm{K}\,\phi\, I_a$$

where
$$K = \frac{1}{2\pi} \times \frac{ZP}{A} = \text{Constant.}$$

3. Derive expression for back emf induced in a DC motor ? **[SBTE June 2006]**

Ans. Emf induced in the armature of a DC motor is called back e.m.f. This voltage acts in opposition to the applied voltage. The applied voltage has to force current through armature conductors against the back e.m.f. Electric work done in overcoming this opposition is converted into mechanical energy.

Expression for back e.m.f:

Let
ϕ = flux per pole in weber

z = Number of armature conductors

P = No of poles

A = No of parallel paths

N = revolutions of armature per minute

E_b = EMF induced per parallel path.

Flux cut per conductor in one revolution = ϕ.P web

Number of revolutions/sec = $\frac{N}{60}$

Time of one revolution of conductor = dt = $\frac{60}{N}$ sec

EMF generated/Conductor = $\frac{d\phi}{dt} = \frac{\phi PN}{60}$ volt

No of conductor in one parallel path = $\frac{Z}{A}$

back emf generated per path = $\frac{\phi PN}{60} \times \frac{Z}{A}$

$$= \frac{\phi ZN}{60} \times \frac{P}{A} \text{ volt}$$

For a given machine Z,P and A are constant. Therefore $E_b = K \phi N$

where $$K = \frac{ZP}{60A} = \text{constant}$$

4. Define Torque Angle. How torque is produced due to alignment of magnetic fields.
[SBTE June 2007]

Ans. Torque angle: If a magnet is placed in the magnetic field cf another magnet, the two field try to align with each other and torque is produced which is directly proportional to sine of the angle between the two fields. This angle is called torque angle.

Production of torque to alignment of fields: Consider a permanent magnet capable of free rotating placed in the magnetic field of two permanent magnets as shown in fig. 4.53.

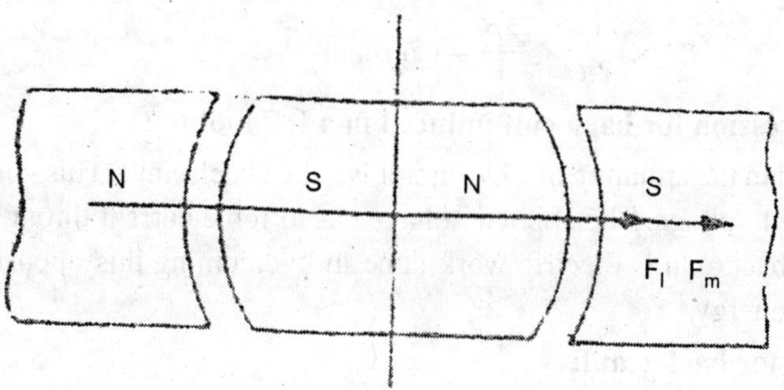

Fig. 4.99

There is force of attraction on the north and south pole of rotating magnet, which being equal and opposite cancel each other. In this position torque produced is zero because the field of rotating magnet F_r and the field of stationary magnet F_m are in line with each other.

When the rotating magnet is rotated through an angle θ as shown in fig. 4.100.

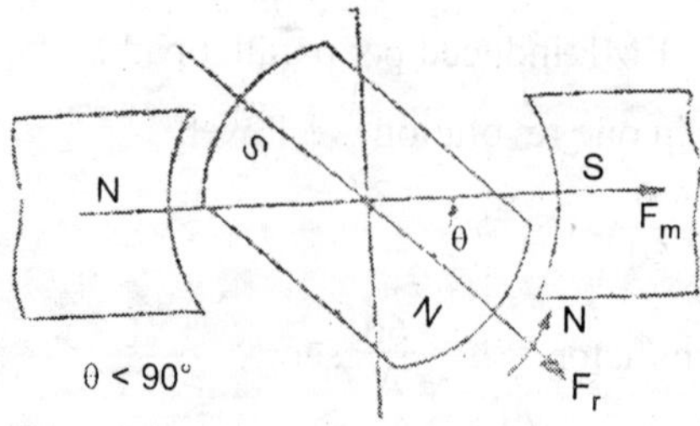

Fig. 4.100

Its north pole will be attracted towards south pole, south will be attracted towards the north pole of stationary magnets. In other words, we can say that rotor field F_r tries to come in line with main field F_m and torque is produced. It is found that torque produced is directly proportional to sine of the angle (θ) between the axis of the two fields *i.e.* magnetic field of stationary magnet and the magnetic field of the movable magnet.

5. Discuss in brief important construction features of a DC motor. ***Imp***

Ans. Fig shows the sectional view of a DC motor

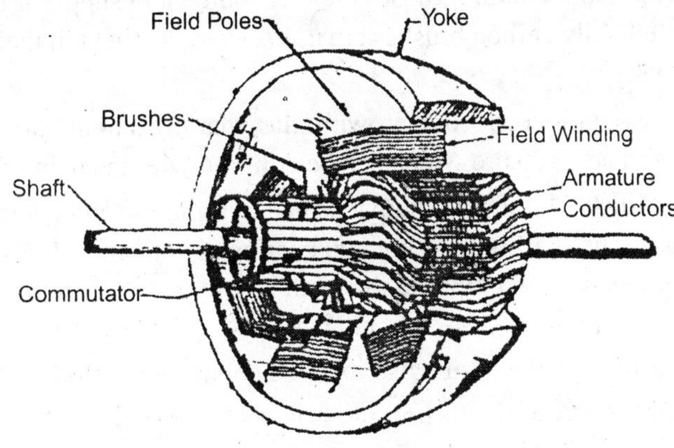

Fig. 4.101

Various motor parts are listed as below.

1. **Yoke:** It is made of cast iron for small machines and cast steel or rolled steel for large machines. Yoke provides space for providing poles for magnetic flux and it carries the magnetic flux produced by the poles. It is also known as frame.
2. **Pole core:** In small d.c. motors magnetic flux is produced by permanent magnets while large d.c. motors use etectro-magnets for production of magnetic flux. Winding is provided on pole core. This field winding is connected to the armature either in series or in shunt (Parallel).

   These are made of stacked laminations made of silicon steel to provide low reluctance magnetic path and to reduce iron losses.
3. **Pole Shoes:** Pole shoes are provided with poles to ensure uniform distribution of magnetic flux in the air gap.
4. **Field coil:** Field coils are provided on the core of poles to work as an electromagnet. These coils are made of copper wire.
5. **Armature:** Armature is provided on the shaft of motor. It is generally made of thin laminations. Slots are provided on the armature to house conductors of armature winding.
6. **Armature winding:** The armature winding is provided on the armature. Armature conductors are placed in the slots provided on the armature. These are then interconnected to form a winding. In d.c. machines, types of winding used are

   (*a*) **Lap winding:** Number of parallel paths in this type of winding are equal to number of magnetic poles.

   (*b*) **Wave winding:** Number of parallel paths in this type of winding is always equal to two.

   Armature winding is supplied d.c. current through commutator and brushes.
7. **Commutator:** Commutator of a d.c. machine supplies d.c. current from supply to the armature windings. It is mounted on the shaft of machine. It has wedge shaped copper segments. These segments are insulated from each other by mica. Every segment of commutator is connected

to the armature coil by using a copper lug. Number of commutator segments is equal to the number of armature coils.

8. **Brushes:** Brushes collect current from the d.c. source and supply it to the armature through commutator. Generally carbon brushes are used. These are held in their position with the help of a brush holder.

   Brushes have a continuous contact with the rotating commutator. These need regular adjustment of contact pressure which can be adjusted with the help of an adjustable spring.

9. **Shaft and Bearings:** All the rotating parts such as armature and commutator are mounted on milod steel shaft. The shaft is supported on bearing at both ends. It also has a pulley mounted on it to transfer mechanical output to the load. Mostly ball bearings are used in D.C. motors.

10. **Terminal box:** Terminal box is mounted on the yoke of machine. Connecting leads are brought from brushes to the terminals box to be connected to the d.c. supply.

6. List various stationary and rotating parts of DC motor.

Ans. **Stationary parts:**

(*i*) Yoke (*ii*) Pole core (iii) Pole shoes

(*iv*) Field coils (*v*) Carbon brushes

Rotating parts:

(*i*) Armature (*ii*) Commutator (*iii*) Shaft.

7. What are motor characteristics. Write down important relations for deriving different characteristics.

Ans. The performance of a d.c, motor can be judged from its characteristic curves known as Motor characteristics. The characteristic curves of a motor are the curves which show the relations between the following quantities.

1. **Torque and Armature current.** (T_d/I_a characteristics.) This curve gives the relation between the torque developed in the armature T_a and armature current, I_a. It is also known as electrical characteristics.

2. **Speed and Armature current.** (N/I_a characteristics). This curve which gives the relation between speed N and the armature current I_a. It is also known as speed characteristics.

3. **Speed and Torque (N/T_a characteristics).** It is the curve which gives 'relation between speed, N and armature torque, T_a. It is also known as mechanical characteristics.

   While discussing the various motor characteristics, the following are the important relations which must be kept in mind.

(*i*) $T_a \propto \phi I_a$ (*ii*) $I_a = \dfrac{V - E_b}{R_a}$ (*iii*) $N \propto \dfrac{E_b}{\phi}$

8. What is a DC series motor. Draw and explain its characteristics. In what applications it is used.

[SBTE June 2004]

Ans. DC series motor: The series motor in which field winding is connected in series with the armature as shown in fig is called DC series motor.

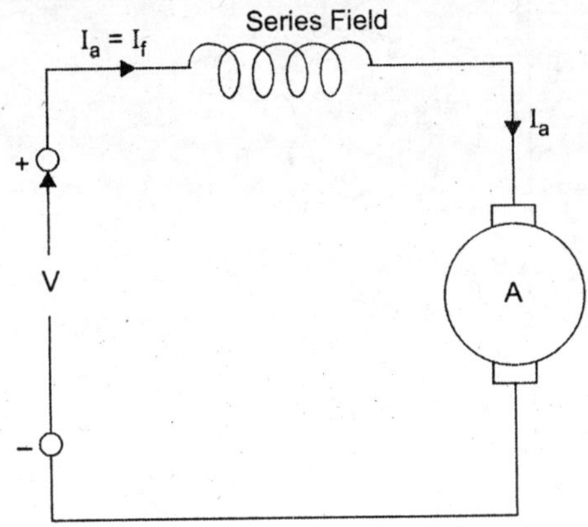

Fig. 4.102

Characteristics of DC series motor:

(a) Torque - current characteristics: As we know that $T = K\phi I_a$. ie $T \propto \phi I_a$. for a DC motor. In DC series motor, field winding is in series with the armature, therefore current flowing through field winding is same as that in Armature winding as field flux is proportional to armature current upto the point of saturation and after saturation it becomes constant. Therefore upto magnetic saturation torque is proportional to square of Armature current and after that torque is proportional to Armature current. Therefore Torque - Armature current curve is a parabola upto point of saturation of fieid and after that it is a straight line as shown in fig. 4.103

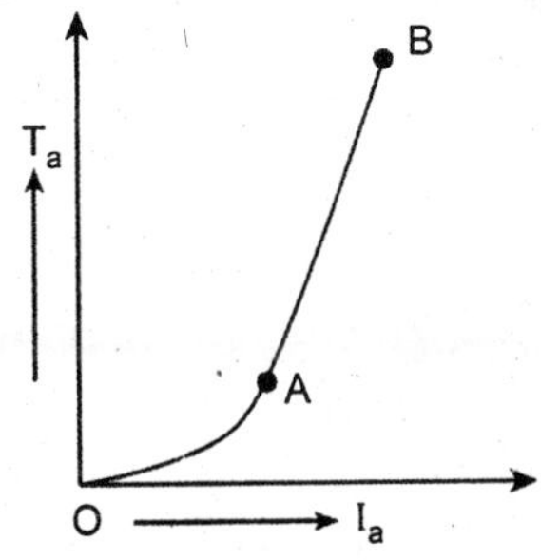

Fig. 4.103

Speed-Armature current characteristics:

As motor speed is given by

$$N = \frac{V - I_a Ra}{\phi}$$

and in a DC series motor $\phi \propto I_a$. Therefore at no load when armature current is negligible field flux ϕ is also very small. Speed of motor is very high. When motor is loaded, armature current increases and hence the field flux also increases. Therefore speed of motor decreases. Fig. 4.104 shows the speed-current characteristics of a DC series motor.

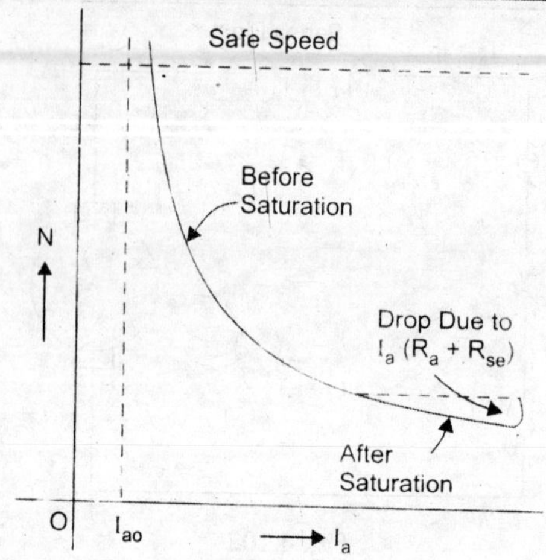

Fig. 4.104

Speed Torque ($N - T_a$) Characteristics: Torque speed characteristics of DC series motor is shown in Fig. 4.105.

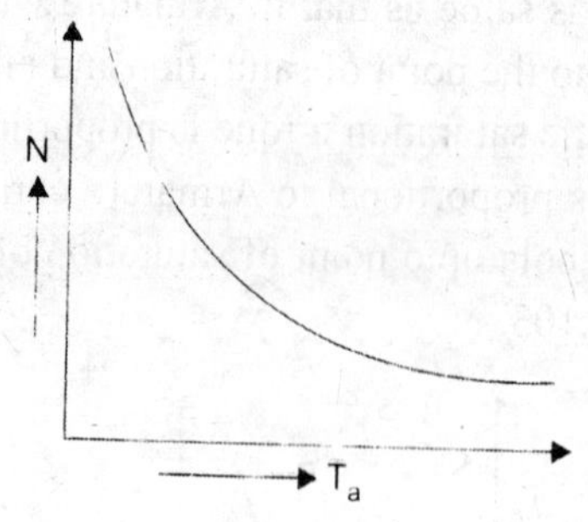

Fig. 4.105

It is clear from the speed Torque characteristics that the motor develops high torque at low speeds and vice versa. As Torque increases, the speed decreases:

Applications of DC series motor:

(*i*) DC series motor is a variable speed motor, and hence best suited for traction work.

(*ii*) The motor develops high starting torque. Therefore it is used in cranes, elevators, hoists, air compressors.

9. What is DC shunt motor? Discuss its characteristics. In what applications it is used.

[SBTE June 2008]

Ans. In a DC shunt motor, field winding is connected in parallel to Armature Winding as shown in fig below.

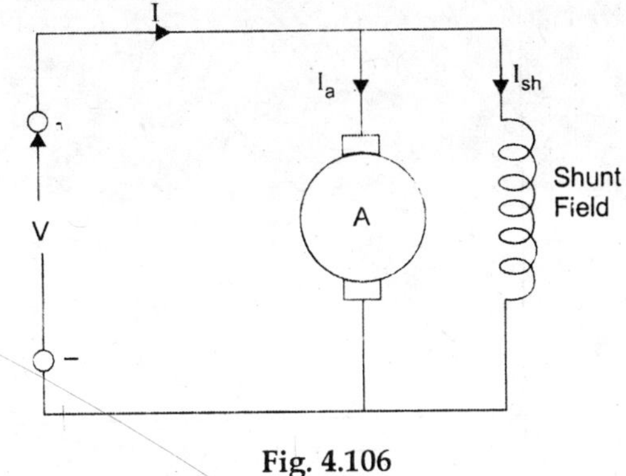

Fig. 4.106

Characteristics of DC shunt motors:

(1) Speed-Armature current (N - I_a) characteristics: Speed - current characteristics of DC shunt motor are shown in fig.

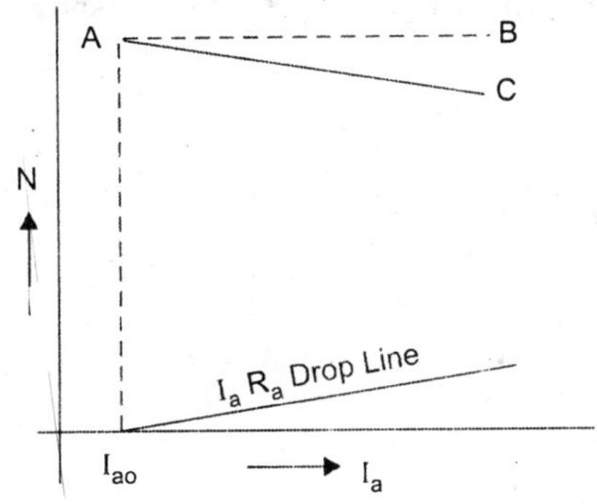

Fig. 4.107

$$\text{We know that } N \propto \frac{E}{\phi} \propto \frac{V - I_a R_a}{\phi}$$

As field flux in DC shunt motor is constant N $\propto$ V - $I_a R_a$. If drop in Armature is negligible, speed of motor will remain practically constant for all values of load as shown in fig by dotted line AB. But as the armature current increases due to increase in load, Armature voltage drop $I_a R_a$ increases and the speed of motor decreases slighly as shown by straight line AC. The characteristic curve does not start from a point of zero armature current because a small current I_{ao} is necessary to maintain the rotation of rotor at no load.

(2) Torque - Armature current (T - I_a) characteristics: We know that, T $\propto \phi I_a$ Since flux is constant, $\therefore T \propto I_a$

Hence, the electrical characteristics (*i.e.* T - I_a) is a straight line passing through the origin as shown in fig. It is clear from the characteristics curve that a large armature current is required at the start if machine is on heavy load. Thus, shunt motor should never be started on load.

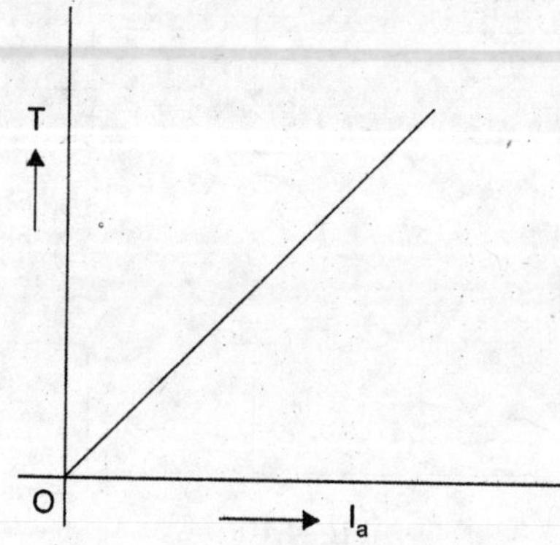

Fig. 4.108

(3) N - T Characteristic: The N - T characteristic is derived from the first two characteristics. When load torque increases, armature current I_a increases but speed decreases slightly. Thus with the increase of torque speed decreases slightly as shown in fig. 4.109.

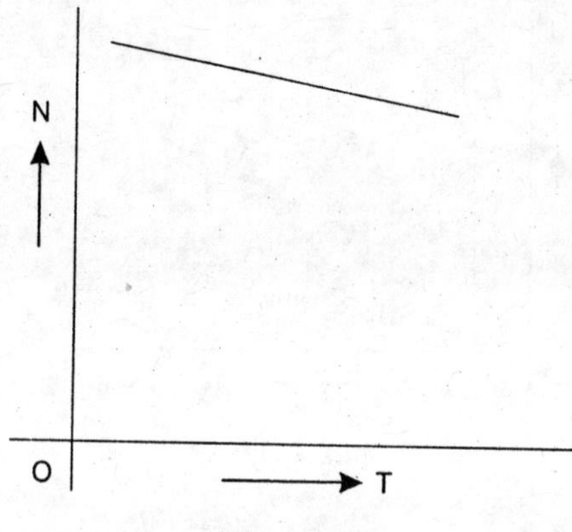

Fig. 4.109

Applications of DC Shunt motor: A DC shunt motor is used in applications where speed from no load to full load is required to be maintained constant such as lathes, grills, grinders, shapers, spinning and weaving machines etc.

10. Compare DC series and DC shunt motors. State three applications. **[*SBTE June* 2007]**

Ans.

DC Series Motor	*DC Shunt Motor*
1. Armature and field windings are connected in series.	1. Armature and field windings are connected in parallel.
2. Starting torque is high.	2. Starting torque is low.
3. At no load Speed is very high and decrease with increase in load.	3. Speed is almost constant and decreases slightly with the increase in load.
4. Torque-current characteristics are not linear.	4. Torque-current characteristics are linear.

Application of DC sereis motor: Used in cranes, hoists, elevators and tractions.

Application of DC series motor: Used in lathe machine, drills grinders, shapers etc.

11. Discuss in brief different methods of speed control of DC motors?

V. Imp [SBTE Dec 2005, 2006, 2007, 2008]

Ans. Speed of DC motor is given by

$$N = K\frac{E}{\phi} = K\frac{V - I_a R_a}{\phi}$$

Where V = Applied voltage

I_a = Armature current

R_a = Armature resistance

ϕ = Field flux

From above equation it is clear that, speed of a DC motor can be controlled by

(*i*) By varying flux per pole ϕ *i.e.* flux or field control method

(*ii*) By varying Armature circuit resistance *i.e.* Armature control method

(*iii*) By varying the applied voltage, *i.e.* voltage control method.

Speed control of DC shunt motors: Speed of DC shunt motor can be controlled by using any of the methods stated above.

(*i*) **Field control method:** In this method a variable resistance is connected in series with the field winding of shunt motor as shown in fig. 4.110 below

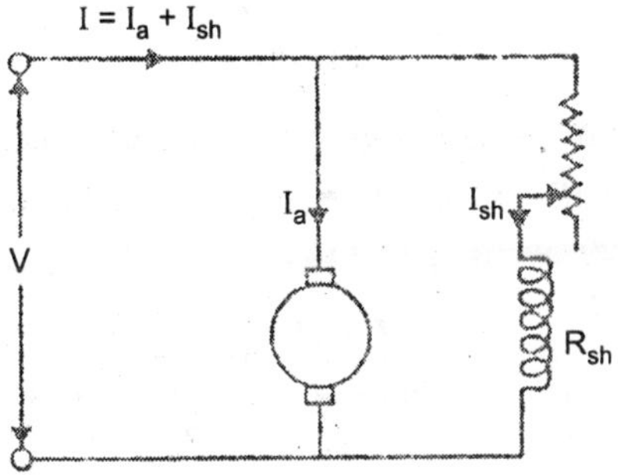

Fig. 4.110

Due to increase in resistance of shunt field, field current and hence field flux reduces thereby increasing the speed. This method is used to obtain speed above normal values.

(*ii*) **Armature control method:** In this method of speed control, a variable resistance is connected in series with the armature of the motor due to increase in resistance of the armature winding voltage drop in the armature increases and hence speed reduces. This method is used to obtain speed below normal.

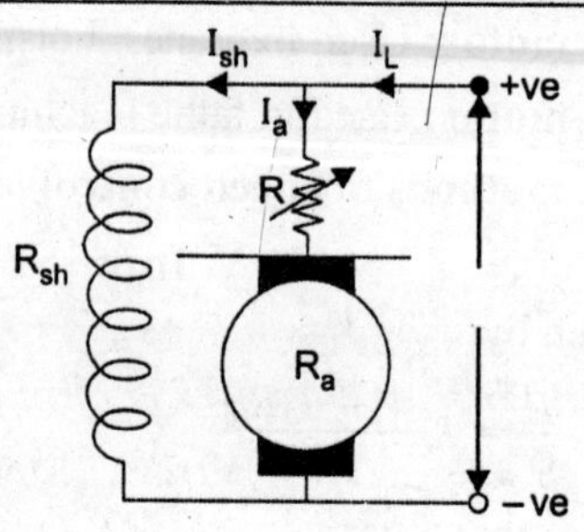

Fig. 4.11

Speed control of DC series motors: *[SBTE June 2008]*

(i) Field control method: In this method a variable resistance *R* is connected in parallel with series field winding as shown in fig. 4.112

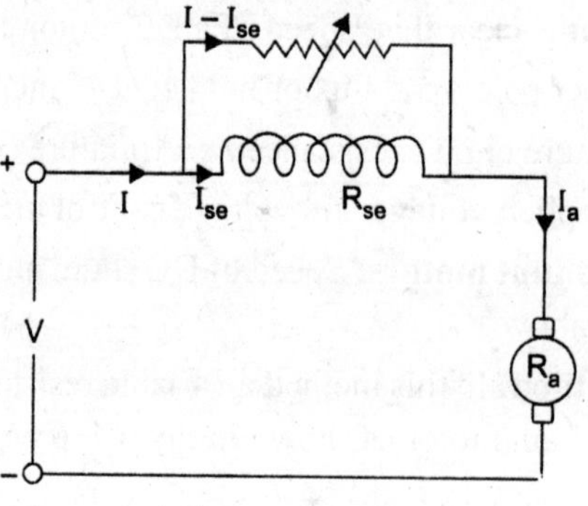

Fig. 4.112

By this method, only speeds above normal can be obtained.

(ii) Armature divertor method: In this method a variable resistance R is connected in parallel with the armature as shown in fig. 4.113

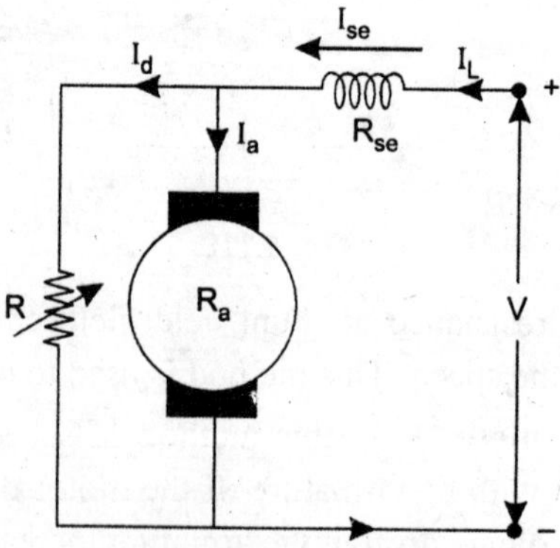

Fig 4.113

By this method, any speed below normal can be obtained

(iii) Tapped field control method: In this method the number of turns of the series field winding can be changed by short circuiting a part of it as shown.

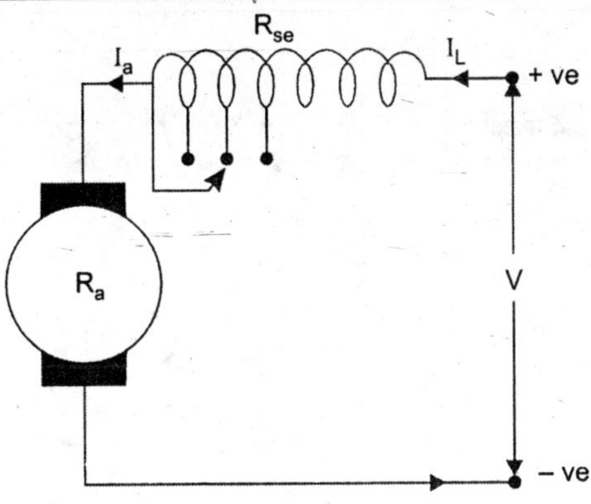

Fig. 4.114

The only speed above normal can be obtained by this method.

(iv) **Armature control method:** In this method a variable resistance, R is connected in series with the armature as shown in fig. 4.115

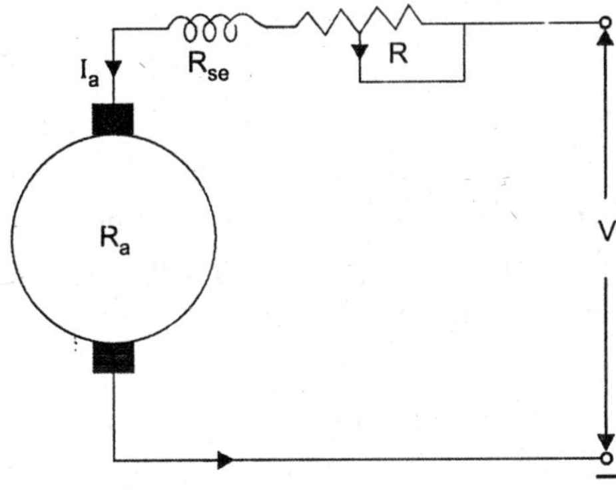

Fig. 4.115

By changing the value resistance any speed below normal can be obtained

12. What is the necessity of starter in DC motors. Explain the working of 3 point starter for DC shunt motor. [SBTE June 2007 V. Imp]

Ans.(*i*) Starting of Direct Current Motors: We know that the armature current, $I_a = \frac{V - E_b}{R_a}$ when the motor is at rest there is no back e.m.f developed in its armature. If full supply voltage is connected across the armature at start, heavy current $\left(I_a = \frac{V}{R_a}\right)$ flows through it. This heavy current may blowout fuses, damages the motor winding and in addition will cause a heavy voltage regulation in the line. To avoid this rush of heavy current, an external resistance is connected in series with the armature, which is gradually cut out as the motor gains speed.

(ii) **Three point D.C. Shunt motor starter:** The three point motor Starter volt release and over load release is shown in the fig.

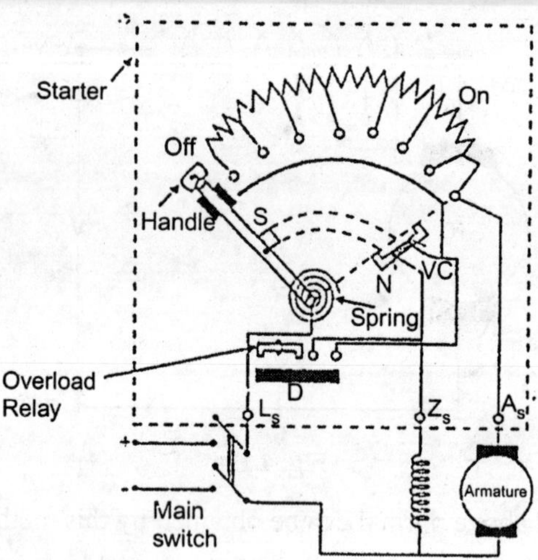

Fig. 4.116

To start the motor, the supply is switched on and the handle is moved in the clock-wise direction. When the handle makes connection with the first stud, the field is connected directly across the line and at the same time the entire starting resistance is put in series with the armature. As the motor picks up speed, the handle is slowly moved and the starting resistance is gradually cut out. When the handle reaches the running position, it is held against the action of the spring by a soft iron magnet called the hold up magnet connected in series with shunt field which attracts the soft iron piece attached to the starting handle.

When the handle reaches "ON" position, the resistance is totally cut off and motor starts running at normal speed, if the supply gets interrupted or disconnected, the handle will spring back to the "OFF" position as the no volt coil gets de-magnetised. Consequently, the motor is disconnected from the supply. This prevents the blowing off of fuses, as it would be, if the supply were restored being the handle in the "ON" position.

Function of Over Load Coil: An over load coil is an electromagnet fitted in the starter. This consists of small number of turns of thick wire. It is connected in series with the motor and carries the line current. If the motor becomes over loaded beyond a certain predetermined value, the strip "D" is lifted up and it short circuits the " No Volt Coil" circuit. Hence the handle is released and pulled back to the off position due to spring action. Thus the motor is disconnected from the supply and is protected against over loading.

13. Why a starter is necessary for a d.c. motor ?

Ans. For protection of motor against the flow of excessive current.

14. In electric traction, voltage control method of speed control of d.c. series motors is employed ? Why ?

Ans. The speed of a d.c. series motor (*traction motor*) can be controlled by *Rheostatic Control Method* and *Voltage Control method.* In rheostatic control method, number of external resistances are connected in series with the armature. At the time of start of motor, heavy current passes through the external resistances, hence a lot of electrical energy is wasted in the external resistances, whereas in voltage control method, the voltage across traction motors can be varied by connecting the motors in series and parallel. Thus the drawback of wasting of energy in rheostatic control is avoided in voltage control method. This is the reason that voltage control method is preferred in the speed control of d.c. series motors.

15. Belt loads are never recommended for d.c. series motors. Why? (Tech Edu. 2007)

Ans. Since on no load, the armature current and hence flux of d.c. series motor is very small, speed being inversely proportional to the flux will be dangerously high. When the motor is loaded, its armature current I_a increases and speed falls. Belt driven loads are never recommended for d.c. series motor because the slip of belt may cause the motor to run without load, which may damage the motor.

16. In electro-mechanical energy conversion device, the angle between main field and the rotor field is called torque angle. Why ? (Tech. Edu 2003 May 2007)

Ans. In the working of electro-mechanical energy conversion device, there are two fields, F_m is the main field and F_r is the rotor field and the angle between these two fields is "θ". The angle "θ", between the two fields, upon which the torque depend is known as "Torque Angle". The torque angle is measured with respect to the direction of rotation of the rotor.

17. D.C. series motors are never started without load? Why? (Tech Edu May 2003)

Ans. On no load, the armature current and series field current are very small. The speed of the motor being inversely proportional to the flux or field current, I_{se} will be dangerously high. It may damage the foundation bolts or may harm to the operator. So it is a main precaution that D.C. series motors should not be started without load.

18. For punching, d.c. compound motor is best suited. Why ?

Ans. D.C. compound motors, particularly cumulative compound wound motors are used in driving machines, which are subjected to sudden applications of heavy loads such as in punching and shearing machines. The other advantage of cumulative compound motor is that it has high starting torque.

19. Compensating winding neutralizes the effect of armature field. How?

(Tech Edu Dec. 2003)

Ans. A compensating winding is an auxiliary winding embedded in slots located in the faces of the main poles as shown in fig. The compensating winding is connected in series with the armature in such a way that the direction of current through the compensating winding in any pole face will be opposite to the direction of current through the adjacent armature conductors.

Fill in the Blanks

1. Outward flow of current in a conductor is represented by .... **Tech. Edu (May 2004)**
2. In case of d.c. .... motor, torque developed is directly proportional to the armature current.
3. The best suited motor for electric traction is ....
4. The efficiency of d.c. machine is maximum when .... **Tech Edu (May 2004)**
5. Armature torque of a d.c. motor is a function of field flux and .... **(Dec. 2003)**
6. The current drawn by a 240 V d.c. motor of armature resistance 0.5 Ω and back e.m.f. 230 V is ....

7. Sparking at the brushes is caused by the self inductance of the coil undergoing .... **(Dec. 2003)**
8. In case of d.c. .... motor, starting torque is approximately proportional to the square of the armature current.
9. The current taken by d.c. motor at the time of start is ....
10. For core, generally .... steel is preferred.
11. The armature shaft is invariably made of ....
12. .... loss least vary with load on the motor.
13. D.C. series motor is used for .... **Tech. Edu (May 2003)**
14. Divertor is used across armature of d.c. motor to .... the speed.
15. When load on d.c. shunt motor is increased, its speed will .... **(–do–May 2003)**
16. Wave winding has .... parallel paths.
17. The resistance of the field winding of a shunt motor is .... than the resistance of the armature winding. **(–do–May 2005)**
18. The commutator segments of d.c. machine are made up of .... **(–do–Dec. 2002)**
19. The wire used for series field winding is .... than the wire used for shunt field winding. **(–do–Dec. 2002)**
20. In d.c. motor, starter is used to .... the starting current. **(–do–Dec. 2002)**
21. The resistance of armature of a d.c. machine is .... **(—— do ——)**
22. By reversing the field current and armature current, direction of rotation of d.c. motor will .... **(–do–Dec. 2002)**
23. Armature reaction demagnetise the ....
24. The current drawn by a 120 V d.c motor of armature resistance 0.5 Ω and back e.m.f of 110 *V* is .... **(–do–May 2002)**
25. Voltage equation of d.c. motor is $V = E_b +$ ....
26. The laminations of d.c. machine armature are provided to reduced .... **(–do–Dec. 2001)**
27. The direction of rotation of a d.c. motor can be determined by Fleming's .... hand rule.
28. The purpose of installing fuses in motor circuit is to provide protection against ....
29. Belt driven load is preferred for a .... motor
30. Inward flow of current is represented by .... **(–do–Dec. 2004)**
31. The d.c. .... motor are best suited where almost constant speed is required.
32. The speed of d.c. motor can be varied by .... method. **(–do–Dec. 2004)**
33. In d.c. motor starters, no volt release coil consists of an electromagnet in .... with shunt field.
34. Over load release coil in d.c. motor starter carries full .... current.

Answers

1. ⊙
2. Shunt
3. D.C. series motor
4. Variable losses = constant losses.
5. Armature current
6. 20 Amps
7. Commutation
8. series
9. Too high
10. Silicon.
11. mild steel
12. friction and windage
13. Traction work.
14. Decrease
15. Decrease
16. Two
17. more
18. Hard drawn copper.
19. Thicker
20. limit
21. $R_a = Pl/_a$ ohm
22. Not change
23. Main field
24. 20 Amps.
25. I_aR_a
26. Eddy current losses
27. Left
28. Overload
29. Shunt
30. ⊕
31. Shunt
32. Flux control and armature control
33. Series
34. Load.

TRUE OR FALSE QUESTIONS

1. In a d.c. motor shunt field copper losses are usually 20-25%
2. A series motor attains its maximum efficiency at a load considerably less than the rated full load.
3. Brushes should have high conductivity and low co-efficient of friction.
4. The speed of a d.c. motor can be varied by controlling the terminal voltage.
5. For a d.c. motor the voltage equation, $E = V - I_aR_a$
6. The stator of a d.c. motor has salient poles.
7. Series motors are preferably directly coupled to load.
8. Sparking at the brushes can be reduced by using inter poles.
9. Swin burn's test is used to determine the efficiency of shunt machines.
10. The d.c. series motors are best suited where almost constant speed is required.
11. The inter pole winding is connected is series with that of armature
12. In a d.c. shunt motor, the shunt field copper losses are practically constant.
13. The armature core of a d.c. motor is made of silicon steel laminations and the pole cores are made of solid iron.
14. D.C. series motor should never be started on no load.
15. The brushes of d.c. motor are made of carbon.

16. The speed of d.c. motor is inversely proportional to the field flux.
17. The commutator is made of carbon.
18. The main field poles of a d.c. motor are on the rotating part.
19. The speed of a d.c. motor is always constant
20. Starters are used in d.c motors to regulate the speed.
21. The speed regulation of d.c. motor is $\frac{\textit{No load speed}}{\textit{Full load speed}}$
22. For large load currents, the armature of a d.c. motor should be provided with lap winding.

Answers

1. False.	2. True	3. True	4. True
5. True	6. True	7. True	8. True.
9. True	10. False	11. True	12. True
13. False	14. True	15. True	16. True
17. False	18. False	19. Fales	20. False
21. False	22. True.		

OBJECTIVE TYPE QUESTIONS

Choose the correct answers.

1. Which of the following motors has high starting torque?
   (*a*) d.c. series motor.
   (*b*) d.c. shunt motor
   (*c*) both series & shunt motor,
   (*d*) none of the above.
2. The direction of rotation of a d.c. series motor can be changed by
   (*a*) inter changing terminals of the field
   (*b*) inter changing terminals of the supply
   (*c*) either '*a*'or '*b*'
   (*d*) none of the above.
3. If d.c. motor is connected across d.c. supply.
   (*a*) The motor will burn.
   (*b*) The motor will run at the rated speed
   (*c*) The motor will run at slow speeds
   (*d*) The motor will not run.
4. As the load on d.c. shunt motor is increased, the speed of the motor will
   (*a*) increase highly,   (*b*) remain constant
   (*c*) reduce   (*d*) increase.

5. A d.c. series motor is preferably started with some mechanical load because
   (*a*) It develops excessive speed otherwise and may be damaged.
   (*b*) It will not run on no-load.
   (c) small load acts as a starter.
   (*d*) All the above.
6. Which of the d.c. motor will be preferred for conveyors
   (*a*) shunt motor
   (*b*) series motor
   (*c*) separately excited d.c. motor
   (*d*) none of the above.
7. Which of the d.c. motor will be preferred for machine tools
   (*a*) Series motor
   (*b*) Shunt motor
   (*c*) Separately excited d.c. motor
   (*d*) None of the above.
8. Which of the d.c. motor will be preferred for constant speed.
   (*a*) Series motor
   (*b*) Shunt motor
   (*c*) Cumulative compound motor
   (*d*) Differential compound motor.
9. Which of the d.c. motor will be preferred for elevators:
   (*a*) Series motor
   (*b*) Shunt motor
   (*c*) Cumulative compound motor
   (*d*) Differential compound motor.
10. If the excitation to the field is constant, then the torque developed by the motor is proportional to:
    (*a*) Field flux (*b*) Speed
    (*c*) Armature current (*d*) Magnetic flux.
11. For d.c. shunt motors the speed is dependent upon the induced e.m.f. because
    (*a*) flux is practically constant
    (*b*) flux is proportional to armature current
    (*c*) armature drop is negligible
    (*d*) none of the above.
12. According to the Fleming's Left Hand Rule, the thumb will point in the direction of
    (*a*) Magnetic field (*b*) E.M.F.
    (*c*) Motion (*d*) None of the above.

13. According to the Fleming's Left hand rule, the fore finger points in the direction of
    (*a*) Magnetic field (*b*) E.M.F.
    (*c*) Motion (*d*) All the above.
14. According to the Fleming's left hand rule, the middle finger points in the direction of
    (*a*) Magnetic field (*b*) E.M.F.
    (*c*) Motion (*d*) None of the above.
15. The self load properties are shown by
    (*a*) D.C. series motor
    (*b*) D.C. shunt motor
    (*c*) D.C. cumulative compound motor
    (*d*) D.C. differential compound motor.
16. If suddenly, the back e.m.f. of a D.C. motor vanishes:
    (*a*) The motor will run continuously
    (*b*) The motor will stop
    (*c*) The armature will burn
    (*d*) The motor will burn
17. In d.c. motor, condition for maximum power is
    (*a*) Supply Voltage = $\frac{1}{2}$ × Back e.m.f.
    (*b*) Supply Voltage = $\sqrt{2}$ × Back e.m.f.
    (*c*) Back e.m.f. = 2 × Supply Voltage
    (*d*) Back e.m.f. = $\frac{1}{2}$ × Supply Voltage
18. If condition for maximum power of a d.c. motor is established, the efficiency of the motor will be
    (*a*) 100% (*b*) 90 to 95%
    (*c*) 81% (*d*) less than 50%.
19. A 200 volt d.c. machine has an armature resistance of 0.5 Ω. If the full load armature current is 30 Amps, the induced e.m.f. when the machine acts as motor will be
    (*a*) 230 V (*b*) 225 V
    (*c*) 215 V (*d*) 210 V.
20. The ratio of starting torque to full load torque is least in case of
    (*a*) Shunt motor (*b*) Series motor
    (*c*) Compound motor.
21. A d.c. motor being full load speed of 800 r.p.m. and speed regulation of 8% will have no load speed of
    (*a*) 864 r.p.m. (*b*) 832 r.p.m.
    (*c*) 768 r.p.m. (*d*) 736 r.p.m.

22. For a series motor, if T_a be the armature torque, I_a the armature current ; then which relation is valid for the condition before saturation

(a) $T_a \propto I_a$ (b) $T_a \propto I_a^2$

(c) $T_a \propto \frac{1}{I_a}$ (d) $T_a \propto \frac{1}{I_a^2}$

23. If the applied voltage of d.c. shunt motor is halved with the load torque doubled, the armature current will be

(a) Unaltered (b) Zero

(c) Doubled (d) Halved.

24. The armature current of a d.c. motor is given by

(a) $I_a = \frac{V + E_b}{R_a}$, when E_b= Back e.m.f

(b) $I_a = \frac{V - E_b}{R_a}$

(c) $I_a = \frac{R_a - E_b}{V}$

25. Which d.c. motor should never run at no-load?

(a) d.c. shunt motor,

(b) d.c. series motor

(c) d.c. compound motor.

26. The amount of flux leakage will depend upon

(a) flux density employed in core & teeth

(b) length of air gap

(c) shape of the magnet core

(d) all the above

27. The function of the starter of a d.c. motor is

(a) To limit the starting current

(b) To limit the starting voltage

(c) To increase field resistance

(d) To reduce armature resistance

28. The generated e.m.f and current are in the opposite direction in case of

(a) d.c. motors

(b) d.c. generators

(c) Both d.c. motors as well as d.c. generators

(d) Neither d.c. motors nor d.c. generators.

29. The brush voltage drop in d.c. motors is usually of the order of

(a) 2 Volts (b) 20 Volts

(c) 50 Volts (d) 100 Volts

30. In a d.c. motor which of the following can sustain the maximum temperature rise?

(*a*) Armature winding (*b*) Field winding

(*c*) Commutators (*d*) Slip rings.

31. In class '*B*' d.c. motors, the maximum temperature rise in armature winding is

(*a*) 45°C (*b*) 55°C

(*c*) 75°C (*d*) 105°C

32. A 250 Volts d.c. motor has external resistance R_1 in the field circuit and R_2 in the armature circuit. The starting armature current for the motor will be minimum, when

(*a*) R_1 is minimum and R_2 is maximum

(*b*) R_1 is maximum and R_2 is minimum

(*c*) R_1 and R_2 both are minimum

(*d*) R_1 and R_2, both are maximum.

33. A 250 V d.c. motor has an armature circuit resistance of 0.6 Ω. If the full load armature current is 30 A and no load armature current is 4 Amp, the change in back e.m.f. from no-load to full load will be

(*a*) 1.5 Volts (*b*) 15.6 Volts

(*c*) 33.2 Volts (*d*) 64 Volts.

34. What would happen, if the field of the d.c. shunt motor is opened

(*a*) The speed of the motor will be reduced

(*b*) It will continue to run at its normal speed

(*c*) The speed of the motor will be enormously high and might destroy itself

(*d*) The current in the armature will increase.

35. Electrical energy converted into mechanical energy by a d.c. motor is given by

(*a*) VI_a (*b*) VI_{sh}

(*c*) E_bI_a (*d*) E_bI_{sh}.

36. Rheostatic speed control method is

(*a*) Economical for varying load

(*b*) Not suitable for varying load

(*c*) Efficient

37. The speed of d.c. motor can be varied by varying

(*a*) Applied voltage (*b*) Field resistance

(*c*) Armature resistance (*d*) All the above.

38. A 220 Volts shunt motor develops a torque of 54 Nm at an armature current of 10 Amps. The torque produced when the armature current is 20 A, is **[A.M.*I.e.* (Sec-B); W'93]**

(*a*) 54 Nm (*b*) 81 Nm

(*c*) 108 Nm (*d*) none of the above.

39. We under by dynamic braking a control function that **[A.M.*I.e.* (Sec B), W'93]**
   (*a*) provides braking by reversing motor line voltage polarity so that motor develops a counter torque and exerts a retarding force.
   (*b*) brakes a drive or motor by dissipating its stored energy in a resistor.
   (*c*) brakes a drive by converting the kinetic energy of the motor and its driven machinery and returning to the power system.
   (*d*) none of the above.

40. A d.c. shunt motor is operating at no-load. If the armature is shunted by a resistance, its speed will **[A.M.*I.e.* (Sec. B) S'94]**
   (*a*) increase (*b*) decrease
   (*c*) remain the same (*d*) be unpredictable.

Answers

1. (*a*)	2. (*b*)	3. (*a*)	4. (*b*)
5. (*a*)	6. (*b*)	7. (*b*)	8. (*b*)
9. (*c*)	10. (*c*)	11. (*a*)	12. (*c*)
13. (*a*)	14. (*b*)	15. (*d*)	16. (*c*)
17. (*d*)	18. (*b*)	19. (*c*)	20. (*a*)
21. (*a*)	22. (*b*)	23. (*c*)	24. (*b*)
25. (*b*)	26. (*d*)	27. (*a*)	28. (*a*)
29. (*a*)	30. (*b*)	31. (*c*)	32. (*a*)
33. (*b*)	34. (*c*)	35. (*c*)	36. (*b*)
37. (*d*)	38. (*d*)	39. (*a*)	40. (*b*).

Assignment Unit-1

1. Prove the expression for the force on a conductor carrying a steady state current in a magnetic field. Hence find the torque on the armature of the motor carrying a total of Z conductors through which a current of I_a flows. Assume diameter of the core as d cm and the length l cm and the flux density in the airgap as B Wb/m^2. **[London University]**
2. Prove that when a current is taken through a magnetic field, work is done.
3. State the various factors on which the speed of a D.C. motor depends.
4. What is the basic difference between a D.C. generator and a D.C. motor ? Explain the working principle of a D.C. motor.
5. Define back e.m.f. What is its significance for a D.C. motor ? State the factors upon which the value of back e.m.f. depends. **[AMIE Section B, Summer 1979]**
6. A D.C. shunt motor is to drive a constant torque load whose speed is required to be controlled over a range 2:1. Compare the following schemes for economy in capital cost:
   (*a*) A motor rated for the higher speed with armature resistance control.

(*b*) A motor rated for the lower speed with field resistance control.

[AMIE Section B, May 1965]

7. Show that in a D.C. motor, torque produced is proportional to the product of quadrature current and flux per pole. **[AMIE Section B, Summer 1979]**
8. Explain the methods of controlling the speed of a D.C. shunt motor and bring out their merits and demerits. Hence state the situations where each method is suitable.

[AMIE Section B, Winter 1979]

9. A motor is driving a mechanical load, the torque-speed characteristics of the motor of the load are given. Hence how will you determine the running speed of the set ?

[AMIE Section B, Winter 1974]

10. Describe with relevant circuit diagrams, the operation of Ward-Leonard system of speed control for D.C. motors. Discuss the main advantages of this system and the industrial field application. **[AMIE Section B, Summer 1975]**
11. Describe the various methods used for control of speed of D.C. shunt and series motors and discuss their relative merits. **[AMIE Section B, May 1966]**
12. Describe the basic principles of the various methods for controlling the speed of a D.C. shunt motor. **[AMIE Section B, Winter 1976, Summer 1977]**
13. How the speed of a D.C. shunt motor can be varied both above and below the speed at which it runs with full load current ? **[AMIE Section B, May 1963]**
14. Draw a diagram of a D.C. shunt motor starter. Explain the function of each component. How does the starter protect the motor from overload and overspeed ?

[AMIE Section B, May 1974]

15. Show that a shunt motor when allowed to speed up with constant field without altering the resistance of the armature, will increase in speed according to an exponential law.

[London University]

16. What is meant by the mechanical characteristics of a D.C. motor ? Sketch the form it takes in the case of a shunt-wound D.C. motor connected to constant voltage mains.

[London University]

17. Give the diagram of connections of a D.C. shunt motor and its associated face plate starter, and explain the mode of operation. Include over-current and under-voltage release.

[AMIE Section B, Winter 1975]

18. Considering magnetisations for generated e.m.f. and developing relevant questions, show and explain the nature of speed-torque characteristics of (*i*) a D.C. shunt motor, and (*ii*) a D.C. series motor. **[AMIE Section B, Winter 1975]**
19. (*a*) Discuss the applications of D.C. series motor.

[AMIE Section B, Summer 1976, Winter 1977]

(*b*) Discuss the applications of a D.C. shunt motors and compound motors.

[AMIE Section B, Winter 1977]

20. (*a*) Explain the torque speed characteristics of the following D.C. motors: (*i*) shunt motor, (*ii*) series motor and (*iii*) cummulatively compound motor.

[AMIE Section B, Summer 1977]

(*b*) Explain why (*i*) starters are used for D.C. motors (*ii*) a fly wheel is used with a D.C. series motor, and (*iii*) a D.C. shunt generator is used for charging a battery.

[AMIE Section B, Winter 1977]

Assignment Unit-2

1. A 230 volt-D.C. motor has an armature circuit resistance of 0.6 ohm. If the full load armature current is 30 A and the no-load armature current is 4 A, find the change in back e.m.f. from no-load to full load.

   [AMIE Section B, May 1953] (**Ans.** 15.6 V)

2. A 25 kW, 250 volt, D.C. shunt generator has armature and field resistances of 0.06 ohm and 100 ohm respectively. Determine the total armature power developed when working (*i*) as a generator delivering 25 kW output and (*ii*) as a motor taking 25 kW input.

   [Punjab University]

   (**Ans.** 26.25 kW, 23.8 kW)

3. Determine the value of torque in N-m units established by the armature of a 4-pole motor having 774 conductors, two paths in parallel, 24 m Wb per pole when the total armature current is 50 amperes.

   [AMIE Nov. 1950] (**Ans.** 295.3 Nw-m.)

4. A 90 h.p. (British), 500 V, 1000 r.p.m., 6-pole, D.C. shunt motor has a 2 circuit wave-connected armature. The shunt field resistance is 500 ohm and the combined armature, commutating field and brush resistance is 0.15 ohm. The motor has a full load efficiency of 90%. If there are 500 conductors on the armature, calculate (*a*) the flux per pole and (*b*) the useful torque for full load. **[AMIE May 1962]** (**Ans.** 0.0191 Wb and 641 Nw.m.)

5. A series motor has a resistance of 0.5 ohm between terminals. It runs at a speed of 1500 r.p.m. when taking 10 A from 200 volts D.C. supply. Find the speed at which it will run when taking 20 A from the same supply. Assume no saturation.

   [P.U. April 1967] (**Ans.** 731 r.p.m.)

6. The armature resistance of a 220 volt D.C. shunt motor is 0.4 ohm and it takes a no-load armature current of 2 A and runs at 1350 r.p.m. Find the speed when taking an armature current of 50 A if the armature reaction weakens the flux by 2 per cent.

   [Kerala Uni. Elect. Tech. 1966]

   (**Ans.** 1257 r.p.m.)

7. A 250 volts series motor has an armature resistance of 0.08 ohm and field resistance of 0.02 ohm and produces full load torque when running at 500 r.p.m. taking a current of 40 amperes. Calculate (*a*) armature current and (*b*) the speed when producing $^1/_2$ full load torque. Neglect effects of armature reaction and saturation.

   [*AMIE* Nov. 1966] **[Ans.** (*a*) 28.28 A, (*b*) 710 r.p.m.]

8. A D.C. series motor running on open circuit at 1000 r.p.m. holds the following voltage-current relationship. The total resistance of the machine (armature and field) is 0.2 ohm. Neglecting

the effects of armature reaction and brush drop, plot the speed-torque curve of the motor when operating on 500 V supply.

Current, amperes	50	100	150	200	250	300
Open circuit voltage, volts	150	295	402	480	530	565

[AMIE Section B, May 1971]

9. A D.C. series motor runs at 500 r.p.m. when taking a current of 60 A at 460 V. The resistance of the armature circuit is 0.2 ohm and the field winding is 0.1 ohm. Calculate the speed when a 0.15 ohm diverter is connected in parallel with the field winding. Assume the torque to remain unaltered and the flux to be proportional to the field current.

[AMIE Section B, Summer 1974]

10. The torque-speed characteristics of a motor is given by the equation $N = 1490 - 2T$, and that of a pump coupled to the motor is given by $T = 0.1206 \times 10^{-4} N^2$, where T is the torque in Newton-metres and N is the speed in r.p.m. Determine the speed at which the set will run.

[AMIE Winter 1974]

11. A D.C. series motor is to drive a load whose torque is proportional to the square of the speed. If with the rated voltage applied the speed is 1400 r.p.m. what must be the applied voltage so that the speed is 1000 r.p.m. ? Neglect armature resistance and saturation.

[AMIE Section B, 1969] (**Ans.** 51% of rated voltage)

12. Explain in detail what happens when the flux is reduced by 10% in a 200 V D.C. motor, having an armature resistance of 0.2 ohm carrying a current of 50 A and running at 960 r.p.m. prior to weakening the field. The total torque may be assumed to remain constant, iron and friction losses may be neglected. **[AMIE Nov. 1966]** (**Ans.** 10.60 r.p.m.)

13. A 30 h.p. shunt motor takes 100 amperes running normally and has to start up against full load torque, the starting current not to exceed 50% of the normal running current. Design a suitable starter. Armature resistance = 0.02 ohm, supply voltage = 200 volts.

[AMIE Section B, Nov. 1962]

(**Ans.** 0.445 Ω, 0.296 Ω, 0.198Ω, 0.132Ω, 0.088Ω, 0.058Ω, 0.038 Ω, 0.026Ω, 0.017Ω, 0.011Ω and 0.004 Ω)

14. A 10 h.p. 220 V shunt motor has a full load speed of 1000 r.p.m. The resistance of the armature and the field circuits are 0.25 Ω and 14.6Ω respectively. The full load efficiency of the motor is 85%. Neglecting brush drop and the effects of armature reaction, calculate:

(*a*) the speed at which the motor will run on no load, if under these conditions its total input is 550 watts.

(*b*) the value of resistance to be added to the armature circuit to reduce the speed to 800 r.p.m. when giving full load torque and full field current.

[AMIE Section B, May 1963] (**Ans.** 1044 r.p.m., 1.113 ohm)

15. A 220 volt shunt D.C. motor has an armature resistance of 0.5 Ω and takes a current of 40 A on full load. By how much the main flux be reduced to raise the speed by 50% if the developed torque is constant. **[Calcutta University, Elect Engg. 1967]** (**Ans.** 37.5%)

16. A 250 volt D.C. series motor takes 40 A when developing in full load torque at 1500 r.p.m. its resistance is 0.5 ohm. If the load torque varies as the square of the speed, determine the resistance to be connected in series with the armature to reduce the speed to 1200 r.p.m. Assume that the flux is proportional to the field current.

[AMIE Section B, May 1966] (**Ans.** 2.7125 ohm)

17. A series motor with an unsaturated magnetic circuit and negligible resistance takes 80 A at 640 V, when running at a certain speed on a given load. If the load torque varies as the cube of the speed find the resistance necessary to reduce the speed by 75%.

[AMIE Section B, November, 1967] (**Ans.** 62 ohm)

18. A D.C. series motor runs at 1000 r.p.m. and takes 25 A from 250 V mains. The armature current is then reduced to 15 A by inserting a series resistance. Find the new speed and the value of the resistance inserted if the load torque varies as the square of the speed and the field flux is reduced by 15% for above change in the armature current. Assume the combined resistance of the armature and the series field to be 1.0 ohm.

[AMIE Section B, November 1968] (**Ans.** 6.56 ohm)

19. A 4-pole series wound fan motor runs normally at 600 r.p.m. on a 250 V supply taking 20 amperes. The field coils are connected all in series. Estimate the speed and the current taken by the motor, if the field coils are reconnected in two parallel groups of two coils in series. The load torque increases as the square of the speed. Assume that the flux is directly proportional to the field current and ignore all losses in the machine.

[AMIE Section B, Summer 1976]

20. A 250 D.C. shunt motor has an armature current 20 amperes when running at 1000 r.p.m. against full load torque. The armature resistance is 0.5 ohm. What resistance must be inserted in series with the armature to reduce the speed to 500 r.p.m. at the same torque, and what will be the speed if the torque is halved with this resistance in circuit? Assume the flux to remain constant throughout. **[AMIE Section B, Winter 1975]**

TRANSFORMERS

5.1. DEFINITION AND INTRODUCTION OF TRANSFORMER

A Transformer is a static machine which transforms a.c. electric power from one circuit to another without change in frequency. This transfer of power may or may not be accompanied by a change in voltage.

If a transformer receives power at one voltage and delivers it at a higher voltage, the transformer is known as step up transformer. If it receives power at one voltage and delivers it at lower voltage, the transformer is known as stepdown transformer. If the transformer receives power at one voltage and delivers it at the same voltage, the transformer is known as one-to-one transformer.

Since transformer is a static machine, it does not have any rotating part. Due to this reason, mechanical losses in the transformer are zero and therefore the efficiency of this machine is quite high. A medium size transformer has a full load efficiency of about 97 to 98%. The Machine also does not need much of maintenance because it has no rotating parts. Transformer is quite useful for transmitting and distributing a.c. power. The generated a.c. voltage at 11 kV can be stepped up with the help of transformer. As many times the voltage is stepped up in a transformer, the current gets stepped down that many times. The reduction in the value of current, reduces the size of the transmission line conductor thus saving the conductor material and also reduces the copper losses many times, thus increasing the efficiency of transmission.

5.1.1 Function of Transformer

The function of a transformer, as the name implies, is to transform the alternating current energy from one voltage into another voltage. The transformer has no rotating part hence it is often called a static transformer.

5.1.2 Constructional Features of a Transformer

A transformer basically consists of two independent windings wound on a common magnetic core made of silicon steel. The winding connected to supply mains is the **primary winding** and the winding connected to the load side is called the **secondary winding**. The core is made of thin laminations of silicon steel sheet (0.33 mm thick). Each lamination is provided with Zinc-oxide coating or varnish insulation layer on both the sides. Such type of construction of core ensures low core losses. The primary and secondary windings are electrically separate but they are magnetically coupled with each other.

5.2. PRINCIPLE OF TRANSFORMER

The transformer is based on the principle of electromagnetic induction. A simple diagram of transformer is shown in Fig. 5.1.

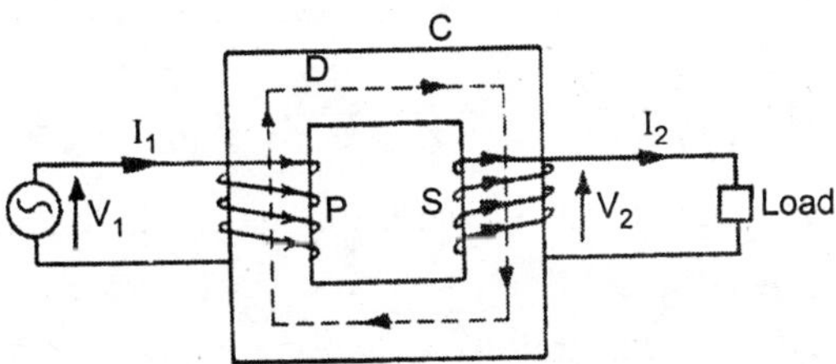

Fig. 5.1. A Simple transformer

It consists of an iron core *C* made of a number of laminated sheets about 0.35 mm. thick each. These laminated sheets are insulated from each other by means of varnish. All these sheets are dipped in varnish, dried and then assembled to form a core. The sheets are laminated in order to reduce eddy current loss which is produced due to eddy currents induced in the core by alternating magnetic flux. The sheets are made of silicon steel material because this type of material has very less hysteresis loss.

The vertical portions of the core are known as limbs whereas top and bottom portions are known as yokes. The coils are wound on the limbs. Coil *P* is connected to the supply as shown in Fig. 5.1 and is known as primary coil whereas coil *S* is connected to the load and is known as secondary coil.

When alternating voltage is applied to the primary of the transformer, alternating current flows in the primary because primary circuit is complete. This primary alternating current produces alternating flux in the iron core, the mean path of which is represented by dotted line *D*. The flux follows the path of iron core because it has the least reluctance. If the flux as a result of leakage is neglected, then whatever flux links primary coil also links the secondary. The primary and secondary flux linkages keep on changing due to changing alternating flux. The changing flux linkages produce e.m.f. both in primary and secondary. Since the same flux links both primary and secondary, so voltage induced per turn in primary and secondary winding is same.

If N_1 is the number of turns in primary and

N_2 is the number of turn in secondary, then

Total e.m.f. induced in secondary winding

$$= N_2 \times \text{Voltage induced per turn}$$

Total e.m.f. induced in primary winding

$$= N_1 \times \text{Voltage induced per turn}$$

$$\frac{\textit{Total e.m.f induced in Secondary S}}{\textit{Total e.m.f. induced in Primary P}} = \frac{N_2 \times \textit{Voltage per turn}}{N_1 \times \textit{Voltage per turn}}$$

$$= \frac{N_2}{N_1} \simeq \frac{V_2}{V_1}$$

When the secondary of the transformer is open, *i.e.* no load is connected across the secondary, then secondary does not draw any current, and therefore its terminal voltage is same as induced voltage. When no current flows in the secondary, very little current flows in the primary. Current in the primary is of magnitude so that it is able to produce flux sufficient to produce required e.m.f. in the primary.

Since primary current is very small, the applied voltage V_1 is practically equal and opposite to the e.m.f. induced in *P*.

$$\text{Therefore } \frac{E.m.f.\ induced\ in\ Secondary}{E.m.f.\ induced\ in\ Primary} = \frac{N_2}{N_1} \simeq \frac{V_2}{V_1} \qquad ...(i)$$

A transformer enables us to transfer a.c. power from one circuit to another with a change in voltage level.

The following points may be noted carefully:

(*i*) The transformer action is based on the laws of electromagnetic induction.

(*ii*) There is no electrical connection between the primary and secondary. The a c power is transferred from primary to secondary through magnetic flux.

(*iii*) There is no change in frequency *i.e.*, output power has the same frequency as the input power,

(*iv*) The losses that occur in a transformer are:

(*a*) core losses → eddy current and hysteresis losses

(*b*) copper losses → in the resistance of the windings

In practice, these losses are very small so that output power is nearly equal to the input primary power. In other words, a transformer has very high efficiency.

5.3. RATINGS OF TRANSFORMER

The different parameters like power, voltage, frequency and efficiency etc. which are mentioned on the name plate of the transformer are known as ratings of the transformer. Out of above mentioned parameters, 'Power' is the quantity, which keeps its utmost importance from expressing point of view. As the rated primary voltage is the maximum value of voltage which a transformer can carry in its primary side, similarly secondary voltage is the maximum value of voltage which a transformer can carry in its secondary side beyond which chances of overheating, hence burning of transformer are set up. Also the rated frequency is the value of frequency in 'Hertz' upon which the transformer can operate with reasonable high efficiency. But the power rated of the transformer is expressed in kVA in place of kW. The reason for expressing power in kVA in place of kW is the power factor. The power factor depends upon the type of load on the transformer. The value of power factor varies from 0 to 1, hence the 'kW' power of the transformer also varies. As the 'kVA' rating is independent of power factor and remains constant for every machine, hence only due to this reason the power rating of the transformer is expressed in kVA.

5.3.1 An Ideal Transformer

Ideal transformer is that which has

(*i*) No winding resistance

(*ii*) No leakage flux (*i.e.*, eddy current and hysteresis losses in the core.)

Actually ideal transformer can not be physically realised, yet its study gives a very strong tool in the analysis of a practical transformer

As such practical transformer have properties that approach very close to an ideal transformer.

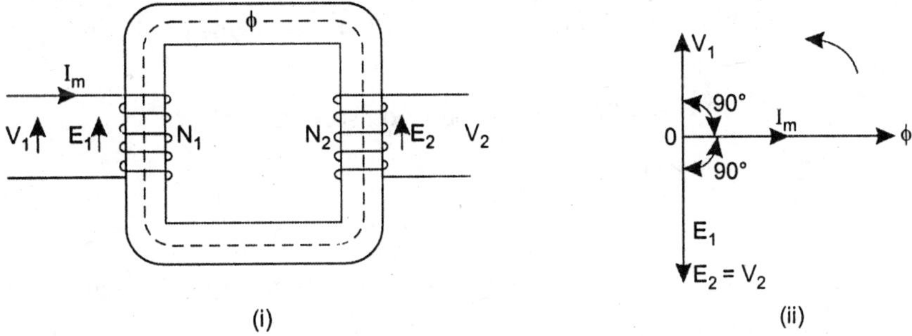

Fig. 5.1.1

Consider an ideal transformer on no load *i.e.* secondary is open-circuited as shown in Fig. 5.1.1 (*i*) Under such conditions the primary is simply a coil of pure inductance. When an alternating voltage V_1 is applied to the primary, it draws a small magnetising current I_m which lags behind the applied voltage by ** 90°. This alternating current I_m produces an alternating flux ϕ which is proportional to and in † phase with it. The alternating flux ϕ links both the windings and induces e.m.f. E_1 in the primary and e.m.f. E_2 in the secondary. The primary e.m.f. E_1 is at every instant, equal to and in opposition to V_1 (Lenz's law). Both e.m.f.s E_1 and E_2 lag behind flux ϕ by 90° (See Art. 5.5) However, their magnitudes depend upon the number of primary and secondary turns.

Fig. 5.1.1 (*ii*) shows the phasor diagram of an ideal transformer on no load. Since flux ϕ is common to both the windings, it has been taken as the reference phasor. As shown in Art. 5.5 the primary e.m.f. E_1 and secondary e.m.f. E_2 lag behind the flux ϕ by 90°. Note that E_1 and E_2 are in phase. But E_1 is equal to V_1 and 180° out of phase with it.

5.4. RELATIONSHIP BETWEEN PRIMARY CURRENT AND SECONDARY CURRENT

When the secondary of the transformer is on open circuit, the primary current known as no-load current is very small as a result no load ampere-turns are also very small. These small no-load ampere-turns are just sufficient to produce flux necessary to induce an e.m.f. that is practically equal and opposite to the applied voltage. This primary current is about 3 to 5% of the full load primary current.

Note: * Since $d\phi/dt$ is common for both the windings.

** In a pure inductive circuit, current lags behind the voltage by 90°.

† Since there are no iron losses, flux ϕ is in phase with I_m.

When the load is connected across the secondary terminals of the transformer, the secondary current flows. This secondary current also produces its own flux which as per Lenz's law produces a demagnetising effect and as a result the main flux in the core gets reduced. This reduced flux in the core produces reduced flux linkages. These reduced flux linkages in the primary produce lesser e.m.f. in the primary. The applied voltage having remained the same, the current in the primary gets increased. The new increased primary current would be approx. 20 times the no-load current. Thus the primary ampere-turns get increased. Thus the decrease in the ampere-turns due to demagnetising effect, on the secondary is neutralised by the increase in the ampere-turns on account of increase in primary current. Thus the flux set up in the core still remains constant.

If the primary ampere turns on no-load which is very small and is neglected, then

Full load ampere-turns on primary

= full load ampere-turns on secondary

∴ Full load ampere turns on primary

$$= I_1N_1$$

Where I_1 = Current in primary corresponding to current I_2 in secondary

Full load ampere-turns on secondary

$$= I_2N_2$$

Where I_2 = Current in the secondary ...(*i*)

$$\therefore \quad I_1N_1 = I_2N_2$$

$$\frac{I_1}{I_2} = \frac{N_2}{N_1} \qquad ...(ii)$$

But
$$\frac{N_2}{N_1} \simeq \frac{V_2}{V_1}$$

$$\therefore \quad \frac{I_1}{I_2} = \frac{N_2}{N_1} \simeq \frac{V_2}{V_1} \qquad ...(iii)$$

It may be mentioned here that although secondary winding and primary winding are not connected with each other electrically but still any change in secondary current is always accompanied by the corresponding change in primary current. This is accomplished magnetically.

5.5. E.M.F. EQUATION OF A TRANSFORMER

Let N_1 be number of turns on primary side and N_2 be the number of turns on secondary side as shown in Fig. 5.2.

Let $\phi = \phi_m \sin \omega t$ be the flux developed as a result of alternating voltage applied across the primary where ϕ is the instantaneous value of flux in webers

and ϕ_m is the max. value of flux in webers.

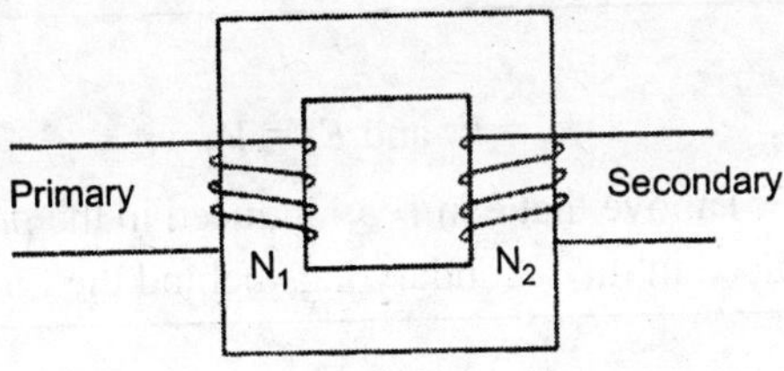

Fig. 5.2

$$e_1 = \text{instantaneous value of e.m.f. induced in the primary winding}$$

$$= -N_1 \frac{d\phi}{dt}$$

but $$\phi = \phi_m \sin \omega t$$

$\therefore$ $$e_1 = -N_1 \frac{d}{dt}(\phi_m \sin \omega t)$$

$$= -N_1 \phi_m \omega \cos \omega t$$

$$= -N_1 \phi_m \omega \sin\left(\frac{\pi}{2} - \omega t\right)$$

$$= N_1 \phi_m \omega \sin\left(\omega t - \frac{\pi}{2}\right) \qquad ...(iv)$$

$$= N_1 \phi_m \omega \sin(\omega t - 90°) \qquad ...(v)$$

Maximum value of e.m.f. shall be induced in primary winding

when $\sin\left(\omega t - \frac{\pi}{2}\right)$ shall have its max. value, *i.e.* equal to one

$$E_{1\max} = N_1 \phi_m \omega$$

R.M.S. value of voltage induced in the primary E_1 is given by

$$E_1 = \frac{E_{1\max}}{\sqrt{2}} = \frac{N_1 \phi_m \omega}{\sqrt{2}}$$

$$\omega = 2\pi f$$

$\therefore$ $$E_1 = \frac{N_1 \phi_m 2\pi f}{\sqrt{2}}$$

But $$\frac{2\pi}{\sqrt{2}} = 4.44$$

$\therefore$ $$E_1 = 4.44\, \phi_m N_1 f = 4 \times 1.11\, \phi_m N_1 f$$

But $$1.11 = K_f \text{ is from factor}$$

$\therefore$ $$E_1 = 4K_{f\,\phi m} N_1 f = 4.44\, \phi_m N_1 f \text{ volts}$$

Similarly e.m.f. induced in the secondary winding is

$$E_2 = 4.44\, \phi_m N_2 f \text{ volts.}$$

In an ideal transformer

$$E_1 = V_1 \text{ and } E_2 = V_2$$

Note: It is clear from exp. (V) above that e.m.f 'e_1' induced in the primary lags behind the flux, ϕ by 90°. Likewise e.m.f. 'e_2' induced in the secondary lags behind the flux ϕ by 90°.

5.6. ALTERNATE METHOD OF. E.M.F. EQUATION OF TRANSFORMER

If ϕ_m is the maximum value of flux in webers varying with time as shown in Fig. 5.3 at frequency f cycles/sec, then the time taken for the flux to change from ϕ_m to $-\phi_m$ is the same as the one taken to complete half cycle.

Time taken to complete half cycle = $\frac{1}{2f}$ seconds

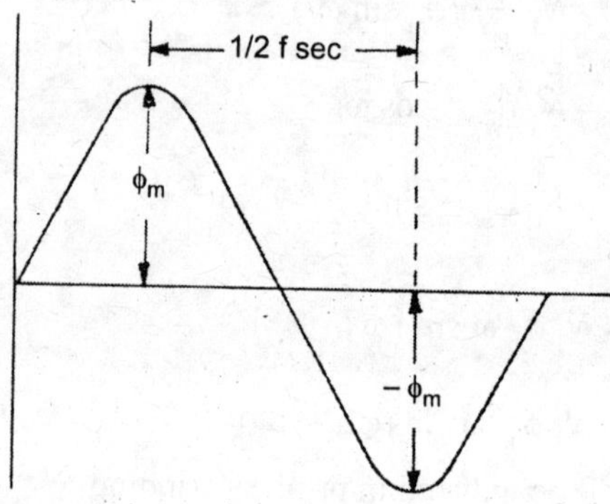

Fig. 5.3. Waveform of flux variation

The flux ϕ_m has changed to $-\phi_m$ in time $\frac{1}{2f}$ seconds.

Average rate of change of flux

$$= \frac{\phi m - (-\phi_m)}{\frac{1}{2f}} = 2\phi_m \times 2f$$

$$= 4\,\phi_m f \text{ webers/sec.}$$

∴ Average e.m.f. induced in each turn

$$= 1 \times \text{Average rate of change of flux}$$

$$= 1 \times 4\,\phi_m f \text{ volts}$$

$$= 4\,\phi_m f \text{ volts}$$

Average e.m.f. induced in the primary of transformer having N_1 number of turns

$$= 4\,\phi_m f N_1$$

∴ R.M.S. value of e.m.f. induced in primary

$$= E_1 = 4\,\phi_m f N_1 \times 1.11$$

$$\left(\frac{R.MS.\ value}{Average\ value} = K_f = form\ factor = 1.11\right)$$

$\therefore$ $$E_1 = 4.44\ \phi_m N_1 f \text{ volts} \qquad ...(v)$$

Similarly R.M.S. value of voltage induced in secondary

$$E_2 = 4.44\ \phi_m N_2 f \text{ volts} \qquad ...(vi)$$

5.6.1. Voltage Transformation Ratio (K)

From the above equations of induced e.m.f., we have (See Fig. 5.3.1).

$$\frac{E_2}{E_1} = \frac{N_2}{N_1} = K$$

The constant K is called voltage transformation ratio. Thus if $K = 5$ (*i.e.* $N_2/N_1 = 5$) then $E_2 = 5\ E_1$.

For an ideal transformer;

(*i*) $E_1 = V_1$ and $E_2 = V_2$ as there is no voltage drop in the windings.

$\therefore$ $$\frac{E_2}{E_1} = \frac{V_2}{V_1} = \frac{N_2}{N_1} = K$$

(*ii*) there are no losses. Therefore, volt-amperes input to the primary are equal to the output volt-amperes *i.e.*

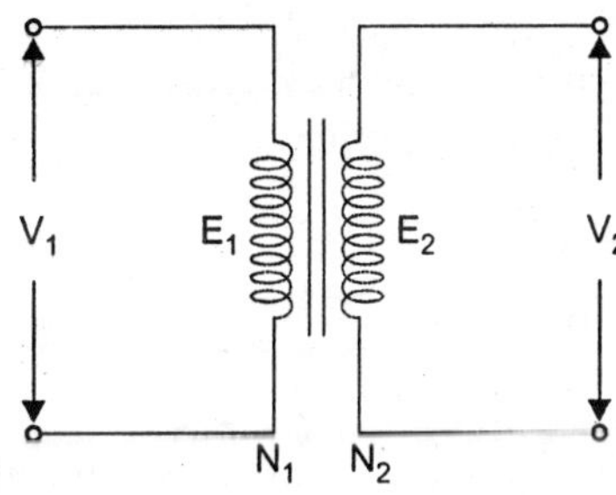

Fig. 5.3.1

$$V_1 I_1 = V_2 I_2$$

or $$\frac{I_2}{I_1} = \frac{V_1}{V_2} = \frac{1}{K}$$

Hence, currents are in the inverse ratio of voltage transformation ratio.

5.6.2. Turn Ratio

The Ratio of primary to secondary turns is called turn ratio, *i.e.*,

$$\text{Turn ratio} = \frac{N_1}{N_2}$$

Note: (*i*) Incase $N_2 > N_1$ the transformer is Step up and

(*ii*) when $N_2 < N_1$ the transformer is step down transformer.

5.6.3. Transformation Ratio

The ratio of Secondary voltage to primary voltage is called voltage transformation ratio of the transformer. It is represented by K.

$$K = \frac{E_2}{E_1} = \frac{N_2}{N_1}$$

5.7. CONSTRUCTION OF TRANSFORMER

A transformer consists mainly of the following components

(*i*) Primary winding. (*ii*) Secondary winding.

(*iii*) An iron core.

To make a successful transformer in practice, however several other parts are necessary. The windings must be insulated properly from each other as well as from the core. This insulation is major insulation. Then each turn of the winding must be insulated from the other turn through insulation known as minor insulation. The windings also must be protected from effects of moisture and as such the windings must be impregnated in suitable solid compound or in fluids which also serve to carry away heat.

The core plates must be firmly clamped together to keep them in place and prevent vibration of excessive noise.

Terminal bushings are needed to bring the winding connections out from the tank in which the transformer is oil immersed for the purpose of cooling.

The Core

Transformers normally are of two types:

(*i*) Core type (*ii*) Shell type.

A core type transformer is one in which there is only one iron path usually rectangular in form and the windings are arranged either around one limb only or on two opposite sides. Two such core type transformers are shown in Fig. 5.4 (*a*) and (*b*).

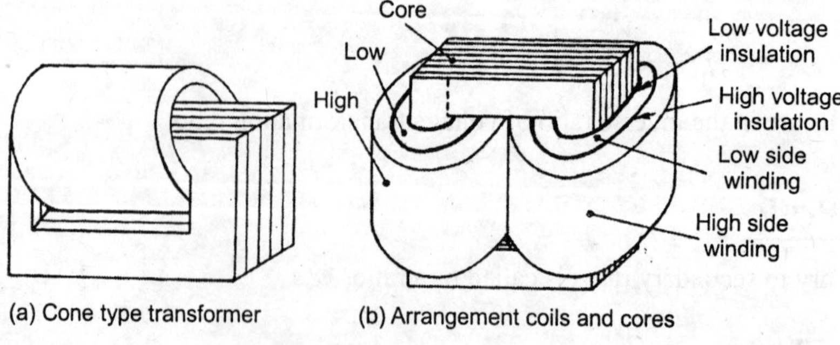

(a) Cone type transformer (b) Arrangement coils and cores

Fig. 5.4

The core type is not often used in small sizes because its shape makes mounting more difficult but, it is advantageous because of the ease of insulation when very high voltages are to be generated on small transformers.

In the shell type the core is distributed around the coils either in a uniform manner or in several blocks of laminations. The simplest shell type core is that built up from *E* and *I* or *T* and *U* stampings, with the windings around the centre limb. There are thus two parallel magnetic paths into which the flux from the central limb can divide. These two paths lie in this case in the same plane but there may be three or more such paths in which case of course they are placed radially round the core as in the radial or Berry pattern illustrated in Fig. 5.5 (*a*) and (*b*).

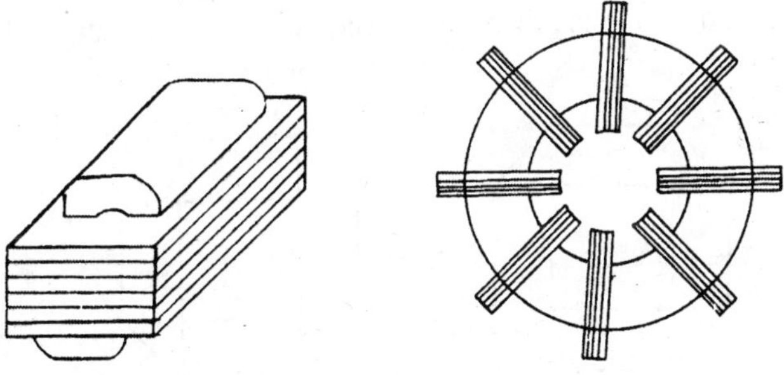

(a) Shell type transformer. (b) Distributed shell or Berry type in plan view.

Fig. 5.5

Laminations: In all types of transformers, the core is constructed of transformer sheet steel laminations assembled to provide a continuous magnetic path with a minimum of air gap. The steel used for the laminations is high grade silicon steel which has a low hysteresis loss at the working flux densities. The eddy current loss is minimised by making the core in the form of laminations and then insulating each lamination from the other by dipping each one in a bath of varnish and then drying and assembling it.

The thickness of each lamination varies from 0.35 to 0.5 mm. depending upon the frequency. For a frequency of 50 c/s, the thickness of lamination may be 0.35 mm. and for a frequency of 25 c/s, the thickness of each lamination may be 0.5 mm. and in between the two ranges of frequency, the thickness varies accordingly.

Core of Core Type Transformer

In order to reduce the air gaps to minimum the joints of these laminations in alternate layers are staggered. If the laminations used are I-type, then the stagging of joints is done in core type transformer as shown in Fig. 5.6.

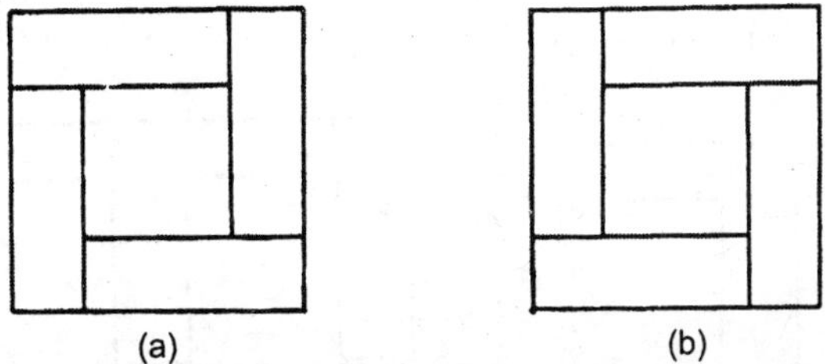

(a) (b)

Fig. 5.6. Arrangement of joints in adjacent lamination layers of I-type laminations

If the first layer has the *I* type laminations arranged as in Fig. 5.6 (*a*) then the second layer has the laminations arranged as shown in Fig. 5.6 (*b*) and the third layer again has laminations arranged as per in Fig. 5.6 (*a*) and 4th layer as per Fig. 5.6 (*b*). This continues till the thickness of the core is obtained as per design. Then all these laminations are pressed together and bolted together.

If the laminations are L-type then the staggering is done as shown in Fig. 5.7 (*a*) and (*b*). The L-type laminations are arranged alternately with first layer as shown in Fig. 5.7 (*a*), second layer as shown in Fig. 5.7 (*b*), third layer again as shown in Fig. 5.7 (*a*) and fourth as shown in Fig. 5.7 (*b*), so on and so forth.

If the transformer were made with the primary and secondary coils on separate legs, an unsatisfactory transformer would result,

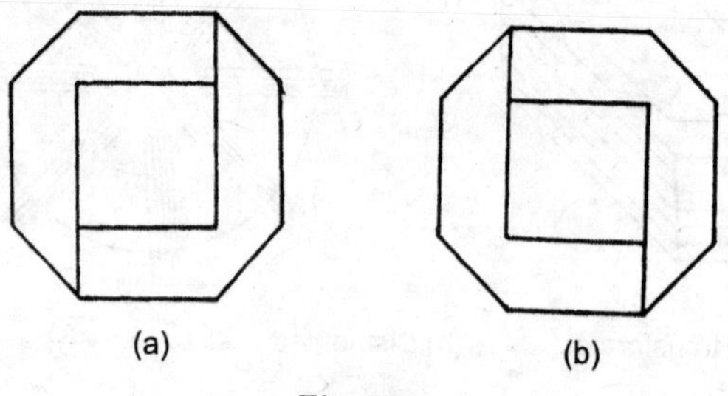

Fig. 5.7

as large leakage flux for both primary and secondary would give very poor regulations. By having both primary and secondary on each leg, the leakage flux is reduced to a small value. If the high voltage winding were placed next to the core, it would be necessary to insulate it from both the core and low voltage winding and two layers of high voltage insulations would be necessary. By placing the high voltage winding outside and around the low voltage winding, only one layer of high voltage insulation, that between the high and low voltage windings is necessary.

Core of Shell Type Transformer

In the shell type transformer, the iron nearly surrounds the copper winding. The core has the form as shown in Fig. 5.8 (*a*). The core is assembled out of E-type and I-type of lamination as shown in Fig. 5.8 (*b*).

The entire flux passes through the central part of the core but outside of this central core, it divides half going in each direction. The coils are usually made of shape of pancakes and are usually wound with strip copper. These coils are taped and primary and secondary are usually stacked so that each primary is adjacent to a secondary. In this way leakage flux of both primary and secondary is reduced to a very low value. The secondaries or low side coils are placed adjacent to the iron in order to minimise the amount of high voltage insulation required.

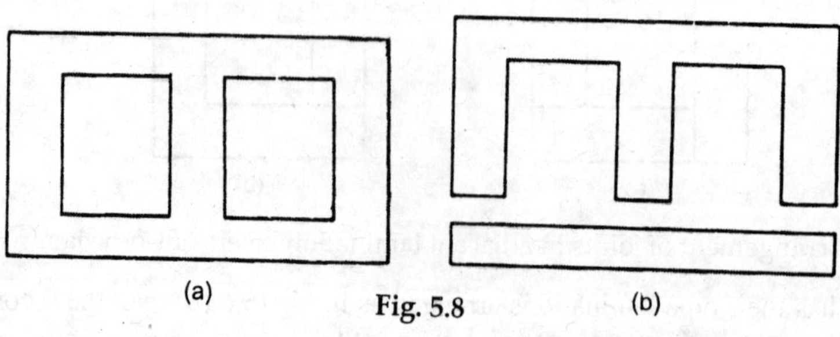

Fig. 5.8

Coils and core of shell type transformer are shown in Fig. 5.9.

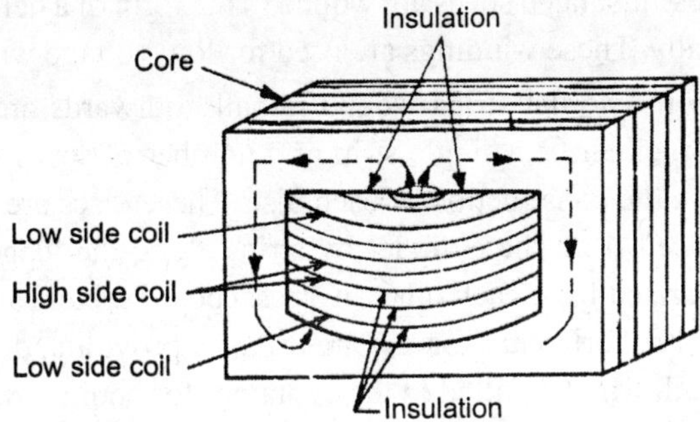

Fig. 5.9. Coils and core shell type transformer

5.8. TRANSFORMER-WINDINGS

The winding of the transformer is also a most important part of the transformer. The different type of windings are given as follows:

1. Concentric windings
2. Sandwich windings.

1. ***Concentric windings:*** These windings are used for core type transformers. Each limb is wound with a group of coils consisting of both primary and secondary turns which may be concentric cylinders. As shown in Fig. 5.10, the low voltage (*L.V.*) winding is placed on the core by 1st providing suitable insulation on the core, then high voltage (*H.V.*) winding is placed.

   The concentric windings are further divided as follows:

   (*i*) ***Cross-over windings:*** The conductors used for this type of winding are cotton covered round wires or copper strips insulated with the paper. The cross over coils having number of layers with a number of turns per layer. Two ends of each coil (one from inside & one from outside) are taken out. The inside end of a coil is connected to the outside end of the adjacent coil. These windings are suitable for high voltage winding of small transformers and currents up to 20 Amps.

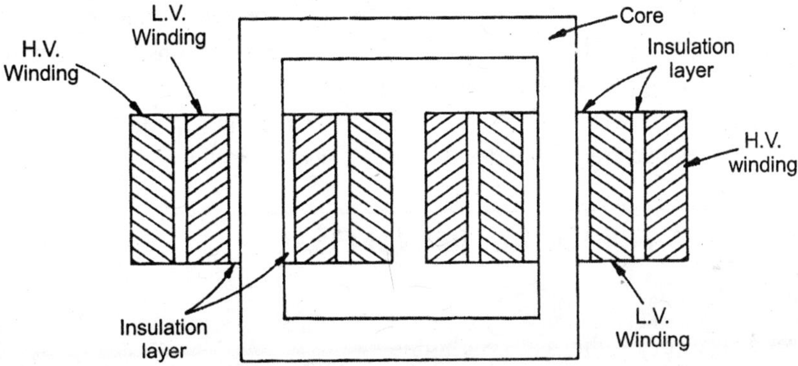

Fig. 5.10. Concentric winding

(*ii*) ***Helical windings:*** In such types of windings the rectangular strips of conducting material are used. These insulated strips are wound in the form of a helix. These strips are wound in parallel radially. These windings are used for low voltage winding of large transformers.

(*iii*) ***Disc-windings:*** The flat strips wound radially outwards are used in this winding. The conductor can either be a single strip or a number of strips in parallel, wound on a flat. This results in the construction of each disc. These discs are wound on the cylinder. The discs are spaced from the cylinder by strips along the length of the cylinder. Also the discs are separated from each other by press–board sectors attached to the vertical strips. These vertical & horizontal spacers are used for providing ducts for proper circulation of transformer oil, which is filled in the container for cooling & insulation purposes.

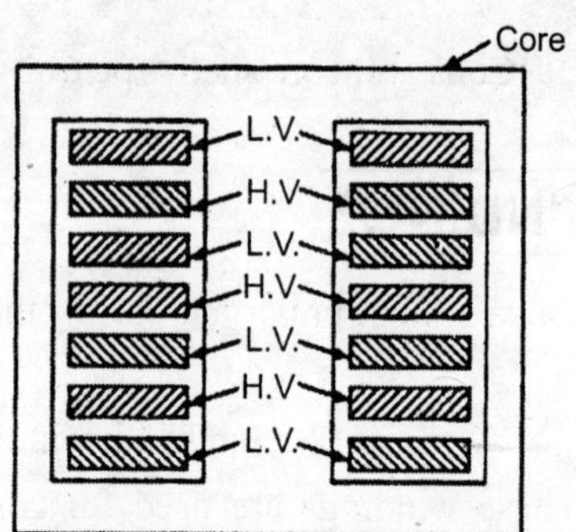

Fig. 5.11. Sandwich winding (Core type transformer)

2. ***Sandwich-Windings***: In these windings both low voltage (*L.V.*) and high voltage (*H.V.*) windings of transformer are split in to number of sections. As shown in Fig. 5.11, the high voltage winding is placed in between low voltage winding. The sandwich winding is applicable for shell type transformers. As there are a number of divisions of windings, the leakage of reactance can be controlled easily.

5.9. COMPARISON BETWEEN CORE TYPE AND SHELL TYPE TRANSFORMERS

To compare the two types of transformer in general, the core type has a longer mean length of core and shorter mean length of the turn. The core type has a lesser cross-section of iron and therefore greater number of turns. The core type is better adopted for high voltage since there is more space for insulation. In the shell type, the coils are better braced mechanically so that they are less easily displaced by high electro-mechanical forces that frequently develop during short circuits.

5.10. THEORY OF AN IDEAL TRANSFORMER

It is assumed that in the ideal transformer:

(*i*) The resistances of windings are negligible.

(*ii*) All the magnetic flux links all the turns of both primary and secondary, *i.e.*, there is no leakage flux.

(*iii*) Eddy current loss and hysteresis loss in the core is negligible.

(*iv*) The permeability of the core material is extremely high and constant.

These assumptions are equivalent to the statement that the transformer has no winding resistance, no magnetising current, no iron losses and no magnetic leakage. In actual practice such like ideal transformers do not exist because any transformer having primary and secondary windings must have some resistance. In addition some of the flux must leak out from the core and losses also must take place although they may be very small. Thus although an ideal transformer is only theoretical interest but still understanding of transformer becomes easier if initially it is assumed to be an ideal transformer. Let us consider the given ideal transformer as shown in Fig. 5.12 (*a*) to be on no load. Thus when the primary winding does not possess any resistance, in that case it is a purely inductive coil. When a sinusoidal alternating voltage V_1 is fed to this primary, a current I_m flows through it. This current lags behind the voltage V_1 by 90°. The current I_m sets up an alternating flux ϕ in the coil and is known as magnetising current. The flux ϕ and current I_m are in phase with each other as there are no iron losses.

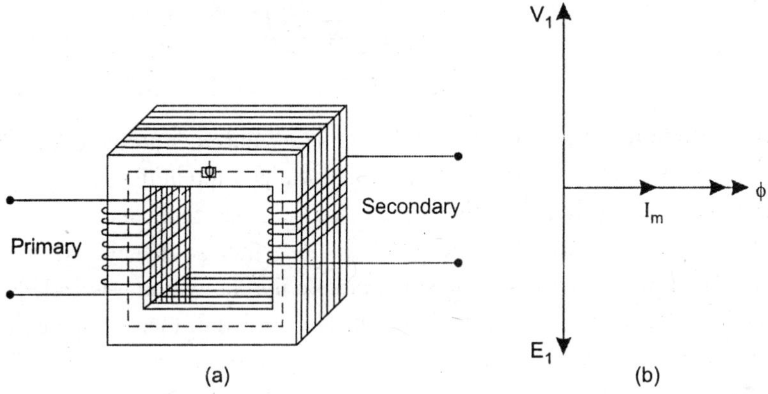

Fig. 5.12. Vector diagram

This is shown in vector diagram drawn at Fig. 5.12 (*b*). This alternating flux links with the primary winding as well as secondary winding and induces e.m.f. in them. The e.m.f. E_1 induced in primary oppose the applied voltage V_1, as a result, the current in the primary is limited down. The e.m.f. E_1 lags behind flux ϕ by 90° as per equation (*iv*).

Had there been no e.m.f. E_1 induced in the primary winding, very heavy current would have passed in the primary when voltage V_1 is applied across it. This is the reason why when transformers are connected across D.C. voltage, get burnt. D.C. voltage applied across transformer primary produces constant flux due to which flux linkages do not change. As such no opposing e.m.f. is induced in the primary. A very heavy current flows due to applied voltage, in the absence of opposing induced e.m.f. and as a result transformer gets burnt.

5.10.1. Practical Transformer

A practical transformer differs from the ideal transformer in many respects. The practical transformer has (*i*) iron losses (*ii*) winding resistances and (*iii*) magnetic leakage, giving rise to leakage reactances.

(*i*) **Iron losses.** Since the iron core is subjected to alternating flux, there occurs eddy current and hysteresis loss in it. Th... two losses together are known as *iron losses or core losses*. The iron losses depend upon the supply frequency, maximum flux density in the core, volume of the core etc. It may be noted that magnitude of iron losses is quite small in a practical transformer.

(*ii*) **Winding resistances.** Since the windings consist of copper conductors, it immediately follows that both primary and secondary will have winding resistance. The primary resistance R and secondary resistance R_2 act in series with the respective windings as shown in Fig 5.12.1 When current flows through the windings, there will be power loss as well as a loss in voltage due to IR drop. This will affect the power factor and E_1 will be less than V_1, while V_2 will be less than E_2.

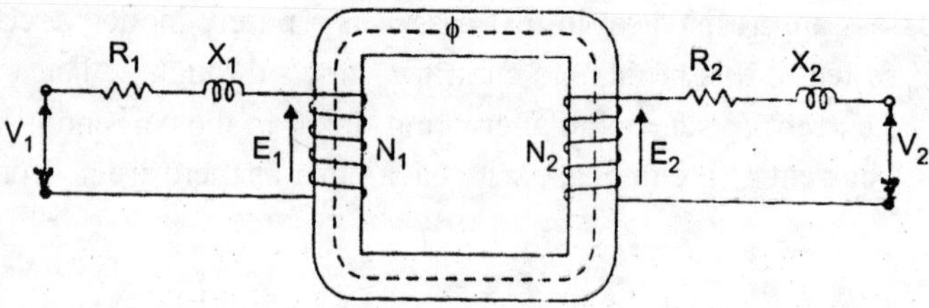

Fig. 5.12.1

(*iii*) **Leakage reactances.** Both primary and secondary currents produce flux. The flux ϕ which links both the windings is the useful flux and is called mutual flux. However, primary current would produce some flux ϕ_1 which would not link the secondary winding (See Fig 5.12.2) Similarly, secondary current would produce some flux ϕ_2 that would not link the primary winding. The flux such as ϕ_1 or ϕ_2 which links only one winding is called leakage flux. The leakage flux paths are mainly through the air. The *effect of these leakage fluxes would be the same as though inductive reactance were connected in series with each winding of transformer that had no leakage flux as shown in Fig. 5.12.2. In other words, the effect of primary leakage flux ϕ_1 is to introduce an inductive reactance X_1 in series with the primary winding as shown in Fig. 5.12.1 Similarly, the secondary leakage flux ϕ_2 introduces an inductive reactance X_2 in series with the secondary winding. There will be no power loss due to leakage reactance. However, the presence of leakage reactance in the windings changes the power factor as well as there is voltage loss due to IX drop.

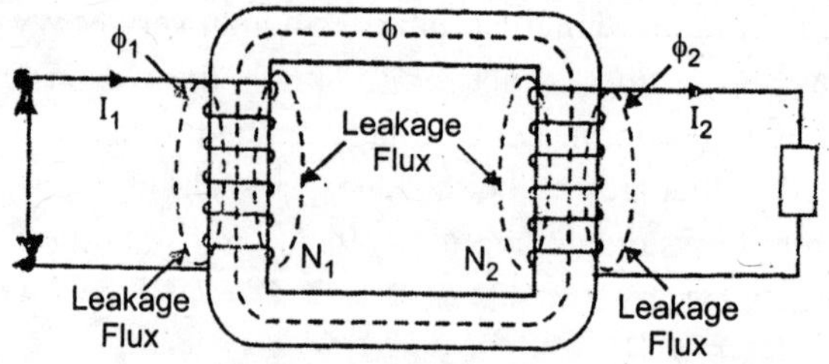

Fig. 5.12.2

Note. Although leakage flux in a transformer is quite small (about 5% of ϕ) compared to the mutual flux ϕ, yet it cannot be ignored. It is because leakage flux paths are through air of high reluctance and hence require considerable m.m.f. It may be noted that energy is conveyed from the primary winding to the secondary winding by mutual flux ϕ which links both the windings.

*The primary leakage flux ϕ_1 is alternating one and hence induces back e.m.f (e_b) in the primary winding.

$$\text{Primary leakage inductance, } L_1 = \frac{\textit{Primary leakage flux linkages}}{\textit{Primary current}}$$

$$= \frac{N_1\,\phi_1}{I_1}$$

$\therefore$ Primary leakage reactance, $X_1 = 2\pi\, f\, L_1$

Also secondary leakage reactance, $X_2 = 2\pi fL_2$

Where $L_2 = N_2 \dfrac{\phi_2}{I_2}$

5.11. TRANSFORMER ON NO LOAD

It has been shown above that in case of an ideal transformer, on no load the magnetising current I_m lags behind the applied voltage V_1 by 90°. But since ideal transformers do not exist and therefore some losses such as iron loss and copper must take place in an actual transformer, therefore, the current I_0 drawn by the primary at no-load does not lag behind the applied voltage V_1 by exactly 90° but by an angle ϕ_0 which is slightly lesser than 90° as shown in Fig. 5.13 (*b*).

E_1 and E_2 are the primary and secondary induced voltages shown to have been drawn in equal magnitude in Fig. 5.13 (*b*), because number of turns in primary and secondary have been taken for simplicity as same.

This current I_0 can be resolved into two components I_m and I_w

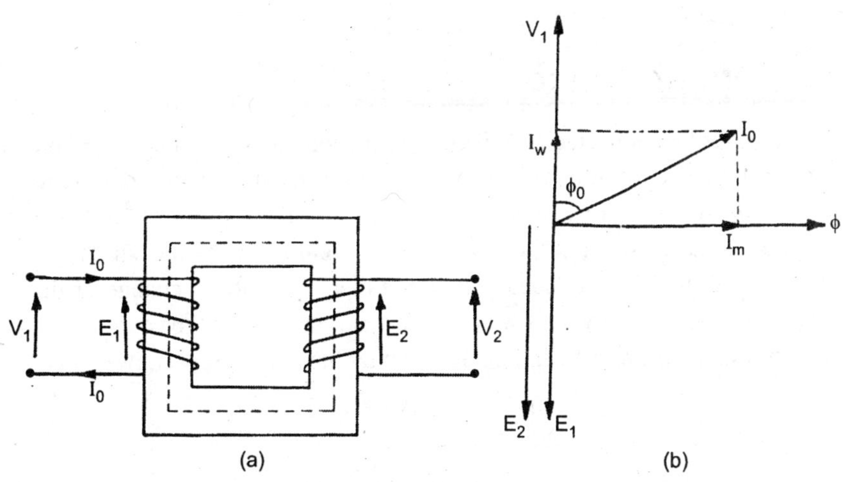

Fig. 5.13

$$I_m = I_0 \sin \phi_0 \qquad \text{...(vii)}$$

This component I_m is known as reactive component or magnetising component of no load current I_0. It is known as reactive because it lags V_1 by 90°. It is known as magnetising component because it is in phase with flux and is responsible for setting up this flux ϕ.

$$I_w = I_0 \cos \phi_0 \quad ...(viii)$$

This component I_w is known as active or power component.

It is known as active component because it is in phase with applied voltage V_1. It is also known as power component because it is responsible for the supply of hysteresis and eddy current loss (Iron loss or core loss) in the core of the transformer and also negligible I^2R loss in the primary winding.

$$\therefore \quad \text{Core loss} = \text{Iron loss} = V_1 I_w$$

$$\text{but} \quad I_w = I_0 \cos \phi_0$$

$$\therefore \quad \text{Core loss} = W_0 = V_1 I_0 \cos \phi_0 \quad ...(ix)$$

When transformer is on no load, output of the transformer is zero,

$$\text{Input} = \text{Output} + \text{Losses} \quad \text{[On no load output is zero]}$$

$$\therefore \quad \text{Input} = \text{Losses}$$

Thus on no load the input to the transformer is nothing else but losses. These losses include core loss and copper loss. On no load, the current drawn by the primary is so small that copper loss (I^2R) is still smaller and therefore is negligible.

Thus the power input to the transformer on no load is nothing else but core loss or iron loss.

From Fig. 5.13 (*b*), no load current

$$I_0 = \sqrt{I_m^2 + I_w^2}$$

$\therefore$ No load power factor on primary

$$= \cos \phi_0 = \frac{I_w}{I_0} \quad ...(x)$$

5.11.1. Transformer Connected to D.C.

Transformer should never be connected to a direct current source as it can not work on d.c supply. If a rated d.c. voltage is applied across the primary winding of a transformer a flux of constant magnitude will be setup in the core and therefore no self induced e.m.f will be produced in the primary winding to oppose the applied voltage except at the moment of switching on the d.c. supply. It should be kept in mind that self induced will be produced only when there is a rate of change of flux linkages .The resistance of the primary winding is very low and the primary current will be quite high (as there will be no back induced e.m.f in the primary) winding as given by the ohm's Law (Law).

$$\text{Primary current} = \frac{D.C.\ applied\ voltage}{Resistance\ of\ primary\ winding}$$

This current is much more than the rated full load current of primary winding. Thus this heavy current will produce lot of heat ($I^2.R$) and burns the insulation of the primary winding due to which transformer will be burnt or damaged. That is why d.c. supply is never applied to a transformer.

Thus the transformer can not be employed for raising or lowering the d.c. voltage.

Example 5.1.1. A 2000/200 V, 20 kVA transformer has 66 turns in the secondary. Calculate (*i*) primary turns (*ii*) primary and secondary full-load currents. Neglect the losses.

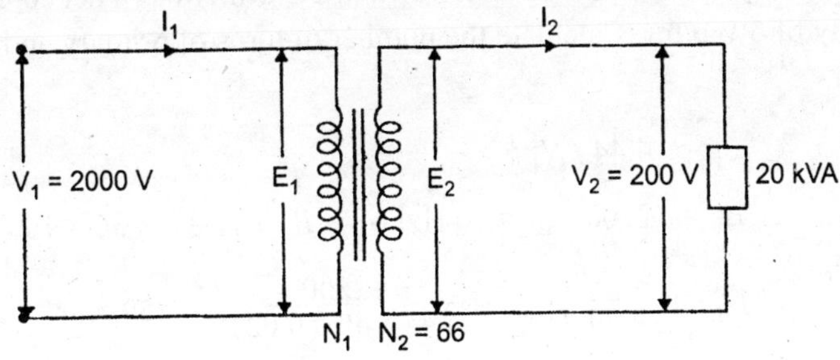

Fig. 5.13.1

Solution. Fig. 5.13.1 represents the conditions of the problem.

$$K = V_2/V_1 = 200/2000 = 1/10$$

(*i*) $$\frac{N_2}{N_1} = K = \frac{1}{10}$$

$\therefore$ $$N_1 = N_2 \times 10 = 66 \times 10 = 660 \textbf{ turns Ans.}$$

(*ii*) $$V_1 I_1 = V_2 I_2 = 20 \times 10^3$$

$\therefore$ $$I_2 = \frac{20 \times 10^3}{V_2} = \frac{20 \times 10^3}{200} = 100 \textbf{ A Ans.}$$

$$I_1 = \frac{20 \times 10^3}{V_1} = \frac{20 \times 10^3}{2000} = 10 \textbf{ A Ans.}$$

Alternatively, $$I_1 = K I_2 = (1/10)\ 100 = 10 \textbf{ A}$$

Example 5.1.2. An ideal 25 kVA transformer has 500 turns on the primary winding and 40 turns on the secondary winding. The primary is connected to 3000 V, 50 Hz supply. Calculate (*i*) primary and secondary currents on full-load (*ii*) secondary e.m.f and (*iii*) the maximum core flux.

Solution.

$$K = \frac{N_2}{N_1} = \frac{40}{500} = \frac{4}{50}$$

(*i*) $$I_1 = \frac{Volt\text{-}amperes}{V_1} = \frac{25 \times 10^3}{3000} = 8.33 \textbf{ A Ans.}$$

$$I_2 = \frac{I_1}{K} = 8.33 \times \frac{50}{4} = 104.2 \text{ A } \textbf{Ans.}$$

(*ii*) $$E_2/E_1 = \text{K}$$

$\therefore$ $$E_2 = K E_1 = (4/50) \times 3000 = 240 \textbf{ V Ans.}$$

(*iii*) $$E_1 = 4.44 f N_1 \phi_m$$

or $$3000 = 4.44 \times 50 \times 500 \times \phi_m$$

$\therefore$ $$\phi_m = \frac{3000}{4.44 \times 50 \times 500} = 27 \times 10^{-3}\ Wb = 27 \textbf{ mWb Ans.}$$

Example 5.1.3. A single phase 2200/250 V, 50 Hz transformer has a net core crea of 36 cm^2 and a maximum flux density of 6 Wb/m^2. Calculate the number of turns of primary and secondary.

Solution:

$$E_1 = 4.44 f N_1 \phi_m$$

Here $E_1 = 2200$ V; $f = 50$ Hz; $\phi_m = B_m \times A = 6 \times 36 \times 10^{-4} = 0.0216$ Wb

$$\therefore \quad N_1 = \frac{E_1}{4.44 f \phi_m} = \frac{2200}{4.44 \times 50 \times 0.0216} = \textbf{459 Ans.}$$

Also
$$N_2 = \frac{E_2}{4.44 f \phi_m} = \frac{250}{4.44 \times 50 \times 0.0216} = \textbf{52 Ans.}$$

Example 5.1.4. A single phase 50 Hz transformer has square core of 20 cm side. The permissible maximum flux density in the core is 1 Wb/m^2. Calculate the number of turns per limb on the high and low voltage sides for a 3000/220 V ratio. To allow for insulation of stampings, assume the net iron length to be 0.9 × gross iron length.

Solution:

$$\text{Net iron length} = 0.9 \times 20 = 18 \text{ cm}$$

$$\text{Net } X\text{-sectional area, } A = 18 \times 20 = 360 \text{ cm}^2 = 0.036 \text{ m}^2$$

$$\text{Max. flux in core, } \phi_m = B_m \times A = 1 \times 0.036 = 0.036 \text{ Wb}$$

$$E_1 = 4.44 f N_1 \phi_m$$

$$\therefore \quad N_1 = \frac{E_1}{4.44 f \phi_m} = \frac{3000}{4.44 \times 50 \times 0.036} = \textbf{375 Ans.}$$

Also
$$N_2 = \frac{E_2}{4.44 f \phi_m} = \frac{220}{4.44 \times 50 \times 0.036} = \textbf{27 Ans.}$$

Note that one length is affected due to stamping.

Example 5.1.5. The no load current of a transformer is 15 A at a power factor of 0.2 when connected to a 460 *V*, 50 *c/s* supply. If primary winding has 550 turns, calculate

(*i*) Magnetising component of no-load current.

(*ii*) The iron loss.

(*iii*) The maximum value of flux in the core.

Solution:

$$I_0 = 15 \text{ A}$$

$$\cos \phi_0 = 0.2$$

when $\cos \phi_0 = 0.2, \sin \phi_0 = 0.98$

(*i*) I_m = Magnetising component of no load current.

$$= I_0 \sin \phi_0$$

$$= 15 \times 0.98 = 14.7 \text{ A } \textbf{Ans.}$$

(*ii*) Iron loss = Power input at no load

$$= V_1 I_0 \cos \phi_0$$

$$= 460 \times 15 \times 0.2$$

$$= 1380 \text{ W} = 1.38 \text{ kW} \quad \textbf{Ans.}$$

(*iii*) At no load $V_1 = E_1$

$\therefore$ $E_1 = 460$ V

$$E_1 = 4.44\,\phi_m N_1 f$$

$$N_1 = 550, f = 50 \ c/s$$

$$460 = 4.44\,\phi_m \times 550 \times 50$$

$$\therefore \quad \phi_m = \frac{460}{4.44 \times 550 \times 50}$$

$$= 0.00377 \ wb = 3.77 \ m\,wb. \quad \textbf{Ans.}$$

Example 5.2. A 10 kVA, 1-phase transformer has 200 turns on the primary and 20 turns on the secondary. The primary is connected to a 1500 V, 50 Hz supply. Find (*i*) Secondary volts on open circuit, (*ii*) The approximate values of currents in the two windings on full load and (*iii*) Maximum value of the flux. (*A.M.I.e.* Section A, Winter 1976)

Solution.

(*i*) $N_1 = 200$

$N_2 = 20$

$V_1 = 1500$

On open circuit $V_2 = E_2$

and $V_1 = E_1$

$$\therefore \quad \frac{V_2}{V_1} = \frac{N_2}{N_1} = \frac{E_2}{E_1}$$

$$\frac{V_2}{1500} = \frac{20}{200}$$

$\therefore$ $V_2 = 150 \ V.$

$\therefore$ Secondary volts on open circuit = 150 V. **Ans.**

(*ii*) Full load current in the secondary

$$= \frac{VI}{V_2} = \frac{10 \times 10^3}{150} = 66.7 \text{ A.} \quad \textbf{Ans.}$$

Full load current in the primary

$$= \frac{VI}{V_1} = \frac{10 \times 10^3}{1500} = 6.67 \text{ A.} \quad \textbf{Ans.}$$

The current shall be approximate as the value of no load current has not been included in it.

(*iii*)
$$E_1 = 4.44\, N_1\, \phi_m f$$
$$1500 = 4.44 \times 200 \times \phi_m \times 50$$
$$\phi_m = \frac{1500}{200 \times 50 \times 4.44} = 0.0338\ wb.\ \textbf{Ans.}$$

Example 5.3. A 25 KVA transformer has 500 turns on the primary and 40 turns on the secondary winding. The primary is connected to 3000 V, 50 Hz mains.

Calculate:

(*i*) Primary and secondary currents on full load.

(*ii*) The max. flux in the core. [*H.S.T.E.*, 4*th* Semester Elect. Diploma Dec'1995]

Solution.

$$N_1 = 500$$
$$N_2 = 40$$
$$V_1 = 3000 \text{ Volts}$$

On open circuit,
$$V_2 = E_2$$
$$V_1 = E_1$$
$$\therefore \quad \frac{V_2}{V_1} = \frac{E_2}{E_1} = \frac{N_2}{N_1}$$
$$\frac{V_2}{3000} = \frac{40}{500}$$

So
$$V_2 = \frac{3000 \times 40}{500} = 240 \text{ Volts.}$$

(*i*) Full load current in the primary
$$\frac{VI}{V_1} = \frac{25 \times 10^3}{3000} = 8.333 \text{ Amp } \textbf{Ans.}$$

Full load current in the secondary
$$\frac{VI}{V_2} = \frac{25 \times 10^3}{240} = 104.16 \text{ Amp} \qquad \textbf{Ans.}$$

(*ii*)
$$E_1 = 4.44\, N_1\, \phi_m f$$
$$\phi_m \Rightarrow \frac{E_1}{4.44\, N_1\, f}$$

So
$$\phi_m \Rightarrow \frac{3000}{4.44 \times 500 \times 50} = 0.027\ Wb.\ \textbf{Ans.}$$

Example 5.3.1. The no load current of a transformer is 5A at 0.2 power factor when supplied at 240 V, 50 Hz. The no. of turns of the primary ωdg is 250. Determine.

(*i*) The max value of flux in core (*ii*) the core loss (*iii*) magnetising current.

Solution:

No load current $I_0 = 5$ A

Power factor, $\cos\phi = 0.2$

Primary induced e.m.f $E_1 = V_1 = 240\ V.$

Supply frequency, $f = 50$ Hz.

Number of turns on primary winding $N_1 = 250$

(*i*) max value of flux in core,

$$\phi\ \text{max} = \frac{E_1}{4.44\ f\ N_1} = \frac{240}{4.44 \times 50 \times 250} = 4.32\ \text{mwb.}$$

(*ii*) core loss $= V_1\ I_0 \cos\phi 0 = 240 \times 5 \times 0.2 = 240$ watts

Energy component of No load current.

$$I_e = I_0 \cos\phi_0 = 5 \times 0.2 = 1\ \text{Amp.}$$

(*iii*) magnetising current $I_m = \sqrt{I_0^2 - I_e^2} = \sqrt{(5)^2 - (1)^2}$

$$= 4.899\ \textbf{A Ans.}$$

Example 5.4. A single phase transformer is required to step down the voltage from 1100 V to 400 V at 50 Hz. The cross sectional area of the core is 25 cm^2 and the maximum value of the flux density is 5 Wb/m^2. Determine the number of turns of the primary and secondary windings.

[*H.S.T.E.* IV*th* Semester (Diploma) June' 94]

Solution.

Here, $V_1 = E_1 = 1100$ Volts

$V_2 = E_2 = 400$ Volts

X-sectional area of core $= 25$ cm^2 or $25 \times 10^{-4}\ m^2$

Maximum flux density $\Rightarrow 5$ Wb/m^2

Supply frequency $= 50$ Hz

Now let max. flux, ϕ_m = Flux density × area

$\Rightarrow 5 \times 25 \times 10^{-4} \Rightarrow 125 \times 10^{-4}\ Wb$ or $0.0125\ Wb$

Also $E_1 \Rightarrow 4.44\ N_1\ \phi_m f$ ...(*i*)

So from equation (*i*)

$$N_1 = \frac{E_1}{4.44\ \phi_m\ f}$$

$$= \frac{1100}{4.44 \times 0.0125 \times 50} \Rightarrow 396.39 \simeq 396\ \text{turns.}$$

Now from transformation ratio

$$\frac{V_1}{V_2} = \frac{N_1}{N_2}$$

$$N_2 \Rightarrow \frac{V_2 N_1}{V_1} \Rightarrow \frac{400 \times 396}{1100} \Rightarrow 144 \text{ turns}$$

Hence primary turns, $N_1 \Rightarrow 396$ & Secondary turns, $N_2 = 144$. **Ans.**

5.12. TRANSFORMER ON LOAD

The effect of winding resistance and leakage reactance of transformer is not taken into account for the time being.

If the secondary winding of the transformer is left on open circuit, the primary acts like an ordinary reactor and takes a small current (I_0) due to its high impedance ; this being called the noload current. It consists of a reactive component (I_m) due to the inter linking flux making the winding inductive together with an active component (I_w) necessary on account of iron losses and small I^2R loss.

Since there is an e.m.f. E_2 induced in the secondary winding, a current I_2 flows if the secondary terminals are connected to the load. The magnitude and phase of I_2 with respect to V_2, the secondary terminal voltage shall depend upon the type of load whether it is resistive, inductive or capacitive. If the load is resistive, the current I_2 shall be in phase with V_2, if the load is inductive, the current, I_2 shall lag behind V_2 and if it is capacitive, the current I_2 shall lead the voltage V_2.

The flux ϕ set up by the primary no load current I_0 is shown in Fig. 5.14 (*a*). The secondary current I_2 sets up its own m.m.f. $N_2 I_2$ and hence its own flux ϕ_2 which is in opposition to the main flux ϕ set up by the no load current I_0. This is shown in Fig. 5.12 (*b*).

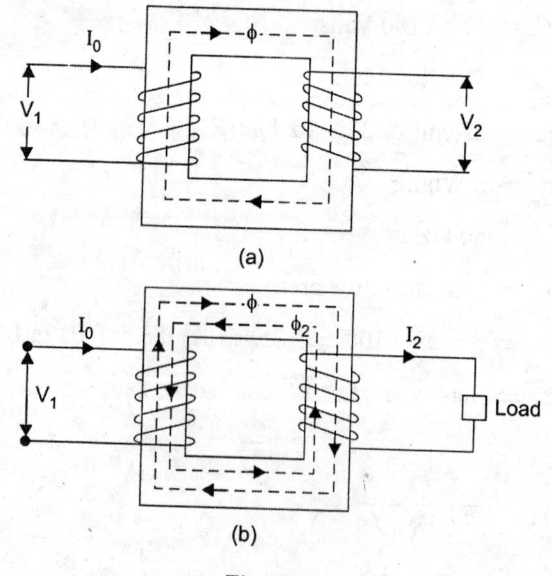

Fig. 5.14

The secondary amp-turns $N_2 I_2$ are accordingly known as demagnetising amp-turns. The flux ϕ_2 on account of the secondary current I_2, when opposes the primary flux ϕ on account of no-load current, I_0, the resultant flux on the primary gets reduced momentarily. This reduced flux induces reduced e.m.f. E_1 on the primary. Applied voltage V_1 having remained the same, since opposing voltage E_1 gets reduced, so current on the primary side gets increased. Thus as soon as there is a current flow of I_2 in the secondary, there is a corresponding flow of current I_1, in the primary. Thus primary current I_1, is the vector sum of two currents I_1 and I_0. This additional primary current I_1, produces additional amp-turns N_1I_1 which sets up its additional flux ϕ_1 which is in opposition to flux ϕ_2 but in the same direction as ϕ. This flux ϕ_1 is equal in magnitude but opposite in direction to flux ϕ_2 and thus neutralises its effect. Thus the resultant flux in the transformer even when the transformer is on load remains constant at ϕ, the one at no load.

Thus the magnitude of flux set up is determined by the applied voltage and its frequency and is independent of load connected and a definite number of amp-turns are needed to maintain it. For a constant applied voltage and at constant frequency, since the flux through the core shall remain constant at all loads ; therefore, the core loss also remains constant practically at all loads.

The vector diagrams of the transformer connected to different types of loads such as resistive, inductive and capacitive are explained and drawn below.

5.13. RESISTANCE LOADING (UNITY POWER FACTOR)

The effect of connecting a unity power factor load to the secondary is to cause secondary current I_2 to flow. This current I_2 shall be in phase with E_2 (As a rule it should be in phase with V_2). As a result of current I_2 in secondary, there shall be corresponding flow of current I_1 in primary. Assuming the turn ratio of transformer $\left(\frac{N_2}{N_1}\right)$ to be one, for simplicity, since

$$\frac{I_2}{I_1} = \frac{N_1}{N_2}$$

and $$\frac{N_2}{N_1} = 1$$

$\therefore$ $$I_2 = I_1$$

This primary current I_1 will be in phase opposition to secondary current I_2 and is shown in Fig. 5.15 (*b*),

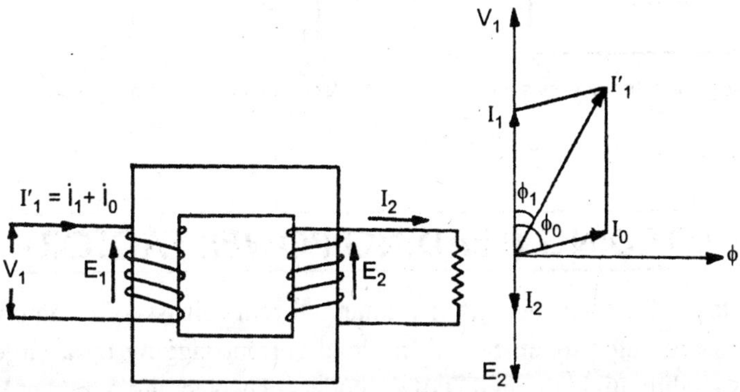

(a) Resistive load connected across secondary (b) Vector diagram for resistive load.

Fig. 5.15

equal in magnitude but opposite in direction. In addition to current I_1, there is no-load current I_0 also in the primary. This current I_0 is shown to have been drawn lagging V_1 by an angle ϕ_0. This angle ϕ_0 is very nearly equal to 90°. The resultant current in the primary is vector sum of the two currents I_1 and I_0 and is shown drawn by the vector I_1' lagging V_1 by angle ϕ_1. Thus resultant current in the primary does not remain in phase on account of the presence of no-load current.

5.14. INDUCTIVE LOADING (LAGGING POWER FACTOR)

If the secondary circuit be connected to inductive load, the secondary current I_2 lags behind the secondary induced voltage E_2 (As a rule it should lag altered the voltage V_2) by angle ϕ_2. The secondary amp-turns are altered in phase and in order that these amp-turns shall be counter-balanced at every instant, the corresponding primary amp-turns must also be altered in phase so as to maintain exact phase opposition. A lagging current in the secondary circuit therefore causes the lagging current to flow in the primary circuit. The actual angle of lag ϕ_1 in the primary is usually greater than that in the secondary, *i.e.* ϕ_2 since the no-load current itself has a very large angle of lag, thus tending to make the power factor cos ϕ_1 of the primary a little lower than cos ϕ_2 of the secondary. The transformer connected with inductive load and the vector diagram thereof is shown to have been drawn in Fig. 5.16. Since turns ratio is assumed one so I_1 is drawn equal and opposite to I_2. No-load current I_0 is shown drawn lagging V_1 by an angle ϕ_0. The resultant current I_1' in the primary is vector sum of current I_1 and I_0 and is shown to have been drawn lagging V_1. by an angle ϕ_1 which is greater than ϕ_2, thus making cos ϕ_1 lower than cos ϕ_2.

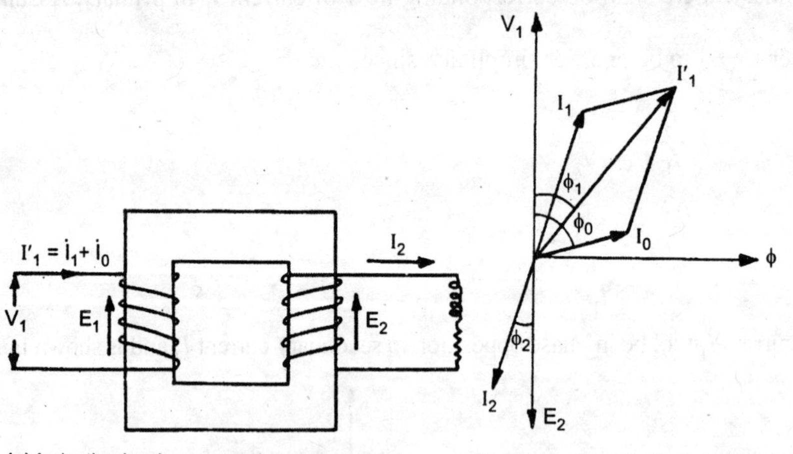

(a) Inductive load connected across secondary. (b) Vector diagram for inductive load.

Fig. 5.16

5.15. CAPACITIVE LOADING (LEADING POWER FACTOR)

When the leading current is taken from secondary, the primary current consists of a component leading the primary voltage by the same angle together with no-load current lagging by a large angle. The primary power factor is now slightly higher than that of secondary. The vector diagram at leading *p.f.* is shown drawn in Fig. 5.17.

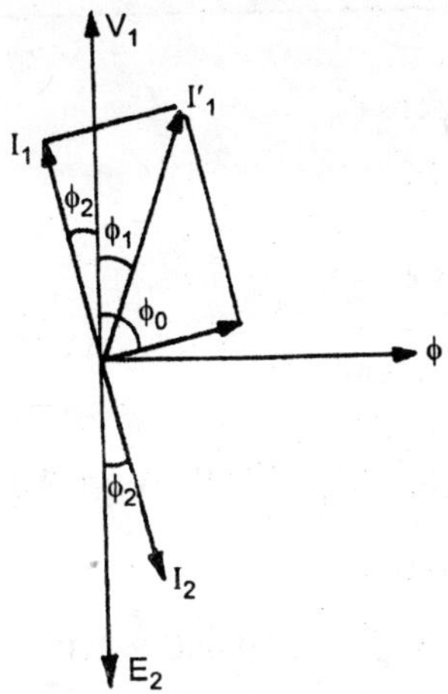

Fig. 5.17. Vector diagram for capacitive load

The primary power factor cos ϕ_1 seems to have improved from secondary *p.f.* cos ϕ_2 as ϕ_1 is lesser than ϕ_2 although on secondary side the *p.f.* is leading whereas on the primary side it becomes lagging.

Example 5.4.1. The no load current of a single phase transformer is 5 Amps at 0.25 p.f. when supplied at 230 V, 50 Hz. The number of turns on primary winding are 200, calculate:

(*i*) Maximum value of flux in the core.

(*ii*) Core loss

(*iii*) magnetising current (A.M.*I.e.*)

Solution: (*i*) Using the relation

$$E_1 = 4.44\, N_1 f \phi_m$$

or

$$230 = 4.44 \times 200 \times 50 \times \phi_m$$

∴ Maximum value of flux, $\phi_m = 5.18\ m.$ wb **Ans.**

(*ii*) Core loss,

$$P_0 = V_1 I_0 \cos\phi_0$$
$$= 230 \times 5 \times 0.25 = 287.5 \textbf{ W} \quad \textbf{Ans.}$$

(*iii*) No load *p.f.*, $\cos\phi_0 = 0.25$

$$\text{Sin}\ \phi_0 = \text{Sin}\cos^{-1} 0.25$$
$$= 0.9682$$

∴ Magnetising current Component

$$I_m = I_0 \sin\phi_0$$
$$= 5 \times 0.9682$$
$$= 4.84 \text{ Amps} \quad \textbf{Ans.}$$

Example 5.4.2. Find (*i*) The active and reactive components of no load current and (*ii*) the no load current of a 400/220 V single phase transformer if the power input to the H.V. winding is 80 Watts. The low voltage side of the transformer is kept open. The power factor of the no-load current is 0.3 lagging.

Solution:

(*i*) $$P_0 = V_1 I_0 \cos \phi_0$$

∴ Active component of no load current

$$I_w = I_0 \cos \phi_0 = \frac{P_0}{V_1}$$

$$= 0.18 \text{ A } \textbf{Ans.}$$

No load current $I_0 = \dfrac{P_0}{V_1 \cos \phi_0} = \dfrac{80}{440 \times 0.3} = 0.606$ Amp. **Ans.**

Reactive Component of no load current.

$$I_m = \sqrt{I_0^2 - I_w^2} = \sqrt{(0.606)^2 - (0.18)^2}$$

$$= 0.578 \text{ A. } \textbf{Ans.}$$

Alternatively $$I_m = I_0 \sin \phi_0 = I_0 \sin (\cos^{-1} \phi_0)$$

$$= 0.606. \sin (72.54°) = 0.578 \text{ A } \textbf{Ans.}$$

Example 5.4.3. A single phase transformer on no load takes 4.5 A at a power factor of 0.25, lagging when connected to a 230 V, 50 Hz supply. The number of turns of the primary winding is 250. Calculate (*i*) the magnetising current (*ii*) the core loss and (*iii*) the maximum value of flux in the core.

Solution. Fig. 5.17.1 shows the phasor diagram of the transformer on no load, $V_1 = 230$ V, $N_1 = 250$ turns, $\cos \phi_0 = 0.25$ lag ; $I_0 = 4.5$ A

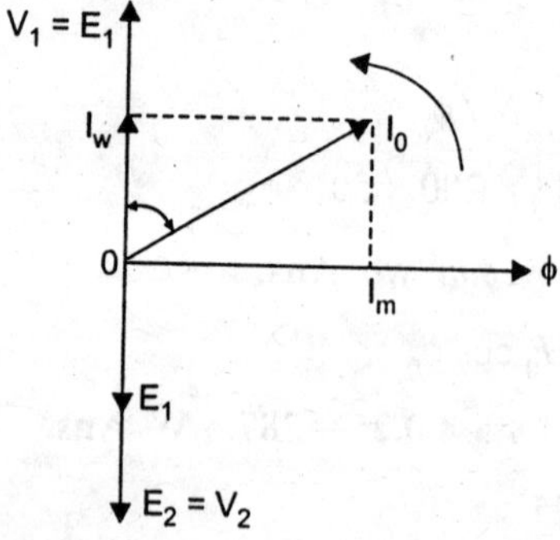

Fig. 5.17.1. Phasor diagram

(*i*) Magnetising current,

$$I_m = I_0 \sin \phi_0$$

$$= 4.5 \sin (\cos^{-1} 0.25)$$

$$= 4.35 \text{ A } \textbf{Ans.}$$

(*ii*) Core loss

$$P_0 = V_1 I_0 \cos \phi_0$$

$$= 230 \times 4.5 \times 0.25 = 259 \text{ W } \textbf{Ans.}$$

(*iii*) Since no load current

$$I_0 \text{ is small, } E_1 = V_1$$

$$\therefore \quad V_1 = 4.44\, \phi_m f N_1 \text{ volts}$$

or

$$230 = 4.44 \times \phi_m \times 50 \times 250$$

$$= \phi_m = \frac{230}{4.44 \times 50 \times 250}$$

$$= 4.14 \times 10^{-3} \text{ Wb. } \textbf{Ans.}$$

Example 5.5. A 400/200 *V*, 1-phase transformer is supplying a load of 50 A at a *p.f.* of 0.866 lagging. The no load current is 2A at 0.208 *p.f.* lagging. Calculate the primary current and primary power factor.

Solution.

$$\text{Secondary current}, I_2 = 50 \text{ A}$$

$$\text{Secondary } p.f., \cos\phi_2 = 0.866$$

when

$$\cos\phi_2 = 0.866, \sin\phi_2 = 0.5$$

$$I_2 = 50(\cos\phi_2 - j\sin\phi_2)$$

$$= 50(0.866 - j\,0.5)$$

$$= 43.3 - j\,25$$

Corresponding current on primary side = I_1

$$\dot{I}_1 = (43.3 - j\,25) \times \frac{200}{400}$$

$$= 21.65 - j\,12.5$$

$$\dot{I}_0 = 2(\cos\phi_0 - j\sin\phi_0)$$

When

$$\cos\phi_0 = 0.208, \sin\phi_0 = 0.978$$

$$\dot{I}_0 = 2(0.208 - j\,0.978)$$

$$= (0.416 - j\,1.956)$$

Current in the primary I_1' is vector sum of I_1 and I_0

$$\therefore \quad I_1' = (21.65 - j\,12.5) + (0.416 - j\,1.956)$$

$$= (22.066 - j\,14.456)$$

Magnitude of current

$$I_1' = \sqrt{(22.066)^2 + (14.456)^2}$$

$$= \sqrt{486.91 + 208.97}$$

$$= 26.4\, A. \textbf{ Ans.}$$

$$\cos\phi_1 = \text{Power factor on primary side}$$

$$= \frac{22.066}{26.4} = 0.836. \textbf{ Ans.}$$

Example 5.6. The number of turns on the primary and secondary windings of a single phase transformer are 350 and 38 respectively. If primary winding is connected to a 2.2 KV, 50 c/s supply, determine

(*a*) Secondary voltage on no load.

(*b*) The primary current when secondary current is 200 A, at 0.8 p.f. lagging if the no load current is 5 A at 0.2 p.f. lagging.

(*c*) The power factor of the primary.

Solution.

(*a*) $N_1 = 350$

$N_2 = 38$

At no load $V_1 \simeq E_1 = 2.2\ kV.$

$$\frac{E_1}{E_2} = \frac{N_1}{N_2} = \frac{350}{38}$$

$$E_2 = \frac{E_1 \times 38}{350} = \frac{2.2 \times 38}{350} = 0.2388\ kV$$

or E_2 = secondary voltage on no load

$= 238.8\ V.$

(*b*) When secondary current is 200 *A*, corresponding value of primary current

$$I_1 = 200 \times \frac{38}{350} = 21.7\ \text{A}$$

No-load current, on primary = 5 A.

When $\cos \phi_2 = 0.8$

$\phi_2 = 36.86°$

$\phi_0 = 78.46°$

The current I_1 and I_0 are drawn on primary side as shown in vector diagram Fig. 5.18.

The angle between I_1 and I_0

$= 78.46 - 36.86$

$= 41.6°.$

$\therefore$ I_1' from vector diagram is given by

$$I_1' = \sqrt{I_1^2 + I_0^2 + 2I_1 I_0 \cos(\phi_0 - \phi_2)}$$

$$= \sqrt{(21.7)^2 + (5)^2 + 2 \times 21.7 \times 5 \cos 41.6}$$

$$= \sqrt{470.89 + 25 + 217 \times 0.747}$$

$$= \sqrt{495.89 + 162.1}$$

$$= \sqrt{657.99} = 25.65\ \text{A}$$

Vertical component of

$$I_1 = I_1 \cos \phi_2 = 21.7 \times 0.8 = 17.36 \text{ A}$$

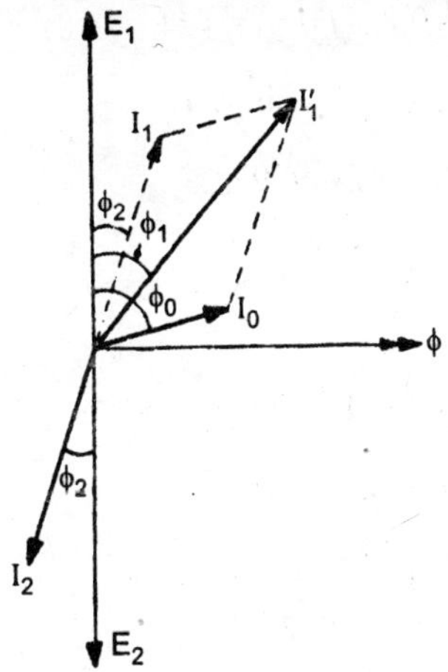

Fig. 5.18

Vertical component of

$$I_0 = I_0 \cos \phi_0 = 5 \times 0.2 = 1.0 \text{ A}$$

Vertical component of I_1' is the sum of these two vertical components

$$= 17.36 + 1$$

$$= 18.36 \text{ A}$$

$$\cos \phi_1 = \frac{18.36}{25.65} = 0.7157 \text{ lag. } \textbf{Ans.}$$

Example 5.7. A single phase transformer with a ratio of $\frac{440}{110}$ *V* takes a no-load current of 5 A at 0.2 power factor lagging. If secondary supplies a current of 120 A at *p.f* of 0.8 lag, estimate the current taken by the primary. *(A.M.I.e. Section B, May 1994)*

Solution:

$$\therefore \quad \frac{N_1}{N_2} = \frac{E_1}{E_2} = \frac{440}{110} = 4$$

Current on secondary side

$$I_2 = 120 \text{ A}$$

Current on primary side corresponding to current 120 A on secondary side

$$I_1 = I_2 \times \frac{N_2}{N_1} = 120 \times \frac{1}{4} = 30 \text{ A}$$

Thus current in the primary side is sum of the current of 30 A at 0.8 p.f. lagging and 5 A at 0.2 p.f. lagging.

Total current in primary side

$$= \dot{I}'_1 = \dot{I}_1 + \dot{I}_0$$

$$\dot{I}_1 = 30' \cos \phi_2 - j \sin \phi_2$$

$$= 30(0.8 - j\,0.6) = (24 - j\,18) \text{ A}$$

$$\dot{I}_0 = 5(\cos \phi_0 - j \sin \phi_0)$$

$$= 5(0.2 - j\,0.979)$$

$$= (1 - j\,4.895)$$

$$\dot{I}'_1 = \dot{I}_1 + \dot{I}_0$$

$$= (24 - j\,18) + (1 - j\,4.895)$$

$$= (25 - j\,22.895)$$

∴ Total current in the primary

$$= \sqrt{(25)^2 + (22.895)^2}$$

$$= \sqrt{625 + 524.18} = \sqrt{1149.18}$$

$$= 33.9 \text{ Amp. } \textbf{Ans.}$$

5.16. TRANSFORMER WITH WINDING RESISTANCE BUT NO MAGNETIC LEAKAGE

The ideal transformers were supposed to have no resistance of its windings but in actual transformers, these resistances do exist. Let R_1 be the resistance of primary windings and R_2 be the resistance of secondary windings. These resistances have been shown to be connected in series with the primary and secondary windings respectively in Fig. 5.19. Once they have been shown separately, the windings should be considered as resistance less in that case.

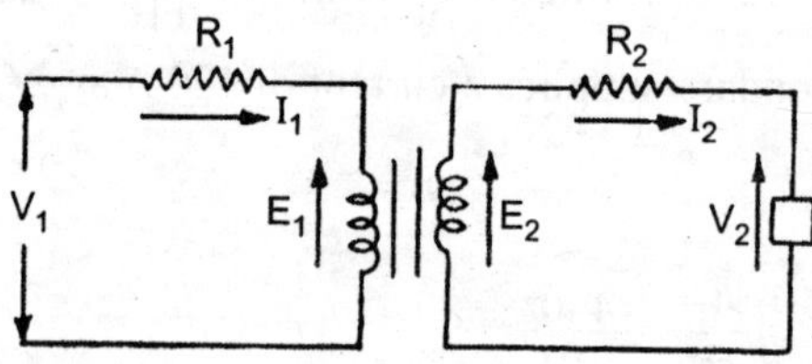

Fig. 5.19

Owing to the resistance of the primary winding, part of the primary applied voltage is absorbed as $I_1' R$ drop in the winding, the remaining component (obtained by vectorial subtraction) producing the flux which generates the voltage in the secondary.

Thus $$\dot{E}_1 = \dot{V}_1 + \dot{I}_1' R_1$$

Or $$\dot{V}_1 = \dot{E}_1 - \dot{I}_1' \dot{R}_1$$

$$\dot{I}'_1 = \dot{I}_1 + \dot{I}_0$$

where E_1 is the voltage induced in the primary winding.

V_1 is the applied voltage to the primary.

I_0 = no-load current.

I_1' = current in the primary corresponding to load current I_2 in the secondary.

In a similar way, due to ohmic resistance R_2 of the secondary-winding, the secondary terminal voltage V_2 is less than the total induced secondary e.m.f. E_2 by an amount equal to I_2R_2. When it is delivering current I_2.

Thus $$\dot{V}_2 = \dot{E}_2 - \dot{I}_2 R_2$$

or $$\dot{E}_2 = \dot{V}_2 + \dot{I}_2 R_2$$

The vector diagrams of transformer having winding resistances at different loads such as resistive, inductive and capacitive have been shown to be drawn in Figs. 5.20, 5.21 and 5.22 respectively.

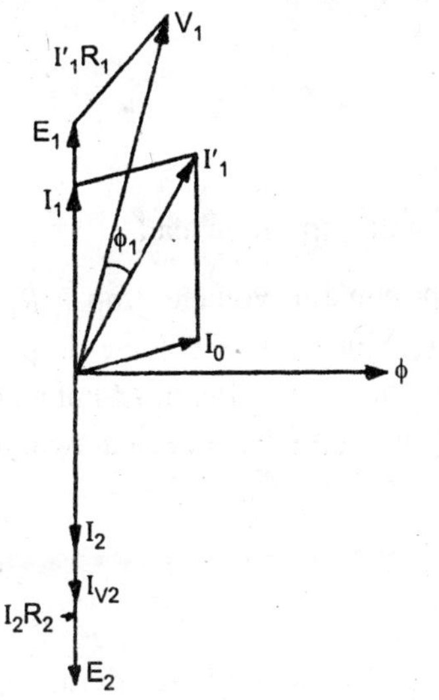

Fig. 5.20. Vector diagram of transformer with resistive load

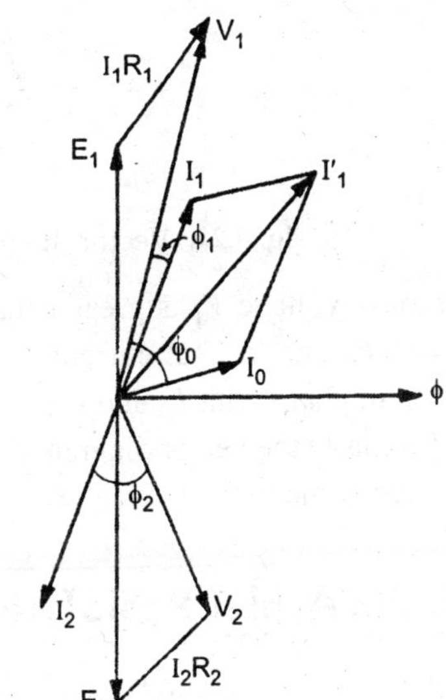

Fig. 5.21. Vector diagram of transformer with inductive load

Induced voltage E_2 lags the flux ϕ by 90°. The induced voltage E_1 has been shown drawn in the opposite direction to E_1 in Fig. 5.20.

The effect of connecting a unity *p.f.* load to the secondary is to cause a secondary current I_2 to flow. This will be in phase with E_2 as shown in Fig. 5.20. The corresponding load component of the primary current I_1 will be in phase opposition to the secondary current I_2. The total primary current I_1' is the resultant of I_1 and I_0. The phase angle ϕ_1 is considerably lesser than ϕ_0, giving a p.f. nearer unity.

Since it is assumed for the sake of simplicity that turns ratio is one, so

$$\begin{Bmatrix} E_1 = E_2 \\ I_1 = I_2 \end{Bmatrix} \text{ in magnitude.}$$

Now terminal voltage V_2 on secondary side is lesser than E_2 by an amount $E_2 R_2$. Since I_2 is in phase with V_2, so I_2R_2, the voltage drop across resistance should be in phase with V_2. V_2 being lesser than E_2 by amount I_2R_2. Thus vector E_2 has been drawn by adding I_2R_2 drop in vector V_2 in the same direction.

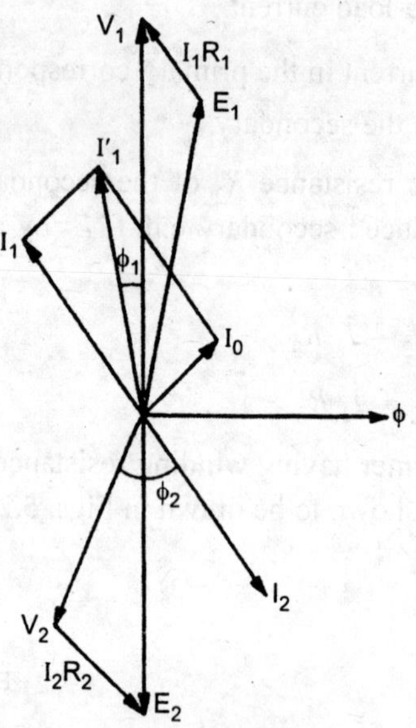

Fig. 5.22. Vector diagram of transformer with capacitive load

Now primary voltage V_1 is greater than E_1 by an amount equal to voltage drop $I_1'R_1$, across the primary resistance due to total current I_1', flowing through it. Since it is a voltage drop across pure resistance, it is in phase with I_1' and hence shown to have been drawn parallel to I_1' but added to E_1 to find out V_1. Similarly the vector diagrams at lagging p.f. and leading p.f. have been drawn in Figs. 5.21 and 5.22 as already mentioned.

5.17. EQUIVALENT RESISTANCE

The transformer with primary resistance R_1 and secondary resistance R_2 is shown drawn in Fig. 5.23. Now that the resistances have been shown separately, the windings may be considered to be without resistance.

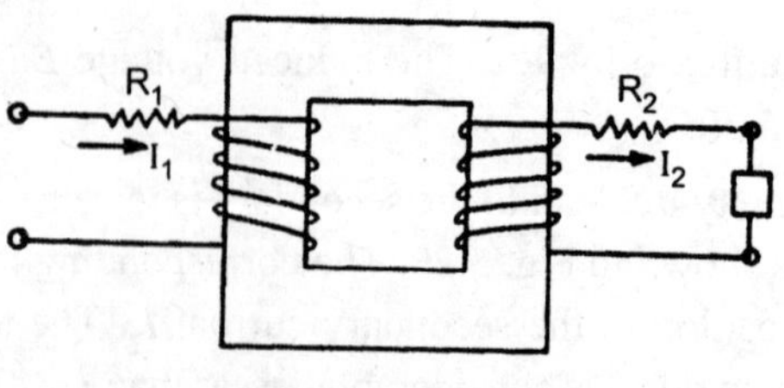

Fig. 5.23

The primary resistance R_1 can be transferred to secondary side and secondary resistance R_2 to primary side. While these resistances are being transferred from primary to secondary and vice versa, care should be taken that performance of the transformer is not affected, *i.e.* overall current in the primary or secondary does not get changed. In fact the transfer of resistance to one side, either primary or secondary makes the calculations quite easy.

Let us consider the conversion of resistance R_2 of secondary to primary side. Let R_2' be the equivalent resistance of secondary or primary side. In that case power loss in R_2' when on primary side and carrying primary current I_1 should be the same as the power loss in resistance R_2' when on secondary side and carrying current I_2.

Thus $$I_1^2 R_2' = I_2^2 R_2$$

(No load current on the primary side is neglected)

$$R'_2 = \frac{I_2^2}{I_1^2} R_2$$

But $$\frac{I_2}{I_1} = \frac{N_1}{N_2} = \frac{1}{K}$$

$\therefore$ $$R'_2 = \frac{R_2}{K^2}$$

where K is turns ratio of transformer.

Thus equivalent resistance of secondary on primary side

$$= R_2/K^2$$

The total resistance on the primary side = Effective resistance of the transformer as referred to the primary side

$$R_{t1} = R_1 + R_2/K^2$$

The total resistance R_{t1} on the primary side is shown to have been drawn in Fig. 5.24. Since secondary resistance has been transferred on the primary side, so secondary is not shown to have any resistance in Fig. 5.24.

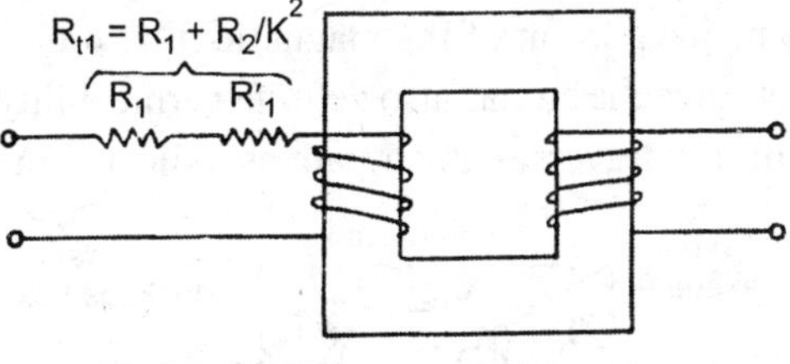

Fig. 5.24

Similarly if R_1' is the resistance of primary when transferred to secondary side, then the total resistance on the secondary side R_{t2} is given by

$$R_{t2} = R_2 + R'_1$$

As already discussed, if primary resistance R_1 is to be transferred to the secondary side, then copper loss in R_1 when carrying a current I_1 on the primary side should be same as in R_1' when carrying a current I_2 on the secondary side

Thus $$I_1^2 R_1 = I_2^2 R_1'$$

$$R'_1 = \frac{I_1^2}{I_2^2} R_1$$

But $$\frac{I_1}{I_2} = \frac{N_2}{N_1} = K$$

$$\therefore \quad R_1' = K^2 R_1$$

Thus total resistance on secondary side

$$R_{t_2} = R_2 + R'_1$$

$$= R_2 + K^2 R_1.$$

Thus total resistance on secondary side R_{t2} is shown to have been drawn in Fig. 5.25. Since primary resistance is transferred on secondary side, so no resistance has been shown on primary side.

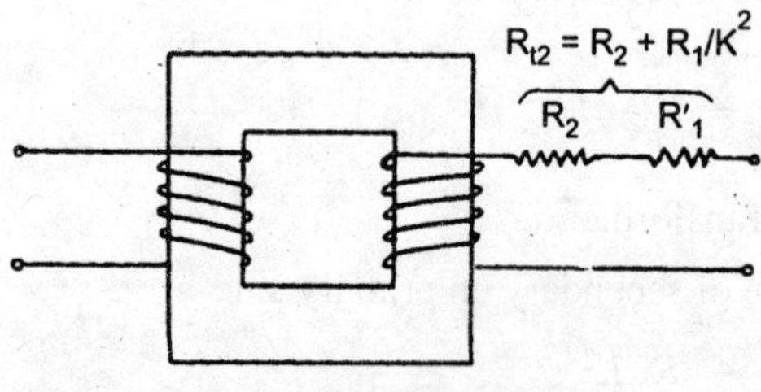

Fig. 5.25

5.18. MAGNETIC LEAKAGE

In the previous discussions on the ideal transformer, it was assumed that all the magnetic flux links all the turns of both primary and secondary and that there is no leakage flux and secondly the core material has the permeability which is extremely high and constant but in actual transformer it is not so.

In actual transformer, the major portion of the magnetic flux, produced by the primary amp-turns passes through the iron core but since the air has also definite permeability, although very much less than that of iron, a certain amount of flux traverses an air path as indicated in Fig. 5.26.

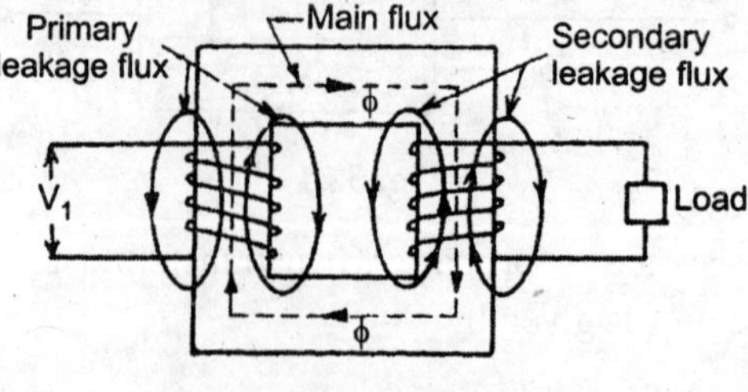

Fig. 5.26

These air paths are in parallel with the iron paths but whereas the flux traversing the iron, cuts the secondary winding, that following air paths serve no useful purpose and form a primary leakage flux. This is as against the main flux following an all iron path and linking with both the windings.

The secondary current sets up amp-turns which oppose the existing main flux, deflecting a portion of it into leakage paths in addition to setting up leakage flux which links only with the secondary winding as shown in the diagram. Flux following these leakage paths constitutes the leakage flux.

These leakage fluxes linking with each winding produce a self-induced e.m.f. in that winding which opposes the applied voltage, thus reducing the resultant voltage applied to the winding. This is equivalent to saying that a small choke of inductive coil has been connected in series with the winding.

Thus the effect of primary leakage flux is to add a certain amount of Inductive reactance to the primary winding, serving no useful purpose and using up a certain amount of primary applied voltage in the same way as does the resistance of the primary winding. The reactance due to this primary leakage flux is ***called the Primary Leakage Reactance.***

The secondary leakage flux acts much in the same manner and has the effect of diverting more and more of main flux into leakage paths as the current is increased, for inside the secondary windings, the secondary amp-turns oppose the main flux. The reactance due to this secondary leakage flux is called the *Secondary Leakage Reactance.*

The main useful flux decreases very slightly as the load increases but the leakage fluxes are practically proportional to the currents in the respective windings.

The effect of magnetic leakage upon the ratio of transformation is thus to reduce the secondary terminal voltage for a given primary applied voltage.

The primary leakage reactance is represented by X_1 and secondary leakage reactance by X_2

$$X_1 = \frac{{}^eL_1}{I_1}$$

$$X_2 = \frac{{}^eL_2}{I_2}$$

where ${}^eL_1$ and ${}^eL_2$ are emfs induced in primary and secondary respectively.

When primary leakage flux and secondary leakage flux have been linking primary and secondary winding respectively. I_1 is current in the primary and I_2 current in the secondary.

Thus a transformer with magnetic leakage is equivalent to an ideal transformer with inductive coils connected both in primary and secondary circuits as shown in Fig. 5.27.

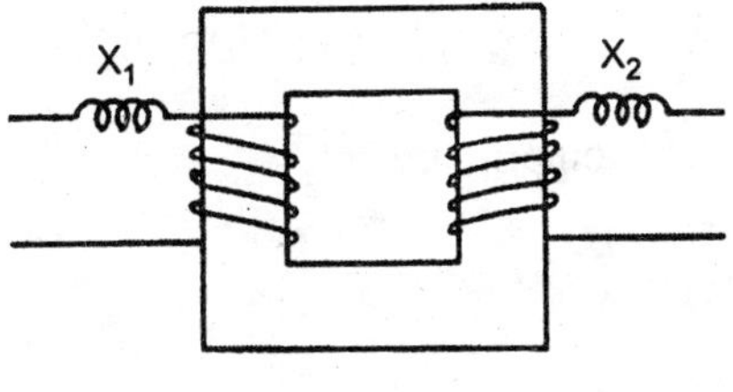

Fig. 5.27

In order to reduce the values of X_1 and X_2, primary winding and secondary windings are not placed on separate legs but as interleaved. If the primary winding and secondary winding are placed on separate limb, large amount of leakage flux both on primary and secondary windings shall result and values of leakage reactances X_1 and X_2 shall increase.

5.19. EQUIVALENT REACTANCE

The transformer with primary reactance X_1 and secondary reactance X_2 is shown drawn in Fig. 5.27. The way resistances of primary and secondary windings can be transferred on each other's side, similarly primary reactance can be transferred on the secondary side and secondary on the primary side. If done so, the calculations on transformers get easy. If the reactance X_1 of the primary is transferred to the secondary side, it shall be denoted by X_1' and shall be known as equivalent reactance of primary on secondary. Similarly if reactance X_2 of the secondary is transferred to the primary side, it shall be denoted by X_2' and shall be known as equivalent reactance of secondary side.

Let us consider the conversion of reactance X_2 of secondary on primary side. When current I_2 flows on the secondary side, it creates a voltage drop of I_2X_2 in the reactance on secondary side. This voltage drop of I_2X_2 when transferred to the primary side becomes $\frac{N_1}{N_2}(I_2X_2)$. The current I_1 in primary corresponding to current I_2 on secondary shall create a voltage drop equal to $I_1X'_2$ in the reactance of secondary transferred to the primary side.

If the performance of the transformer is to remain same with this transfer, then

I_1X_2' must be equal to $\frac{N_1}{N_2}(I_2X_2)$

Thus
$$(I_2X_2') = \frac{N_1}{N_2} I_2X_2$$

$$X_2' = \frac{N_1}{N_2} \times \frac{I_2}{I_1} \times (X_2)$$

But
$$\frac{I_2}{I_1} = \frac{N_1}{N_2}$$

∴
$$X'_2 = X_2\left(\frac{N_1}{N_2}\right)^2 = \frac{X_2}{K^2}$$

On the same line it can be proved that equivalent reactance of primary, when taken on the secondary side is given by

$$X_1K^2 = X_1'$$

Thus total reactance of transformer on primary side

$$X_{t1} = X_1 + X'_2$$
$$= X_1 + \frac{X_2}{K^2}$$

Similarly total reactance of transformer on secondary side

$$= X_{t2}$$
$$= X_2 + X_1'$$
$$= X_2 + X_1K^2.$$

The transformer with resistance and reactance of secondary transferred to the primary side has been shown drawn in Fig. 5.28.

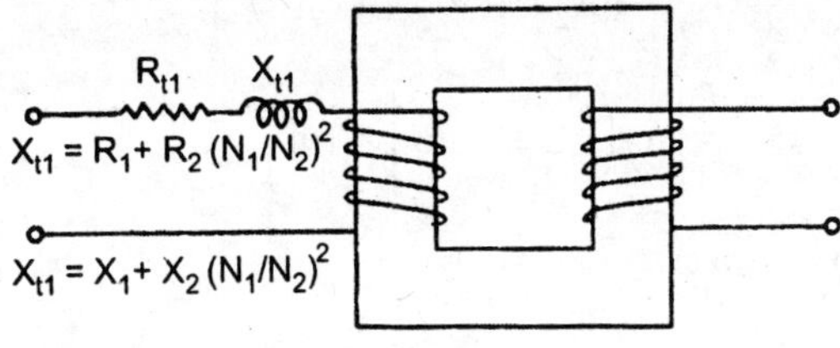

Fig. 5.28

Whereas with resistance and reactance of primary transferred to the secondary side is shown drawn in Fig. 5.29.

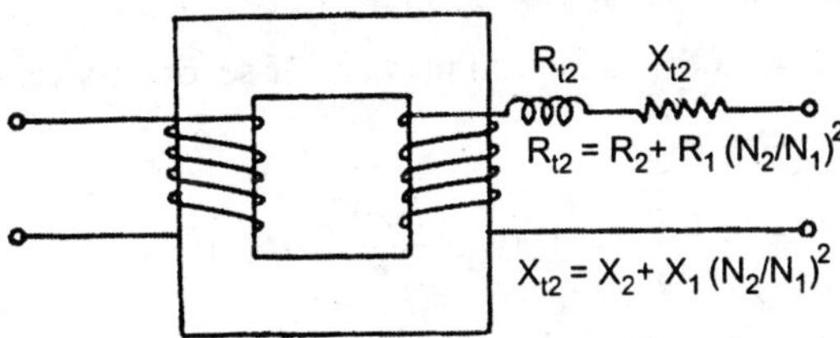

Fig. 5.29

5.20. PERCENTAGE RESISTANCE, REACTANCE AND IMPEDANCE

Percentage Resistance. It is defined as the voltage drop across the resistance expressed as percentage of full load terminal voltage. Thus of total resistance of transformer on secondary side is R_{t2} and value of full load current is I_2, then percentage resistance is given by

Percentage resistance

$$= \frac{I_2 R_{t2}}{V_2} \times 100$$

where V_2 is the value of terminal voltage on secondary side.

Now $$I_2 = I_1 \left(\frac{N_1}{N_2}\right)$$

and $$V_2 = V_1 \left(\frac{N_2}{N_1}\right)$$

$\therefore$ $$\text{\%age resistance} = \frac{I_2 R_{t2}}{V_2} \times 100 = \frac{I_1 \left(\frac{N_1}{N_2}\right)}{V_1} \left(\frac{N_2}{N_1}\right) R_{t2} \times 100$$

$$= \frac{I_1}{V_1} \times \left(\frac{N_1}{N_2}\right)^2 R_{t2} \times 100$$

But $$R_{t2} = R_2 + R_1 \left(\frac{N_2}{N_1}\right)^2$$

∴ percentage resistance

$$= \frac{I_1}{V_1} \times \left(\frac{N_1}{N_2}\right)^2 \left[R_2 + R_1\left(\frac{N_2}{N_1}\right)^2\right] \times 100$$

$$= \frac{I_1}{V_1}\left[R_2\left(\frac{N_1}{N_2}\right)^2 + R_1\right] \times 100$$

But $\quad R_2\left(\frac{N_1}{N_2}\right)^2 + R_1 = R_{t1}$

∴ percentage resistance

$$= \frac{I_1}{V_1} \times R_{t1} \times 100$$

But R_{t1} is total resistance of transformer on primary side.

Thus percentage resistance whether taken on primary or secondary remains same.

Similarly % reactance

$$= \frac{I_2 . X_{t2}}{V_2} \times 100 \text{ or } \frac{I_1 . X_{t1}}{V_1} \times 100$$

Percentage reactance is defined as voltage drop across reactance when full load current flows through it expressed as a percentage of full load terminal voltage.

Similarly % Impedance

$$= \frac{I_2 Z_{t2}}{V_2} \times 100$$

$$= \frac{I_1 Z_{t1}}{V_1} \times 100.$$

Example 5.8. A single phase transformer has 180 and 90 turns respectively in its secondary and primary windings. The respective resistances are 0.233 Ω and 0.067 Ω. Calculate the equivalent resistance of

(*a*) The primary in terms of secondary winding

(*b*) The secondary in terms of primary winding

(*c*) The total resistance of transformer in terms of primary.

Solution.

Number of turns on secondary = N_2 = 180

Number of turns on primary = N_1 = 90

Resistance of secondary = R_2 = 0.233 Ω

Resistance of primary = R_1 = 0.067 Ω

(*a*) Equivalent resistance of primary on secondary side

$$= R_1\left(\frac{N_2}{N_1}\right)^2$$

$$= 0.067\left(\frac{180}{90}\right)^2$$

$$= 0.067 \times 4 = 0.268\ \Omega.\ \textbf{Ans.}$$

(*b*) Equivalent resistance of secondary on primary side

$$= 0.233\left(\frac{N_1}{N_2}\right)^2$$

$$= 0.233\left(\frac{90}{180}\right)^2 = \frac{0.233}{4}$$

$$= 0.0582\ \Omega\ \textbf{Ans.}$$

(*c*) Total resistance of transformer in terms of primary

$$= R_{t1} = R_1 + R_2\left(\frac{N_1}{N_2}\right)^2 = R_1 + R'_2$$

$$= 0.067 + 0.233\left(\frac{90}{180}\right)^2$$

$$= 0.067 + 0.0582 = 0.1252\ \Omega\ \textbf{Ans.}$$

Example 5.9. Calculate in terms of primary the effective (equivalent) resistance and leakage reactance of a transformer which gave the following data on test with secondary terminal short circuited:

Applied voltage, 60 *V*; Current, 100 A, Power input = 1.2 KW.

Solution.

Power input on short circuit test = copper loss = 120 W

$$\text{Current} = 100\text{ A}$$

Total resistance of transformer on primary side = R_{t1}

$$\therefore \quad I_1^2 R_{t1} = 1200$$

$$100^2 \times R_{t1} = 1200$$

$$R_{t1} = \frac{1200}{100 \times 100} = 0.12\ \Omega$$

Total impedance on primary side

$$Z_{t1} = \frac{V}{I} = \frac{60}{100}$$

$$= 0.6\ \Omega\ \textbf{Ans.}$$

Total reactance on primary side

$$= X_{t1} = \sqrt{Z_{t1}^2 - R_{t1}^2}$$

$$X_{t1} = \sqrt{(0.6)^2 - (0.12)^2} = 0.59\ \Omega\ \textbf{Ans.}$$

Example 5.10. A 230/110 V single phase transformer has *a* primary resistance of 0.35 ohm and primary leakage reactance of 0.6 ohm and secondary resistance of 0.07 Ω and secondary leakage reactance of 0.12 Ω. Determine the ohmic loss and output voltage when a current 20 A is taken from the secondary at lagging *p.f* of 0.85 and the primary side is supplied at rated voltage. Ignore magnetising current.

(A.M.I.e. Section B, Summer 1975)

Solution.

Total resistance on primary side

$$= R_{t1} = R_1 + R_2 \left(\frac{N_1}{N_2}\right)^2$$

$$= 0.35 + 0.07 \left(\frac{230}{110}\right)^2$$

$$= 0.35 + 0.306 = 0.656\ \Omega$$

Total reactance on primary side

$$= X_1 + X_2 \left(\frac{N_1}{N_2}\right)^2$$

$$= 0.6 + 0.12 \times \left(\frac{230}{110}\right)^2$$

$$= 0.6 + 0.524$$

$$= 1.124\ \Omega$$

Current I_2 = Current on secondary side = 20 A

Current I_1 = Current on primary side = $20 \times \frac{110}{230} = 9.56$ A

Total copper loss on the primary side = $I_1^2 R_{t1}$

$$= (9.56)^2 \times 0.656 = 59.95 \text{ watts } \textbf{Ans.}$$

Let V_2' be terminal voltage of secondary expressed on the primary side as shown in Fig. 5.30.

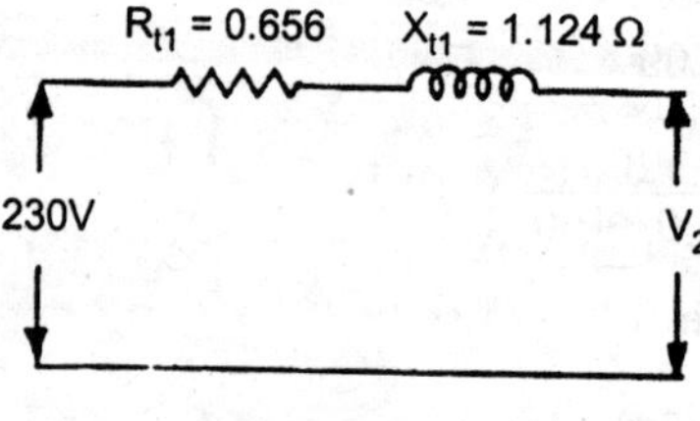

Fig. 5.30

Voltage drop across resistance and reactance on the primary side when current of 9.56 A at *p.f.* 0.85 lagging flows through the primary

$$= I_1 (R_{t1} \cos \phi_1 + X_{t1} \sin \phi_1)$$

when $\cos \phi_1 = 0.85$, $\sin \phi_1 = 0.5268$

$$= 9.56(0.656 \times 0.85 + 1.124 \times 0.5268)$$

$$= 9.56(0.5576 + 0.5921) = 10.991$$

$\therefore \quad V_2' = 230 - 10.991 = 219.002$ volts

$= 219.01$ **V**

Terminal voltage of secondary expressed on secondary side

$$= 219.01 \times \frac{110}{230} = 104.74 \text{ V. } \textbf{Ans.}$$

Example 5.11. A 40 KV A transformer with a ratio of 2000/250 *V* has a primary resistance of 1.15 Ω and secondary resistance of 0.0155 Ω. Calculate (*a*) Total resistance in terms of secondary windings, (*b*) The total resistance drop on full load, (*c*) The total copper loss on full load.

Solution.

(*a*) Total resistance in terms of secondary

$$R_{t2} = R_2 + R_1\left(\frac{N_2}{N_1}\right)^2 \quad \Bigg| \text{ Now } R_1 = 1.15\,\Omega$$

$$= 0.0155 + 1.15\left(\frac{250}{2000}\right)^2 \quad \Bigg| \; R_2 = 0.0155\,\Omega, \quad \frac{N_1}{N_2} = \frac{2000}{250}$$

$= 0.0155 + 0.0179$

$= 0.0334\ \Omega$. **Ans.**

(*b*) Full load current on secondary side

$$= I_2 = \frac{40 \times 1000}{250} = 160 \text{ A}$$

$\therefore$ Total resistance drop on full load on secondary side

$= I_2 R_{t2}$

$= 160 \times 0.0334$

$= 5.34$ **V. Ans.**

(*c*) Total copper loss on full load

$= I_2^2 R_{t2}$

$= (160)^2 \times 0.0334$

$= 856.04\ W$. **Ans.**

5.21. EQUIVALENT CIRCUIT OF A TRANSFORMER

It has now been established that in the practical transformer:

(*i*) Resistance of both primary and secondary windings exists.

(*ii*) The core permeability is not infinitely high, *i.e.* a magnetising current is required to produce the flux.

(*iii*) The whole of magnetic flux does not link the windings as there is definite some flux leakage which links primary and secondary winding independently due to which primary leakage reactance and secondary leakage reactance is produced.

(*iv*) There is an appreciable amount of hysteresis loss and eddy current loss in the core.

The practical transformer accordingly takes the following equivalent shape as shown in Fig. 5.31.

In Fig. 5.31, the resistance R_0 is of such value that power dissipated in it when current, I_w flows through it is equal to the combined hysteresis and eddy current losses. The reactance X_0 is there because an appreciable M.M.F. is now needed to produce the required flux since the permeability is assumed to be finite. To produce this M.M.F, a magnetising current is necessary and its magnitude determines the value X_0 which is assumed to pass this value of current. Thus X_0 carries that part of no load current which produces flux, *i.e.* it carries current I_m. Owing to the variation in characteristics of iron core with the degree of magnetisation, the values of R_0 and X_0 change with the change in the frequency of supply voltage.

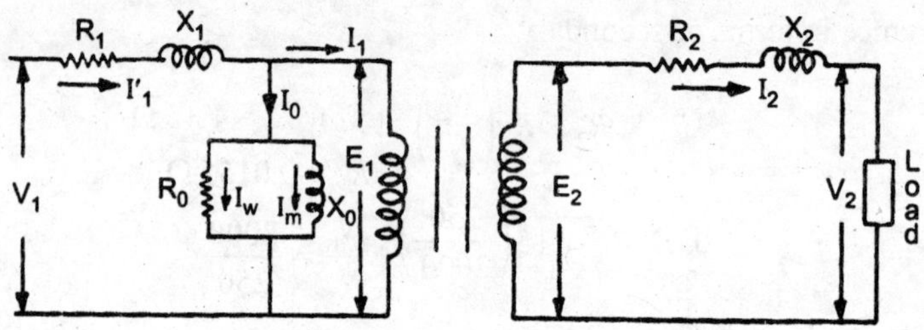

Fig. 5.31. Equivalent circuit of transformer

This of course does not apply to the other component whose values are largely independent of frequency.

From the equivalent circuit it is clear that primary current is composed of

(*i*) Magnetising component (I_m)

(*ii*) Iron loss component (I_w)

(*iii*) Load component I_1 corresponding to current I_2 in the secondary.

As far as first two components are concerned they remain unchanged in magnitude whether transformer is supplying load or not and together they make up the exciting current but the load component is proportional to secondary current.

R_1 and R_2 are resistances equal to the resistances of the primary and secondary windings of actual transformer. Similarly inductive reactances X_1 and X_2 represent, the reactance of the windings due to leakage flux in the actual transformer as already explained.

Total impedance of the primary

$$Z_1 = R_1 + jX_1 = \sqrt{R_1 + X_1^2}$$

Total impedance of the secondary

$$Z_2 = R_2 + jX_2 = \sqrt{R_2^2 + X_2^2}$$

The value of E_1 is obtained by subtracting vectorially the voltage drop I_1Z_1 from V_1.

The value of $\quad X_0 = \dfrac{E_1}{I_m}$

and value $\quad R_0 = \dfrac{E_1}{I_w}$

Now $$\frac{E_1}{E_2} = \frac{N_1}{N_2} = \frac{1}{K}$$

It has already been mentioned that calculations become quite easy if all voltages, currents and impedances are either transferred to the primary or to secondary. In that case one is to work with one winding only, which is very convenient.

When secondary induced e.m.f. E_2 is taken on primary side, it is represented as

$$E'_2 = E_2 \times \frac{N_1}{N_2} \text{ but } E_2 \times \frac{N_1}{N_2} = E_1$$

$$\therefore \quad E'_2 = E_2 \times \frac{N_1}{N_2} = \frac{E_2}{K} = E_1$$

Similarly when secondary terminal or output voltage transferred on the primary side, it is represented as V_2'

and $$V'_2 = \frac{V_2}{K}.$$

Similarly primary equivalent of secondary current is

$$I'_2 = I_2 K = I_1$$

$$R'_2 = \frac{R_2}{K^2}, X'_2 = \frac{X_2}{K_2}$$

Thus when whole of secondary circuit is transferred to primary side, the equivalent circuit is shown in Fig. 5.32.

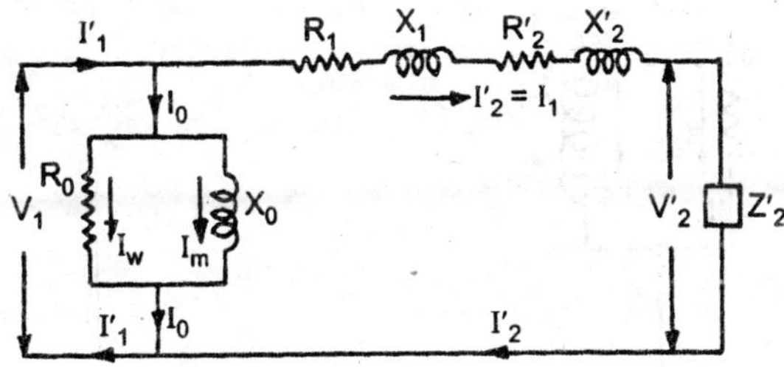

Fig. 5.32. Equivalent circuit simplified

5.22. APPROXIMATE EQUIVALENT CIRCUIT

It is clear from above discussion that E_1 differs from V_1 by a very small amount. Also no load current I_0 is a small fraction of full load primary current, so that I_2' is equal to I_1 practically. So the equivalent circuit can be simplified by transferring the parallel branch consisting of R_0 and X_0 to the extreme left position of the circuit.

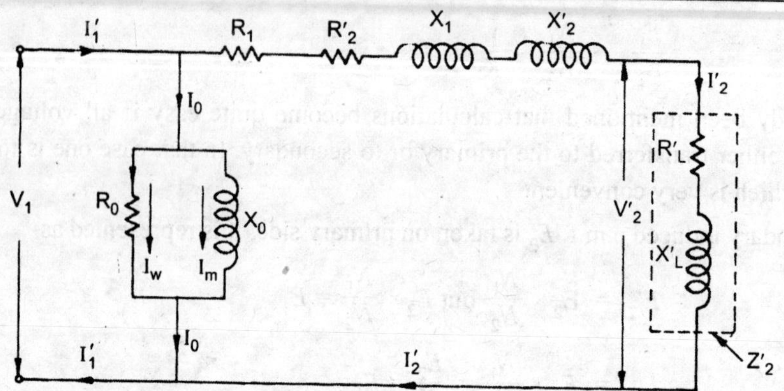

Fig. 5.33. Approximate equivalent circuit of transformer

It is shown in the Fig. 5.33, it is known as an approximate circuit of the transformer. The overall analysis of the equivalent circuit and approximate equivalent circuit is same. But the analysis of the approximate equivalent circuit is simpler than that of the equivalent circuit because in approximate equivalent circuit the resistances R_1 and R_2' and leakage reactances X_1 and X_2' can be combined which is not possible in equivalent circuit. The values of R_1 and R_2' and that of X_1 and X_2' can be shown lemped together in Fig. 5.34 and approximate equivalent circuit appears to be simpler.

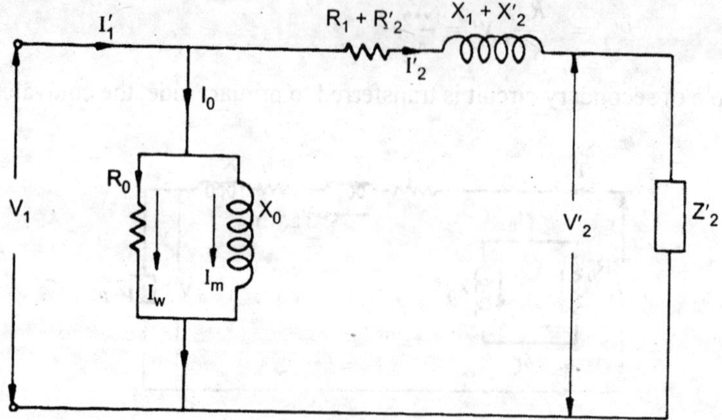

Fig. 5.34. Equivalent circuit

Example 5.12. A 440/120 V, single phase 50 cycles per second transformer supplies a load whose impedance is $(2 + j\,1.5)$ ohms. The H.V. winding has and impedance of $(0.028 + j\,0.012)$ ohms, and L.V. winding has impedance of $(0.55 + j\,0.22)$ ohms.

Calculate the values of the primary and the secondary currents, the load voltage and the power consumed by the load.

Solution.

Given, the transformer is single phase.

$$V_1 = 440 \text{ Volts.}$$

$$V_2 = 120 \text{ Volts}$$

$$f = 50 \text{ cycles/second}$$

$$Z_l = (2 + j\,1.5) \text{ ohms.}$$

$$Z_1 = (0.55 + j\,0.22) \text{ ohms.}$$

$$Z_2 = (0.028 + J\,0.012) \text{ ohms.}$$

We have, K = the ratio of transformation.

$$= \frac{V_2}{V_1}$$

$$= \frac{120}{400} = 0.3$$

The load and secondary impedances referred to primary,

$$= [(2 + j\,1.5) + (0.028 + j\,0.012)] \left(\frac{1}{0.3}\right)^2$$

$$= (2.028 + j\,1.512) \times 11.11$$

$$= 22.5 + j\,16.8 \text{ ohms.}$$

Adding the primary impedance, the total impedance becomes

$$Z = (22.5 + j\,16.8) + (0.55 + j\,0.22)$$

$$= (23.05 + j\,17.02) = 28.6 \text{ ohms.}$$

$\therefore$ Primary current $= \frac{400}{28.6} = 13.96$ A **Ans.**

and secondary current $= 13.96 \times \frac{400}{120}$

$$= 46.53 \text{ A Ans.}$$

The secondary terminal voltage

= Secondary current × load impedance.

$$= 46.53 \times 2.5$$

= 116.326 V **Ans.**

The load p.f. $= \frac{2}{2.5} = 0.8$ (lag)

Power consumed by the load

$$= 116.326 \times 46.33 \times 0.8 \times 10^{-3} \text{ KW}$$

= 4.31 KW **Ans.**

Example 5.13. The ratio of turns of a single phase transformer is 8. The resistances of primary and secondary windings are 0.85 ohms and 0.012 ohms respectively. The leakage reactances of these windings are 4.8 ohms and 0.07 ohm respectively. Determine the voltage to be applied to the primary to obtain a current of 150 A in the secondary when the secondary terminals are short circuited. Ignore the magnetising current. *(Haryana, July 1974)*

Solution.

Given,

$$K = \text{turns ratio} = 8$$
$$R_1 = 0.85\ \Omega$$
$$R_2 = 0.012\ \Omega$$
$$X_1 = 4.8\ \Omega$$
$$X_2 = 0.07\ \Omega$$
$$I_2 = 150\ \text{Amp.}$$

The secondary is short circuited. So, the load impedance is zero, and hence whole of the applied voltage appears across the primary equivalent impedance.

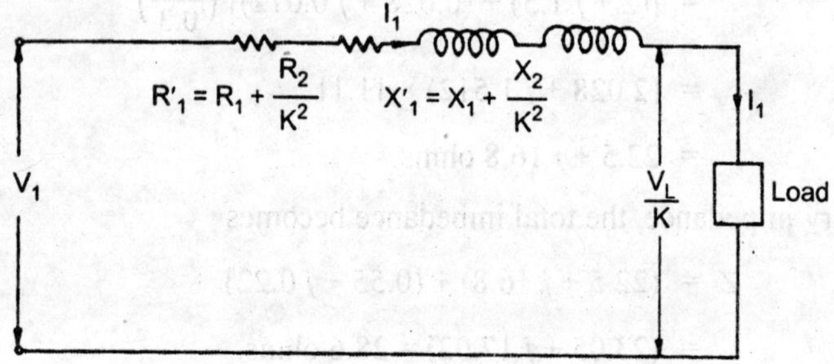

Fig. 5.35. Simplified equivalent circuit

Refer Fig. 5.35

Here

$$I_1 = KI_2$$
$$= 8 \times 150 = 1200\ \text{Amp.}$$
$$R_1 = R_1 + \frac{R_2}{K^2}$$
$$= 0.85 + \frac{0.012}{64}$$
$$\simeq 0.85\ \Omega$$
$$X'_1 = X_1 + \frac{X_2}{K^2}$$
$$= 4.8 + \frac{0.07}{64}$$
$$= 4.8044.$$
$$Z'_1 = \sqrt{(R'_1)^2 + (X'_1)^2}$$
$$\Rightarrow \quad \sqrt{(0.85)^2 + (4.8044)^2}$$
$$= \sqrt{0.172 + 23.1}$$
$$= 4.81\ \text{ohms.}$$

$$V_1 = I_1 Z_1' \text{ ; Since load impedance is zero.}$$
$$= 1200 \times 4.81 = 5772 \text{ Volts. } \textbf{Ans.}$$

5.23. PHASOR DIAGRAM OF TRANSFORMER ON LOAD

(Taking into consideration the effect of resistance and reactance of the windings.)

In drawing the vector diagram of a transformer, it is convenient to start with the flux vector ϕ as being the connecting link between primary and secondary. The drawing of the vector diagram becomes quite easy if the ratio of transformation is taken as 1: 1. For the time being load connected is considered to be inductive *i.e. p.f.* is considered to be lagging.

In the e.m.f. equation of transformer, induced e.m.f. e_1 on the primary side was given by

$$e_1 = N_1 \phi_m \omega \sin\left(\omega t - \frac{\pi}{2}\right)$$

Similarly e.m.f. e_2 induced on secondary side is given by

$$e_2 = N_2 \phi_m \omega \sin\left(\omega t - \frac{\pi}{2}\right)$$

When the flux was given by

$$\phi = \phi_m \sin \omega t$$

These two equations show that e.m.f. E_2 induced on the secondary side lags behind the flux ϕ which links both primary and secondary winding by 90°. Since flux ϕ remains constant, so flux ϕ has been taken as a reference vector in the vector diagram drawn in Fig. 5.36 and e.m.f. E_2 lagging behind ϕ by 90°.

In developing this vector diagram, the quantities are all lettered in a similar way as in the equivalent circuit diagram of Figs. 5.33 and 5.34.

When the secondary of the transformer is on open circuit the terminal voltage V_2 is equal to the induced e.m.f. E_2 but when secondary is connected to the load, the terminal voltage falls slightly (In case of leading currents the terminal voltage may rise also).

Now
$$E_2 = V_2 + I_2 (R_2 + jX_2)$$
$$= V_2 + I_2 Z_2$$
$$V_2 = E_2 - I_2 Z_2$$

when secondary is open, $I_2 = 0$

$$\therefore \quad V_2 = E_2 \text{ as already mentioned on open circuit.}$$

Since *p.f.* is considered to be lagging, thus secondary current I_2 has been shown to be lagging behind V_2 by an angle ϕ_2. The magnitude and phase of current I_2 depending upon the character of the load.

This current I_2 flows through the secondary resistance R_2 and causes a voltage drop I_2R_2 which is in phase with current I_2 as shown in vector diagram. A further voltage drop takes place when current I_2 passes through secondary reactance X_2. This is a voltage drop across reactance and therefore it leads the current I_2 by 90°. The combination of these two drops I_2R_2 and I_2X_2 gives an impedance drop I_2Z_2. This impedance drop I_2Z_2 is subtracted vectorially from E_2 to get secondary terminal voltage V_2. The power factor of secondary load circuit is given by cos ϕ_2. It should be borne in mind that ϕ_2 is the angle between secondary current and secondary terminal voltage and not between secondary current and secondary induced voltage E_2.

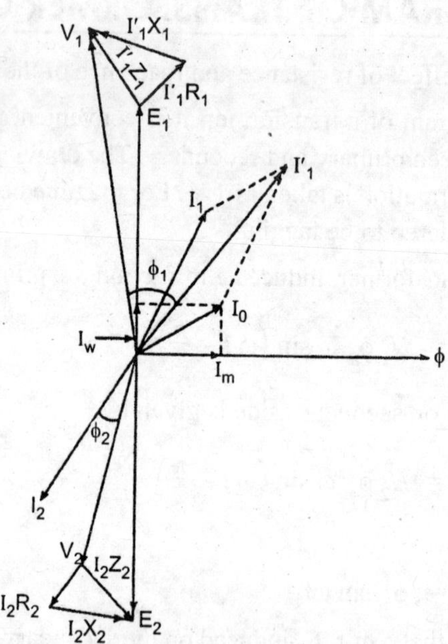

Fig. 5.36. Vector diagram of transformer on lagging p.f. load

When secondary is on open circuit, the primary has only no load current. I_0 flowing through it which is very small compared with full load circuit. This no load current I_0 consists of two components, I_w and I_m. I_w is known as core loss component and it supplies the core loss consisting of hysteresis and eddy current loss. I_m is known as magnetising current and is necessary for magnetising the core. This component is in phase with flux and thus lags 90° behind the e.m.f. E_1. The core loss component I_w is in phase with E_1, since it represents the power loss.

When the secondary delivers a current I_2, a corresponding cu.. nt I_1 flows in the primary equal in magnitude (In a 1: 1 transformer) and exactly opposite in phase. The total primary current is now I_1' which is vector sum of I_1 and I_0. Normally majority of transformers have ratios that differ greatly from unity and as such there shall be great disparity in the lengths of the vectors I_2 and I_1 if they were drawn to the same scale.

The alternating flux sets up a back e.m.f. E_1 in the primary winding which is drawn equal in magnitude but opposite in direction to E_2 (In a 1: 1 transformer). In addition a voltage $I_1' R_1$ has to be applied to provide for the resistance drop and this should be in phase with primary current I_1'.

A further voltage $I_1' X_1$ has to be supplied to provide for the reactance drop produced in primary reactance flux X_1. This $I_1' X_1$ drop leads current I_1' by 90°. The combination of the resistance and reactance drops gives the primary impedance voltage drop $I_1'Z_1$. The resultant applied voltage V_1 is the vector seem of E_1 and $I_1'Z_1$ where $I_1' Z_1$ is the vector sum of $I_1'R_1$ and $I_1'X_1$.

$$\mathbf{V_1 = E_1 + I_1'(R_1 + j X_1) = E_1 + I_1' Z_1}$$

The primary power factor is cos ϕ_1 where ϕ_1 is the phase angle between V_1 and I_1'.

When the load is inductive which is normally the case, the primary power factor is always lesser than that of secondary except when it is less than on no load which is not likely to occur in practice.

When the secondary current is a leading one, the vector diagram for that is shown in Fig. 5.37.

The power factor of the primary in that case is higher than that of the secondary. This is quite evident from the vector diagram also. The reason for the increased value of power factor on the secondary side is that part of no load magnetising current is neutralised side is that part of no load magnetising current is neutralised by a portion of the capacitive current required to balance the secondary current. In fact for one particular value of the secondary current at leading power factor, the primary power factor is unity. For lower values of secondary currents, the primary current lags while that in the secondary leads.

At leading power factor, the secondary terminal voltage V_2 of the transformer on load is more than the secondary induced voltage E_2.

This is also quite evident from the vector diagram of Fig. 5.37.

The vector diagram of transformer at unity p.f. load is shown drawn in Fig. 5.38.

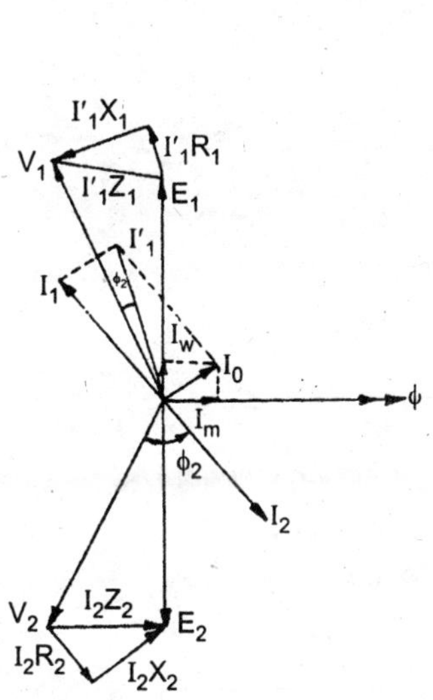

Fig. 5.37. Vector Diagram of transformer on leading p.f. load

Fig. 5.38. Vector diagram of transformer on unity p.f. load

Example 5.14. A 10 KVA single phase transformer for 2000 V/400 V at no load has resistances and leakage reactances as follows:—

Primary winding resistance, 5.5 Ω, reactance 12 Ω,

Secondary winding ; resistance 0.2 Ω ; reactance 0.45 Ω.

Determine the approximate value of the secondary voltage at full load, 0.8 *p.f.* lagging when primary supply voltage is 2000 V.

Solution: Equivalent circuit of transformer, neglecting the no load part is drawn on the primary side as shown in Fig. 5.39.

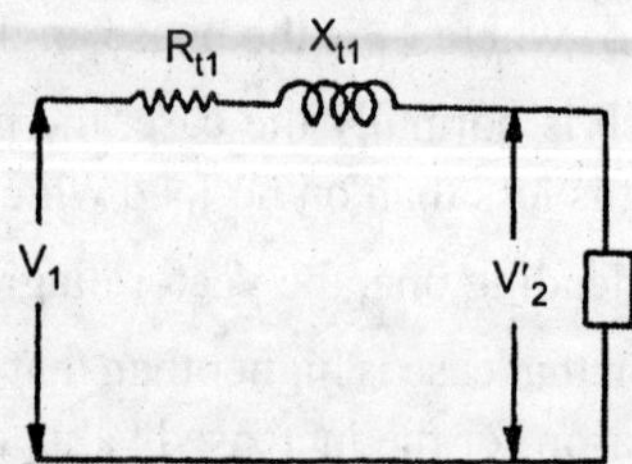

Fig. 5.39

$$R_{t1} = R_1 + R_2\left(\frac{N_1}{N_2}\right)^2$$

$$= 5.5 + 0.2\left(\frac{2000}{400}\right)^2$$

$$R_{t1} = 10.5\ \Omega$$

$$X_{t1} = X_1 + X_2\left(\frac{N_1}{N_2}\right)^2$$

$$= 12 + 0.45\left(\frac{2000}{400}\right)^2$$

$$= 12 + 11.25 = 23.25\ \Omega$$

$$V'_2 = V_1 - (I_1 R_{t1}\cos\phi_1 + I_1 X_{t1})$$

Full load primary current

$$= \frac{10 \times 1000}{2000} = 5\text{ A}$$

$$\cos\phi_1 = 0.8$$

$$\therefore \quad \sin\phi_1 = 0.6$$

$$\therefore \quad V_2' = 2000 - 5\,(10.5 \times 0.8 + 23.25 \times 0.6)$$

$$= 2000 - 5(8.4 + 13.95)$$

$$= 2000 - 5 \times 22.35$$

$$= 2000 - 111.75$$

$$= 1888.25 \text{ volts}$$

$$\frac{V_2'}{V'_2} = \frac{N_2}{N_1} = \frac{400}{2000}$$

$\therefore$ V_2 = secondary voltage on full load

$$= 1888.25 \times \frac{400}{2000}$$

$$= 377.65\text{ V}$$ **Ans.**

5.24. OPEN CIRCUIT AND SHORT CIRCUIT TESTS ON A TRANSFORMER

The performance of a transformer is best judged if the parameters of its equivalent circuit are known. The four parameters of the equivalent circuit are:

(*i*) Total equivalent resistance of transformer on primary side. *i.e.* R_{e_1}

Or

Total equivalent resistance of transformer on secondary side. *i.e.* R_{e_2}

(*ii*) Total equivalent reactance of transformer on primary side, *i.e.* X_{e_1}

Or

Total equivalent reactance of transformer on secondary side, *i.e.* X_{e_2}.

(*iii*) The resistance of the parallel circuit, *i.e.* R_0 where no load losses take place.

(*iv*) The reactance of the parallel circuit, *i.e.* X_0 which takes the magnetising current to produce the requisite flux.

All these four parameters are determined from the two tests.

(*i*) Open circuit test (*ii*) Short circuit test.

These two tests are very economical and convenient and when they determine the four constants or parameters of equivalent circuit enable the voltage regulation and efficiency to be determined without actually loading the transformer and with accuracy far higher than is possible by the direct measurement of input and output powers and voltages. In addition, the power required to carry out these tests is very small compared with the full load output of the transformer.

5.25. OPEN CIRCUIT TEST

This test helps to find out the no load current of transformer, *i.e.* I_0, which further helps in finding R_0 and X_0, no load losses, *i.e.* iron losses which remain practically constant, so long as the applied voltage and frequency remain same.

The transformer is connected to a supply at rated voltage and frequency namely the voltage and frequency given on the name plate as shown in Fig. 5.40.

A wattmeter *W*, an ammeter *A* and a voltmeter *V* are connected to the low voltage winding which incidentally in this case is primary winding. Since normal voltage at normal frequency is applied to the transformer, so normal flux is set up in the core and hence normal iron losses take place in the core of the transformer.

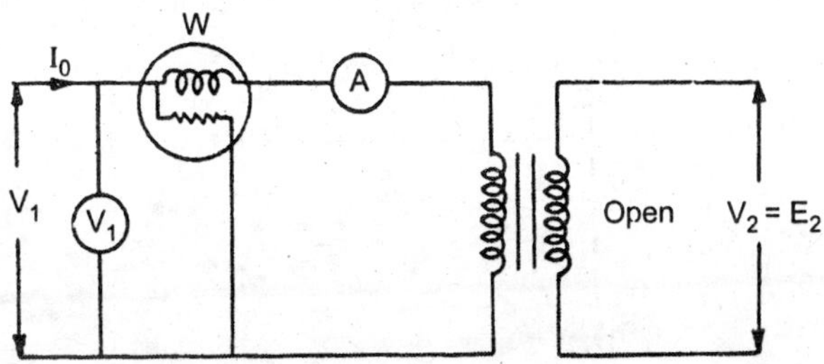

Fig. 5.40. Open circuit test

Since secondary of transformer is open, so output of transformer is zero.

But Input to the transformer = output + losses

But output = zero

∴ Input to the transformer = losses.

Input to the transformer is measured by the wattmeter W in this case. Thus wattmeter W in this case measures nothing else but losses.

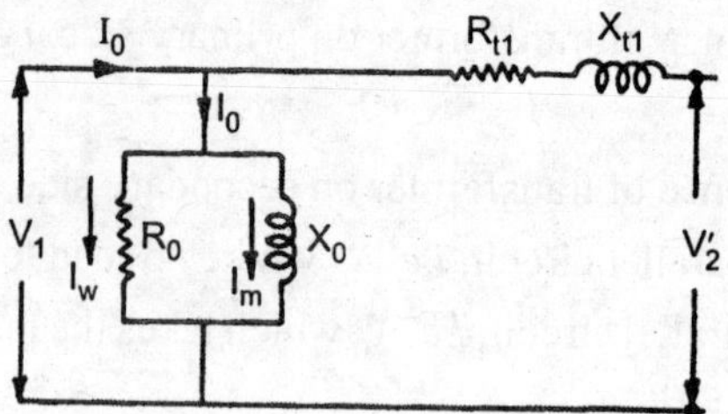

Fig. 5.41. Equivalent circuit of transformer on Primary side in open circuit condition

Losses in the transformer are iron losses and copper losses. When the secondary of the transformer is open, *i.e.* no load is connected across secondary and current drawn by the primary is very small and is normally less than 5% of the full load current. Thus if the current is less than $\frac{1}{20}$*th* time the full load current, the copper losses shall be much lesser than $\left(\frac{1}{20}\right)^2$ or $\frac{1}{400}$ times the copper losses on full load and therefore are so small as compared to iron losses that they can be neglected.

Hence the wattmeter reading can be taken as iron loss of the transformer. Thus on open circuit test, the input to the transformer is nothing else but iron loss.

Now input to the transformer

$$W = V_1 I_0 \cos \phi_0$$

or
$$\cos \phi_0 = \frac{W}{V_1 I_0}$$

From Fig. 5.42 power loss component of no load current

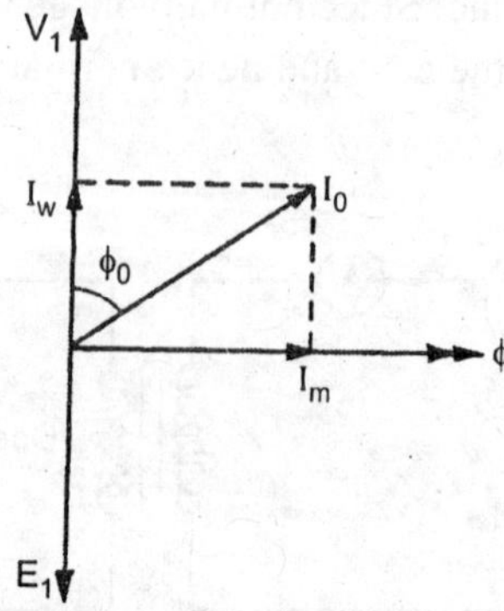

Fig. 5.42. Vector diagram of transformer on no load

$$= I_w = I_0 \cos \phi_0$$

and magnetising component of no load current

$$= I_m = I_0 \sin \phi_0$$

Now from equivalent circuit of Fig. 5.37.

$$R_0 = \frac{V_1}{I_w} = \frac{V_1}{I_0 \cos \phi_0}$$

and $$X_0 = \frac{V_1}{I_m} = \frac{V_1}{I_0 \sin \phi_0}$$

5.26. SHORT CIRCUIT TEST ON A TRANSFORMER

Short circuit test on a transformer helps us to find out

(*i*) Total copper loss in a transformer at full load

(*ii*) Total resistance of transformer either on primary or on secondary side.

(*iii*) Total reactance of transformer either on primary or on secondary side.

(*iv*) From (*ii*) and (*iii*) total impedance of transformer either on primary or on secondary side.

The circuit diagram of short circuit test on transformer is shown in Fig. 5.43. The secondary of the transformer is shorted through ammeter A_2 of suitable range as shown in Fig. 5.43. The short circuited winding should be low voltage winding. The voltage to the primary is fed through autotransformer, starting from minimum. The voltage to the primary is increased slowly till full load current I_2 flows through secondary as shown by ammeter A_2. When full load current flows through secondary, full load current, flows through primary also. This full load current when secondary is shorted starts flowing when the applied voltage is about 5 to 10% of the primary applied voltage. At this small voltage, the flux set up is also small and hence core losses taking place become so small that they can be neglected.

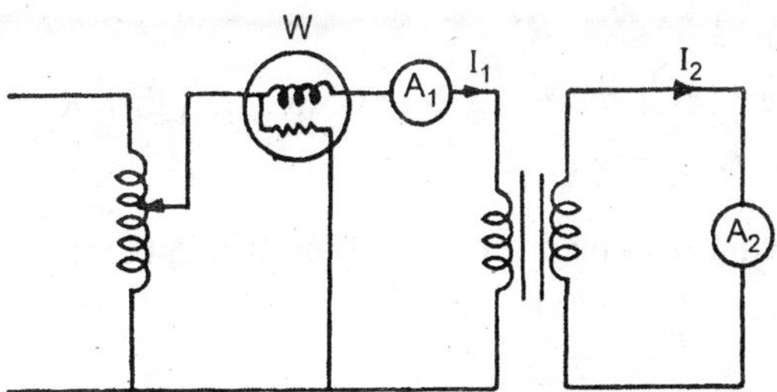

Fig. 5.43. Short circuit test on transformer

Now Input to the transformer = output + losses.

On short circuit output is zero.

Since terminal potential difference on secondary is zero.

∴ Input to the transformer = Losses.

$$\text{Losses} = \text{Copper loss} + \text{Iron loss}$$

The iron loss at the voltage short circuit test performed is negligible.

$$\therefore \quad \text{Losses} = \text{copper loss}$$

Therefore, input to the transformer at the time short circuit test is performed is equal to copper losses.

Thus wattmeter W which measures input, measures copper loss. Since the current flowing in the transformer at this time is full load current, therefore, wattmeter W reads full load copper loss both on primary as well as on secondary side.

The equivalent circuit of transformer, with secondary under short circuit condition is shown in Fig. 5.44. Since no load losses are negligible at the time of short circuit test, so no load portion of the equivalent circuit is removed.

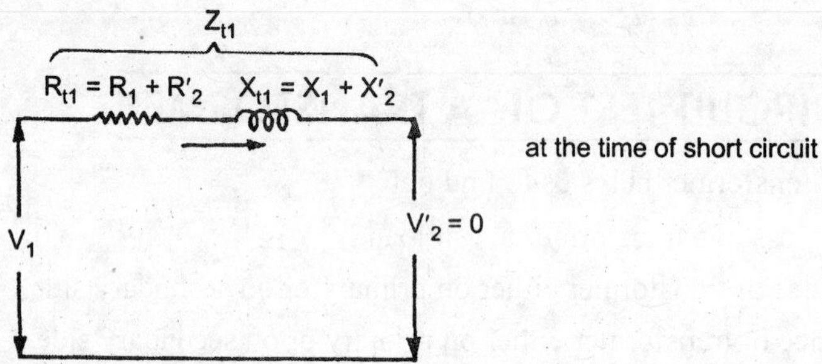

Fig. 5.44. Equivalent circuit of transformer under short circuit condition

Now total loss taking place in the transformer

$$= I_1^2 R_{t1} = W$$

$$\therefore \quad R_{t1} = \frac{W}{I_1^2}$$

$$Z_{t1} = \frac{V_1}{I_1}$$

$$\therefore \quad X_{t1} = \sqrt{Z_{t1}^2 - R_{t1}^2}$$

Now if primary resistance R_1 is determined from Ohm's law, then R_2' can be found out

$$R'_2 = R_{t1} - R_1$$

when R_2' is found out, then R_2 can be determined from the fact that

$$R'_2 = R_2 \left(\frac{N_1}{N_2}\right)^2.$$

5.26.1. Polarity of Transformers

In a transformer each of the primary terminals becomes alternately positive and negative with respect to the other and the same is true about the secondary terminals. If the transformer is to be used alone, the polarity is not important but if the transformer is to be used in parallel with another transformer the *instantaneous polarity is important* because the terminals having identical instantaneous polarity have to be connected together.

Refer Figs. 5.44.1 and 5.44.2. The terminals of the high voltage (h.v.) winding (*i.e.* H_1 and H_2) and the terminals of the low voltage (l.v.) winding (*i.e.* X_1 and X_2) are so marked that when the instantaneous voltage is directed from H_1 to H_2 in the high voltage winding, it is directed from X_1 to X_2 in the low voltage winding. In other words if the high voltage terminal H_1 is positive with respect to H_2 at any instant when the low voltage terminal X_1 will be positive with respect to X_2 at the same instant. It follows that when the terminals are arranged as in Fig. 5.44.1 polarity is subtractive whereas the additive polarity is represented as in Fig. 5.44.2.

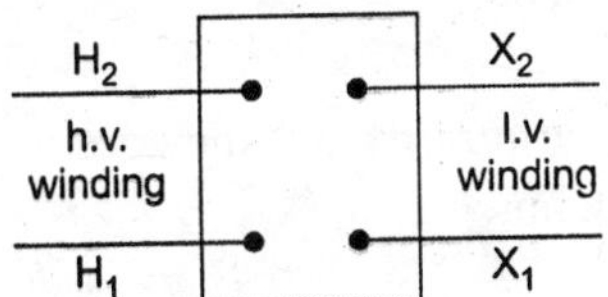

Fig. 5.44.1. Subtractive polarity

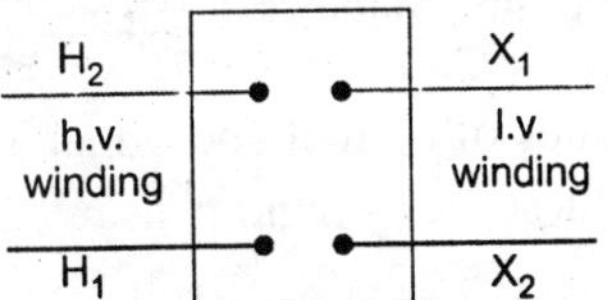

Fig. 5.44.2. Additive polarity

5.26.2. Polarity Test

A polarity test is carried out to *find out the terminals having the same instantaneous polarity assuming* that the terminals are not marked. The connections are shown in Fig. 5.44.3.

- One H.T. and one L.T. terminals are joined together. A volt-meter is placed between the remaining two terminals.
- A convenient moderate voltage is impressed on the H.T. winding.

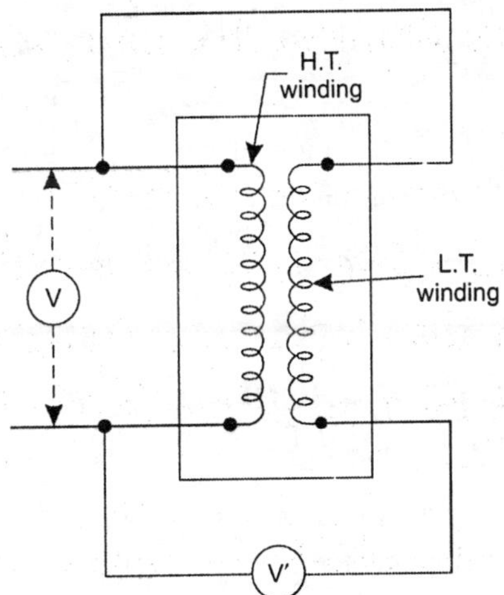

Fig. 5.44.3. Polarity test

*If the voltage V', is '**greater**' than the applied voltage V, then the trønsformers has '**additive**' polarity.*

*If V' is '**less**' than V, the transformer has '**subtractive**' polarity.*

The terminals are then marked accordingly.

5.26.3. Per Unit Values

Per unit system is found often. convenient to carry out calculations relating to electrical machines and other equipments. All the quantities are expressed as fractions of chosen base values. Per unit system entails the following *two main advantages*:

1. The constants of transformers and other equipments fall within very narrow limits when expressed in per units of their ratings.
2. In computations involving transformers the need to refer quantities from one side of the transformer to other side is eliminated.

$$\text{Per unit value} = \frac{\text{Actual value}}{\text{Base value}} \quad ...(1)$$

The base values of current and voltage may be chosen arbitrarily but they are usually chosen as equal to rated values. For a single-phase system the base volt amperes are

$$(\text{Volt ampere})_{base} = (V_{base})(I_{base}) \quad ...(2)$$

In practice it is more usual to choose the base voltage and base volt. Amperes and then calculate I_{base} from eqn. (2). The ratio of V_{base} to I_{base} is known as base impedance.

The transformer resistance, leakage reactance and impedance are also expressed in per unit. If the rated voltage V is taken as V_{base} and rated current I is taken as I_{base}, then

$$\text{Per unit resistance} = \frac{RI}{V} \quad ...(3)$$

$$\text{Per unit reactnce} = \frac{XI}{V} \quad ...(4)$$

$$\text{Per unit impedance} = \frac{ZI}{V} \quad ...(5)$$

When per unit system is used for calculation of regulation, efficiency etc. for transformers, *the transformer raring is taken as the base volt ampere. The respective voltages of high and low voltage sides are taken as the base voltages for the two sides. Then per unit resistance, reactance and impedance referred to high voltage side are the same as referred to low voltage side.*

5.26.4. Separation of Components of Core Losses i.e. Separation of Hysteresis and Eddy Current Losses

The core losses (or iron losses) comprises of hysteresis loss and eddy current loss. Sometimes it is desirable to find the hysteresis loss component and eddy current loss component in the total core losses.

Hysteresis Loss, $P_h = khf B_{max}$ watts/m³

Eddy current loss, $P_e = K_e f^2 B^2_{max} t^2$ watts/m³

Where B_{near} = Maximum flux density, f = frequency,

K_h, k_e = constants can be determined by carrying out two experiments using two different frequencies.

For a given machine having maximum flux-density, B_{max}

$$P_h \propto f \text{ and } P_e \propto f^2$$

$$P_n = a_f \text{ and } P_e = bf^2$$

Where a and b are the constants.

Total core loss, $P_i = af + bf^2$

Hence, if the total core loss for given B_m is known at two frequencies, the constants a and b can be calculated. Knowing the values of a and b, the hysteresis loss component and eddy current loss component of the core loss can be determined.

P_i/f and f curve

$$P_i = af + bf^2$$

or

$$\frac{P_i}{f} = a + bf$$

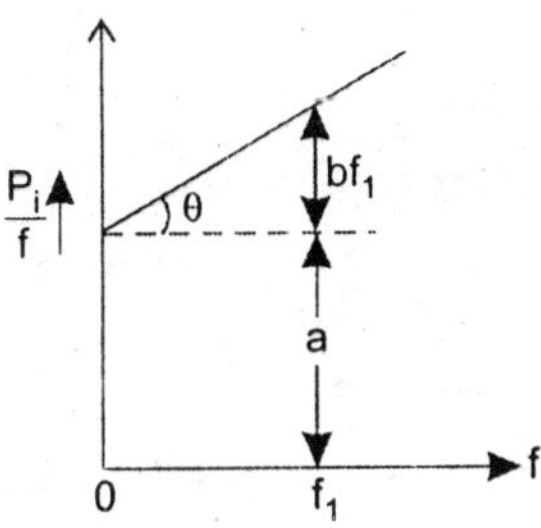

Fig. 5.44.4

The total core losses are measured at various frequencies while the other factors upon which core losses depend are maintained constant. If a graph is plotted between P_i/f and f, it will be a straight line with slope tan $\theta = b$ (See Fig. 5.44.4). Therefore, constants a and b can be evaluated. Hence the hysteresis and eddy current losses at a given frequency (say f_1) can be found out.

Example 5.14.1. *The iron loss in a certain transformer is 80 W at 25 Hz and 204 W at 60 Hz, the maximum flux density being the same. Calculate the total iron losses at 100 Hz at the same maximum flux density.*

Solution.

Total iron losses, $P_i = af + bf^2$ ...(*i*)

or

$$\frac{P_i}{f} = a + bf$$

At 25 Hz: $\frac{80}{25} = a + 25\,b$; At 60 Hz: $\frac{204}{60} = a + 60\,b$

On solving these two equations, we have $a = 107/35$; $b = 1/175$. Total iron loss at 100 Hz can be obtained by putting the values of a, b and f (= 100 Hz) in eq (*i*).

Total iron loss, $P_i = \frac{107}{35} \times 100 + \frac{1}{175} \times (100)^2 = \mathbf{362.85\ W}$

Example 5.14.2. *In a test for determination of losses of a 440 V, 50 Hz transformer, the total iron losses were found to be 2500 W at normal voltage and frequency. When the applied voltage and frequency were 220 V and 25 Hz, the iron losses were found to be 850 W. Calculate the eddy current loss at normal voltage and frequency.*

Solution. In a transformer, $\phi_m \propto V_1/f$. Since in the second case, voltage as well as frequency is halved,the ratio V_1/f remains the same. Therefore, maximum flux density in the two cases is the same.

Total iron losses, $P_i = af + bf^2$

or $\frac{P_i}{f} = a + bf$

For the first case, $\frac{2500}{50} = a + 50\,b$

For the second case, $\frac{850}{25} = a + 25\,b$

Solving the these two equations, we have, $b = 0.64$.

$\therefore$ Eddy current loss $= bf^2 = 0.64 \times 50^2 =$ **1600 W**

We can also find the hysteresis loss by subtracting 1600 W from 2500 W.

Example 5.14.3. *The iron loss in a transformer core at normal flux density was measured at 30 Hz and 50 Hz, the results being 30 W and 54 W. Calculate the hysteresis and eddy current loss at 50 Hz.*

Solution.

Total iron loss, $P_i = af + bf^2$

For the first case, $30 = 30\,a + b \times (30)^2$

For the second case, $54 = 50\,a + b \times (50)^2$

Solving these two equations, we have, $a = 44/50$; $b = 1/250$.

$\therefore$ Hysteresis loss at 50 Hz $= af = \frac{44}{50} \times 50 =$ **44 W**

Eddy current loss at 50 Hz $= bf^2 = \frac{1}{250} \times (50)^2 =$ **10 W**

Example 5.14.4. *The total iron loss in a 460 V, 50 Hz, single-phase transformer is 2400 W. When a 230 V, 25 Hz supply is applied, the total iron loss is 800 W. Calculate the hysteresis loss and eddy current loss at normal voltage and frequency.*

Solution. In a transformer, $\phi_m \propto V_1/f$. Since in the second case, voltage as well as frequency is halved, the ratio V_1/f remains the same. Therefore, maximum flux density in the two cases is the same.

$\therefore$ Total iron loss, $P_i = af + bf^2$

or $\frac{P_i}{f} = a + bf$

For the first case, $\frac{2400}{50} = a + 50\,b$

For the second case, $\frac{800}{25} = a + 25\,b$

Solving these two equations, we get, $a = 16$; $b = 16/25$.

$\therefore$ Hysteresis loss at 50 Hz = $af = 16 \times 50 =$ **800 W**

Eddy current loss at 50 Hz = $bf^2 = \frac{16}{25} \times (50)^2 = 1600$ W

5.26.5. WHY TRANSFORMER RATING IN KVA?

An important factor in the design and operation of electrical machines is the relation between the life of the insulation and operating temperature of the machine. Therefore, temperature rise resulting from the losses is a determining factor in the rating of a machine. We know that copper loss in a transformer depends on current and iron loss depends on voltage. Therefore, the total loss in a transformer depends on the volt-ampere product only and not on the phase angle between voltage and current *i.e.,* it is independent of load *power factor. For this reason, the rating of a transformer is in kVA and not kW.

5.26.6. SUMPNER OR BACK-TO-BACK TEST

This test is conducted simultaneously on two identical transformers and provides data for finding the efficiency, regulation and **temperature rise. The main advantage of this test is that the transformers are tested under full-load conditions without much expenditure of power. The power required to conduct this test is equal to the losses of the two transformers. It may be noted that two identical transformers are needed to carry out this test.

Circuit. Fig. 5.44.5 shows the connections for back-to-back test on two identical transformers T_1 and T_2. The primaries of the two transformers are connected in parallel across the rated voltage V_1 while the two secondaries are connected in phase opposition. Therefore, there will be no circulating current in the loop formed by the secondaries because their induced e.m.f.s are equal and in opposition. There is an auxiliary low-voltage transformer T which can be adjusted to give a variable voltage and hence current in the secondary loop circuit. A wattmeter W_1, an ammeter A_1 and voltmeter V_1 are connected to the input side. A wattmeter W_2 and ammeter A_2 are connected in the circuit.

* Rating in kW = kVA × load p.f.
The load p.f. depends upon the nature of load. Thus kW rating of transformer will be different for different load p.f.

* No doubt the open-circuit and short-circuits tests provide data for determining the efficiency and regulation of a transformer but they indicate no information regarding temperature rise. It is because in each of these tests, the power loss is either the core loss or copper loss but not both.

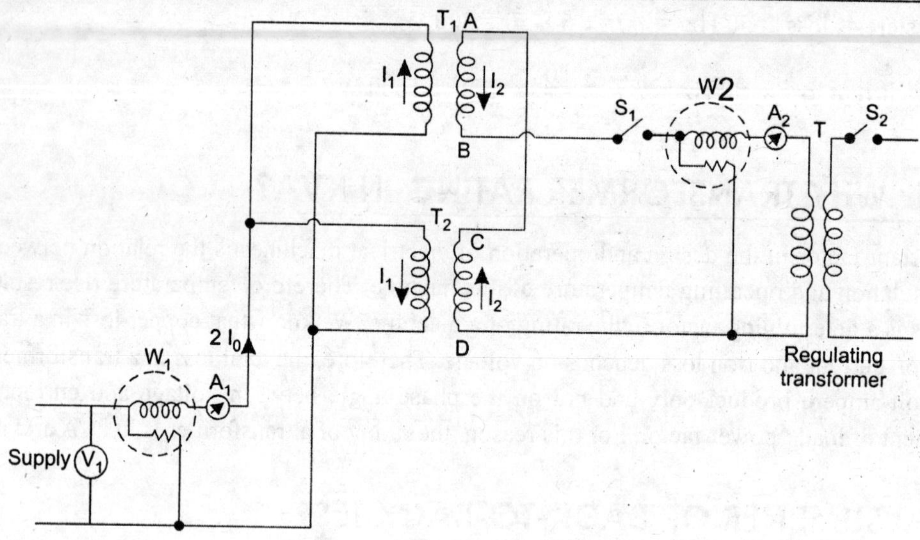

Fig. 5.44.5. Back-to-Back Test

Operation

(i) The secondaries of the transformers are in phase *opposition. With switch S_1 closed and switch S_2 open (*i.e.*, regulating transformer not in the circuit), there will be no circulating current z($I_2 = 0$) in the secondary loop circuit. It is because the induced e.m.f.s in the secondaries are equal and in opposition. This situation is just like an open-circuit test. Therefor, the current drawn from the supply is 2 I_0 is the no-load current of each transformer. The reading of wattmeter W_1 Will be equal to the core losses of the two transformers.

$$W_1 = \text{Core losses of the two transformers}$$

(ii) Now switch S_2 is also closed and output voltage of the regulating transformer is adjusted till full-load current I_2 flows in the secondary loop circuit. The full-load secondary current will cause full-load current I_1 (= $K I_2$) in the primary circuit. The primary circuit I_1 circulates in primary winding **only and will not pass through W_1. Note that full-load currents are flowing through the primary and secondary windings. Therefore, reading of wattmeter W_2 will be equal to the full-load copper losses of the two transformers.

$$W_2 = \text{Full-load Cu losses of two transformers}$$

$$\therefore \quad W_1 + W_2 = \text{Total losses of transformers at full load}$$

* This can be done by first connecting any two terminals (say A and C) together and a high-pressure voltmeter (of twice the rated secondary voltage) is connected to the remaining terminals B and D. For correct back-to-back connection, the voltmeter should give zero reading. If the voltmeter gives large reading, the terminal connections should be reversed.

** The primary windings are virtually short-circuited so far as I_1 is concerned. The injection of I_2 resembles the short-circuit test with the roles of primary and secondary windings reversed.

The following points may be noted:

(*a*) The wattmeter W_1 gives that core losses of the two transformers while wattmeter W_2 gives the full-load copper losses (or at any other load current I_2) of the two transformers. Therefore, power required to conduct this test is equal to the total losses of the two transformers.

(*b*) Although transformers are not supplying any load, yet full iron loss and full-load copper losses are occurring in them.

(*c*) There are two voltage sources (supply voltage and regulating transformer) and there is no interference between them. The supply voltage gives only 2 I_0 while regulating transformer supplies I_2 and hence I_1 (= $K I_2$).

Advantages

(*i*) The power required to carry out the test is small.

(*ii*) The transformers are tested under full-load conditions.

(*iii*) The iron losses and full-load copper losses are measured simultaneously.

(*iv*) The secondary current I_2 can be adjusted to any current value. Therefore, we can find the copper loss at full-load or at any other load.

(*v*) The temperature rise of the transformer can be noted.

Example 5.14.5. *In a back-to-back test (See Fig. 5.44.5), the wattmeter W_1 reads 4 kW while wattmeter W_2 (at full-load current) reads 6 kW. Find the full-load efficiency of each transformer. The transformer are rated at 200 kVA. Assume p.f. to be unity.*

Solution.

Iron loss of each transformer = $W_1/2 = 4/2 = 2$ kW

F.L. Cu loss of each transformer = $W_2/2 = 6/2 = 3$ kW

Total F.L. losses of each transformer = 2 + 3 = 5 kW

F.L. output of each transformer = 200 × 1 = 200 kW

F.L. efficiency of each transformer = $\frac{200}{200+5} \times 100 =$ **97.56%**

5.26.7. Harmonics

(*a*) **Wave shape of No Load Current:** Consider hysteresis loop for transformer core material as shown in Fig. 5.44.6. Here, let us call Fig. 5.44.6 as Fig. X for convenience. The B-H loop is plotted in terms of flux ϕ(= *Bx* area) and no-load current i_o (= $\frac{Hl}{N}$), instead of usual flux density B and magnetic field intensity H. A graphical procedure for determining the wave shape of current i_o for sinusoidal flux is as shown in Fig. X. For obtaining no-load current wave form for sinusoidal flux (and therefore sinusoidal supply voltage to primary), proceed as under.

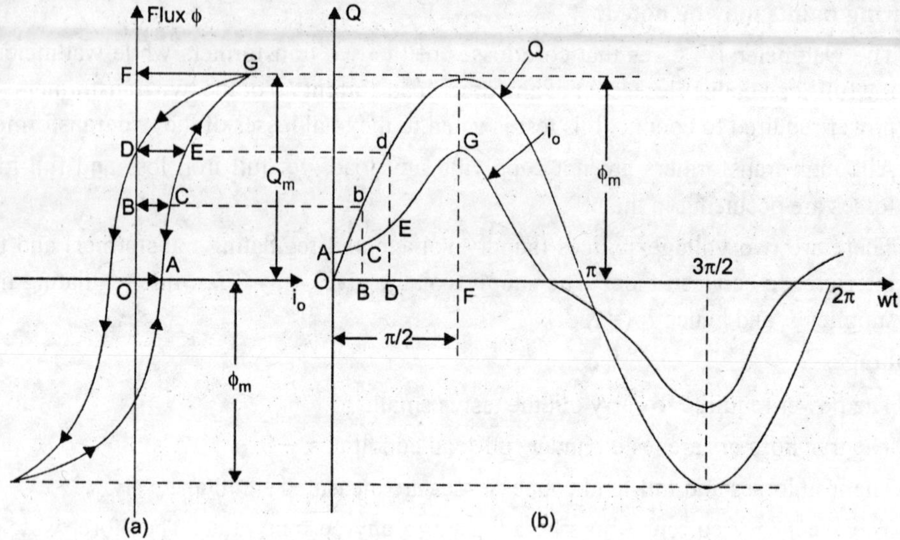

Fig. 5.44.6 (*a*) B-H loop and (*b*) wave form of no-load current of a transformer.

At instant $\omega t = O$ in Fig. *X* (*b*), flux is zero and the corresponding current for zero flux seen from hysteresis loop is *OA* in Fig. *X*(*a*). This current *OA* is now plotted as *OA* in Fig. *X*(*b*) at $\omega t = O$. At instant $\omega t = OB$ in Fig. *X*(*b*), core flux is *Bb* in Fig. *X*(*b*) and *OB* in Fig. *X*(*a*) and the corresponding current is *BC* in Fig. *X*(*a*). This current is now plotted as *BC* in Fig. *X*(*b*) at instant *B*. At instant *OD*, flux is *Dd* in Fig. *X*(*b*) and *OD* in Fig. *X*(*a*) and the corresponding current is *DE* in Fig. *X* (*a*). This current is plotted as *DE* in Fig. *X*(*b*) at instant *D*. For maximum flux ϕ_m at $\omega t = \frac{\pi}{2}$, the maximum flux is shown as *OF* Fig. *X*(*a*) and the corresponding current is *FG* in Fig. *X*(*a*). Now this current is plotted as *FG* in Fig. *X*(*b*). When flux is maximum, no-load current is also maximum. After $\omega t = \frac{\pi}{2}$, both flux and no-load current begin to decrease. Following the above procedure for different values of flux, the value of no-load current i_o can be obtained from Fig. *X*(*a*) and plotted in Fig. *X*(*b*). A line passing through *ACEG*... etc. gives the wave shape of no-load current as shown in Fig. *X*(*b*).

It is seen from Fig. *X*(*b*) that

(i) the flux waveform is symmetrical about its peak and is sinusoidal,

(*ii*) the no-load current waveform is unsymmetrical about its peak and is non-sinusoidal,

(*iii*) the flux and current waveforms have their maximum values at the same instant.

The analysis of the no-load current wave form shows that it consists of fundamental component and third, fifth and higher order odd harmonics. The amplitude of harmonic decreases as the order of harmonic increase. Out of various harmonic components, third harmonic is the most dominant. Sometimes, the third harmonic may be as high as 40% of the fundamental component.

(*b*) **Harmonics in Three-phase Transformers:** Here we discuss about harmonics in three-phase transformers at an elementary level.

1. **Y-connected Primary:** Let us consider the case when four-wire supply is given to primary winding of a star-connected transformer. The third harmonic currents in 3-phases are co-phasal. Therefore, current in the neutral wire is the sum of the three components and thus third harmonic current in the neutral wire is 3 times the third-harmonic component in each phase. The third harmonic current and sinusoidal magnetizing current can exist in both the lines and transformer windings. As a result, flux is sine wave and therefore phase voltages are also sinusoidal. So the line voltage = $\sqrt{3}$ phase voltage.

   The main disadvantages of the third harmonic currents in the lines is that these may cause considerable interference with the communication circuits running parallel to the transmission lines.

   If the secondaries are star-connected, third harmonic emfs are not present in the secondary phase and line voltages and line voltage = $\sqrt{3}$ phase voltage.

   If the secondary winding is delta-connected, the phase as well as line voltages are free third harmonic emfs.

   If the supply to tranformer primary winding is **without neutral wire,** then third harmonic current cannot flow but sinusoidal magnetizing current can flow in phase windings. As a result, the flux contains third harmonic component. Therefore, third harmonic emfs, as large as 40% of fundamental voltage may be present in phase voltages. Net phase voltage $= \sqrt{1^2 + 0.4^2} = 1.077$ times the fundamental component of phase voltage. Therefore, with both windings in star, line voltage $\neq \sqrt{3} \times$ phase voltage. However, line to line voltages are free from third harmonic emfs.

   If the secondary is delta-connected, even then third harmonic current cannot flow in the primary star. As a result, third harmonic flux is present in the core. This third harmonic flux induces third harmonic emf in both primary and secondary windings. In the secondary delta, third harmonic emfs give rise to the flow of third harmonic current. Thus the magnetizing current in the secondary winding consists of third harmonic current only. Combined action of fundamental current in primary and third harmonic current in secondary closed delta causes the resultant flux in the core to be sine wave. As a result, no third harmonic emfs are present in primary and secondary emfs in star-delta transformer.

2. **Delta-connected Primary:** In delta-connected primary winding, the third harmonic magnetizing current cannot flow in the lines, therefore magnetizing current is sinusoidal. As a result, flux is flat-topped and therefore third harmonic emfs are induced in the closed delta. These third harmonic emfs are additive in closed delta and therefore third harmonic current is established in delta. Thus, the transformer primary delta has sinusoidal magnetizing current plus third harmonic magnetizing current. Presence of third harmonic component in the magnetizing current requires sinusoidal flux. Therefore, emfs induced in both primary and secondary windings are almost sine waves.

   The third harmonic magnetizing current can flow in the closed delta only due to third harmonic emf and therefore presence of third harmonic flux ϕ_3 is essential. As flux ϕ_3 has low value, a very small amount of third harmonic emf (= 1% of rated phase voltage or even less) is induced in both primary and secondary windings.

   If the secondary is in star, low third harmonic voltage components are present in line to neutral voltage but not in line-to-line voltage.

If the secondary is in delta, the third harmonic voltages produce a very low value of circulating current around the closed delta.

5.27. LOSSES IN A TRANSFORMER

Since transformer is a static machine, so mechanical losses such as friction and windage losses do not exist.

Mainly there are two types of losses taking place in a transformer

(*i*) Core loss or iron loss (*ii*) Copper loss.

(*i*) **Core loss.** Core loss takes place in the core of transformer and it is further made of two parts

(*i*) Hysteresis loss (*ii*) Eddy current loss.

Hysteresis loss takes place in the core due to the magnetisation and demagnetisation of the core due to the reversal of current and then flux after every half cycle in the core. Due to this magnetisation and demagnetisation, the molecules in the core keep on moving periodically which results in consumption of power known as Hysteresis loss.

Hysteresis loss $\propto B_{max}$ $1.6 f$, where B_{max} is the max. value of flux density and f is the frequency.

This loss can be reduced by choosing a particular type of material for the core which has the smallest B-H curve such as manganese steel or silicon steel.

Eddy current loss takes place due to the varying flux linking the core in addition to the windings. This flux linkage with the core induces emfs in the core which sends circulating current in the core known as eddy currents. These eddy currents when flow through the core which has a resistance produce loss known as eddy current loss.

Eddy current loss $\propto B^2_{max} f^2 t^2$

where B_{max} is the max value of flux density, f is the frequency and t is the thickness of laminations.

The eddy current loss can be reduced by laminating a core with each lamination insulated from the other through a coating of varnish. The thickness of the lamination should be quite small to further reduce the eddy current loss.

Iron losses can be determined from open circuit test.

(*ii*) **Copper loss.** The copper loss occurs because of the resistance of the both primary and secondary windings. It is given by I^2R. This loss is proportional to the square of current. It can be determined from short circuit test.

$$\text{Total copper loss} = I_1^2 R_1 + I_2^2 R_2$$

These losses, as is evident, are proportional to square of current or kVA^2.

Example 5.15. Calculate the values of R_0, X_0, R_t and X_t in the diagram for the equivalent circuit of a 1-phase, 4 KVA, 200/400 V, 50 c/s transformer of which following are test results:

Open circuit: 200 V, 0.7 A, 70 W on low voltage side (Primary)

Short circuit: 15 V, 10 A, 80 W on high voltage (Secondary side)

Solution.

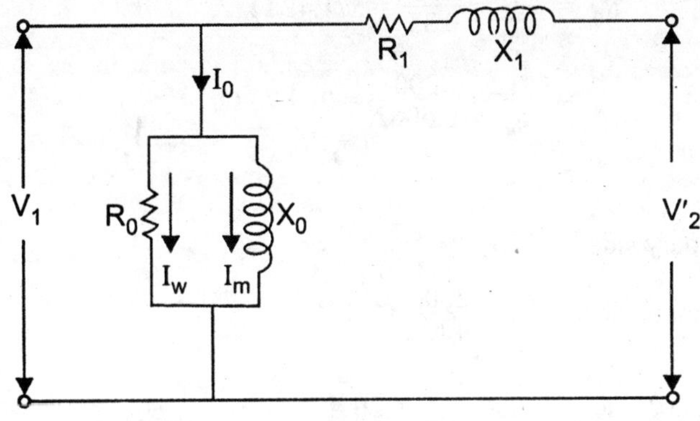

Fig. 5.45

Open circuit lest:

$$V_1 I_0 \cos \phi_0 = \text{Power input on open circuit}$$
$$= 70\text{W}$$

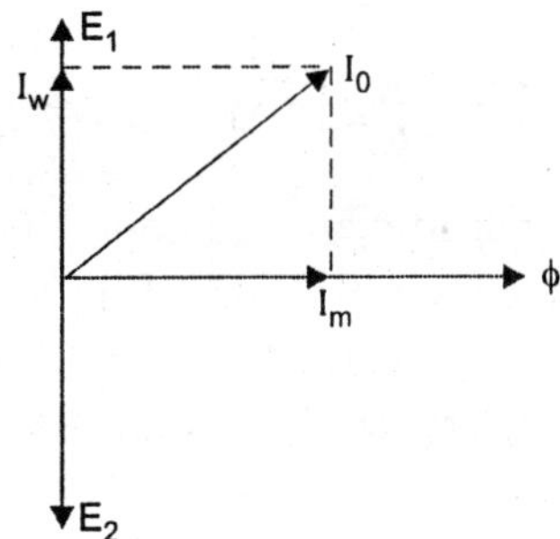

Fig. 5.46

$$V_1 = 200\ V, I_0 = 0.7 \text{ Amp}$$

$$\therefore \quad 200 \times 0.7 \times \cos \phi_0 = 70$$

$$\cos \phi_0 = \frac{70}{200 \times 0.7} = 0.5$$

$$\sin \phi_0 = 0.866$$

$$I_w = \text{Power loss component}$$
$$= I_0 \cos \Phi_0 = 0.7 \times 0.5$$
$$= 0.35 \text{ Amp.}$$

$$\text{Magnetising component} = I_m = I_0 \sin \Phi_0 = 0.7 \times 0.866$$
$$= 0.6062.$$

$$R_0 = \frac{V_1}{I_w} = \frac{200}{0.35} = 571.42\ \Omega$$

$$X_0 = \frac{V_1}{I_m} = \frac{200}{0.6062} = 329.92\ \Omega.$$

Short circuit test:

Voltage on secondary side = $15\ V$

$\therefore$ Voltage on primary side = $15 \times \frac{200}{400} = 7.5\ V$

Current on primary side = $10 \times \frac{400}{200} = 20\ A$

$$\therefore \quad I_1^2 R_t = 80$$

or

$$(20)^2 R_t = 80$$

$$R_t = \frac{80}{400} = 0.2\ \Omega$$

$$Z_t = 7.5/20 = 0.375\ \Omega$$

$$X_t = \sqrt{Z_t^2 - R_t^2} = \sqrt{(0.375)^2 - (0.2)^2} = 0.317\ \Omega \textbf{ Ans.}$$

Example 5.16. A 200 V/2000 V transformer is fed from a 200 V supply. The total winding resistance and leakage reactance as referred to low voltage side is 0.15 Ω. and 0.6 Ω respectively. The resistance representing core loss is 450 ohm and magnetising reactance is 2500 *m.m.* A load of impedance (600 + *j* 400 Ω) is connected across the secondary terninals. Calculate:

(*i*) Input current.

(*ii*) Secondary terminal voltage.

(*iii*) Primary power factor.

Solution:

Transformation ratio, $K = \frac{2000}{200} = 10.$

The total winding resistance referred to *LV* side

$$R_{01} = 0.15\ \Omega.$$

Total winding reactance referred to *LV* side

$$X_{01} = 0.6\ \Omega$$

Resistance representing the core loss

$$R_0 = 450\ \Omega$$

Magnetising Reactance, $X_0 = 250\ \Omega.$

Load impedances connected across the secondary terminals,

$$Z_L = (600 + j\,400\ \Omega)$$

$$R_L = 600\ \Omega$$

$$X_L = 400\ \Omega$$

Load resistance referred to primary (*LV*),

$$R'_L = \frac{R_L}{K^2} = \frac{600}{(10)^2} = 6\ \Omega$$

Load reactance referred to primary (*LV*),

$$X'_L = \frac{X_L}{K^2} = \frac{400}{(10)^2} = 4\ \Omega$$

The magnetising component of no-load current I_0,

$$I_m = \frac{200 < 0^\circ}{j\,250} = -j\,0.8\ \text{A}$$

The wattful component of no-load current I_0

$$I_w = \frac{200 < 0^\circ}{450} = 0.444\ \text{A}$$

(*i*) Input current, $I_1 = ?$

Secondary current referred to primary,

$$I'_2 = \frac{V_1}{(R_1 + R'_2) + R'_L + J(X_1 + X'_2 + X'_L)}$$

$$= \frac{200 < 0^\circ}{R_{01} + R'_L + j(X_{01} + X'_L)} = \frac{200 < 0^\circ}{0.15 + 6 + j\,(0.6 + 4)}$$

$$= \frac{200 < 0^\circ}{6.15 + j\,(4.6)} = \frac{200(6.15 - j\,4.6)}{(6.15 + j\,4.6)(6.15 - j\,4.6)}$$

$$= \frac{200(6.15 - j\,4.6)}{58.98} = 20.85 - \text{j}\ 15.6\ \text{A}$$

So, $$I_1 = I_2' + I_m + I_w$$

$$= (20.85 - j\,15.6) + j\,0.8) + 0.444$$

$$= 21.294 + j\,16.44$$

$= 26.9 < -37.67^\circ$ A. **Ans.**

(*ii*) Secondary terminal voltage, $V_2 = ?$

Secondary terminal voltage referred to primary,

$$V_2' = I_2'\,(R_L' + j\,X_L') = (20.85 - j\,15.6)\,(6 + j\,4)$$

$$= (26.04 < 36.8^\circ)\,(7.21 < 33.7^\circ)$$

$$= 187.75 < -3.1^\circ\ \text{V}$$

Secondary terminal voltage, $V_2 = KV_2' = 10 \times 187.75$

$$= 1877.5\ \text{V}.$$

(*iii*) Primary power factor, $\cos \phi_1 = ?$

$$\cos \phi_1 = \cos (37.67°) = 0.791 \text{ (lagging) } \textbf{Ans.}$$

Example 5.17. A 50 c/s 1-phase transformer has a turn ratio of 6. The resistances are 0.9 Ω and 0.03 Ω. and the reactances 5 Ω and 0.13 Ω. for high voltage and low voltage windings respectively. Find (*a*) the voltage to be applied to high voltage side to obtain full load current of 200 A in the low voltage winding on short circuit (*b*) p.f. on short circuit.

Solution.

Total resistance on high voltage side

$$= R_{12} = R_2 + R_1 \left(\frac{N_2}{N_1}\right)^2 \left(\because \frac{N_2}{N_1} = 6\right)$$

$$= 0.9 + 0.03 \times (6)^2$$

$$= 0.9 + 0.03 \times 36$$

$$= 0.9 + 1.08 = 1.98 \ \Omega.$$

Total reactance on high voltage side

$$X_{12} = X_2 + X_1 \left(\frac{N_2}{N_1}\right)^2$$

$$= 5 + 0.13 \ (6)^2$$

$$= 5 + 4.68 = 9.68 \ \Omega.$$

Total impedance on high voltage side

$$= \sqrt{(1.98)^2 + (9.68)^2}$$

$$= \sqrt{3.92 + 93.70} = \sqrt{97.62}$$

$$= 9.88 \ \Omega$$

Short circuit current on high voltage side

$$= 200 \times \frac{1}{6} = \frac{100}{3} \text{ A}$$

On short circuit, short circuit current

$$= \frac{\textit{Applied voltage}}{\textit{Impedance}}$$

∴ Voltage applied to high voltage side

$$= \frac{100}{3} \times 9.88$$

$$= 329.3 \text{ V. } \textbf{Ans.}$$

Since there is no other load on short circuit except the impedance of transformer, therefore,

$$\cos \phi_2 = \text{power factor} = \frac{R_{12}}{Z_{12}} = \frac{1.98}{9.88} = 0.2$$

Example 5.18. A 100 KVA, 3300/230 V, single phase transformer takes a no-load current of 1.5 A and power of 1.1 KW at rated voltage and frequency at the primary (*H.T.*) side. On short circuit with full load secondary (*L. T.*) current flowing, it takes 1.4 KW at a primary terminal voltage of 150 V and rated frequency.

Estimate the efficiency and primary p.f. for 75% of full load secondary current at 0.9 p.f. lagging p.f. Ignore the effect of temperature rise. (*A.M.I.e. Section B, Dec. 1995*)

Solution:

(*i*) Output of transformer at 75% full load at 0.9 p.f. lagging

$$= 100 \times 0.75 \times 9$$

$$= 67.5 \text{ kW}$$

From short circuit test full load copper loss

$$= 1.4 \text{ kW.}$$

Copper loss at 75% of full load

$$= 1.4 \times \left(\frac{75}{100}\right)^2$$

$$= 0.7875 \text{ kW}$$

From open circuit test, iron loss

$$= 1.1 \text{ kW}$$

Input to the transformer at 75% full load

$$= 67.5 + 0.7875 + 1.1$$

$$= 69.3875 \text{ kW}$$

∴ Efficiency of transformer at 75% full load

$$= \frac{67.5}{69.3875} \times 100$$

$$= 97.28\%$$

(*ii*) At no load

$$V_0 I_0 \cos\phi_0 = 1.1 \times 10^3$$

$$3300 \times 1.5 \times \cos\phi_0 = 1100$$

$$\therefore \quad \cos\phi_0 = \frac{1100}{3300 \times 1.5} = 0.22$$

P.f. of primary current on no load = 0.22

Corresponding to full load secondary current, there is full load primary current

$$= \frac{100 \times 10^3}{3300} = 30.30 \text{ A at p.f. 0.9 lag.}$$

$$\dot{I}_1 = 30.30 (\cos\phi - j\sin\phi)$$

when $\cos\phi = 0.9, \sin\phi = 0.436$

$$= 30.30\,(0.9 - j\,0.436)$$

$$= (27.270 - j\,13.21)$$

No load current $\dot{I}_0 = I_0(\cos\phi_0 - j\sin\phi_0)$

$$= 1.5\,(0.22 - j\,0.975)$$

$$= (0.33 - j\,1.46)$$

Total current on primary,

$$= \dot{I}_1 + \dot{I}_0 = (27.27 - j\,13.21) + (0.33 - j\,1.46)$$

$$= 27.6 - j\,14.67$$

Magnitude of primary current

$$= \sqrt{(27.6)^2 + (14.67)^2}$$

$$= \sqrt{761.75 + 215.20}$$

$$= \sqrt{976.95} = 31.25$$

Power factor of primary current

$$= \frac{27.6}{31.25} = 0.8832 \text{ lagging.}$$ **Ans.**

5.28. VOLTAGE REGULATION OF A TRANSFORMER

Regulation of a transformer is the difference between the no-load secondary voltage and the secondary voltage when delivering full load current with constant primary voltage. It is expressed as a percentage of no-load secondary voltage.

Mathematically it is given by:

Percentage regulation

$$= \frac{E_2 - V_2}{E_2} \times 100$$

where E_2 = Secondary terminal voltage on no load.

and V_2 = Secondary terminal voltage on full load.

As the current taken from the secondary of the transformer is increased, the voltage at the terminals of the secondary tends to drop due to voltage drop across its resistance and reactance. This behaviour is referred to as regulation of a transformer. A small variation of output voltage with load is considered as a good regulation.

When secondary is loaded, corresponding current flow is there in the primary. This current flowing in primary causes a voltage drop in the resistance and reactance of the primary as a result voltage induced in the primary gets reduced. When the primary induced voltage is reduced, secondary induced voltage is reduced accordingly Then there occurs a voltage drop in the resistance and reactance of the secondary winding due to this current flow, thus further reducing the terminal voltage of the secondary.

Thus both primary and secondary impedances are responsible for changing the voltage at the terminals of the secondary.

Full load regulation can be found out experimentally by measuring the voltage across the terminals of the secondary by voltmeter when no load is connected across it. This voltage is induced voltage E_2. Then full load is connected across the secondary and secondary terminal voltage again measured. This voltage is terminal voltage V_2, percentage regulation is given by

$$= \frac{E_2 - V_2}{E_2} \times 100.$$

5.29. CALCULATION OF REGULATION

The regulation can be determined mathematically by drawing the vector diagram.

The vector diagram of equivalent circuit of Fig. 5.47 has been drawn in Fig. 5.48. For calculating the regulation, it has already been affirmed that resistance and reactance of both primary and secondary has to be taken into consideration. Whenever there is an increase in current on secondary side, there is a corresponding increase in the current on the primary which increases the drop across resistance and reactance of primary, thus reducing the induced voltage in primary. Reduced primary voltage induces reduced voltage in secondary. Then there is again a voltage drop in secondary resistance and reactance due to increased current on the secondary side thus reducing the terminal voltage further on secondary side. This clearly shows that resistance and reactance of both primary and secondary help in changing the secondary terminal voltage.

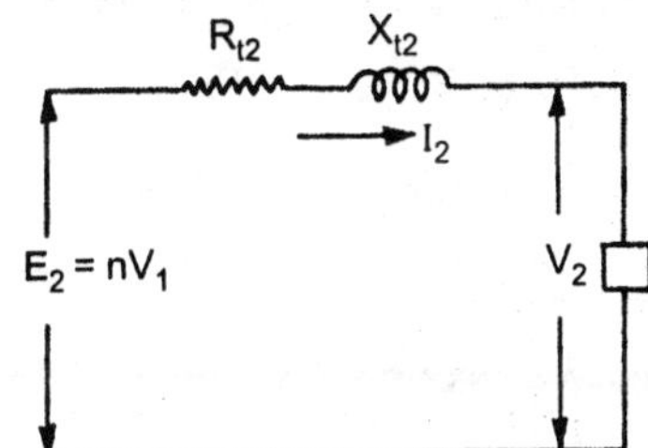

Fig. 5.47. Equivalent circuit of transformer on secondary side

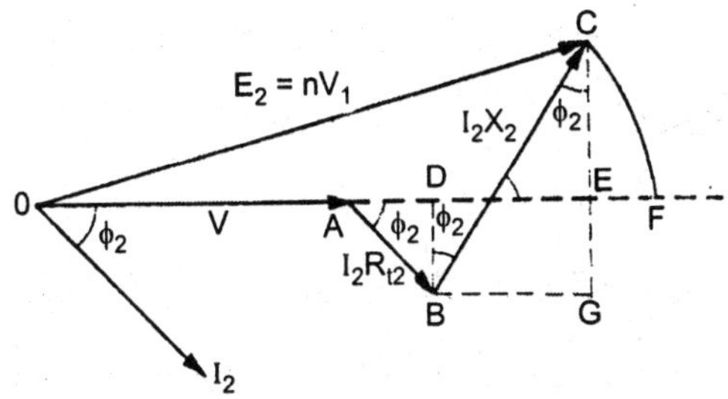

Fig. 5.48. Vector diagram of transformer of equivalent circuit of Fig. 5.47 at lagging p.f.

Referring to Fig. 5.48 with *O* as centre and radius equal to *OC* drawn, an arc cutting the line *OA* produced at point *F*. From *C*, a perpendicular *CE* is drawn on *OF* and also perpendicular *BD* is drawn on *OF*. Then another perpendicular is drawn from *E* on *BG* which is parallel to *DE*.

Now EF is so small that for approximate formula, this can be neglected and OE can be considered approx. equal to OF.

As $OC = E_2$

$\therefore$ $OE \simeq E_2$

$OE = OA + AD + DE$

$= OA + AD + BG$ as $DE = BG$

$OA = V_2$

In right angled triangle ADB

$$\frac{AD}{AB} = \cos \phi_2$$

$\therefore$ $AD = AB \cos \phi_2$ but $AB = I_2 R_{t2}$

$\therefore$ $AD = I_2 R_{t2} \cos \phi_2$

In right angled triangle BGC

$$\frac{BG}{BC} = \sin \phi_2$$

$\therefore$ $BG = BC \sin \phi_2$ but $BC = I_2 X_{t2}$

$\therefore$ $BG = I_2 X_{t2} \sin \phi_2$

Now $OE = OA + AD + BG$

$= V_2 + I_2 R_{t2} \cos \phi_2 + I_2 X_{t2} \sin \phi_2$

But $OE = E_2$

$\therefore$ $E_2 = V_2 + I_2 R_{t2} \cos \phi_2 + I_2 X_{t2} \sin \phi_2$

$\therefore$ $E_2 - V_2 = I_2 R_{t2} \cos \phi_2 + I_2 X_{t2} \sin \phi_2$

Percentage regulation

$$= \frac{E_2 - V_2}{E_2} \times 100$$

$$= \frac{(I_2 R_{t2} \cos \phi_2 + I_2 X_{t2} \sin \phi_2)}{E_2} \times 100$$

$$= \frac{I_2 R_{t2}}{E_2} \times 100 \cos \phi_2 + \frac{I_2 X_{t2} \sin \phi_2}{E_2} \times 100$$

but $\frac{I_2 R_{t2}}{E_2} \times 100$ = percentage resistance

and $\frac{I_2 X_{t2}}{E_2} \times 100$ = percentage reactance

∴ Approximate value of percentage regulation.

$$= \text{percentage resistance} \times \cos \phi_2 + \text{percentage reactance} \times \sin \phi_2$$

For finding the exact value of regulation ; portion *EF* in vector diagram of Fig. 5.48 should be neglected.

In right angled triangle *OEC*

$$CE^2 = OC^2 - OE^2 = (OC + OE)(OC - OE)$$

But *EF*, the portion already neglected

$$= OF - OE$$

$$= OC - OE$$

$$\therefore \quad EF = OC - OE = \frac{CE^2}{OC + OE}$$

but

$$CE = CG - EG = CG - BD$$

$$= I_2 X_{t2} \sin \phi_2 - I_2 R_{t2} \sin \phi_2$$

$$\therefore \quad EF = \frac{(I_2 X_{t2} \sin \phi_2 - I_2 R_{t2} \sin \phi_2)^2}{OC + OE}$$

If *OC* and *OE* are taken as 100% each.

Then $\quad OC + OE = 200$

$$\therefore \quad EF = \frac{(I_2 X_{t2} \sin \phi_2 - I_2 R_{t2} \sin \phi_2)^2}{200}$$

Adding this term to approximate expression, the percentage regulation becomes

$$= \left[\frac{(I_2 R_{t2} \cos \phi_2 + I_2 X_{t2} \sin \phi_2) + \dfrac{(I_2 X_{t2} \sin \phi_2 - I_2 R_{t2} \sin \phi_2)^2}{200}}{100} \right] \times 100$$

∴ Exact value of percentage regulation

$$= (I_2 R_{t2} \cos \phi_2 + I_2 X_{t2} \sin \phi_2) + \frac{(I_2 X_{t2} \sin \phi_2 - I_2 R_{t2} \sin \phi_2)^2}{200}$$

5.30. APPROXIMATE FORMULA FOR REGULATION OF LEADING POWER FACTOR

The vector diagram of transformer equivalent circuit of Fig. 5.47 at leading *p.f.* has been drawn in Fig. 5.49.

With *O* as centre and radius = $OC = E_2$, an arc is drawn, cutting the line *OA* at point *F*. There is very little difference between *OE* and *OF* and hence for practical purposes *OC* can be considered equal to *OE*, neglecting the portion *EF* which is quite small.

Now $\quad OE = OA + AD - ED$

$$= OA + AD - GB$$

Now $OA = V_2$

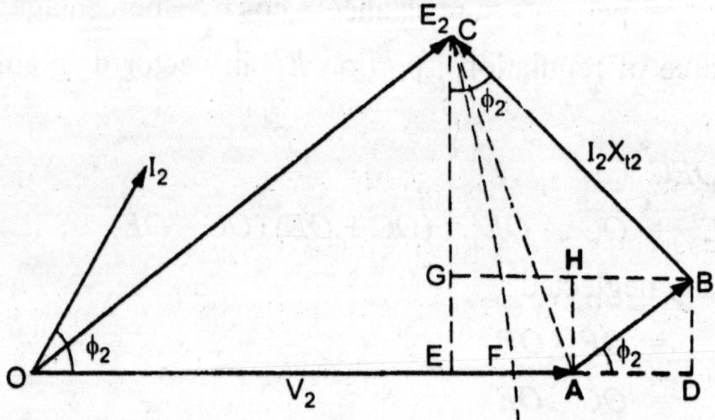

Fig. 5.49. Vector diagram of transformer equivalent circuit, of Fig. 5.47 at leading *p.f.*

In right angled triangle ADB,

$$\frac{AD}{AB} = \cos\phi_2$$

$$AD = AB\cos\phi_2$$

But $AB = I_2R_{t2}$

$$AD = I_2R_{t2}\cos\phi_2$$

Similarly in right angled triangle CGB

$$\frac{GB}{CB} = \sin\phi_2$$

or $GB = CB\sin\phi_2$

But $CB = I_2X_{t2}$

$\therefore$ $GB = I_2X_{t2}\sin\phi_2$

$\therefore$ $OE = V_2 + I_2R_{t2}\cos\phi_2 - I_2X_{t2}\sin\phi_2$

But $OE \simeq E_2$

$\therefore$ $E_2 = V_2 + I_2R_{t2}\cos\phi_1 - X_{t2}\sin\phi_2$

$\therefore$ $E_2 - V_2 = I_2R_{t2}\cos\phi_2 - I_2X_{t2}\sin\phi_2$

$\therefore$ Percentage regulation at leading *p.f.*

$$= \frac{E_2 - V_2}{E_2} \times 100$$

$$= \frac{I_2R_{t2}\cos\phi_2 - I_2X_{t2}\sin\phi_2 \times 100}{E_2}$$

Thus approximate formula for percentage regulation of transformer

$$= \frac{I_2 R_{t2} \cos \phi_2 \pm I_2 X_{t2} \sin \phi_2}{E_2} \times 100$$

Where plus sign stands for lagging p.f.

And –ive sign stands for leading p.f.

Example 5.19. Calculate the voltage regulation at 0.8 lagging p.f. for a transformer which has an equivalent resistance of 2% and an equivalent reactance of 4%.

Solution:

Percentage regulation at lagging p.f.

= %age equivalent resistance × cos ϕ

+%age equivalent reactance x sin ϕ

$= 2 \times 0.8 + 4 \times 0.6$

$= 1.6 + 2.4$

= 4% **Ans.**

Example 5.20. The open circuit test and short circuit test on a 5 *KVA*, 250/125 *V*, 50 Hz single phase transformer gave the following results:

O.C. Test (H.T. side) 250 *V*; 0.7 A ; 90 W

S. C. Test (L. T. side) 12 V ; 30 A ; 90 W

Calculate (*i*) the full load efficiency and (*ii*) the full load regulation at unity power factor.

(A.M.I.e. Section B, Summer 1977)

Solution.

(*i*) Rating of the transformer

= 5 kVA

Rated secondary terminal voltage

= 125 V

Full load current on secondary side

= Rated secondary current

$$I_2 = \frac{5 \times 1000}{125} = 40 \text{ A}.$$

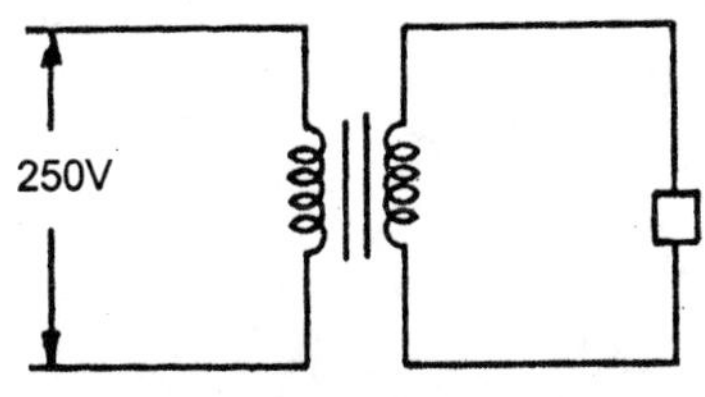

Fig. 5.50

Copper loss in transformer when secondary current is 30 A

= 90 W

Copper loss in transformer when secondary current is 40 A

$$= 90 \times \left(\frac{40}{30}\right)^2$$

$$= 160 \text{ W}$$

Iron loss in transformer

$$= 90 \text{ W}$$

Full load output of transformer at unity power factor

$$= 5 \times 1 = 5 \text{ kW}$$

Full load copper loss

$$= 160 \text{ W} = 0.16 \text{ kW}$$

Iron loss $= 90 \text{ W} = 0.09 \text{ kW}$

Input to the transformer

$$= \text{Output} + \text{Losses}$$

$$= 5 + 0.16 + 0.09$$

$$= 5.25 \text{ kW}$$

Full load efficiency of transformer

$$= \frac{Output}{Input} \times 100$$

$$= \frac{5}{5.25} \times 100$$

or $= 95.23\%$. **Ans.**

(*ii*) Equivalent resistance R_{t2} of transformer on secondary side from short circuit test is given by

$$I_2^2 R_{t2} = \text{Copper loss}$$

$$(30)^2 R_{t2} = 90$$

$$R_{t2} = \frac{90}{900} = 0.1 \text{ ohm.}$$

Percentage regulation of transformer is given by

$$\frac{I_2(R_{t2}\cos\phi_2 + X_{t2}\sin\phi_2)}{E_2} \times 100$$

where X_{t2} = Total reactance of transformer on secondary side.

Full load current, $I_2 = 40 \text{ A}$

$$\cos\phi_2 = 1$$

$$\sin\phi_2 = 0$$

$$E_2 = 125 \text{ V}$$

$\therefore$ Percentage regulation

$$= \frac{40(0.1 \times 1 + X_{t2} \times 0)}{125} \times 100$$

$$= \frac{40 \times 0.1}{125} \times 100$$

$$= \frac{400}{125} = \frac{16}{5} = 3.2\% \textbf{ Ans.}$$

5.31. CALCULATION OF EFFICIENCY FROM THE OPEN CIRCUIT AND SHORT CIRCUIT TESTS

The efficiency of transformer is given by

$$\eta = \frac{\textit{Output in watts}}{\textit{Input in watts}}$$

Since transformer is a machine which is quite efficient, hence it has very small amount of losses. Therefore, there is very little difference between input and output of transformer. It is very difficult to mark this difference of input and output from direct measurement. As such it is advisable to find out the efficiency by indirect method, *i.e.* from open circuit test and short circuit test.

Let P_0 be the input power in watts on open circuit test

$$= \text{Iron loss}$$

P_c be the input power in watts on short circuit test with full load current = Total copper loss on full load

Total loss on full load

$$= P_0 + P_c$$

Output of transformer on full load $V_2 I_2 \cos \phi_2$

$$= \text{Full load } VA \times p.f.$$

where I_2 = full load secondary current

Input to transformer on full load

Percentage η of transformer on full load

$$= V_2 I_2 \cos \phi_2 + P_0 + P_c$$

$$= (\text{Full load } VA \times p.f.) + P_0 + P_c$$

$$= \frac{V_2 I_2 \cos \phi_2}{V_2 I_2 \cos \phi_2 + P_0\ P_c} \times 100$$

$$= \frac{\textit{Full load VA} \times \cos \phi_2}{(\textit{Full load VA} \times \cos \phi_2) + P_0 + P_c} \times 100$$

If the load is n times the full load where n is lesser than 1,

then Output $= n \times$ Full load output

Copper losses at this load

$$= n^2 \times (\text{Full load copper loss})$$

$$= n^2 P_c$$

Iron loss at this load is still the same

$$= P_0$$

∴ Percentage efficiency at n times the full load

$$= \frac{n \times Full\ load\ V.A. \times p.f.}{(n \times Full\ load\ V.A. \times p.f.) + P_0 + n^2 P_c}$$

$$= \frac{n \times V_2 I_2 \cos \phi_2}{(n \times V_2 I_2 \cos \phi_2 + P_0 + n^2 P_c)} \times 100$$

5.32. CONDITION FOR MAX. EFFICIENCY

Full load output of transformer

$$= V_2 I_2 \cos \phi_2$$

Full load copper loss $= I_2^2 R_{t2} = I_1^2 R_{t1}$

Iron loss $= P_0$.

∴ Input to the transformer

$$= V_2 I_2 \cos \phi_2 + I_2^2 R_{t2} + P_0$$

η of the transformer

$$= \frac{V_1 I_2 \cos \phi_2}{V_2 I_2 \cos \phi_2 + I_2^2 R_{t2} + P_0}$$

$$y = \frac{1}{\eta\ of\ transformer} = \frac{V_2 I_2 \cos \phi_2 + I_2^2 R_{t2} + P_0}{V_2 I_2 \cos \phi_2}$$

$$= 1 + \frac{I_2 R_{t2}}{V_2 \cos \phi_2} + \frac{P_0}{V_2 I_2 \cos \phi_2}$$

If η is to be maximum, y must be minimum.

The condition for y to be minimum is that $\frac{dy}{dI_2} = 0$

$$\therefore \quad \frac{dy}{dI_2} = \frac{R_{t2}}{V_2 \cos \phi_2} - \frac{P_0}{V_2 I_2^2 \cos \phi_2} = 0$$

or
$$\frac{R_{t2}}{V_2 \cos \phi_2} = \frac{P_0}{V_2 I_2^2 \cos \phi_2}$$

or
$$P_0 = I_2^2 R_{t2}$$

Thus the condition for the efficiency of the transformer to the maximum is that iron loss should be equal to copper loss.

In some cases efficiency of transformer occurs at full load but in many other cases, this is not so. When this happens, the full load copper losses exceed the iron losses and maximum efficiency occurs at load lower than full load.

Let $\frac{Full\ load\ copper\ losses}{Iron\ losses} = \frac{P_c}{P_0} = K$

and let maximum efficiency occur at x per cent of full load. Then copper loss at max. efficiency.

$$= \left(\frac{x}{100}\right)^2 \times P_c = P_0$$

or $$x = \sqrt{\frac{P_0}{P_c}} \times 100 = \frac{100}{\sqrt{K}}$$

If the full load copper losses

$$= 2 \times \text{iron losses}$$

Then $$\frac{P_c}{P_0} = 2$$

Then $$x = \frac{100}{\sqrt{2}} = 70.7\%$$

Thus maximum efficiency occurs at 70.7% of full load.

5.33. VARIATION OF EFFICIENCY WITH POWER FACTOR

We know that transformer efficiency,

$$\eta = \frac{Output}{Input} = \frac{Input - Losses}{Input} = 1 - \frac{Losses}{Input} = 1 - \frac{Losses}{(V_2 I_2 \cos\phi + Losses)}$$

Let, $$\frac{Losses}{V_2 I_2} = \beta.$$

$\therefore$ $$\eta = 1 - \left(\frac{Losses/V_2 I_2}{\cos\phi + Losses/V_2 I_2}\right) \quad \text{or} \quad = 1 - \frac{\beta}{(\cos\phi + \beta)}$$

or $$\eta = 1 - \frac{(\beta/\cos\phi)}{(1 + \beta/\cos\phi)}$$

The variations of efficiency with power factor at different loadings on a transformer is as shown in Fig. 5.51.

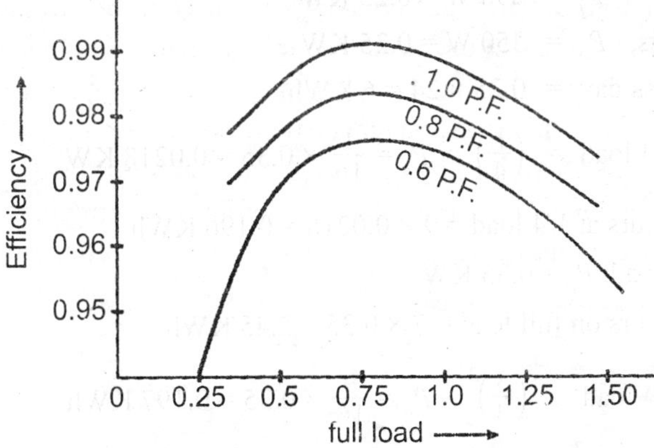

Fig. 5.51. Variation of efficiency with power factor at different loadings

5.34. ALL DAY EFFICIENCY OF TRANSFORMER

The performance of transformers which are used for supplying lighting load and for general net work, *i.e.* Distribution transformers etc. cannot be judged by the ordinary efficiency which is defined as the ratio of power output to power input in watts. Since these transformers have their primaries always energised for all the 24 hours irrespective of the fact whether its secondary is supplying any load or not, as such iron loss keeps on taking place for all the 24 hours whereas copper loss occurs when transformer is loaded. The performance of such a transformer is judged from its all day efficiency. All day efficiency is defined as the ratio of the total watt-hour output of transformer to the total watt-hour input taken over a working day.

$$\eta_{\text{all day}} = \frac{\textit{Output in kWh for 24 hr.}}{\textit{Input in kWh for 24 hr.}} \text{ or } \frac{\textit{output}}{\textit{output + losses}} \times 100$$

Since core loss in distribution transformers is to keep on taking place throughout the day, so such transformers are designed for low value of core loss.

Example 5.20.1: A 15 KVA, 2000/200 V transformer has an iron loss of 250 W and full-load copper loss 350 W. During the day it is loaded as follows:

Number of hours	*Load in KW*	*Power factor*
9	1/4 load	0.6
7	full load	0.8
6	3/4 load	1.0
2	no load	–

Calculate the all-day efficiency.

Solution: Rating of transformer = 15 KVA

Iron loss, P_i = 250 W = 0.25 KW

Full load copper loss, P_c = 350 W = 0.35 KW

Iron loss/day = 0.25 × 24 = 6 KWh

$$\text{Copper loss at 1/4 load} = \left(\frac{1}{4}\right)^2 \times P_c = \frac{1}{16} \times 0.35 = 0.0218 \text{ KW}$$

Copper loss for 9 hours at 1/4 load = 9 × 0.0218 = 0.196 KWh

Copper loss at full load, P_c = 0.35 KW

Copper loss for 7 hours on full load = 7 × 0.35 = 2.45 KWh

$$\text{Copper loss at 3/4 load} = \left(\frac{3}{4}\right)^2 \times P_c = \frac{9}{16} \times 0.35 = 0.197 \text{ KWh}$$

Copper loss for 6 hours at 3/4 load = 0.197 × 6 = 1.18 KWh

Copper loss/day = 0.196 + 2.45 + 1.18 = 3.826 KWh

Total loss/day = Iron loss/day + copper loss/day

= 6 + 3.826 = 9.826 KWh

Total output /day

$$= \frac{1}{4} \times 15 \times 0.6 \times 9 + 15 \times 0.8 \times 7 + \frac{3}{4} \times 15 \times 1.0 \times 6$$

$$= 20.25 + 84 + 67.5 = 171.75 \text{ KWh}$$

$$\text{All-day efficiency} = \frac{Output}{Output + losses} \times 100$$

$$= \frac{171.75}{171.75 + 9.826} \times 100 = 94.59\% \textbf{ Ans.}$$

5.34.1. Isolation Transformers

When a transformer is used only to isolate the electronic circuits (devices) from main electrical source without changing the voltage level, such transformers are called ***Isolation Transformers***.

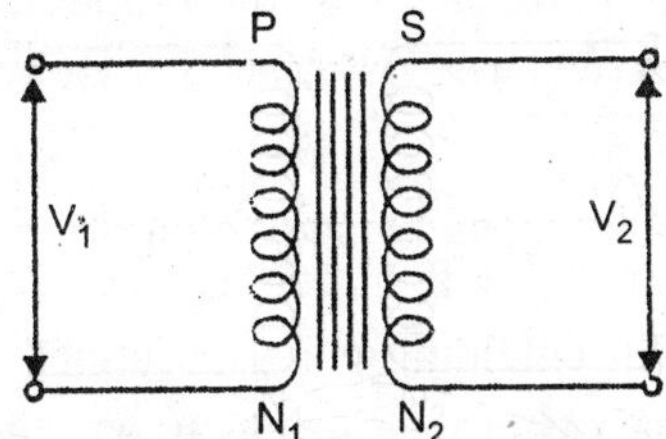

Fig. 5.51.1. Isolation Transformer

The isolation transformer is similar to ordinary transformer with the difference that it cannot step up or step down the voltage as desired. The level of the voltage is same in primary and secondary side *i.e.*, the output voltage is equal to input voltage.

The number of turns in such type of transformers are same on primary and secondary side. The size of conductor used for windings is same. This is also called one to one transformer *i.e.*, transformation ratio (K) is one.

The windings of such transformers are electrically insulated from each other. It is available in different ratings.

Uses:

1. It is used to isolate the electronic devices from actual connections of power lines.
2. It can be employed in electronic circuit to protect the sophisticated devices from unwanted surges.

Disadvantages. It cannot be used to raise or lower the voltage.

5.35. AUTO TRANSFORMER

A transformer in which part of the winding is common to both the primary and secondary circuits is known as an auto-transformer. The primary is electrically connected to the secondary, as well as magnetically coupled to it.

In Fig. 5.52 'AB' is the primary winding having N_1 turns and 'CB' is the secondary winding having N_2 turns. Here transformation ratio is

$$\frac{V_2}{V_1} = \frac{N_2}{N_1} = \frac{I_1}{I_2} \Rightarrow K,$$

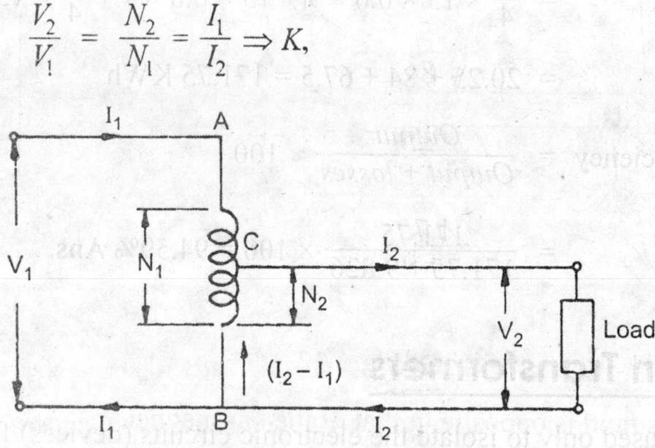

Fig. 5.52. Auto transformer

The amount of flow of Current in the section BC is the vector difference of I_1 & I_2 but as the two currents (practically) are in phase opposition the resultant is $I_2 - I_1$ (if $I_2 > I_1$).

An auto-transfomer is a transformer with only one winding wound on a laminated core. A part of this winding is common to both primary and secondary sides. On load, a part of the load current is obtained direct from the supply and remaining part is obtained by transformer action. In an ordinary transformer the primary and secondary windings are electrically insulated from each other but connected magnetically (see Fig. 5.52.1) whereas in an auto-transformer the primary and secondary windings are connected magnetically and electrically. Fig. 5.52.2 shows the primary winding AB from which a tapping at C is taken, such that CB acts as a secondary winding. The supply voltage is applied across AB and the load is connected across CB. The tapping may be fixed or variable.

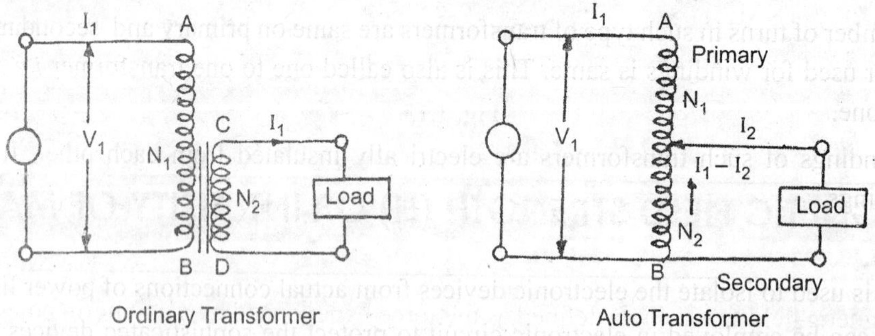

Fig. 5.52.1 **Fig. 5.52.2**

When $a.c.$ voltage V_1 is applied across AB, an alternating flux is set up in the core, it induces e.m.f. E_1 in the winding AB. The part of this e.m.f. is taken in the secondary circuit.

Let, V_1 = primary applied voltage

V_2 = secondary voltage across the load

I_1 = primary current

$$I_2 = \text{load current}$$

$$N_1 = \text{number of turns between A and B}$$

and $$N_2 = \text{number of turns between C and B.}$$

Neglecting no-load current, leakage reactance and losses,

$$V_1 = E_1 \text{ and } V_2 = E_2.$$

$$\therefore \text{ Transformation ratio, } K = \frac{V_2}{V_1} = \frac{N_2}{N_1} = \frac{I_1}{I_2}.$$

As the secondary ampere turns are opposite to primary- ampere turns so the current I_2 is in phase opposition to I_1. The secondary voltage is less than the primary, therefore, current I_2 is more than I_1. The resultant current flowing through section BC is $(I_2 - I_1)$

Now, ampere turns due to section BC = current × turns

$$= (I_2 - I_1) N_2$$

$$= \left(\frac{I_1}{K} - I_1\right) \times N_1 K$$

$$= I_1 N_1 (1 - K). \qquad ...(i)$$

Ampere turns due to section $AC = I_1 (N_1 - N_2)$

$$= I_1 N_1 \left(1 - \frac{N_2}{N_1}\right)$$

$$= I_1 N_1 (1 - K). \qquad ...(ii)$$

Equation (*i*) and (*ii*) show that the ampere turns due to section BC and AC balance each other which is the characteristic of transformer action.

Saving of copper: Volume, and hence weight of copper, is proportional to the length and area of X-section of the conductors. The length of conductor is proportional to number of turns and area of X-section is proportional to the current flowing through it. Hence the weight of copper is proportional to the product of current and number of turns.

Now, with reference to Fig. 5.52.2 weight of copper required in an auto-transformer,

$$Wa = \text{weight of } Cu \text{ in section } AC + \text{weight of } Cu \text{ in section } CB$$

$$\therefore \quad Wa \propto I_1(N_1 - N_2) + (I_2 - I_1)N_2$$

or $$Wa \propto I_1 N_1 + I_2 N_2 - 2 I_1 N_2.$$

If an ordinary two winding transformer is to perform the same duty, then with reference to Fig. 5.52.1

Total weight of copper required in the ordinary transformer,

$$W_0 = \text{weight of } Cu \text{ on its primary} + \text{weight of } Cu \text{ on its secondary}$$

$$\therefore \quad W_0 \propto I_1 N_1 + I_2 N_2.$$

Now, the ratio of weight of copper in auto-transformer to the weight of copper in an ordinary-transformer.

$$\frac{W_a}{W_0} = \frac{I_1 N_1 + I_2 N_2 - 2I_1 N_2}{I_1 N_1 + I_2 N_2}$$

$$= \frac{I_1 N_1 + I_2 N_2}{I_1 N_1 + I_2 N_2} - \frac{2I_1 N_2}{I_1 N_1 + I_2 N_2}$$

$$= 1 - \frac{2\, I_1 N_2 / I_1 N_1}{I_1 N_1 / I_1 N_1 + I_2 N_2 / I_1 N_1} = 1 - K$$

or $$W_a = (1 - K)\, W_0.$$

Saving of copper affected by using an auto-transformer

= Wt. of Cu required in an ordinary transformer – wt. of copper required in an auto-transformer

$$= W_0 - Wa = W_0 - (1 - K)\, W_0 = KW_0.$$

∴ Saving = K × Wt. of copper required for two winding transformer.

Hence, saving in copper increases as the transformation ratio approaches to unity, therefore, auto-transformers are used when K is nearly equal to unity.

Uses of auto-transformer: (*i*) It is used as an auto-transformer starter to give upto 50 to 60% of full voltage to the stator of a squirrel cage induction motor during starting.

(*ii*) It is used to give a small boost to a distribution cable to correct the voltage drop.

(*iii*) It is used as a regulating transformer (the tap point C is variable in this case).

Disadvantages: Though auto-transformers have less cost, better regulation and low losses as compared to the ordinary two winding transformer of same rating. But still they are not widely used due to one major disadvantage that the secondary winding is not insulated from the primary. If an auto transformer is used to supply low voltage from a high voltage and there is a break in the secondary winding, the full primary voltage comes across the secondary terminals which may be dangerous to the operator and equipment (load). Therefore, it is advisable not to use an auto-transformer for inter-connecting high voltage and low voltage system. The use is only limited to the places where slight variation of output voltage from the input voltage is required.

Example 5.20.2. The primary and secondary voltage of an auto transformer are 500 V and 400 V respectively. Show with the aid of diagram the current distribution in the windings when the secondary current is 100 A. Calculate the economy of copper in this particular case. (*P.S.B.* Sep., 1984)

Solution. Primary voltage, $V_1 = 500$ V

Secondary voltage, $V_2 = 400$ V

Secondary current, $I_2 = 100$A

Transformation ratio, $K = \frac{V_2}{V_1} = \frac{400}{500} = 0.8$

Using the relation, $\frac{I_1}{I_2} = K$

Primary current. $I_1 = KI_2 = 0.8 \times 100 = 80$ A **Ans.**

Current in section $BC = I_2 - I_1 = 100 - 80$

$= 20$ A **Ans.**

The current distribution in the winding is shown in Fig. 5.52.3.

Economy or saving of Copper = $KW_0 = 0.8\ W_0$

$\therefore$ Percentage saving = $0.8 \times 100 = 80\%$ **Ans.**

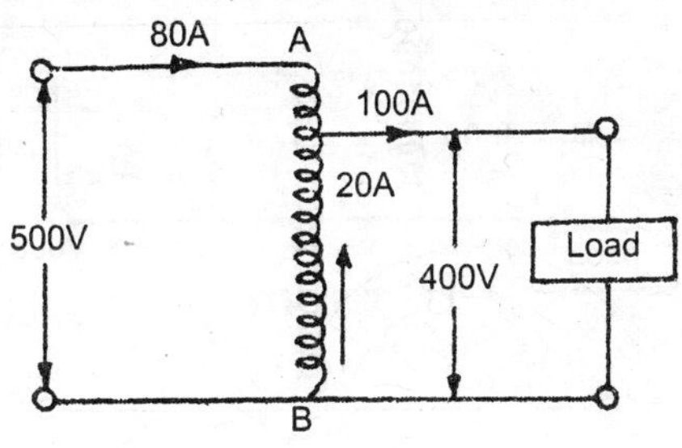

Fig. 5.52.3

Example 5.20.3: An auto-transformer is required to step up a voltage from 225 V to 250 V. The total number of turns is 2000. Find (*i*) the position of the tapping point, (*ii*) current in each winding when the output is 10 kVA and (*iii*) the economy in copper over the two winding transformer.

Solution:

Transformer output, = 10 kVA = 10×10^3 VA

Primary voltage, $V_1 = 225$ V

Secondary voltage, $V_2 = 250\ V$

Secondary turns $N_2 = 2000$

Transformation ratio, $K = \frac{V_2}{V_1} = \frac{N_2}{N_1}$

$$K = \frac{250}{225} = \frac{10}{9}$$

(i) $\therefore$ Primary turns, $N_1 = \frac{N_2}{K} = 2000 \times \frac{9}{10} = 1800$ **Ans.**

(*ii*) Primary current, $I_1 = \frac{10 \times 10^3}{225} = 44.44$ A **Ans.**

Secondary current, $I_2 = \frac{10 \times 10^3}{250} = 40$ A **Ans.**

$\therefore$ Current in common section $CB = I_1 - I_2$

$= 44.44 - 40 = 4.44$ A **Ans.**

The current distribution in the winding is shown in Fig. 5.52.4.

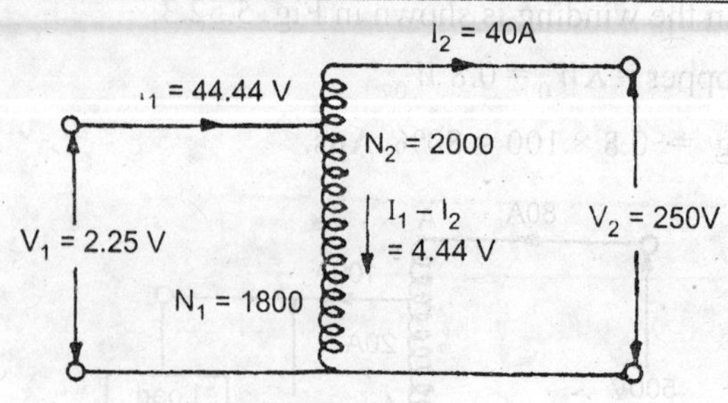

Fig. 5.52.4

(*iii*) Economy or saving in copper = KW_0.

As the economy cannot be more than 100%, hence for economy consideration.

$$K = \frac{\textit{low voltage}}{\textit{high voltage}} = \frac{225}{250} = 0.9$$

$\therefore$ Saving of copper $= 0.9\ W_0$

Percentage saving $= 0.9 \times 100 = 90\%$ **Ans.**

5.35.1. Comparison Between Auto-Transformer and Two-Winding Transformer

1. **VA ratings.** In Fig. 5.52 two-winding transformer is connected as an auto-transformer. Let us compare the volt-ampere ratings of two transformers.

Voltage rating as two winding transformer,

$$= (V_1 - V_2)I_1 = (I_2 - I_1)V_1$$

When used as an auto-transformer voltage rating as an auto transformer

$$= V_1 I_1 = V_2 I_2$$

V-A rating as two winding transformer,

= V-A rating of an auto-transformer.

$$= \frac{V_1 I_1}{(V_1 - V_2)I_1} = \frac{V_2 I_2}{V_2(I_2 - I_1)} = \frac{1}{1-K}$$

From the equation obtained it is obvious that two-winding transformer of a given volt-ampere rating when connected as an auto-transformer can handle high volt-amperes.

2. **Conductor material requirements.** Volume and hence weight of copper, is proportional to the length and area of cross-section of the conductors. But length of conductor is proportional to the product of the current and number of turns *i.e.*

Weight of *cu* $\propto$ No. of turns $\times$ current with reference to Fig 5.52.

Weight of copper in section *AC* is $\propto (N_1 - N_2)\ I_1$

Weight of copper in section *BC* is $\propto N_2(I_2 - I_1)$

$\therefore$ Total weight of copper in auto-transformer is proportional to $(N_1 - N_2)I_1 + N_2(I_2 - I_1)$

If a two-winding transformer were to perform the same duty then

Weight of copper on its primary $\propto N_1 I_1$

Weight of copper on its secondary $\propto N_2 I_2$

$\therefore$ Total weight of copper $\propto N_1 I_1 + N_2 I_2$

$$= \frac{\textit{Weight of copper in auto transformer}}{\textit{Weight of copper in ordinary transformer}}$$

$$\frac{W_a}{W_0} = \frac{(N_1 - N_2)I_1 + N_2(I_2 - I_1)}{N_1 I_1 + N_2 I_2}$$

$$\frac{W_a}{W_0} = \frac{N_1 I_1 - N_2 I_1 + N_2 I_2 - N_2 I_1}{N_1 I_1 + N_2 I_2}$$

$$\frac{W_a}{W_0} = \frac{N_1 I_1 + N_2 I_2}{N_1 I_1 + N_2 I_2} - \frac{2N_2 I_1}{N_1 I_1 + N_2 I_2}$$

(Dividing Denominator and Numerator by $N_1 I_1$)

$$\frac{W_a}{W_0} = 1 - \frac{2\frac{N_2}{N_1}}{1 + \frac{N_2}{N_1} \times \frac{I_2}{I_1}} = 1 - \frac{2K}{1 + \left(K \times \frac{1}{K}\right)}$$

$$\frac{W_a}{W_0} = 1 - \frac{2k}{1+1} = -\frac{2K}{2} = 1 - K \qquad \left(\because \frac{N_2}{N_1} = K; \frac{I_2}{I_1} = \frac{1}{K}\right)$$

$\therefore$ Weight of Cu in auto transformer,

$$W_a = (1 - K)W_0$$

$$= K \times (wt.\text{ of } Cu \text{ in ordinary transformer})$$

$\therefore$ Saving in $Cu = W_0 - W_a = W_0 - (1 - \text{K})\, W_0 = KW_0$

$= K \times$ ($Wt.$ of Cu in ordinary transformer W_0)

The saving in copper with an auto-transformer goes on increasing as the value of 'K' increases. The maximum saving is more effective when $K = 1$.

3. **Core size.** With the reduction in conductor material core length is reduced. Thus for the same core area, the size and weight of the core of the auto-transformer is reduced. Accordingly the si̇ze and weight of the auto-transformer is reduced.

   The two winding transformer when used as auto-transformer is less costly of the same

5. **Higher efficiency.** Due to reduction in conductor and core materials, the ohmic losses in conductor and the core loss are lowered. Thus an auto-transformer has lower losses and, therefore, higher efficiency as compared to two-winding transformer of the same output.

6. **Better Regulation.** An auto-transformer has lower value of leakage impedance and has better regulation than a two winding transformer of the same volt-amperes output.

5.35.2. Step-Down Auto-Transformer

Fig. 5.52.5 shows a step down auto transformer. The output voltage V_2 is less than input voltage V_1 and the output current I_2 is more than input current I_1. If ideal conditions are assumed then

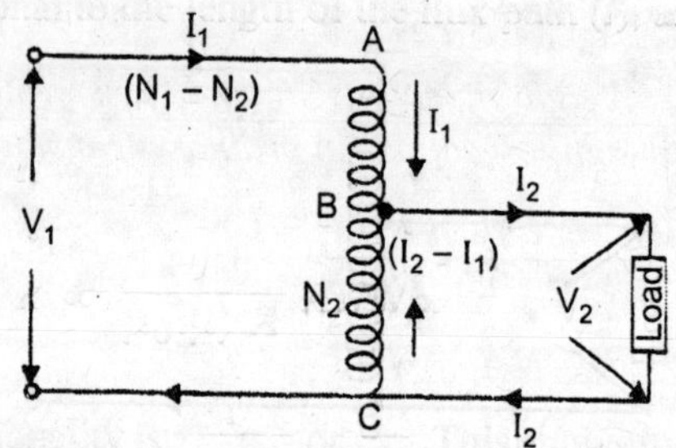

Fig. 5.52.5. Step down auto-transformer

$$\frac{V_1}{V_2} = \frac{N_1}{N_2} = \frac{I_2}{I_1} = K$$

The current distribution is shown in Fig. 5.52.4. The volt-ampere delivered to the load is V_2I_2 and written as

$$V_2I_2 = V_2I_1 + V_2(I_2 - I_1)$$

where V_2I_1 = Volt-amperes transferred conductively to the load through winding portion AB and $V_2(I_2 - I_1)$ = volt amperes transferred inductively to the load through winding portion BC. It also represents the rating of 2-winding transformer.

$$\frac{\text{Output } VA \text{ of auto -- transformer}}{\text{Output } VA \text{ of equivalent 2--winding transformer}}$$

$$\frac{V_2I_2}{V_2(I_2 - I_1)} = \frac{K}{K-1}$$

Thus a 2-winding transformer when connected as an auto-transformer will have a volt-ampere rating $\frac{K}{K-1}$ times its rating as 2-winding transformer.

5.35.3. Step-Up Auto-Transformer

Step up auto-transformer is shown in Fig. 5.52.6. The number of turns in portion AB is $(N_1 - N_2)$ and the number of turns in portion BC is N_2.

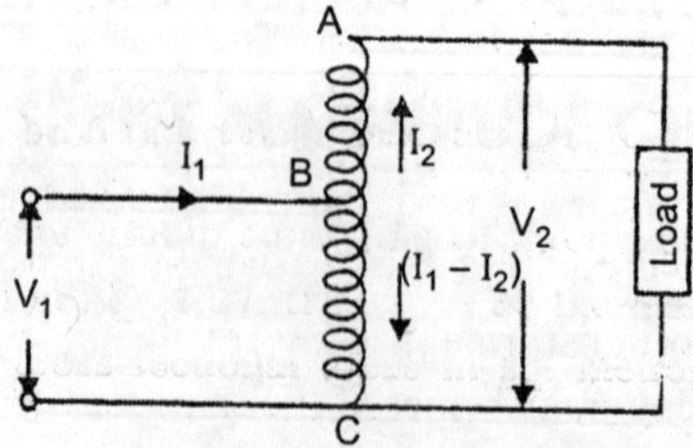

Fig. 5.52.6. Step up auto-transformer

V_2 is more than V_1 and I_1 is greater than I_2.

ideal conditions

$$\frac{V_2}{V_1} = \frac{N_2}{N_1} = \frac{I_1}{I_2}$$

Volt-ampere input, $V_1 I_1 = V_1 I_2 + V_1(I_1 - I_2)$

$V_1 I_2$ = Volt-ampere transferred conductively from input to the load $V_1(I_1 - I_2)$ = Volt-ampere transferred inductively from input to load

$$\therefore \frac{\textit{Output VA of auto transformer}}{\textit{Volt - ampere transferred inductively}} = \frac{V_1 I_1}{V_1(I_1 - I_2)} = \frac{K}{K-1}$$

Hence power rating in this case is also the same as in the case of step down transformer.

Example 5.20.4: A 10 KVA, 2400/240V two winding transformer is connected as an auto-transformer as shown in Fig. 5.52.7 and excited by 2500V source. The transformer is loaded so that the rated currents of the winding are not exceeded. Determine:

(*a*) Currents in different sections of the auto-transformer.

(*b*) KVA output.

(*c*) Power transferred inductively

(*d*) Power transferred conductively from input to output

(*e*) Saving in copper as compared to a 2640/2400 V two-winding transformer for the same output.

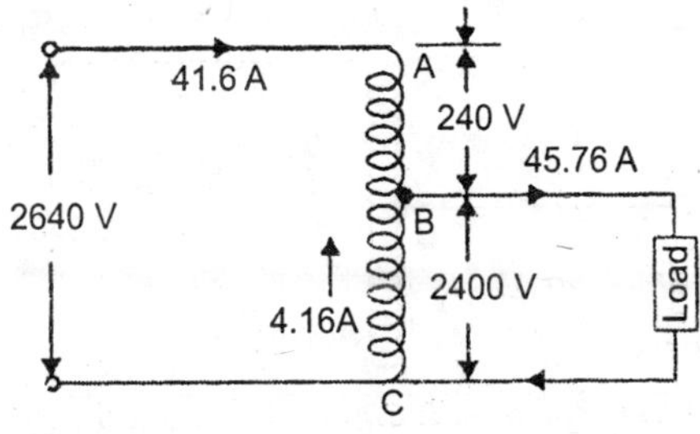

Fig. 5.52.7

Solution: Current rating of 240 V winding $= \frac{10,000}{240} = 41.6$ A

Current rating of 2400 *V* winding $= \frac{10000}{2400} = 4.16$ A

(*a*) The current distribution is shown in Fig. 3.49. The load current is 41.6 + 4.16 = 45.76 A at 2400 V.

(*b*) KVA rating $= \frac{2400 \times 45.76}{1000} = 109.82$ KVA

(*c*) Power transferred inductively = 2400 × 4.16 = 9984 *VA* **Ans.**

(*d*) Power transferred conductivity = 2400 × 41.6 = 99840 *VA* **Ans.**

(e) $K = \frac{N_1}{N_2} = \frac{2640}{2400} = 1.1$

$$\text{Saving in copper} = \frac{1}{K} = \frac{1}{1.1} = 0.909 \text{ or } 90.9\% \text{ Ans.}$$

Example 5.20.5: A 25 KVA, 2200/220 V, 2 winding transformer is to be used as an auto-transformer with source voltage of 2200 V. At full load of 0.8 power factor. Calculate:

(a) Power output,

(b) Power transformed and power conducted. If the efficiency of the two-winding transformer at power factor 0.85 is 90%, find the efficiency of the auto-transformer.

Solution: Current rating of 2200 V winding = $\frac{25 \times 1000}{2200} = 11.36$ A

Current rating of 220 V winding = $\frac{25 \times 1000}{220} = 113.63$ A

Output voltage = 2200 + 220 = 2420 V

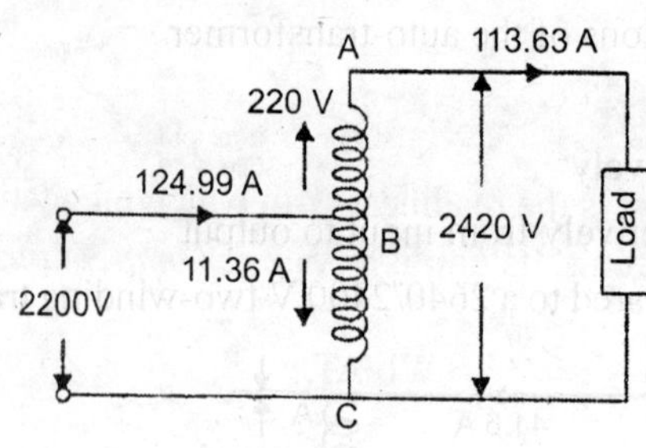

Fig. 5.52.8

Input line current = 113.63 + 1 1.36 = 124.99 A

Output current of auto transformer I_L = 113.63 A

KVA rating of auto transformer = $\frac{2420 \times 113.63}{1000} = 274.98$ KVA

Power output at full load and 0.8 power factor = KVA × cos ϕ

= 274.98 × 0.8 = 219.98 KW

$$\text{KVA transformed} = \frac{V_{AB}\, I_{AB}}{1000} = \frac{220 \times 113.63}{1000} = 24.99 \text{ KVA}$$

$$\text{Also KVA transformed} = \frac{V_{BC} \times I_{BC}}{1000} = \frac{2200 \times 11.36}{1000} = 24.99 \text{ KVA}$$

Power transformed = KVA × cos ϕ = 24.99 × 0.8 = 19.99 KW

$$\text{KVA conducted} = \frac{2200 \times 113.63}{1000} = 249.39 \text{ KVA}$$

Power conducted = 249.39 × 0.8 = 199.5 KW

Calculation of efficiency

$$\eta = \frac{Output}{Output + Losses}$$

$$\therefore \quad \text{Losses} = \left(\frac{1}{\eta} - 1\right) \times \text{Output}$$

Losses in a 2-winding transformer

$$= \left(\frac{1}{0.9} - 1\right) \times 25000 \times 0.85 = 2361.11 \text{ W}$$

Since auto-transformer operates at rated voltage and rated currents, the loss in auto-transformer = losses in two-winding transformer = 2361.11 W.

Efficiency of auto-transformer

$$\%\eta = \frac{Output}{Output + Losses}$$

$$= \frac{274.98 \times 1000 \times 0.85}{274.98 \times 1000 \times 0.85 + 2361.11} \times 100$$

$$= \frac{233733}{233733 + 2361.11} \times 100 = \frac{233733}{236094.11} \times 100$$

$$= 98.99 \textbf{ Ans.}$$

5.36. APPLICATION OF AN AUTO TRANSFORMER

The auto-transformer has the following applications:

1. These can be used to obtain partial line voltages for starting induction and synchronous motors with squirrel cage windings.
2. To minimise the voltage drop in distribution lines, these can be used in giving small boost to the distribution cables.
3. These can be used as regulating transformers.
4. These can be used as furnace transformers for getting a convenient supply to suit the winding of the furnace.
5. The continuously variable auto-transformers are widely used in electrical-testing laboratories.

5.37. INSTRUMENT TRANSFORMERS

The instrument transformers are intended to supply low values of voltage or current to measuring instruments. It is not practicable to connect instruments directly to the lines in high voltage circuits. It may become dangerous to the operator if measuring instruments are connected directly to the *H.V.* system. By means of instrument transformers like current transformer and potential transformer, the instruments can be completely insulated from the high voltage system and hence measure the current & voltage of high voltage circuits.

The working principle of the instrument transformer is same as that of the power transformer. These can be classified as follows:

1. Potential Transformer (**P.T.**) 2. Current Transformer (**C.T.**)

1. ***Potential transformer (P.T.):*** The potential transformer is similar to the power transformer except that the power rating of the potential transformer is low. A potential transformer is a step down transformer, the primary of which having many number of turns as compared to its secondary winding. The primary winding is connected across the high voltage system whose voltage is to be measured.

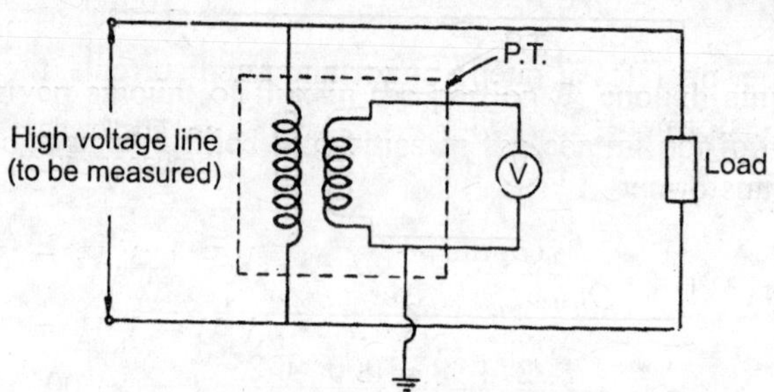

Fig. 5.53. Connections of potential transformer

These transformers are made with high quality iron core operating at very low flux densities so that the magnetising current may be very small. The secondary winding of these transformers is usually rated for 110 V irrespective of the primary voltage rating. The primary winding of the transformer is wound for the voltage which is to be measured. Let the voltage to be measured is 220 kV. The turn ratio of the transformer will be 2,20,000/110 $\Rightarrow$ 2000: 1. The connections of the potential transformer are shown in Fig. 5.53. It may be noted that the secondary is grounded, so that if the insulation breaks down, the high voltage does not endanger the operator, who may be reading the meter.

The potential transformers are extremely accurate-ratio step down transformers. The primary winding having large number of turns is always connected across the supply system and the secondary winding having few number of turns is connected to the standard low range voltmeter as shown in Fig. 5.5.1. The deflection of the low range voltmeter when divided by the transformation ratio ($K = N_2/N_1$), gives the true voltage of the supply system.

Let the voltage to be measured of a system is 11 kV. It would be very risky to use the voltmeter directly on this voltage and moreover the voltmeter size would be bulky and uneconomical. Thus, a potential transformer having secondary to primary turn ratio 1: 100 is used in conjunction with the low range voltmeter which steps down the voltage from 11 kV to 110 V as shown in Fig. 5.53.1.

Such transformers are similar to that of ordinary two winding transformers. Since the secondary windings of these transformers are required to operate instruments or relays, their ratings are usually very small (– 40 to 100 W). For safety purposes, the following two points should be noted:

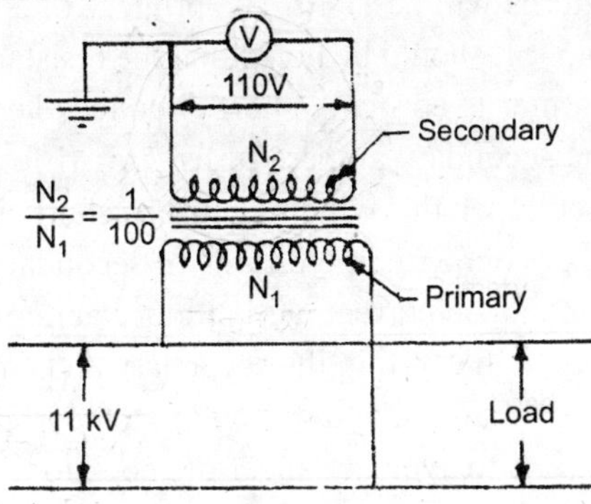

Fig. 5.53.1

(*i*) The secondary should be completely insulated from the high voltage primary.

(*ii*) The secondary should be earthed to protect the operator from high voltage hazard when he by chance comes in contact with the live wire. These transformers are made shell type because this condition develops a higher degree of accuracy. For medium voltages *i.e.* upto 6.6. *kV* the potential transformers are usually of dry type, between 6.6 to 11 *kV*, they may be either dry type or oil immersed, but for voltages more than 11 *kV* they are always oil immersed type.

2. *Current transformers (C.T):* A high magnitude alternating current can be easily measured by a combination of a current transformer and a low range ammeter.

The primary winding of a current transformer consists of a few turns and is connected in series with the line whose current is to be measured. The secondary has comparatively more number of turns. A low range ammeter generally of rating 0.5 A is connected in the secondary circuit as shown in Fig. 5.54.

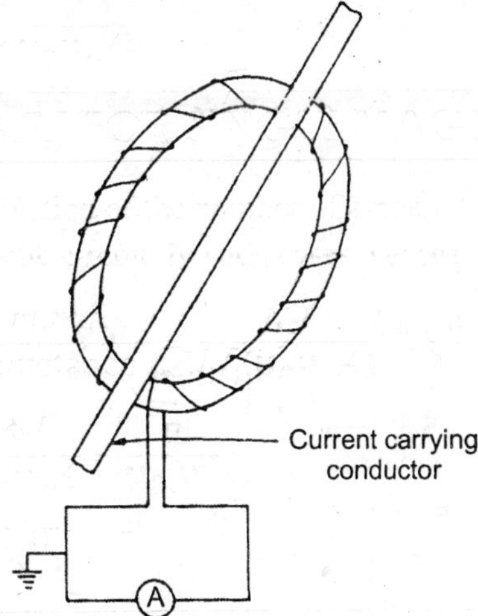

Fig. 5.54. Connections of current transformer

The current transformer ratio is not equal to the ratio of secondary to primary turns, mainly due to the effect of the magnetising current. The secondary of all the current transformers are rated at 5 A irrespective of the primary current ratings. A 200 Amp. current transformer has a ratio of 40: 1. The ratio of primary and secondary turns will be 1: 40. The primary of a current transformer may be of the form of a bar as shown in Fig. 5.54. It should be noted that the resistance if the ammeter is very low, the secondary of the current transformer is normally short circuited. Therefore the primary ampere-turns, I_1N_1 are counter balanced by the secondary ampere-turns I_2N_2. If for any reason, the ammeter is to be removed from the secondary circuit then this winding must be short circuited by fairly thick wire. If this is not done then due to absence of counter ampere-turns of secondary the unopposed primary ampere-turns or m.m.f. which depends upon load current, will produce abnormally high value of flux. This high value of flux induces dangerously high e.m.f. in the secondary and enormous core loss producing lot of heat. This may cause accident to human life and damage to the current transformer. The usual practice to earth the secondary side of C.T. is to avoid a danger of shock to the operator if the secondary side is accidentally open-circuited.

The current transformers are the step up transformers. The primary winding having one or two turns of thick wire is connected in series with the line whose current is to be measured as shown in Fig. 5.54.1 The secondary winding having large number of turns of fine wire is connected across the ammeter (usually of 5A range).

Let the current to be measured in a system is 200 A. The size of an ammeter to measure this current directly would be very bulky and uneconomical. Thus a current transformer (C.T.) having secondary to primary turn ratio of 40: 1 is used in conjunction with the low range ammeter which basically steps down the current from 200 A to 5 A as shown in Fig. 5.54.1

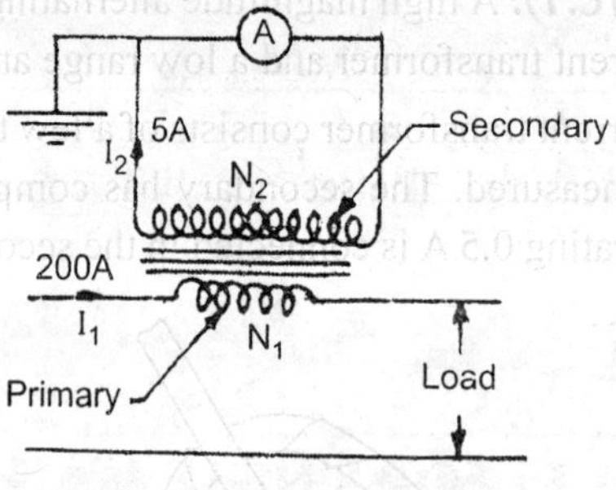

Fig. 5.54.1

It should be noted that the resistance of the ammeter is very low, the secondary of current transformer is normally short circuited. Therefore, the primary ampere turns I_1 N_1 are counter balanced by the secondary ampere turns I_2 N_2. If for any reason the ammeter is to be removed from the secondary circuit, then this winding must be short circuited by fairly thick wire. If this is not done then due to absence of counter ampere turns of secondary (I_2 N_2) the unopposed primary ampere turns or m.m.f. I_1 N_1, which depends upon load current I_1, will produce abnormally high value of flux. This high value of flux induces dangerously high e.m.f. in the secondary and enormous core loss producing lot of heat. This may cause accident to human life and damage to the current transformer. The usual practice is to earth the secondary side of the C.T. to avoid a danger of shock to the operator if the secondary side is accidentally open-circuited and he (the operator) comes in contact with the live wire.

The practical design of current transformers are clamp on or clip on type and bar type which are shown in Figs. 5.54.2 and 5.54.3 respectively.

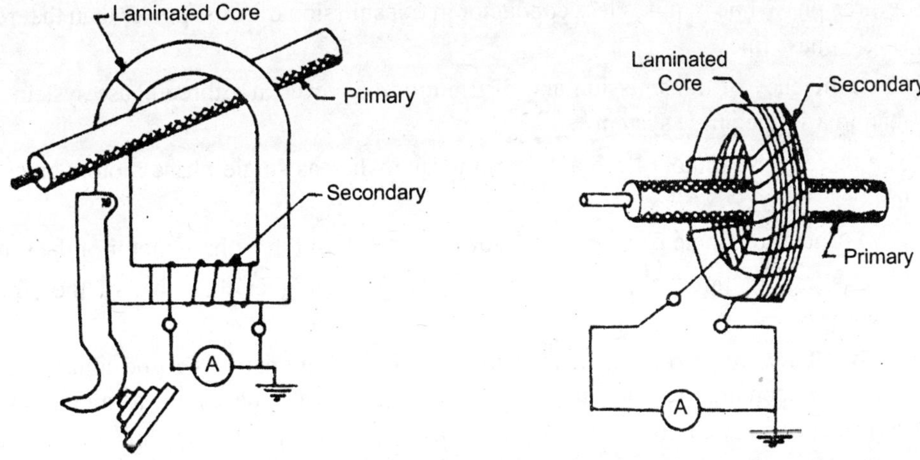

Fig. 5.54.2. Clip on type C.T. **Fig. 5.54.3.** Bar type C.T.

For measurement of power or energy in a high voltage power systems both P.T. and C.T. are used. P.T. is used to step down the system voltage and C.T. is used to step down the system current upto the required value. The potential coil (P.C.) of the wattmeter or the energy meter is connected across the secondary of P.T. and current coil (C.C.) of the wattmeter or energy meter is connected across the secondary of C.T. as shown in Fig. 5.54.4

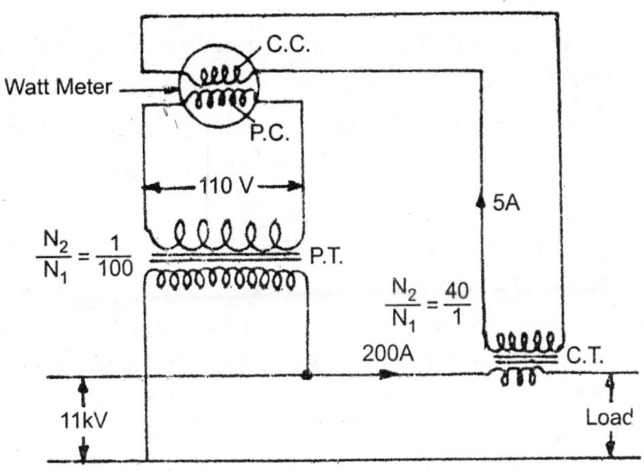

Fig. 5.54.4

The wattmeter or energy meter is calibrated so that it gives full scale deflection for the rated power or energy in the main circuit.

5.38. INTRODUCTION TO THREE PHASE SYSTEM

Nearly all alternating current electrical energy is generated by three phase a.c. generators or alternators. In this system, each voltage source consists of a group of voltages having relative magnitudes and phase angles. This three phase system is also used to transmit and distribute the electrical energy. The several advantages of a three-phase system over a single phase system are:

1. A three phase line requires less conductor in transmission of some power than that required in single phase line.
2. The efficiency of transmission and distribution of power in a three phase system are better than in a single phase system.
3. The three phase motors have a uniform torque whereas single phase motors have pulsating torque.
4. Power factor of single phase motor is lower than that of three phase motor of the same rating.
5. kVA ratings of three phase electrical machines are higher than that of the single phase machines.

In this way alternating current generated by three phase alternator is to be transmitted at high voltages due to the economic reasons and at the receiving end it is necessary to transform this high voltage electrical energy to required low voltage for distribution purposes. In a three phase transformer, the three phase electrical energy can be transformed from one three phase circuit to another three phase circuit by changing its voltage and current levels, but not changing its power and supply frequency.

Voltage transformation may be carried out by using three single phase transformers in three phase system by making their connections in Star and Delta as per the requirements, but now a days three phase transformers are increasingly being adopted for transformation of voltages to step up or step down purposes due to the following reasons.

1. For the same kVA rating, the cost of one three phase transformer is less than the cost of three single phase transformers.
2. A three phase transformer weighs less and occupies less space than that of the three single phase transformers.

So from the above discussion we can conclude that the three phase transformers are mostly preferred and used everywhere in transmission and distribution of three phase *ac* electrical energy.

5.38.1. Energy Transformers

The transformer used in the power system for transfer of power or energy from one circuit to the other are called energy transformers. The rating of a transformer includes voltage, frequency and kVA. The kVA rating is the kVA output that a transformer can deliver at the rated voltage and frequency under general service conditions without exceeding the standard limit of temperature rise (usually 45° to 60°). The energy transformer has the following important parts:

1. **Magnetic circuit.** The magnetic circuit comprises of transformer core. The transformer core may be core type or shell type in construction (as explained in previous article). The energy transformers used in the power system are mostly three-phase transformers. In a core type 3-phase transformer core has three limbs of equal area of cross section as shown in Fig. 5.54.5.
2. **Electrical circuit.** In three-phase transformers there are three primary (H.V.) windings and three secondary (L.V.) windings. Whole of the L. V. winding is wound over one limb next to the core, then whole of the H.V. winding is wound over the L. V. winding as shown in Fig. 5.54.5. In between the L.V. winding and H.V. winding and between core and L.V. winding insulation is provided.

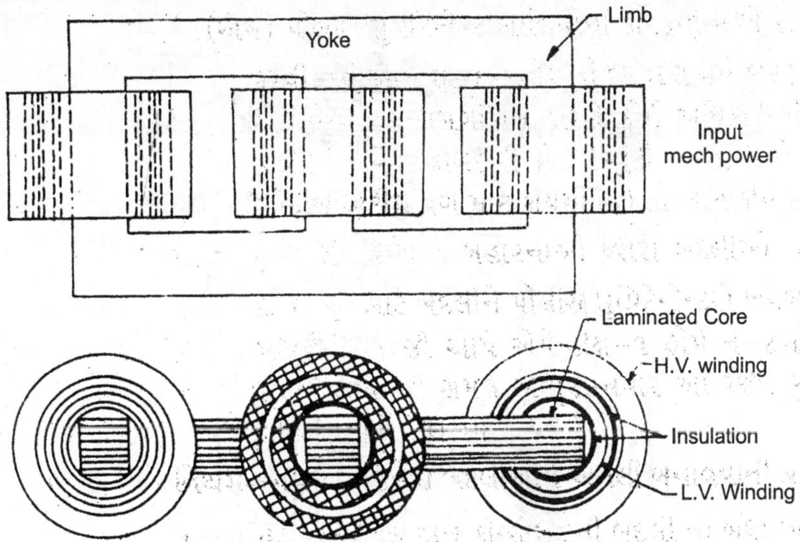

Fig. 5.54.5. Core type 3-phase transformer

3. **Transformer oil.** Transformer oil is a mineral oil obtained by fractional distillation of crude petroleum. The oil is used only in the oil cooled transformer. The oil not only carries the heat produced due to losses in the transformer, by convection from the windings and core to the transformer tank, but also has even more important function of insulation.

   When transformer delivers power, heat is produced due to the iron and the copper losses in the transformer. This heat must be dissipated effectively otherwise the temperature of the winding will increase. The rise in temperature further increases the losses. Thus, the efficiency of the transformer will decrease. As there is no rotating part in the transformer it is difficult to cool down the transformer as compared to rotating machines . Various methods are adopted to cool down the transformers of different rating. The common methods are air natural cooling, oil immersed natural cooling, oil immersed forced oil circulation natural cooling, oil immersed forced oil circulation with air blast cooling, oil immersed forced oil circulation with water cooling etc.

   Generally for cooling of distribution transformers oil immersed natural cooling method is adopted. Cooling tubes or small cooling radiators are used with the main tanks, as shown in Fig. 5.54.6, to increase the surface area for the dissipation of heat.

4. **The Tank Cover.** A number of parts are arranged on the tank cover of which most important are:

   (*i*) **Bushings.** The internal windings of the transformer are connected to the lines through copper rods or bars which are insulated from the tank cover, these are known as bushings. Upto 33 kV ordinary porcelain bushings can be used. Above this voltage oil filled bushings or condenser bushings are required.

   (*ii*) **Oil conservator.** Oil conservator is also known as an oil expansion chamber. It is a small cylindrical air tight and oil tight vessel. The oil conservator is connected with a tube to the main transformer tank at the tank cover. This tank is partially filled with oil. The expansion and contraction of oil, changes the oil level in the conservator.

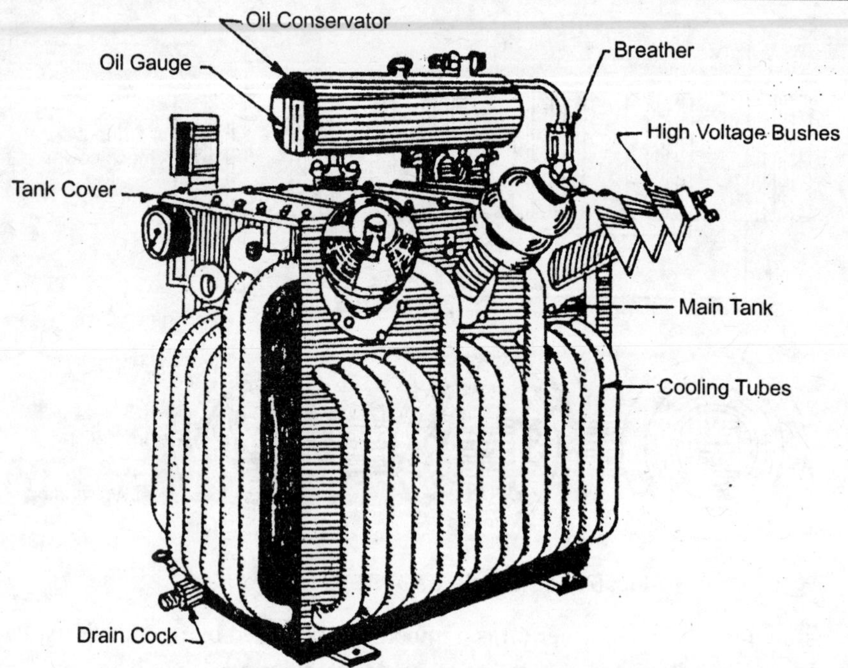

Fig. 5.54.6. Pictorial view of a 100 kVA, 11 kV/400 V oil immersed natural cooled distribution transformer

(*iii*) **Breather.** The transformer oil should not be allowed to come in contact with atmospheric air, since a small amount of moisture causes a great decrease in the dielectric strength of transformer oil. All the tank fittings are made air tight. When oil level in the oil conservator changes, air moves in and out of the conservator. This action is known as **breathing**.

The breathed-in air is made to pass through an apparatus called breather to abstract the moisture. Breather contains Silicagel or some other drying agent such as calcium chloride. This ensures that only dry air enters the transformer.

(*iv*) **Buchholz Relay.** This is installed in between the main tank and the oil conservator. It is a gas relay which gives warning of any fault developing inside the transformer, and if the fault is dangerous the relay disconnects the transformer circuit. This relay is installed in the transformer having capacity more than 750 kVA.

All the important parts of a 100 kVA, 11 kV/400 *V* oil immersed natural cooled distribution transformer are shown in Fig. 5.54.6.

Shell type transformers: In shell type transformers, the core construction is such that the windings are embedded in the core instead of surrounding the iron as shown in fig. 5.54.7. The area of cross section of the central limbs is double to that of the side limbs and horizontal members.

The low voltage and high voltage windings of the three-phases are wound on the central limbs. These windings are placed vertically in the three portions as shown in Fig. 5.54.7. The low voltage (LV) winding is always placed nearer to the core and high voltage (HV) winding is placed over the low voltage winding. To obtain uniform distribution of flux in the core, usually second winding placed on the central limb is wound in the reverse direction as shown in Fig. 5.54.8.

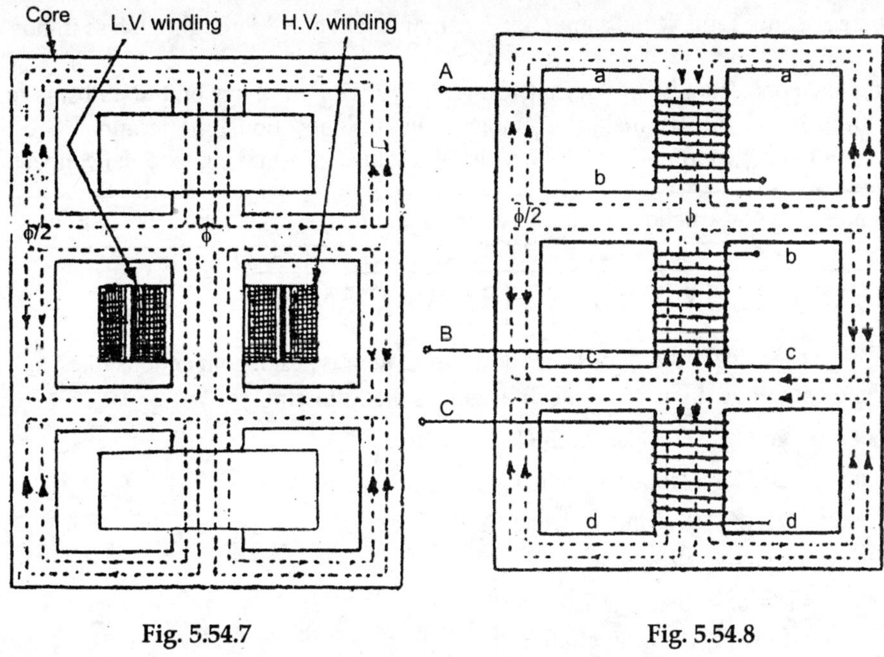

Fig. 5.54.7 Fig. 5.54.8

5.39. CONSTRUCTION OF THREE PHASE TRANSFORMERS

The construction of a 3 ϕ transformer is shown in Fig. 5.55.

Fig. 5.55. Arrangement of placing high voltage and low voltage coils on the core limbs of a three phase transformer

As shown in Fig. 5.55 it is clear that both windings are placed on the similar limbs. The windings are the same as that of the windings of single phase transformers. Both low voltage windings and high voltage windings are placed on each limb. The six ends of low voltage winding and similar six ends of high voltage winding are brought out and connections are made star or delta as per the requirements. The low voltage windings are placed nearer the core limb because it is easier to insulate the low voltage winding from the core than the high voltage winding. The high voltage coils are wound in one direction and the low voltage coils are wound in the opposite direction from the direction of the high voltage coils.

The flux in the common core area between adjacent phases is thus equal to the difference of two of the phase fluxes. Since the fluxes are 120° apart in time. This mutual flux is equal to $\sqrt{3} \times (\frac{1}{2}\,\phi)$ or 0.866 of the flux in the central limb. If the same flux density is maintained throughout, less iron is required in the common limb.

The complete core structure of the transformer along with windings on the limbs, is placed in the tank full of transformer oil. By making suitable required connections, the terminals are brought out distinguishly high voltage terminals and low voltage terminals for making external connections.

Note: Remaining all constructional detail has been explained earlier in the articles from 5.7 to 5.10.

5.40. TYPES OF THREE PHASE TRANSFORMERS

Basically, three phase transformer types are known from their types of connections like Star-Star, Delta-Delta etc. The most frequently used connections are as the following:

(*i*) Primary Star (*Y*)–Secondary Star (*Y*)

(*ii*) Primary Star (*Y*)–Secondary Delta (Δ)

(*iii*) Primary Delta (Δ)–Secondary Delta (Δ)

(*iv*) Primary Delta (Δ)–Secondary Star (*Y*)

The above connections are explained as follows:

1. The Star-Star (*Y-Y*) connections:

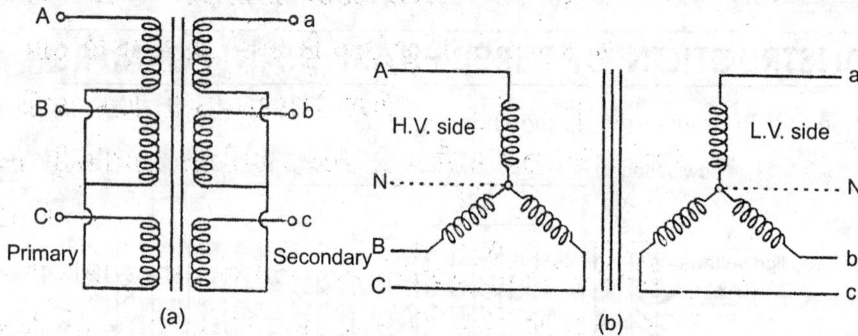

Fig. 5.56. *Y-Y* connections

As shown in Fig. 5.56 ; in Star-Star (*Y-Y*) connections of a transformer, the primary winding of a transformer is connected in star (*Y*), as well as the secondary winding is connected in star (*Y*) too. Here let the transformation ratio is '*K*' the same ratio will be there in primary and secondary voltages. Most conveniently these connections of transformers can be used for good results, where three phase balanced load is to be supplied.

Merits of Star-Star connections

1. These connections give better results, where balanced load is to be supplied.
2. The phase or line current in both the windings is equal, the winding is stronger to bear the stresses because the cross-section of the winding wire is kept large.
3. It is cheaper because less number of turns are required per winding as the voltage across each is $1/\sqrt{3}$ times the line voltage.

Demerits of Star-Star connections

1. These connections are not applicable, when load is unbalanced. If unbalanced load is connected the electrical neutral point will shift from its exact centre to a point that will make the line to neutral voltage unequal. Also this may impose full line voltage on the secondary. So it is must to avoid shifting of the neutral point which is only possible by making the connections of alternators star point to the star point of primary winding of the transformer.
2. In case of distribution network, generally load is unbalanced, hence the regulation of the phases will be very poor too, if star points of both primary and secondary windings are not earthed.
3. If there exists third harmonic in the alternators voltage, this will appear in the secondary of the transformer too which will cause triple frequency currents. The result of these currents is additive in the neutral wire which will cause interferences in the telephone lines located along the transmission lines of electrical energy.

2. The Star-Delta (Y-Δ) connections

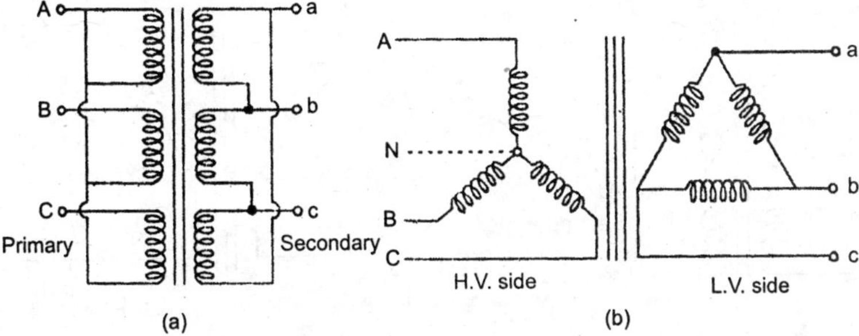

Fig. 5.57. Y-Δ connections

As shown in Fig. 5.57, these Y-Δ connections are used where the voltage is to be stepped up *e.g.* these connections are used at the beginning of high voltage transmission lines.

In this system of connections the ratio of secondary voltage to primary voltage is $\sqrt{3}$ times the transformation ratio K.

The main draw back of these connections is, the Delta (Δ) connections allow a path for the third harmonic currents. Also it is desirable that primary & secondary line voltages & currents are out of phase with each other by 30°. Due to this the parallel operation of such transformers with Δ-Δ and Y-Y connected transformers is not possible.

3. Delta-Star (Δ -Y) connections

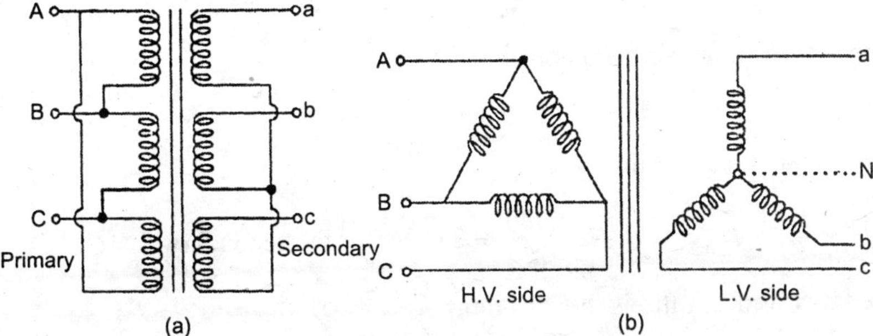

Fig. 5.58. Δ-Y connections

As shown in Fig. 5.58, these connections are mainly used where the voltage is to be stepped down *e.g.* at the end of transmission line.

Here Y-point has one of the good merit that it is convenient to have line to neutral voltage. Here line to neutral voltage is less than the line to line voltage by $\sqrt{3}$ factor.

The similar drawback like (Y-Δ) system also exists in this system that Y-Δ has a phase shift between the primary and secondary voltages which is 30° and only reason that these transformers can not be made parallel either Y-Y or Δ-Δ connected transformers.

4. Delta-Delta (Δ–Δ) connections

As shown in Fig. 5.59, in these connections the primary winding as well as secondary winding both are connected in delta (Δ). Here if transformation ratio is K, the same ratio will exist in secondary to primary voltages. This system is conveniently adopted where voltages are not very high, continuity of service must be maintained and neutral is not needed.

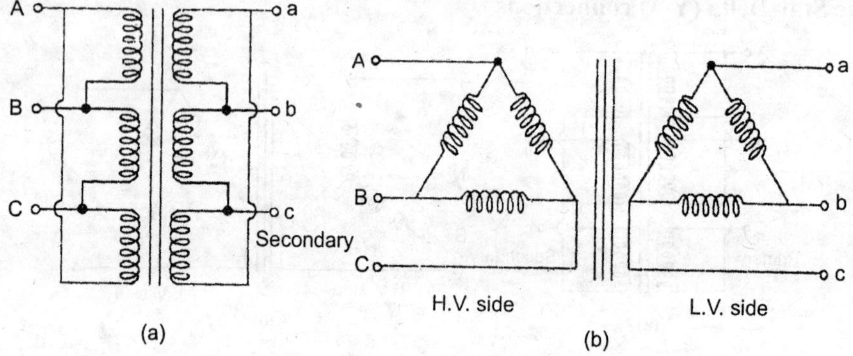

Fig. 5.59. Δ-Δ connections

This system can be used where unbalanced load is to be supplied. Also there exists no any distoration of flux because third harmonic component of current can flow in delta connected windings without flowing in the transmission & distribution lines.

The main demerit of this system is that more insulation is required as compared to star-star (*Y-Y*) connections and this is also disadvantageous that there is no any star point, due to which maximum voltage between windings and core will be there if due to any faulty reason one of the line gets earthed.

Example 5.20.6. A three phase, 50 Hz transformer has a delta-connected primary and star-connected secondary, the line voltage being 22000 V and 400 V respectively. The secondary has a star-connected balanced load at 0.8 power factor lagging. The line current on the primary side is 5 A. Determine the current in each coil of the primary and in each secondary line. What is the output of the transformer in *kW*?

(A.M.*I.e.*, May 1953)

Solution. Since the primary is delta connected.

$$\therefore \quad V_{ph} = V_l = 22000\ V \text{ (for the primary)}$$

and as the secondary is star-connected,

$$\therefore \quad V_{ph} = \frac{V_l}{\sqrt{3}} = \frac{400}{\sqrt{3}} = 231 \text{ V (for the secondary)}$$

As the phase transformers ratio is the turn ratio

$$n = \frac{V_{ph}\,(Secondary)}{V_{ph}\,(\text{Pr}\,imary)} = \frac{231}{22000}$$

or $\qquad n = \dfrac{231}{22000}$

Primary line current, $\quad I_l = 5\text{ A}$

$$\therefore \qquad I_{ph} = \frac{I_l}{\sqrt{3}} = \frac{5}{\sqrt{3}} = 2.887\text{ A (for primary)}$$

∴ Secondary phase current is

$$\therefore \qquad = \frac{I_{ph}\,(primary)}{n}$$

$$= \frac{2.887}{21/2000} = 275\text{ A}$$

Since the secondary is star-connected

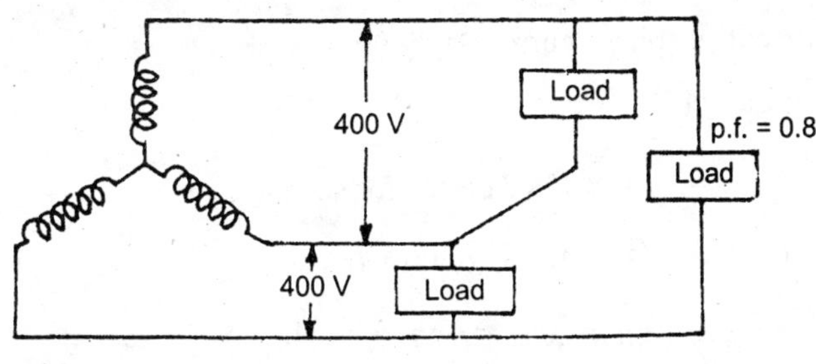

Fig. 5.59.1

∴ Secondary line current

$$= \text{secondary phase current} = 275\text{ A}$$

Output of the transformer

$$= \sqrt{3}\ V_l.\ I_l \cos\phi$$

Here $\qquad V_l = 4000\text{ A}$

$\qquad I_l = 275\text{ A}$

and $\qquad \cos\phi = 0.8\text{ (given)}$

$$\therefore \qquad \text{output} = \sqrt{3} \times 400 \times 275 \times 0.8 = 15240\text{ W}.$$

Example 5.20.7. A 6600/440, 3 phase, 50 Hz transformers has a delta-connected primary and a star-connected secondary. The line current on the primary side is 6 amperes. The secondary has a balanced load of 0.8 *p.f.* lagging. Calculate: (1) Line and phase currents of the secondary and (2) Transformer output.

Solution. (1) The primary being delta-connected.

$$\therefore \qquad \text{Phase voltage} = \text{line voltage} = 6600\text{ V}$$

The secondary being a star-connected

$$\therefore \qquad \text{Phase voltage} = \frac{\textit{line voltage}}{\sqrt{3}} = \frac{440}{\sqrt{3}} = 254.1\text{ V}$$

∴ The transformation ratio

$$n = \frac{254.1}{6600} = 0.0385$$

$$\text{Primary line current} = 6\text{ A}$$

$$\therefore \text{ Primary phase current} = \frac{6}{\sqrt{3}} = 3.465\text{ A}$$

$$\therefore \text{Secondary phase current} = \frac{I_{ph}\,(Primary)}{n}$$

$$= \frac{3.465}{0.0385} = 89.99\text{ A}$$

Secondary being a star-connected one,

$$\text{line current} = \text{phase current} = 89.99\text{ A},$$

(2) The transformer output

$$= \sqrt{3} \times V \times I \cos\phi \text{ (for secondary)}$$

$$= \sqrt{3} \times 440 \times 89.99 \times 0.8\text{ W}$$

$$= 54870\text{ W or } 54.87\text{ kW.}$$

5.40.1. Open Delta or Vee-Vee Connections

The Vee-Vee or open delta connection is sometimes used in place of the normal delta. One might think on superficial considerations that the removal of one transformer winding would seriously unbalance the system voltages but to a great extent this is not so in reality.

In a delta connection the voltage of any one phase at any instant is equal and opposite to the sum of the voltages in the other two phases, so that if one transformer A of a system of delta connected transformers is disconnected, the difference of potential between the lines *a* and *b* remains unchanged. It is being maintained by the transformers *B* and *C* in series, so the three-phase power can still be obtained from the lines *a*, *b* and *c*. This type of connection is called the Vee-Vee or open-delta connection. (Fig. 5.59.2)

If the rated full-load secondary current of each transformer is *I* amperes, then the full-line current with the delta-delta connection is $\sqrt{3}\ I$, being the vector difference of two currents which are equal to *I* and which are 120° out of phase from each other.

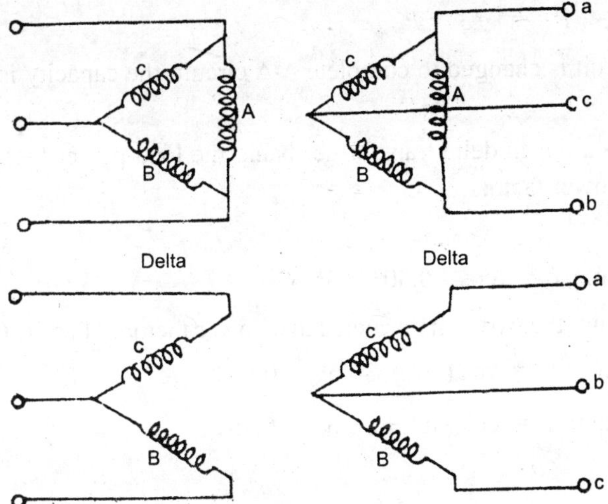

Fig. 5.59.2. Vee-Vee or open delta connections

The kVA rating of each transformer is $\frac{VI}{1000}$ kVA. The total power transmitted by the line is $\sqrt{3}$ $V_l I_l \cos \phi$ where V_l = line voltage and I_l line current. As shown already by here $V_l = V$ and $I_l = \sqrt{3}\ I$ and therefore kVA rating of the three-phase transformer is

$$\frac{\sqrt{3}\, V_l I_l}{1000} = \frac{3\, VI}{1000} \text{ kVA}$$

or three times the rating of one transformer.

But if now one transformer is removed from the delta combination, each of the two remaining transformers is able to carry its rated full-load current I, but the line current is now the current from a single transformer winding. Consequently removal of one transformer reduces the full-load current from $\sqrt{3}\ I$ to I amperes which is a reduction of 42.3% instead of $33\frac{1}{3}$%.

The open-delta connection is very extensively used on distribution systems, for instance, during the initial stages of rural electrification when the load is small but is expected to grow later on.

5.40.2. Applications of Open-Delta Or V-V Connection

The V-V circuit has a number of features that are advantageous. A few applications are given below by way of illustration:

(*i*) The circuit can be employed in an emergency situation when one transformer in a complete Δ - Δ circuit must be removed for repair and continuity of service is required.

(*ii*) Upon failure of the primary or secondary of one transformer of a complete Δ - Δ circuit, the system can be operated as V-V circuit and can deliver 3-phase power (with reduced capacity) to a 3-phase load.

(*iii*) A circuit is sometimes installed as V-V circuit with the understanding that its capacity may be increased by adding one more transformer to form complete Δ-Δ circuit. As shown earlier,

$$\frac{P_V}{P_\Delta} = \frac{1}{\sqrt{3}} = 0.577$$

$\therefore \quad P_\Delta = \sqrt{3} \times P_V$

Thus if a V – V circuit is changed to complete Δ-Δ circuit, the capacity is increased by a factor of $\sqrt{3}$ (= 1.732).

Example. 5.20.8. In an open delta transformer bank, the load power factor is 0.803. What are the individual transformer power factors ?

Solution.

$$\text{Load p.f. angle, } \phi = \cos^{-1} 0.803 = 36.6°$$

In an open delta circuit, the two transformers have power factors of cos (30° – ϕ) and cos (30° + ϕ).

$$\therefore \quad \text{p.f. of transformer 1} = \cos(30° - 36.6°) = 0.993$$

$$\text{p.f. of transformer 2} = \cos(30° + 36.6°) = 0.397$$

Example. 5.20.9.

(*i*) Two identical 1-phase transformers are connected in open delta across a 3-phase mains and deliver a balanced load of 3000 kW at 11 kV and 0.8 p.f. lagging. Calculate the phase currents and the average power factor at which they operate,

(*ii*) If one more identical unit is added and the open delta is converted to close delta, calculate the additional load at the same power factor that can now be supplied for the same temperature rise. Also calculate the phase and line currents.

Solution.

(*i*) If *I* is the line current, then.

$$\sqrt{3} \times 11000 \times I \times 0.8 = 3000 \times 10^3$$

$$\therefore \quad I = \frac{3000 \times 10^3}{\sqrt{3} \times 11000 \times 0.8} = 197 \text{ A}$$

Since line current has the same magnitude as the phase current,

∴ Secondary phase current = 197 A

The average power factor at which V - V bank operates is less than that of the load. This power factor is actually 86.6 % of the balanced load power factor.

$$\therefore \quad \text{Transformer } p.f. = 86.6\% \text{ of } 0.8 = \mathbf{0.693}$$

$$(ii) \quad \text{Additional load} = 72.5\ \% \text{ of } 3000\ kW = \mathbf{2175\ kW}$$

$$\text{Total load} = 3000 + 2175 = 5175 \text{ kW}$$

$$\text{Now} \quad \sqrt{3}\ V\ I_L \cos\phi = 5175 \times 10^3$$

$$\text{or} \quad I_L = \frac{5175 \times 10^3}{\sqrt{3} \times 11000 \times 0.8} = \mathbf{340\ A}$$

$$\text{Phase current} = I_L / \sqrt{3} = 340 / \sqrt{3} = \mathbf{196\ A}$$

5.40.3. Tee-Tee Scott Connection *(Two-phase to three-phase conversion)*

The Tee-connection is very little used in three-phase to three-phase transformations, but in the form of the Scott-connection, it is important in three-phase to two-phase conversion and vice-versa.

The Tee arrangement resembles some what with star-connection. Fig 5.59.3 shows the Scott-connection used to transform energy from two phase to three phase. The primaries of the two transformers *A* and *B* are wound for the same voltage, namely, the voltage V_1 of the two-phase line. The secondary of transformer A is wound to give the desired three-phase voltage of V_2 while the secondary of transformer *B* is wound to give a voltage $\sqrt{3}/2\ V_2$. One end of the secondary of transformer *B* is connected to the mid-point *O* of the secondary of transformer A.

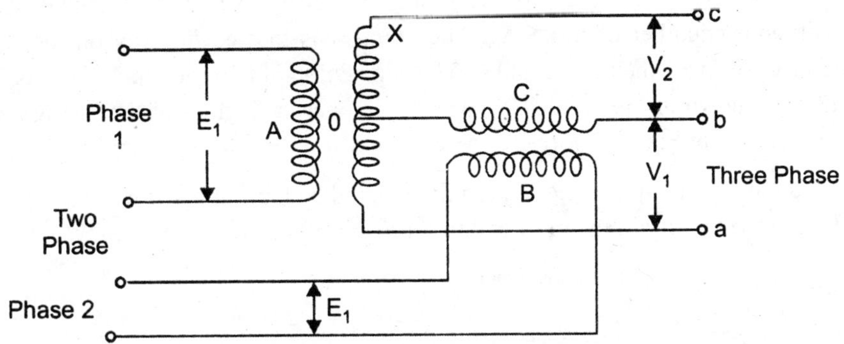

Fig. 5.59.3. Tee Tee scott connection

When the windings *A* and *B* are fed from a two-phase system the e.m.fs. induced in the secondaries have a phase displacement of 90° and if f.m.s. values of the e.m.f. in *XY* is E_2 that is the portions *XO* and Y_0 is $V_2/2$ and that in the secondary winding of *B* is $\sqrt{3}/2\ V_2$. Then the e.m.fs. between the lines bc is the vector difference between the e.m.fs. between *XO* and *OC*, *i.e.*,

$$V_{bc} = V_{xo} + V_{oc}$$

$$= -\frac{V_2}{2} + \frac{\sqrt{3}}{2} V_2.$$

Similarly $$V_{ca} = -\frac{\sqrt{3}}{2} V_2 - \frac{V_2}{2}$$

and $$V_{ab} = \frac{V_2}{2} + \frac{V_2}{2} = V_2$$

$$V_{bc} = V_{ca}^2 \sqrt{\left(\frac{V_2}{2}\right)^2 + \left(\frac{\sqrt{3}\,V_2}{2}\right)^2} = V_2$$

and the voltages are equally displaced from each other *i.e.* by 120°.

5.40.4. Phase Conversion

Three/Two-phase Conversion (Scott Connection)

Phase conversion from three to two phase is needed in special cases, such as in supplying 2-phase electric are furnaces.

The concept of 3/2-phase conversion follows from the voltage phasor diagram of balanced 3-phase supply shown in Fig. 5.59.4 (b). If the point M midway on V_{BC} could be located, then V_{AM} leads V_{BC} by 90°. A 2-phase supply could thus be obtained by means of transformers; one connected across AM, called the *teaser transformer* and the other connected across the lines B and C. Since $V_{AM} = \frac{\sqrt{3}}{2} V_{BC}$, the transformer primaries must have $\sqrt{3}\, N_1/2$ (teaser) and N_1 turns; this would mean equal voltage/turn in each transformer. A balanced 2-phase supply could then be easily obtained by having both secondaries with equal number of turns, N_2. The point M is located midway on the primary of the transformer connected across the lines B and C. The connection of two such transformers, known as the Scott connection, is shown in Fig. 5.59.4 (a), while thee phasor diagram of the 2-phase supply on the secondary side is shown in Fig. 5.59.4 (c).

The neutral point on the 3-phase side, if required, could be located at the point N which divides the primary winding of the tertiary in the ratio 1: 2 (refer Fig. 5.59.4. (b).

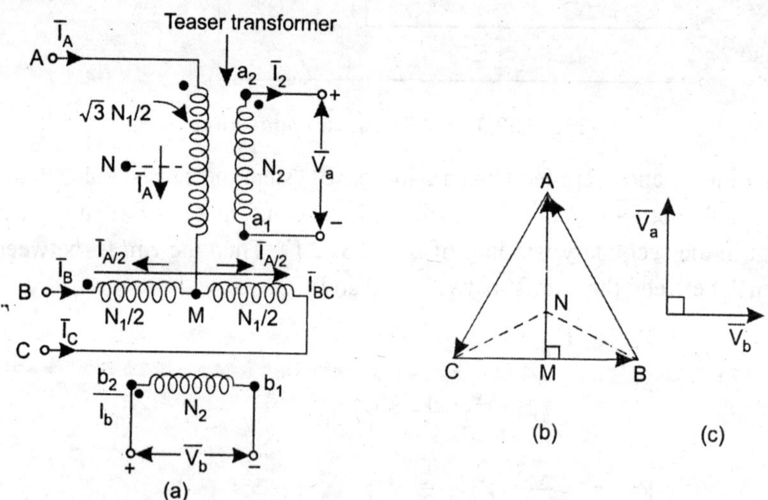

Fig. 5.59.4. Scott connection

Load Analysis

If the secondary load currents are $\bar{I}_a$ and $\bar{I}_b$, the currents can be easily found on the 3-phase side from Fig. 5.59.4. (a).

$$\bar{I}_A = \frac{2N_2}{\sqrt{3}N_1}\bar{I}_a = \frac{2}{\sqrt{3}}\bar{I}_a \text{ (for } N_1/N_2 = 1)$$

$$\bar{I}_{BC} = \frac{N_2}{N_1}\bar{I}_b \text{ (for } N_1/N_2 = 1)$$

$$\bar{I}_B = \bar{I}_{BC} - \bar{I}_A/2$$

$$\bar{I}_C = -\bar{I}_{BC} - \bar{I}_A/2$$

The corresponding phasor diagram for balanced secondary side load of unity power factor is drawn in Fig. 5.59.5 from which it is obvious that the currents drawn from the 3-phase system are balanced and cophasal with the star voltages. The phasor diagram for the case of an unbalanced 2-phase load is drawn in Fig. 5,59.6.

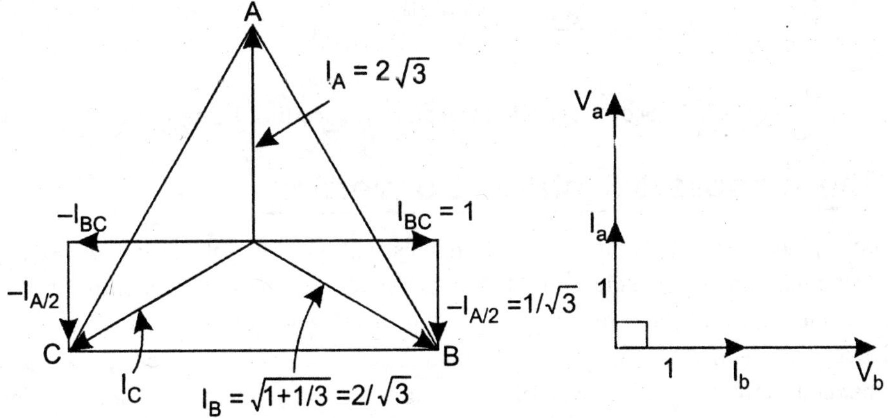

Fig. 5.59.5. Scott connection, balanced load (unity power factor)

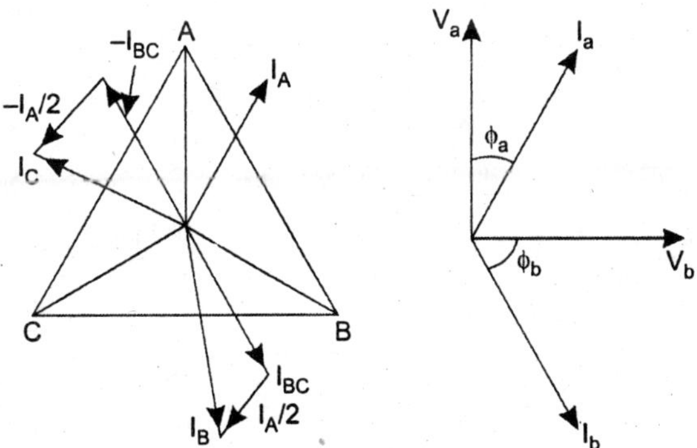

Fig. 5.59.6. Scott connection, unbalanced load

Three/One-phase Conversion

A single-phase power pulsates at twice the frequency, while the total power drawn by a balanced 3-phase load is constant. Thus a 1-phase load can never be transferred to a 3-phase system as a balanced load without employing some energy-storing device (capacitor, inductor or rotating machine). Suitable transformer connections can be used in distributing a 1-phase load on all the three phases though not in a balanced fashion. For large 1-phase loads, this is better than allowing it to load one of the phases of a

3-phase system. A variety of transformer connections are possible. Figure 5.59.7. (a) shows how Scott-connected transformers could be used for this purpose and Fig. 5.59.7. (b) shows the corresponding phaseor diagram.

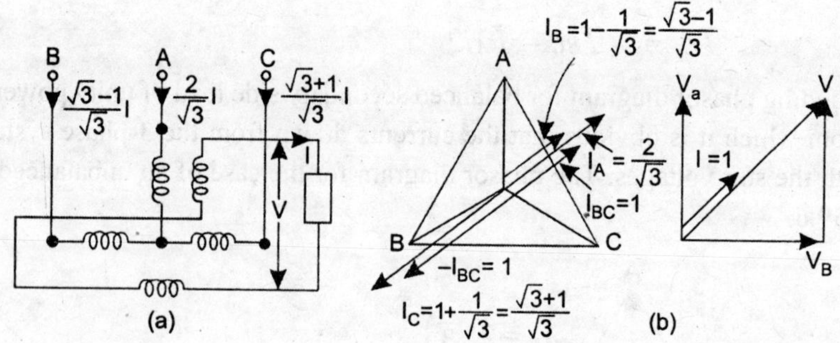

Fig. 5.59.7. Scott-connected transformers feeding 1-phase load

5.40.5. Three Phase/Six-phase Conversion

Each secondary phase is divided into two equal halves with polarity labelling as in Fig. 5.59.8. The winding of each phase on the star side is divided in its two equal haives with labelling as in Fig. 5.59.8. Each leg of the star connection is formed by using halves from two different phases. The phasor diagram for this connection is given in Fig. 5.59.9. from which the connection diagram easily follows. obviously it is the 0° connection from back. Reversal of connection the solar side gives us the 180° connection.

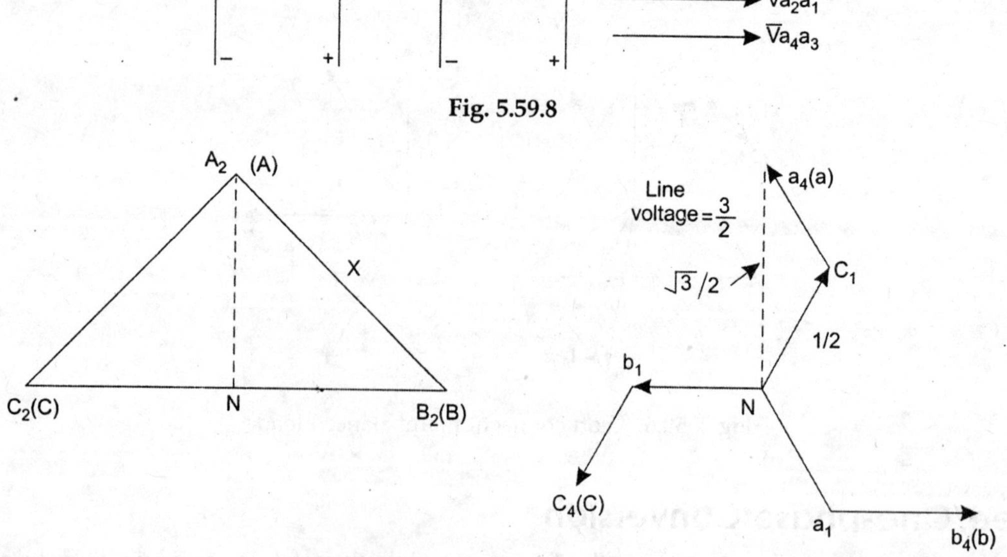

Fig. 5.59.9. Della/Zig Zag slar 0° connection

$$\text{Phase transformation} = x : 1$$

$$\text{Line transformation} = x : \frac{3}{2} \text{ or } \frac{2}{x} x : 1$$

Six-phase voltages (characteristic angle 360°/6 = 60°) are obtained by means of two stars in phase opposition, each star being formed from three respective half-windows as shown in Fig. 5.59.10. This connection is employed in rectifiers and thyristor circuits where a path for the dc current is needed.

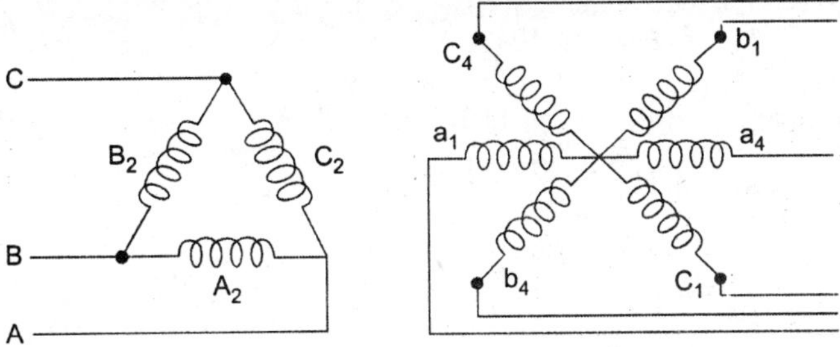

Fig. 3.59.10. (a) 3-phase delta to 6-phase star connection

Example. 5.20.9. (*a*) Two single-phase furnaces *A* and *B* are supplied at 100 V by means of a Scott-connected transformer combination from a 3-phase 6600 V system. The voltage of furnace *A* is leading. Calculate the line currents on the 3-phase side, when the furnace *A* takes 400 kW at 0.707 pf of lagging and *B* takes 800 kW at unity pf.

Solution.

With reference to Fig. 5.59.4 (*a*)

$$\frac{N_1}{N_2} = \frac{6600}{100} = 66$$

$$\therefore \quad \frac{\frac{\sqrt{3}}{2} N_1}{N_2} = 57.16$$

Furnace currents are

$$I_a = \frac{400 \times 1000}{100 \times 0.707} = 5658 \text{ A}; \ \phi_a = 45° \text{lagging}$$

$$I_b = \frac{800 \times 1000}{100 \times 1} = 8000 \text{ A}; \ \phi_b = 0°$$

Furnace voltages and currents are drawn in the phasor diagram of Fig. 5.59.11.(a).

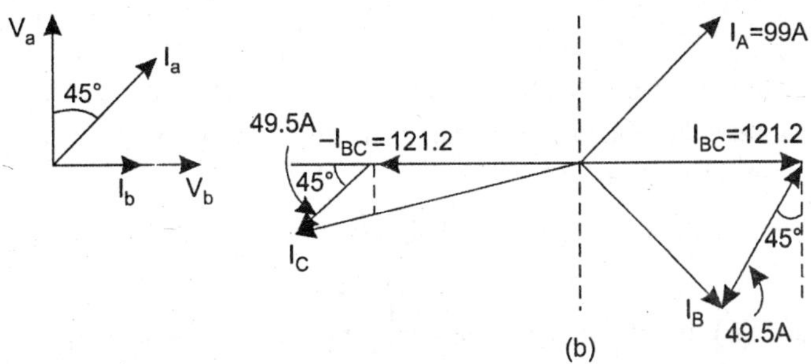

Fig. 5.59.11

On the 3-phase side

$$I_A = \frac{5658}{57.16} = 99 \text{ A}$$

$$I_{BC} = \frac{8000}{66} = 121.2 \text{ A}$$

From the phase or diagram of Fig. 5.59. 11(b)

$$\overline{I}_B = 121.2 - 49.5(0.707 + j\,0.707)$$

$$= 86.2 - j\,35$$

or

$$\overline{I}_B = 93 \text{ A}$$

$$\overline{I}_C = 121.2 + 49.5\ (0707 - 90.707)$$

$$= 156.2 - j\,35$$

$$I_C = 160 \text{ A}$$

5.40.6. (b) Tap Changing Transformers

Voltage variation in power systems in a normal phenomenon owing to the rapid growth of industries and distribution network. System voltage control is therefore essential for:

(*i*) Adjustment of consumers' terminal voltage within prescribed limits.

(*ii*) Control of real and reactive power flow in the network.

(*iii*) Periodical adjustment (1 – 10%) to check off-set load variations.

Adjustment is normally carried out by off-circuit tap changing, the common range being 5% in 2.5% steps. Daily and short-time control or adjustment is carried out by means of on-load tap changing gear.

Besides the above, tapping are also provided for one of the following purposes:

(*i*) For varying the secondary voltage.

(*ii*) For maintaining the secondary voltage constant with a varying primary voltage.

(*iii*) For providing an auxiliary secondary voltage for a special purpose, such as lighting.

(*iv*) For providing a low voltage for starting rotating machines.

(*v*) For providing a neutral point, *e.g.* for earthing.

The principal tapping is one to which the rating of the winding is related. A positive tapping means more, and a negative tapping implies less turns than those of the principal tap. Tap changing may be achieved in one of the three conditions, viz.

(*i*) voltage variation with constant flux and constant voltage turn,

(*ii*) with varying flux,

(*iii*) a mix of (*i*) and (*ii*). In (*i*) the percentage tapping range is same as the voltage variation.

Location

The tap may be placed on the primary or secondary side which partly depends on construction. If tappings are near the line ends, fewer bushing insulators are required. If the tappings are placed near the neutral ends, the phase-to-phase insulation conditions are eased.

For achieving large voltage variation, tappings should be placed near the centres of the phase windings to reduce magnetic asymmetry. However, this arrangement cannot be put on LV windings placed next to the core (as in core type transformer) because of accessibility and insulation considerations. The HV winding placed outside the LV winding is easily accessible and can, thus, be tapped easily.

It is not possible to tap other than an integral number of turns and this may not be feasible with LV side tappings. For example 250 V phase winding with 15 V/ turn cannot be tapped closer than 5%. It is therefore essential to tap the HV windings which is advantages in a step-down transformer.

Some of the methods of locating tappings are depicted in Fig. 5.59.12. (*a*) and (*b*).

(a) Taps at one for small transformers

(b) Large transformer taps centrally placed for both delta and star transformer.

Fig. 5.59.12. Location of transformer tappings

Axial mmf unbalance is minimized by thinning out the LV winding or by arranging parts of the winding more symmetrically. For very large tapping ranges a special tappings coil may be employed.

Tap changing causes changes in leakage reactance, core loss, I^2R loss and perhaps some problems in parallel operation of dissimilar transformers.

5.40.7. Three Winding Transformers

Transformers are built with a third winding, called the tertiary winding, in addition to the primary and secondary windings. Various purposes which impel the use of a tertiary winding are given below:

(*i*) For supplying the substation auxiliaries at a voltage different from those of the primary and secondary windings.

(*ii*) Synchronous condensers or static capacitors may be connected to the tertiary winding for reactive power injection in to the system for voltage control.

(*iii*) A Delta connected tertiary reduces the impedance offered to the zero sequence currents thereby allowing a larger earth-fault current to flow for proper operation of protective equipment. Further it limits voltage in balance when the load is unbalanced. It also permits the third harmonic current to flow thereby reducing third-harmonic voltages.

(*iv*) Three windings may also be used for interconnecting three transmission lines at different voltages.

(*v*) Tertiary can serve the purpose of measuring voltage of an High voltage (HV) testing transformer.

When it is used for purpose (*iii*) above the tertiary winding is called a stabilizing winding.

5.40.8. Stabilization by Tertiary Winding

The star/star transformer comprising single-phase units or a single unit with a 5-limb core offers high reactance to the flow of unbalanced load between the line and neutral. Any unbalanced load can be divided into three 3-phase sets (positive, negative and zero sequence components). The zero-sequence component (cophasal currents on three lines, $I_0 = 1/3I_n$) caused by a line-to-neutral load on the secondary side cannot be balanced by primary currents as the zero-sequence currents cannot flow in the isolated neutral star-connected primary. The zero-sequence currents on the secondary side therefore set up magnetic flux in the core. Iron path is available for the zero sequence flux* in a bank of single-phase units and in the 5-limb core and as a consequence the impedance offered to the zero-sequence currents is very high (0.5 to 5 pu) inhibiting the flow of these currents. The provision of a delta-connected tertiary permits the circulation of zero-sequence currents in it, thereby considerably reducing the zero-sequence. This is illustrated in Fig. 5.59.13.

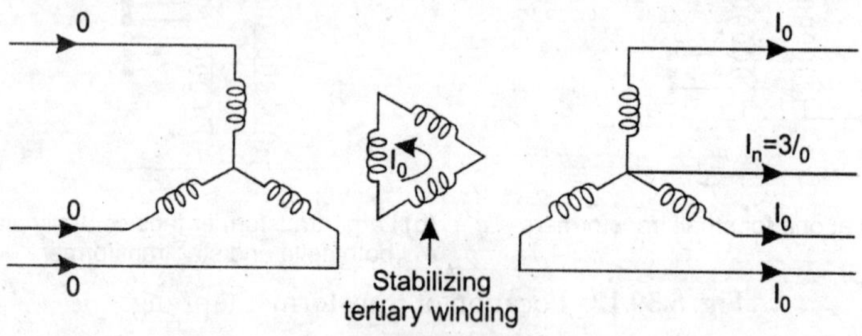

Fig. 5.59.13

5.40.9. Equivalent Circuit

The equivalent circuit of a 3-winding transformer can be represented by the single-phase equivalent circuit of Fig. 5.59.14. wherein each winding is represented by its equivalent resistance and reactance. All the values are reduced to a common rating base and respective voltage bases. The subscripts 1, 2 and 3 indicate the primary, secondary and tertiary respectively. For simplicity, the effect of the exciting current is ignored in the equivalent circuit. It may be noted that the load division between the secondary and tertiary is completely arbitrary. Three external circuits are connected between terminals 1, 2 and 3 respectively and the common terminal labelled 0. Since the exciting current is neglected, $\bar{I}_1 + \bar{I}_2 + \bar{I}_3 = 0$.

*In a 3-limb core the zero-sequence flux (directed upwards or downwards in all the limbs) must return through the air path, so that only a small amount of this flux can be established; hence a low zero-sequence reactance.

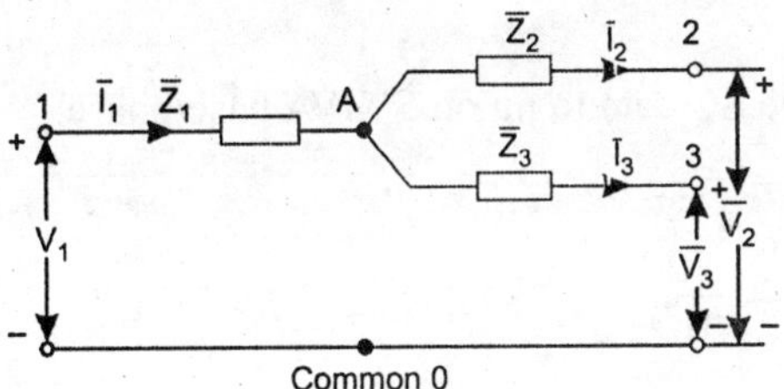

Fig. 5.59.14. Single-phase equivalent circuit of 3-winding transformer

The impedance of Fig. 5.59.12 can be easily obtained from three simple short-circuit tests. If $\bar{Z}_{12}$ indicates the SC impedance of winding 1 and 2 with winding 3 open, then from the equivalent circuit.

$$\bar{Z}_{12} = \bar{Z}_1 + \bar{Z}_2 \quad (1)$$

Similarly
$$\bar{Z}_{23} = \bar{Z}_2 + \bar{Z}_3 \quad (2)$$

$$\bar{Z}_{13} = \bar{Z}_1 + \bar{Z}_3 \quad (3)$$

where $\bar{Z}_{23}$ = SC impedance of windings 2 and 3 with winding 1 open.

$\bar{Z}_{13}$ = SC impedance of windings 1 and 3 with winding 2 open.

All the impedances are referred to a common base.

Solving Eqs (1) – (3) yields

$$\bar{Z}_1 = \frac{1}{2}(\bar{Z}_{12} + \bar{Z}_{13} - \bar{Z}_{23}) \quad (4)$$

$$\bar{Z}_2 = \frac{1}{2}(\bar{Z}_{23} + \bar{Z}_{12} - \bar{Z}_{13}) \quad (5)$$

$$\bar{Z}_3 = \frac{1}{2}(\bar{Z}_{13} + \bar{Z}_{23} - \bar{Z}_{12}) \quad (6)$$

The open-circuit test can be performed on any one of the three windings to determine the core-loss, magnetizing impedance and turn-ratio.

Example. 5.20.9. (*b*) The primary, secondary and tertiary windings of a 50-Hz, single-phase, 3-winding transformer are rated as 6.35 kV, 5 MVA; 191 kV, 2.5 MVA; 400 V, 2.5 MVA respectively. Three SC tests on this transformer yielded the following results:

(*i*) Secondary shorted, primary excited: 500 V, 393.7 A

(*ii*) Tertiary shorted, primary excited: 900 V, 393.7 A

(*iii*) Tertiary shorted, secondary excited: 231 V, 21 312.1 A

Resistances are to be ignored.

(*a*) Find the pu values of the equivalent circuit impedances of the transformer on a 5 MVA, rated voltage base.

(*b*) Three of these transformers are used in a 15 MVA, Y-Y-Δ, 3-phase bank to supply 3.3 kV and 400 V auxiliary power circuits in a generating plant. Calculate the pu values of steady-state short-circuit currents and of the voltage at the terminals of the secondary windings for a 3-phase balanced short-circuit at the tertiary terminals. Use 15 MVA, 3-phase rated voltage base.

Solution.

(*a*) Let us first convert the SC data to pu on 5 MVA base/phase.

For primary, $V_B = 6.35$ kV

$$I_B = \frac{5000}{6.35} = 787.4 \text{ A}$$

For secondary, $V_B = 1.91$ kV

$$I_B = \frac{5000}{1.91}$$

Converting the given test data to pu yields:

Test No.	*Winding involved*	*V*	*I*
1	*P* and *S*	0.0787	0.5
2	*P* and *T*	0.1417	0.5
3	*S* and *T*	0.1212	0.5

From test 1, 2 and 3, respectively.

$$X_{12} = \frac{0.0787}{0.5} = 0.1574 \text{ pu}$$

$$X_{13} = \frac{0.1417}{0.5} = 0.2834 \text{ pu}$$

$$X_{23} = \frac{0.1212}{0.5} = 0.2424 \text{ pu}$$

From eqs 4 – 6

$$X_1 = 0.5(0.1574 + 0.2834 - 0.2424) = 0.0992 \text{ pu}$$

$$X_2 = 0.5(0.2424 + 0.1574 - 0.2834) = 0.05825) \text{ pu}$$

$$X_3 = 0.5(0.2834 + 0.2424 - 0.1574) = 0.1842 \text{ pu}$$

(*b*) The base line-to-line voltage for the *Y*-connected primaries is $\sqrt{3} \times 6.35 = 11$ kV, *i.e.* the bus voltage is 1 pu. From Fig. 5.59. 15 for a short-circuit at the terminals of the tertiary, $V_3 = 0$. Then

$$I_{SC} = \frac{V_1}{X_1 + X_3} = \frac{V_1}{X_{13}} = \frac{1.00}{0.2834} = 3.53 \text{ pu}$$

SC current primary side $= 3.53 \times 787.4 = 2779.5$ A

SC current tertiary side $= 3.53 \times \dfrac{5000 \times 1000}{400/\sqrt{3}} = 76424$ A (line current)

Neglecting the voltage drops due to the secondary load current, the secondary terminal voltage is the voltage at the junction point *A* (Fig. 5.59.15), *i.e.*

$$V_2 = I_{SC} X_3 = 3.53 \times 0.1842 = 0.6502 \text{ pu}$$

$$V_2(\text{actual}) = 0.6502 \times 1.91\sqrt{3} = 2.15 \text{ kV (line-to-line)}$$

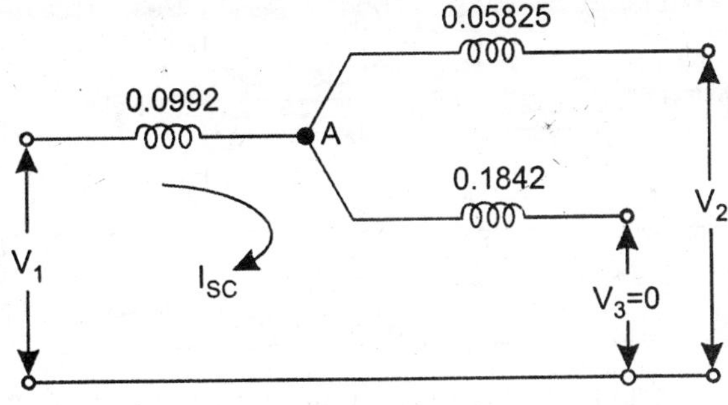

Fig. 5.59.15

5.41. PARALLEL OPERATION OF TRANSFORMERS

When load on the transformer from its existing load, is increased or when the power to be transformed is greater than that which can be handled by one transformer, there are two solutions for the said problem *i.e.* either replacing the existing transformer by another of a higher rating or by connecting another transformer in parallel with the existing one. But practically, we connect transformers in parallel because of the reason that if we install one transformer of higher power rating in spite of more than one transformer of different ratings to meet the said power rating, then if this transformer being faulty due to any reason, all the supply connected to this transformer, fails. And on the other hand if there are more than one transformers in parallel, then if one of the transformer fails, some of the supply can be continued from other transformers. The main draw back of system is that, the system is costly but then also this system of parallelising more than one transformers is very much beneficial.

Keeping in view the above article, first of all we will discuss about parallel operation of single phase transformers.

5.42. PARALLEL OPERATION OF SINGLE PHASE TRANSFORMERS

As discussed, about the advantage of parallel operation of transformers in article 5.41, there are certain conditions for parallel operation of transformers. These are stated as follows:

1. The voltage ratings of primary and secondary of all the transformers, should be same, obviously it is important that transformation ratio *i.e.* '*K*' for all the transformers should be same.
2. The transformers must be properly connected with regard to their polarity.
3. The percentage impedances of all of the transformers should be equal.
4. Equivalent resistance to equivalent reactance ratio of all the transformers should be same.

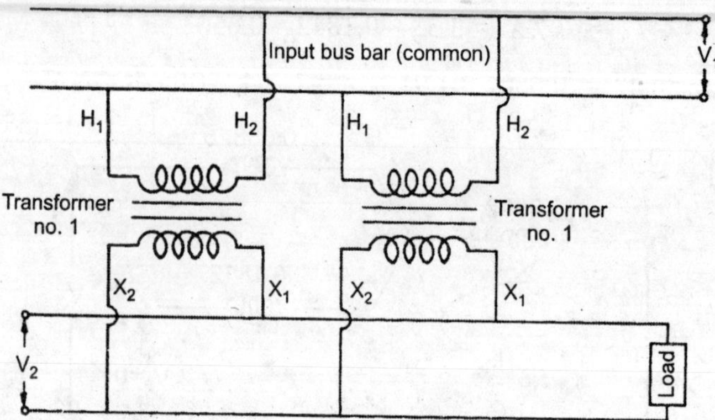

Fig. 5.59.16 Parallel operations of 1-ϕ transformers

If the two step down transformers in Fig. 5.59.16 are identical as to voltage ratings, percentage impedance values and both have additive polarities it is a simple matter to connect them in parallel. The two similar HV leads (H_1) of both transformers are connected to one line wire and the other two primary leads (H_2) are connected to the other line wire. The two similar low voltage leads (X_1) are connected to the one secondary line wire, while the other two low voltage leads are connected to the other low voltage line wire. These two transformers comply with the four requirements previously listed and they will both deliver secondary currents to the load in proportion to their kVA ratings.

In case the transformers are of different manufacture and it is not known whether they are of additive or subtractive polarity, the following test procedure may be used:

In this procedure it will be assumed that one transformer is already operating as a step down transformer to supply energy to the bus bars at lower voltage level. This transformer will be called transformer 1. A second transformer, 2, is to be parallelled with the 1st transformer. This 2nd transformer has the same voltage ratings and percentage impedance, but it is not known whether it has additive or subtractive polarity as the tags on the transformer's terminals are missing.

Fig. 5.61 shows that transformer 1 has additive polarity. Regardless of the polarity of the transformer 2, the H_1 lead of this transformer is always on the left hand side when observed from low voltage side of the case. Therefore this lead is connected to the same high voltage line wire as the H_1 lead of transformer 1.

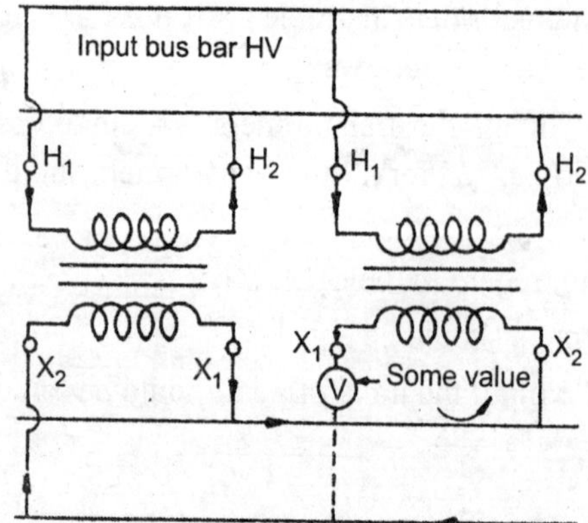

Fig. 5.59.17. Checking polarity of transformers previous to paralleling

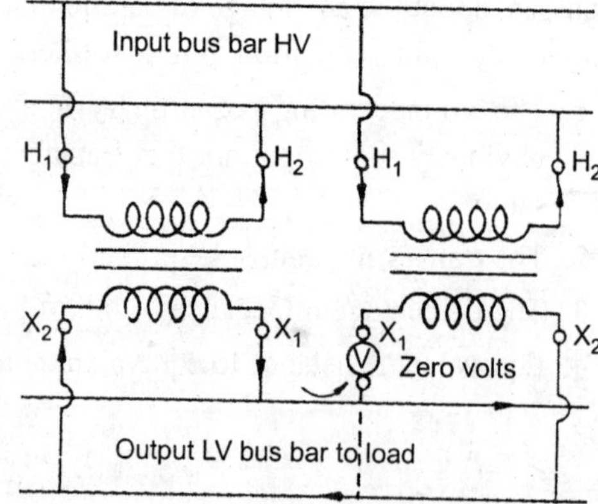

Fig. 5.59.18. Checking polarity of transformers previous to paralleling

Obviously the H_2 lead of transformer 2 is connected to the other side of the high voltage line. One of the low voltage leads is connected to one side of the low voltage secondary. A voltmeter is next connected between the other side of low voltage secondary and the secondary load of transformer 2, which is still disconnected. If transformer 2, is of substractive polarity, the voltmeter will indicate twice the secondary coil voltage.

In Fig. 5.59.17. instantaneous directions of voltage have been indicated. A check of the instantaneous directions of the voltage in this figure will show why the voltmeter indicates twice the voltage. If an attempt were made to connect this lead to the secondary line wire where the voltmeter is connected there would be a potential difference of twice the voltage at the connection point which would result in a short circuit.

Fig 5.59.18. shows the right hand, low voltage lead of transformer 2, changed to the other secondary line wire. Now the voltmeter indicates zero potential which shows that the instantaneous polarity of the secondary leads of both transformers is the same. The voltmeter can now be removed and the final connection made without fear of a short circuit.

5.43. PARALLEL OPERATION OF THREE PHASE TRANSFORMERS

The conditions for parallel operation of three phase transformers are the same as required for parallel operation of single phase transformers with some of the additions which are mentioned here as under:

1. The phase sequence and vector grouping of the transformers to be parallelled, should be the same.
2. The voltage ratio should refer to the terminal voltage of primary winding and secondary winding of the transformers.

The phase sequence is known as the order in which the given three phases reach their maximum positive value, must be same for all the transformers to be parallelled. On the other hand during the cycle each pair of phases will be short circuited, resulting in disturbance and ultimately dangerous harm to all the system.

5.43.1. Load Sharing Between Two Transformers Connected In Parallel

The load sharing between two transformers connected in parallel depends upon the various conditions as discussed below:

(*i*) When the two transformers have the same voltage ratios and their impedance voltage triangles are identical in size and shape.

The condition for which the transformers have the same voltage ratio and impedance voltage triangle is known ideal condition or ideal case. Let E be the no load secondary voltage of each transformer and V the terminal voltage. Fig 5.60.1 shows the equivalent circuit in which I_1 and I_2 are the currents supplied by the transformers A and B. I be the total load current lagging behind the voltage V by an angle ϕ. The impedance voltage triangles of the individual transformers are identical in shape and size and are therefore, represented by a single triangle VAB with the resistance drop side VA parallel to the load current vector OI as shown in fig. 5.61.2 The current I_1 and I_2 in the individual transformers are both in phase with the load current I and are inversely proportional to the respective impedances.

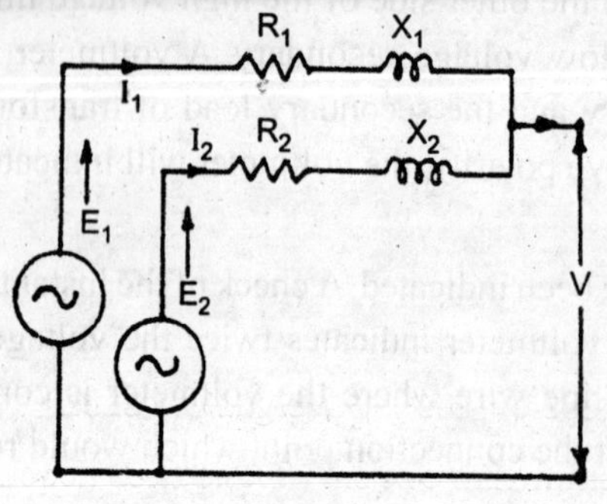

Fig. 5.60

Fig. 5.61

$$\bar{I} = \bar{I}_1 + \bar{I}_2 \qquad ...(i)$$

Also
$$\bar{I}_1 \bar{Z}_1 = \bar{I}_2 \bar{Z}_2 \qquad ...(ii)$$

or
$$\frac{\bar{I}_1}{\bar{I}_2} = \frac{\bar{Z}_2}{\bar{Z}_1}$$

Substituting the value of I_1 in eq. (*i*), we get,

$$\bar{I} = \bar{I}_2 \frac{\bar{Z}_2}{\bar{Z}_1} + \bar{I}_2 = \bar{I}_2 \left[\frac{\bar{Z}_2 + \bar{Z}_1}{\bar{Z}_1}\right]$$

or
$$\bar{I}_2 = \bar{I} \cdot \frac{\bar{Z}_1}{\bar{Z}_1 + \bar{Z}_2} \qquad ...(iii)$$

Similarly,
$$\bar{I}_1 = \frac{\bar{Z}_2}{\bar{Z}_1 + \bar{Z}_2} \times \bar{I} \qquad ...(iv)$$

Multiplying both sides by the common terminal voltage V, we get,

$$\bar{I}_1 \bar{V} = \frac{\bar{Z}_2}{\bar{Z}_1 + \bar{Z}_2} \bar{V} \bar{I}\text{; similarly } \bar{I}_2 \bar{V} = \frac{\bar{Z}_1}{\bar{Z}_1 + \bar{Z}_1} \bar{V} \bar{I}$$

$\therefore$
$$\overline{kVA_1} = \frac{\bar{Z}_2}{\bar{Z}_1 + \bar{Z}_2} \times \overline{kVA} \qquad ...(v)$$

and
$$KVA_2 = \frac{\bar{Z}_1}{\bar{Z}_1 + \bar{Z}_2} \times \overline{kVA} \qquad ...(vi)$$

(*ii*) **When the two transformers have the same voltage ratios but different voltage triangles.**

In this case, no load voltages of both secondary windings are equal in magnitude as well as in phase *i.e.* there is no phase difference between E_1 and E_2 which will only be possible if the magnetising currents of the two transformers are not very different from each other or nearly the same. Under these conditions, both sides of two transformers can be connected in parallel, and no current will circulate between them on no load.

Fig. 5.62. shows the equivalent circuit diagram when the parallel connected transformers are sharing the load current I, and it represents two impedances in parallel. The impedance voltage triangles are now represented by two triangles *VAB*, *VA'*, *B* having common hypotenuse *VB* as shown in fig. 5.62.1 The resistance drop sides of the triangles VA, VA' are parallel to the phasors OI_1 and OI_2 of the respective secondary currents. The sum of these vectors OI_1 and OI_2 represent the load current OI.

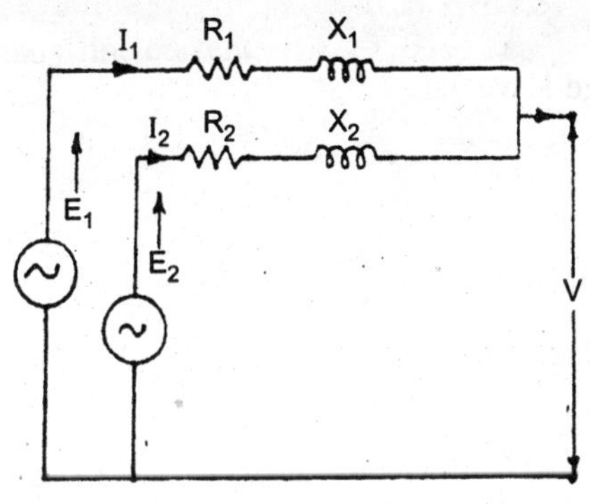

Fig. 5.62

Fig. 5.62.1

$$\overline{Z_1} \text{ and } \overline{Z_2} = \text{impedances of the two transformers}$$

$$\overline{I_1} \text{ and } \overline{I_2} = \text{the currents of the two transformers}$$

$$\overline{I} = \text{total load current}$$

$$\overline{V} = \text{common terminal voltage.}$$

The total current $\overline{I}$ is given by

$$\overline{I} = \overline{I_1} + \overline{I_2}$$

From the equivalent circuit diagram, it is seen that

$$\overline{E_1} = \overline{E_2} = \overline{E}\text{, the common terminal voltage}$$

$$\therefore \quad \overline{I_1}\,\overline{Z_1} = \overline{I_2}\,\overline{Z_2} = \overline{v} \qquad \text{...(i)}$$

Since $\overline{Z_1}$ and $\overline{Z_2}$ are in parallel, we have the equivalent impedance $\overline{Z}$

$$\frac{1}{\overline{Z}} = \frac{1}{\overline{Z_1}} + \frac{1}{\overline{Z_2}}$$

$$\therefore \quad \overline{Z} = \frac{\overline{Z_1}\,\overline{Z_2}}{\overline{Z_1} + \overline{Z_2}}$$

$\therefore$ The total combined current

$$\overline{I} = \frac{\overline{v}}{\overline{Z}} = \frac{\overline{v}(\overline{Z_1} + \overline{Z_2})}{\overline{Z_1}\,\overline{Z_2}}$$

or

$$\overline{v} = \frac{\overline{Z_1 Z_2}}{(\overline{Z_1} + \overline{Z_2})}\,\overline{I}$$

$$\therefore \quad \overline{I_1}\,\overline{Z_1} = \frac{\overline{Z_1 Z_2}}{\overline{Z_1} + \overline{Z_2}} \cdot \overline{I}$$

or

$$\overline{I_1} = \frac{\overline{Z_2}}{\overline{Z_1} + \overline{Z_2}} \cdot \overline{I} \qquad \text{...(ii)}$$

Similarly

$$\overline{I_2} = \frac{\overline{Z_1}}{\overline{Z_1} + \overline{Z_2}} \cdot \overline{I} \quad ...(iii)$$

Multiplying both sides by the common terminal voltage V we get,

$$\overline{I_1}\,\overline{V} = \frac{\overline{Z_1}}{\overline{Z_1} + \overline{Z_2}}\,\overline{V}\,\overline{I}$$

Similarly

$$\overline{I_2}\,\overline{V} = \frac{\overline{Z_1}}{\overline{Z_1} + \overline{Z_2}}\,\overline{V}\,\overline{I}$$

Let $\quad V \times I \times 10^{-3}$ = kVA, the combined load in kVA.

$V \times I_1 \times 10^{-3}$ = kVA_1 load shared by transformer 'A' in kVA,

$V \times I_2 \times 10^{-3}$ = kVA_2 load shared by transformer 'B' in kVA.

$$\overline{kVA_1} = \frac{\overline{Z_2}}{\overline{Z_1} + \overline{Z_2}} \times \overline{kVA} \quad ...(iv)$$

$$\overline{kVA_2} = \frac{\overline{Z_1}}{\overline{Z_1} + \overline{Z_2}} \times \overline{kVA} \quad ...(v)$$

$\therefore \quad \dfrac{kVA_1}{kVA_2} = \dfrac{\overline{Z_2}}{Z_1}$ *i.e.* the load shared by each transformer is inversely proportional to their impedances

Again from equation (*ii*) or (*iii*), we get,

$$I_1 = \frac{1}{\dfrac{Z_1}{Z_2} + 1} \times I \text{ or } I_2 = \frac{1}{\dfrac{Z_2}{Z_1} + 1} \times I \quad ...(vi)$$

Equation (*vi*) shows that the load shared by each transformer depends upon ratio of impedances, so the unit in which they are measured does not matter.

Note. The expression derived above are vectorial so that kVA_1 and kVA_2 are obtained in magnitude as well as in direction.

Example 5.20.10 Two transformers are connected in parallel to supply a load requiring 500 A, at 0.8 power (lagging), at a terminal voltage of 400 V. The equivalent impedances of the two transformers referred to the secondary sides are $(2 + j3)$ ohms and $(2.5 + j5)$ ohms respectively. Calculate the current and kVA supplied by each transformer and the power factor at which they operate.

Solution:

Let $\quad \overline{Z_1} = 2 + j3$ and $\overline{Z_2} = 2.5 + j5$

R_1 = 2 ohms R_2 = 2.5 ohms

X_1 = 3 ohms X_2 = 5 ohms.

$$\overline{Z_1} + \overline{Z_2} = 2 + j3 + 2.5 + j5$$

$$= 4.5 + j8$$

Load current shared by first transformer,

$$\overline{I_1} = \frac{\overline{Z_2}}{\overline{Z_1} + \overline{Z_2}} \times \overline{I}$$

$$\overline{I} = \text{I} (\cos \phi - j \sin \phi) = 500(0.8 - \text{j}0.6) \quad (\textit{Given})$$

$$I_1 = \frac{2.5 + j5}{4.5 + j8} \times 500\ (0.8 - j\,0.6)$$

$$= \frac{500(0.8 - j0.6)(2.5 + j5)(4.5 - j8)}{4.5^2 + 8^2} = 252 - \text{j}170.6$$

$$I_1 = \sqrt{(252)^2 + (170.6)^2} = \mathbf{304\ A\ \ Ans.}$$

$$\text{Cos}\ \phi_1 = \frac{252.0}{304.0} = \mathbf{0.829\ lag\ Ans.}$$

$$\overline{I_2} = \frac{\overline{Z_1}}{\overline{Z_1} + \overline{Z_2}} \times \overline{I} = \frac{2 + j3}{4.5 + j8} \times 500(0.8 - j0.6)$$

$$= \frac{500(0.8 - j0.6)(2 + j3)(4.5 - j8)}{4.5^2 + 8^2} = 148 + j\,129.4$$

$$I_2 = \sqrt{(148)^2 + (129.4)^2} = \mathbf{197\ A\ Ans.}$$

$$\text{Cos}\ \phi_2 = \frac{148.0}{197.0} = \mathbf{0.75\ Lag\ Ans.}$$

Example 5.20.11: Two single-phase transformers connected in parallel supply a load of 1000 A at 0.8 p.f. lagging. For each transformer, the secondary e.m.f. on open circuit is 3300 V and the total leakage impedances in terms of the secondary are (0.1 + j 0.2) and (0.05 + j 0.4) ohm respectively. Determine the output current for each transformer and the ratio of the kW output of the two transformers.

Solution. $\overline{Z_1} = 0.1 + j0.2\ ;\ \overline{Z_2} = 0.05 + j\,0.4$

$$\therefore \quad \overline{Z_1} + \overline{Z_2} = 0.1 + j\,0.2 + 0.05 + j\,0.4$$

$$= 0.15 + j\,0.6$$

Taking secondary terminal voltage as reference vector, the expression of the current is

$$\overline{I} = I\,(\cos \phi - j \sin \phi)$$

$$= 1000\ (0.8 - j0.6)$$

$$\therefore \quad \overline{I_1} = \frac{\overline{Z_2}}{\overline{Z_1} + \overline{Z_2}} \times \overline{I}$$

$$= \frac{0.05 + j0.4}{(0.15 + j0.6)} \times 1000(0.8 - j0.6) = 564.5 - j325.5$$

$$I_1 = \sqrt{(564.5)^2 + (325.5)^2}$$

$$= \mathbf{652\ A\ Ans.}$$

$$\text{Cos } \phi_1 = \frac{564.5}{652} = 0.865 \text{ lagging}$$

$$\overline{I_2} = \frac{\overline{Z_1}}{\overline{Z_1} + \overline{Z_2}} \times \overline{I}$$

$$= \frac{0.1 + j\,0.2}{0.15 + j\,0.5} \times 1000\,(0.8 - j\,0.6) = 235 - j\,274.5$$

$$I_2 = \sqrt{(235.5)^2 + (274.5)^2}.$$

$$= \mathbf{362.0\ A\ Ans.}$$

$$\text{Cos } \phi_2 = \frac{235.5}{362.0} = 0.648 \text{ lagging}$$

Ratio of the outputs of the two transformers.

$$\frac{kW_1}{kW_2} = \frac{VI_1 \cos \phi_1}{VI_2 \cos \phi_2} = \frac{I_1 \cos \phi_1}{I_2 \cos \phi_2}$$

$$= \frac{652 \times 0.865}{362 \times 0.648} = \mathbf{2.4\ Ans.}$$

Example 5.20.12. Two single-phase transformers *I* and *II* rated at 250 kVA, each are connected in parallel on both sides. Resistance and reactance drops for *I* and *II* are 1% and 6% and 1.2% and 4.8% respectively. Calculate the load shared by each and the respective power factors, if the total load is 500 kVA at 0.8 power factor lagging. Their no load emfs are equal.

Solution:

$$\overline{Z_1} = (1 + j6)\%,\ \overline{Z_2} = 1.2 + j\,4.8)\%$$

$$\overline{Z_1} + \overline{Z_2} = (1 + \text{j}\,6)\% + (1.2 + \text{j}\,4.8)\%$$

$$= (2.2 + \text{J}\,10.8)\%$$

$$\overline{kVA} = \text{KVA}\,(\cos \phi - \text{j} \sin \phi)$$

$$= 500\,(0.8 - j0.6)$$

$$\therefore \quad \overline{kVA_1} = \frac{\overline{Z_2}}{\overline{Z_1} + \overline{Z_2}}\,\overline{kVA}$$

$$= \frac{1.2 + j4.8}{(2.2 + j10.8)} \times 500\,(0.8 - j\,0.6)$$

$$= (173.26 - j\,142.32)$$

$$\text{kVA}_1 = \sqrt{(173.26)^2 (+142.32)^2} = \mathbf{223\ kVA\ Ans.}$$

$$\text{Cos } \phi_1 = \frac{173.26}{223} = \mathbf{0.776\ Ans.}$$

$$\overline{kVA_2} = \frac{\overline{Z_1}}{\overline{Z_1} + \overline{Z_2}} \times \overline{kVA}$$

$$= \frac{1+j6}{(2.2+j10.8)} \times 500(0.8-j0.6)$$

$$= (226.74 - j\,157.68)$$

$$KVA_2 = \sqrt{(226.74)^2 + (157.68)^2} = \mathbf{277\ kVA\ Ans.}$$

$$\text{Cos}\,\phi_2 = \frac{226.74}{277} = \mathbf{0.814\ Ans.}$$

5.44. DIFFERENCE BETWEEN POWER AND DISTRIBUTION TRANSFORMER

1. *Power Transformer*: The rating of these transformers is kept above 200 kVA, and these are installed at generating stations or sub-stations of factories etc. having load beyond 200 kVA. These transformers are installed at the end of transmission lines either to step-up or to step down the voltage. These transformers show high efficiency as the transformers are operated at their full kVA ratings and the leakage reactance of these transformers is less as compared to that of the distribution transformers.
2. *Distribution Transformers*: These transformers are basically step-down transformers, which transform standard 11 kV or 6.6 kV to serviceable voltage of 440 Volts. These transformers are always connected with supply lines and the iron loss in these occur continuously every time. So these are designed in this manner that iron losses should be minimum in the transformers. The efficiency of these transformers is kept good enough, even upon the 50% load of the transformers the rating of these transformers is kept up to 200 kVA only.

5.45. CLASSIFICATION AND COOLING OF TRANSFORMERS

Since there is no rotating part in the transformer which may induce a ventilating draught, so transformers are more difficult to cool than rotating electrical machines. In small output transformers the external surface is sufficient to dissipate heat by radiation to the atmosphere but in larger-size transformers, additional means of carrying away, the heat from the windings are provided in the different ways and the transformers are classified according to the method of cooling which are given below:

1. Natural Cooling

(*a*) *Air natural cooling.* In this method, the cooling is affected by the circulation of air around the transformer tank. The cores of the transformer and the windings are kept open all round to the air. This method is applicable to very small unit of a few kVA at low voltage.

(*b*) *Oil immersed natural cooling.* In this method, the Cooling is affected by natural circulation of oil through the cooling ducts which are provided between winding coils and transformer cores.

The cooling is more affected by (*a*) Corrugating the sides of the transformer tank; (*b*) attaching a number of fins of the tank; (*c*) providing number of external corrugating tubes on the side of the tanks.

If further additional cooling is required, the external tubes are replaced by radiators provided with transformer tank.

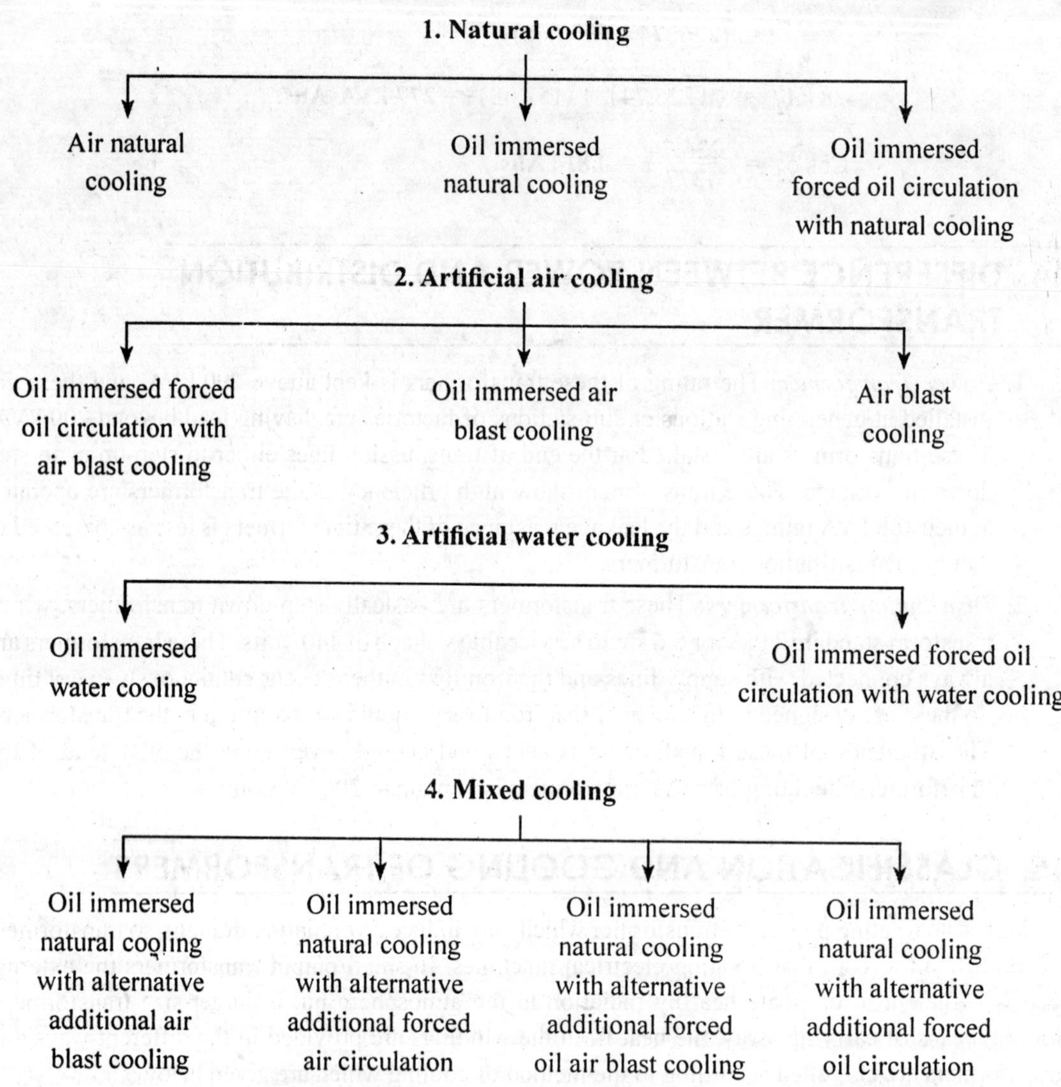

(c) Oil immersed forced oil circulation with natural cooling. In this method, the cores and winding coils are immersed in the oil and the cooling is affected by forced oil circulation through motor driven oil pump. This method is employed with the radiators separately installed from the transformers and connected to them with the headers at the top and bottom.

A pump in the power header forces the oil through the windings and tank and back to the radiators.

2. Artificial Air Cooling

(a) *Oil immersed forced oil circulation with air blast cooling.* In this method, the cooling is achieved by means of fans running under the radiators. The radiators may be kept at some little distance from the transformer tank.

(b) *Oil immersed air blast cooling.* In this method, the winding coils and cores are immersed in the oil and the cooling is increased by forced air over radiators. This additional cooling is provided by motor driven fans mounted directly on the radiators.

(c) *Air blast cooling.* In this method, the transformer upto 5000 KVA is housed in a thin sheet metal box open at both ends through which air is blown from the bottom to top by means of external fan or blower. In this method, the filtered cooling air is supplied to remove dust and dirt otherwise the ducts will be covered with a film of dust which would considerably decrease the heat dissipation from the transformer's winding and core to the cooling air.

3. Artificial Water Cooling

(a) *Oil immersed water cooling.* In this case, the winding coils and the cores are immersed in oil the cooling is effected by the circulation of water through tubes, installed in the transformer tank and immersed in the oil. Cold water is passed through the system of pipes fitted inside the upper portion of the tank. The heat of the oil is carried away by this water passing through the pipes.

(b) *Oil immersed, forced oil circulation water cooling.* In this method, the oil is circuited by pump from the top of the transformer to a radiator where it is cooled by low pressure water. This cooled oil then returns to the bottom of the transformer tank.

4. Mixed Cooling Systems

In large substations, a mixture of natural and forced cooling is used. In any of the mixed cooling systems, oil circulates through the radiators by natural connection upto about half load and provides sufficient cooling. For the higher loads, the oil pump and fan, both are employed to achieve the forced cooling. The phenomenon is obtained automatically.

5.46. CHARACTERISTIC OF INSULATING OIL

1. It should have a high dielectric strength *i.e.* not less than 40 kV (R.M.S.) in drums and 30 KV (R.M.S.) in the transformer tank for new untreated and for the gap of 4 mm of the electrodes.
2. It should be free from moisture contents and water vapours.
3. The oil should be perfectly clear and pale in colour, transparent and free from suspended matter of sediments.
4. Acidity contents should be very low in the oil.
5. It should have higher flash point *i.e.* 104°C and lower pour point as per specifications laid down.
6. The oil should be chemically stable.
7. It should possess low viscosity.
8. The sludge value of the oil after treating should be 1.2%.
9. Density of the oil at 20°C should be 0.89 gm/cm^2.
10. Mineral oil grade B should be used.

5.47. TAP CHANGER

The modern electrical equipment are normally designed to operate satisfactorily at fixed voltage level. It is, therefore, of great importance to keep the consumer's terminal voltage within the specified limits. The transformer output voltage and, hence, the consumer's terminal voltage may be varied, on the one hand, in steps or, on the other hand, by stepless control. However, in most cases it has been found that system voltage variation can be carried out quite effectively in steps without creating objectionable disturbances on the system. This stepped variation of voltage is generally achieved by means of tappings provided on the transformer windings.

There are three common types of tappings from the point of view of construction.

Tapping Inside the Tank. This is the simplest and also the cheapest type of tapping arrangement and is usually employed when tapping changes are likely to be infrequent. To operate this type of tap changer the tank cover or hand hole cover must be removed. If the transformer has an oil conservator, then it is also necessary to drain out part of the oil for changing this type of tapping.

Tappings Outside the Tank. The tap changers which are located outside the tank are very convenient but are also very expensive, particularly for high voltage transformers. The several tapping leads which are approximately at the same potential are brought out through a single terminal bushing to reduce the cost. This type of tap changers also become essential in the cases where two or more voltages are to be used simultaneously.

Selector Operated Tappings. Using selector switches is the most convenient method of dealing with changes of tap position. Tap changers having tappings outside the tank and operated by an external selector are suitable for on-load operation and are regarded as an integral part of the transformer. On the other hand, tap changers having tappings inside the tank and connected to an internal selector which is operated by an external handle are most widely used for off-circuit operation.

From the point of view of operation, transformer tap changers fall into two categories: (*a*) Off-load tap changers by which the tapping changes are made when the transformer is isolated from the supply on both sides and (*b*) On-load tap changers by which tap positions are changed without interrupting the load current.

No-load (off-load or off circuit) Tap Changer. The simplest arrangement is that the transformer tappings are terminated just below oil level and are changed by means of swinging links or plugs mounted on a suitable terminal board operated by an external handle.

These tap-changers are used for seasonal voltage variations. The schemetic diagram of a no-load tap-changer is shown in Fig. 5.63. A winding is topped and its leads are connected to six studs marked 1 to 6. The studs are stationary and are arranged in a circle. The face plate carrying the studs can be mounted anywhere on the transformer, say on the yoke or on any other convenient place (say a separate box). The rotatable arm 'A' is attached to a handwheel which is kept outside the tank and can be rotated.

Sometimes, in case of large transformers, the rotatable arm is rotated with the help of a motor (with gear drive) and the controls of the motor are placed on the panel board although handwheel is also provided for manual operation.

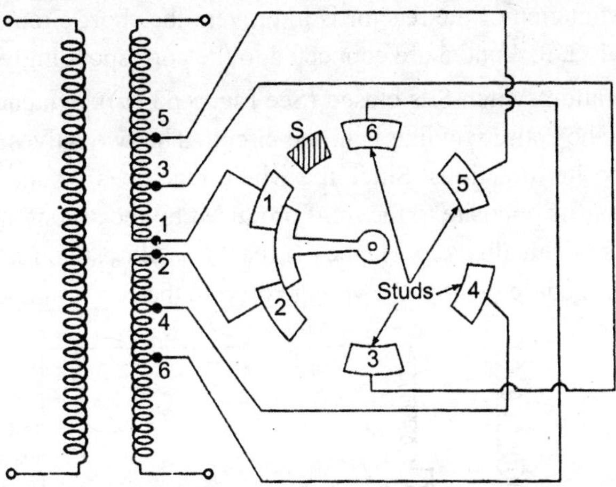

Fig. 5.63. No-load tap changer

The active number of turns of the winding which remain in the circuit depends upon the position of rotating arm. If the winding is tapped at 2% interval, then at various positions of the rotatable arm 'A', the winding in the circuit will be as under:

(*i*) at studs 1-2: Full winding is in the circuit.

(*ii*) at studs 2-3: 98% of the winding is in the circuit.

(*iii*) at studs 3-4: 96% of the winding is in the circuit.

(*iv*) at studs 4-5: 94% of the winding is in the circuit.

(*v*) at studs 5-6: 92% of the winding is in the circuit.

A stopper *S* is placed in between the stud 1 and 6. It fixes the final position of the arm 'A' at stud 5-6. Moreover, it prevents the clockwise rotation of the arm 'A' from stud 1. It prevents the connections of studs 1 and 6 through arm A. If studs 1 and 6 are connected then only the lower part of the winding is cut out of circuit which is undesirable from mechanical stress considerations.

In this case, the tap-changing is carried out only after the transformer is disconnected from the supply. For instance, let the arm 'A' is at stud 1 and 2 and the whole winding is in the circuit. Now, if we want to reduce the winding to 96%, we have to rotate the arm in anticlockwise direction to bridge stud 3 and 4 through arm 'A'. While doing so, the transformer is disconnected from the supply, arm is rotated to the desired position and then the transformer is energised.

This tap-changer is never operated on load. If it would be operated on load, there would be heavy sparking at the studs when arm 'A' is separated from them. It may damage the tap-changer and the transformer winding.

This tap-changer is used for daily or short period voltage regulations. The output voltage can be regulated with the help of this tap-changer without any supply interruptions. During the operation of an on-load tap-changer the following points must be kept in mind:

(*i*) Never open the main circuit during the operation of tap-changer otherwise dangerous sparking will occur, and

(*ii*) No part of the topped winding should get short circuited.

One form of an on-load tap-changer provided with a centre-tapped reactor is shown in Fig.

5.63 (*a*). The function of the reactor is to prevent the short-circuiting of the tapped winding. The switches 1, 2, 3, 4 and 5 are connected to the correspondingly marked taps.

During normal operation switch S is closed (See Fig. 5.63 (*a*)), switches 2, 3, 4 and 5 are opened and switch 1 is closed. The entire winding is in the circuit. The two halves of the reactor carry half of the total current in opposite directions. Since the whole reactor is wound in the same direction, the mmf produced by one-half is opposite to the mmf produced by the second half. These mmfs are equal, therefore, the net mmf is practically zero. Hence the reactor is almost non-inductive and the impedance offered by it is very small, consequently, the voltage drop in the centre-tapped reactor is negligible.

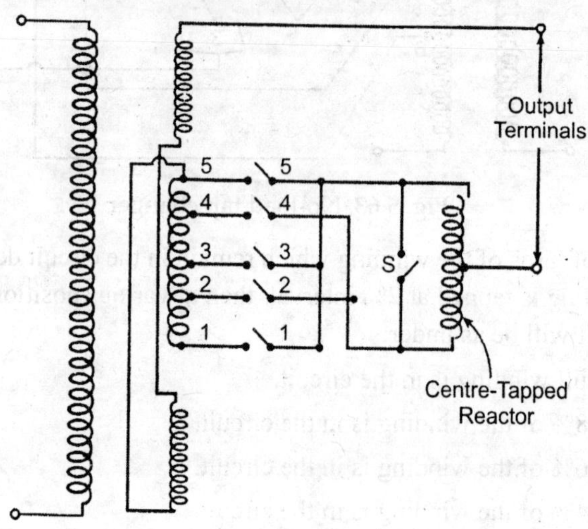

Fig. 5.63. (*a*) Schematic diagram of a no load tap changer.

When a change in voltage is required, the following sequence of operations are adopted:

(*i*) *Open the switch S*: By opening this switch, total current flows through the upper half of the reactor and there is more voltage drop. Since reactor is to carry full load current momentarily, the reactor must be designed accordingly.

(*ii*) *Close the switch 2:* When switch 2 is closed, the winding between taps 1 and 2 is connected across the reactor. Since the impedance offered by the reactor is high for a current flowing in only one direction, the local circulating current flowing through the reactor and tapped winding is quite small. Thus reactor prevents the tapped winding from getting short circuited. The terminal voltage at this instant is mid-way between the potentials of tappings 1 and 2.

(*iii*) Open the switch *I*: The entire current now flows through the lower half of the reactor which causes more voltage drop.

(*iv*) *Close the switch S*: By closing the switch, current is divided equally in the upper and lower part of the reactor which causes almost negligible voltage drop.

The same sequence of operations is repeated if the tapping is to be changed from stud 2 to 3.

On-load Tap Changing

On-load tap changers are used to change the turn ratio of transformer to regulate system voltage while the transformer is delivering load. With the introduction of on-load tap changer, the operating efficiency of electrical system gets considerably improved. Now a days almost all the large power transformers are fitted with on-load tap changer. During the operation of an on-load tap changer the main circuit should not be opened to prevent (dangerous) sparking and no part of the tapped winding should get short-circuited. All forms of on-load tap changing circuits are provided with an impedance, which is introduced to limit short-circuit current during the tap changing operation. The impedance can either be a resistor or centre-tapped reactor. The on-load tap changers can in general be classified as resistor or reactor type. In modern designs the current limiting is almost invariably carried out by a pair of resistors.

On-load tap changing gear with resistor transition, in which one winding tap is changed over for each operating position, is depicted in Fig. 5.63.(*b*) The figure also shows the sequence of operations during the transition from one tap to the next (adjoining)(in this case from tap 4 to tap 5). Back-up main contractors are provided which short-circuit the resistor for normal operation.

To ensure that the transition once started gets completed, an energy (usually a spring device) storage is provided which acts even if the auxiliary power supply happens to fail. In resistor-aided tap changing the current break is made easier by the fact that the short-circuit resistor causes the current to be opened to have unity power factor.

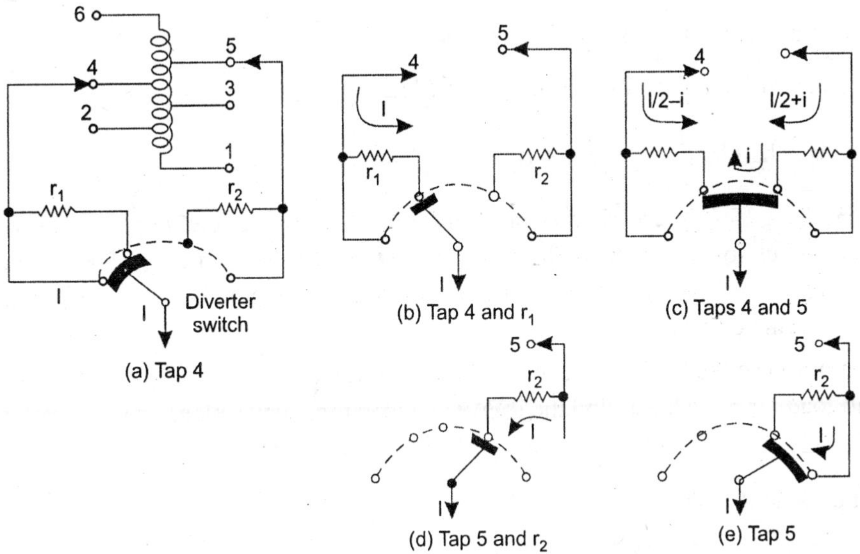

Fig. 5.63. (*b*) Simple switching sequences for on-load tap changing

On-load tap changer control gear can be from simple push-button initiation to complex automatic control of several transformers operating in parallel. The aim is to maintain a given voltage level within a specified tolerance or to raise it with load to compensate for the transmission line voltage drop. The main components are an automatic voltage regulator, a time delay relay, and compounding elements. The time delay prevents unwanted initiation of a tap change by a small transient voltage fluctuation. It may be set for a delay unto 1 min.

At present tap changers are available for the highest insulation level of 1475 kV (peak) impulse and 630 kV power frequency voltage. Efforts are underway to develop tap changers suitable for still higher insulation levels. More compact tap changers with high reliability and performance are being made by employing vacuum switches in the diverter switch. Also, now thyristorized tap changers are available for special applications where a large number of operations are desired.

Example 5.22. A 240 V/400 V, single phase transformer absorbs 35 *W* when its primary winding is connected to a 240 *V*, 50 Hz supply, the secondary being on open circuit.

When the primary is short circuited and a 10 V, 50 Hz supply is connected to the secondary winding, the power absorbed is 48 *W* when current has the full load value of 15 A.

Estimate the efficiency of transformer at half load and 0.8 *p.f.* lagging.

Solution. Iron loss = 35 W

Full load copper loss = 48 W

Full load current = 15 A

Full load output of the transformer at 0.8 *p.f.*

$$= 400 \times 15 \times 0.8 = 4800 \text{ W}$$

Output at half load = 2400 W

Copper loss at half load $= 48 \times (1/2)^2 = 12$ W

$\therefore$ Input at half load $= 2400 + 35 + 12 = 2447$ W

$$\therefore \quad \eta \text{ at half load} = \frac{2400}{2447} \times 100 = 98.1\% \textbf{ Ans.}$$

Example 5.23. A 75 *k*VA transformer rated at 6600/230 *V* on no load requires 310 V across the primary to circulate full load currents on short circuit, the power absorbed being 1.6 KW. Determine (*a*) the percentage voltage regulation and (*b*) the full load secondary terminal voltage for power factors of (*i*) unity (*ii*) 0.8 lagging (*iii*) 0.8 leading.

If the input power to the transformer on no load is 0.9 KW, calculate the per unit efficiency at full load and at half load for *p.f.* 0.8 and find the KVA at which efficiency is max.

Solution.

Full load Rating = 75 kVA

$E_1 = 6600$ V

$E_2 = 230$ V

I_2 = full load current on secondary

$$= \frac{75 \times 1000}{230} = 326.08 \text{ A}$$

This full load current flows in primary when secondary is short and primary is applied with voltage of 310 V.

310 volts on primary are equivalent to $310 \times \dfrac{230}{6600}$

$= 10.8$ V on secondary.

∴ Total impedance of transformer on secondary side

$$= \frac{10.8}{326.08} = 0.033\ \Omega$$

$$\text{Copper loss} = \text{Power absorbed on short circuit test}$$

$$= 1.6\text{ kW}$$

$$\text{Copper loss} = I_2^2 R_{t2} = 1600$$

$$\therefore \quad R_{t2} = \frac{1600}{I_2^2} = \frac{1600}{(326.08)^2} = 0.015$$

$$X_{t2} = \sqrt{Z_{t2}^2 - R_{t2}^2} = \sqrt{(0.033)^2 - (0.015)^2}$$

$$= \sqrt{0.00109 - 0.000225} = \sqrt{0.000765} = 0.0276\ \Omega$$

%age voltage regulation at 0.8 p.f lagging

$$= \frac{I_2(R_{t2}\cos\phi_2 + X_{t2}\sin\phi_2)}{E_2} \times 100$$

$$= \frac{326.08(0.015 \times 0.8 + 0.0276 \times 0.6)}{230} \times 100$$

$$= \frac{326.08(0.012 + 0.0165) \times 100}{230}$$

$$= \frac{326.08 \times 0.0285 \times 100}{230} = 4.04\%\ \textbf{Ans.}$$

Percentage regulation at unity p.f.

$$= \frac{326.08(0.015 \times 1 + 0)}{230} \times 100 \quad \left[\begin{array}{l}\text{when } \cos\phi_2 = 1\\ \sin\phi_2 = 0\end{array}\right.$$

$$= 2.12\%$$

Percentage regulation at 0.8 p.f. leading

$$= \frac{I_2(R_{t2}\cos\phi_2 + X_{t2}\sin\phi_2)}{E_2} \times 100$$

$$= \frac{326.08 \times (-0.0045) \times 100}{230} = -0.638\%$$

Secondary terminal voltage at 0.8 p.f. lagging

$$= 230 - I_2(R_{t2}\cos\phi_2 + X_{t2}\sin\phi_2)$$

$$= 230 - 326.08\ (0.015 \times 0.6 - 0.0276 \times 0.06)$$

$$= 230 - 9.3 = 220.7\text{ V } \textbf{Ans.}$$

Secondary terminal voltage at unity p.f.

$$= 230 - 326.08\ (0.015 \times 1 - 0.0276 \times 0)$$

$$= 230 - 4.89 = 225.11\text{ V } \textbf{Ans.}$$

Secondary terminal voltage at 0.8 p.f. leading

$$= 230 - I_2(R_{t2} \cos \phi_2 - X_{t2} \sin \phi_2)$$

$$= 230 - 326.08\ (0.015 \times 0.8 - 0.0276 \times 0.6)$$

$$= 230 - 326.08\ (-0.0045)$$

$$= 230 + 1.467 = 231.467 \text{ V } \textbf{Ans.}$$

Input to the transformer on no load

$$= \text{Iron loss} = 0.9 \text{ kW} = 900 \text{ W}$$

$$\text{Full load copper loss} = 1600 \text{ W} = 1.6 \text{ kW}$$

Full load output at 0.8 p.f.

$$= 75 \times 0.8 = 60 \text{ kW}$$

$$\text{Full load input} = 60 + 1.6 + 0.9 = 62.5 \text{ kW}$$

∴ Full load per unit efficiency

$$= \frac{60}{62.5} = 0.96 \textbf{ Ans.}$$

Output of transformer at half load, 0.8 *p.f.*

$$= \frac{75 \times 0.8}{2} = 30 \text{ kW}$$

$$\text{Iron loss} = 0.9 \text{ kW}$$

Copper loss at half load

$$= 1.6 \times (1/2)^2 = 0.4 \text{ kW}$$

Input to transformer at 1/2 load

$$= 30 + 0.9 + 0.4 = 31.3 \text{ kW}$$

Per unit efficiency at half load

$$= \frac{30}{31.3} = 0.9584 \textbf{ Ans.}$$

At maximum efficiency, Copper loss = Iron loss

$$\text{Iron loss} = \text{constant} = 900 \text{ W}$$

At max. η, copper loss is also = 900 W

$$\text{Copper loss at full load,} = 1600 \text{ W}$$

∴ kVA at which efficiency is max.

$$= 75 \times \sqrt{\frac{900}{1600}} = \frac{75 \times 30}{40} = 56.25 \text{ KVA } \textbf{Ans.}$$

Example 5.24. A 200 kVA single phase transformer has an efficiency of 98 per cent at full load 0.8 *p.f.* lagging. If maximum efficiency occurs at three quarters of a full load, calculate (*i*) Iron loss (*ii*) Copper loss at full load (*iii*) Efficiency at half load. Ignore magnetising current and assume a power factor of 0.8 at all loads. (*A.M.I.e. Section B, Winter 1974*)

Solution.

Full load output of transformer at 0.8 *p.f.*

$$= 200 \times 0.8 = 160 \text{ kW}$$

$$\eta = 0.98$$

∴ Input to the transformer

$$= \frac{160}{0.98} = 163.26 \text{ kW}$$

Losses in the transformer = 163.26 – 160 = 3.26 kW

Losses in transformer = Copper loss + Iron loss

At max. efficiency, Copper loss = Iron loss

$$= \frac{3.26}{2} = 1.63 \text{ KW.}$$

Since max. η takes place at 3/4 th of full load.

∴ Copper loss at 3/4 of full load = 1.63 kW

Copper loss at full load = $1.63 \times (4/3)^2 = \frac{1.63 \times 16}{9} = 2.89$ kW

Copper loss at half load = $2.89 \times (1/2)^2 = 0.725$ kW

Iron loss = 1.63 kW

Output at half load and 0.8 p.f.

$$= \frac{200}{2} \times 0.8 = 80 \text{ kW.}$$

Input to the transformer at half load

$$= 80 + 1.63 + 0.725 = 82.355 \text{ kW.}$$

∴ Efficiency of transformer at half load

$$= \frac{80}{82.355} = 97.14\%$$ **Ans.**

Example 5.25. In a 25 kVA, 3300/230 V single phase transformer, the iron and full load copper losses are respectively 350 W and 400 W. Calculate (*i*) the efficiency at half load, 0.8 *p.f.* and (*ii*) the load at which efficiency is maximum. (*A.M.I.e., Section A, Nov., 1974*)

Solution.

(*i*) Output of transformer at half load at 0.8 p.f.

$$= \frac{25}{2} \times 0.8 = 10 \text{ W}$$

Iron loss = 350 W

Full load copper loss = 400 W

Copper loss at 1/2 load = $400 \times (1/2)^2 = 100$ W

Input to transformer at half load

$$= 10 + \frac{350 + 100}{1000} = 10.45 \text{ kW}$$

$\therefore$ η of transformer at half load

$$= \frac{10}{10.45} \times 100 = 95.7\% \textbf{ Ans.}$$

(*ii*) Efficiency is max. when,

Copper loss = Iron loss.

Since iron loss is constant = 350 W

$\therefore$ Copper loss at max. η = 350 W

Full load copper loss = 400 W

Load at which efficiency is max.

$$= \sqrt{\frac{350}{400}} \times 25$$

$$= \frac{18.7}{20} \times 25 = 23.375 \text{ kVA } \textbf{Ans.}$$

Example 5.26. A transformer has its. max. efficiency of 0.98 at 15 KVA at unity p.f. During the day it is loaded as follows:

12 hours: 2 KW at 0.5 *p.f.*

6 hours: 12 KW at 0.8 *p.f.*

6 hours: 18 KW at 0.9 *p.f.*

Find the all day efficiency.

Solution:

Full load output of transformer at unity p.f.

$$= 15 \times 1$$

$$= 15 \text{ kW}$$

$$\eta = 0.98$$

$\therefore$ Input to transformer

$$= \frac{15}{0.98} = 15.3 \text{ kW}$$

$\therefore$ Total losses = $15.3 - 15$

$= 0.3 \text{ kW} = 300$ W

At max efficiency, copper loss = Iron loss

$$= \frac{300}{2} = 150 \text{ W}$$

For 12 hours, output

$$= \frac{2}{0.5} = 4 \text{ kVA}$$

Copper loss at load of 4 kVA

$$= 150 \times \left(\frac{4}{15}\right)^2$$

$$= \frac{32}{3} \text{ Watts}$$

$$\text{For 6 hours output} = \frac{12}{0.8} = 15 \text{ kVA}$$

Copper loss at a load of 15 kVA

$$= 150 \text{ W.}$$

For another 6 hours output

$$= \frac{18}{0.9} = 20 \text{ kVA}$$

Copper loss at a load of 20 kVA

$$= 150 \times \left(\frac{20}{15}\right)^2 = \frac{800}{3} \text{ W}$$

Energy consumed by copper loss in 12 hours

$$= \frac{32}{3} \times 12 = 128 \text{ Wh}$$

Energy consumed by copper loss in 6 hours

$$= 150 \times 6 = 900 \text{ Wh}$$

Energy consumed by copper loss in next 6 hours

$$= \frac{800}{3} \times 6 = 1600 \text{ Wh}$$

Iron loss takes place for all the 24 hours

$\therefore$ Energy consumed by iron loss for 24 hours

$$= 150 \times 24 = 3600 \text{ Wh.}$$

Output of transformer in 24 hours

$$= 2 \times 12 + 6 \times 12 + 6 \times 18$$

$$= 24 + 72 + 108 = 204 \text{ kWh}$$

Losses of transformer in 24 hours in kWh

$$= 128 + 900 + 1600 + 3600$$

$$= 6228 \text{ Wh}$$

$$= 6.228 \text{ kWh}$$

$\therefore$ Input to transformer in 24 hours

$$= 204 + 6.228$$

$$= 210.228 \text{ kWh}$$

All day efficiency of transformer

$$= \frac{\textit{Output in kWh}}{\textit{Input in kWh}} \times 100$$

$$= \frac{204}{210.228} \times 100$$

$$= 97\%. \textbf{ Ans.}$$

HIGHLIGHTS

1. **Transformer:** It is an electrical apparatus which transfers electrical power from one circuit to another without change is frequency. The working of the transformer is based upon the principle of electromagnetic induction
2. **E.M.F. Equation of a transformer:**

$$E_1 = 4.44 f N_1 \phi_m \text{ volts}$$

$$E_2 = 4.44 f N_2 \phi_m \text{ volts} \qquad [\phi_m = B_{max} \times A]$$

3. **Transformation Ratio**: K, the Ratio of secondary voltage to Primary voltage or Ratio of Primary current to secondary current is called transformation ratio.
4. **Types of transformers:**
   (*i*) Core type
   (*ii*) Shell type.
5. **Ideal transformer:** is that in which the losses are neglected.

i.e. Power input = Power output

or $E_1 I_1 \cos\phi = E_2 I_2 \cos\phi$

6. **Transformer on D.C.** the transformer should never be connected to d.c. source otherwise due to the absence of opposing e.m. f. primary will draw large current from the supply lines due to constant magnitude of flux which may burn the primary winding of the transformer.
7. **Transformer on no load.** At no load transformer draws power to meet with iron losses.
   (*i*) Active component $I_w = I_0 \cos \phi_0$

(*ii*) Reactive component $I_m = I_0 \sin \phi_0$

$$P_0 = V_1 I_0 \cos \phi_0$$

$$I_0 = (I_m^2 + I_w^2)$$

8. Voltage Regulation. The change in secondary terminal voltage from no load to full load is known as voltage Regulations.

$$\% \text{ Regulation} = \frac{E_2 - V_2}{E_2} \times 100$$

E_2 = Secondary Terminal voltage at no load.

V_2 = Secondary Terminal voltage at full load.

When all the quantities are referred to the primary side of the transformer:

Then: $$\%\text{Regulation} = \frac{V_1 - E_1}{V_1} \times 100$$

9. Losses in a transformer: Two types of losses in a transformer are:

(*i*) Iron losses P_i

(*ii*) Copper losses P_c

10. Efficiency of transformer:

$$\eta = \frac{V_2 I_2 \cos \phi_2}{V_2 I_2 \cos \phi_2 + P_i + P_c}$$

11. Copper losses = Iron losses, is the condition for maximum efficiency of the transformer.

12. Mutual flux: the flux which links with both the windings *i.e.* Primary and secondary of a transformer is called mutual flux.

13. Leakage flux. Some part of flux produced by one winding does not link with the other winding is called leakage flux.

14. Equivalent reactance of a transformer.

$$R_{01} = R_1 + \frac{R_2}{K^2}$$

$$R_{02} = R_2 + k^2 R_1$$

15. Equivalent reactance of a transformer.

$$X_{01} = X_2 + K^2 X_1$$

$$X_{02} = X_1 + \frac{X_2}{K^2}$$

SHORT ANSWER TYPE QUESTIONS

1. What is a transformer? *[SBTE June 2004]*

Ans. Transformer is a device which transforms electrical power from one circuit to another at the same frequency by changing its voltage/current level.

2. What is a step up transformer ? *[SBTE Dec. 2006]*

Ans. When voltage at the output terminals of a transformer is more than the voltage at input terminals, transformer is called step up transformer.

3. What is step down transformer ? *[SBTE June 2005]*

Ans. When the output voltage of transformer is less than the input voltage, the transformer is called step down transformer.

4. What is the principle of transformer ? *[SBTE June 2006]*

Ans. When an A.C. supply is given to the windings of transformers current flows through it. This AC current produces an alternating flux in the core. This flux which is altrenating in nature links with the secondary windings through the soft iron core, and an e.m.f. induced in secondary windings due to mutual induction. The frequency of e.m.f is induced in secondary winding is same as the frequency of supply voltage. When a load is connected across the second terminals, a current flows in secondary circuit.

5. Transformer is based on the principle of...............induction? *(self / Mutual)*

Ans. Mutual.

6. Write EMF equation of a transformer? *(V. Imp)*

Ans. $E = 4.44\,\phi_m f N$

Where f = frequency of supply

N = No. of turns

ϕ_m = Maximum flux linking the core

7. Name the material used in the manufacture of core of transformer? *[SBTE June 2006]*

Ans. Silicon steel.

8. Define transformation ratio of a transformer? *V. Imp [SBTE Dec 2005, 2007]*

Ans. It is ratio of secondary voltage to primary voltage of a transformer and is called transformation ratio. It is given by

$$K = \frac{V_2}{V_1} = \frac{E_2}{E_1} = \frac{I_1}{I_2} = \frac{N_2}{N_1}$$

9. Define primary and secondary winding of a transformer?

Ans. Primary Winding: The winding of transformer to which voltage is applied is called primary winding.

Secondary Winding: The winding of transformer from which output is taken is called secondary winding.

10. Which current causes losses in the core of a transformer? *[SBTE June 2006]*

Ans. Eddy Current.

11. Iron losses in a transformer consist of......and..... . *[SBTE Dec. 2007]*

Ans. Hysteresis, eddy currents.

12. Why transformer is rated in KVA? *V. Imp [SBTE Dec. 2007]*

Ans. Copper losses in the transformer depend upon current and core loss depend upon voltage. Therefore total loss in the transformer depend upon volt-Ampere and not the phase angle between voltage and current. That is why the transformers are rated in KVA not in KW.

13. A 25 KVA transformer having 500 turns on primary is connected to 40 turns on secondary winding. The primary is connected to 3000V, 50 Hz mains. The secondary voltage will be...........? *[SBTE June 2008]*

Ans.

$$\frac{V_2}{V_1} = \frac{N_2}{N_1}$$

$$\frac{V_2}{3000} = \frac{40}{500}$$

$$V_2 = \frac{40}{500} \times 3000 = 240 \text{ V}$$

14. Transformer cannot be used on DC. Why? *[SBTE Dec. 2006]*

Ans. Transformer cannot be used on DC because it is based on the principle of electromagnetic induction. No e.m.f. is induced in its windings, when connected to DC.

15. What is an instrument transformer? *[SBTE Dec. 2006]*

Ans. The transformer which is used with Am-metres/volt meters to measure high current/voltage is called instrument transformer.

16. Name the losses which occur in a transformer? *V. Imp*

Ans. Losses occuring in a transformer are

(*i*) Core losses *i.e.* hysteresis and current loss (*ii*) Copper loss

17. State two applications of an auto transformer? *[SBTE Dec. 2006]*

Ans. (*i*) It is used in laboratory to get variable AC supply.

(*ii*) It is used in the starting of three phase induction motor to give upto 50 to 60% of rated voltage during starting.

18. What is the function of conservator in a transformer? *[SBTE June 2004]*

Ans. Conservator tank is provided at the top of tank of the transformer and is partly filled with transformer oil and is connected to the main tank by a pipe. Oil in the main tank expands on heating and rises to the conservator tank. On cooling the oil contracts and comes back to the main tank. The function of conservator tank is thus to take up expansion and contraction of oil in the main tank.

19. What is the function of breather in a transformer? *Imp*

Ans. During contraction and expansion of oil in tank air is breathed in and out. The air entering the conservator tank must be dry. Silica gel breather absorbs moisture from air.

20. Name the relay used for the protection of transformer from internal short circuits?

Ans. Buchholtz relay.

21. What is an isolation transformer?

Ans. In a transformer primary and secondary windings are electrically insulated from each other. Therefore a transformer can be used to isolate one circuit from the other. Such transformer is called isolation transformer and is used to couple the two amplifier stages.

Medium Long Answer Type Questions:

1. Derive e.m.f equation of a transformer. **[SBTE June 2005]**

Ans. Let ϕ_m = Maximum value of flux in core = $(B_m \times A)$ Web

f = Frequency of A.C. supply in Hertz.

N_1 = No. of turns in primary winding.

N_2 = No. of turns in secondary winding.

E_1 = e.m.f induced in primary winding

E_2 = e.m.f induced in secondary winding.

The flux increases from zero to its maximum value in one quarter of the cycle *i.e.* in $\frac{1}{4f}$ second shown in fig. 1.

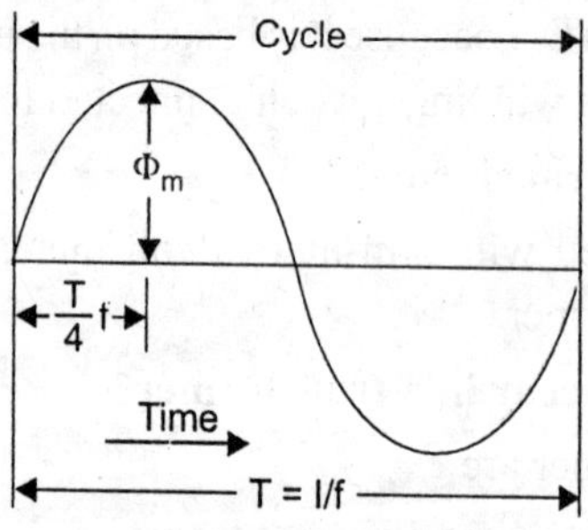

Fig. 1.

$$\Rightarrow \text{Average change of flux} = \frac{\phi_m}{1/(4f)} = 4\phi_m \text{ f wb/sec}$$

Now, Rate of change of flux per turn = induced e.m.f in volts.

$\therefore$ Average emf/turn = $4\phi_m f$ volts

Also, for a sinusoidal quantity

$$\text{Form Factor} = \frac{r.m.s\ value}{average\ value} = 1.11.$$

$\therefore$ r.m.s value of emf/turn = (Form factor) × (Average value)

$$= (1.11) \times (4\phi_m f)$$

$$= 4.44 f\phi_m \text{ volts}$$

The r.m.s value of emf induced in primary winding

$$E_1 = \text{(emf induced/turn)} \times \text{(No of primary turns)}$$
$$= (4.44 f \phi_m)(N_1)$$
$$= 4.44 f \phi_m N_1$$
$$= 4.44 f N_1 B_m A \text{ Volts}$$

Similarly. r.m.s value of induced e.m.f in secondary winding is given by

$$E_2 = 4.44 f N_2 \phi_m$$
$$= 4.44 f N_2 B_m A \text{ Volts}$$

For an ideal transformer, $V_1 = E_1$ and $V_2 = E_2$ where V_1 and V_2 are terminal voltages at primary and secondary windings.

2. Discuss in brief the different types of losses occuring in a transformer?

V. Imp. (SBTE, June 2008)

Ans. There are mainly two types of losses which occur in transformers. They are (*i*) Core or Iron Losses:- The losses which occur in the core of transformer are known as core or iron losses. These losses are constant in nature and donot vary with load. They are further of two types:

(*i*) Hysteresis loss $W_h = \eta B^{1.6}_{max.}$ f.v watt.

(*ii*) Eddy current loss $W_e = P. B^2_{max.} f^2 t^2$ watt

The hysteresis loss can be reduced by using Silicon steel material for construction of cores, Whereas Eddy current loss can be minimized by using laminations. Laminations are very thin strips of *E*, *L* and *I* shapes having thickness ranging between 0.35 to 0.5 mm.

(*ii*) **Copper Losses:-** This loss occurs in the windings of transformers which are made up of Copper that's why the name Copper loss. This loss is due to the ohmic resistance of transformer windings.

$$\text{Copper Loss} = I^2 R$$

Where I = Current in Amperes R = Ohmic resistance of windings. Thus, copper losses are variable and are proportional to the square of current flowing in the windings.

3. What is a transformer. Discuss in brief its principle and construction. (SBTE, June 2006)

Ans. Transformer is an electrical device which transforms electrical power from one circuit to another at same frequency by changing its voltage/current level. When the voltage at output terminals is more than the input voltage, it is called step-up transformer. When voltage at output terminals is less than the input voltage, it is called step-down transformer.

Working Principle:- When an A.C supply is given to the windings of transformer current flows through it. This A.C current produces an alternating flux in the core. This flux which is alternating in nature links with the secondary windings through the soft iron core, and an e.m.f is induced in secondary windings due to mutual induction. The frequency of e.m.f induced in secondary winding is same as the frequency of supply voltage. When a load is connected across the secondary terminals, a current flows in secondary circuit.

Construction:- A simple transformer consists of silicon steel or soft iron core. Two windings insulated from each other and also from core are placed on soft iron core as shown in fig. 2.

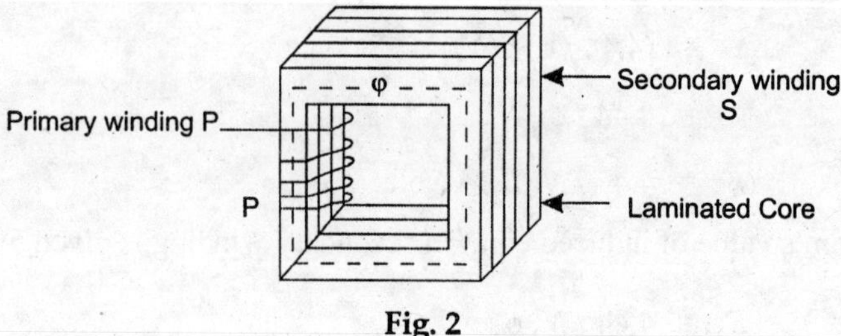

Fig. 2

The core of transformer is made up of very thin soft iron or silicon steel laminations. The laminations provide a path of low reluctance to the magnetic flux. The winding to which A.C supply is connected, is known as primary winding and the winding connected to load circuit is called secondary winding.

The thickness of laminations varies from 0.35 mm. to 0.5 mm The core laminations (in the form of strips) are joined as shown in fig. 3.

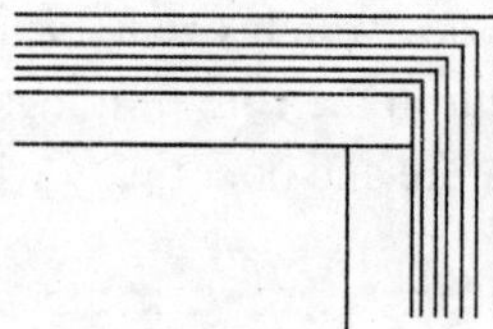

Fig. 3

The joints in the alternate layers are staggered in order to avoid the presence of narrow gaps through the cross section of the core

On the basis of construction, transformers can be divided into two types. They are core type and shell-type. In core-type transformers, the windings surround considerable part of the core. The primary and secondary windings are on side limbs as shown in fig. 4.

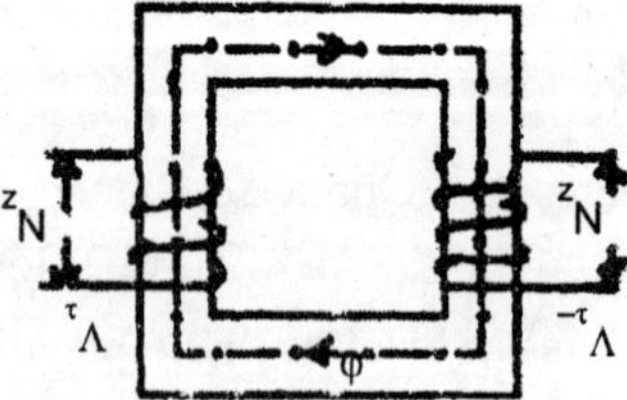

Fig. 4

In a shell-type transformer, the core surround considerable portion of the winding. Both the primary and secondary windings are on the central-limb as shown in fig. 5.

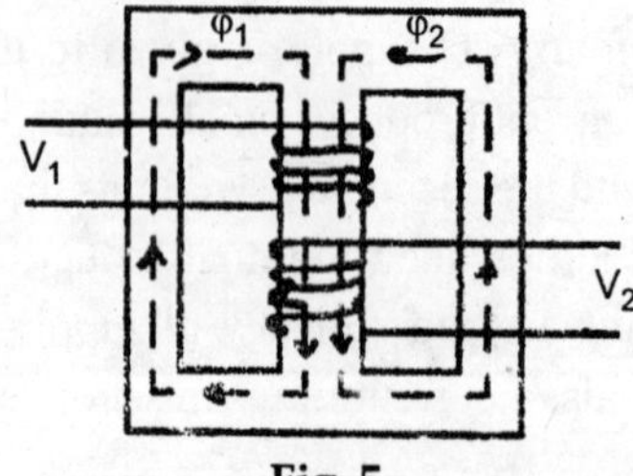

Fig. 5

4. Define voltage regulation of a transformer. What is its significance.

V. Imp [SBTE, June 2008]

Ans. When a transformer is loaded, voltage drops in the resistance and reactance of windings and there is a change in the secondary terminal voltage from no load secondary terminal voltage to full load secondary terminal voltage. This change in secondary terminal voltage from no load to full load expressed as a percentage of no toad secondary voltage is called regulation of transformer.

$$\% \text{ regulation} = \frac{V_{nl} - V_{fl}}{V_{nl}} \times 100$$

Significance of voltage regulation: As per Indian electricity rules, the supply voltage should be maintained with in ±5 % of declared value. The voltage regulation signifies changes in the output voltage of a transformer from no load to full load. Therefore voltage regulation has great significance in the design of transmission and distribution system to maintain the supply voltage within the declared limits. A good transformer should keep the secondary terminal voltage as constant as possible under all conditions of load. The lesser the value of voltage regulation, the better is the transformer.

5. What are the conditions of parallel operation of three phase transformer.

[SBTE June 2006]

Ans. For supplying a load in excess of the rating of an existing transformer,; a second transformer may be connected in parallel. There are certain conditions that are to be satisfied for successful parallel operation of transformers.

(1) Transformers must be connected properly with regard to polarity.

(2) Transformers should have the same turn ratio.

(3) The percentage impedence should be equal in magnitude and have the same X/R ratio.

(4) The phase displacement between primary and secondary voltages must be same for all the transformers which are to be connected in parallel.

(5) Phase sequence must be the same.

(6) All the transformers connected in a parallel bank shall be of same construction *i.e* either shell or core type.

6. Discuss in brief various three phase transformer connections.

Ans. Three phase transformer connections: The windings of three phase transformers may be connected in Y or Δ in the same manner as for three single phase transformers. Since the secondaries may be connected either-in Y or Δ regardless of which connection is used on the primaries, there must be four ways of connecting the windings of a 3-phase transformer, namely Y - Y, Δ - Δ, Y - Δ, and Δ - Y. The interconnections are made inside of the case so that only the terminal leads need to be brought outside the case.

1. **Star-Star (Y-Y) connections:** It gives line voltage $\sqrt{3}$ times the phase voltage. It is economical for small high voltage transformers as the number of turns per phase and the amount of insulation required is less. Fig. 6 shows the star-star connections of a three phase transformer

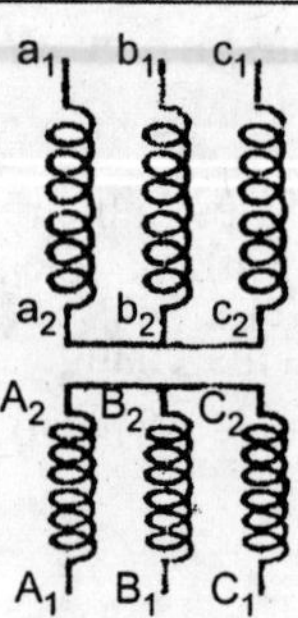

Fig. 6

2. **Delta-Delta (Δ - Δ) connections:** The arrangement is generally used in systems which carry large currents on low voltages and specially when continuity of service is to be maintained even though one of the phases develops fault. The conductor required is of smaller *x*-section as the phase current is $\frac{1}{\sqrt{3}}$ times the line current. No difficulty is experienced due to unbalancing of loads on the secondary side. The disadvantages are that more insulation is required and the voltage appearing between windings and core will be equal to full in voltage in case of earth fault on one phase Fig shows Δ – Δ connection of a 3 phase transformer

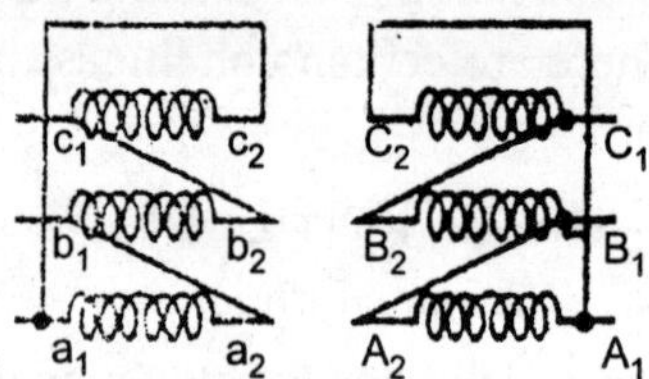

Fig. 7

3. **Star-Delta (Y - Δ) connections:** Such connections are used principally where the voltage is to be stepped down, as for example, at the end of a transmission line. The neutral of the primary winding is earthed. In this system, line voltage ratio is $1/\sqrt{3}$ times of transformer turn-ratio and secondary voltage lags behind primary voltage by 30°. Transformer at the generating end is connected in star-delta. Fig shows star-delta connection of 3 phase transformer *i.e.* primary winding is connected in star and secondary winding is connected in delta.

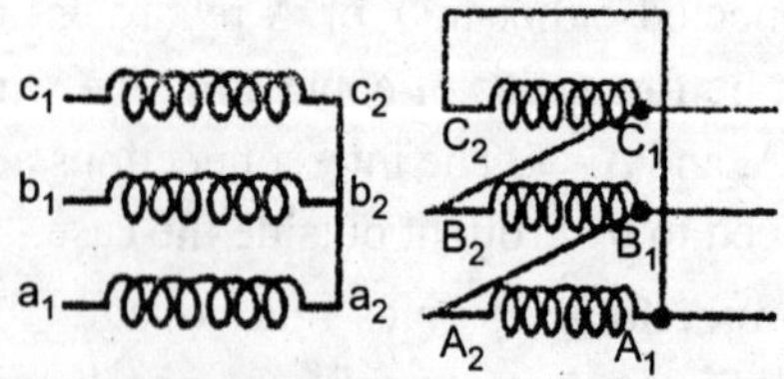

Fig. 8

4. **Delta-Star (Δ – Y) connections:** Such connections are used where it is necessary to step-up the voltage, as for example, at the beginning of a H.T transmission line. The line

voltage ratio is $\sqrt{3}$ times of transformer turn-ratio. This arrangement has become very popular for low voltage distribution system.

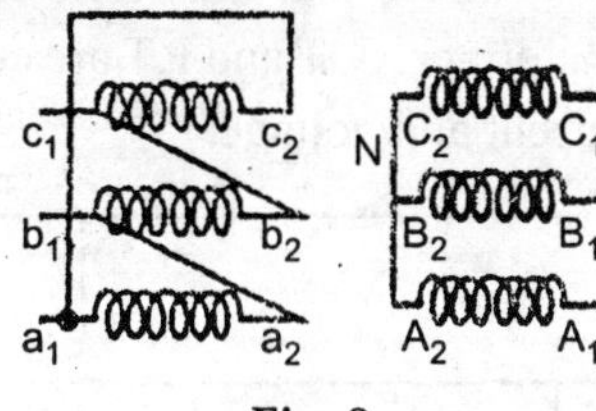

Fig. 9

7. List the specifications to be given on the terminal plate of transformer.

[SBTE June 2006]

Ans. All the manufacturers are required to give following information / specifications on the terminal plate of the transformer.

(*i*) BIS no
(*ii*) Rated KVA
(*iii*) No. of phases
(*iv*) Frequency
(*v*) Rated voltage on no load
(*vi*) Rated current
(*vii*) winding connection (Y or Δ)
(*viii*) cooling system adopted
(*ix*) total weight
(*x*) Max permissible temperature of oil used
(*xi*) Year of manufacture
(*xii*) serial number of transformer
(*xiii*) Name of manufacturer with address.

8. Write a short note on instrument transformer. *[SBTE June 2008]*

Ans. Instrument transformers are made with the low range Am - meters and volta meters for the measurement of high value of currents and voltages. Accordingly there are two types of instrument transformers.

(*i*) Current Transformer (CT)
(*ii*) Potential Transformer (PT)

(*i*) **Current Transformer (CT):** A CT has few turns on primary winding and large number of turns on secondary winding. Primary winding is connected in series with the line and secondary winding is connected to low range Ammeter as shown in fig. 10

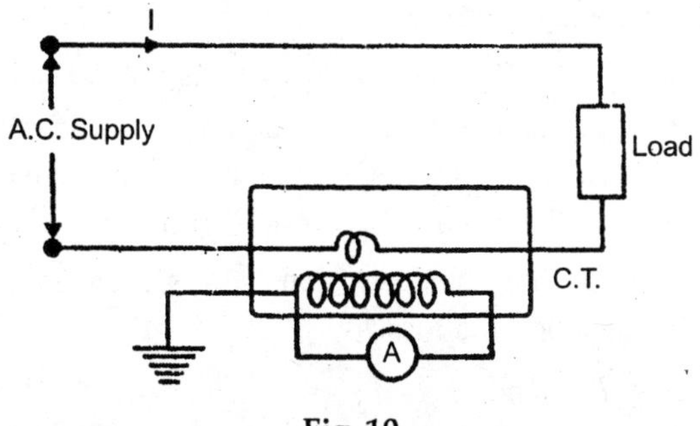

Fig. 10

Secondary of CT is earthed.

(*ii*) **Potential Transformer (PT):** A potential transformer is a two winding, low power transformer. It has large number of turns on the primary winding while there are very few turns on the secondary winding. The primary winding is connected to H.V. Supply. The secondary winding is normally rated for 110 V The number of turns on primary winding depends upon input voltage. Secondary of P.T is earthed for the safety of operator. Fig. 11 shows a potential transformer. C. T and P.T are commonly used in H.V. substations for measurement of high current and voltage.

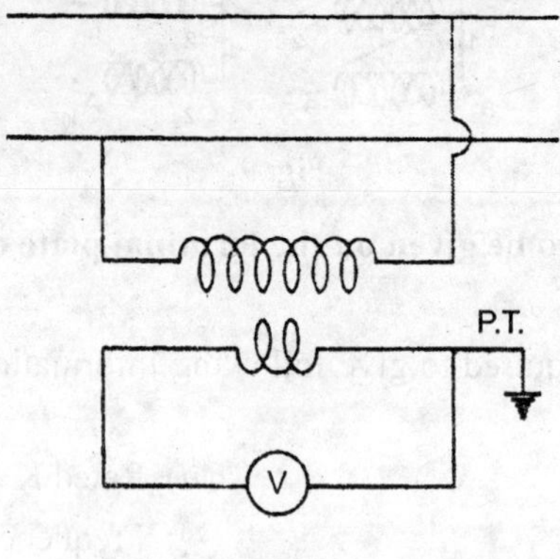

Fig. 11

Q. 9 What is an auto - Transformer. In what applications it is used.

Ans. An auto - transformer is a transformer having a part of its winding common to the primary and secondary circuits. Thus in fig. winding AB has a tappling at C, the load being connected across BC and the supply voltage across AB.

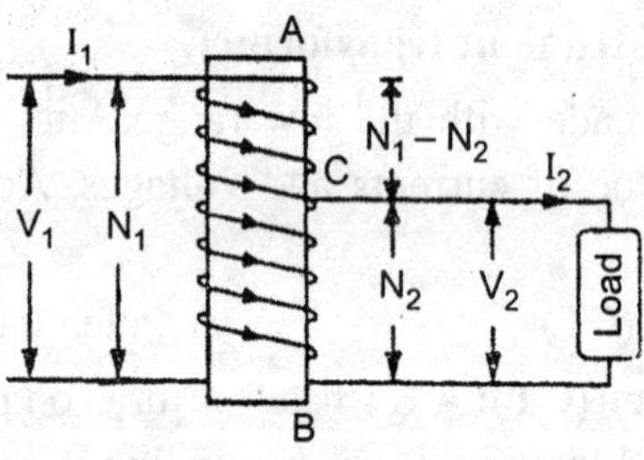

Fig. 12

Auto transformers are mainly used for:

(*i*) Interconnecting systems that are operating roughly at the same voltage

(*ii*) Starting squirrel cage induction motor. If an auto - transformer is used to supply a low voltage system from a high voltage system, it is essential to earth the common connection *i.e.* point *B*, otherwise there is a risk of serious shock.

As in ordinary transformer, the transformation ratio is equal to the turn ratio Neglecting no load current, leakage reactance and losses.

$$V_1 = E_1 \quad \text{and} \quad E_2 = V_2$$

$$\therefore \quad \frac{E_2}{E_1} = \frac{V_2}{V_1} = \frac{N_2}{N_1} = \frac{I_1}{I_2} = K$$

For same capacity and voltage ratio, the auto - transformer requires less copper than an ordinary transformer.

Since the cross-section of a conductor is proportional to the current carried and the length of conductor in a winding is proportional to the number of turns. Hence weight of copper in a winding is proportional to the product of current and number of turns.

Fill in the Blanks in the Following

1. Efficiency of 3-phase transformer is .... than a single phase transformer.
2. Next to the core .... winding is placed.
3. For a given line voltage the number of turns required in a winding is .... when windings are connected in delta than when the windings are connected in star.
4. In star-star connected transformer, if one of the windings fails to supply, the whole supply will be ....
5. The load current shared by one transformer is given by the relation $\overline{I}_1$ = ... $\overline{I}$, when the two transformers connected in parallel have the same voltage ratios and percentage impedances.
6. Distribution transformers are designed for low .... losses.
7. Power transformers are designed for low .... losses.
8. Tap changers are provided on the .... voltage winding of the transformer.
9. There are two types of tap-changers provided on the transformers called .... and ....
10. To avoid moisture to enter the transformer tank .... is placed in the breather.
11. Distribution transformers are designed to have maximum efficiency nearly ....
12. When two transformers of different kVA ratings are connected in parallel, they divide total load in proportion to their respective kVA rating only, when their .... are equal.
13. In any transformer, the voltage per turn in primary and secondary remains ....
14. The full load copper loss in a transformer is 400 W. At half load, the copper loss will be ....
15. For no-load tap changing, the best method is to use ....
16. .... is placed in between the tank and conservater.
17. Transformer oil is used as ....
18. For large power transformers, it is preferable to use ....
19. Winding to earth faults may be caused due to ....
20. The combinations of 3-phase transformers which can successfully operate in parallel are ....
21. The num in a transformer is due to ....
22. The primary and secondary coils of a standard transformer are coupled together ....
23. The no load current in a transformer is usually .... percent of the full load current.
24. An auto transformer finds its applications extensively as ....
25. The primary current in a current transformer is determined by the ....
26. In terms of primary to secondary turn ratio a current transformer is a .... transformer.

27. For parallel operation of two transformers, they must have .... phase sequence.
28. At lower frequency .... laminations can be used.
29. The transformer tanks are usually made of ....
30. A transformer has no .... losses.
31. Bushings are used for insulating and bringing out .... from the container to the external circuit.
32. Eddy current loss ultimately appears in the form of ....
33. In case of negative regulation of a transformer full load voltage is more than ....

Answers

Fill in the blanks:

1. more 2. LV 3. more 4. interrupted
5. $\dfrac{Z_2}{Z_1 + Z_2}$ 6. iron 7. copper 8. high
9. Off load ; on load-tap-change 10. Silicagel or calcium chloride 11. at 50% of full load
12. per unit impedences are equal 13. Always same 14. 1000 W
15. tap changers out side the tank operated by selector switch 16. Buchholz relay
17. Both insulant and coolant 18. tanks with separate coolers
19. Both surge voltages and current chopping 20. $\Delta - Y$ and $\Delta - Y$
21. Magnetostriction 22. Magnetically 23. Five
24. Variable voltage device 25. External circuit 26. Step up
27. Same 28. Thicker 29. Mild steel
30. Frictional windage 31. Terminals of winding 32. Heat
33. No. load voltage

Say 'Yes' or 'No' Type Questions

1. When a transformer raises the voltage it is called the step-up transformer.
2. A transformer must not be connected to D.C. source.
3. The ratio of primary voltage to secondary voltage is known as transformation ratio.
4. An ideal transformer is one in which the resistance of the windings is negligible and the core has no losses.
5. Primary and secondary currents are directly proportional to their respective turns.
6. The function of the magnetising component of no-load current is to sustain the alternating flux in the core.
7. The no-load primary input is practically equal to the iron loss in the transformer.

8. A transformer is said to be loaded when the secondary circuit of a transformer is completed through an impedance load.
9. Magnetic flux can be confined into a designed path.
10. When shifting resistance to the secondary, divide it by K^2:
11. An open-circuit test is conducted to find no-load or core loss.
12. Short-circuit test is conducted to find full-load copper loss.
13. The change in voltage when rated load at a specified power is removed is termed as voltage regulation.
14. Iron or core losses include copper loss and eddy current loss.
15. Iron or core losses are found from short-circuit test.
16. The efficiency of a transformer at a particular load and power factor is defined as the ratio of power output to power input.
17. Copper losses = Iron losses is the condition for maximum efficiency of a transformer.
18. η all-day = $\frac{Output\ in\ kWh}{Input\ in\ kWh}$ (for 24 hours)
19. A transformer in which part of the winding is common to both the primary and secondary circuits is known as auto-transformer,
20. The Δ-Δ connection is generally used in systems in which the voltages are not very high and especially when continuity of service must be maintained even though one of the transformers should fail.
21. The Y- Δ connection is principally used where the voltage is to be stepped up.
22. The Δ- Y connection is employed where it is necessary to step-up the voltage.
23. The *V-V* circuit is frequently used for two auto-transformers.
24. It is practicable to connect instruments and meters directly to the lines in high voltage circuits.
25. A potential transformer is a step down transformer used along with a low range voltmeter for measuring a high voltage.
26. The current transformer ratio is not equal to the ratio of secondary to primary turns, mainly because of the effect of the magnetising current.
27. A constant-current transformer is used to supply power to street lights which are connected in series.
28. In case of an induction regulator primary winding is stationary.

Answers

1. Yes	**2.** Yes	**3.** No	**4.** Yes
5. No.	**6.** Yes	**7.** Yes	**8.** Yes
9. No	**10.** No	**11.** Yes	**12.** Yes
13. Yes	**14.** No	**15.** No	**16.** Yes
17. Yes	**18.** Yes	**19.** Yes	**20.** Yes
21. No	**22.** Yes	**23.** Yes	**24.** No
25. Yes	**26.** Yes	**27.** Yes	**28.** No

SELECT THE BEST ALTERNATIVES FOR THE FOLLOWING

1. In a transformer the copper loss at half load as compared to that at full load will be
(*a*) 4 times (*b*) 2 times
(*c*) half (*d*) one fourth.

2. Which of the following is used to absorb moisture from air entering the transformer ?
(*a*) Sodium chloride (*b*) Silica sand
(*c*) Felt pad (*d*) Silica gel.

3. The desirable properties of transformer core material are
(*a*) low permeability and low hysteresis loss
(*b*) high permeability and high hysteresis loss
(*c*) high permeability and low hysteresis loss
(*d*) low permeability and high hysteresis loss.

4. In a distribution transformer normally
(*a*) Core losses are equal to copper losses (*b*) Core losses are more than copper losses
(*c*) Core losses are less than copper losses (*d*) Core losses are half of the copper losses.

5. An auto transformer has
(*a*) only one winding (*b*) two windings of the same gauge of wire
(*c*) two windings of different materials (*d*) more than two windings.

6. Which of the following conditions should be fulfilled for the parallel operation of two transformers ?
(*a*) Percentage impedance should be the same
(*b*) Polarities of both secondaries should be same
(*c*) Voltage rating should be the same
(*d*) All of the above.

7. For an ideal transformer the windings should have
(*a*) maximum resistance on primary side and least resistance on secondary side
(*b*) least resistance on primary side and maximum resistance on secondary side
(*c*) equal resistance on primary and secondary side
(*d*) no ohmic resistance on either side.

8. Three-to-three phase transformer connection possible for parallel operation is
(*a*) $\Delta - Y$ to $\Delta - Y$ (*b*) $\Delta - \Delta$ to $\Delta - X$
(*c*) $Y - Y$ to $\Delta - Y$ (*d*) $\Delta - Y$ to $Y - \Delta$.

9. Three-to-three phase transformer connections not feasible for parallel operation is
(*a*) $Y - Y$ to $Y - Y$ (*b*) $Y - Y$ to $\Delta - \Delta$
(*c*) $Y - \Delta$ to $\Delta - \Delta$ (*d*) $Y - \Delta$ to $\Delta - Y$.

10. Which of the following loss in a transformer is zero even at full load ?
(*a*) eddy current loss (*b*) hysteresis loss
(*c*) core loss (*d*) friction loss,

11. Which of the following part is likely to suffer maximum damage due to excessive temperature rise ?

(*a*) Core laminations (*b*) Copper winding

(*c*) Dielectric strength of oil (*d*) Winding insulation.

12. The maximum load that a power transformer can carry is limited by its

(*a*) Voltage ratio (*b*) Copper loss

(*c*) Temperature rise (*d*) Dielectric strength of oil.

Write True or False for the Following Statements:

13. Copper loss occurs in primary winding only.
14. Copper loss is proportional to the square of the current in the winding.
15. Eddy current losses are resistive heating losses in the core of the transformer.
16. Hysteresis losses are associated with the rearrangement of the magnetic domains in the core during each half cycle.
17. The transformer noise depends on flux density.
18. Scott connections are used for 2 phase to 3 phase conversion.
19. A transformer operates on the principles of mutual electromagnetic induction.
20. Breather is used in the transformer to cool the oil.
21. Eddy current and hysteresis loss in a transformer are minimised by laminating the core.
22. In a transformer under no load conditions the eddy current loss is negligible.
23. Transformer rating is usually expressed in terms of kVA.
24. Iron losses of a transformer can be determined by open circuit test.
25. Copper losses of a transformer can be determined by short circuit test.
26. The main reason for using an auto transformer is saving in copper.

Answers

1. (*d*)	2. (*d*)	3. (*c*)	4. (*c*)	5. (*a*)	6. (*d*)	7. (*d*)
8. (*a*)	9. (*c*)	10. (*d*)	11. (*d*)	12. (*a*)		

Answers

13. False	14. True	15. True	16. True
17. True	18. False	19. True	20. False
21. False	22. False	23. True	24. True
25. True	26. True		

OBJECTIVE TYPE QUESTIONS

Choose the correct answers:

1. Which of the following does not change in an ordinary transformer:
   (*a*) Voltage (*b*) Current
   (*c*) Frequency (*d*) All the above.
2. The material used in construction of core is usually,
   (*a*) Wood (*b*) Aluminium
   (*c*) Carbon (*d*) Silicon Steel.
3. Which of the following is minimised by laminating the core of a transformer,
   (*a*) Hysteresis losses (*b*) Eddy current losses
   (*c*) Heat losses (*d*) All the above.
4. In a transformer the energy is conveyed from primary to secondary,
   (*a*) Through cooling coil (*b*) Through air
   (*c*) By the flux (*d*) None of the above.
5. Under no-load conditions, which of the following loss is negligible,
   (*a*) Hysteresis loss (*b*) Eddy current loss
   (*c*) Copper loss (*d*) All losses have same magnitude.
6. For a transformer, the condition for maximum efficiency is
   (*a*) Hysteresis losses = Eddy current losses. (*b*) Core losses = Hysteresis losses
   (*c*) Copper losses = Iron losses (*d*) Total losses = $\frac{2}{3}$ × copper losses.
7. In case there are burrs on the edges of the laminations of the transformer, it is likely to result in
   (*a*) Vibrations (*b*) Noise
   (*c*) Higher eddy current loss (*d*) Higher hysteresis loss.
8. No load test on a transformer is carried out to determine
   (*a*) Copper loss (*b*) Magnetising current.
   (*c*) Magnetising current 4 loss (*d*) Efficiency of the transformer
9. The dielectric strength of transformer oil is expected to be
   (*a*) 1 kV (*b*) 33 kV
   (*c*) 100 kV (*d*) 330 kV.
10. The purpose of providing an iron core in a transformer is to
    (*a*) Provide support to windings.
    (*b*) Reduce hysteresis loss.
    (*e*) Decrease the reluctance of the magnetic path.
    (*d*) Reduce eddy current losses.

11. The following side is short-circuited, while short circuit test is conducted on the transformer

(*a*) High voltage side (*b*) Low voltage side

(*c*) Primary side (*d*) Secondary side.

12. In a transformer, the tappings are generally provided on

(*a*) Primary side (*b*) Secondary side

(*c*) Low voltage side (*d*) High voltage side.

13. An ideal transformer has infinite values of primary and secondary inductances ; The statement is

(a) True (*b*) False

14. The transformer ratings are usually expressed in terms of

(*a*) Volts (*b*) Amperes

(*c*) kW (*d*) kVA.

15. The function of conservator in a transformer is

(*a*) To protect against internal fault

(*b*) To reduce copper as well as core losses

(*c*) To cool the transformer oil

(*d*) To take care of the expansion and contraction oil due to variation of temperature of surroundings.

16. The transformer oil must be free from

(*a*) Sludge (*b*) Odour

(*c*) Gases (*d*) Moisture.

17. A buchholz relay can be installed on

(*a*) Auto-transformer (*b*) Air cooled transformers

(*c*) Welding transformer (*d*) Oil-cooled transformers.

18. Which of the following property is not necessarily desirable in the material for transformer core ?

(*a*) Mechanical strength (*b*) Low hysteresis loss

(*c*) High thermal conductivity (*d*) High permeability.

19. Helical coils can be used on

(*a*) Low voltage side of high kVA transformers.

(*b*) High frequency transformers.

(*c*) High voltage side of small capacity transformers.

(*d*) High voltage side of high kVA rating transformers.

20. High frequency transformers sometimes make use of ferrite cores because it has,

(*a*) High specific gravity (*b*) High resistance

(*c*) High hysteresis (*d*) Low permeability.

21. Cross over windings are used on

(*a*) Low voltage side of high kVA rating transformers

(*b*) Current transformers
(*c*) High voltage side of high kVA rating transformers
(*d*) High voltage side of low kVA rating transformers.

22. Tertiary winding is provided in transformers having.
(*a*) Mesh/star winding (*b*) Mesh/mesh winding
(*c*) Star/star winding (*d*) Any of the above.

23. Laminations used are generally made from silicon steel, because it reduces
(*a*) Hysteresis losses (*b*) Eddy current losses
(*c*) Copper losses (*d*) All the above.

24. Which of the following is the main advantage of an auto transformer over a two winding transformer ?
(*a*) Hysteresis losses are reduced (*b*) Saving in winding material
(*c*) Copper losses are negligible (*d*) Eddy current losses are eliminated.

25. During open circuit test of a transformer
(*a*) Primary is supplied rated voltage
(*b*) Primary is supplied full-load current
(*c*) Primary is supplied current at reduced voltage
(*d*) Primary is supplied rated kVA.

26. During short-circuit test iron losses are negligible because
(*a*) The current on secondary side is negligible
(*b*) The voltage on secondary side does not vary
(*c*) The voltage applied on primary side is low
(*d*) Full load current is not supplied to the transformer.

27. The function of breather in a transformer is
(*a*) To provide oxygen inside the tank
(*b*) To cool the coils during reduced load
(*c*) To filler the transformer cooling oil
(*d*) To arrest flow of moisture when outside air enters the transformer.

28. The size of a transformer core will depend upon
(*a*) Frequency (*b*) Area of the core
(*c*) Flux density of the core material. (*d*) (*a*) & (*b*) both.

29. Which of the following is not the standard voltage for power supply in India ?
(*a*) 11 kV (*b*) 33 kV
(c) 66 kV (*d*) 122 kV.

Answers

1. (*c*)	**2.** (*d*)	**3.** (*d*)	**4.** (*c*)	**5.** (*c*)	**6.** (*c*)
7. (*c*)	**8.** (*c*)	**9.** (*b*)	**10.** (*c*)	**11.** (*b*)	**12.** (*c*)

13. (*b*)	**14.** (*d*)	**15.** (*d*)	**16.** (*d*)	**17.** (*d*)	**18.** (*c*)
19. (*a*)	**20.** (*b*)	**21.** (*d*)	**22.** (*c*)	**23.** (*a*)	**24.** (*b*)
25. (*a*)	**26.** (*c*)	**27.** (*d*)	**28.** (*d*)	**29.** (*d*)	

EXERCISE

1. (*a*) Draw and explain the no load phasor diagram for a single phase transformer.

(*b*) A 2200/200 V transformer draws a no load primary current of 0.6 A and absorbs 400 Watts. Find the magnetising and iron loss component. [**Ans.** 0.572 A, 0.182 A]

(*c*) A 2200/250 V transformer takes 0.5 A at a p.f. of 0.3 on open circuit, find magnetising and working component of no load primary current. [**Ans.** 0.442 A, 0.15 A]

2. The no load current of a transformer is 4.0 A at 0.25 p.f. when supplied at 250 V, 50 c/s. The number of turns on primary winding is 200. Calculate

(*i*) R.M.S. value of flux in the core (Assume sinusoidal flux)

(*ii*) The core loss

(*iii*) The magnetising current. [**Ans.** (*i*) 3.98 *m* Wb (*ii*) 250 W (*iii*) 13.87 A]

3. A 2200/200 V transformer takes 1 A at the H.T. side on no load at a p.f. of 0.385 lagging. Calculate the iron losses.

If a load of 50 A at a p.f. of 0.8 lagging is taken from the secondary of a transformer, calculate the actual primary currents and power factor. [**Ans.** 847 W, 5.44 A, 0.74 lag]

4. The diagram shows the equivalent circuit for a single phase transformer. Figure gives resistances and reactances in ohms in terms of the primary side. The ratio of secondary to primary turns is 10 and the load is inductive. Find

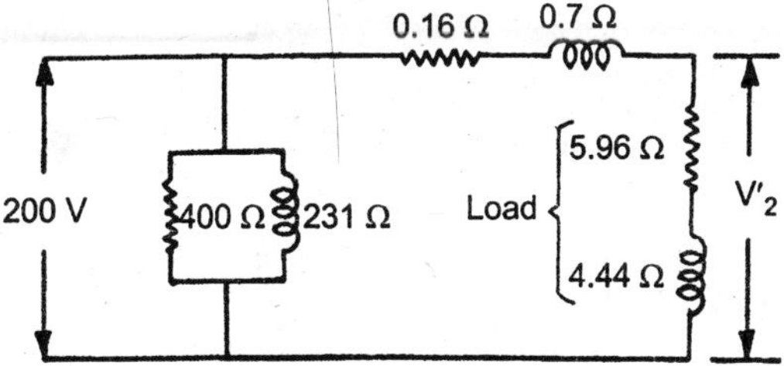

(*a*) The secondary terminal voltage.

(*b*) The primary current.

(*c*) The efficiency. [**Ans.** (*a*) 1860 V, (*b*) 25.9 A, (*c*) 94.9%]

5. A 100 kVA, 6600/330 V, 50 c/s single phase transformer took 10 A and 436 W at 100 V in a short circuit test, the figures referring to the high voltage side. Calculate the voltage to be applied to the high voltage side on full load at p.f. 0.8 lagging when secondary terminal voltage is 330 V. [**Ans.** 6734 V]

6. In a 25 kVA 2000/200 V transformer, the iron and copper losses are 350 and 400 W respectively. Calculate the efficiency on unity p.f. at (*a*) full load (*b*) half load (*c*) determine the load at max. efficiency and iron and copper loss in this case. [**Ans.** (*a*) 97.1% (*b*) 96.5% (*c*) 23.4 kVA]

7. A 50 kVA distribution transformer has a full load efficiency of 94% and the full load copper loss is just equal to the constant iron loss. Calculate its all day efficiency if it is loaded as per the following schedule:

   (*i*) no load for 10 hours (*ii*) 25% of full load at 6 hours

   (*iii*) half load at 5 hours (*iv*) full load for 3 hours **[Ans.** 88.4%]

8. The primary and secondary windings of a 50 kVA, 6600/220 V transformer have resistances of 7.8 ohms and 0.0085 ohms respectively. The transformer draws no load current of 0.328 A at a p.f. 0.3. Calculate efficiency at full load assuming the p.f. of load to 0.8. **[Ans.** 96.3%]

9. A 100 kVA, 6600/250 V, 50 c/s transformer gave the following test results:

   O.C. test: 900 W, normal voltage

   S.C. test: (data on h.v. side); 12 A, 290 V, 860 W.

   Calculate (*i*) the efficiency and percentage regulation at full load of 0.8 *p.f.* lagging.

   (*ii*) the load at which max. efficiency occurs and the value of this efficiency at p.f. 0.8 lagging. **[Ans.** (*a*) 97.3%, 4.32% (*b*) 81 kVA, 97.3%]